Finding God

Following Jesus

Parish Catechist Guide

As I open this book, I open myself
to God's presence in my life.
When I allow God's grace to help me,
I see with truth, hear with forgiveness,
and act with kindness.
Thank you, God, for your presence in my life.

Barbara F. Campbell, M.Div., D.Min.
James P. Campbell, M.A., D.Min.

LOYOLA PRESS.
A JESUIT MINISTRY
Chicago

Imprimatur	In Conformity
In accordance with c. 827, permission to publish is granted on August 1, 2012 by Rev. Msgr. John F. Canary, Vicar General of the Archdiocese of Chicago. Permission to publish is an official declaration of ecclesiastical authority that the material is free from doctrinal and moral error. No legal responsibility is assumed by the grant of this permission.	The Subcommittee on the Catechism, United States Conference of Catholic Bishops, has found the doctrinal content of this manual, copyright 2014, to be in conformity with the *Catechism of the Catholic Church*.

Finding God: Following Jesus is an expression of the work of Loyola Press, a ministry of the Chicago-Detroit Province of the Society of Jesus.

Senior Consultants
Joe Paprocki, D.Min.
Tom McGrath, M.A.
Robert Fabing, S.J., D.Min.
Richard Hauser, S.J., Ph.D., S.T.L.
Jane Regan, Ph.D.

Advisors
George A. Aschenbrenner, S.J., S.T.L
Most Reverend Gordon D. Bennett, S.J., D.D.
Paul Brian Campbell, S.J., Ph.D.
Paul H. Colloton, O.P., D.Min.
Gerald Darring, M.A.
Eugene LaVerdiere, S.S.S., Ph.D., S.T.L.

Catechetical Staff
Jeanette L. Graham, M.A.
Jean Hopman, O.S.U., M.A.

Grateful acknowledgment is given to authors, publishers, photographers, museums, and agents for permission to reprint the following copyrighted material. Every effort has been made to determine copyright owners. In the case of any omissions, the publisher will be pleased to make suitable acknowledgments in future editions. Acknowledgments continue on page T-403. Young People's Book acknowledgments begin on page 331.

Cover design: Loyola Press
Cover Illustration: Rafael López
Interior design: Loyola Press

ISBN-13: 978-0-8294-3673-0
ISBN-10: 0-8294-3673-1

LOYOLA PRESS.
A JESUIT MINISTRY

3441 N. Ashland Avenue
Chicago, Illinois 60657
(800) 621-1008

www.loyolapress.com
www.ignatianspirituality.com
www.other6.com

12 13 14 15 16 17 18 19 RRD 10 9 8 7 6 5 4 3 2 1

Contents

CONTENTS

Finding·God

"Yes, dear young people, Christ gave himself for each one of you and loves you in a unique and personal way."

*Address of His Holiness Pope Benedict XVI to Young People
of the Archdiocese of Madrid, Spain, April 6, 2009*

Welcome to *Finding God* Grades 7–8!

Reaching young people—mind and heart, body and soul, *Finding God* Grades 7–8 helps every young Catholic

Know Your Faith

▶ **Full and authentic teachings** of the Catholic Church

▶ **Rooted in Ignatian spirituality** to foster a life of prayer

▶ **Grade 7: faith formation** with a focus on the life, Death, and Resurrection of Jesus Christ

▶ **Grade 8: faith formation** with a focus on the Church and what it means to be Church

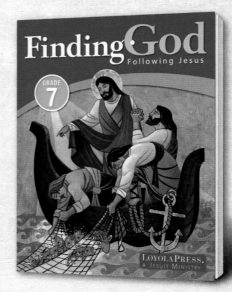

Grow in Faith

▶ **Experiential learning** and "Adventures in Faith": *so much more* than read and discuss

▶ **Prayer integrated** into every session at least three times: traditional, meditative, contemplative, and more

▶ **Parent components** that keep the faith growing at home and in parish life

Go in Faith

▶ **Discipleship is key:** call to action in every session

▶ **Faith in Action projects** to end each unit

▶ **Service-project suggestion** included in every session

▶ **Grade 8: Ready for Confirmation** feature that helps young people understand what it means to live a life of faith

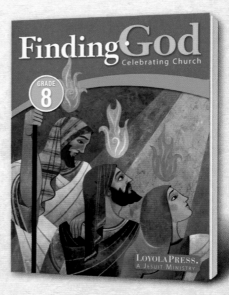

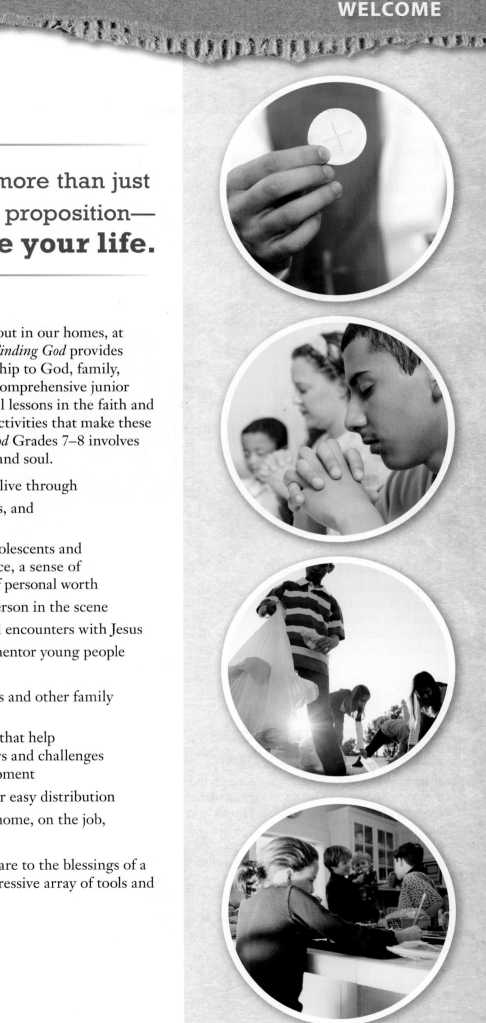

Catholicism is more than just an interesting theological proposition— it's the way you live your life.

OUR FAITH is meant to be lived out in our homes, at school, in our jobs, and in the community. *Finding God* provides an invitation into a way of living in relationship to God, family, parish, and neighbor. This compelling and comprehensive junior high program provides sound and substantial lessons in the faith and delivers those lessons through experiential activities that make these lessons part of a lifelong practice. *Finding God* Grades 7–8 involves the whole individual: mind and heart, body and soul.

With *Finding God* Grades 7–8, faith comes alive through

- **Active experiences** for the feasts, seasons, and liturgical life of the Church
- **Where Do I Fit In?** articles geared to adolescents and their need for trust, respect, independence, a sense of belonging in a valued group, and a sense of personal worth
- **Scripture stories** that place the young person in the scene
- **Guided reflections** that lead to prayerful encounters with Jesus
- **Diverse opportunities for prayer** that mentor young people toward a life of prayer

And *Finding God* engages junior high parents and other family members through

- *Seasons of Family and Faith* **magazines** that help parents and young people navigate the joys and challenges of this unique time of growth and development
- **Family e-newsletters** delivered online for easy distribution
- **Online resources** for living faith in the home, on the job, and in the community

You want to lead the young people in your care to the blessings of a lifelong faith. *Finding God* offers you an impressive array of tools and resources to help you do just that.

Program Components

Soundly grounded in Scripture, Church Tradition, and prayer, *Finding God* Grades 7–8 offers catechists everything they need to inspire and guide young people's faith formation. Engaging, developmentally appropriate content and faith experiences for young people have been paired with easy-to-use, supportive catechist tools and materials to create a comprehensive, integrated, relevant program.

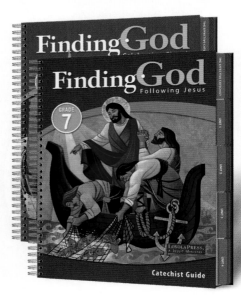
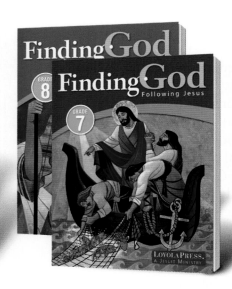

Catechist Guide

Each guide includes complete catechetical background, clear plans, step-by-step support, and additional activities—with custom guides for parish and school.

Young People's Book

The truth and beauty of the Catholic faith is shared through prayer, Scripture, articles, story, song, illustration, and experience. In **Grade 7,** themes develop around the life, Death, and Resurrection of our Lord, Jesus Christ. In **Grade 8,** Church history provides the context and springboard for learning.

CDs: Scripture Stories, Guided Reflections, and Reflective Music

Dramatized recordings of Scripture stories bring the Bible to life; reflections mentor young people to live a life of prayer; and reflective music reveals the diversity and unity of the Catholic Church (two CDs per grade).

Poster Sets

Posters at each grade level include relevant topics and beautiful visuals (17 x 22 in.).

Grade 7 Posters

- Time Line of the New Testament
- Prologue of the Gospel of John
- The Beatitudes
- Saint Paul's Missionary Journeys
- The Four Evangelists
- The Liturgical Year

Grade 8 Posters

- The Early Christian Communities
- The Early Ecumenical Councils
- The Great Cathedrals
- Ignatian Spirituality
- Catholic Social Teaching
- The Liturgical Year

Seasons of Family and Faith Magazines

These 32-page "geared to the grade" magazines help parents and family members meet the unique needs of adolescents through inspiring articles, practical advice, and pathways to honest discussion about faith and life.

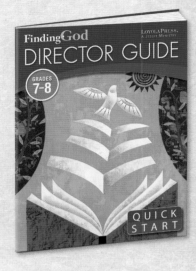

Director Quick-Start Guide

It's easy to begin with clear, concise plans for step-by-step program implementation. A variety of implementation models are provided, including full-year, half-year, summer intensive, and at-home catechesis.

Technology—*Online Resources for Everyone*

DRE/Principal
- Director Guide Supplements
- Family E-Newsletters

Catechist/Teacher
- Activity Finder
- Prayer Services
- Blackline Masters
- Lesson Planner
- Links to Other Resources
- Assessments
- Faith in Action Projects

Families
- *Finding God:* At-Home Edition
- Spanish Support

Children
- Spanish and English Glossaries
- Session Reviews
- Study Guides
- Games

 www.findinggod.com

To take full advantage of the secured items on the site, directors of religious education, principals, catechists, and teachers should register online with this **access code: FG-JrHigh**

Spiral Curriculum

An integrated curriculum that spirals through the grades, *Finding God* provides support when and how it is needed. As children are introduced to and revisit concepts and vocabulary from one year to the next, their knowledge and experience both broaden and deepen.

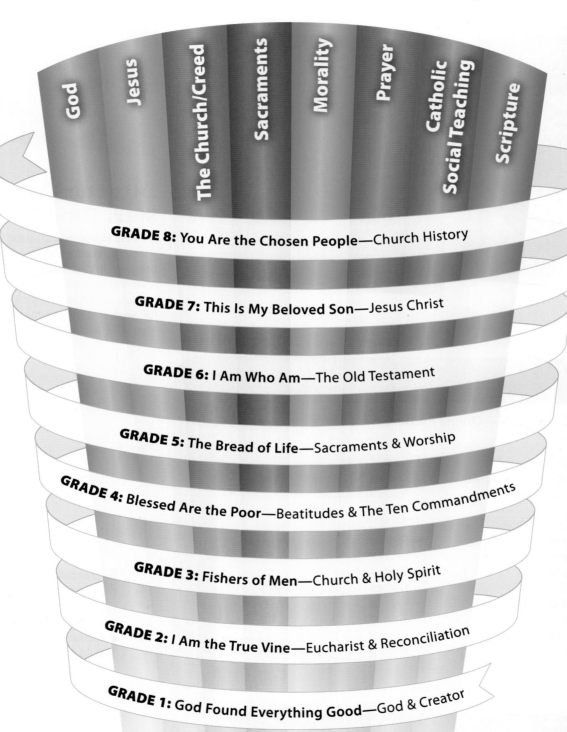

God · Jesus · The Church/Creed · Sacraments · Morality · Prayer · Catholic Social Teaching · Scripture

GRADE 8: You Are the Chosen People—Church History

GRADE 7: This Is My Beloved Son—Jesus Christ

GRADE 6: I Am Who Am—The Old Testament

GRADE 5: The Bread of Life—Sacraments & Worship

GRADE 4: Blessed Are the Poor—Beatitudes & The Ten Commandments

GRADE 3: Fishers of Men—Church & Holy Spirit

GRADE 2: I Am the True Vine—Eucharist & Reconciliation

GRADE 1: God Found Everything Good—God & Creator

Note: An optional Unit 6, The Year in Our Church, is offered for all grades.

Varied Catechetical Approaches

Finding God Grades 7–8 offers catechists and teachers a variety of catechetical approaches so that all needs are met and so that young people, families, parishes, and schools are nurtured to grow in faith and become living examples of God's love.

Core Content as Catechesis

This program presents the Church's doctrine and Tradition accurately, comprehensively, and with approval by the United States Conference of Catholic Bishops. Direct references to the *Catechism of the Catholic Church* and *General Directory for Catechesis* are included in the Catechist Preparation section of each session.

Prayer as Catechesis

Finding God nourishes a relationship with God through traditional prayer, meditation, liturgical prayer, and praying with Scripture. At least three opportunities to pray are woven into each of the 25 sessions. Prayer Service opportunities are provided for each Seasonal Session and online for each unit.

Liturgical Experiences as Catechesis

This series echoes our belief that the Eucharist is the "source and summit of the Christian life" (*CCC* 1324). For example, each Celebrating Session (Sessions 5, 10, 15, 20, and 25) helps young people connect to their faith through the celebration of faith at Mass and to join in a more meaningful participation in the Church's sacramental and liturgical life.

Scripture as Catechesis

Scripture sets the foundation for the truths that are reflected on in each session. The authentic teaching of the Church is revealed through Scripture and presented with ample opportunities for reflection and discussion.

Service/Catholic Social Teaching as Catechesis

Every session in this program provides young people and adults with opportunities to explore and act on their commitment to the principles of Catholic Social Teaching. Faith in Action projects close each unit.

Classroom-Based or Youth Ministry-Based Catechesis

Finding God Grades 7–8 is filled with active-learning opportunities that can take place in a variety of settings so that catechesis can be conducted in either a classroom or a youth-ministry setting.

Young People's Book

Catholic content is shared in a rich context, with beautiful images, thoughtful prayer, and engaging experiences that draw in young people to fully learn and express their faith.

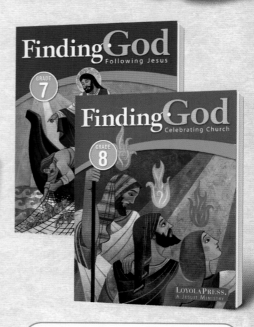

Unit Opener

Each unit opens with a saint whose holy life and response to God's love reflects the unit theme.

Fact-filled biographies bring to life our Catholic faith, history, and Tradition.

Engage

Each session begins at a crucial starting point for an adolescent—his or her own life. Thought-provoking questions and an opening prayer lead young people into the session.

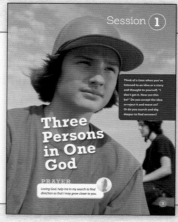

Special Features

These special features help young people make content connections:

- Our Catholic Character
- Past Meets Present
- Sacred Art
- Study Corner
- Ready for Confirmation (Grade 8)

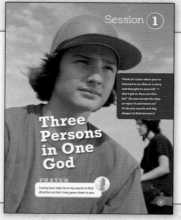

Our Catholic Character

Our belief in the mystery of the Trinity—Three Pers in one God— does not imply that we believe in more than one God. Christianity, Judaism, and Islam are al major monotheistic religions, which means they are based on a belief in one God. Other religions, such as Hinduism, Buddhism, Jainism, and Shinto, have varying degrees of polytheism, the worship of mar gods. Despite this fundamental difference, the C Church respects other faith traditions.

Explore

Young people deepen their understanding of the Catholic faith as they read, discuss, experience, and pray. Activities abound so that young people can record their reflections and learning.

Reflect

Helpful background information prepares young people for prayer.

Various forms of prayer draw young people into a personal relationship with God.

As they read and discuss Where Do I Fit In? articles, young people are invited to express thoughts and ideas as another way to understand and reflect.

Respond

Young people review what they've learned and are invited to respond to God's call in daily life. Each Respond page concludes with a call to action that invites young people to live out their faith as it relates to the session theme.

Additional Content

Prayers and Practices and the **Glossary** help young people reinforce and extend their learning and practice their faith.

Faith in Action

Each unit closes with a choice of two Faith in Action projects that invite small groups to live out the principles of Catholic Social Teaching.

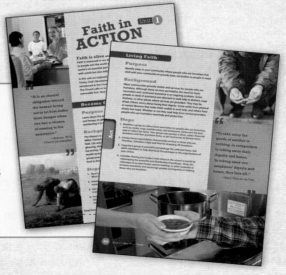

Seasonal Sessions

The Year in Our Church Seasonal Sessions provide options for learning more about the liturgical year and its feast days.

Celebrating the Liturgical Year

Celebrating Sessions highlight Catholic life and practices throughout the liturgical year.

Catechist Guide

So easy to use, the Catechist Guide is the perfect companion for catechists and teachers of every experience level.

Catechist Preparation

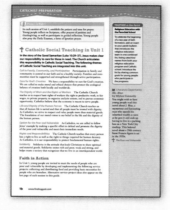

Overview
To begin each unit, catechists are introduced to the unit theme, session descriptions, and the unit-opener saint.

Catholic Social Teaching
For each unit, catechists are provided with an overview of the prayer experiences and Catholic Social Teaching themes.

Together as One Parish
This idea provides an opportunity for the parish to come together when both the religious education program and the parochial school are using the *Finding God* curriculum.

Literature Opportunity
Catechists can incorporate popular and classic literature as another way to explore the unit theme.

Retreat/Background
To begin each session, catechists are invited to pray in preparation. Then they read to gain background knowledge in Scripture, Tradition, and catechesis that young people will experience.

One-Hour Planner
This easy-to-follow, one-hour lesson planner guides catechists to implement the session. (A five-day session planner is also provided in the school edition Catechist Guide.)

Unique Ways to Open and Close the Unit

Unit Openers
Because adolescents often look to role models for guidance and direction, each unit opens by highlighting the life of a saint or holy person. Step-by-step instructions guide catechists to make connections between the saints and unit themes.

Faith in Action
With these "call to action" projects, catechists close the unit as they guide groups of young people to choose a project that revolves around social justice and a Catholic Social Teaching theme.

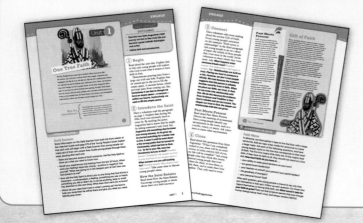

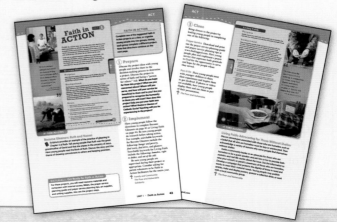

Start at the Heart of a Young Person's Life

Every session opens by inviting young people to reflect on or talk about themselves, their friends, and their family—to tell their own stories as an entry point for discovering the session theme.

Engage

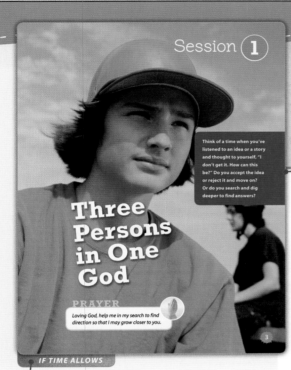

A helpful list informs catechists of desired outcomes.

Young people can write or share their responses to the questions provided.

Meaningful demonstrations, activities, and discussion lead each young person to reflect on his or her own life and understand how it ties in to the session theme.

Special Features

Look for these icons, which highlight special learning opportunities throughout the Catechist Guide:

- 3-Minute Retreat
- Adventures in Faith
- Audio CDs
- Catholic Social Teaching
- Prayer Opportunities
- Scripture References

If Time Allows suggestions lead catechists to help young people complete these hands-on, minds-on extension activities.

Session Extenders provide catechists with helpful Loyola Press Web links to session-related articles, prayers, activities, and more.

Simple instructions guide catechists to pray with young people and set the tone for the session.

Rich Instruction in Three Simple Steps

Finding God Grades 7–8 teaches concepts in context—through Scripture, story, articles, engaging images, and interactive writing and drawing opportunities. In addition to definitions and facts, this program makes connections that translate into a life of faith.

Explore

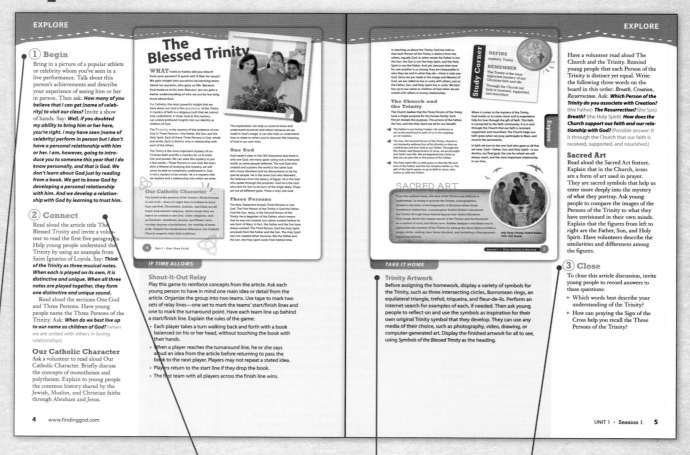

① Begin
Before jumping into the page, catechists are guided to tap young people's prior knowledge and build background with active openings.

② Connect
Catechists lead young people through the core content on the pages, questioning, discussing, demonstrating, and interacting along the way.

③ Close
Each article closes with an opportunity for young people to reflect on and deepen their faith experience.

Take It Home
Homework suggestions are included if catechists wish to extend learning beyond group meeting times.

Catechists and teachers are supported every step of the way. The guides are so easy to navigate that even first-year catechists and teachers can use them with confidence.

Explore Further

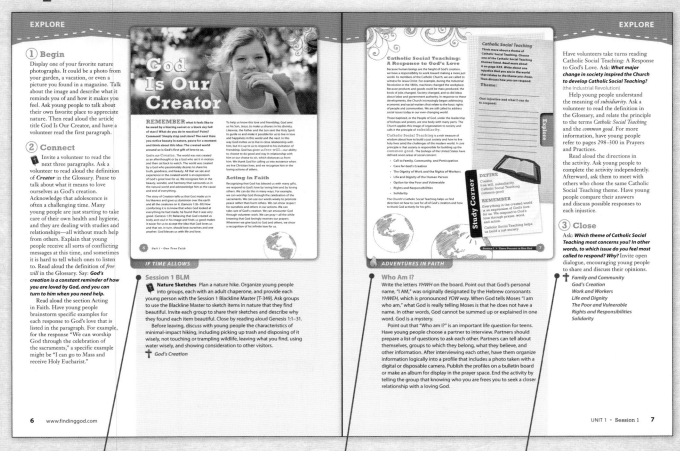

Blackline Masters
Each session includes a Blackline Master found in the back of each Catechist Guide or online for easy reproduction.

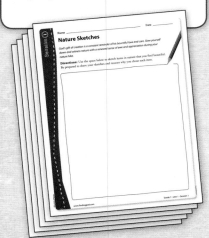

Adventures in Faith
Each session includes an extension activity that invites young people to challenge themselves in significant ways. Catechists will see a flame icon each time an Adventures in Faith activity is suggested.

Catholic Social Teaching
Catechists will see a cross icon each time young people work with a Catholic Social Teaching theme.

Helping Young People Enter into a Deeper Relationship with God

Finding God **consistently provides opportunities** for catechists and young people to experience and cherish prayer as a deeply important, always-present opportunity to grow in relationship with God.

Pray

Approach 1

Many Prayer pages include an option to use a recorded guided reflection found on the program CD. When a recording is included, catechists are provided with two options for leading young people in prayer.

Approach 2

These simple instructions help catechists guide young people through the prayer on the page without the use of a recording.

REFLECT

Prayer

Choose an approach and pray with young people.

APPROACH 1

Guided Reflection

Prepare Listen in advance to the recorded guided reflection "Living in Relationship" [CD 1, Track 1]. Decide if you will play the recording or pray aloud the reflection yourself. If you choose to lead, listen to the recording a second time, following the script [pages T-339–T-340] and noting pauses and tone. You can then follow the script exactly or adapt it as you wish.

Pray During the session, have volunteers read aloud the paragraphs in the left column. Discuss the meaning of *disciple*. Read aloud the definition in the Glossary. Then introduce meditation as a form of prayer in which one thinks reflectively, in this case about being in relationship with God. Play the recording or lead using the script, joining the young people in meditative prayer. If you pray aloud the script, play reflective music softly in the background [CD 1, Track 7].

APPROACH 2

Young People's Page

Prepare Pray the prayer in advance to become familiar with it.

Pray Have volunteers read aloud the paragraphs in the left column. Discuss the idea of being a disciple. Ask: *What is more important for a disciple—words or actions?* (both) Then pray together the vocal prayer in Reflect on the Sign of the Cross. Designate the Leader part. Have the rest of the group respond at the All part. Pause briefly between parts.

8 www.findinggod.com

Prayer

Signs of Love

As Catholics we begin our day and our prayers with the Sign of the Cross. It's a simple reminder that our whole life is lived under the sign that saved us, the Cross of Jesus, by the power of the Trinity—one God, who is Father, Son, and Holy Spirit.

It is an important sign that places before us and on us the shape of the cross that saves us. It is the sign traced on our foreheads when we become a Christian in Baptism, and it is made over us in death as we complete our Christian life.

When we bless ourselves with the Sign of the Cross, we remember the God who created us, the one who saves us, and the Spirit whose wisdom guides us. This sacramental helps us grow in our spiritual life because it reminds us of our core beliefs.

The Sign of the Cross is also a visible sign of a *disciple*, a person who accepts Jesus' message and tries to live as he did, including sharing his mission. Jesus' words in Luke 9:23 remind us to take up his cross daily and follow him. Though short and simple, the Sign of the Cross lets the whole world see that we belong to God—Father, Son, and Holy Spirit.

8 *Unit 1 • One True Faith*

Reflect on the Sign of the Cross

Leader: Let's pause for a moment to become aware of God's presence with us as we prepare ourselves for prayer. Trace a small cross on your forehead. Reflect on the ways you use your mind to know and understand God better.

All: Faithful God, you created us with a mind that we might seek and know you. Help us recognize you in all the people and events of our lives.

Leader: Next, trace a small cross on your chest. Pause for a moment to thank God for all the ways he has shown you how much he loves you. Let's pray together.

All: God of love, thank you for the gift of your Son, Jesus, who died on the cross for love of us. Help us know how to love others the way you love us.

Leader: Now slowly trace a small cross on each shoulder. Reflect on anything in your life that feels heavy to you, or reflect on a burden that you could use help carrying. Now let's pray together.

All: Merciful God, your Son bore the weight of our human suffering on his shoulders. Help us take up our cross each day and follow you. Inspire us through your Holy Spirit to be generous in offering help to others who carry heavy burdens.

IF TIME ALLOWS

Pray Again
If you used the recorded guided reflection, you might conclude the session by praying the Sign of the Cross.

FYI

Coaching Young People to Pray

Before praying, emphasize to young people that prayer is communication with God about every part of our lives. Prayer is an essential part of our daily lives that helps us grow closer in our relationship to God. Encourage young people to focus their attention on a specific image or idea to help them concentrate and reflect.

If Time Allows

This feature gives catechists the option of expanding the prayer experience in meaningful ways.

Coaching Young People to Pray

To help catechists and young people enter confidently and more fully into prayer, a coaching tip is offered for each prayer.

Where Do I Fit In?

These reflective essays, penned by Catholics from all walks of life and all regions of the United States, encourage young people to take time to reflect and recognize God's presence in their lives and in the world.

Reflect

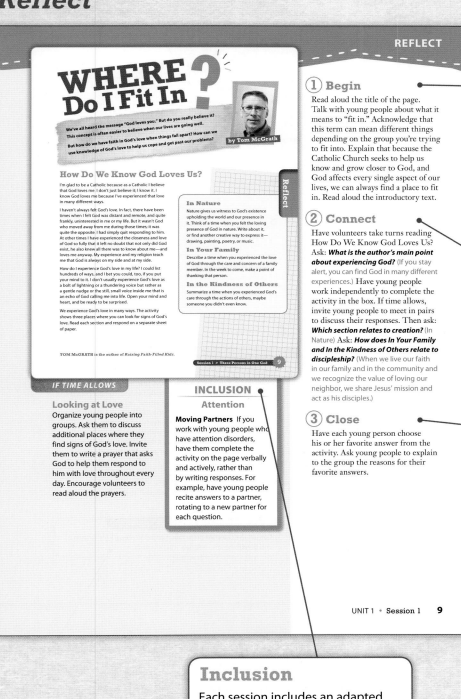

① Begin

To make the author's narrative relevant, catechists are guided to help young people tap into what they have experienced in their own lives.

② Connect

Catechists lead young people through reading and discussing the narrative.

③ Close

Catechists close the page by having young people complete an activity that makes connections between the narrative and living their faith.

Inclusion

Each session includes an adapted activity for young people with special needs. See page EC-11 for more information about inclusion.

Look Back and Send Forth

Through a review of key concepts and vocabulary, young people identify how they can respond to God's invitation as they live each day.

What's What?

① Begin

During this step, catechists lead young people to complete the review activity.

② Connect

Important vocabulary is discussed in this section. Catechists then lead young people in an exercise that invites them to go forth and live out their faith.

③ Go in Peace

The session closes with clear directions and a call to action.

Service Suggestion

Every session includes an idea for serving others, a real-life application of Catholic Social Teaching themes.

RESPOND

① Begin

What's What? Have a volunteer read aloud the directions and the first main idea. Read aloud the example of supporting details. Have young people turn back to pages 1–2 to verify the details in the text. Invite volunteers to give other possible supporting details. Then have young people complete the page independently or with a partner. Afterward, share responses as a group.

② Connect

Say What? Ask volunteers to read aloud and define the terms. Review each term in the Glossary if necessary.

Now What? Read aloud the section. Invite each young person to answer the question independently.

③ Go in Peace

Collect materials and return them to their appropriate places. Encourage young people to follow through with their Now What? idea during the week. Draw a triangle on the board and write *Father* at the top. Add *Son* to the second point, and *Holy Spirit* at the third point. Starting at the apex, trace your finger from word to word on the triangle. Say: *If I stop before I reach the next Person of the Trinity, I weaken my chance to live a life of holiness. Let's ask God for an increase in our faith and strength to live in the name of the Father, the Son, and the Holy Spirit.*

 **3-Minute Retreat**
Give young people an opportunity for quiet meditation at **www.loyolapress.com/retreat**.

10 www.findinggod.com

What's What?

For each main idea, write a supporting detail.

1. Saint Augustine's faith journey led him to live a holy life and become a great Catholic theologian and writer. (PAGES 1–2)
   Example: Saint Augustine made mistakes, but he kept searching and eventually had experiences that helped him have faith in God.

2. The Trinity is the most important mystery of our Christian faith and life. (PAGES 4–5)

3. Through the Church our faith is received, supported, and nourished. (PAGE 5)

4. God sent us his Son so that we would know his love. (PAGE 6)

5. We can respond to God's love through prayer, word, and action. (PAGE 6)

6. Catholic Social Teaching gives us direction on how to show love for others and to care for all of God's creation. (PAGE 7)

7. We pray the Sign of the Cross to remind us that our lives are lived under the sign that saved us—the Cross of Jesus. (PAGE 8)

Say What?
Know the definitions of these terms.

Catholic Social Teaching	free will
common good	mystery
Creator	sacramentals
disciple	subsidiarity
faith	Trinity

Now What?
Through faith in the Holy Trinity, we can learn to live a life of holiness. What can you do this week to live as a holy person?

10 Unit 1 • One True Faith

IF TIME ALLOWS

Service: Set Up a Junior's Department
Explain that through the Catholic Social Teaching theme of "option for the poor and vulnerable," we are called to help combat poverty. Together, do research to find a local Catholic organization that works to clothe families who are in need, especially families with adolescent children. Solicit help from adult volunteers and organize a long-term project in which young people work with the organization to collect, wash, mend, and attractively display a department store-type junior's department for needy adolescents to go and obtain clothing.
✝ *The Poor and Vulnerable*

Session-Assessment Option
An assessment for this session can be found at www.findinggod.com.

PLAN AHEAD: Get Ready for Session 2
Consult the catechist preparation pages to prepare for Session 2 and determine any materials you will need.

🕯 *3-Minute Retreat*
Catechists can give young people an opportunity for quiet meditation at **www.loyolapress.com/retreat**.

Assessment Options
Catechists are provided with the option to have young people complete a formal assessment.

Plan Ahead
This box leads catechists to find the materials and plans for their next session.

Assessment

The ability to monitor progress helps catechists know when young people need further reinforcement of concepts and thus guides future instruction. Formal assessment also helps teachers gather information for progress reports. *Finding God* Grades 7–8 provides both session and unit assessments to monitor immediate progress as well as retention over time.

Session Assessments

Available as PDFs on the Web, these assessments track young people's progress for all 25 sessions.

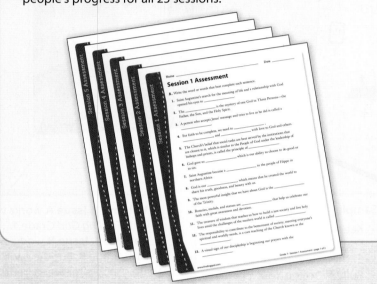

Games, Reviews, and Study Guides

Online games, interactive reviews, and study guides help young people prepare for assessment.

Unit Assessments

Five unit assessments are bound in the Catechist Guide as Blackline Masters or available online as PDFs.

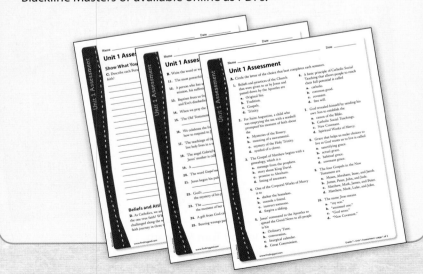

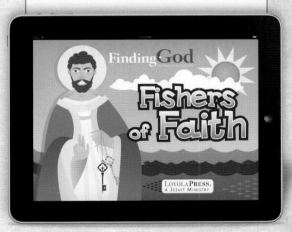

Seasons of Family and Faith

Magazines that support parents of adolescents and meet them in the midst of their busy lives

To everything there is a season, and the season of raising middle schoolers can be exhilarating, challenging, and filled with opportunities to nurture faith. *Seasons of Family and Faith* engages and inspires parents of young adolescents, recognizing that this is a time of major change for everyone.

Sample Topics:
- Keeping the Sabbath
- Forgiveness
- Catholic Identity
- Bully-Proofing Your Child
- Welcoming and Letting Go

Volume 1, Issue A works well with *Finding God* Grade 7. **Volume 1, Issue B** works well with Grade 8. But the contents are suitable for any parents of young people ages 12–16.

The "Seasons"

- **Challenge and Opportunity**
- **Togetherness and Autonomy**
- **Sorrow and Hope**
- **Joy and Celebration**

Each magazine is organized into four "seasons" that parents and young people experience. The articles show how the Catholic faith responds to real-life challenges.

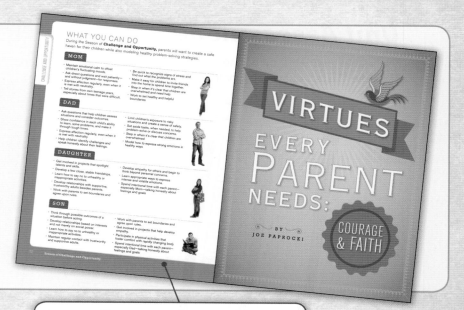

Conceived by a team led by Tom McGrath, each season offers five practical and content-rich articles plus a helpful "what you can do" guide for moms, dads, daughters, and sons.

More for the Family

Because support for families is so important, *Finding God* offers these additional components.

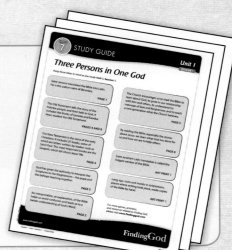

Finding God: At-Home Edition

Parents can go to www.findinggod.com to find an at-home lesson adaptation for each session in *Finding God*. Perfect for groups that meet only a few times a year or for long absences due to illness or extended vacation.

Faith Moves

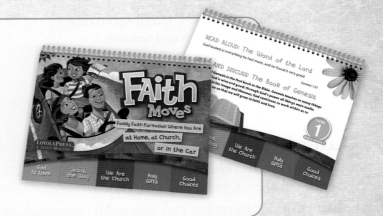

**Faith Formation Where You Are—
At Home, at Church, or in the Car!**

Geared for families with children of all ages, this action-packed deck makes family faith formation accessible and fun for everyone. It's the take-anywhere answer to "How do I get my families involved?" **Available in English and Spanish.**

Finding God Family E-Newsletters

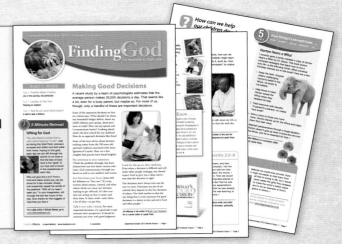

Provided seven times a year, these e-newsletters give parents inspiring suggestions to help bring faith alive. Articles and special features on topics such as saints, what it means to be Catholic, and media reviews make these newsletters relevant and inviting. **Available in English and Spanish.**

www.findinggod.com

Loyola Press's Web site offers a wealth of resources to support and enhance the program—www.findinggod.com has the entire faith community in mind.

To access secured materials such as assessments, directors of religious education, principals, catechists, and teachers should register online with this **access code: FG-JrHigh.**

Directors of Religious Education and Principals

▶ **Director Guide Supplements:** Retreat plans for introducing the program.

▶ **Family E-Newsletters:** Offered seven times a year. **Available in English and Spanish.**

▶ **Catechist Training Plans:** A wonderful retreat that helps prepare catechists for the upcoming year.

Catechists and Teachers

▶ **Activity Finder:** Hundreds of activities for every grade level, grouping, and learner.

▶ **Blackline Masters:** For easy access, all program Blackline Masters are also available as PDFs online. In addition, vocabulary development blackline masters are provided.

▶ **Lesson Planner:** Fast and easy to use. Takes the guesswork out of lesson planning.

▶ **Assessments:** Session and unit assessments are available as printable PDFs.

▶ **Faith in Action Projects:** Additional ideas for each unit.

▶ **Faith in Action Prayer Services:** Printable PDFs for Prayer Services for every Faith in Action theme.

Families

▶ **Finding God: At-Home Edition:** For homeschoolers or for long absences. Provides everything for families to complete the program independently at home.

▶ **Glossaries in English and Spanish:** A definition for every vocabulary word in the program.

▶ **Family E-Newsletters:** Offered seven times a year. **Available in English and Spanish.**

Young People

▶ **Interactive Session Reviews:** To test comprehension and prepare for upcoming assessments.

▶ **Online Games:** An entertaining and educational way to reinforce content.

▶ **Glossaries in English and Spanish:** A definition for every vocabulary word in the program.

Loyola Press Web Sites

LOYOLAPRESS.com

- ▶ **3-Minute Retreats online:** Available in English and Spanish for your computer, iPhone®, or iPad®. Great for personal use or to open sessions or meetings.
- ▶ **Sunday Connection:** Useful background and activities to explain the upcoming Sunday's Scripture readings.
- ▶ **Family, Faith, and Fun:** Fun activities to help parents see family life as an opportunity to recognize the grace of God.
- ▶ **Saint Resources:** Activities, biographies, reflections, and stories.
- ▶ **Our Catholic Faith Resources:** Articles, activities, and facts about Catholic life.
  Note: Be sure young people are closely supervised by adults when on the Internet.

Ignatian Spirituality.com

- ▶ **What Is Ignatian Spirituality?** Relevant articles and information about Saint Ignatius of Loyola and his teachings.
- ▶ **Ignatian Prayer:** A variety of prayers developed or inspired by Saint Ignatius.
- ▶ **Making Good Decisions:** Information on discernment, spiritual direction, and life vocations.
- ▶ **Ignatian Voices:** Articles and biographies about those inspired by Ignatian spirituality.
- ▶ **Ignatian Community:** Connections to Jesuit and Ignatian organizations and communities.

Other 6.com

- ▶ **Online Community:** An inspirational place to connect with other Catholics and to answer two profound questions:
  - Where have you found God today?
  - Where do you need to find God today?

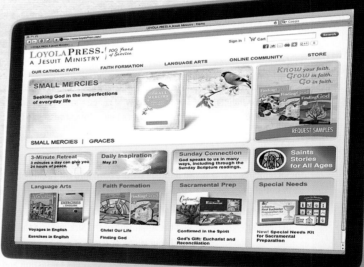

Other Online Offerings

- ▶ DREConnect.com
- ▶ CatechistsJourney.com
- ▶ DeepeningFriendship.com
- ▶ PeopleforOthers.com

Unit	Session	Session Theme	Scripture	CCC References	
1 God, Our Creator and Father	**1** The Bible, God's Story	In the Bible, God reveals himself to us, especially in the life, Death, and Resurrection of Jesus Christ.	2 Peter 1:20–21; Deuteronomy 30:19–20	121–123, 128–130	
	2 God Creates the World	The human family is created in the image and likeness of God.	Genesis 1:1—3:24; Psalm 8:5–7	282–289	
	3 Sin and Salvation	The root of sin is lack of trust in God and disobedience to his commands.	Genesis 2:15—3:24, 3:15, 4:1–16, 6:5—9:17; Proverbs 3:5–6; 1 John 1:9; Jeremiah 17:7	402–411	
	4 Abraham Listens to God	God calls Abraham and Sarah to believe in him.	Genesis 15:1–5, 18:1–10, 22:1–13; Galatians 3:7; Matthew 1:18–21; Luke 2:8–14; Mark 1:12–13	59, 72, 165, 762, 992, 1819, 2571	
	5 Celebrating Ordinary Time	Ordinary Time is a time to grow in the love of Jesus Christ.	Psalm 25:5		
2 Jesus, Our Lord and Savior	**6** God Is Faithful	God helps people overcome sinful choices.	Genesis 25:19–34, 27:1–45, 29:15–30	207, 211, 302–314	
	7 Passover and the Eucharist	Jesus calls us to a new covenant.	Exodus 1:1—2:10, 2:11—3:17; Psalm 23	1322–1405	
	8 God Leads His People	The Exodus describes the covenant between God and the Israelites.	Exodus 12:31—13:22, 14:5–31; Psalm 51	2056–2063	
	9 Being Faithful to God	David and Ruth made choices that helped prepare the way for Jesus.	2 Samuel 11:1–27; Matthew 20:30	1731–1738	
	10 Celebrating Advent	Advent is a time to appreciate the people who accompany us as we travel toward Jesus and plan to celebrate his birth.	Isaiah 11:9; James 5:8		
3 The Church, Our Community in the Spirit	**11** God's Presence in the Temple	The Church is the new temple of the Holy Spirit.	1 Kings 6:1—8:26, 7:13–51; John 2:19,22	308, 1373–1377	
	12 Psalms, the Prayers of Jesus	The psalms help us learn how to pray, and Wisdom Literature gives us practical advice on how to live.	Psalm 20, 104:30, 51:4, 118:17, 96:12–13, 23:1–4; Genesis 31:40; Sirach 18:11–12	2585–2589	
	13 The Mission of the Church	The mission of the Church is to proclaim Jesus' presence today.	Matthew 5:16; Acts of the Apostles 2:1–41	783–786	
	14 Marks of the Church	The Church is one, holy, catholic, and apostolic.	Luke 1:46–55, 1:49; Jeremiah 31:33; Ephesians 4:1–6,15–16	811–865	
	15 Celebrating Christmas	Christmas is a time to celebrate Jesus' birth and the coming of the Wise Men.	Matthew 2:1–2, 2:10–11		
4 Sacraments, Our Way of Life	**16** Prophets Challenge the People	The prophets who called the Chosen People to repentance and conversion were powerful witnesses to God.	Isaiah 6:1–8, 40:1	61, 64, 218	
	17 Prophets Give Hope	The prophets bring words of hope and encouragement.	Isaiah 40:1, 7:14, 40:3, 53:4, 53:7, 50:6, 9:1; Psalm 143; Matthew 4:16	128–130	
	18 Sacraments of Initiation	In Baptism we are born into the family of Jesus; this bond is strengthened in the Eucharist and Confirmation.	John 6:53–54; Ephesians 2:21–22; 1 Peter 2:4–5; Psalm 118:22	1213–1314	
	19 Sacraments of Healing	In celebrating the Sacraments of Penance and Reconciliation and the Anointing of the Sick, we find the healing presence of God in our everyday lives.	Isaiah 35:5–6, 66:18	1420–1525	
	20 Celebrating Lent and Holy Week	Lent and Holy Week are times for fasting and prayer.	Matthew 22:39		
5 Morality, Our Lived Faith	**21** Jesus' Way of Love	Jesus calls us to practice the virtues of faith, hope, and charity.	I Corinthians 13:1–13; Deuteronomy 6:4–5	1812–1829	
	22 Sacraments of Service	In the Sacraments of Holy Orders and Matrimony, Christians are called to holiness.	Leviticus 11:44	1536–1666	
	23 Caring for the Earth	All of creation is a gift from God, and the goods of the earth are to be used in ways that honor God.	Genesis 1:28–31; Psalm 96:11–13	339–343, 2415–2418	
	24 Jesus' Call for Justice	As Christians we are called to support the common good and the fundamental rights of each person.	I John 4:21; James 2:14–26	1868–1869, 1905–1917	
	25 Celebrating Easter	Easter is a time to celebrate the great story of our Salvation from the time of our ancestors in faith into the future.	Genesis 1:28		

A sixth unit includes separate sessions for these liturgical seasons and feast days: Advent, Christmas, Lent, Holy Week, Easter, Pentecost, and All Saints Day.

Words Learned	Saints and Holy People	Prayers / Parts of the Mass	Catholic Social Teaching Themes	Service Suggestion
inspired, interpretation, Magisterium, scriptorium, Vulgate	St. Jerome St. Frances Xavier Cabrini Abraham Sarah Adam Eve Noah Cain Abel Isaac	Prayer to the Holy Spirit	Family and Community	Share a Bible Passage
culture, exile, racism, sexism			God's Creation, Poor and Vulnerable, Solidarity, Life and Dignity	A Class Service Project
Garden of Eden		Hail Mary	Family and Community	Community Cards
Chosen People, Patriarchs		Act of Hope	Life and Dignity	Pen-Pal Project
		Liturgy of the Word	Poor and Vulnerable	Organize a Shoe Drive
Divine Providence	St. John Neumann Jacob Esau Abraham Moses King David	Morning Offering	Family and Community, Rights and Responsibilities	Tutor Children
Eastern Catholic Churches, Eucharistic Liturgy, Israelite, Pharaoh, Sabbath, Yahweh		Psalm 23	Solidarity	Donate Items
Canaan, Exodus, manna		Ten Commandments	Solidarity, Rights and Responsibilities	Serve a Meal
Jerusalem		Prayer of Forgiveness	Solidarity, Rights of Workers	Research Fair Trade
Jesse tree			Life and Dignity	Homemade Recording
Ark of the Covenant, discrimination, Holy of Holies, sacrifice	St. Helena Solomon Mary Three Magi	Dwell in Us, O Holy Spirit, The Sacrament of Holy Orders	Family and Community	Parish Cleanup
communal prayer, Liturgy of the Hours, personal prayer, Wisdom Literature		Liturgy of the Word	Family and Community	Psalm Card
crucified		The Lord's Prayer	Family and Community	Thank-You Cards
Nicene Creed		Nicene Creed	Solidarity	Letter-Writing Campaign
Epiphany			Poor and Vulnerable	Used Coat Drive
prophets, reform, seraphim	St. Ignatius of Loyola Dorothy Day Amos Jeremiah Isaiah Matthew	Send Me, Lord	Solidarity, Poor and Vulnerable	"I Care" Kits
Promised Land		Praying a Psalm	Solidarity	Donate Toys
catechumen, Easter Vigil		Eucharist, Holy Communion	Family and Community	Letter to Catechumen
euthanasia		Act of Contrition	Life and Dignity	Prayer Cards
fasting			Family and Community	Nursing-Home Letters
canonize, Doctor of the Church	St. Benedict of Palermo St. Catherine of Siena St. Thérèse of Lisieux St. Teresa of Ávila Pope John Paul II	Act of Faith	Life and Dignity, Poor and Vulnerable	Donate to Child
presbyter		Sacrament of Matrimony, Holy Orders, Prayer of Guidance	Family and Community, Solidarity	Prayers for Clergy
encyclical		Act of Love, *Magnificat*	Solidarity, God's Creation	Conserve Energy
natural law			Life and Dignity, Rights and Responsibilities, Family and Community	Letter Defending Human Rights
			Family and Community	Spring Cleanup

Unit	Session	Session Theme	Scripture	CCC References
1 One True Faith	**1** Three Persons in One God	The Trinity is the central mystery of our Christian faith and life.	Genesis 1:26–31; Luke 9:23	232–260
	2 Jesus Is the Answer to a Promise	John the Baptist announced the coming of Jesus, the promised Messiah.	Genesis 17:1–8; Luke 1:5–13,39–41, 3:1–6,9–14, 7:24–35; Matthew 11:7–19; Mark 1:3,7–8,10–11; John 1:1–5,29,34; Ezekiel 1:10; Revelation 4:78; Exodus 3:14, 6:30—7:1	101–133
	3 Jesus Reveals God to Us	Jesus fulfills the Revelation of God found in the history of the Chosen People.	Genesis 9:16, 17:5, 22:17; Exodus 19—20, 32:1–30; Matthew 1:1–17, 2:15; Luke 22:20; Mark 15:39; John 15:15; 2 Samuel 11	238, 781, 1102, 1612, 2058
	4 Jesus Calls Us to Say Yes	Mary was the first person to say yes to Jesus and experience God's grace.	Luke 1:26–38,42, 10:29–37; Isaiah 7:14; Genesis 6:8, 17:19, 18:2–3; Exodus 33:12–17; 2 Samuel 15:25; Psalm 28:7, 121:1–2; Ephesians 1:2	484–511
	5 Celebrating Ordinary Time	Ordinary Time is a time to grow as a disciple of Christ.	James 1:19–22; Matthew 10:8, 16:24, 25:40, 28:19	1397, 1928–1942, 2425–2426
2 The Early Life of Jesus	**6** Jesus Became One of Us	The Incarnation is Jesus Christ, the Son of God, made flesh. Jesus is our model of humanity.	Mark 2:1–12, 8:27, 12:28–34, 14:36; Matthew 5:13–14, 11:25, 14:22–33, 26:36–46; John 1:1–5,14, 2:13–16, 3:16, 10:30, 11:34–35,41–44, 14:6–7, 15:12–17; Luke 5:5–11, 8:1–3, 11:2–4; Philippians 2:6–7	456–478
	7 Jesus Is God with Us	The names for Jesus are connected to Salvation History. God calls us by name and speaks to us.	Matthew 1:18–21,23, 18:20, 28:20; Isaiah 7:13–14, 9:5–6, 11:1–2, 43:1; Genesis 15:1; Psalm 77	430–451
	8 Jesus Is for All People	The hardships in Jesus' early life fulfilled prophecies.	Luke 1:33, 2:1,4–5,7,13–14, 17:21; Wisdom 7:4–6; John 10:11; 1 Corinthians 1:27–29; Matthew 2:6,15,18,23; Psalm 22, 34:4–8	522–524
	9 Jesus Grew in Wisdom, Age, and Grace	Jesus begins to understand that God, his Father, is calling him to a special mission.	Luke 2:41–52; Mark 3:21,31–35; Matthew 10:7–8; Ephesians 4:25	532–534
	10 Celebrating Advent and Christmas	We prepare our hearts during the season of Advent to celebrate the birth of Jesus at Christmas.	Isaiah 42:16; John 8:12; 1 Timothy 6:11–16; 2 Samuel 22:29; Job 12:22; Romans 13:11–12; Luke 2:1–7,11,19; Psalm 96:1–2,7–8,11–13	522–534
3 The Public Life of Jesus	**11** Jesus Prepares for His Ministry	Jesus accepted his mission as Messiah and renounced Satan's temptations.	Luke 3:11,13–14,16,21–22, 4:1–13; Hebrews 4:15; Matthew 4:1–11, 13:3–9,18–23; Romans 13:1	1803–1811
	12 Jesus Performs Signs	Jesus' signs reveal that he is the one who fulfills the Father's promise to humankind with abundance.	John 2:1–12, 6:9–13, 10:10, 20:23; Genesis 2:24, 41:55; Matthew 18:21–35, 19:8, 28:19; Luke 22:19	1145–1162
	13 Jesus Is Our Teacher	In the Beatitudes, Jesus invites everyone to happiness in this life and eternal joy in the next.	Matthew 5:3–10,23–24, 6:32, 13:18–33,36–50, 23:27; John 14:6; Luke 8:10, 15:3–7, 17:21; Mark 4:30–32; 1 Corinthians 2:6–16	1716–1724
	14 Jesus Heals and Forgives	Forgiveness, a key message of Jesus' ministry, is given to us in the Sacrament of Reconciliation.	Mark 1:29–31, 2:1–12, 5:35–43, 6:6–13, 9:27–31; Matthew 18:22; John 9:1–41, 20:22–23; Numbers 21:8; James 5:14–15	1420–1532
	15 Celebrating Lent	We imitate the life of Christ by performing Lenten practices of prayer, fasting, and almsgiving.	Philippians 2:5; Matthew 20:34, 26:39, 28:20; Luke 22:25–26; John 13:15, 14:18; Mark 1:15, 8:37; Joel 2:12–17	541–553
4 Jesus the Christ	**16** Jesus Gives Us Himself	In the Eucharist, we recognize the Real Presence of Jesus Christ at the consecration.	Luke 9:11–17, 14:12–14, 22:7–20; Matthew 25:31–46; Acts of the Apostles 2:42; Psalm 46:11	1356–1381
	17 Jesus Makes a Choice	We are called to stay true to our identities as sons and daughters of God.	Genesis 2:18; Mark 14:34,36; Luke 22:44–46; Matthew 26:38–39; 1 Corinthians 8; Romans 12:9–12; Numbers 6:24–26	1750–1754
	18 Jesus Redeems Us	Jesus' glory is revealed through his suffering, Death, and Resurrection.	1 Corinthians 5:7; Mark 8:29,33–35, 9:7, 15:33–39; Isaiah 53:11; Luke 23:34; Matthew 25:31–46	571–635
	19 Jesus Brings Us New Life	We find Christ's presence in prayer, in the Christian community, and in the sacraments.	Mark 8:34, 10:45, 16:1–7; 1 Corinthians 15:54–55; Luke 18:22, 22:19–20, 24:48–49; John 3:5, 15:12–15; Acts 8:14–17; Matthew 22:36–40	1210–1419
	20 Celebrating Holy Week and Easter	Jesus' Resurrection opens the promise of eternal life with him in Heaven.	John 13:15; 1 Corinthians 2:9	638–655, 1020–1050
5 Jesus Lives On	**21** Jesus Opens Our Eyes	Jesus' pathway through his life, Death, Resurrection, and Ascension is our path.	John 3:18–19, 15:13, 20:16,26–28, 21: 4–7; Luke 24:13–35; Acts of the Apostles 1:9–11; Ben Sira 14:3–19; Genesis 2:15; 1 Corinthians 3:9, 12:4–6; Matthew 5:14–16	282–289, 378, 901, 1609, 1914, 2427
	22 Jesus Sends Us Forth with His Spirit	We celebrate the Holy Spirit's presence within us and within the Church.	Acts of the Apostles 1:8, 2:3; Isaiah 11:2; Romans 8:14; Matthew 5:16	737–747
	23 We Are Called and Sent	Like Saint Paul, God calls us to conversion. Saint Paul's words are also meant for us.	Acts of the Apostles 9:4; Colossians 3:12–13; 1 Corinthians 13:13; Ephesians 4:31–32	1533–1666
	24 Jesus Calls Us to Eternal Life	Mary's Assumption reflects her exalted place in the Communion of Saints.	Revelation 21:3–4, 22:20; Matthew 25:31–32; Luke 4:18–19, 24:50–53; John 11:17–27	963–972
	25 Celebrating Pentecost	The Church began with the sending of the Holy Spirit on Pentecost.	John 14:18,26; Acts of the Apostles 2:2–3, 17:28; Galatians 5:22–23	2623–2625, 2670– 2672

An additional section, The Year in Our Church, includes sessions for these liturgical seasons and feast days: Advent, Christmas, Lent, Holy Week, Easter, Pentecost, and All Saints Day. The Scope and Sequence for this section is on page 221a.

Words to Know	Saints and Holy People	Prayers / Parts of the Mass	Catholic Social Teaching Themes
Catholic Social Teaching, common good, Creator, disciple, faith, free will, mystery, sacramentals, subsidiary, Trinity	St. Augustine, Pope Benedict XVI, John the Baptist, Mary, Zechariah and Elizabeth, Abraham, Isaac, Jacob, David, Joseph, Pope John Paul II, Moses, Noah, the angel Gabriel, Sarah, St. Ignatius of Loyola, St. Paul, the Apostles, St. Thérèse of Lisieux, St. Vincent de Paul	Daily Examen, Sign of the Cross	All seven Catholic Social Teaching themes
Acts of the Apostles, Ascension, canon, Covenant, Gospels, Original Sin, precursor, prophet, priest, Resurrection, Son of God, Tradition		Scripture reflection and petitions, Lord's Prayer	Rights and Responsibilities, Solidarity
Abraham, genealogy, Israelites, Revelation		Litany of Thanksgiving	Work and Workers
actual grace, Annunciation, grace, habitual grace, Immaculate Conception, intercession, sanctifying grace		guided reflection, Hail Mary, *Suscipe*	Life and Dignity
convocation, Corporal Works of Mercy, Great Commission, Ordinary Time, Spiritual Works of Mercy		Prayers of Intention for Those Who Are Sick	Family and Community, Life and Dignity, Solidarity
catholic, consubstantial, dignity of the human person, Great Commandment, heresy, Incarnation, *lectio divina*, miracle, missionary, novices	Blessed Marie of the Incarnation, St. Paul, St. Damien of Molokai, the angel Gabriel, Mary, Joseph, the Magi, Moses, the Apostles, Jacob, David, St. Francis of Assisi, Pope John Paul II, St. John Bosco	Daily Examen, Nicene Creed, Lord's Prayer, *lectio divina*	Life and Dignity
adoration, Christ, Emmanuel, Infancy Narrative, monstrance		guided reflection	Family and Community, Life and Dignity
census, Magi, novena, prophecy, refugees, solidarity, swaddling		novena, Psalm 34:4–8	Solidarity
Cardinal Virtues, domestic church, Passover		guided reflection	Family and Community
Advent, Christmas, feast days, Feast of Our Lady of Guadalupe, Holy Day of Obligation, Nativity, sanctuary		Christmas novena *Simbang Gabi*, Psalm 96:1–2,7–8,11–13	Family and Community, Life and Dignity
bishops, epiphany, Evangelists, ministry, parable, pope, Satan, temptation	the Evangelists, Matthew, Mark, Luke, and John; John the Baptist; St. Thomas Becket; Pedro Arrupe, S.J.; St. Thomas Aquinas; Joseph, son of Jacob; Mary; Blessed Miguel Pro; Moses; the Apostles; St. Peter; St. Paul	Daily Examen, Prayer of Saint Thomas Aquinas	Rights and Responsibilities, God's Creation
penance, repentance, rite, sacraments, signs		the Rosary, *lectio divina*	Family and Community, Rights and Responsibilities
Beatitudes, Kingdom of God, Kingdom of Heaven, Magisterium, Sermon on the Mount		Prayer to See as God Sees	Life and Dignity, Family and Community
blasphemy, capital sins, contrition, imperfect contrition, mortal sins, perfect contrition, sacramental seal, Second Vatican Council, venial sins		*lectio divina*, Act of Contrition	Life and Dignity
abstain, Advocate, almsgiving, Ash Wednesday, conversion, fasting, Lent, Pentecost		Prayer of Renewal, Jesus Prayer, *Kyrie*, the Rosary, Stations of the Cross, Lord's Prayer	Poor and Vulnerable, Solidarity, Family and Community
Institution Narrative, Last Supper, liturgy, Mystical Body of Christ, Pharisees, Real Presence, transubstantiation	St. Teresa Benedicta of the Cross; St. John Chrysostom; Pope John Paul II; the Apostles; St. Katharine Drexel; St. Paul; John the Baptist; St. Peter; James and John; Elijah; Moses; Mary Magdalene; Mary, the mother of James; Salome; Nicodemus	Daily Examen, petition, Institution Narrative	Family and Community, Solidarity
Agony in the Garden, conscience, moral choice, social sin		Prayer to Act in Good Conscience	Rights and Responsibilities
Apostles' Creed, Paschal Mystery, Passion, Transfiguration		Apostles' Creed, guided reflection, Lord's Prayer	Family and Community
doxology, marginalized, social justice		Eucharistic Prayer in the Concluding Doxology, petitions	Solidarity, Family and Community
Easter Vigil, *Exsultet*, indulgence, particular judgment, Purgatory, Stations of the Cross, Triduum		Daily Examen, Stations of the Cross, Liturgy of the Word, Liturgy of the Eucharist	Family and Community, Poor and Vulnerable, Life and Dignity
consumerism, dignity of work, Epistle, the Way	St. Maximilian Mary Kolbe, Monsignor George Higgins, Pope Benedict XVI, the Emmaus disciples, St. Julie Billiart, the Apostles, St. Paul, Mary, St. Juan Diego, Pope Pius XII, St. John Vianney	Daily Examen, Litany of Gratitude	Family and Community, God's Creation
Chrism, Gifts of the Holy Spirit, Good News		virtuous circle reflection, Prayer to the Holy Spirit	Solidarity
chastity, deacons, Holy Orders, justification, Matrimony, obedience, poverty, righteousness		Prayer for Conversion, Lord's Prayer	Rights and Responsibilities, Family and Community
apocalyptic literature, Assumption, Communion of Saints, infallibly, Last Judgment, literary forms, Theological Virtues		Prayer for Faith, Hope, and Charity	Rights and Responsibilities
Paraclete		Petitions to the Holy Spirit, Saint Augustine's Prayer to the Holy Spirit	Family and Community

Suggestions for service projects appear at the end of each session.
Faith-in-Action opportunities conclude each unit.

Unit	Session	Session Theme	Scripture	CCC References
1 The Early Church	**1** Jesus' Message	We are called to follow Peter's example by proclaiming the Good News to others.	John 21:15–19; Matthew 6:9–14; Acts of the Apostles 2:1–13	696, 731, 1287, 2623, 2769–2865
	2 The Church Grows	Following the example of the Church leaders at the Council of Jerusalem, we are called to welcome all those who want to join the Church.	Acts 10:11–15,44–48; Ephesians 4:1–6; Psalm 145:9–11; Isaiah 49:16	839–848
	3 Witnesses to the Faith	The early Christian martyrs were faithful to Jesus, even in the face of adversity.	Acts of the Apostles 6:5, 7:60	946–962, 1173, 2113, 2473–2474
	4 The Catechumenate in the Early Church	The Sacraments of Initiation welcome us into the community of believers known as the Church.	Matthew 28:19; John 3:5	1113–1134
	5 Celebrating Ordinary Time	During Ordinary Time we reflect on our call to discipleship.	Luke 1:46–55	165, 272, 437, 456, 484–485, 490, 501
2 We Belong	**6** We Believe	During the early ecumenical councils, Church leaders reflected on Jesus' relationship with God the Father. The fruit of their reflection is contained in the Nicene Creed, a prayer through which we profess our love and devotion to God.	Matthew 5:1–12, 28:1–10	464–478
	7 Praise God in Worship	We grow in our relationship with God when we live by the first three commandments.	Genesis 1:28; Psalm 8:2,4–10; Matthew 6:19–21	2084–2167
	8 Monasteries and Community	Practicing the virtues of poverty, chastity, and obedience helps us follow Jesus' example and live peacefully with others.	Matthew 5:3; Ben Sira 6:14–16	914–927
	9 Sent on a Mission	Just like early missionaries, we are called to spread the Good News to others.	Mark 4:21; John 4:4–42, 20:11–18	849–865
	10 Celebrating Advent and Christmas	During Advent we prepare for Jesus' coming, which we celebrate during the Christmas season.	Romans 10:10–13; Book of Isaiah; Luke 1:26–38	522–530
3 We Worship	**11** The Church and Society	The Marks of the Church are one way we express our unity as a community of believers.	Psalm 133:1, 100:2–3	813–865
	12 The Great Cathedrals and Worship	For generations, Catholics have gathered in churches and cathedrals to celebrate the sacraments—the foundation of Catholic life.	John 1:1–5; 1 Corinthians 6:19	1113–1134
	13 Nourished by the Eucharist	Participating in the celebration of the Eucharist unites us as members of the Body of Christ.	Acts of the Apostles 2:42–47, 4:32–37; Matthew 26:26–30	1322–1419
	14 Serving Physical and Spiritual Needs	We care for people's physical and spiritual needs by following the example of the Church. The Sacraments of Service give people the grace to do so in unique ways.	1 Samuel 3:1–9; John 2:1–11	1554–1580, 1601–1632
	15 Celebrating Lent	During Lent, we prepare for the coming of the Lord by asking for forgiveness and praying for strength to live as the People of God.	1 John 1:5–10	540, 1095, 1438
4 We Are Called	**16** The Protestant Reformation	We find our calling from God by focusing our hearts and minds on listening to what God asks of us.	James 2:21–24,26; Psalm 138:1,3,7,8	1020–1050
	17 Renewal in the Church	Making good, moral decisions is not always easy, but we can find support and forgiveness in God.	Matthew 5:23–24; Numbers 6:24–26	1420–1470
	18 The Church Reaches Out	We cultivate our relationship with God by living his will every day.	Psalm 1:1–3	2258–2283, 2331–2400, 2514–2533
	19 Faith and Reason	Faith is possible because we believe God is the truth, and we trust him wholeheartedly.	Exodus 20:1–17	1749–1761, 2401–2425, 2464–2499, 2534–2557
	20 Celebrating Holy Week and Easter	The Church celebrates Jesus' life, Passion, Death, and Resurrection during Holy Week and Easter so that we may be reminded of Jesus' sacrifice for our Salvation.	Matthew 5:69–75, 25:35–40; 26:14–16,47–56	1168–1171, 1813, 1817–1821
5 We Are Sent	**21** Truth Revealed by God	In response to the modernism movement, the Church developed new ways to reach followers.	Matthew 9:16–17	2477, 2479, 2507, 2479
	22 Acting on Behalf of Justice	We build up the Kingdom of God by working to end injustices and answering God's call to serve.	Matthew 5:3–12, 25:35–36,40; John 13:1; Romans 5:5	1397, 1928–1942, 2425–2426
	23 Called by God	We respond to God's call of holiness by serving others and spreading God's grace.	1 Peter 2:4–5; 1 Corinthians 12:4–11; Matthew 9:35–38	9–10
	24 People for Others	We respond to God's call using our unique talents.	Luke 4:18–19; Matthew 25:34–40	1458, 1473, 1815, 1879, 1853, 2044, 2447
	25 Celebrating Pentecost	Pentecost reminds us that as members of the Church, we support one another in fulfilling the Church's mission.	Acts of the Apostles 2:2–4; John 10:10; Matthew 10:26–35; Isaiah 61:1–2	731–747

An additional section, The Year in Our Church, includes sessions for these liturgical seasons and feast days: Advent, Christmas, Lent, Holy Week, Easter, Pentecost, and All Souls Day. The Scope and Sequence for this section is on page 221a.

Words to Know	Saints and Holy People	Prayers / Parts of the Mass	Catholic Social Teaching Themes
Beatitudes, Church, Gentiles, Kingdom of God, Lord, martyr, Messiah, mission, Pentecost, Salvation, Transfiguration	St. Peter, St. James, St. John, St. Matthias, Pope Benedict XVI, Mary, St. Paul, St. Cornelius, St. Barnabas, St. Augustine, Tertullian, St. Stephen, St. Polycarp, St. Perpetua, St. Felicity, Adam and Eve, St. Nicodemus, St. Teresa of Ávila, Pope Gregory III, Pope Gregory XII, St. Francis de Sales, St. Aloysius Gonzaga, St. Teresa Benedicta of the Cross, St. Frances Xavier Cabrini	Daily Examen	Solidarity, Rights and Responsibilities, Family and Community, God's Creation
converts, Council of Jerusalem, Eucharist, grace, Pharisee		Nicene Creed	Family and Community, Solidarity
blasphemy, catechumen, charism, Communion of Saints, Gifts of the Holy Spirit, intercessors, relics, Sanhedrin		Litany of the Saints	Rights and Responsibilities, Family and Community, Solidarity
age of reason, catechumenate, character, justice, liturgy, neophyte		Liturgy of the Word, Liturgy of the Eucharist, baptismal promises	Family and Community, Rights and Responsibilities, Solidarity
Assumption, canonization, *Magnificat*, sacramentals, venerate		*Magnificat*	Rights and Responsibilities, Family and Community, Solidarity
communal prayer, consubstantial, ecumenical councils, faith, heresies, incarnate, Magisterium, monastery, Mother of God, Nicene Creed, Paschal Mystery, Trinity	St. Benedict; St. Scholastica; Constantine; Mary; St. Gregory the Great; Pope Leo I the Great; Moses; St. Basil; St. Augustine; St. Albert; St. Robert; St. Dominic; St. Ignatius of Loyola; St. Anthony; St. Peter; St. Paul; St. Patrick; St. Columban; St. Boniface; St. Priscilla; St. Phoebe; Sisters Maura Clarke, Ita Ford, and Dorothy Kazel; Jean Donovan; Pope Benedict XVI; St. Thérèse of Lisieux; Isaiah; St. Gabriel; St. John the Baptist; St. Hildegard of Bingen; St. Francis of Assisi	baptismal promises, Nicene Creed, Daily Examen	Solidarity
adoration, Doctor of the Church, doctrine, Gregorian chant, idolatry, Real Presence, Sabbath		Eucharistic adoration	Rights and Responsibilities, Family and Community, God's Creation, Solidarity
consecrate, culture, evangelical counsels, monasticism, temperance, theologian		Lord's Prayer	Family and Community, Rights and Responsibilities, Poor and Vulnerable
meditation, missionaries, New Evangelization, personal prayer		meditation	Family and Community
antiphon, apologists, crèche, Emmanuel, heralds, Liturgy of the Hours, repentance, Second Coming		O Antiphons, Liturgy of the Hours, Prayer of Saint Richard of Chichester	Poor and Vulnerable
apostolic, atoned, holy, infallibility, Mendicant Orders, one, Orthodox Church, patriarch, *Summa Theologiae*, transubstantiation, Truce of God	St. Thomas Aquinas, Pope John Paul II, St. Francis of Assisi, St. Peter, Pope Innocent III, St. Catherine of Siena, Melchizedek, Abraham, Samuel, Pope Benedict XVI	Liturgy of the Eucharist, Daily Examen	Life and Dignity, Family and Community, Solidarity
cathedrals, piety, prayers of intercession, rites, Rosary, sanctify, spirituality		prayers of intercession, Rosary, Lord's Prayer	Family and Community
absolution, dogma, mortal sin, Precepts of the Church, Second Vatican Council		Liturgy of the Word, Liturgy of the Eucharist, Litany of the Blessed Sacrament of the Altar	Rights and Responsibilities, Poor and Vulnerable
annulment, deacon, Great Schism, Holy Orders, mystic, ordination, Sacraments at the Service of Communion		Prayer for Vocations	Family and Community, Life and Dignity, Solidarity
Rite of Christian Initiation of Adults, solidarity, temptation		baptismal promises, Act of Contrition	Family and Community
actual grace, free will, indulgences, Last Judgment, particular judgment, Purgatory, sanctifying grace	St. Angela Merici, Adam and Eve, Mary, St. Francis de Sales, St. Jeanne de Chantal, Pope John Paul II, St. Ignatius of Loyola, St. Frances Xavier, Blessed Peter Faber, St. Aloysius Gonzaga, St. Edmund Campion, St. Isaac Jogues, St. Peter Claver, Archbishop Oscar Romero, St. Vincent de Paul, St. Louise de Marillac, Blessed Frederick Ozanam, St. Peter	Responsorial Psalm, Liturgy of the Hours, Daily Examen	Poor and Vulnerable, Solidarity
catechism, personal sin, seminary, social sin, Ten Commandments, venial sin		Liturgy of the Eucharist, Lord's Prayer	Family and Community, Rights and Responsibilities, God's Creation
abortion, adultery, asceticism, chastity, covet, euthanasia, moral law, Spiritual Exercises		Spiritual Exercises, Daily Examen, Lord's Prayer	God's Creation, Life and Dignity
Age of Enlightenment, calumny, detraction, divine law, Fruits of the Holy Spirit, fundamentalists, rationalists		reflective prayer	Life and Dignity, God's Creation, Family and Community
Crucifixion, *Exsultet*, hope, Judaism, Triduum		Liturgy of the Eucharist, *Exsultet*	Poor and Vulnerable, Solidarity
evangelization, pantheism, *Syllabus of Errors*	Pope John XXIII, Pope Pius IX, Mary, Father Isaac Hecker, St. Ignatius of Loyola, Pope Leo XIII, Pope Benedict XVI, Pope John Paul II, Blessed Teresa of Calcutta, St. Martin of Tours, St. Louise de Marillac	Peace Prayer, Daily Examen	Life and Dignity, Family and Community
encyclical, Industrial Revolution, living wage, participation, subsidiarity		Litany to Heal Injustices	Life and Dignity, Family and Community, Solidarity, Work and Workers, Rights and Responsibilities
laity, synod		prayers of intercession	Poor and Vulnerable, Solidarity, Family and Community
beatified, contemplative, superior		Beatitudes, Peace Prayer	Rights and Responsibilities, Solidarity, Family and Community, Poor and Vulnerable
Fruits of the Holy Spirit, Jubilee Year		Sequence for Pentecost	Family and Community, Poor and Vulnerable

Suggestions for service projects appear at the end of each session.
Faith-in-Action opportunities conclude each unit.

The Daily Examen
in *Finding God* Grades 7–8

Approximately 500 years ago, Saint Ignatius of Loyola developed a daily way of praying that invited people to examine their lives so that they could better serve God. This prayer, the Daily Examen, is part of the *Spiritual Exercises*, a guide that includes retreats, meditations, prayers, and contemplative practices developed by Saint Ignatius.

Saint Ignatius believed that the key to healthy spirituality is to find God in all things and live in a way that helps people cooperate with God's will. The Daily Examen helps people develop a deeper relationship with God by inviting him to speak to their hearts as they discern his will in their lives. Prayed widely all over the world, this prayer is well-suited for anyone, including young people who are eager to reflect on and connect their thoughts and actions in daily life to God's will for them.

In the spirit of Saint Ignatius, *Finding God* Grades 7–8 opens each unit with a customized examen. Following are the basic steps of the Daily Examen as described by Jim Manney in *A Simple, Life-Changing Prayer*:

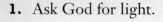

1. **Ask God for light.**

   I want to look at my day with God's eyes, not merely my own.

2. **Give thanks.**

   The day I have just lived is a gift from God. Be grateful for it.

3. **Review the day.**

   I carefully look back on the day just completed, being guided by the Holy Spirit.

4. **Face your shortcomings.**

   I face up to what is wrong—in my life and in me.

5. **Look toward the day to come.**

   I ask where I need God in the day to come.

More information about the Daily Examen can be found in the Praying Our Faith section of Prayers and Practices in the *Finding God* Young People's Book. Catechists are guided to lead young people through this explanation at the beginning of each unit so that young people are appropriately introduced to the prayer. Catechist scripting provides support through each prayer experience.

The Effective Catechist

A Catechist's Role

As a junior high catechist, you are responding to a call to share the gift of faith with a very special group of people—young people who are in the midst of great change. This call may have reached you through your child, pastor, the director of your parish's religious education program, or through your role as Catholic school teacher. But know this calling ultimately comes from God whose Holy Spirit inspires and guides you, and that this *Finding God* Catechist Guide was designed to accompany you every step of the way with abundant resources, practical tips, and support.

Fundamental Characteristics of Your Role

As catechists we yearn for the knowledge and skills that help us gently nurture young people to experience their faith. We ground our efforts in these fundamentals:

▶ a basic understanding of Catholic teaching, Scripture, and Catholic Tradition

▶ honest and respectful relationships with young people

▶ effective teaching methods and techniques

Qualities of an Effective Catechist

As catechists we share our personal faith and humanity. The ability to share authentically requires certain qualities that include

▶ a desire to grow in our faith

▶ an awareness of God's grace and the desire to respond to that grace

▶ a commitment to the Church's liturgical and sacramental life and moral teachings

▶ a strength of character built on patience, responsibility, confidence, and creativity

▶ required or voluntary training to protect God's children, such as Virtus training

▶ an understanding of the developmental level of the young people with whom you work. (See pages EC-2–EC-3.)

▶ a generosity of spirit, respect for diversity, and a habit of hospitality and inclusion

As you reflect on your role as a catechist, know that support abounds in *Finding God* Grades 7–8. Through the catechist preparation pages in this guide, the resources on **www.loyolapress.com**, and professional-development opportunities such as webinars and workshops, Loyola Press is your partner on the journey.

> As catechists we yearn for the knowledge and skills that help us gently nurture young people to experience their faith.

Junior High: A Time of Rapid Growth and Change

Young people in junior high are experiencing unparalleled developmental changes when compared to any other stage in their lives. Emotional, physical, and cognitive growth is sure to happen, yet at varying times and rates for each person. During this time of rapid transition, healthy relationships, moral guidance, and our faith tradition can provide young people with structure and stability. Here is a snapshot of traits common to many young people in junior high.

> Young people in junior high are experiencing unparalleled developmental changes.

Intellectual and Psychological Development

Young people often

- are increasingly capable of abstract thinking in regard to life and faith
- have an increased desire for approval and recognition from either peers or adults other than their parents
- have a high need to avoid failure or achieve in specific tasks
- strive to formulate a sense of identity and achieve balance between uniqueness and conformity, which can sometimes lead to inconsistency in behavior or low self-esteem
- seek autonomy while still wanting support and encouragement
- are hungry for active-learning experiences and higher-level reading material
- show high levels of curiosity
- display short attention spans
- experience anxiety, uneasiness, or moodiness due to physical and emotional changes

Moral Development

Young people often

- rely on a sense of trust, loyalty, and concern as a basis for making moral judgments
- define *justice* as "good actions should be rewarded, and bad actions should be punished"
- become increasingly sensitive to issues of right and wrong as they begin to encounter decisions that have serious moral consequences
- use independent thinking and acting while still relying on others to follow rules, sometimes causing the questioning of authority
- take notice of gaps between the moral conduct and Christian faith of adults, sometimes causing them to show resentment toward authority
- experience tension in the formation of conscience due to physical or sexual development

Social Development

Young people often

- have a high need for relatedness, to be connected socially to others—which can lead to making socializing a priority, trying to impress certain groups of peers, or showing concern for others

- have a high need for affiliation with peer groups, distancing themselves from family; those with an extremely high need for affiliation may be more susceptible to peer pressure

- are capable of serving others, but sometimes need to be encouraged to be more generous or purposeful with their time

- focus on their appearance and require great amounts of affirmation and support

- maintain respect for parents and other adults while beginning to question their authority

- develop close friends

- become increasingly interested in the opposite sex

- want to be viewed as unique while still conforming to current trends

- begin to face challenging issues concerning money, smoking, alcohol, drugs, or sex

Spiritual Development

Young people often

- show increased conscience formation and the ability to form a strong personal relationship with Jesus

- see Jesus as a model and an ideal, one who guides them in struggle and offers unshakable hope in the Kingdom of God

- display newfound independence by doubting, questioning, or challenging faith while at the same time seeking a deeper understanding of the same

- begin to reject childhood notions of society, faith, Church, and God while at the same time embracing their faith roots, religious heritage, and Tradition

- develop their own sense of spiritual identity based on personal experience

- seek to discover their place in the Church and show eagerness to participate in projects that build up the Body of Christ

- desire more freedom for self-expression while still needing some structure and encouragement

Knowing that you will work with young people who are at such a critical stage in their development, use pages EC-4 to EC-14 to discover practical ways to motivate, inspire, and guide throughout the year.

> Young people often have a high need for relatedness.

Preparing a Sacred Space

When Jesus planned a special meal with his Apostles during Passover, he sent Peter and John ahead of him, saying, "Go and make preparations for us . . ." (Luke 22:8) In the same way, preparing the physical space for faith formation is important—especially for the often curious, active, and sometimes easily distracted young people in junior high. Here are some ideas for creating an inspiring learning environment.

Resources and Supplies

Every learning space provides its challenges. Whether you meet in a multipurpose room, a home, or your classroom, consider these suggestions to provide young people with what they want and need.

▶ Provide enough Bibles, books, and writing supplies so that each young person can have his or her own.

▶ When possible, provide technology tools.

▶ Have available facial tissues, bandages, trash cans, and perhaps a mirror (such as for young people who have just gotten contacts or braces). Invite young people to use the items independently, without calling attention to themselves.

▶ Place common art supplies, such as crayons, glue, and scissors, in a central area or in tubs. Label containers clearly.

▶ Designate a file box or drawer for extra handouts and assignments, sorted by date. When young people are absent, they can quietly retrieve their own work.

Lighting

Each person responds differently to lighting. To find the optimum lighting for your group, try one or more of the following suggestions over a period of time and adapt to your group's needs.

▶ Use half the lights in the space. Allow young people to sit where they feel most comfortable.

▶ When weather permits, teach outdoors or in a space with natural light.

▶ Cover bright white surfaces with colored paper or fabric.

▶ Permit young people to wear caps or sun visors if they seem to prefer low light.

▶ Use opaque curtains to shade window panes for young people who need soft illumination.

Audio

As with lighting, the need for quiet or noise varies among young people. Consider these suggestions as you experiment with audio for your group.

▶ During quiet times, permit young people who prefer background sound to use headphones and listen to the reflective music provided on the *Finding God* CDs.

▶ Allow young people to wear soft cotton or rubber ear plugs or headphones during assessments, reflections, or meditation.

▶ Encourage young people who need quiet to sit away from traffic and activity patterns.

▶ Carpet heavy traffic areas.

▶ Use tennis balls to cover the bottom of the legs of each young person's chair or desk.

▶ Provide private spaces for young people easily distracted by noise. Offer seats near the door or activity centers for young people who prefer sound.

Temperature

Each person has a different preference regarding room temperature. Young people who seem either lethargic or too energetic may be responding to temperature without even realizing it. To accommodate young people's varying needs, consider these ideas.

▶ Provide drinking water.

▶ Turn on a fan. Allow young people to sit near it if they wish.

▶ Use curtains to block the sun or drafts.

▶ Allow young people to wear a sweater or jacket.

Prayer Space and Table

Be sure to arrange a focal point with symbols that express the presence of the Word of God and communicate a sense of the sacred. Set up your own prayer space and table, using these suggestions.

▶ Display a small table prominently.

▶ Change the table cover for each liturgical season.

▶ Place on the table a Bible, small plant or flowers, and a candle.

▶ Consider adding one or more of the following elements to the table: bowl of holy water, crucifix, or religious image or statue.

Seating

Develop a seating arrangement that fosters community and is appropriate for the activity being experienced. Consider these ideas.

▶ Arrange seats in a large circle or semicircle for whole-group discussions.

▶ Organize several chairs around tables for small-group work.

▶ Provide for relaxed "open seating" of choice for silent reading or guided reflections.

▶ Allow young people to rotate through established "stations" to complete segments of a long assignment.

▶ Allow young people to take a 60-second break from time to time so that they can take time out and then return to an assignment.

Visuals

To give young people a sense of belonging and an awareness of sacred space, no matter your environment, consider the following ideas.

▶ Display a cross or crucifix prominently.

▶ Allow young people to decorate a door, wall, or bulletin board with themes from their learning.

▶ Display a *Finding God* poster, chosen from the set.

▶ Allow young people to bring in and display photographs or objects relevant to session topics.

"Go and make preparations for us . . ."

Luke 22:8

Motivating Young People

You can tell when a young person is motivated and engaged. Aside from obvious smiles or looks of satisfaction, these characteristics are also present—motivated young people are attracted to the subject matter and their experiences with that subject matter; they work through challenges and obstacles with persistence; and they show pride and obvious happiness in their accomplishments. So what can a catechist do to increase the motivation of young people and keep them engaged? Following are some suggestions.

Competence and Self-Worth

- Develop lessons that center around the interests and needs of young people.
- Clearly define expectations each time you meet.
- Clearly explain criteria for success and provide clear, immediate, and constructive feedback.
- Provide affirmation so that young people know they are important to you and to others, and that success in your group and in life is within their grasp.
- Model the behavior you'd like to see.
- With young people, establish reasonable rules.
- Allow water and restroom breaks.
- Acknowledge young people's achievements both inside and outside of your group.
- Keep an orderly setting.
- Invite young people to participate in daily tasks.
- Tell young people specifically what to remember for assessments.

Curiosity

- Avoid a consistent "read and discuss" format throughout an entire session. Change classroom activities frequently.
- Take young people's lead—when they show interest in a topic, pursue the topic further, even if it means going beyond the textbook.
- Provide information about a topic in a variety of ways—through word, song, video, and experience.
- Relate topics to young people's lives. Be sure connections are authentic and not superficial.

Originality and Self-Expression

- Build in time for creative projects that invite young people to express ideas and concerns.
- Encourage young people to share their talents, even if they do not directly relate to the subject matter.
- Know that even an audience of one is acceptable for sharing ideas. Not every project needs a production to be shared.
- Consider giving young people more choice in what they learn and how they learn.
- Celebrate ethnic diversity by inviting young people to share ideas and traditions from ancestral origins.

Healthy Relationships

- Attend young people's parish events and extra-curricular events outside of religious education.
- Show interest in young people's lives. Ask about a young person's day—and then listen.
- Let young people know that you and everyone else in the group have something to offer.
- Allow group activities such as discussion with a partner, cooperative learning in small groups, skits, and peer evaluation.
- Address bullying.

Presentation Tips

Jesus had a positive presence and the ability to communicate with enthusiasm, confidence, authority, hospitality, and sensitivity. Here are some ways that you can present your sessions in a similar way.

Use Technology and Media

Use media to enrich your presentations. Here are some ideas.

▶ During prayer or reflective experiences, play reflective music featured in the *Finding God* program.

▶ Project the daily **3-Minute Retreat** found at **www.loyolapress.com** and lead young people through it.

▶ Invite young people to experience the online activities at **www.findinggod.com**.

▶ Show movie clips or short films to bring concepts to life. The USCCB provides a list of recommended films. For movies with a rating of A-II, obtain parental permission for viewing and show only preselected scenes. Always preview films to be sure they are appropriate for the young people with whom you work.

Communicate with Care

As you work with young people, be sure to communicate with care by following these suggestions.

▶ Refer to each young person by name.

▶ Move around the room and use gestures and body movements.

▶ Make eye contact with each young person.

▶ Use facial expressions to show your enthusiasm, compassion, and kindness.

▶ Speak gently, confidently, and respectfully.

▶ Speak clearly and appropriately, varying your tone and volume.

Lead Lively Discussions

Try these tips to lead lively discussions.

▶ Read your session in advance, and highlight the questions you will ask. Think about the best way to ask the questions. For example, will you use a prop or a gesture to help illustrate the concept?

▶ Ask questions with enthusiasm.

▶ Rephrase questions if only a few young people raise their hands.

▶ Give young people "think time" (10–15 seconds) before calling on someone to answer.

▶ Affirm acceptable responses, and gently redirect incorrect responses.

Communicate with enthusiasm, confidence, authority, hospitality, and sensitivity.

Be Prepared

Scripture tells us, "[P]roclaim the word; be consistent whether it is convenient or inconvenient; convince, reprimand, encourage through all patience and teaching." (2 Timothy 4:2) And so it is with catechizing young people in junior high—catechists and teachers need to be prepared as well as patient. Preparedness is one of the best ways to assure good group management so that the time you spend with young people can be fun and worthwhile.

Develop Procedures

Young people feel safe when they know what is expected of them. Before meeting with young people, prepare a written list of procedures and routines that you can consistently reinforce. Here are some areas in which you may wish to establish processes.

▶ absence and tardy policies

▶ drop-off/pick-up

▶ acceptable items to bring to class

▶ setting up the space before you meet

▶ entering the class

▶ assigning seats

▶ conduct during prayer

▶ working in groups

▶ moving around the room

▶ answering questions

▶ getting coats or items from backpacks

▶ sharpening pencils

▶ leaving for restroom breaks

▶ turning in assignments

▶ cleaning up after class

> ...proclaim the word; be consistent whether it is convenient or inconvenient; convince, reprimand, encourage through all patience and teaching.
>
> *2 Timothy 4:2*

Implementing New Processes

Once procedures and routines have been developed and recorded, be sure to share the list with young people on the first day you meet as well as intermittently as needed. Take the time to go over the rules carefully and to model them. Time taken in the beginning of the year will make the rest of the year go more smoothly. Display posters for rules that are often forgotten. Teaching and practicing the processes expected of young people is essential to a successful classroom-management plan. Frequently praise young people for their adherence to the rules. Begin each session with group prayers of petition to develop a caring community and to help young people center on the love of Christ.

Worthwhile Incentives

Incentives are often useful to keep a group focused and learning. Try these ideas to keep your group motivated and on task.

▶ Develop and vote for a group name or motto that reflects discipleship or stewardship. Post the name or motto on the wall. With parental permission, take photos during significant experiences or service projects and post them on the wall. From time to time, discuss how your group lives up to its motto or name. Consider ordering or making T-shirts for the group.

▶ Develop a simple Web site to showcase young people's poetry, essays, drawings, or photos related to *Finding God*. Control content by posting the items yourself and not allowing comments.

▶ Offer young people a special "open discussion day" as a reward for behavior of your choice. On this special day, provide topics for discussion and allow young people to share their ideas freely for the entire meeting time.

Gentle Intervention and Redirection

When the catechist or teacher is calm and patient in reacting to situations and acts in carefully planned ways, conflicts can sometimes resolve themselves. As you get to know the group you're working with, consider these proactive means of intervention if a problem arises.

▶ Diffuse anxiety or conflict with well-meaning humor. Empathize, smile, and joke when appropriate.

▶ Be consistent and fair. Don't treat one young person's behavior different from another's.

▶ Allow young people to sit near friends as long as they don't disrupt the group. Separate young people as soon as they show they have difficulty maintaining respectful behavior. Allow a second chance the next time you meet.

▶ During discussion or quiet reflection time, walk around the room. Stand near young people who may be apt to disrupt the group.

▶ Use simple nonverbal cues to gain the group's attention. For example, you might establish a hand signal, turn on and off the lights, or play music to focus young people's attention.

▶ Naturally interject a young person's name into your scripting. For example, you might say: **It's easy to see, Tom, why we need to be a follower of Jesus'.**

▶ Begin directives with the word *I* rather than *You*. For example, you might say: **I need you to line up at the door so we're not late.** Follow up with a silent pause and wait for the desired behavior.

▶ Ignore harmless attention-seeking behavior, such as silly comments or other actions. Take this as a cue to make learning more active.

> Incentives are often useful to keep a group focused and learning.

Diversity

As a catechist you can help all young people recognize themselves in the story of Salvation History and celebrate the Church's diversity. This richness in diversity is reflected and celebrated throughout *Finding God*. Here are some examples.

Art

▶ Photographs in the Young People's Book portray people of various cultures and backgrounds.

▶ Sacred Art features display artworks from different heritages and time periods throughout Church history.

▶ Featured artists reflect the ethnic and cultural diversity of the Church.

Saints and Holy People

▶ Featured saints and holy people show diversity in culture, personality, and gifts from God.

▶ Brief biographies and informational sections honestly examine what it means to be part of a diverse Church and society.

Music

▶ Melodies and instrumental arrangements represent music styles from across the globe.

▶ Musical activities invite young people from all backgrounds to participate.

Ritual and Tradition

▶ A rich variety of traditions are integrated throughout the program.

▶ Draw on the popular devotions and prayer expressions in your community that respond to the needs of various ethnic and cultural groups.

▶ Catechist preparation pages include Together as One Parish features to help religious education programs and Catholic schools come together as one while celebrating the uniqueness of each situation.

> As a catechist you can help all young people recognize themselves in the story of Salvation History and celebrate the Church's diversity.

Inclusion: Special Needs

Among the young people you serve, some may have special needs. *Finding God* Grades 7–8 has Inclusion activities in each Catechist Guide that adapt teaching approaches so that all young people are included and can successfully enter into the faith experience. In addition, these Catholic resources offer suggestions for helping young people with special needs.

Inclusion Activities in the Guide

Inclusion: Look for the title *Inclusion* in the Catechist Guide to find lesson adaptations for young people with special needs in the following categories: attention disorders, autism spectrum disorders, chronic illness, cognitive differences, communication disorders, emotional needs, gifted, hearing impairments, physical challenges, vision challenges, and specific learning disorders.

Additional Resources

Autism Spectrum

Autism resources from the **National Catholic Partnership on Disability:**
www.ncpd.org/ministries-programs/specific/autism

Chronic Illness

An Apostolate of Persons with Chronic Illness or Disability:
www.cusan.org

Cognitive Differences

Resources from the **National Apostolate for Inclusion Ministry:**
www.nafim.org

Hearing Challenges

National Catholic Office for the Deaf:
www.ncod.org

Physical Challenges

Resources from the University of Dayton Institute for Pastoral Initiatives, **The Network of Inclusive Catholic Educators:**
http://ipi.udayton.edu/nice.htm

Vision Challenges

Xavier Society for the Blind:
www.xaviersocietyfortheblind.org

> Among the young people you serve, some may have special needs.

Long-Range Planning

The following is a sample long-range plan for faith formation sessions that take place from the end of August to early June. Additional implementation models can be found in the Director Quick-Start Guide. You can modify this plan to fit your needs, using page EC-13 or by accessing the customizable online lesson planner at **www.findinggod.com**.

AUGUST

Unit 1
Session 1 plus related Blackline Masters
The Year in Our Church Introduction
Optional Session Assessment (www.findinggod.com)

SEPTEMBER

Unit 1
Sessions 2 to 5 plus related Blackline Masters
Optional Session Assessments (www.findinggod.com)
Unit 1 Assessment

OCTOBER

Unit 2
Sessions 6 to 8 plus related Blackline Masters
All Saints Day / All Souls Day Seasonal Session
Optional Session Assessments (www.findinggod.com)

NOVEMBER

Unit 2
Sessions 9 and 10 plus related Blackline Masters
Advent Seasonal Session
Optional Session Assessments (www.findinggod.com)
Unit 2 Assessment

DECEMBER

Unit 3
Session 15 plus related Blackline Masters
Christmas Seasonal Session
Optional Session Assessment (www.findinggod.com)

JANUARY

Unit 3
Sessions 11 and 12 plus related Blackline Masters
Optional Session Assessments (www.findinggod.com)

FEBRUARY

Unit 3
Sessions 13 and 14 plus related Blackline Masters
Optional Session Assessments (www.findinggod.com)
Unit 3 Assessment

MARCH

Unit 4
Sessions 16 to 18 plus related Blackline Masters
Optional Session Assessments (www.findinggod.com)
Lent Seasonal Session

APRIL

Unit 4
Sessions 19 and 20 plus related Blackline Masters
Holy Week Seasonal Session
Easter Seasonal Session
Optional Session Assessments (www.findinggod.com)
Unit 4 Assessment

MAY

Unit 5
Sessions 21 to 24 plus related Blackline Masters
Pentecost Seasonal Session
Optional Session Assessments (www.findinggod.com)

JUNE

Unit 5
Session 25 plus related Blackline Masters
Optional Session Assessment (www.findinggod.com)
Unit 5 Assessment

Your Long-Range Plan

Use the example on page EC-12 and modify that plan to fit your calendar year. Or you may wish to use the customizable online lesson planner at **www.findinggod.com**.

AUGUST	FEBRUARY
Week 1	Week 1
Week 2	Week 2
Week 3	Week 3
Week 4	Week 4

SEPTEMBER	MARCH
Week 1	Week 1
Week 2	Week 2
Week 3	Week 3
Week 4	Week 4

OCTOBER	APRIL
Week 1	Week 1
Week 2	Week 2
Week 3	Week 3
Week 4	Week 4

NOVEMBER	MAY
Week 1	Week 1
Week 2	Week 2
Week 3	Week 3
Week 4	Week 4

DECEMBER	JUNE
Week 1	Week 1
Week 2	Week 2
Week 3	Week 3
Week 4	Week 4

JANUARY	JULY
Week 1	Week 1
Week 2	Week 2
Week 3	Week 3
Week 4	Week 4

The First Day

Beginnings are always important. Here are some tips to help make your first day a good experience.

Prepare in Advance

Advance preparation is important to a successful session. You can get ready by doing the following:

▶ Read the Catechist Preparation pages for Unit 1, Session 1.

▶ Gather materials for the lesson and the If Time Allows activities that you choose to do.

▶ Survey the room in which the session will take place. Plan for the best seating arrangement. Adorn the space with suggestions from pages EC-4 and EC-5.

Set the Stage

To begin the session, consider incorporating the following suggestions:

▶ Greet young people warmly and explain the purpose of your time together.

▶ Arrange young people according to your preplanned seating arrangement and play a "get to know your name" game if young people are unfamiliar to you or to one another.

▶ Invite each young person to tell one thing he or she wants to learn or experience in Catholic faith formation. Say: **As we spend time together this year, let's remember these ideas and explore them further as they come up during our sessions.**

Present the Books

Follow this plan to help young people appreciate the value of this special, sacred time together:

▶ Call each young person by name to receive a book. Say: **May your life be changed by recognizing God in all things.**

▶ When all books are distributed, read aloud the book title and explain what it means.

▶ Have young people open their books and fill in the nameplate on the inside front cover.

▶ Slowly and prayerfully pray aloud the Scripture verse below the nameplate. Then pray together the prayer on the title page: **As I open this book . . .**

▶ Invite pairs of young people to look through the book and discuss what they see. Invite young people to share their ideas with the group.

> Beginnings
> are always
> important.

Unit 1

Catechist Preparation pages open each unit and session.

Unit Opener   1

UNIT 1

One True Faith

Unit 1 focuses on the Trinity and the core Catholic belief that Jesus is the Savior, the fulfillment of God's promise to his people. In this unit, young people will learn the following concepts.

SESSION 1 ## Three Persons in One God

In this session, young people learn that the Trinity is the core mystery of the Catholic faith. As Catholics, we are called to respond to God's love in important ways, such as through prayer, living out the themes of Catholic Social Teaching, and living as disciples for Jesus in the world.

SESSION 2 ## Jesus Is the Answer to a Promise

The Bible, consisting of the Old and New Testaments, is the inspired Word of God. The Bible tells us that John the Baptist announced the coming of Jesus, the Messiah, a Savior promised to God's people. The message of Jesus' life, Death, Resurrection, and Ascension is shared with us through the Gospels. Young people learn that we can meditate on the Word of God as a form of prayer.

SESSION 3 ## Jesus Reveals God to Us

The genealogy of Jesus in the Old and New Testaments reveals that God worked through Jesus' ancestors to prepare for the Salvation that Jesus brought to humanity. As Catholics, we believe Jesus himself fulfills the Revelation of God found in the Old Testament. We believe that Jesus is the Son of God, a God for all people, and a God who forgives our sins and invites us into his kingdom.

SESSION 4 ## Jesus Calls Us to Say Yes

Throughout Scripture, many people say yes to God. But Mary, the Mother of God, holds a special place in the minds and hearts of Catholics because she said yes to God when she was asked to be the Mother of Jesus. Mary lives wholly and fully in the grace of God. We, too, receive God's grace in the forms of sanctifying and actual grace.

SESSION 5 ## Celebrating Ordinary Time

In this session, young people learn the meaning of Ordinary Time, explore how Ordinary Time is celebrated in our Church, and learn that Ordinary Time is a time to grow as a disciple of Christ and deepen our commitment to him.

UNIT SAINT

Saint Augustine

Saint Augustine took time to discover that Christianity is the one true faith. He eventually responded with love for God and for others. As a result of his abiding faith, Saint Augustine became one of the great leaders of the early Church.

Prayer in Unit 1

In each session of Unit 1, establish the pattern and tone for prayer. Young people reflect on Scripture, offer prayers of petition and thanksgiving, as well as participate in guided reflection. Young people also pray the Daily Examen, a form of Ignatian prayer.

✝ Catholic Social Teaching in Unit 1

In the story of the Good Samaritan (Luke 10:29–37), Jesus makes clear our responsibility to care for those in need. The Church articulates this responsibility in Catholic Social Teaching. The following themes of Catholic Social Teaching are integrated into this unit.

Call to Family, Community, and Participation   Participation in family and community is central to our faith and to a healthy society. Families and communities must be supported and strengthened through active participation.

Care for God's Creation   We have a responsibility to care for God's creation. We are called to make moral and ethical choices that protect the ecological balance of creation both locally and worldwide.

The Dignity of Work and the Rights of Workers   The Catholic Church teaches us to respect basic rights of workers: the right to productive work, to fair wages, to private property, to organize and join unions, and to pursue economic opportunity. Catholics believe that the economy is meant to serve people.

Life and Dignity of the Human Person   The Catholic Church teaches us that all human life is sacred and that all people must be treated with dignity. As Catholics, we strive to respect and value people more than material goods. The foundation of our moral vision is our belief in the life and the dignity of the human person.

Option for the Poor and Vulnerable   As Catholics, we are called to follow Jesus' example by making a specific effort to defend and promote the dignity of the poor and vulnerable and meet their immediate needs.

Rights and Responsibilities   The Catholic Church teaches that every person has a right to live as well as the right to things required for human decency. As Catholics, it is our responsibility to protect fundamental human rights.

Solidarity   Solidarity is the attitude that leads Christians to share spiritual and material goods. Solidarity unites rich and poor, weak and strong, and helps create a society that recognizes that we live in an interdependent world.

Faith in Action

In Unit 1, young people are invited to meet the needs of people who are poor and vulnerable by developing and implementing the following service projects: collecting and distributing food and providing basic necessities for people who are homeless. Alternative service-project ideas also appear on the last page of each session in this guide.

TOGETHER *as One Parish*

Religious Education with the Parochial School

To celebrate the beginning of a new year of faith formation, add an insert to your parish bulletin that introduces the religious education team in one combined list, listing catechists' names from both your religious education program and Catholic school. Introduce the list by sharing common goals for young people who participate in the programs.

📖 **Literature Opportunity**
Mr. Blue
by Myles Connelly
You might wish to have young people read this novel about J. Blue, a mysterious and fascinating man who spends his inherited wealth as soon as he gets it and ends up having to live in a packing box on a New York City rooftop. This beloved novel about a 20th century Saint Francis figure is set in the 1920s.

✝ *The Poor and Vulnerable*

Three Persons in One God

3-Minute Retreat

Before you prepare the session, pause and be still. Take three deep breaths and be aware of the loving presence of God, who is with you on this journey.

John 3:16

"For God so loved the world that he gave his only Son, so that everyone who believes in him might not perish but might have eternal life."

Reflection

God is a model of selfless love for us. There was no need for God to create our planet or the creatures that inhabit it. Creation was an act of selfless love. There was no need for God to send his only Son to save us. It was an act of selfless love. As we learn about God's love, we draw closer to God and the mystery of the Trinity. God has lavished us with love in the Persons of the Son and the Spirit, who in turn nurture in us the desire to do the same for others.

Questions

In what ways do I live out God's selfless love for me in my caring for others? When has someone shared an act of selfless love with me? Recall the experience and say a silent prayer for that person.

 Concluding Prayer

Speak to God, using the words of this prayer or your own.

Triune God, your love for us is beyond our ability to comprehend. May I grow in my desire to share your love with the people I meet today.

Knowing and Sharing Your Faith in Session 1

Consider how Scripture and Tradition can deepen your understanding of session content.

Scripture

Genesis 1:26–31 tells us that God made us in his likeness, that he gave us dominion over the earth and the creatures on it, and that God found his creation to be good.

Luke 9:23 reminds us to take up Jesus' cross daily and to follow him.

Tradition

God has made the Trinity known to us by revealing himself as Father, Son, and Holy Spirit. As the Trinity, the Three Persons are inseparable in what they are and what they do. The word *Person* is used to designate the Father, Son, and Holy Spirit as really distinct from one another. The word *relation* is used to designate that their distinction lies in the relationship of each to the other two. When the Father sends his Word, he always sends his breath, the Spirit. In their joint mission, the Son and the Holy Spirit are distinct but inseparable. Christ is the one who is seen, the visible image of the invisible God, but the Spirit is the one who reveals him.

Catholic Social Teaching

In this session all seven themes of Catholic Social Teaching are introduced. See page 1b for an explanation of these themes.

Window on the Catechism

The mystery of the Trinity is described in *CCC* 232–260.

General Directory for Catechesis

The Trinitarian nature of the Gospel message is described in *GDC* 99 and 100.

One-Hour Session Planner

SESSION 1 Three Persons in One God

Session Theme: *The Trinity is the central mystery of our Christian faith and life.*

Before This Session

▶ Prepare a prayer space. See pages EC-4–EC-5 for ideas.

▶ Establish group rules and procedures. See page EC-8 for ideas.

▶ Bookmark your Bible to Genesis 1:26–31 and Luke 9:23. Place the open Bible in your prayer space.

▶ Read the Guide for this session, choose any additional If Time Allows activities that you might have time to complete, and gather the listed materials.

STEPS	APPROXIMATE TIME
Engage *Unit Saint:* Saint Augustine PAGES 1–2 *Daily Examen* PAGE 1 *Three Persons in One God* PAGE 3	10–20 minutes
Explore *The Blessed Trinity* PAGES 4–5 *God Is Our Creator* PAGES 6–7	30–40 minutes
Reflect *Prayer:* Signs of Love PAGE 8 *Where Do I Fit In?* PAGE 9	10–15 minutes
Respond *What's What?* PAGE 10	10–15 minutes

Prayer in Session 1

In this session, set a precedent for the pattern and tone for prayer throughout the program. Point out that young people will experience different forms of prayer in the sessions. A short prayer on the opener page invites young people to reflect on the session's theme. At the end of the session, young people are invited to access an online 3-Minute Retreat that reflects on Scripture. This session includes an extended guided reflection. Follow the Prepare directions on the Catechist Guide page before sharing with young people.

TAKE IT HOME

Homework options:

Trinity Artwork	PAGE 5
Blessed with Life and Love	PAGE 7

Materials

REQUIRED

▶ Can of juice, can opener (page 1)

▶ Sacramentals (page 2)

▶ Picture of a popular athlete or celebrity (page 4)

▶ Nature photograph (page 6)

▶ Writing supplies (pages 7, 9, 10)

▶ CD player (page 8)

▶ CD 1, Track 1: "Living in Relationship" (10:48) (page 8)

▶ CD 1, Track 7: Reflective Music (page 8)

▶ Computers with Internet access (page 10)

OPTIONAL

▶ Painter's tape (page 2)

▶ Bible (page 3)

▶ Tape, books (page 4)

▶ Session 1 BLM, T-349 (page 6)

▶ Magazines and computers with Internet access (page 9)

▶ Session 1 Assessment, www.findinggod.com (page 10)

Unit 1

One True Faith

Saint Augustine grew up in northern Africa around A.D. 350. His mother was a Christian, and his father was a pagan. Augustine was intelligent, but like all of us, this did not stop him from making bad choices. It is said that he and his friends once stole pears from a farm, not because they were hungry, but for no good reason. At the time, Augustine didn't seem to care that he and his friends were stealing. He didn't think about how his choices affected other people, who may have sold the pears for a living or who needed them for food. Some of his actions were thoughtless and hurtful to others. But his ideas would change over time.

How the Saint Relates { Saint Augustine represents a person who needed to take some time to discover the one true faith—Christianity. In the same way as Saint Augustine, we are on a faith journey that leads us closer to God.

①

UNIT OPENER

OUTCOMES

► Describe how Saint Augustine's faith journey led him to live a holy life and become a great Catholic theologian and writer.

► Define *faith* and *sacramentals*.

① Begin

Read aloud the unit title. Explain that in this unit young people will explore who God is and what it means to have faith in him.

Demonstrate pouring juice from a large can with one hole. Explain that air cannot get in the can to fill the empty space. A vacuum forms, which prevents juice from coming out. Say: ***Sometimes it can feel as though we have an empty space—a vacuum— within our hearts. Instinctively, we seek to fill this empty space.***

② Introduce the Saint

Have a volunteer read the paragraph on page 1. Explain that during the 300s, food was extremely hard to come by. By stealing the pears, Augustine had to know that he might be taking someone's only food. Say: ***Augustine did something that he knew was wrong anyway. As he grew up, he started searching for a better way to live. It wasn't until he went down a few wrong paths that he turned to Christianity, which led him to God.*** Ask: ***So far in your life, how has Christianity led you to God?*** (Possible answer: Christianity has taught me how to pray and how to act toward others.) ***What answers are you still looking for?*** (Possible answer: Why doesn't God stop wars?) Take some time to discuss young people's ideas.

How the Saint Relates

Read aloud How the Saint Relates. Encourage young people to think about their own faith journeys.

OPENING PRAYER

Daily Examen

Share information on the Daily Examen from both the front matter of the Catechist Guide and page 279 of the Young People's book. Explain that each unit will begin with a Daily Examen that young people can make part of their own prayer lives. Guide young people through these steps, pausing after each one.

• Relax and become aware of God's presence. Ask the Holy Spirit to show you what you need to know now.

• Recall your experiences and feelings from the last 24 hours. When were your feelings especially strong—positive or negative? Ask yourself, "What was going on in the deepest part of me? How was God present to me?"

• Now ask the Holy Spirit to direct you to one thing that God thinks is important—a conversation, a feeling, something you saw or heard, something you did or didn't do. It can be anything, large or small. Pay attention to this one thing. What does God want you to know?

• Where do you need God most in what's coming up? Ask God to help you remember he will be there and give you what you need. Silently pray *Amen*.

③ Connect

Have volunteers take turns reading aloud the section Gift of Faith. Focus young people's attention on the sentence "Faith exists in relationships" in the third paragraph. Ask young people to jot on a sheet of paper the initials of three people they trust most in the world. Invite volunteers to share whom they trust most. Ask: **What happens when someone breaks trust?** (Possible answer: The relationship is damaged or ended.) Say: **Relationships are built on trust. Placing our trust in someone is a risk. However, we don't trust people blindly. We trust because the evidence suggests that this person is reliable. Another word for trust is faith. When we place our faith, our trust, in God, we can enter into relationship with him. We do this because the evidence from Scripture and Tradition is that God is reliable and can be trusted. The deeper our trust in God, the deeper our relationship with him can grow.**

Past Meets Present

Read aloud Past Meets Present. Discuss the meaning of *sacramentals*. Have young people identify any sacramentals in the room, such as a crucifix, rosary, or statue. Ask volunteers to name other sacramentals.

④ Close

Read aloud this quotation from Saint Augustine: "When I am completely united to you, there will be no more sorrow or trials; entirely full of you, my life will be complete." Ask young people what they think this means. Remind young people that God is there for them, to love them, to guide them, and to make their lives complete. They only need to trust.

Past Meets Present

PAST: Sometimes insights into our faith come when we least expect them. According to legend, as Augustine reflected on the Trinity while walking along the seashore, he saw a child drawing water out of the sea with a seashell and pouring the water into a sand pit. When he asked the child what he was doing, the child answered that he was emptying the sea into the pit. Augustine commented that such a task was impossible. The child responded, "So too is it impossible for the human mind to understand the mystery of the most Holy Trinity." Augustine turned away to ponder this. When he looked back, the child was gone. This mysterious event revealed to Augustine that the human mind can no more fully understand the mystery of the Trinity than a seashell can empty out the sea.

PRESENT: Cardinal Joseph Ratzinger chose a seashell as part of his coat of arms when he was appointed archbishop in 1977. The seashell was a reminder of the story of Saint Augustine. Elected pope in 2005, Cardinal Ratzinger, now Pope Benedict XVI, had seashells embroidered on the vestments he wore at his installation Mass. This sign and other **sacramentals**, such as rosaries, medals, and statues, are given by the Church to help us celebrate our faith with greater awareness and devotion.

2   *Unit 1 • One True Faith*

ADVENTURES IN FAITH

Gift of Faith

As a young man, Augustine began to question his thoughtless actions. He sought to learn from a religious group that seemed to have the answers about the meaning of life. Eventually he became disappointed in what they taught. Augustine tried reading the Old Testament but thought it was too simplistic to tell a real story about God and how he relates to us. Following the custom of his time, Augustine put off being baptized until he figured out what he believed. Throughout it all his mother, Saint Monica, prayed for him and encouraged him in his search for the true **faith**.

Augustine kept searching, and gradually he developed some important friendships, especially with Saint Ambrose, bishop of Milan, Italy. These new relationships, as well as a series of life-changing personal experiences, helped Augustine learn about Jesus and his Revelation of God the Father. Augustine's faith in Jesus and in the Church blossomed, and he chose to be baptized. He became a famous theologian and spiritual writer. The people of Hippo in northern Africa made Augustine their bishop.

Augustine's journey opened his eyes to faith. Faith means saying yes to God when he reveals himself and gives himself to us. Faith is a gift from God that helps us believe in him. Faith exists in relationships. In our relationship with God, faith enables us to respond with love to God and to others. For faith to be complete, we need to believe, accept, and respond.

Augustine's life shows us that God doesn't force us to believe. Faith is a free human choice. Faith grows in people through different experiences and at different times in their lives. To grow in faith, we need to be open to what God has in store for us. Faith grows when we watch, listen, and search for God. Our faith grows stronger when we love and serve others. When we are honest, open, and willing, our faith can grow.

Faith Meter

In advance, use blue painter's tape to line the floor with a large semicircle. Add ten tape strips inside the semicircle to create a large meter. Ask each of the following questions, and have young people stand on the line that corresponds to their level of faith. The first line means little faith; the 10 line means total faith. If they have no faith at all, they should not stand on a line. Ask: **How much faith do you have in . . .**

- your ability to make good decisions on your own?
- our government leadership?
- your teachers at school? your parents? your parish leaders?
- the goodness of strangers?
- your personal future? God?

After each question, give young people a chance to say why they put themselves in that spot. Follow up each question. For those who regard themselves as having little faith, ask: **What would it take for your faith to grow?** Point out that Scripture teaches that even though human beings betray God's trust, God always remains faithful.

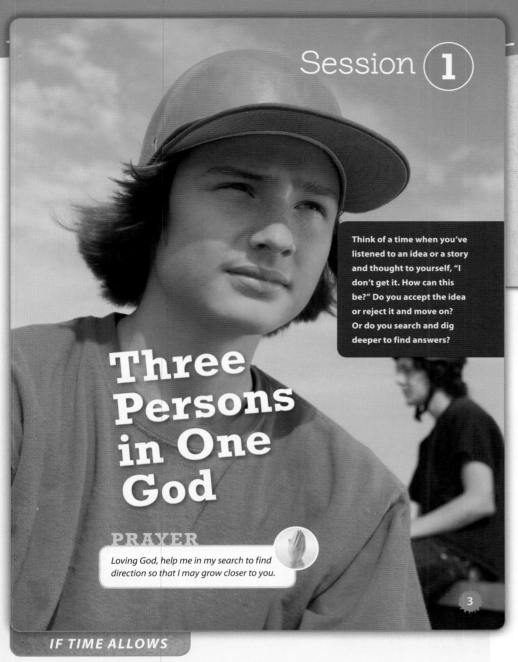

Session ①

Think of a time when you've listened to an idea or a story and thought to yourself, "I don't get it. How can this be?" Do you accept the idea or reject it and move on? Or do you search and dig deeper to find answers?

Three Persons in One God

PRAYER

Loving God, help me in my search to find direction so that I may grow closer to you.

③

IF TIME ALLOWS

Asking for Answers

Read aloud one of the designated Scripture readings for the upcoming Sunday Mass. Ask: **What part of this reading makes you think, "I don't get it" or "How can this be?"** Record young people's ideas and inform them that you will bring their questions to your pastor or a pastoral leader for answers. Invite this guest to visit the group and answer the questions in person, after they have had time to go over them. To close, remind young people that asking questions about God is one of the ways that we build our faith—our trust—in God. Tell them that they should not be afraid to ask questions of Church leaders. Church leaders are there to help.

➜ Go to **www.findinggod.com/sessionextenders** for Catholic beliefs about the Apostles' Creed. You may wish to share this with the group.

OUTCOMES

▸ Explain that the Trinity is a core mystery of our faith.

▸ Define Catholic Social Teaching as a response to God's love.

▸ Meditate on the Sign of the Cross.

▸ Define *Catholic Social Teaching, common good, Creator, disciple, free will, mystery, subsidiarity,* and *Trinity.*

① Set the Stage

Read aloud the text in the box. Have young people record their ideas and then share them with a partner.

② Get Started

Pose the following mystery. Say: *A man was found murdered one Sunday morning. The police questioned his wife and household staff. Here are the alibis:*

▸ The wife said she was reading a book.

▸ The cook claimed she was preparing breakfast.

▸ The gardener claimed he was planting seeds.

▸ The maid said she was getting the mail from the letter carrier.

▸ The butler claimed he was polishing the silver.

Say: *Who did it, and how do you know?* Invite volunteers to solve the mystery. (It was the maid. She couldn't have gotten the mail because there is no mail on Sunday.) Read aloud the session title. Ask: *How do you think the idea of mystery and the session title might be related?* (It's a mystery that there are Three Persons in one God.) Emphasize the difference between a murder mystery and a faith mystery.

Prayer

Say: *Let's pray together to prepare ourselves for life's journey.* Pray aloud the prayer. Conclude by praying the Sign of the Cross.

1 Begin

Bring in a picture of a popular athlete or celebrity whom you've seen in a live performance. Talk about this person's achievements and describe your experience of seeing him or her in person. Then ask: **How many of you believe that I can get [name of celebrity] to visit our class?** Invite a show of hands. Say: **Well, if you doubted my ability to bring him or her here, you're right. I may have seen [name of celebrity] perform in person but I don't have a personal relationship with him or her. I am, however, going to introduce you to someone this year that I do know personally, and that is God. We don't learn about God just by reading from a book. We get to know God by developing a personal relationship with him. And we develop a relationship with God by learning to trust him.**

2 Connect

Read aloud the article title The Blessed Trinity and invite a volunteer to read the first five paragraphs. Help young people understand the Trinity by using an example from Saint Ignatius of Loyola. Say: **Think of the Trinity as three musical notes. When each is played on its own, it is distinctive and unique. When all three notes are played together, they form one distinctive and unique sound.**

Read aloud the sections One God and Three Persons. Have young people name the Three Persons of the Trinity. Ask: **When do we best live up to our name as children of God?** (when we are united with others in loving relationships)

Our Catholic Character

Ask a volunteer to read aloud Our Catholic Character. Briefly discuss the concepts of monotheism and polytheism. Explain to young people the common history shared by the Jewish, Muslim, and Christian faiths through Abraham and Jesus.

The Blessed Trinity

WHAT traits or habits did you inherit from your parents? A quick wit? A flair for music? We gain insight into ourselves by learning more about our parents, who gave us life. Because God made us in his own likeness, we can gain a better understanding of who we are by learning more about God.

For Catholics the most powerful insight that we have about our God is the **mystery** of the Trinity. A mystery of faith is a religious truth that we cannot fully understand. A closer look at this mystery can unlock profound insights into our identity as children of God.

The **Trinity** is the mystery of the existence of one God in Three Persons—the Father, the Son, and the Holy Spirit. Each of these Three Persons is God, whole and entire. Each is distinct only in relationship with each of the others.

The Trinity is the most important mystery of our Christian faith and life, a mystery for us to enter into and ponder. We can state this mystery in just a few words—Three Persons in one God. But even after a lifetime of studying this mystery, we will never be able to completely understand it. God is not a mystery to be solved. He is a mystery that we explore and a relationship into which we enter.

This exploration can help us come to know and understand ourselves and others because we are made in God's image. It can also help us understand how to relate to others and to discover the meaning of God in our own lives.

One God

God made it clear in the Old Testament that there is only one God, not many gods ruling over a fractured world, as some people believed. The one God who created and sustains the world is the same God who chose Abraham and his descendants to be his special people. He is the same God who liberated the Hebrews from the slavery of Egypt. He is the God who spoke through the prophets. And he is the God who sent his Son to be born of the Virgin Mary. These are not all different gods. There is only one God.

Three Persons

The New Testament reveals Three Persons in one God. The First Person of the Trinity is God the Father. God the Son, Jesus, is the Second Person of the Trinity. He is begotten of the Father, which means that he was not created, but rather, existed before he was born of Mary. In fact, the Father and the Son have always existed. The Third Person, God the Holy Spirit, proceeds from the Father and the Son. The Holy Spirit was not created either because, like the Father and the Son, the Holy Spirit exists from before time.

Our Catholic Character

Our belief in the mystery of the Trinity—Three Persons in one God— does not imply that we believe in more than one God. Christianity, Judaism, and Islam are all major monotheistic religions, which means they are based on a belief in one God. Other religions, such as Hinduism, Buddhism, Jainism, and Shinto, have varying degrees of polytheism, the worship of many gods. Despite this fundamental difference, the Catholic Church respects other faith traditions.

4 *Unit 1 • One True Faith*

IF TIME ALLOWS

Shout-It-Out Relay

Play this game to reinforce concepts from the article. Ask each young person to have in mind one main idea or detail from the article. Organize the group into two teams. Use tape to mark two sets of relay lines—one set to mark the teams' start/finish lines and one to mark the turnaround point. Have each team line up behind a start/finish line. Explain the rules of the game:

- Each player takes a turn walking back and forth with a book balanced on his or her head, without touching the book with their hands.
- When a player reaches the turnaround line, he or she says aloud an idea from the article before returning to pass the book to the next player. Players may not repeat a stated idea.
- Players return to the start line if they drop the book.
- The first team with all players across the finish line wins.

In teaching us about the Trinity, God has told us that each Person of the Trinity is distinct from the others, equally God. In other words the Father is not the Son, the Son is not the Holy Spirit, and the Holy Spirit is not the Father. And yet, because their love for one another is so strong, they are inseparable in who they are and in what they do—there is only one God. Since we are made in the image and likeness of God, we are called to live in unity with others, just as the Father, Son, and Holy Spirit live in unity. We best live up to our name as children of God when we are united with others in loving relationships.

The Church and the Trinity

The Church realizes that the Three Persons of the Trinity have a single purpose for the human family. Each Person reveals this purpose. The actions of the Father, the Son, and the Holy Spirit are all for our benefit.

➜ The Father is our loving Creator. He continues to act in the world and in each of us in the ongoing act of creation.

➜ The Son, the Second Person of the Trinity, shared in our humanity without loss of his divinity so that we could know and love God as our Father. Through the life, Death, and Resurrection of Jesus, we are brought into God's own life. We are baptized into Christ so that we can join him in the praise of the Father.

➜ The Holy Spirit fills us with grace so that the life and love of the Father and the Son breathe within us. The gift of the Spirit opens us up to faith in Jesus, who unites us with the Father.

Study Corner

DEFINE
mystery, Trinity

REMEMBER
The Trinity is the most important mystery of our Christian faith and life.

Through the Church our faith is received, supported, and nourished.

When it comes to the mystery of the Trinity, God invites us to come closer and to experience fully his love through the gift of faith. This faith is connected to the faith community. It is in and through the Church that our faith is received, supported, and nourished. The Church helps our faith grow when we pray, participate in Mass, and receive the sacraments.

In faith we turn to the one God who gave us all that we have. God—Father, Son, and Holy Spirit—is our destiny, our final goal, the one for whom we will always reach, and the most important relationship in our lives.

SACRED ART

From the earliest times, the idea of the Trinity was difficult to understand. In trying to portray the Trinity, iconographers turned to the story of the hospitality of Abraham when three wanderers visited him. Iconographer Andrei Rublev represents the Trinity through three haloed figures that visited Abraham. This image shows the unique nature of the Trinity and the Eucharist as a symbol of unity and divine love. Rublev designs a wordless way to appreciate the mystery of the Trinity by setting the three figures within a single circle, making their faces identical, and including a blue garment, signifying divinity.

Holy Trinity (Troitsa), Andrei Rublev, 1425–1427, Russia.

Session 1 > Three Persons in One God **5**

TAKE IT HOME

Trinity Artwork

Before assigning the homework, display a variety of symbols for the Trinity, such as three intersecting circles, Borromean rings, an equilateral triangle, trefoil, triquetra, and fleur-de-lis. Perform an Internet search for examples of each, if needed. Then ask young people to reflect on and use the symbols as inspiration for their own original Trinity symbol that they develop. They can use any media of their choice, such as photography, video, drawing, or computer-generated art. Display the finished artwork for all to see, using *Symbols of the Blessed Trinity* as the heading.

Have a volunteer read aloud The Church and the Trinity. Remind young people that each Person of the Trinity is distinct yet equal. Write the following three words on the board in this order: *Breath, Creation, Resurrection*. Ask: **Which Person of the Trinity do you associate with Creation?** (the Father) **The Resurrection?** (the Son) **Breath?** (the Holy Spirit) **How does the Church support our faith and our relationship with God?** (Possible answer: It is through the Church that our faith is received, supported, and nourished.)

Sacred Art

Read aloud the Sacred Art feature. Explain that in the Church, icons are a form of art used in prayer. They are sacred symbols that help us enter more deeply into the mystery of what they portray. Ask young people to compare the images of the Persons of the Trinity to what they have envisioned in their own minds. Explain that the figures from left to right are the Father, Son, and Holy Spirit. Have volunteers describe the similarities and differences among the figures.

③ Close

To close this article discussion, invite young people to record answers to these questions:

▶ Which words best describe your understanding of the Trinity?

▶ How can praying the Sign of the Cross help you recall the Three Persons of the Trinity?

① Begin

Display one of your favorite nature photographs. It could be a photo from your garden, a vacation, or even a picture you found in a magazine. Talk about the image and describe what it reminds you of and how it makes you feel. Ask young people to talk about their own favorite place to appreciate nature. Then read aloud the article title God Is Our Creator, and have a volunteer read the first paragraph.

② Connect

 Invite a volunteer to read the next three paragraphs. Ask a volunteer to read aloud the definition of *Creator* in the Glossary. Pause to talk about what it means to love ourselves as God's creation. Acknowledge that adolescence is often a challenging time. Many young people are just starting to take care of their own health and hygiene, and they are dealing with studies and relationships—all without much help from others. Explain that young people receive all sorts of conflicting messages at this time, and sometimes it is hard to tell which ones to listen to. Read aloud the definition of *free will* in the Glossary. Say: **God's creation is a constant reminder of how you are loved by God, and you can turn to him when you need help.**

Read aloud the section Acting in Faith. Have young people brainstorm specific examples for each response to God's love that is listed in the paragraph. For example, for the response "We can worship God through the celebration of the sacraments," a specific example might be "I can go to Mass and receive Holy Eucharist."

God Is Our Creator

REMEMBER what it feels like to be awed by a blazing sunset or a black sky full of stars? What do you do in reaction? Point? Comment? Simply stop and stare? The next time you notice beauty in nature, pause for a moment and think about this idea: The created world around us is God's first gift of love to us.

God is our **Creator.** The world was not created as an afterthought or by a God who set it in motion and then sat back to watch. The world was created by a God who passionately desires to share his truth, goodness, and beauty. All that we see and experience in the created world is an expression of God's great love for us. We recognize him in the beauty, wonder, and harmony that surrounds us in the natural world and acknowledge him as the cause and end of everything.

The story of Creation tells us that God made us in his likeness and gave us dominion over the earth and all the creatures on it. (Genesis 1:26–30) How comforting it is to know that when God looked at everything he had made, he found that it was very good. (Genesis 1:31) Believing that God created us body and soul in his image and finds us good makes it easier for us to accept the idea that God loves us and that we, in turn, should love ourselves and one another. God blesses us with life and love.

To help us know this love and friendship, God sent us his Son, Jesus, to make us sharers in his divinity. Likewise, the Father and the Son sent the Holy Spirit to guide us and make it possible for us to live in love and happiness in this world and the next. In this way God invites us to live in close relationship with him, but it is up to us to respond to his invitation of friendship. God has given us **free will**—our ability to choose to do good and stay in relationship with him or our choice to sin, which distances us from him. We thank God for calling us into existence when we live Christian lives, and we recognize him in the loving actions of others.

Acting in Faith

Recognizing that God has blessed us with many gifts, we respond to God's love by loving him and by loving others. We can do this in many ways. For example, we can worship God through the celebration of the sacraments. We can use our words wisely to promote peace rather than harm others. We can show respect for ourselves and others in our actions. We can take care of God's creation. We can encounter God through volunteer work. We can pray—all the while knowing that God lovingly receives our prayers. Whenever we give back to God and others, we show a recognition of his infinite love for us.

6   *Unit 1 • One True Faith*

IF TIME ALLOWS

Session 1 BLM

 Nature Sketches Plan a nature hike. Organize young people into groups, each with an adult chaperone, and provide each young person with the Session 1 Blackline Master [T-349]. Ask groups to use the Blackline Master to sketch items in nature that they find beautiful. Invite each group to share their sketches and describe why they found each item beautiful. Close by reading aloud Genesis 1:1–31.

Before leaving, discuss with young people the characteristics of minimal-impact hiking, including picking up trash and disposing of it wisely, not touching or trampling wildlife, leaving what you find, using water wisely, and showing consideration to other visitors.

✝ *God's Creation*

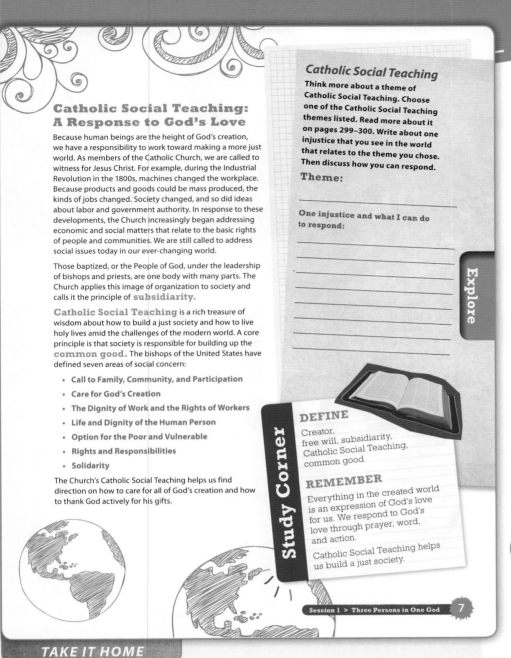

Catholic Social Teaching: A Response to God's Love

Because human beings are the height of God's creation, we have a responsibility to work toward making a more just world. As members of the Catholic Church, we are called to witness for Jesus Christ. For example, during the Industrial Revolution in the 1800s, machines changed the workplace. Because products and goods could be mass produced, the kinds of jobs changed. Society changed, and so did ideas about labor and government authority. In response to these developments, the Church increasingly began addressing economic and social matters that relate to the basic rights of people and communities. We are still called to address social issues today in our ever-changing world.

Those baptized, or the People of God, under the leadership of bishops and priests, are one body with many parts. The Church applies this image of organization to society and calls it the principle of subsidiarity.

Catholic Social Teaching is a rich treasure of wisdom about how to build a just society and how to live holy lives amid the challenges of the modern world. A core principle is that society is responsible for building up the common good. The bishops of the United States have defined seven areas of social concern:

- Call to Family, Community, and Participation
- Care for God's Creation
- The Dignity of Work and the Rights of Workers
- Life and Dignity of the Human Person
- Option for the Poor and Vulnerable
- Rights and Responsibilities
- Solidarity

The Church's Catholic Social Teaching helps us find direction on how to care for all of God's creation and how to thank God actively for his gifts.

Catholic Social Teaching

Think more about a theme of Catholic Social Teaching. Choose one of the Catholic Social Teaching themes listed. Read more about it on pages 299–300. Write about one injustice that you see in the world that relates to the theme you chose. Then discuss how you can respond.

Theme:

_____

_____

One injustice and what I can do to respond:

_____

_____

_____

_____

_____

_____

_____

Study Corner

DEFINE
Creator, free will, subsidiarity, Catholic Social Teaching, common good

REMEMBER
Everything in the created world is an expression of God's love for us. We respond to God's love through prayer, word, and action.

Catholic Social Teaching helps us build a just society.

Session 1 > Three Persons in One God   **7**

TAKE IT HOME

Blessed with Life and Love

Ask young people to spend the next day literally counting their blessings. On that day, young people should take notice of each time they feel blessed or loved. Provide examples, such as "Today I felt loved when my daughter made me a cup of coffee." Ask young people to write one sentence describing each blessing. Encourage young people to record as many blessings as possible. When young people turn in their work, invite two or three volunteers to share the number of blessings they felt they received.

Have volunteers take turns reading Catholic Social Teaching: A Response to God's Love. Ask: **What major change in society inspired the Church to develop Catholic Social Teaching?** (the Industrial Revolution)

Help young people understand the meaning of *subsidiarity*. Ask a volunteer to read the definition in the Glossary, and relate the principle to the terms *Catholic Social Teaching* and the *common good*. For more information, have young people refer to pages 298–300 in Prayers and Practices.

Read aloud the directions in the activity. Ask young people to complete the activity independently. Afterward, ask them to meet with others who chose the same Catholic Social Teaching theme. Have young people compare their answers and discuss possible responses to each injustice.

(3) Close

Ask: **Which theme of Catholic Social Teaching most concerns you? In other words, to which issue do you feel most called to respond? Why?** (Answers will vary.) Invite open dialogue, encouraging young people to share and discuss their opinions.

✝ *Family and Community*
God's Creation
Work and Workers
Life and Dignity
The Poor and Vulnerable
Rights and Responsibilities
Solidarity

Prayer

Choose an approach and pray with young people.

APPROACH 1

Guided Reflection

Prepare Listen in advance to the recorded guided reflection "Living in Relationship" [CD 1, Track 1]. Decide if you will play the recording or pray aloud the reflection yourself. If you choose to lead, listen to the recording a second time, following the script [pages T-339–T-340] and noting pauses and tone. You can then follow the script exactly or adapt it as you wish.

Pray During the session, have volunteers read aloud the paragraphs in the left column. Discuss the meaning of *disciple*. Read aloud the definition in the Glossary. Then introduce meditation as a form of prayer in which one thinks reflectively, in this case about being in relationship with God. Play the recording or lead using the script, joining the young people in meditative prayer. If you pray aloud the script, play reflective music softly in the background [CD 1, Track 7].

APPROACH 2

Young People's Page

Prepare Pray the prayer in advance to become familiar with it.

Pray Have volunteers read aloud the paragraphs in the left column. Discuss the idea of being a disciple. Ask: **What is more important for a disciple—words or actions?** (both) Then pray together the vocal prayer in Reflect on the Sign of the Cross. Designate the Leader part. Have the rest of the group respond at the All part. Pause briefly between parts.

Prayer

Signs of Love

As Catholics we begin our day and our prayers with the Sign of the Cross. It's a simple reminder that our whole life is lived under the sign that saved us, the Cross of Jesus, by the power of the Trinity—one God, who is Father, Son, and Holy Spirit.

It is an important sign that places before us and on us the shape of the cross that saves us. It is the sign traced on our foreheads when we become a Christian in Baptism, and it is made over us in death as we complete our Christian life.

When we bless ourselves with the Sign of the Cross, we remember the God who created us, the one who saves us, and the Spirit whose wisdom guides us. This sacramental helps us grow in our spiritual life because it reminds us of our core beliefs.

The Sign of the Cross is also a visible sign of a **disciple,** a person who accepts Jesus' message and tries to live as he did, including sharing his mission. Jesus' words in Luke 9:23 remind us to take up his cross daily and follow him. Though short and simple, the Sign of the Cross lets the whole world see that we belong to God—Father, Son, and Holy Spirit.

 8 *Unit 1 • One True Faith*

Reflect on the Sign of the Cross

Leader: Let's pause for a moment to become aware of God's presence with us as we prepare ourselves for prayer. Trace a small cross on your forehead. Reflect on the ways you use your mind to know and understand God better.

All: Faithful God, you created us with a mind that we might seek and know you. Help us recognize you in all the people and events of our lives.

Leader: Next, trace a small cross on your chest. Pause for a moment to thank God for all the ways he has shown you how much he loves you. Let's pray together.

All: God of love, thank you for the gift of your Son, Jesus, who died on the cross for love of us. Help us know how to love others the way you love us.

Leader: Now slowly trace a small cross on each shoulder. Reflect on anything in your life that feels heavy to you, or reflect on a burden that you could use help carrying. Now let's pray together.

All: Merciful God, your Son bore the weight of our human suffering on his shoulders. Help us take up our cross each day and follow you. Inspire us through your Holy Spirit to be generous in offering help to others who carry heavy burdens.

IF TIME ALLOWS

Pray Again

If you used the recorded guided reflection, you might conclude the session by praying the Sign of the Cross.

FYI

Coaching Young People to Pray

Before praying, emphasize to young people that prayer is communication with God about every part of our lives. Prayer is an essential part of our daily lives that helps us grow closer in our relationship to God. Encourage young people to focus their attention on a specific image or idea to help them concentrate and reflect.

WHERE Do I Fit In?

We've all heard the message "God loves you." But do you really believe it? This concept is often easier to believe when our lives are going well. But how do we have faith in God's love when things fall apart? How can we use knowledge of God's love to help us cope and get past our problems?

by Tom McGrath

How Do We Know God Loves Us?

I'm glad to be a Catholic because as a Catholic I believe that God loves me. I don't just believe it; I know it. I know God loves me because I've experienced that love in many different ways.

I haven't always felt God's love. In fact, there have been times when I felt God was distant and remote, and quite frankly, uninterested in me or my life. But it wasn't God who moved away from me during those times; it was quite the opposite. I had simply quit responding to him. At other times I have experienced the closeness and love of God so fully that it left no doubt that not only did God exist, he also knew all there was to know about me—and loves me anyway. My experience and my religion teach me that God is always on my side and at my side.

How do I experience God's love in my life? I could list hundreds of ways, and I bet you could, too, if you put your mind to it. I don't usually experience God's love as a bolt of lightning or a thundering voice but rather as a gentle nudge or the still, small voice inside me that is an echo of God calling me into life. Open your mind and heart, and be ready to be surprised.

We experience God's love in many ways. The activity shows three places where you can look for signs of God's love. Read each section and respond on a separate sheet of paper.

TOM McGRATH is the author of *Raising Faith-Filled Kids.*

In Nature

Nature gives us witness to God's existence upholding the world and our presence in it. Think of a time when you felt the loving presence of God in nature. Write about it, or find another creative way to express it—drawing, painting, poetry, or music.

In Your Family

Describe a time when you experienced the love of God through the care and concern of a family member. In the week to come, make a point of thanking that person.

In the Kindness of Others

Summarize a time when you experienced God's care through the actions of others, maybe someone you didn't even know.

Session 1 > Three Persons in One God 9

Reflect

IF TIME ALLOWS

Looking at Love

Organize young people into groups. Ask them to discuss additional places where they find signs of God's love. Invite them to write a prayer that asks God to help them respond to him with love throughout every day. Encourage volunteers to read aloud the prayers.

INCLUSION

Attention

Moving Partners If you work with young people who have attention disorders, have them complete the activity on the page verbally and actively, rather than by writing responses. For example, have young people recite answers to a partner, rotating to a new partner for each question.

---

① Begin

Read aloud the title of the page. Talk with young people about what it means to "fit in." Acknowledge that this term can mean different things depending on the group you're trying to fit into. Explain that because the Catholic Church seeks to help us know and grow closer to God, and God affects every single aspect of our lives, we can always find a place to fit in. Read aloud the introductory text.

② Connect

Have volunteers take turns reading How Do We Know God Loves Us? Ask: ***What is the author's main point about experiencing God?*** (If you stay alert, you can find God in many different experiences.) Have young people work independently to complete the activity in the box. If time allows, invite young people to meet in pairs to discuss their responses. Then ask: ***Which section relates to creation?*** (In Nature) Ask: ***How does In Your Family and In the Kindness of Others relate to discipleship?*** (When we live our faith in our family and in the community and we recognize the value of loving our neighbor, we share Jesus' mission and act as his disciples.)

③ Close

Have each young person choose his or her favorite answer from the activity. Ask young people to explain to the group the reasons for their favorite answers.

① Begin

What's What? Have a volunteer read aloud the directions and the first main idea. Read aloud the example of supporting details. Have young people turn back to pages 1–2 to verify the details in the text. Invite volunteers to give other possible supporting details. Then have young people complete the page independently or with a partner. Afterward, share responses as a group.

② Connect

Say What? Ask volunteers to read aloud and define the terms. Review each term in the Glossary if necessary.

Now What? Read aloud the section. Invite each young person to answer the question independently.

③ Go in Peace

Collect materials and return them to their appropriate places. Encourage young people to follow through with their Now What? idea during the week. Draw a triangle on the board and write *Father* at the top. Add *Son* to the second point, and *Holy Spirit* at the third point. Starting at the apex, trace your finger from word to word on the triangle. Say: *If I stop before I reach the next Person of the Trinity, I weaken my chance to live a life of holiness. Let's ask God for an increase in our faith and strength to live in the name of the Father, the Son, and the Holy Spirit.*

3-Minute Retreat
Give young people an opportunity for quiet meditation at **www.loyolapress.com/retreat**.

What's What?

Respond

For each main idea, write a supporting detail.

1 Saint Augustine's faith journey led him to live a holy life and become a great Catholic theologian and writer. (PAGES 1–2)

Example: Saint Augustine made mistakes, but he kept searching and eventually had experiences that helped him have faith in God.

2 The Trinity is the most important mystery of our Christian faith and life. (PAGES 4–5)

Possible answer: The Trinity is Three Persons in one God.

3 Through the Church our faith is received, supported, and nourished. (PAGE 5)

Possible answer: Our faith is connected to the faith community.

4 God sent us his Son so that we would know his love. (PAGE 6)

Possible answer: We are sharers in his divinity.

5 We can respond to God's love through prayer, word, and action. (PAGE 6)

Possible answer: We can participate in the sacraments and act with respect for ourselves and others.

6 Catholic Social Teaching gives us direction on how to show love for others and to care for all of God's creation. (PAGE 7)

Possible answer: There are seven areas of social concern.

7 We pray the Sign of the Cross to remind us that our lives are lived under the sign that saved us—the Cross of Jesus. (PAGE 8)

Possible answer: It is a visible sign of discipleship.

Say What?
Know the definitions of these terms.

Catholic Social Teaching	free will
common good	mystery
Creator	sacramentals
disciple	subsidiarity
faith	Trinity

Now What?
Through faith in the Holy Trinity, we can learn to live a life of holiness. What can you do this week to live as a holy person?

Answers will vary.

10 *Unit 1 • One True Faith*

IF TIME ALLOWS

Service: Set Up a Junior's Department

Explain that through the Catholic Social Teaching theme of "option for the poor and vulnerable," we are called to help combat poverty. Together, do research to find a local Catholic organization that works to clothe families who are in need, especially families with adolescent children. Solicit help from adult volunteers and organize a long-term project in which young people work with the organization to collect, wash, mend, and attractively display a department store-type junior's department for needy adolescents to go and obtain clothing.

✝ *The Poor and Vulnerable*

Session Assessment Option

An assessment for this session can be found at www.findinggod.com.

PLAN AHEAD: Get Ready for Session 2

Consult the catechist preparation pages to prepare for Session 2 and determine any materials you will need.

Jesus Is the Answer to a Promise

3-Minute Retreat

Before you prepare the session, pause and be still. Take three deep breaths and be aware of the loving presence of God, who is with you on this journey.

John 1:14

And the Word became flesh
>   and made his dwelling among us,
>   and we saw his glory,
>   the glory as of the Father's only Son,
>   full of grace and truth.

Reflection

Can we feel the awe that lies beneath these words? The Evangelist is overwhelmed by the experience of seeing God with his own eyes. He has walked and talked and eaten and shared life with the Word made flesh for three years. He uses words such as *glory* and *grace* and *truth* to describe his experience. We, too, are gifted with glimpses of God's glory and grace and truth. In our experiences of love, we see the Word become flesh with our own eyes. By sharing our experiences, we act as witnesses to the glory of the Word become flesh.

Questions

What glimpses of God's glory, grace, and truth have you seen recently? How would you describe these glimpses to someone?

 Concluding Prayer

Speak to God, using the words of this prayer or your own.

Jesus, Word made flesh, thank you for revealing God's glory to us. Grant me the grace to share my experiences freely with others.

Knowing and Sharing Your Faith in Session 2

Consider how Scripture and Tradition can deepen your understanding of session content.

Scripture

John 1:29 reveals John the Baptist's testimony to Jesus, announcing him as the long-awaited Savior.

Mark 1:10–11 shows Jesus' identity as God the Father's beloved Son.

Tradition

God is the author of Sacred Scripture, which was recorded by human authors under the inspiration of the Holy Spirit. The Evangelists used their own faculties and powers to write in their own words what God wanted written. The Church accepts as inspired 46 books of the Old Testament and 27 books of the New Testament. The Scriptures teach faithfully and without error the truth that God wishes us to know for our Salvation. The task of reading and interpreting the Scriptures in an authentic way has been entrusted to the Magisterium, the living teaching office of the Church.

Catholic Social Teaching

In this session the integrated Catholic Social Teaching themes are **Rights and Responsibilities** and **Solidarity.** See page 1b for an explanation of these themes.

Window on the Catechism

The formation and interpretation of Sacred Scripture is presented in *CCC* 101–133.

General Directory for Catechesis

The relationship between Sacred Scripture and catechesis is presented in *GDC* 127 and 128.

One-Hour Session Planner

SESSION 2 Jesus Is the Answer to a Promise

Session Theme: *John the Baptist announced the coming of Jesus, the promised Messiah.*

Before This Session

▶ Display the *Finding God* poster The Time Line of the New Testament.

▶ Bookmark your Bible to Genesis 17:1–8, Luke 1:5–13, Luke 1:39–41, Luke 3:1–6, Luke 3:9–14, Luke 7:24–35, Matthew 11:7–19, Mark 1:3, Mark 1:7–8, Mark 1:10–11, John 1:1–5, John 1:29, John 1:34, Ezekiel 1:10, Revelation 4:78, Exodus 3:14, Exodus 6:30—7:1. Place the open Bible in your prayer space.

▶ Read the Guide for this session, choose any additional If Time Allows activities that you might have time to complete, and gather the listed materials.

STEPS	APPROXIMATE TIME
Engage *Jesus Is the Answer to a Promise* PAGE 11	10 minutes
Explore *John the Baptist* PAGES 12–13 *The Inspired Word of God* PAGES 14–15	30–40 minutes
Reflect *Prayer:* Praying the Gospel PAGE 16 *Where Do I Fit In?* PAGE 17	10–15 minutes
Respond *What's What?* PAGE 18	10–15 minutes

Prayer in Session 2

This session continues the pattern and tone for prayer in the program. A short prayer on the opening page invites young people to reflect on this session's theme. An online 3-Minute Retreat concludes the session. Session 2 invites young people to offer prayers of thanks to God for his Word in Scripture. Follow the Prepare directions on the Catechist Guide page before sharing with young people.

TAKE IT HOME

Homework options:

Faithful Citizenship	PAGE 13
Time Capsule	PAGE 15

Materials

REQUIRED

▶ Magazine or newspaper advertisements (page 11)

▶ Bible (page 12)

▶ Writing supplies (pages 13, 17, 18)

▶ Copy of terms of agreement for a product or service (page 14)

▶ *Finding God* poster: The Time Line of the New Testament (page 15)

▶ CD player (page 16)

▶ CD 1, Track 7: Reflective Music (page 16)

▶ Computers with Internet access (page 18)

OPTIONAL

▶ Bibles, art supplies (page 12)

▶ Session 2 BLM, T-350 (page 12)

▶ Writing supplies, digital or disposable camera, photo album (page 14)

▶ Sticky notes, Bibles (page 15)

▶ Bible (page 16)

▶ Writing supplies, stationery, envelopes, stamps (page 17)

▶ Session 2 Assessment, www.findinggod.com (page 18)

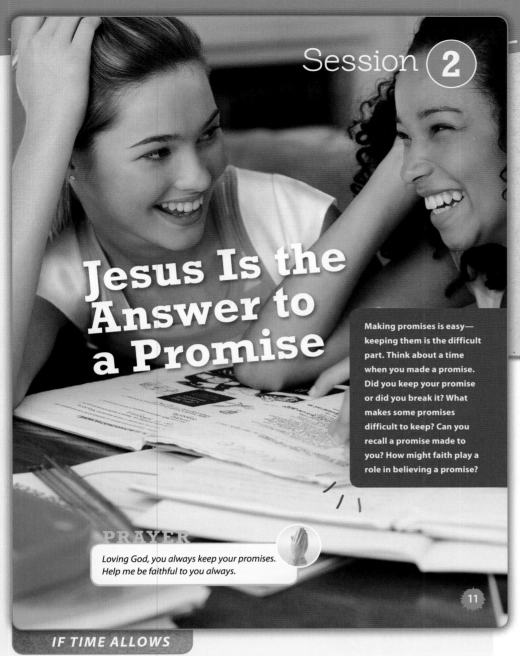

Session 2

Jesus Is the Answer to a Promise

Making promises is easy—keeping them is the difficult part. Think about a time when you made a promise. Did you keep your promise or did you break it? What makes some promises difficult to keep? Can you recall a promise made to you? How might faith play a role in believing a promise?

PRAYER

Loving God, you always keep your promises. Help me be faithful to you always.

11

SESSION 2

OUTCOMES

▶ Explain that John the Baptist was a prophet who announced the coming of Jesus, the Messiah.

▶ Explain that the Gospels in the New Testament tell the stories of Jesus' life, Death, Resurrection, and Ascension.

▶ Offer prayers of thanks to God for his Word in Scripture.

▶ Define *Acts of the Apostles, Ascension, canon, Covenant, Gospels, Original Sin, precursor, priest, prophet, Resurrection, Son of God,* and *Tradition.*

① Set the Stage

Read aloud the questions on page 11. Give young people time to discuss aloud or record their ideas.

② Get Started

Display side by side several magazine or newspaper advertisements for products that promise amazing results or offer something of great value. Ask volunteers to read aloud the claims made for each product. Ask: ***Do you believe the promises made in each ad? Why or why not?*** (Answers will vary.) Read aloud the Session 2 title. Say: ***Promises are easier to believe when they come from a trusted source.*** Ask: ***How do you think the idea of trust and the title might be related?*** (Possible answer: We can put trust in God.) Tell young people that they will learn about a promise God made and kept.

Prayer

Say: ***Let's pray together to remind ourselves about God's faithfulness to his people.*** Pray aloud the prayer. Conclude by praying the Sign of the Cross.

IF TIME ALLOWS

Do You Promise?

Allow young people some time to talk about promises they have made. Record their ideas on the board. Ask: ***Which do you think is harder—promising to feed and walk a neighbor's dog for a day or promising to care for the dog for two weeks while they are on vacation?*** (caring for the dog for two weeks) ***What makes some promises hard to keep?*** (Possible answer: Some promises require more time or effort.) To close, remind young people that even if they fail to keep a promise, or someone breaks a promise made to them, it is possible to take positive steps to restore trust and faith in their relationships.

➤ Go to **www.findinggod.com/sessionextenders** for an article about John the Baptist. You may wish to share this with the group.

① Begin

Ask young people to think about current events around the world. Ask: *Who are some people who have had a major impact, for better or for worse, on national and international issues?* (Answers will vary.) Ask: *What do we expect from famous people in society?* (Possible answers: to influence change, gain wealth or power, or improve lives) Say: *Whether leaders do good or bad work in the world, they are usually impressive in terms of worldly power. As you read this article, consider what God might think about certain influential people in the world today.*

② Connect

Invite volunteers to read aloud the title and first three paragraphs. Use the Glossary and define the terms *prophet* and *precursor*. Say: *Think of a prophet as a spokesperson, not a foreteller of the future.* Read aloud Exodus 6:30—7:1. Explain that Moses believes he is a poor public speaker. God replies that "Aaron your brother shall act as your prophet."

Read aloud the section Miraculous Beginnings. Have volunteers read aloud the Bible passages. Say: *God had special plans for John from the start.* Ask: *What is God's plan for you?* Say: *Pray about this during personal prayer.*

Ask a volunteer to read aloud the last section. Discuss where John taught and how he lived. Say: *John not only looked different; his message was different too.* Ask: *Who raises eyebrows today because of their look or message? What about them makes you uncomfortable?* (Answers will vary.) Say: *Each of us is a child of God, made in God's image and likeness.*

Our Catholic Character

Read aloud the feature. Read the definitions of *Original Sin* and *priest* in the Glossary. Then read about Baptism on page 287 of Prayers and Practices and discuss the ideas.

John the Baptist

THE Old Testament tells us that the Jewish people had already been waiting several centuries for the promised Messiah, the Son of David. *Messiah* is a title that means "anointed one."

Someone called to speak for God is a **prophet.** Scripture captures times when God spoke to his people through prophets so that they would remember, keep in mind his promises, and be prepared to accept the Salvation that he was going to bring for all people.

John the Baptist is the prophet who announced the coming of the Messiah, so he is often considered the last of the prophets, the bridge between the Old Testament and the New Testament. God chose John to be the **precursor,** or immediate forerunner, sent to prepare the Messiah's way.

Our Catholic Character

Even though Jesus chose to be baptized by John in the Jordan River, he was free from sin, As Jesus rose from the waters of the Jordan, the Holy Spirit came to rest upon him.

As Catholics we celebrate Baptism, which frees us from **Original Sin,** the consequence of Adam and Eve's disobedience when human beings lost God's blessing and became subject to sin and death. In Baptism, we receive new life in Jesus Christ through the Holy Spirit. Baptism makes us sons and daughters of God, fills us with grace, and makes us members of the Church. The **priest** or deacon pours water, a reminder of both death and life, over us at Baptism and says, "I baptize you in the name of the Father, and of the Son, and of the Holy Spirit."

Miraculous Beginnings

The Gospel of Luke tells us that John the Baptist's parents, Zechariah and Elizabeth, were a righteous, elderly couple who had no children. Zechariah, a Jewish priest, was performing duties in the Temple when the angel Gabriel appeared to him. The angel told Zechariah that his prayers had been heard and that Elizabeth would bear a son to be named John. (Luke 1:5–13) When Mary visited and greeted her pregnant cousin Elizabeth, the infant John leaped in her womb. (Luke 1:39–41)

A Voice in the Desert

John grew up and became the "voice . . . in the desert" announced by the prophet Isaiah. (Mark 1:3) John kept things simple—his clothes, his diet of locusts and wild honey, and his message to repent. He was not worldly, rich, or politically powerful. John admonished the people, saying "[E]very tree that does not produce good fruit will be cut down and thrown into the fire." (Luke 3:9) He instructed them on how to repent. (Luke 3:10–14) Luke's Gospel shows the great importance of John the Baptist's supporting role in proclaiming God's Word and preparing the way for Jesus. Everyone, even those who are not thought of as great or powerful, can take part in proclaiming the Word.

12 *Unit 1 • One True Faith*

IF TIME ALLOWS

Prepare the Way

Have partners read about John the Baptist in Luke 3:1–6. Ask: *Why do you think John was preaching the prophet Isaiah's words? How would you put Isaiah's message into ordinary words?* Have partners make a poster that illustrates the words of at least one verse.

Session 2 BLM

Mark the Evangelist—The Lion Arrange young people in small groups and have them brainstorm a list of sports teams that are named after animals. Direct them to identify characteristics that each animal represents, such as speed for a jaguar or ferocity for a bull. Allow time for each group to report aloud. Then provide each young person with the Session 2 Blackline Master [T-350]. Ask them to use the Blackline Master to learn more about the Gospel of Mark.

SACRED ART

It is said that John the Baptist's voice resembled that of a roaring lion like those found in the Judean wilderness. A winged lion is used to represent the Gospel of Mark. Mark's Gospel account begins with John the Baptist "crying out" in the wilderness that "[o]ne mightier" than he is coming. (Mark 1:3,7)

Stained glass at St. Thérèse Church in Appleton, Wisconsin.

The Promise of the Messiah

Because John the Baptist was a charismatic and popular preacher, he attracted many followers. Some of his followers believed that he might be the one promised by the prophets. But John was not confused about his role in God's plan. He pointed the way to Jesus and announced "One mightier than I is coming after me. I am not worthy to stoop and loosen the thongs of his sandals." (Mark 1:7)

A Sign of Repentance

As a way to show that they had heard and accepted John's message of repentance, many followers allowed him to baptize them in the Jordan River. When John baptized, the act of washing was a symbol of forgiveness and a willingness to start a new life. John continued to instruct that his baptizing was not the fulfillment that is found in the Messiah. "I have baptized you with water; he will baptize you with the holy Spirit." (Mark 1:8)

John Baptizes Jesus

John's testimony to Jesus raised interest. "Behold, the Lamb of God, who takes away the sin of the world." (John 1:29) At hearing these words, two disciples, one being Andrew, the brother of Simon Peter, began to follow Jesus. These early disciples told others about Jesus, and as Jesus' reputation grew, so did the number of his disciples.

Jesus began his public life on the banks of the Jordan River when John baptized him. Jesus had no need to repent for sins. He was without sin and totally faithful to the will of his Father. By submitting to the baptism given by John the Baptist, Jesus set the example of how we should empty ourselves in obedience to

God's will as a way to reconcile with the Father. Mark wrote "On coming up out of the water [Jesus] saw the heavens being torn open and the Spirit, like a dove, descending upon him. And a voice came from the heavens, 'You are my beloved Son; with you I am well pleased.'" (Mark 1:10–11) God fulfilled his promise of the Messiah in Jesus.

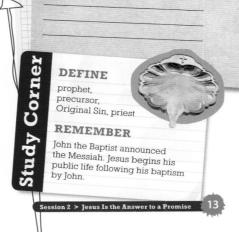

Jesus' Testimony to John

Read Jesus' testimony concerning John the Baptist in Matthew 11:7–19 and Luke 7:24–35. Summarize the key ideas here or on another sheet of paper.

_____

_____

_____

_____

Study Corner

DEFINE

prophet, precursor, Original Sin, priest

REMEMBER

John the Baptist announced the Messiah. Jesus begins his public life following his baptism by John.

Session 2 > Jesus Is the Answer to a Promise **13**

TAKE IT HOME

Faithful Citizenship

Before assigning this long-range homework project, remind young people that John the Baptist was a true prophet. Suggest that he was somewhat of a rebel, preaching in the desert and living a severe ascetic life. His preaching ultimately angered King Herod, who had him imprisoned and beheaded. Have young people choose from among a list of significant witnesses of the Catholic social movement in the last century, such as Dorothy Day, César Chávez, or Archbishop Oscar Romero. Assign young people to research one person's life. Have them identify the stand the person took in response to contemporary political thought in light of the call to social justice. Ask them to choose a format in which to present their findings to the group. For example, they may want to tape a mock interview, give a slide-show presentation, or set up a learning station that displays the research.

✝ *Rights and Responsibilities*

Sacred Art

Ask a volunteer to read aloud Sacred Art. Briefly discuss the image of the lion as a symbol of strength and courage. Mention that a winged lion is included in the vision of four winged creatures in Ezekiel 1:10 and in Revelation 4:78.

Have young people read The Promise of the Messiah and A Sign of Repentance. Ask: **Why was John's act of baptizing a powerful sign?** (The washing was a sign of forgiveness.) Ask: **What are some other signs of forgiveness that you know?** (Possible answers: the priest laying his hands on the head of a penitent during Reconciliation, a handshake, a hug or smile) Record ideas on the board.

Read aloud John Baptizes Jesus. Ask: **Why is Jesus' baptism significant?** (He sets an example of obedience and reconciliation with God.) Say: **In Jesus' time, news traveled slowly and by word of mouth.** Ask: **How then did the numbers of disciples grow?** (John, Andrew, and Simon Peter told others about Jesus.) Ask: **What happened when Jesus came out of the water?** (The heavens opened and the Spirit descended on him. A voice came from the heavens.) Ask: **What promise is fulfilled in Jesus?** (God's promise of the Messiah)

Give young people time to read and respond to the activity Jesus' Testimony to John. Then lead a class discussion about the key ideas.

(3) Close

To close, say: **Jesus called John the Baptist a prophet.** Explain that the *Catechism of the Catholic Church* tells us that in John, "the Holy Spirit concludes his speaking through the prophets. John completes the cycle of prophets begun by Elijah." [*CCC* 719] Through John, the ultimate message about Jesus is clear: "Now I have seen and testified that he is the Son of God." [John 1:34]

1 Begin

Bring in a copy of the terms of agreement for a product or service that you purchased. Read aloud parts of the contract, asking young people to point out any complicated words or language. Contrast this with the simple solemn agreement, or Covenant, that God entered into with Abraham. Read aloud Genesis 17:1–8. Point out that God promises to do far more for us than he asks in return.

2 Connect

Read aloud the article title and invite volunteers to read the first two paragraphs. Read aloud the definition of *Covenant* in the Glossary. Acknowledge that keeping your end of a bargain can be difficult. Say: ***It may be hard to wake up early to go to Mass, attend band practice, or give up weekend time to visit a sick grandparent. When keeping an agreement gets hard, it is tempting to forget about it or pretend it doesn't matter.*** Remind young people that God is loving. He is always faithful and invites them to renew their agreement with him at any time.

Have a volunteer read aloud the third paragraph. Ask young people to open their Bibles to the table of contents and review the sections. Refer them to page 254 in Prayers and Practices for tips on navigating the Bible. Ask a volunteer to read the definition of *canon* in the Glossary.

Have volunteers take turns reading aloud the section The Old Testament. In the table of contents of your Bible, point out the first five books. Say: ***This part of the Bible was originally written in Hebrew for the Jewish people. The word old describes it as the original, or former, testament—it does not suggest that it is obsolete or no longer relevant.***

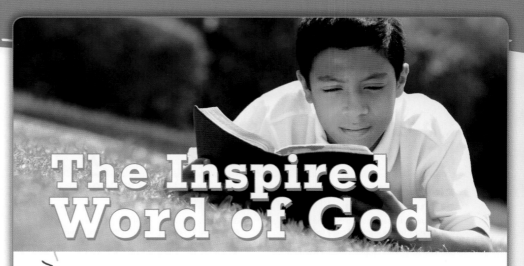

The Inspired Word of God

IN a variety of ways, both the Old Testament and the New Testament tell a single story of God's love for us.

The Old Testament records how God made a promise to Abraham, our father in faith, and his descendants. This **Covenant** was a solemn agreement between God and his people. The New Testament tells us how this plan came to completion in Jesus Christ. Everything we need to know about what it means to live in relationship with God our Father is revealed in Jesus. Throughout many generations, God was faithful to the Covenant. God kept his promise, a promise fulfilled in Jesus.

We read about God's covenants throughout the ages in the Bible. The Bible is the collection of books containing the truths of God's Revelation to us. The Bible, written by human beings, is the inspired Word of God. Because of this, God is really the author of the Bible. The two main parts of the Bible are the Old Testament and the New Testament. After several centuries the Church established the official list of the 73 books that make up the Old and New Testaments of the Bible. This official list is called the **canon,** which comes from a Greek word meaning "measuring stick" or "rule," because the writings contained within the Bible are our rule of faith.

The Old Testament

The Old Testament contains 46 books that tell stories about the Jewish people and their faith in God before Jesus was born. The first five books are referred to as the Torah, meaning "instruction" or "law." The central story in the Torah is the Exodus, the liberation of the Hebrew slaves as Moses led them out of Egypt. During the journey God gave the Ten Commandments to Moses and the people. Many prophets, such as John the Baptist, were called by God to speak for him and to urge the Jewish people to be faithful to the Covenant. A total of 18 books in the Old Testament present the messages and actions of the prophets.

This part of the Bible was originally written for the Jews. The books of the Old Testament were their Scriptures. Jesus and his disciples grew up studying Scripture and praying the psalms. The early Christians began to refer to these writings as the old covenant, or Old Testament, as they began to understand that God was forming a new relationship with them through Jesus—the New Covenant.

The Bible is God's personal message to us. It is important for us to know the Old Testament in order to understand fully the New Testament. Both the Old and New Testaments tell about God's great plan for the human family.

14 *Unit 1 • One True Faith*

ADVENTURES IN FAITH

Who Am I?

Write the letters *YHWH* on the board. Point out that God's personal name, "I AM," was originally designated by the Hebrew consonants *YHWEH,* which is pronounced *YOW way.* When God tells Moses, "I am who I am" in Exodus 3:14, what God is really telling Moses is that he does not have a name. In other words, God cannot be summed up or explained in one word. God is a mystery.

Point out that "Who am I?" is an important life question for teens. Have young people choose a partner to interview. Partners should prepare a list of questions to ask each other. Partners can tell about themselves, groups to which they belong, what they believe, and other information. After interviewing each other, have them organize information logically into a profile that includes a photo taken with a digital or disposable camera. Publish the profiles on a bulletin board or make an album for display in the prayer space. End the activity by telling the group that knowing who you are frees you to seek a closer relationship with a loving God.

The New Testament

The New Testament consists of 27 books. For Christians the most important books of the New Testament are the four **Gospels:** Matthew, Mark, Luke, and John. Even though each Gospel gives a unique portrait of Jesus, together they teach the essential truth that Jesus is the **Son of God** become man, sent by the Father for the sake of our Salvation. The end of the Gospel of John states that if all the stories about Jesus were told, there would not be enough books to record them. What we do have is a special treasure, helping us know Jesus.

The books of the New Testament tell the story of Jesus' life, Death, **Resurrection** from the dead, and **Ascension** into Heaven, and the experience of the early Christians. For about 25 years after these events, just about everything we know about Jesus was passed on through word of mouth. The Apostles and the other disciples preached the Gospel, and followers of Jesus gathered in their homes to worship God. Then, around the year A.D. 51, the apostle Paul began writing letters to communities of Christians in different parts of the Roman Empire. The four Gospels followed. In its final form, the New Testament is made up of the Gospels according to Matthew, Mark, Luke, and John; the **Acts of the Apostles;** the letters of Saint Paul to the Romans; 1 and 2 Corinthians; Galatians; Ephesians; Philippians; Colossians; 1 and 2 Thessalonians; 1 and 2 Timothy; Titus; Philemon; the Letter to the Hebrews; the Letters of James; 1 and 2 Peter; 1, 2, and 3 John; Jude; and Revelation. The Church accepts and venerates as inspired both the Old and New Testaments.

Scripture tells us much that we need to know about our faith. The beliefs and practices of the Church that Christ entrusted to the Apostles continues to be passed down from generation to generation under the guidance of the Holy Spirit. This **Tradition,** together with Scripture, makes up the single deposit of faith which remains present and active in the Church.

Study Corner

DEFINE

Covenant, canon, Gospels, Son of God, Resurrection, Ascension, Acts of the Apostles, Tradition

REMEMBER

The Bible is the inspired Word of God. Together the Old Testament and the New Testament reveal God's message. Faithful accounts of Jesus' life are presented in the Gospels of Matthew, Mark, Luke, and John.

Past Meets Present

PAST: For centuries monks and nuns living and working in monasteries copied the Bible by hand. The process was painstaking, sometimes taking almost a year to complete a single copy. A calligrapher would try very hard not to make mistakes and would have a companion check all the work. The Catholic Church developed a tradition of adding elaborate illuminations to the sacred text. These beautiful illustrations brought to life the story or theme of the sacred text. The invention of the printing press around the middle of the fifteenth century helped make Bibles accessible to more people.

PRESENT: The Bible is the all-time best-selling book in the world. Today you can read a Bible in book form, online, on a smartphone, or on another electronic device. You can listen to it as you exercise or while riding the bus to school. No matter what form the Bible takes, it is the Word of God, so it should be received with respect.

TAKE IT HOME

Time Capsule

Explain that a time capsule is a container used to store objects that represent life at a particular time and place. The container is sealed and buried with the intent for it to be opened years later by a future generation. Tell young people that when they read the Bible, it is in some ways like opening a time capsule. In other words, we can look to it when we want to better understand the experiences of people who lived in biblical times. For homework, ask young people to develop a list of things they would place in a time capsule that tells about your parish. Back in class have young people share their lists with the entire group. Suggest they assemble a time capsule to bury for a future generation.

INCLUSION
Specific Learning

Bible Search If you work with young people who have specific learning difficulties, assign a partner to help them understand how to use their Bible. Have them practice finding verses, attaching a sticky note to each page.

Display the *Finding God* poster The Time Line of the New Testament. Have volunteers take turns reading the section The New Testament. Ask volunteers to read aloud the definitions of the terms in the Glossary. Say: *If your favorite performer released a new CD, you wouldn't throw away the old CDs. You would just recognize them as coming before the new release. In the same way, the New Testament is God's newer way of speaking to us through his Son, Jesus Christ.* Discuss the Gospels in the New Testament. Ask: *Why is each Gospel unique?* (Each was written for a different audience and at a different time.) Display different versions of a recent news event. Ask: *What does perspective mean?* (a specific point of view; a way of looking at things) Say: *Reporters see or interpret events in a variety of ways. We have different perspectives on people, songs, movies, athletes, and so on. In the New Testament, we have received more than one perspective on Jesus— we have four Gospels.* Have young people open their Bibles and locate the four Gospels.

Past Meets Present

Read aloud Past Meets Present. Say: *Before people had access to the printed word, they relied on memorization.* Ask: *What verse or verses from the Bible do you know by heart?* (Answers will vary.) Invite young people to discuss their preferred way to read the Bible. Ask: *What are the advantages or disadvantages of each way?* (Answers will vary.)

③ Close

Invite young people to reflect on their personal use of the Bible and record their responses. Ask: *How frequently do you read the Bible? How can you make it a bigger part of your everyday life?* Invite young people to learn more about the Bible by reading pages 253–255 in Prayers and Practices.

Prayer

Follow the steps to guide young people through the prayer on page 16.

Young People's Page

Prepare Pray the prayer in advance to become familiar with it.

Pray Ask a volunteer to read aloud the paragraphs on the left. Discuss our opportunity to meet God in new ways every time we read the Bible. Point out that the Bible is like a library filled with stories, poems, and letters. We see how God works in the world, mostly through the everyday experiences of his people.

✝ Invite young people to prepare for prayer. Say: *Let's ask God to open our hearts and minds to hear his Word.* Read aloud John 1:1–5. Allow time for reflection.

💿 Ask three volunteers to take the Reader parts. Point out the places labeled All where everyone responds. Say: *Quiet your minds, relax, and prepare for prayer.* Play reflective music quietly [CD 1, Track 7]. Invite young people to join in a procession to show respect and reverence for God's Word in the Bible. Have a volunteer carry the Bible, leading a procession and ending at the prayer space where the Bible is enthroned.

Read aloud the Leader part and pause. Have Reader 1 pray, and invite everyone to pray aloud the All part. Continue the same way with the remaining parts and pray aloud the Lord's Prayer as indicated. Conclude by reading the part of the Leader and pause for a moment to meditate. Pray together the Sign of the Cross. Say: *As you go through life and hear so many conflicting messages, remember to pray with Scripture and ask God to keep you close to his truth.*

Prayer

Praying the Gospel

Reflecting on Scripture is a form of prayer. Each time we open the Bible, we have an opportunity to meet God in a new way.

When we read or listen attentively to the Gospel, we become open to receiving the Word of God and allowing it to form us. Just as the Apostles preached the Good News of God's mercy and love, we learn religious truths by experiencing the stories of Jesus' life, Death, Resurrection, and Ascension through the Gospels.

And the Word Was God

Leader: The Word of God is like a light that shines in the darkness. It shows us the way to God by teaching us to live as followers of his Son, Jesus. Aware of God's presence with us as we gather in Jesus' name, let's pause to prepare ourselves to offer our prayers to God in thanksgiving for this gift of light.

Reader 1: God of all creation, through you all things came to be. Through our study of Scripture, help us grow closer to Jesus, your Word. Let us pray to the Lord.

All: Lord, hear our prayer.

Reader 2: God of love, in Scripture you reveal how close you are to us. Through our study of Scripture, open our hearts to accept your friendship with us. Let us pray to the Lord.

All: Lord, hear our prayer.

Reader 3: God of all truth, in Scripture you teach us all we need to know for our Salvation. Through our study of Scripture, guide us along your path of truth. Let us pray to the Lord.

All: Lord, hear our prayer.

Leader: And now let us pray in the words that Jesus taught us.

Together pray the Lord's Prayer.

Leader: Your Word, O God, became flesh and made his dwelling among us. We thank you for the gift of your Word. Help us recognize your presence in the Scripture we study. We ask this through Christ, our Lord. Amen.

16   *Unit 1 • One True Faith*

IF TIME ALLOWS

Active Listening

✝ Emphasize that the first step in understanding God's Word is to listen attentively. Lead a simple exercise to promote active listening. Choose a Bible passage to read aloud while young people listen. Then tell them you are going to read the same passage a second time. Ask them to notice any words or ideas that they missed while listening to the reading the first time. Invite volunteers to share their thoughts with the group. Encourage young people to make it a habit to listen to God's Word actively so they can take it to heart.

FYI

Coaching Young People to Pray

Before praying, emphasize to young people that Jesus, the Word of God, speaks to us through Scripture. Say: *God is our greatest teacher. When you read or listen to his Word, open your heart and mind to hear what he is telling you. Pray for understanding.*

WHERE Do I Fit In?

I think many people believe that trusting God involves no effort—that no matter what, God will work out your problems for you. Truly trusting in God requires effort. You have to do the work and have faith that what happens is part of his plan.

by Daniel Kennedy

Trust in God

I have never had an easy time trusting God, but one night a few years ago I learned how. It was mid-January, and I was driving my two best friends home from basketball practice. The temperature was slightly above freezing, and it was raining. The temperature of the ground was colder than the air, which is a dangerous condition, as was explained to me later. When rain hits the ground under these conditions, it freezes, causing what is known as black ice.

I was driving about 70 miles per hour on the freeway when I noticed something unusual. I saw one taillight on a car in the lane up ahead, like a left-turn signal. This struck me as odd because we were in the left-most lane, and there wasn't anywhere to turn further left. I suddenly realized that this car was completely stopped. I hit my brakes hard, but nothing happened. The freeway was covered with black ice. We started to skid. I realized that we were going to hit the car.

Instantly, my head was full of so many thoughts that I couldn't keep track of them: my parents, my friends, my car, my future, my past. My life really was flashing before my eyes. Just before impact, my mind emptied out. I gave up. There was nothing more I could do. "God, save us," I prayed.

DANIEL KENNEDY is a college sophomore from Ann Arbor, Michigan, who hopes to combine his interests in history and travel with study abroad in Rome.

Impact. My car spun off the road. Five more cars piled up after mine. All but one of the cars was totaled, but no one was critically hurt.

Before my crash, I didn't really know how to trust God. Now I've learned how to pray "God, save me" practically every day. After I have done all I can to help myself, I've learned that I must trust that God will take care of the rest.

Learning to Trust

Think about a time in your life when you resisted trusting either God or others. Describe this experience. Then write a trusting response. Continue on a separate sheet of paper, if needed.

No Trust

_____

_____

_____

Trust

_____

_____

_____

_____

Reflect

Session 2 > Jesus Is the Answer to a Promise 17

IF TIME ALLOWS

A Trusted Friend

Have young people think of a friend or a relative they trust profoundly and write a thank-you note to that person. Encourage them to explain in detail what makes the person such a comforting presence. Ask them to refer to specific events in their relationship that have helped build trust. Invite young people to express gratitude for making the presence of God known to them. Suggest that young people mail the note to the friend or relative.

✝ *Family and Community*

---

① Begin

Ask: *What does it really mean to trust in God?* (Answers will vary.) Say: *When we hear the word* trust, *we generally think of a feeling or an attitude. But trusting in God requires action on our part.* Invite a volunteer to read aloud the introductory text. Say: *Sometimes the hardest work is "letting go and letting God."* Ask young people why they think this is so. (Answers will vary.)

② Connect

Have volunteers take turns reading Trust in God. Say: *Trusting in God doesn't mean getting behind the wheel and just sitting there. If we did this with the events in our own lives, we would never get anywhere. We have to do what we know how to do; we have to drive the car. But there are limits to our knowledge and powers.* Invite young people to describe times in which they came face-to-face with the limits of their own powers. Explain that this realization may not be as dramatic as the author's close call in a car. A realization of the need to trust God may involve someone's physical, emotional, or spiritual life. Say: *Thankfully, events like car crashes are rare.* Ask: *Nevertheless, what does the author pray every day?* ("God, save me.") Ask: *Why?* (He knows that in spite of his best efforts, there are some things he can't do on his own.)

Have young people complete the Learning to Trust activity independently. Afterward, invite volunteers to share what they wrote.

③ Close

Invite young people to pray silently and ask God to increase their ability to trust him so that they may overcome any fears that are slowing them down from living as God wishes them to live.

① Begin

What's What? Read aloud the directions. Remind young people to use the referenced page to develop the best response. Have young people either complete the page at home or with a partner in class. Afterward, discuss responses as a group.

② Connect

Say What? Ask volunteers to read aloud and define the terms. Review each term in the Glossary if necessary.

Now What? Read aloud the section. Invite each young person to answer the question independently.

③ Go in Peace

Collect materials and return them to their appropriate places. Encourage young people to put at least one of their ideas for strengthening their relationship with God into action during the week. Say: ***Remember that a healthy friendship is reciprocal and requires equal effort from both parties. Even so, God is always present for you, even at times when you fail to meet your end of the bargain. Because of his great love for you, God invites you back to relationship with him over and over.***

Respond

What's What?

Complete each sentence with details from the text.

1 John the Baptist is called the bridge between the Old Testament and the New Testament because _____ . (PAGE 12)

he was the last of the prophets who announced the coming of the Messiah

2 John fulfilled the prophecy of Isaiah when he became _____ . (PAGE 12)

the voice in the desert

3 Jesus began his public life when _____ . (PAGE 13)

John baptized him on the banks of the Jordan River

4 We know that God is faithful to his promise of the Messiah because _____ . (PAGES 14–15)

the New Testament tells us how Jesus fulfills the Covenant

5 The two main parts of the Bible are _____ . (PAGE 14)

the Old Testament and the New Testament

6 These two main parts work together because _____ . (PAGE 14)

they reveal God's story of Salvation

7 The books of the New Testament tell about _____ . (PAGE 18)

Jesus' life, Death, Resurrection, and Ascension

Say What?

Know the definitions of these terms.

Acts of the Apostles	precursor
Ascension	priest
canon	prophet
Covenant	Resurrection
Gospels	Son of God
Original Sin	Tradition

Now What?

Because God keeps his promises, we are free to share in his plan of Salvation for us. What is something you can do this week to strengthen your relationship with God?

Answers will vary.

18 *Unit 1 • One True Faith*

IF TIME ALLOWS

Service: United We Stand

Young Catholics who attend different schools may not know each other very well. Promote unity between those who attend different schools. Encourage solidarity by having young people work with both the school principal and the director of religious education to organize cooperative projects throughout the year that encourage friendship and care. Ask young people to brainstorm ideas that allow them to socialize, build goodwill, or promote good causes.

✝ *Solidarity*

Session Assessment Option

An assessment for this session can be found at www.findinggod.com.

3-Minute Retreat
Give young people an opportunity for quiet meditation at **www.loyolapress.com/retreat**.

PLAN AHEAD: Get Ready for Session 3

Consult the catechist preparation pages to prepare for Session 3 and determine any materials you will need.

Jesus Reveals God to Us

 3-Minute Retreat

Before you prepare the session, pause and be still. Take three deep breaths and be aware of the loving presence of God, who is with you on this journey.

Matthew 19:20–22

The young man said to him, "All of these I have observed. What do I still lack?" Jesus said to him, "If you wish to be perfect, go, sell what you have and give to [the] poor, and you will have treasure in heaven. Then come, follow me." When the young man heard this statement, he went away sad, for he had many possessions.

Reflection

We never learn the young man's name, but we know that he has observed the commandments and that he is wealthy and attached to his possessions. Jesus, knowing this, invites him to do something more—to live for God. The young man's observance of the commandments and his Jewish heritage has prepared him for this moment. But he is unable to take the step toward greater freedom. All our religious education is to prepare us to make a similar step with Jesus, who challenges us to look beyond what we have and see an even bigger picture.

Questions

Is there anything in your life today that is preventing you from following Jesus more closely? How will you respond when Jesus asks you for something more?

 Concluding Prayer

Speak to God, using the words of this prayer or your own.

Jesus, source of freedom, keep inviting me to let go of the things that keep me from following you wholeheartedly.

Knowing and Sharing Your Faith in Session 3

Consider how Scripture and Tradition can deepen your understanding of session content.

Scripture

Matthew 1:1–17 traces the genealogy of Jesus from God's Covenant with Abraham through 42 generations.

Luke 22:20 reveals Jesus as the New Covenant and the Divine Revelation.

Tradition

The foundation for our Christian faith is the Covenant that God established long ago with Abraham. A covenant is a sacred relationship, a kinship with God into which he invites us to enter. Unlike a modern-day contract, which is a legal agreement between equals, our covenant with God is an expression of our total dependence on him. We can remain faithful to the covenant only through God's help. Despite our unfaithfulness, God's mercy continually invites us to return to the relationship he has established and to live by the law of love in order that we may reap the benefits of the covenant—eternal life.

Catholic Social Teaching

In this session the integrated Catholic Social Teaching theme is **The Dignity of Work and the Rights of Workers.** See page 1b for an explanation of this theme.

Window on the Catechism

God and his Covenant with his people are discussed in *CCC* 238, 781, 1102, 1612, 2058.

General Directory for Catechesis

Revelation and Covenant are discussed in *GDC* 40.

One-Hour Session Planner

SESSION 3 Jesus Reveals God to Us

Session Theme: *Jesus fulfills the Revelation of God found in the history of the Chosen People.*

Before This Session

▶ Bookmark your Bible to Genesis 9:16, Genesis 17:5, Genesis 22:17, Exodus 19—20, Exodus 32:1–30, Matthew 1:1–17, Matthew 2:15, Luke 22:20, Mark 15:39, John 15:15, and 2 Samuel 11. Place the open Bible in your prayer space.

▶ Read the Guide for this session, choose any additional If Time Allows activities that you might have time to complete, and gather the listed materials.

STEPS	APPROXIMATE TIME
Engage *Jesus Reveals God to Us* PAGE 19	10 minutes
Explore *The Genealogy of Jesus* PAGES 20–21 *God Makes Himself Known* PAGES 22–23	30–40 minutes
Reflect *Prayer:* The Family and Prayer PAGE 24 *Where Do I Fit In?* PAGE 25	10–15 minutes
Respond *What's What?* PAGE 26	10–15 minutes

Materials

REQUIRED

▶ Family photos or heirlooms (page 19)
▶ Thomas Merton's book *No Man Is an Island* (page 20)
▶ Poster or copy of a familiar work of art (page 22)
▶ Bibles (page 22)
▶ Art supplies (page 25)
▶ Writing supplies (pages 25, 26)
▶ Computers with Internet access (page 26)

OPTIONAL

▶ Magnifying glasses, small objects to examine (page 19)
▶ Family photos or heirlooms (page 19)
▶ Session 3 BLM, T-351 (page 20)
▶ Plastic interlocking building pieces or other building materials, blindfolds (page 23)
▶ Plastic storage tub (page 24)
▶ Writing supplies (pages 24, 25)
▶ Video camera (page 26)
▶ Session 3 Assessment, www.findinggod.com (page 26)

 Prayer in Session 3

This session continues the pattern and tone for prayer established earlier and reinforced in each session. The short opening prayer invites young people to reflect on this session's theme. An online 3-Minute Retreat concludes the session with a reflection on Scripture. Session 3 invites young people to pray petitions that offer thankful praise to God for their families. Follow the Prepare directions on the Catechist Guide page before sharing with young people.

TAKE IT HOME

Homework options:

Hall of Fame	PAGE 21
Passover Seder	PAGE 22

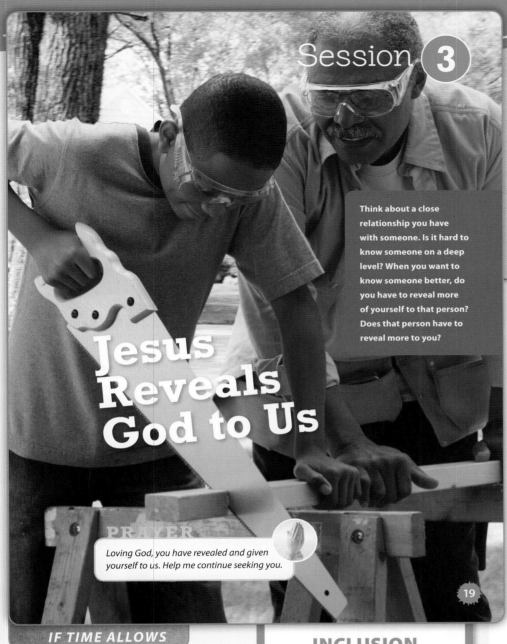

Session **3**

Think about a close relationship you have with someone. Is it hard to know someone on a deep level? When you want to know someone better, do you have to reveal more of yourself to that person? Does that person have to reveal more to you?

Jesus Reveals God to Us

PRAYER

Loving God, you have revealed and given yourself to us. Help me continue seeking you.

19

▶ Explain the significance of Jesus' genealogy to Salvation History.

▶ Discuss ways that Jesus fulfills the Revelation of God.

▶ Pray petitions of thankful praise to God for our families.

▶ Define *Abraham, genealogy, Israelites,* and *Revelation.*

① **Set the Stage**

Read aloud the text in the box. Give young people time to discuss their responses with a partner or write them on paper.

② **Get Started**

Display family photos or a family heirloom. Share related stories that shed light on your family history. Ask: *What things might a family member pass along to another generation? Why do you think valued family possessions are passed down?* (Answers will vary.) Say: *A photo or an heirloom tells only a small part of the story of your family's history.* Ask: *What do you know about your family tree?* Invite young people to share experiences. Say: *The stories in the Bible are like heirlooms of the Church.* Read the session title aloud. Ask: *In what ways do you think Jesus reveals God?* (Possible answers: through his stories; through his life, Death, and Resurrection) Explain that in this session they will learn about God's Revelation.

Prayer

Invite young people to reflect on ways God reveals himself to us. Say: *As we pray, remember everything we need to know is in God's Word.* Pray aloud the prayer. Conclude by praying the Sign of the Cross.

IF TIME ALLOWS

Take a Closer Look
Tell young people to examine a simple object, such as the palm of their hand, a pencil point, or a strand of hair, and take notes about what they see with the unaided eye. Then provide magnifying glasses to groups and ask them to repeat each examination. Point out that when you magnify something, you see it in a new way. Have groups compare their observations and remind them that reading Scripture thoughtfully and carefully reveals God's Word in a deeper, fuller way.

INCLUSION
Emotional

Sharing in a Group If you have young people with emotional or behavioral disorders, encourage their participation by asking them to bring in family photos or heirlooms. When they share with the group, help them stay on task by standing nearby. Use positive words to promote good behavior. Encourage them to follow any group rules for discussion.

Go to **www.findinggod.com/sessionextenders** for information about Jesus' genealogy. You may wish to share this with the group.

① Begin

Share any information you know about your family tree. Suggest ways the information has been helpful.

② Connect

Read aloud the article title and invite volunteers to read the paragraphs on the page. Ask volunteers to read aloud the definitions of the terms *Abraham* and *genealogy* in the Glossary. Discuss Jesus' ancestors. Ask: **When were you chosen for something that you wanted to do?** (Answers will vary.) **In that case, how did you feel when you were chosen?** (Possible answers: special, grateful, anxious, excited, surprised) Explain that the idea of being chosen by God is not outdated. Because we read the Old Testament in light of Christ crucified and risen, we are people of the New Covenant.

Our Catholic Character

Read aloud the feature. Explain that we grow and become fully human only if we develop relationships. Say: **The way people communicate and stay connected has changed over the years. Today we use technology such as e-mails, text messages, and video chats in addition to face-to-face and telephone encounters. But staying connected means far more than simple communication.** Ask: **What does staying connected mean to you?** (Answers will vary.) Ask: **What do you think Pope John Paul II meant when he said, "... the happiness to which we aspire cannot be obtained without an effort and commitment on the part of all, nobody excluded?"** (Answers will vary.)

If desired, extend the discussion by reading chosen passages from Thomas Merton's book *No Man Is an Island* to emphasize the importance of community and interconnectedness for a healthy spiritual life.

The Genealogy of Jesus

The Nativity, Bartolome Esteban Murillo (1618–1682).

PEOPLE are often curious to know where they came from and how they are related to others. For many it seems that the more they learn about their families, the more they learn about themselves. As Catholics what might we learn from Jesus' heritage?

As a Jew, Jesus shared in a Jewish religious heritage. The Gospel of Matthew begins with the promise that God made to **Abraham,** our father in faith, centuries before Jesus was born. "I will bless you and make your descendants as countless as the stars of the sky and the sands of the seashore; . . ." (Genesis 22:17) God promised Abraham that he would always be his God and that his descendants would be his people. Through this Covenant with Abraham, the Chosen People were set apart by God to have a special relationship with him.

The Gospel of Matthew begins with a **genealogy,** which is a listing of ancestors. The genealogy of Jesus, described in Matthew 1:1–17, traces the Covenant from the time of Abraham through 42 generations, including Abraham's son, Isaac; Isaac's son, Jacob; and Jacob's 12 sons. The 12 sons would become the 12 tribes of Israel. God revealed his Law through Moses. Kings ruled at this time, the greatest being King David. David's son, King Solomon, built a Temple in Jerusalem. The genealogy ends with Joseph, the husband of Mary and foster father of Jesus. God worked through Jesus' ancestors to prepare them for the Salvation that Jesus would bring to humanity.

Our Catholic Character

People are social beings. We are born into a family, our first example of how to live in a larger society. Participation in family life and life in society is important to our formation as people. Pope John Paul II expressed in the encyclical *On Social Concern* in 1987 that it is vital that people work together to ensure that families and individuals have the ability to participate in the life of society. He wrote: "Today perhaps more than in the past, people are realizing that they are linked together by a common destiny, which is to be constructed together, if catastrophe for all is to be avoided. . . . The idea is slowly emerging," he stressed, "that the good to which we are all called and the happiness to which we aspire cannot be obtained without an effort and commitment on the part of all, nobody excluded."

20 *Unit 1 • One True Faith*

IF TIME ALLOWS

Session 3 BLM

 Grand Genes Explain that the Gospel of Matthew was written in a Jewish Christian community in Syria about the year A.D. 85. Jesus' genealogy is prominently placed as the opening chapter in the Gospel of Matthew. Have young people work independently or with a partner to complete Session 3 Blackline Master [T-351]. Ask them to use the Blackline Master to learn more about how promises made in the Old Testament are fulfilled in Jesus.

We All Belong

The genealogy of Jesus includes Gentiles and Jews, people who are upright, and people who are immoral. The genealogy of Jesus reveals not only examples of faith and fidelity but also examples of imperfect people who made poor choices. Some are the most well-known members of the Jewish family, and some are obscure. God keeps his promise—a promise now fulfilled in Jesus—for better or for worse, even when some of the ancestors of Jesus were undeserving. In a similar way, each of us is part of a story that began long before we were born and will continue long after we die.

Your Family

Ask family members about yourself and your family history. Record the responses on another sheet of paper.

1. Where and when were you born?
2. What do you remember about growing up?
3. Where did you go to school?
4. What did you want to be when you grew up?
5. How did your parents meet?
6. What do you know about your grandparents? Your great-grandparents?
7. Were any of your ancestors born in a different country? If so, who and where?
8. What are some of your family traditions?
9. Was anyone well-known in your family?
10. What is your favorite family memory?

Study Corner

DEFINE

Abraham
genealogy

REMEMBER

God is revealed to us through the history of the Chosen People.

We all belong to Jesus' family tree.

Session 3 > Jesus Reveals God to Us   21

TAKE IT HOME

Hall of Fame

Explain that the purpose of a Hall of Fame is to identify people considered to be outstanding in their field. Often a building is dedicated to honoring such people. Tell young people to choose an ancestor that they want to honor in their personal Hall of Fame. Ask young people to write a descriptive essay that tells why their ancestor is or was an outstanding person. They should note any important contributions the person made to family, Church, or society. Have young people use print or digital media, and encourage creativity, such as video or voice-recorded interviews. Photographs, drawings, clip art, or significant objects can be incorporated into the display. Arrange an area of the room as a Hall of Fame display. Allow young people to present their work to the group. As a group, conduct a prayer service that thanks God for the people nominated in the Hall of Fame.

Read aloud the section We All Belong. Remind young people that Gentiles, the name given to those who didn't receive God's law, were part of Matthew's audience. Explain that Jesus has many titles, one being Son of David, which is a direct reference to his genealogy. This title connects Jesus to David, an ordinary shepherd until he defeats the mighty Goliath and is revealed as a faithful warrior for God.

Say: *King David was not perfect, and his faith and fidelity were shaky at times. He coveted the wife of Uriah the Hittite, Joab's armor-bearer, and arranged for him to be killed during a battle* [2 Samuel 11]. *With Uriah out of the way as a husband, David married the woman. God sent the prophet Nathan to David, who accused David of being like a rich man who steals the only lamb of a poor man. David became very angry at Nathan but eventually realized his sinfulness and repented.* Ask: *Why might God choose someone sinful as an ancestor of Jesus?* (God loves and acts on behalf of all kinds of people. We are all part of God's family, imperfections and all.)

Read aloud the directions in the activity Your Family. Ask young people to take the questions home and prepare responses to share the next time the group meets. Ask volunteers to share some of their favorite responses with the whole group.

③ Close

Say: *In the early days of television, many families were portrayed unrealistically as nearly perfect.* Remind young people that even Jesus' family tree was imperfect. Invite them to write answers to these questions:

▶ When or where do you find God's grace where you least expect it?

▶ In what imperfect or improbable places can it be found?

① Begin

Bring in a large poster or a copy of a familiar work of art, such as *American Gothic* or the *Mona Lisa*. Before you display the picture, obstruct all but a small section of it. Say: *I am only revealing a tiny part of the whole picture.* Ask: *Can you tell what you are looking at?* Discuss reasonable answers. Slowly reveal more and more of the picture until something identifiable is recognized. Say: *Just like this demonstration, God reveals himself to us over and over again. It's up to us to recognize him.* Then read aloud the article title. Have a volunteer read the opening paragraphs.

② Connect

Read aloud the definition of *Revelation* in the Glossary. Say: *In a way, God's plan for Salvation is similar to the excitement an audience feels while awaiting a performance. Slowly the curtain rises, and it gets even more exciting! Every minute of the performance unifies and contributes to the whole of the masterpiece. Similarly, God's plan for Salvation was revealed slowly. It took a long while before the full, magnificent picture emerged.*

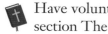 Have volunteers read aloud the section The Covenant with Noah.
Ask: *How does God's covenant with Noah show his faithfulness to his people?*
(God provides a way to restore wholeness. He wants to be with his people.)

Sacred Art

Read aloud Sacred Art. Explain that Moses used three arguments to persuade the Lord to remain faithful to the Sinai Covenant after the people turned unfaithful. Have volunteers read aloud Exodus 32:1–30. Ask young people to recall the three arguments. (They are God's own people. God's reputation will suffer if they are destroyed. The covenant with Abraham still stands.)

God Makes Himself Known

SACRED ART

Michelangelo's marble statue of Moses was the last of his projects for the tomb commissioned by Pope Julius in 1506. The unusual small horns on Moses's head are symbols of wisdom and enlightenment. In Exodus 32:1–30 we read about Moses's 40 days on Mount Sinai with God and how the Israelites turned to the worship of a false god, a golden calf. Moses becomes so infuriated with the people that he breaks the tablets containing the Ten Commandments. The artist captures an angry Moses as seen in the tense face, posture, and flexed arm of the sculpture.

Sculpture of Moses from the tomb of Pope Julius II, Michelangelo Buonarroti, ca. 1513–16.

GOD is a loving God. He seeks a loving relationship with all people.

Revelation is God's communication of himself to us. Revelation occurs through the words and deeds that God has used throughout history to show us the mystery of his plan for our Salvation.

The process of Revelation took centuries to unfold. In the Creation story, we learn that God entered a personal relationship with humanity through Adam and Eve. God set all happiness before them and asked only one thing—that they not eat the fruit of the tree of good and evil. Adam and Eve found the temptation hard to resist. When they lost their battle to temptation and ate the fruit, they broke their agreement with God. This resulted in all their descendants being born with Original Sin. Because God is merciful, he restored the human family so that we could live fully with him as he had intended. God had his plan of Salvation. He promised to send a descendant from Eve who would conquer the Devil.

The Covenant with Noah

As we read Genesis, we realize that God continued to reveal himself and lead all people back to him. When the sinfulness of humanity separated the unity of the human race, God made a covenant with Noah and all living beings. God promised that never again would the waters of a flood destroy the creatures on earth. God gave a sign of the covenant. "When the bow appears in the clouds, I will see it and remember the everlasting covenant between God and every living creature—every mortal being that is on earth." (Genesis 9:16)

22 *Unit 1 • One True Faith*

TAKE IT HOME

Passover Seder

Point out that the Book of Exodus describes the Hebrew people's enslavement under the Egyptian pharaoh, the 10th plague "passing over" the Israelite homes marked with the blood of the lamb, and Moses leading the Israelites out of Egypt. Passover, the memorial feast observed to remember these events, includes a Seder meal that is still observed today in Jewish homes. Have young people research and report on the meaning of the Jewish word *seder,* the food served and what each food signifies, and the rituals performed during the meal.

The Covenant with the Chosen People

Eventually God chose Abraham to become the father of a great nation. (Genesis 17:5) Over the course of many generations, the Israelites, the descendants of Abraham, Isaac, and Jacob, would suffer many trials and hardships.

The Book of Exodus tells us how God called Moses to lead the people, who were enslaved in Egypt, to freedom and the Promised Land, the land first promised by God to Abraham. At Mount Sinai, God gave Moses the Ten Commandments, the rules that sum up God's Law and show us what is required to love God and our neighbor. The Old Testament tells how God revealed his plan through Abraham and his descendants. The New Testament tells how this plan came to completion in Jesus Christ.

Jesus, the Divine Revelation

As Catholics we believe that Jesus fulfills the Revelation of God found in the Old Testament. When God helped Moses lead the Israelites across the Red Sea, it was a preview of the Salvation and freedom Jesus would bring. Jesus is the fulfillment of the promises made to Moses. Matthew describes how Jesus retraced the steps of Moses' journey. He tells how Joseph and Mary took Jesus to Egypt to save him from King Herod. Like his Hebrew ancestors, Jesus was called out of Egypt, and he retraced his journey to the Holy Land. (Matthew 2:15)

In both the Book of Exodus and in the Gospel of Matthew, God is at work saving his people. Chapters 19 and 20 of Exodus describe how Moses went up on Mount Sinai to receive the Law from God. Chapters 5–7 of Matthew recount how Jesus went up a mountain to deliver the new Law. Moses spoke with God's authority, but Jesus spoke with his own authority as the Son of God. As the Son of God, Jesus understands and proclaims the true meaning of the Law. Matthew knew that God used the Passover to help create a people of his own. Now Jesus would create a new People of God.

When the people agreed to the Covenant at Mount Sinai, it was sealed with an animal sacrifice and a meal. Moses united the people to God and his Covenant by sprinkling them with the blood of the sacrifice. At the Last Supper, Jesus explained to the Apostles that he was going to be the New Covenant. "This cup is the new covenant in my blood, which will be shed

for you." (Luke 22:20) God completed everything he wanted to say about himself by sending his own Son and establishing in him a New Covenant. Jesus' Crucifixion revealed the meaning of who he is. Looking at the bruised and battered Jesus on the cross, the Roman centurion recognizes Jesus. "Truly this man was the Son of God!" (Mark 15:39)

Jesus Helps Us Know God

Jesus helps us understand the kind of father we have in God. He tells us to go to God the Father for everything we need. Even if we run away from him, our Father will throw his arms around us and welcome us back just as a father would greet his children. Jesus calls us to friendship. "I no longer call you slaves, because a slave does not know what his master is doing. I have called you friends, because I have told you everything I have heard from my Father." (John 15:15)

In Jesus we see a God who is for all people. Jesus recognized human imperfections and sinfulness. He showed a special concern for sinners, not just the righteous, and could see beyond human failures. Jesus' forgiveness for those who repented and had a conversion of heart demonstrates the mystery of God's deep and infinite love for us.

Explore

Study Corner

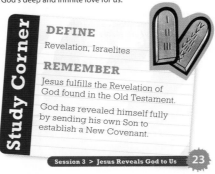

DEFINE
Revelation, Israelites

REMEMBER
Jesus fulfills the Revelation of God found in the Old Testament.

God has revealed himself fully by sending his own Son to establish a New Covenant.

Session 3 > Jesus Reveals God to Us   23

Building a Relationship with God

Remind young people that they are in a covenant relationship with God. Relationships develop over time. Suggest that starting a relationship is easy, but maintaining it is more difficult. Divide the class into groups of four or five. Distribute plastic interlocking building pieces or other building materials to each group and tell them to make a sculpture from the pieces. Next, have groups dismantle the sculpture and mix up the pieces. With blindfolds or eyes closed, have groups reassemble the sculpture. Pose discussion questions for each group to answer. Ask: *How important was listening when you tried to rebuild? How important was communicating with respect? Did rebuilding take more time than you expected? Did your group have a system of communicating? What strategies did you use when you were blindfolded?* Point out that God is there for them, but they need to listen, communicate through prayer, be patient, and show love and respect.

Read aloud The Covenant with the Chosen People and the definition of the word *Israelites* in the Glossary. Ask: *Why is it important to know about God's covenants?* (to understand that Jesus fulfilled them)

Have volunteers take turns reading the next section. Ask: *How is Jesus revealed as the new Moses?* (Possible answers: in escaping from King Herod as a baby, in delivering God's law, at the Last Supper) Draw two parallel lines on the board. Point out that the lines extend in the same direction. Say: *Things in parallel share similarities.* Explain that Matthew's Gospel shows parallels between Moses and Jesus. Write *Moses* next to one line and *Jesus* next to the other. Ask volunteers to write parallel events on each line. Then read aloud the Scripture references in the text. Say: *Without the covenant relationships of the Old Testament and the understanding that grew from them, the human race would never have recognized the Good News revealed through Jesus Christ. As Jesus ate the Passover meal with his disciples the night before he died, so today in remembrance we receive Christ's Body and Blood in the Eucharistic celebration at Mass. We use all the understandings of our ancestors in faith to celebrate the New Covenant.*

Read aloud the last section. Ask: *How does Jesus, the Son of God, help us know God the Father?* (Jesus reveals a God who wants an intimate relationship with us. He reveals a forgiving God who invites all people, even the imperfect ones, into a loving relationship.)

(3) Close

Say: *Jesus taught that he did not come to destroy the Law and the prophets but to fulfill them.* Ask: *How does the Bible reflect a process of coming to knowledge, or Revelation, through Jesus?* Invite discussion, encouraging young people to share and defend their positions.

Prayer

Follow the steps to guide young people through the prayer on page 24.

Young People's Page

Prepare Pray the prayer in advance to become familiar with it. Explain that everyone should read the parts labeled Response. Be sure young people understand that the symbol at the end of many Leader's lines is a prompt to repeat the response.

Pray Ask a volunteer to read aloud the paragraphs in the left column. Ask volunteers to explain how taking prayers to heart is different from memorizing prayers.

Have young people bring their books to the prayer space. Ask them to prepare for prayer by quieting themselves. Say: ***Take a few slow breaths and know that God is present here.*** Pause. Invite young people to pray with you the litany of thanksgiving for who they are today. Prayerfully lead the litany by praying the Leader parts. Pause briefly after each petition and prompt young people to respond as indicated.

After praying the last petition, say: ***Reflect on the words you just prayed in the silence of your hearts.*** Pause briefly in silence. Say: ***Together, let's pray aloud the closing prayer.*** Then conclude by asking everyone to pray aloud the All part.

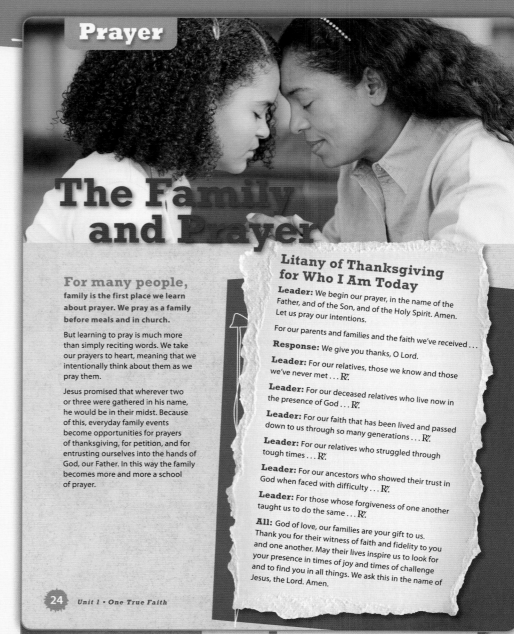

Prayer

The Family and Prayer

For many people,

family is the first place we learn about prayer. We pray as a family before meals and in church.

But learning to pray is much more than simply reciting words. We take our prayers to heart, meaning that we intentionally think about them as we pray them.

Jesus promised that wherever two or three were gathered in his name, he would be in their midst. Because of this, everyday family events become opportunities for prayers of thanksgiving, for petition, and for entrusting ourselves into the hands of God, our Father. In this way the family becomes more and more a school of prayer.

Litany of Thanksgiving for Who I Am Today

Leader: We begin our prayer, in the name of the Father, and of the Son, and of the Holy Spirit. Amen. Let us pray our intentions.

For our parents and families and the faith we've received . . .

Response: We give you thanks, O Lord.

Leader: For our relatives, those we know and those we've never met . . . ℟.

Leader: For our deceased relatives who live now in the presence of God . . . ℟.

Leader: For our faith that has been lived and passed down to us through so many generations . . . ℟.

Leader: For our relatives who struggled through tough times . . . ℟.

Leader: For our ancestors who showed their trust in God when faced with difficulty . . . ℟.

Leader: For those whose forgiveness of one another taught us to do the same . . . ℟.

All: God of love, our families are your gift to us. Thank you for their witness of faith and fidelity to you and one another. May their lives inspire us to look for your presence in times of joy and times of challenge and to find you in all things. We ask this in the name of Jesus, the Lord. Amen.

24 *Unit 1 • One True Faith*

IF TIME ALLOWS

Prayer Space

Arrange small groups and ask them to develop a plan for showing respect for the Bible in the room. If the room already has a prayer space, instruct them to work on a plan to improve its functionality or appeal as a sacred place to gather to pray. Allow groups to present and explain their ideas to the group. Have them vote on the best overall design or incorporate the best ideas from different presentations into the new prayer space. If you do not have a permanent prayer space, consider using a plastic storage tub to house your items.

FYI

Coaching Young People to Pray

Invite young people to enter more deeply into prayer by contemplating the concept of gratitude and the many blessings they have in their lives. Assure them that God is present, inviting them to speak to him with open hearts. Encourage young people to avoid any distractions as they pray with their whole hearts and minds.

WHERE Do I Fit In?

Where does God make himself known? God is everywhere. He is in the song of a spring chickadee and in the arms of a winter tree. He is in our times of joy and in our times of suffering and hardship.

by Suzanne Ecklund

God Makes Himself Known

When I was a little girl growing up on a farm in Pennsylvania, I used to put God to the test. I would lie on my bed, look up at the ceiling and pray, "God, if you are there, please place a bird in the tree outside my bedroom window." I would then peel myself off my bed and peer out the window. And there in the thin, gray arms of the tree, I would either find a bird, or I would not. Thinking back on this time, I realize that I was using my prayer as a kind of test. The kind of test that began, "God, if you are there . . ." And I never stopped looking.

I'm much older now, and although birds continue to serve as winged reminders of God's presence for me, I realize that God extends far beyond the branches of that little Pennsylvanian tree. And God doesn't even have to wait for tests from little farm girls to make his presence known. On the farm, work was defined by what nature brought—and the seasons gave this work its shape. There was a season for planting, a season for growth, a season for harvest, and a season for rest. And God's pulse was at the center of each turning.

To be human is to follow a similar path. Spiritual seasons bring joy and sadness—and everything in between! But just as God is at the center of nature's changing essence, he is also at the center of our turnings of the soul. Sometimes it's hard to imagine that God is with us during times of loss and hardship. It's easier to imagine God's presence in our lives when things are going well. But summer and winter are born out of the same mystery; autumn and spring dance in the same wind. God is present throughout our rich, colorful journey, no matter what it brings.

God Is Present

Take a picture, draw a sketch, or find pictures in magazines that show places, people, or events where God makes himself known. Explain your ideas below or on another sheet of paper.

_____
_____
_____
_____

SUZANNE ECKLUND is working toward a master of divinity at Emory University's Candler School of Theology in Atlanta, Georgia.

Reflect

IF TIME ALLOWS

God in All Seasons

Remind young people that a haiku is a short poem that often describes something in nature. It consists of three lines of five, seven, and five syllables, respectively. Then have young people work in small groups to write haiku, each capturing the presence of God in one of the four seasons. Invite groups to share their completed haiku with the group. Encourage them to add an illustration that reflects the message. If possible, display the haiku.

---

1 Begin

Read aloud the introductory text. Invite young people to answer the question, and list their responses on the board. Discuss whether the list on the board includes instances of sorrow or suffering, and if not, ask why. Remind young people that God is present not only in times of joy and beauty but in every conceivable human experience—including pain and sorrow.

2 Connect

Have volunteers take turns reading God Makes Himself Known. On the board, write the headings *spring, summer, fall,* and *winter* in separate columns. Elicit from young people words and phrases that describe each season, and write their ideas in the appropriate column. Then discuss how the descriptors could apply to the rhythms of human life. For example, trees losing their leaves in autumn remind us that we may have to let go of certain things in our lives. Point out that in nature and in life, every season of loss is followed by a season of new birth. Say: ***Hardship paves the way for joy. If we didn't have one, we couldn't have the other. God is present in different types of experiences, but it is up to us to do the looking and the finding.***

Have young people complete the God Is Present activity independently. The next time you meet, invite volunteers to share their visual representations and their reasoning with the group.

3 Close

Have partners swap stories about a time they "tested" God. Encourage them to discuss how the response they received—or an apparent lack of one—might have been an invitation to deepen their faith.

① Begin

What's What? Read aloud the directions. Emphasize that young people should circle the letter of the best choice. Have young people complete the page independently.

② Connect

Say What? Ask volunteers to read aloud and define the words. Review each word in the Glossary if necessary.

Now What? Read aloud the section. Invite young people to answer the question independently. Ask volunteers to share responses.

③ Go in Peace

Collect materials and return them to their appropriate places. Encourage young people to realize God's presence during the week by making observations in daily life not only with their physical senses but with their hearts and minds. Say: *Prayerful meditation is an opportunity to separate yourself from distractions, speak to God from your heart, and listen for his response.*

3-Minute Retreat
Give young people an opportunity for quiet meditation at **www.loyolapress.com/retreat**.

What's What?

Respond

Circle the letter of the choice that best completes each sentence.

1. God promised _____ that his descendants would be "as countless as the stars of the sky." (PAGE 20)
   - a. Jesus
   - **b. Abraham** (circled)
   - c. Moses
   - d. Adam and Eve

2. We can read about Jesus' genealogy in _____. (PAGE 20)
   - a. the Book of Genesis
   - b. the Book of Exodus
   - **c. the Gospel of Matthew** (circled)
   - d. the Gospel of Mark

3. After Adam and Eve's fall from grace, _____. (PAGE 22)
   - a. God breaks his promise
   - b. the Devil is defeated
   - c. the human family is restored
   - **d. God promises a plan of Salvation** (circled)

4. God called _____ to lead the Israelites to freedom. (PAGE 23)
   - **a. Moses** (circled)
   - b. Abraham
   - c. Noah
   - d. Isaac

5. The Revelation of God found in Old Testament events is fulfilled with _____. (PAGE 23)
   - a. the Ten Commandments
   - b. King David
   - **c. Jesus** (circled)
   - d. Moses

6. At the Last Supper, Jesus explained that he was going to be the _____. (PAGE 23)
   - a. new king
   - **b. New Covenant** (circled)
   - c. last apostle
   - d. greatest prophet

Say What?
Know the definitions of these terms.

Abraham	Israelites
genealogy	Revelation

Now What?
God has revealed himself fully to us by sending his own Son. What is something you can do this week to help you find God or realize his presence in your daily life?
Answers will vary.

_____
_____
_____
_____
_____
_____
_____
_____
_____

26   *Unit 1 • One True Faith*

IF TIME ALLOWS

Service: Fair-Trade Initiative

Explain that Catholics believe the economy is meant to serve all people. Plan time for young people to learn more about fair trade by researching or working with a local not-for-profit organization dedicated to fair trade. Have young people work with leaders to implement a plan for purchasing fair-trade products for use in the school or community, such as coffee, tea, sports equipment, or clothing. Have young people plan and produce a video to convince the school board, parish leaders, or community leaders of the idea's value.

✝ *Work and Workers*

Session Assessment Option

An assessment for this session can be found at www.findinggod.com.

PLAN AHEAD: Get Ready for Session 4

Consult the catechist preparation pages to prepare for Session 4 and determine any materials you will need.

Jesus Calls Us to Say Yes

3-Minute Retreat

Before you prepare the session, pause and be still. Take three deep breaths and be aware of the loving presence of God, who is with you on this journey.

Luke 1:26–28

In the sixth month, the angel Gabriel was sent from God to a town of Galilee called Nazareth, to a virgin betrothed to a man named Joseph, of the house of David, and the virgin's name was Mary. And coming to her, he said, "Hail, favored one! The Lord is with you."

Reflection

The story is familiar. The angel Gabriel delivers God's message to Mary. In that brief encounter, Mary's life is changed forever and so is ours. She is invited into a unique relationship with God, and after questioning the angel, accepts God's invitation to give birth to his Son. Just when she may have been thinking that she knew how her life would unfold—marry Joseph and live a simple life together in Nazareth—her whole life is turned upside down. Her freely given yes brings God closer to the human family than had even been imagined. As the first disciple, Mary is our model of what entrusting our lives to God means.

Questions

How do I freely say yes to Jesus in my ordinary day-to-day life? What do I want to learn from Mary about being a disciple of her Son?

 Concluding Prayer

Speak to God, using the words of this prayer or your own.

Loving God, we honor Mary as the Mother of God and our mother. Help us follow her example of complete trust in you.

Knowing and Sharing Your Faith in Session 4

Consider how Scripture and Tradition can deepen your understanding of session content.

Scripture

Luke 1:26–38 tells us that the angel Gabriel announced to Mary that she would conceive a child through the Holy Spirit and name him Jesus.

Psalm 28:7 recognizes the gift of God's grace as a source of protection and help.

Tradition

To become the mother of the Savior, Mary was prepared by God from the moment of her conception. The angel Gabriel salutes Mary as "favored one." [Luke 1:28] In order for Mary to assent freely to her calling, it was necessary that she be born full of God's grace. Through the centuries, the Church has become increasingly aware that Mary was redeemed from the moment of her conception and preserved from Original Sin. This is what Pope Pius IX defined in 1854 when he proclaimed the dogma of the Immaculate Conception.

Catholic Social Teaching

In this session the integrated Catholic Social Teaching theme is **Life and Dignity of the Human Person.** See page 1b for an explanation of this theme.

Window on the Catechism

The mysteries of the Annunciation and the Immaculate Conception are discussed in *CCC* 484–511.

General Directory for Catechesis

Catechesis on the Blessed Virgin Mary is discussed in *GDC* 196.

One-Hour Session Planner

SESSION 4 Jesus Calls Us to Say Yes

Session Theme: *Mary was the first person to say yes to Jesus and experience God's grace.*

Before This Session

▶ Bookmark your Bible to Luke 1:26–38, Luke 1:42, Luke 10:29–37, Isaiah 7:14, Genesis 6:8, Genesis 17:19, Genesis 18:2–3, Exodus 33:12–17, 2 Samuel 15:25, Psalm 28:7, Psalm 121:1–2, and Ephesians 1:2. Place the open Bible in your prayer space.

▶ Read the Guide for this session, choose any additional If Time Allows activities that you might have time to complete, and gather the listed materials.

STEPS	APPROXIMATE TIME
Engage *Jesus Calls Us to Say Yes* PAGE 27	10 minutes
Explore *The Annunciation: Will You Say Yes?* PAGES 28–29 *Grace* PAGES 30–31	30–40 minutes
Reflect *Prayer:* Favored by God PAGE 32 *Where Do I Fit In?* PAGE 33	10–15 minutes
Respond *What's What?* PAGE 34	10–15 minutes

Prayer in Session 4

Continue the same pattern and tone for prayer in this session. Young people pray a short prayer at the beginning of the session and conclude with an invitation to access a 3-Minute Retreat that is based on Scripture verses. Session 4 includes an extended guided reflection for young people, which is a special approach to meditative prayer. Follow the Prepare directions on the Catechist Guide page before sharing with young people.

TAKE IT HOME

Homework options:

Basilica of the Annunciation   PAGE 28

A Model of Grace   PAGE 31

Materials

REQUIRED

▶ Slips of paper with temptation scenarios written on them (page 27)

▶ Bibles (pages 28, 29)

▶ Writing supplies (pages 29, 31, 33, 34)

▶ Small tokens or healthy snacks (page 30)

▶ Saint Ignatius of Loyola's *Suscipe* (page 31)

▶ CD player (page 32)

▶ CD 1, Track 7: Reflective Music (page 32)

▶ Computers with Internet access (page 34)

OPTIONAL

▶ Bible (page 27)

▶ Tape, empty boxes, parking cones, labels for imaginary hazards, blindfold (page 29)

▶ Session 4 BLM, T-352 (page 30)

▶ Suggestion box (page 32)

▶ Note cards, writing supplies (page 33)

▶ Voice recorders (page 33)

▶ Writing supplies, stationery, stamps (page 34)

▶ Session 4 Assessment, www.findinggod.com (page 34)

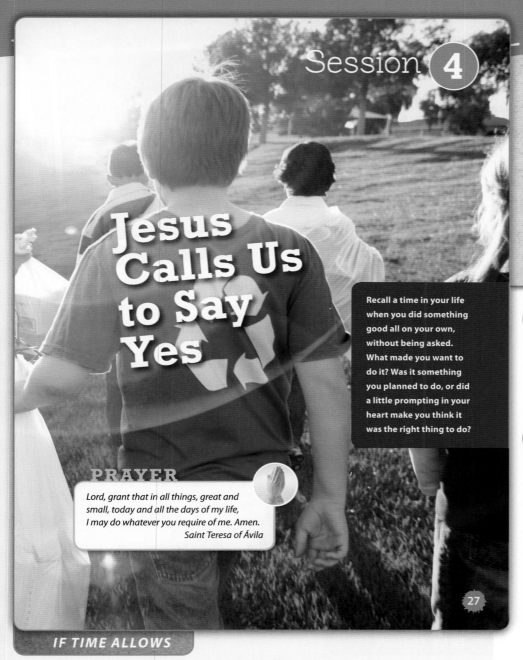

Session 4

Jesus Calls Us to Say Yes

Recall a time in your life when you did something good all on your own, without being asked. What made you want to do it? Was it something you planned to do, or did a little prompting in your heart make you think it was the right thing to do?

PRAYER

Lord, grant that in all things, great and small, today and all the days of my life, I may do whatever you require of me. Amen.
Saint Teresa of Ávila

27

SESSION 4

OUTCOMES

▶ **Explain why Mary's trust in God makes her a model of faith.**

▶ **State that grace is a free gift from God.**

▶ **Practice meditative prayer.**

▶ **Define** *actual grace, Annunciation, grace, habitual grace, Immaculate Conception, intercession,* **and** *sanctifying grace.*

① Set the Stage

Read aloud the questions on page 27. Give young people a few minutes to record their ideas or share them with a partner.

② Get Started

Write different temptation scenarios on slips of paper. The scenarios should suggest situations that require some kind of response. For example:

▶ You see money fall unnoticed from a woman's wallet as she pays for her lunch.

▶ Your brother, with whom you've been fighting, needs help with his homework.

▶ Your classmate's answers to a test are easily visible.

Give groups time to prepare different responses to the scenarios. Ask groups to role-play their responses for the group. Then read aloud the session title. Ask: ***How do you think our responses in life and the session title might be related?*** (Possible answer: When we respond to situations the way Jesus would, we are saying yes to him.)

 Prayer

Say: ***Close your eyes, fold your hands, and pray silently as I pray aloud.*** Pray aloud the prayer. Conclude by praying the Sign of the Cross.

IF TIME ALLOWS

The Good Samaritan

Say: ***Jesus is always calling us to put faith into action.*** Read aloud the story of the Good Samaritan in Luke 10:29–37. Ask: ***What is Jesus teaching us about saying yes?*** (Jesus is saying it is our responsibility to care for everyone in need, not just our friends and family, or others who love us without question. Sometimes it takes courage and risk that requires trust in God.) Ask: ***How might the message be different if the person who stopped to help hadn't been a Samaritan?*** (The message might be to help people who are like us.) Ask: ***How might a good deed affect the future?*** (A good deed can have a ripple effect, inspiring others or leading to further good outcomes.)

➤ Go to **www.findinggod.com/sessionextenders** for Catholic beliefs about Mary. You may wish to share this with the group.

① Begin

Say: *Catholics believe that angels are messengers of God and a reminder of God's constant love and protection for each and every person. I'm going to read three statements about angels. Show me a thumbs up if the statement is true or a thumbs down if the statement is false.* Say: *Angels appear in the Bible.* (thumbs up) *Angels are never identified by name in the Bible.* (thumbs down) *Angels have no choice but to obey God.* (thumbs down) Continue as time allows.

② Connect

Read aloud the article title and the first four paragraphs. Say: *Mary was a teenager and a betrothed wife, living apart from her husband for up to a year, as was the custom. Gabriel's announcement was amazing.*

Have a volunteer read aloud the section Mary's Act of Faith. Ask young people to read the full Bible account in Luke 1:26–38. Point out Gabriel's words, "The Lord is with you." Say: *These words are more than a pleasant greeting.* Explain that Mary recognized that God used these same words to call great leaders in Scripture, such as Moses, Isaac, and David. She knew God had singled her out for something extraordinary. Say: *We'll never know what went through Mary's mind, but she accepted freely and with utter faith. She knew God would be with her, protecting her.* Point out that it is okay to feel frightened or confused by events in daily life. We can live as best we know how and trust God.

Our Catholic Character

Ask a volunteer to read Our Catholic Character. Explain that in this same apostolic letter, Pope John Paul II said the mistreatment of women has resulted in "a spiritual impoverishment of humanity." Ask young people to discuss what he means.

The Annunciation: Will You Say Yes?

The Annunciation, Francesco Furini.

IN the Gospel of Luke (1:26–38), the young Mary is given a glimpse into the future, one in which she gives birth to the Savior. This announcement is delivered by the angel Gabriel, who is acting as a messenger of God.

Gabriel's announcement, called the **Annunciation,** reveals to Mary that her Son will be named Jesus. The word *Jesus* means "God saves."

Gabriel tells Mary that she will conceive a child through the Holy Spirit. This fulfills a prophecy in the Book of Isaiah (Isaiah 7:14), which says that the Messiah will be born of a virgin and be a descendant of King David's.

Mary asks Gabriel how this is possible. Although she and Joseph were betrothed, she was living with her family and apart from Joseph. Gabriel assures Mary that "nothing will be impossible for God." (Luke 1:37) With God—through God and with God's help—nothing is impossible. Nothing is closed to possibility.

Mary's Act of Faith

Mary accepts the announcement that Gabriel describes. She chooses it. She embraces it. The future will hold bright moments (Jesus' healing ministry) and sorrowful moments (Jesus' Crucifixion), but such is Mary's faith. She says yes to God. "Behold, I am the handmaid of the Lord. May it be done to me according to your word." (Luke 1:38) In saying yes to God, Mary shows complete faith and trust in him. In saying yes to becoming the mother of Jesus, she becomes Jesus' first disciple.

Gabriel tells Mary that her cousin Elizabeth has also conceived a child. This child, Jesus' cousin, is John the Baptist. Because Elizabeth is pregnant in her old age, she reminds us of Sarah, the wife of Abraham, who conceived her only son, Isaac, in her old age. (Genesis 17:19)

Our Catholic Character

During the time that Jesus lived, women were not treated with equality. Jesus set a new example. Unlike many people of that time, Jesus treated women with openness, respect, acceptance, and tenderness.

Likewise, our Catholic character is to treat all people with justice and equality. In his 1995 apostolic letter *Letter to Women,* Pope John Paul II acknowledged that the Church, along with the rest of society, had not always followed Jesus' lead in his treatment of women. He thanked all women for their contributions in every area—social, economic, cultural, artistic, and political. The pope continued to say that it is a matter of justice, but also of necessity, that social systems be redesigned in a way that favors the processes of humanization that mark the "civilization of love."

28 Unit 1 • One True Faith

TAKE IT HOME

Basilica of the Annunciation

Have young people use reliable Catholic Web sites to conduct online research on the Basilica of the Annunciation in Nazareth. Explain that the basilica contains the grotto that is said to contain the home of Mary and the site of the Annunciation. Tell them that the basilica contains sacred works of art, including images of Mary that reflect the cultures of countries or regions from five continents. Have young people find an example of Marian art found in the Basilica of the Annunciation and make a color copy. Back in class, have each young person present his or her research and Marian image. Have the group discuss the similarities and differences among the images. Incorporate the topic of enculturation in the Catholic Church into the discussion. Explain that enculturation roots the Gospel in the lives of people worldwide by showing respect and valuing different cultures. This helps to explain different ways that Mary is portrayed in art.

Celebrating Mary

Throughout Scripture many people say yes to God, but Mary's yes gives profound insight into how we as Catholics see and celebrate Mary. The Catholic teaching of the **Immaculate Conception** proclaims Mary free from sin at the moment her parents conceived her and teaches that she remained free from personal sin all her life. In this light, Mary's yes to God truly does fulfill who she is, from the moment she is given life.

Gabriel's announcement and Mary's acceptance change the course of her life. Her yes to Gabriel is sometimes called her *fiat*, a Latin word that means "let it be done." Mary's willingness to respond to God's call is why we as Catholics hold her in high regard and with such devotion. Her yes to becoming the mother of Jesus makes her a model of discipleship. When we respond to God with our own fiat, we embrace a direction that centers around Jesus.

The Gospel account of the Annunciation ends with the words "Then the angel departed from her." (Luke 1:38) We might imagine Mary as being quite alone to contemplate this startling announcement, this Annunciation. But in making her choice, Mary is not alone. She has Jesus, and he will be with her during her journey of faith.

Explain the Annunciation

Write a scene for a movie or play that uses the words from Luke's account of the Annunciation. Continue on another sheet of paper if needed.

_____
_____
_____
_____
_____
_____
_____

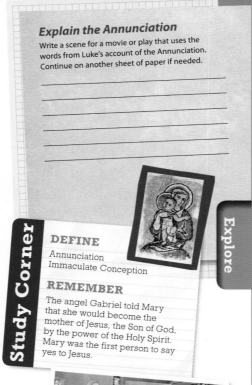

Study Corner

DEFINE

Annunciation
Immaculate Conception

REMEMBER

The angel Gabriel told Mary that she would become the mother of Jesus, the Son of God, by the power of the Holy Spirit. Mary was the first person to say yes to Jesus.

Explore

SACRED ART

At age 15 French painter Maurice Denis was sure about what he wanted to do. He felt a calling and said yes to it. He wrote in his journal, "I have to be a Christian painter and celebrate all the miracles of Christianity; I feel that it has to be so." In this painting, the figures are in a modern setting rather than a historically accurate one. The artist wanted to use color and symbols to communicate emotion or intimacy. The Virgin Mary was one of his favorite subjects.

The Annunciation, Maurice Denis, 1913.

Session 4 > Jesus Calls Us to Say Yes   29

ADVENTURES IN FAITH

Obstacle Course

Arrange an obstacle course before class starts. Choose an outdoor or indoor area. Use tape to set course boundaries and include twists and turns along the way. Label imaginary hazards, such as water, quicksand, rough road, or deer crossing. Make sure other hazards on the path are safe, soft, and light, such as empty boxes or parking cones. Remind young people that Mary fully embraced the idea of becoming the mother of the Messiah, even though she must have been afraid and had no idea what was ahead of her. With this idea in mind, assign partners roles of "walker" or "talker." Walkers wear a blindfold while talkers guide them through the course using verbal directions only. After all walkers have had a turn, have partners reverse roles, but take time to rearrange the obstacle course so the course remains new and unknown. Ask them to discuss the following: *Which is easier—seeing the course with your own eyes or trusting directions while blindfolded? Why? How does this "journey" relate to Mary's saying yes to God?*

Have volunteers read aloud Celebrating Mary. Write on the board *Annunciation* and *Immaculate Conception* and read aloud the definitions in the Glossary. Say: ***The Annunciation celebrates Gabriel's announcement that Mary, through the Holy Spirit, would conceive Jesus. So Jesus had no human, biological father. The Immaculate Conception recognizes that Mary, whose biological parents were Anne and Joachim, was free from Original Sin from the moment of her conception and remained free of sin throughout her life.***

Have young people use their Bibles to read Luke 1:30. Explain Gabriel's words, "Do not be afraid, Mary, for you have found favor with God." Say: ***Being favored was no small thing. These words parallel the accounts of Old Testament people who found favor with God: Noah, Abraham, Moses, and David.*** Have young people find and read Genesis 6:8, Genesis 18:2–3, Exodus 33:12–17, and 2 Samuel 15:25. Discuss God's favor in each account.

Read aloud the directions in the activity. Before young people write, tell them to imagine the most important feelings or ideas they want to impart in their scene.

Sacred Art

Ask a volunteer to read aloud the Sacred Art feature. Say: ***Maurice Denis used art to say yes to God.*** Ask: ***What are some other ways to use talents to say yes to God?*** (Possible answers: song, dance, prayer, poetry, speaking skills, service, volunteer work)

③ Close

To close this article discussion, invite young people to record answers to these questions:

▶ When have you made a leap of faith?

▶ How did you feel after making your decision?

① Begin

Bring small tokens or healthy snacks to pass out to winners of simple challenges. For example, say: **The first person who raises both hands gets this gift. The person sitting with the best posture gets this gift. The first person to smile gets this gift.** After several demonstrations, say: **God's gift of grace does not work like this; God's grace is free and undeserved. It is an invitation to participate in the life of God—it is not a reward or something we earned. Even though God's grace is free, it's up to us to accept the invitation.**

② Connect

 Read aloud the article title and the opening paragraphs that follow. Say: **Mary is "full of grace," meaning favored by God. Favor is something given; she simply receives. Mary sets aside worries and trusts God. She experiences God acting in her life.** Ask a volunteer to read aloud the definition of *grace* in the Glossary. Point out the verses from the Book of Psalms. Challenge young people to find other verses in the Bible that recognize God's grace as a source of strength and help.

Have volunteers read the section Actual Grace. Say: **Grace is God's favor. Actual grace is God's assistance that allows us participation in life as his adopted children.** Refer young people to the term in the Glossary. Suggest that one way they can deepen their awareness of God's grace is through reflective prayer, such as the Daily Examen. Point out that acknowledging moments of grace throughout the day helps them see where God is leading them and what actions he prompts them to take. Refer young people to more information about the Daily Examen on page 279 in Prayers and Practices.

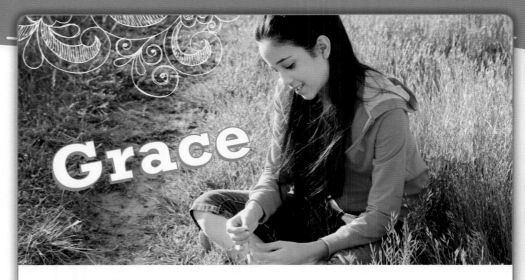

Grace

MARY believed; she had faith. Complete faith requires a response, a yes, when God reveals himself and gives himself to us.

When we pray the Hail Mary, the first thing we say about the Mother of God is that she is "full of grace." By **grace** we don't mean that Mary has poise or is graceful in movement. We mean that she lives wholly and fully in the grace of God.

We recognize the Lord God as a source of human help in the many professions of faith found in the Book of Psalms. For example, Psalm 28:7 recognizes God's grace as a source of protection and help:

> The Lord is my strength and my shield,
>   in whom my heart trusts.
> I am helped, so my heart rejoices;
>   with my song I praise him.

Psalm 121:1–2 acknowledges the Lord as guardian:

> I raise my eyes toward the mountains.
>   From whence shall come my help?
> My help comes from the Lord,
>   the maker of heaven and earth.

Actual Grace

When we need help, strength, and support to accomplish a task or endure a difficult time, God is there to bestow on us his grace—that is, a share in his divine power and life. Grace that helps us make choices to live as God wants us to live is called **actual grace.** We don't need to be going through hardship to ask for and receive God's grace. We may, for example, begin our day by asking God for his grace to help us do his work throughout the day. We may ask for God's grace to help us concentrate in class or to lend depth of feeling to our praying.

Grace is a deep and intimate connection between God and us. Grace is the gift of God's own self to humans. It makes us capable of living in God's love and acting in that love in our daily lives.

"Grace is the gift of God's own self to humans."

30 *Unit 1 • One True Faith*

IF TIME ALLOWS

Session 4 BLM

Cardinal Virtues Let young people know that the word *cardinal* comes from the Latin *cardo,* for *hinge,* meaning "that on which other things depend." Explain that the Cardinal Virtues are human virtues that are acquired through grace when people practice good actions. Provide each young person with the Session 4 Blackline Master [T-352]. As they complete the Blackline Master, ask young people to consider why a hinge is a good way to think about the Cardinal Virtues.

Sanctifying, or Habitual, Grace

The word *sanctify*, meaning "to make sacred," has a similar root word in Latin as the word *saint* and refers to holiness as a state of being in the human soul. **Sanctifying grace** is imparted to us first through the Sacrament of Baptism and produces in us a permanent condition in which we are pleasing to God as God's children. Through the state of sanctifying grace, we participate in God's divine spirituality. The Catholic Church teaches that without this grace, we cannot achieve this participation in God's spirituality.

Our sanctified soul predisposes us to live in goodness in God's eyes and to follow God's Law. This predisposition becomes a condition of our character, or in Latin, *habitus*. Sanctifying grace, then, as it refers to our God-given inclination and capacity for good, is sometimes called **habitual grace.**

God's gift of grace to us, his children, is unique and special. It cannot be bought, bargained for, traded for, or even earned by a particular number of good deeds. God alone bestows the gift of grace freely and unconditionally, because God gives this gift out of abundant love for us.

Grace is without limit and without quantity. Imagine a candle receiving a flame from another lit candle. The first flame is not diminished, and yet now there is twice the light and twice the warmth.

Although grace is not ours to give, we may certainly wish God's grace on other people. Saint Paul wishes God's grace and peace to the Philippians, the Ephesians, and the Galatians: "grace to you and peace from God our Father and the Lord Jesus Christ." (Ephesians 1:2)

Study Corner

DEFINE

grace, actual grace, sanctifying grace, habitual grace

REMEMBER

God's grace is a gift, freely given and not earned. With God's grace we live in his love and make decisions about our actions that will lead us to do what is good.

Past Meets Present

PAST: Saint Ignatius of Loyola was born in Spain in 1491. A nobleman who became a soldier, his life changed when he was injured in battle and began to read the Bible and about the lives of saints. He became a priest and founded a religious order called the Society of Jesus (the Jesuits). One of his greatest contributions to Catholicism is a book he wrote called the *Spiritual Exercises*, which includes a special prayer. Through the prayer a person dedicates all of himself or herself to God. The prayer asks to use all of one's talents to do what God wills. It asks that God give his love and grace because that is all a person wants in life. God's love and grace are enough.

PRESENT: Matt Maher is one of the most critically acclaimed Catholic musicians today. He has received several awards, and young people especially find that his vibrant music speaks to the heart. One of his most popular songs, "Your Grace Is Enough," is included on *Empty and Beautiful*. Saint Ignatius knew that God's grace is enough, and Matt Maher's song with the same phrase gives us the chance to pray it and sing it at the same time.

Explore

TAKE IT HOME

A Model of Grace

Remind young people that although Mary is a model of grace, she was also a real person. Mary experienced tough times. She lived in Nazareth, part of an occupied state under the rule of imperial Rome. She lived with the constant threat of violence. She gave birth while she and Joseph were homeless, and they had to flee like refugees to a strange land to escape being killed by a jealous king.

Ask young people to think about someone they know who acts in keeping with God's call. For homework, have them write character traits, anecdotes, or other descriptions of this person on slips of paper. Then have them trace and cut out an outline of Mary onto mural paper and attach their descriptions to the outline. Display their ideas of people who represent contemporary models of grace.

Have volunteers take turns reading the section Sanctifying, or Habitual, Grace. Read aloud the definitions of the terms *sanctifying grace* and *habitual grace* in the Glossary. Point out that sanctifying grace is first received in Baptism. Explain that we receive the grace that Jesus made possible through his suffering and Death in order to secure our own Salvation. Baptism is our call to Christian life. Say: ***Baptism is a gift from God that opens the door to life in the Spirit and access to the other sacraments.*** Be sure young people understand that Original Sin is cleansed in the Sacrament of Baptism. Say: ***Unfortunately, the tendency to sin is an ongoing human battle. Even after being baptized, people continue to sin. We need the healing grace we receive in the Sacrament of Penance and Reconciliation and the other sacraments.***

Past Meets Present

Read the feature. Refer young people to page 278 in Prayers and Practices. Pray together Saint Ignatius of Loyola's *Suscipe* and discuss the meaning of the prayer.

> *Take, Lord, and receive all my liberty, my memory, my understanding, and my entire will. All I have and call my own.*
>
> *You have given all to me. To you, Lord, I return it.*
>
> *Everything is yours; do with it what you will. Give me only your love and your grace. That is enough for me.*

③ Close

Ask: ***During what times of grace have you become more aware than usual of God's presence in your life? How are you a better person because of this surprise moment?*** Invite young people to write answers to these questions.

Prayer

Follow the steps to guide young people through the prayer on page 32.

Young People's Page

Prepare Pray the prayer in advance to become familiar with it. Remind everyone to respond at the All parts.

Pray Have volunteers take turns reading aloud the paragraphs in the left column. Invite a volunteer to read aloud the definition of *intercession* in the Glossary. Allow time for young people to respond aloud to the question in the final paragraph.

Then have young people bring their books to the prayer space and sit quietly. Say: **Empty your mind of needless worries and distractions. Ask God for his grace to lead you to what is good.**

Explain that they will pray a meditation based on Luke 1:26–38. Slowly pray aloud the guided reflection, or have young people silently pray the text. Play reflective music quietly [CD 1, Track 7]. If you read aloud, pause after each paragraph to allow time for meditation. If young people are reading themselves, allow sufficient time.

Pray the Hail Mary together as indicated. Say: **Reflect on the words we just prayed in the silence of your hearts, listening closely for what God is telling you.**

Conclude by praying aloud the Leader part. Pause and pray together the Sign of the Cross. Say: **As we continue the session, ask God to help you become more aware of his grace in your daily life and to guide you to respond with loving actions.**

Prayer

Favored by God

Most hymns and prayers to Mary contain two elements. The first element is praising God for the great things he did for her and through her for all human beings. The second element is entrusting our needs to her.

Because Mary knows our needs, we rely on her **intercession.** These elements are found in the Hail Mary. The angel Gabriel greets her with the words "Hail, favored one! The Lord is with you," and we pray "Hail Mary, full of grace, the Lord is with you." (Luke 1:28) Mary is wholly given to God, who has come to dwell in her. God promises she will not be alone.

When Mary visits Elizabeth, she greets Mary with the words "Most blessed are you among women." (Luke 1:42) Because of her faith, Mary becomes the mother of all believers. All the nations of the earth receive the blessing of God through Mary. Then we pray "Holy Mary, Mother of God." We entrust all our cares and petitions to her. Like Mary, whose response to God was "May it be done to me according to your word," we abandon ourselves to the will of God. (Luke 1:38) We ask her to "Pray for us sinners, now and at the hour of our death." We acknowledge our weakness and ask for her support. We look for her to welcome us into God's presence.

What do you think of when you think of Mary's Annunciation? This meditation may help you better understand the place of honor she holds for followers of her Son, Jesus.

Annunciation Meditation

Imagine yourself in Mary's place. What would you think if an angel appeared to you? Would you be surprised? Would you be nervous or even laugh? Would you be so filled with awe at seeing an angel standing before you that you'd be afraid? What would you want to ask the angel?

Now imagine that the angel Gabriel speaks to you. Hear the angel say "Hail, favored one! The Lord is with you." Reflect on this message. How does it feel to be favored by God?

Imagine pondering the message the angel tells you. Think of the many feelings and questions you would have. Now hear yourself saying yes. Feel a sense of calm wash over you.

As you pray the Hail Mary, meditate about each line's meaning to your life.

Pray the Hail Mary.

Take note. What is God asking you to do at this time in your life? Be still and see if anything surfaces in your heart. Hear yourself respond with the same words that Mary spoke: "May it be done to me according to your word." Now become aware of your acceptance of God's call. Remember that Mary is our mother and that she is always ready to help us grow as disciples of her Son.

IF TIME ALLOWS

Marian Devotion

Provide a suggestion box and ask young people to write ideas about how they might honor Mary on a regular basis throughout the year. As a group, decide how to change one idea into an action plan. For example, young people might honor Mary by placing her statue in the prayer space, including her in daily intercessions, or praying the Rosary regularly as a group.

FYI

Coaching Young People to Pray

Before praying, ask young people to imagine their favorite image of Mary. Explain that when we pray the Hail Mary, we ask our Blessed Mother to be present to us, to pray for us, and to help us as we ask for the grace to do God's work.

WHERE Do I Fit In?

Life is a roller-coaster ride of changes and challenges. When you find yourself in a difficult situation and you are not quite sure what to do, how do you respond? Do you worry? Get angry? Avoid the problem altogether? God invites you to respond to challenges with faith, courage, strength, and generosity.

by Claire Gillen

Waiting

I was just a day away from finishing my first semester in college. Soon I would be traveling home to spend Christmas with my family. So why was I miserable? Maybe it was because I still had to take an exam in my least favorite subject, and I panicked every time I thought about it. To be honest, I thought about this class as little as possible. I knew that I hadn't studied with the same diligence that I had applied to the classes that I liked.

Weary, I reported to my part-time job in the library. I usually found the task of shelving books tedious, but on this day I discovered that the time passed more quickly, and I was enjoying the work. I began to think about reasons *why*. Shelving books was a job I had to do, but this time I threw myself into it and focused carefully—something I *didn't* do all the time. It occurred to me that my failure to throw myself wholeheartedly into the work right in front of me was part of a broader pattern. For example, in eighth grade, if I encountered a challenging class, I would reassure myself that high school was the real time to buckle down. In high school, I daydreamed about buckling down in college. I wasn't dealing with the present so much as I was imagining an easier future.

If I kept waiting for tomorrows instead of meeting my todays with faith, I would never become the kind of person God wanted me to be. If I didn't respond positively to the challenges right in front of me, I was not living fully as God intended. It was a moment of grace. God used my simple work at the library to remind me that some of life's larger battles can be conquered by facing the work right in front of me. During this moment of grace, I realized the exhilarating truth—the present moment is the only moment that I have to say yes to God and to ask for his help so that I may follow him better.

CLAIRE GILLEN is a history major at the University of Notre Dame.

YES to God

Saying yes to God is an act of faith. Copy and complete this idea web on another sheet of paper. Make the surrounding ovals large enough to write your ideas. Then write ways to say yes in each one.

Session 4 > Jesus Calls Us to Say Yes   33

---

① Begin

Read aloud the introductory text. Invite young people to share their typical responses to difficult situations. Then discuss which responses seem healthiest. Point out that we are tempted to sin. Anger is a capital sin, a vice that can lead us into greater sinfulness. We can let ourselves lapse into this temptation because it looks like the easy path. Say: ***God is always calling us into relationship and away from the "easy choices" that lead to greater sinfulness. The harder lesson is to let go of our selfish motives and to open ourselves up to the grace continually offered to us by our patient God.***

② Connect

Have volunteers take turns reading aloud Waiting. Discuss young people's experiences performing tedious tasks such as washing dishes, raking leaves, or folding laundry. Ask: ***What makes the tasks more enjoyable?*** (Possible answers: working with others instead of alone, listening to music, noticing the progress being made) Say: ***When we put off an unpleasant task, we multiply our own misery by creating a longer period of dread and anxiety for ourselves. On the other hand, when we tackle a task head-on, we reduce the amount of time and energy it takes. We drain the task of its power to make us miserable.***

Have young people complete the YES to God activity with a partner. Encourage them to be specific. When all pairs are done, invite them to share what they wrote with the group.

③ Close

Have young people think of a specific task, issue, or challenge to which they consistently respond with a no. Invite them to explain how they might respond yes the next time the challenge presents itself.

IF TIME ALLOWS

God Is in the Details

Arrange young people in groups and give each group a note card on which is written one of the following tasks: *tidying one's room, walking the dog, chatting with an elderly neighbor, taking out the trash, completing a math assignment, flossing one's teeth.* Make additional cards as needed. Then have group members brainstorm ways their given task can bring them closer to God. Write on the board: *When I fold the laundry, I pay attention to different textures and thank God for my hands and their ability to feel. I thank God for my ability to fold. I am grateful for having clothes to wear and for the appliances that keep them clean.* Invite groups to share their ideas. Encourage young people to adopt these attitudes whenever they perform everyday tasks.

INCLUSION

Physical

Expressing Ideas If you have young people with limitations in movement, they may have difficulty writing responses in the idea web described in the Connect step. Provide voice recorders so they can speak their responses. Be sure to provide prompt feedback.

① Begin

What's What? Have volunteers read aloud the directions. Remind them to refer to the pages shown to find the answers. Have young people complete the page independently or with a partner.

② Connect

Say What? Ask volunteers to read aloud and define the terms. Review each term in the Glossary if necessary.

Now What? Ask a volunteer to read aloud the directions. Invite each young person to reflect and gather their thoughts before composing a prayer independently.

③ Go in Peace

Collect materials and return them to their appropriate places. Encourage young people to pray their prayer each day of the week. Say: **Consider praying your prayer at the same time each day. Feel free to express new thoughts or feelings in your prayer as your week unfolds. Consider what is happening around you and within you to make your prayer meaningful and to bring you closer to God.**

What's What?

Respond

Use details from the text to answer each question.

1. Who delivered a message to Mary, telling her that she would have a Son named Jesus? (PAGE 28)
   the angel Gabriel

2. Mary is our model in faith. As the first of Jesus' disciples, what was she the first to do? (PAGE 28)
   She was the first to say yes to God.

3. What does the word *Jesus* mean? (PAGE 28)
   Jesus means "God saves."

4. What does the Immaculate Conception mean? (PAGE 29)
   It means that Mary was conceived without sin and remained sinless throughout her life.

5. How does actual grace help us? (PAGE 30)
   Actual grace helps us make choices to live as God wants us to live.

6. How is sanctifying, or habitual grace, first given to us? (PAGE 31)
   Sanctifying, or habitual grace, is imparted to us first through the Sacrament of Baptism.

Say What?

Know the definitions of these terms.

actual grace
Annunciation
grace
habitual grace
Immaculate Conception
intercession
sanctifying grace

Now What?

Compose a brief prayer. In your prayer dedicate yourself to God, telling God that you say yes to what he wants you to do. Think of one or two talents or gifts God has given you that you can use in God's service. Then pray the completed pray in the silence of your heart.

34   *Unit 1 • One True Faith*

IF TIME ALLOWS

Service: Advocate for Women

In Jesus' time, women had few domestic or religious rights and relied on the protection and authority of men. In contrast, Jesus welcomed women. Ask a community educator to speak on the topic of domestic violence and its effects on women and children. After the visit, guide a letter-writing campaign to community merchants, requesting goods and services for a local shelter. Enlist adult helpers to deliver goods.

✝ *Life and Dignity*

Session Assessment Option

An assessment for this session can be found at www.findinggod.com.

3-Minute Retreat
Give young people an opportunity for quiet meditation at **www.loyolapress.com/retreat**.

PLAN AHEAD: Get Ready for Session 5

Consult the catechist preparation pages to prepare for Session 5 and determine any materials you will need.

Celebrating Ordinary Time

3-Minute Retreat

Before you prepare the session, pause and be still. Take three deep breaths and be aware of the loving presence of God, who is with you on this journey.

James 2:14–17

What good is it, my brothers, if someone says he has faith but does not have works? Can that faith save him? If a brother or sister has nothing to wear and has no food for the day, and one of you says to them, "Go in peace, keep warm, and eat well," but you do not give them the necessities of the body, what good is it? So also faith of itself, if it does not have works, is dead.

Reflection

The Letter of James presents in strong terms the relationship between faith and social justice. Words of comfort alone will not do; there also has to be action on behalf of those in need. James's letter calls on all Christians to reflect on the social concerns of their time and to take concrete steps to address the needs of their community. It also calls for discernment and prayer to the Holy Spirit to direct our contributions to specific needs based on how these speak to our hearts.

Questions

What social concerns speak to your heart and can help direct your contributions? What needs of the world do you bring to God in prayer?

Prayer

Speak to God, using the words of this prayer or your own.

Jesus, you care for all. Help me recognize ways in which I may share in ministering to those in need, whom you love so much.

Knowing and Sharing Your Faith in Session 5

Consider how Scripture and Tradition can deepen your understanding of session content.

Scripture

Matthew 28:19 tells us Jesus' words to the disciples as he sent them into the world to make disciples of all nations.

James 1:19–22 reminds us that it is not enough to simply hear the Word. We also must be doers of the Word.

Tradition

In the fourth century, Saint John Chrysostom wrote "Not to enable the poor to share in our goods is to steal from them and to deprive them of life." In solidarity we unite ourselves with our neighbor in his or her need. Solidarity with all people calls us to pay special attention to the relief, defense, and liberation of those who are poor. To do so, we look to the inspiration and the spirit of the Beatitudes, the poverty of Jesus, and his concern for the poor.

Catholic Social Teaching

In this session the integrated Catholic Social Teaching themes are **Call to Family, Community, and Participation; Life and Dignity of the Human Person;** and **Solidarity.** See page 1b for an explanation of these themes.

Window on the Catechism

The relationship between the Eucharist and concern for the poor is discussed in *CCC* 1397. Catholic teaching in social justice is found in *CCC* 1928–1942, 2425–2426.

General Directory for Catechesis

Moral formation as one of the fundamental tasks of catechesis is discussed in *GDC* 85–87.

One-Hour Session Planner

SESSION 5 Celebrating Ordinary Time

Session Theme: *Ordinary Time is a time to grow as a disciple of Christ.*

Before This Session

- Display the *Finding God* poster The Liturgical Year.
- Determine whether you will use the Unit Assessment option listed on page 42.
- Determine whether you will also discuss the Ordinary Time seasonal pages in the back of the Young People's Book.
- Bookmark your Bible to James 1:19–22, Matthew 10:8, Matthew 16:24, Matthew 25:40, and Matthew 28:19. Place the open Bible in your prayer space.
- Read the Guide for this session, choose any additional If Time Allows activities that you might have time to complete, and gather the listed materials.

STEPS	APPROXIMATE TIME
Engage *Celebrating Ordinary Time* PAGE 35	10 minutes
Explore *Helping Faith Grow* PAGES 36–37 *Responding to the Gospels* PAGES 38–39	30–40 minutes
Reflect *Prayer:* For Those Who Are Sick PAGE 40 *Where Do I Fit In?* PAGE 41	10–15 minutes
Respond *What's What?* PAGE 42	10–15 minutes

Prayer in Session 5

Continue the pattern and tone for prayer that is used throughout the program. The short prayer at the start of the session invites young people to reflect on this session's theme. An invitation to access an online 3-Minute Retreat concludes the session. Session 5 shows young people how prayers of intention give support to those who are sick or suffering. Follow the Prepare directions on the Catechist Guide page before sharing with young people.

TAKE IT HOME

Homework options:

Discipleship Personal Narrative PAGE 37

Mercy Mobiles PAGE 39

Materials

REQUIRED

- *Finding God* poster: The Liturgical Year (page 35)
- Picture of a famous athlete or a musician/singer (page 36)
- Parish bulletins (page 36)
- Writing supplies (pages 37, 41, 42)
- Media player (page 38)
- Song about answering God's call, such as "We Are Called" by David Haas (page 38)
- Bible (page 39)
- Computers with Internet access (page 42)

OPTIONAL

- Poster board, writing supplies, newspapers, tape (page 35)
- Service pictures (page 35)
- Writing supplies, slips of paper, box (page 36)
- Session 5 BLM, T-353 (page 38)
- Writing supplies (page 41)
- Session 5 Assessment, www.findinggod.com (page 42)
- Unit 1 Assessment, T-354–T-356 (page 42)

Session ⑤

Celebrating Ordinary Time

JUST as we use a calendar to mark important days in our lives, the Church's liturgical calendar helps us remember and celebrate important events from Jesus' life. From the time before his birth to his Death, Resurrection, and Ascension, the liturgical calendar helps us celebrate the life of Jesus.

Ordinary Time occurs twice a year and lasts a total of 33 or 34 weeks. The first period begins after the Christmas season and ends on Ash Wednesday, and the second period begins after the Easter season and ends in late fall. All Saints Day and All Souls Day are celebrated during Ordinary Time.

The "ordinary" in Ordinary Time means "counted time." We number the days and weeks to remind us that all time belongs to God. A good way for us to celebrate Ordinary Time is by growing as a disciple of Christ and deepening our commitment to him. In the Gospel of Matthew, Jesus tells his followers "Whoever wishes to come after me must deny himself, take up his cross, and follow me." (Matthew 16:24)

But what does this mean? A disciple is a person who accepts Jesus' message and tries to live as he did, sharing his mission, his suffering, and his joys. Because you are one-of-a-kind, with your own talents, gifts, personal circumstances, and challenges, the way you grow in discipleship will also be unique. Denying yourself might mean putting someone else first. Taking up the cross might mean working in the parish food pantry, even though some of your friends might pressure you to do something else.

As disciples we are called to live out our faith. Every word, thought, and action show others and Jesus our commitment to living the life we're called to live as one of his followers.

Take a moment and think about your first thoughts and words today. Jesus lived his life as an example of how we should live. How did your first thoughts and words mirror the way Jesus calls you to live? How can you remind yourself to live the way Jesus asks?

PRAYER

Jesus, guide my words and actions so that I may live my life according to your will.

35

IF TIME ALLOWS

Discipleship Chart

Draw a two-column chart on poster board and display it. Label the left side *Following Jesus*. Label the right side *Turning Away*. Distribute newspapers. Ask young people to work in pairs to cut out stories or pictures that exemplify each side of the chart. Have pairs tape their examples in the correct column of the chart. As a group, discuss each side and the importance of being a disciple.

INCLUSION

Autism Spectrum

Disciple Photos Show pictures of young people performing acts of service, such as helping a child with homework or helping the elderly. Discuss what it means to be a disciple and display a picture of Jesus. Say: *When you are a disciple, you try to live as Jesus lived.* Then display more service pictures and invite volunteers to describe how discipleship is shown in each one.

SESSION 5

OUTCOMES

▶ Explain that Ordinary Time is a time to grow as a disciple of Christ and deepen our commitment to him.

▶ Name the Works of Mercy.

▶ Pray prayers of intention.

▶ Define *convocation, Corporal Works of Mercy, Great Commission, Ordinary Time,* and *Spiritual Works of Mercy.*

① Set the Stage

Read aloud and discuss the questions in the purple box. Display a blank wall calendar showing the current month. Ask young people to name special events they celebrate during this month. Say: *Just as we mark important occasions in our lives, the Church marks time according to important events in the life of Jesus, Mary, and the saints.* Read aloud the session title. Ask: *What do you think Ordinary Time means?* (Answers will vary.)

② Get Started

Display the *Finding God* poster The Liturgical Year. Read the paragraph about Ordinary Time on page 222. Ask volunteers to read page 35. Point out the Scripture verse from Matthew. Ask: *What does the Church invite us to do during Ordinary Time?* (grow as a disciple of Jesus) *In what ways are young people today asked to deny themselves for Jesus? What are the benefits? What are some challenges?* (Answers will vary.)

Prayer

Say: *Let's pray together and ask Jesus to be present in our hearts during Ordinary Time.* Pray aloud the prayer. Conclude by praying the Sign of the Cross.

➜ Go to **www.findinggod.com/sessionextenders** to find resources for Ordinary Time. You may wish to share this with the group.

1 Begin

Bring in a picture of a famous athlete or a musician/singer. Talk about this person's achievements. Then ask: **How do you suppose this person achieved his or her goals? Do you think that this person is done growing in his or her skills? Why or why not?** (Answers will vary.) Say: **It's likely that this person practiced thousands of hours. This person probably made many sacrifices and some mistakes but didn't give up. Like most activities that are worthwhile, practice and dedication are the keys to growing.**

2 Connect

Read aloud the article title and invite volunteers to take turns reading the page. Ask: **Why do you think James says that we should be slow to speak and slow to wrath?** (Possible answer: so we have time to think before we do or say something we regret) Point out the last paragraph and reread Jesus' Great Commission. Explain that as doers of the Word, like the Apostles, we try to act and speak in ways that honor him. Say: **Because all of us are on our own unique faith journey through life, we all react differently to Jesus' call. It is okay to feel unsure or even overwhelmed in the realization that each one of us is called personally to live as Christ in the world. But remember, the Holy Spirit is always with you, guiding your steps as you practice and build your faith.**

Our Catholic Character

Ask a volunteer to read aloud Our Catholic Character. Refer young people to the Glossary and discuss the meaning of the word *convocation*. Distribute parish bulletins. Arrange small groups to read the bulletin to find the names of different parish ministries. Have volunteers share stories of ministries that they know about or have been involved in.

Helping Faith Grow

DO you play an instrument or participate in a sport? Think back to when you first began. You probably didn't feel very confident about your abilities at first. You may not have been able to play an entire song or dribble a basketball the first time you tried. You probably set small goals for yourself, working to gain little skills that would add up to success over time.

Similar to sports or music, we need to practice our faith too, so it grows, so we're confident in it, and so it "feels natural." Faith is a beautiful gift from God that helps us believe in him. It is our responsibility to nurture it and help it grow.

Doers of the Word

We can practice our faith in thought, word, and action. We can turn to our Church and to Scripture for guidance as we practice our faith. In a letter to early Christians, James says, "Know this, my dear brothers: everyone should be quick to hear, slow to speak, slow to wrath, for the wrath of a man does not accomplish the righteousness of God. Therefore, put away all filth and evil excess and humbly welcome the word that has been planted in you and is able to save your souls. Be doers of the word and not hearers only, deluding yourselves." (James 1:19–22)

The original doers of Jesus' Word were the Apostles. After Jesus died and rose from the dead, he appeared to the Apostles and sent them out into the world to make disciples of all nations—the **Great Commission**. "Go, therefore, and make disciples of all nations, baptizing them in the name of the Father, and of the Son, and of the holy Spirit. . . ." (Matthew 28:19) They did as Jesus asked, spreading his message, even when it meant putting their lives in danger. Not everyone was ready to hear what they had to say. Some became frightened and turned away. Others became angry. Many people did not understand what it meant to become a follower. As the disciples shared Jesus' message of love and compassion, people began to open their minds and hearts. They accepted Jesus and became living examples of how Jesus asks us to live our lives.

Our Catholic Character

The *Catechism of the Catholic Church* (767) tells us "As the 'convocation' of all men for salvation, the Church in her very nature is missionary, sent by Christ to all nations to make disciples of them." All over the world, the Church reaches out through various ministries and in everyday parish life to bring Christ's help, healing, and love, and to inspire individuals to take up Christ's mission.

36 Unit 1 • One True Faith

ADVENTURES IN FAITH

Humbly Welcome the Word

Invite young people to describe the positive traits of humble people they know. Together discuss what James means by the phrase "humbly welcome the word." Ask each person to write words or phrases on slips of paper that apply to personal discipleship and what it means to humbly welcome the word. Put the slips of paper into a box. Organize young people into small groups and ask a volunteer from each group to draw several slips from the box. As a group, have young people use the slips of paper to write a poem about discipleship. Ask them to add movement and gestures to words or lines and perform their poem for the whole group.

SEASONAL SESSION

All Saints Day
Work with young people through pages 247–250 to learn more about All Saints Day. This special session can take up to one hour to complete.

Everyday Disciple

The Gospels tell us about many people who followed Jesus. We too are called to be disciples of Jesus. Like the disciples in the Gospels, we realize that following Jesus is not always easy. We may experience worries and fears and question ourselves, others, and God. How can we be doers of the Word and practice our faith? How do we experience Jesus in our daily lives? In Jesus' time the disciples traveled, spoke, and set examples. They actively and passionately practiced their faith.

You are called to do the same. To be a disciple means to be bold and to have trust that God is with you. With the help of the Holy Spirit, you find the courage to do good deeds, such as sharing a kind word with someone you might not normally speak with, lending a hand without expecting a thank-you, or beginning each day in prayer asking Jesus to guide you. Each time your thoughts, words, and actions reflect Jesus' teaching, you are a disciple because you are actively engaging your faith and experiencing Jesus in your life. Just as a musician or athlete practices to play better, the more you practice your faith, the stronger it becomes.

The decisions you make every day and the actions that become habits shape your faith over time. Think how you interact with people you meet. Opportunities to practice your faith are everywhere. Your chances to be an everyday disciple may not be obvious, but they are there if you are alert and watch for them.

Study Corner

DEFINE
convocation
Great Commission

REMEMBER
Ordinary Time means "counted time." It's a time for us to grow in discipleship.

As disciples we are called to live out our faith.

Practice Your Faith

Write what you would do to practice your faith in each scene that follows.

School

The math teacher just announced he is giving a surprise quiz. The boy next to you is on the yearbook staff. You know that he has been struggling in math, and his parents told him that if he does not improve, he has to quit the staff. During the test he tries to copy from your paper. What do you do?

_____

_____

_____

_____

Grocery Store

A mother is pushing a cart full of groceries with a baby in the infant seat and two toddlers walking alongside her. As she opens the refrigerated dairy door and pulls out a gallon of milk, she knocks another carton down. It explodes on the ground. What do you do?

_____

_____

_____

_____

Library

A group of students is finishing a project. They discuss taking a break outside. One girl sits quietly and continues her work. The others gather their belongings and leave without saying good-bye. The girl is alone and upset at being excluded. What do you do?

_____

_____

_____

_____

_____

Explore

Have volunteers take turns reading aloud the section Everyday Disciple. Say: *Every action we take and every thought we have are opportunities to grow in faith and make God's presence visible in the world.*

Read aloud the directions and have young people complete the Practice Your Faith activity independently. Encourage them to extend their answers on another sheet of paper, if necessary. Then organize young people into three groups. Ask each group to choose one scene and one response. Have groups develop a skit to show how they would practice their faith through action. Invite groups to perform their skits. After each skit, ask: *What effect might the positive actions have on others?* (Answers will vary.) Say: *Living out your faith in public can have positive effects on people long after the initial experience.*

(3) Close

Organize young people into pairs. Ask each pair to discuss the following questions:

▶ Whom do you know who is the best example of a disciple of Jesus?

▶ Why did you choose this person?

Encourage young people to think about this person as they continue Session 5.

TAKE IT HOME

Discipleship Personal Narrative

Invite each young person to write a personal narrative that tells about a time when he or she was an "everyday disciple." Narratives should tell about *everyday* events, meaning "ordinary," that offer opportunities to follow Jesus' footsteps *every day,* meaning "at least once in a 24-hour period." Encourage them to add dialogue and illustrations to their narratives. Make a bulletin board with a title "Everyday Disciples," and display their work.

① Begin

Invite young people to listen to a song about answering God's call such as "We Are Called" by David Haas from *With You By My Side*. Together discuss the song's meaning.

Explain that during Ordinary Time, we hear many stories that teach us what it means to be called as a disciple of Jesus. Then read aloud the article title and the first two paragraphs.

② Connect

Invite volunteers to name some extra-ordinary disciples and cite qualities that make them so. Then read aloud the section Works of Mercy. Say: **Corporal is an adjective that means "having to do with the body."** Explain that the Corporal Works of Mercy aid the physical needs of a person. Say: **The Spiritual Works of Mercy aid the emotional or spiritual needs.** Ask volunteers to read aloud the definitions of both terms in the Glossary. Explain to young people that when a person's physical, emotional, and spiritual needs are met, they are often better prepared to learn in school, have a job, and live peacefully in their family and in society. Therefore, as disciples of Jesus, we are called to help one another in these ways.

Have a volunteer read aloud the section Saints Respond. Ask: **How can you respond to Jesus' call to follow him?** (Answers will vary.)

Have volunteers read aloud the Works of Mercy box on the page. Help young people understand the meaning of each one. Invite a discussion about different ways to practice each Work of Mercy.

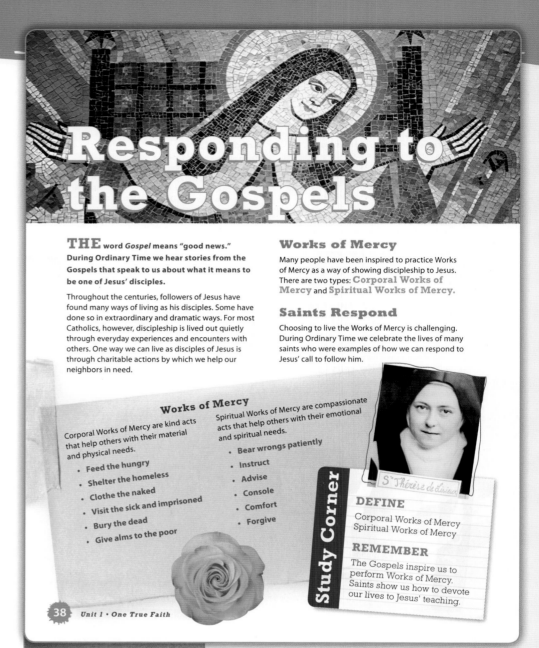

Responding to the Gospels

THE word *Gospel* means "good news." During Ordinary Time we hear stories from the Gospels that speak to us about what it means to be one of Jesus' disciples.

Throughout the centuries, followers of Jesus have found many ways of living as his disciples. Some have done so in extraordinary and dramatic ways. For most Catholics, however, discipleship is lived out quietly through everyday experiences and encounters with others. One way we can live as disciples of Jesus is through charitable actions by which we help our neighbors in need.

Works of Mercy

Many people have been inspired to practice Works of Mercy as a way of showing discipleship to Jesus. There are two types: **Corporal Works of Mercy** and **Spiritual Works of Mercy**.

Saints Respond

Choosing to live the Works of Mercy is challenging. During Ordinary Time we celebrate the lives of many saints who were examples of how we can respond to Jesus' call to follow him.

Works of Mercy

Corporal Works of Mercy are kind acts that help others with their material and physical needs.

- Feed the hungry
- Shelter the homeless
- Clothe the naked
- Visit the sick and imprisoned
- Bury the dead
- Give alms to the poor

Spiritual Works of Mercy are compassionate acts that help others with their emotional and spiritual needs.

- Bear wrongs patiently
- Instruct
- Advise
- Console
- Comfort
- Forgive

Study Corner

St Thérèse de Lisieux

DEFINE

Corporal Works of Mercy
Spiritual Works of Mercy

REMEMBER

The Gospels inspire us to perform Works of Mercy. Saints show us how to devote our lives to Jesus' teaching.

38   *Unit 1 • One True Faith*

IF TIME ALLOWS

Session 5 BLM

Saint Thérèse of Lisieux Have young people complete Session 5 Blackline Master [T-353], which asks them to choose from a selection of statements about Saint Thérèse and write a paragraph explaining why he or she agrees or disagrees with that statement.

Saint Thérèse of Lisieux

Thérèse was born in 1873, the youngest of nine children, to devout Catholic parents. At a young age, Thérèse's mother died, and she was raised by her father and older sisters. Years later, her oldest sister left home to enter a Carmelite convent, and Thérèse became very sick. Through prayers and intercession to Mary, Thérèse was healed. After a pilgrimage to Rome, Thérèse knew she wanted to devote her life to God.

When Thérèse was 15, she entered the Carmelite Order. Always honest about her feelings, Thérèse realized there were things in life she would never like, such as certain chores. But her devotion to God inspired her to show love and compassion in quiet, little ways. She would smile at people she did not like or aid another sister who was not kind to her. She learned that any small task done in God's name brought her joy.

Throughout her life Thérèse prayed spontaneously. Whether she was sad and sick or happy and well, she carried on conversations with God. The head of her convent asked Thérèse to write about her faith and how she lived her life. Her autobiography is called *The Story of a Soul,* and it is read today by people all over the world. Here is some of what Thérèse tells us in her work: "Then, beside myself with joy, I cried out: 'O Jesus, my Love, at last I have found my vocation. My vocation is love! Yes, I have found my place in the bosom of the Church, and this place, O my God, Thou hast Thyself given to me: in the heart of the Church, my Mother, I will be LOVE!'..."

In 1925 Pope Pius XI declared Thérèse a saint. Pope John Paul II declared her a Doctor of the Church in 1997.

Saint Vincent de Paul

Vincent de Paul was born in Gascony, France, in the late 1500s. He was ordained in 1600. Vincent led an exemplary life. He began his ministry by visiting prisoners in jail. Barely surviving in damp, dark cells and given very little food, these prisoners were in terrible health and had little or no faith in God. Deeply moved by their condition, Vincent tended to their needs and showed them tremendous compassion. Many prisoners, overwhelmed by his kindness, became followers of Jesus. Years later Vincent helped found a hospital for people suffering such hardship.

Later, Vincent founded the Congregation of the Priests of Mission. This is not a special order but an institute with special vows. These priests, who add the letters C.M. to their names, help the poor in Jesus' name. Vincent also founded the Sisters or Daughters of Charity, a congregation devoted to performing Corporal and Spiritual Works of Mercy. They care for those who are poor, sick, and orphaned. To this day the Sisters or Daughters of Charity perform their ministry in schools, hospitals, and orphanages.

Vincent was canonized a saint on June 16, 1737. Today the Society of St. Vincent de Paul still helps those in need. Volunteers provide services through thrift stores, food pantries, home and hospital visits, and lend support wherever needed. A very strong and vital youth movement exists within the Society. Young adults across the country are working together to serve others.

Explore

SACRED ART

The Paupers' Meal on a Winter Day in Paris, Norbert Goeneutte, 1881.

Images of hunger bypass language and time barriers. This painting portrays the emotion and need of those who experience hunger. Painted in the late 1800s by Norbert Goeneutte, a French artist, we still understand the concept 100 years later. The expressions in the painting range from quietly resigned to fearful and wounded, and even contentment. Feeding the hungry, one of the Corporal Works of Mercy, is a universal theme.

Session 5 > Celebrating Ordinary Time   **39**

TAKE IT HOME

Mercy Mobiles

Ask young people to make note cards that include writing and drawings as a way to explain how they, a family member, or a friend lived out each Work of Mercy. Have young people use a hole punch to string the cards together with yarn and assemble them into a "Mercy Mobile" to display.

Read aloud Saint Thérèse of Lisieux. Ask: **What sacrifices do you think Thérèse had to make to be in community with the other sisters?** (Answers will vary.) Say: **Yet she entered the convent and lived a full life of joy and love.** Ask young people to name times in their lives when they were worried about a new challenge, but the situation turned out well. Say: **Which of these situations reminds you of Saint Thérèse?** (Answers will vary.)

Have volunteers take turns reading aloud the section Saint Vincent de Paul. Say: **Saint Vincent de Paul humbly responded to the Gospel and answered Jesus' call. Good works in his name continue today.** Say: **God blessed Vincent de Paul with the ability to effect great change. We are called to do good work, not to please or impress God, but to discover his presence in those we serve.**

Sacred Art

Read aloud the Sacred Art feature. Ask young people if they have ever volunteered in a soup kitchen or food pantry. Invite one or two volunteers to share their experience. Explain that art often tells a story without using words. Ask: **Which Work of Mercy does this painting portray?** (Feed the hungry.)

③ Close

 Ask a volunteer to open the Bible and read aloud Matthew 25:40. Say: **We are all brothers and sisters in Christ. God our Father reminds us that when we do something for one another, we are also doing it for him.** Remind young people to try and see God in one another. Say: **Sometimes it's good to step outside your social circle or regular routine in order to discover God's presence in other people around you.**

Prayer

Follow these steps to guide young people through the prayer on page 40.

Young People's Page

Prepare Pray the prayer in advance to become familiar with it.

Pray Have volunteers read aloud the title and the paragraphs in the left column. Point out that one way to share in Jesus' healing ministry is to pray for those who are ill. Explain that we have this opportunity every day, not just on Sunday during Mass. Encourage young people to include prayer for the sick in their daily prayers.

Have young people bring their books to the prayer space. Invite them to get comfortable, grow still, and close their eyes. Ask young people to think about those who are ill. Perhaps they are relatives, friends, or neighbors. Point out that maybe they are people they've never met.

Say: *Take a moment to still yourselves. Relax your shoulders, hands, and feet. Prepare your hearts and minds to spend some time with Jesus.* Pray aloud the Leader part. Pause briefly between each paragraph, allowing time for the words to sink in. After the last paragraph, invite young people to pray aloud their own intentions, followed by the response "Jesus, heal us." After all intentions have been prayed aloud, read the second Leader part. Invite everyone to pray aloud the final All part. Afterward, allow time for silent meditation. Say: *Remember to keep these names in your daily prayers. As you ask Jesus each day to guide and protect you, ask him to extend his healing grace to those who are sick and their families.*

Prayer

For Those Who Are Sick

Regarding those who are sick, Jesus gives the Apostles this commission in Matthew 10:8: "Cure the sick. . . . Without cost you have received; without cost you are to give."

The Church carries out this commission in the Sacrament of the Anointing of the Sick. This sacrament, a way through which God's life enters our lives, also calls all of us to care for those who are sick and to be present with them in their illness through prayer and physical care.

Sunday is a special day for reflection, silence, and meditation that can help us grow in our Christian life. When we go to Mass on Sunday, we pray the Prayer of the Faithful. This prayer is a special time to pray for family members, relatives, and friends who are ill or who are in need in some other way.

Have you ever thought of illness as an opportunity for grace? Most people don't. But Jesus sees things differently. He sent his Apostles to anoint and cure those who were sick. Today the Church continues to anoint those who are seriously ill. We, as his disciples, are called to care for those who are sick. By doing so, we help them experience God's healing grace. Through our prayers we can support and serve those who are sick and suffering.

40 *Unit 1 • One True Faith*

Prayers of Intention

Leader: Think about relatives, friends, or neighbors who are ill. Also recall media reports that you've seen or heard from around the world that tell about those who are ill. In your imagination, picture God's healing love surrounding each person.

Become aware of the power of prayer and the promise of Jesus to be in the midst of those who gather in his name.

Let's join together in prayer for those who are sick. Feel free to speak aloud the first name of someone you want to pray for, and, if you wish, describe the situation he or she faces.

Pray aloud intentions and respond after each.

Response: Jesus, heal us.

Conclude praying aloud intentions.

Leader: Let us pray aloud together.

All: God of Mercy, your Son, Jesus, walked our earth and shared our humanity. In his name we ask you to hear our prayers and to comfort all those who are ill in body, mind, or spirit. Amen.

IF TIME ALLOWS

On Human Suffering
Read aloud and discuss this excerpt from *On the Christian Meaning of Human Suffering* by Pope John Paul II. "Suffering is present in the world in order to release love, in order to give birth to works of love toward neighbor, in order to transform the whole of human civilization into a 'civilization of love.'"

Invite young people to discuss the alleviation of suffering in individuals, families, communities, and nations. Explain that love can be released and good can happen when suffering is transformed.

FYI

Coaching Young People to Pray

Before the prayer, invite a priest to come to class to discuss the Sacrament of the Anointing of the Sick. When engaging in the prayer experience, remind young people about what they have learned.

WHERE Do I Fit In?

From the tiniest mustard seed, a magnificent tree springs, giving shade to all. Every ordinary day is an opportunity for extraordinary discipleship. Your choices in daily life, whether big or small, are powerful, and you are completely free to make them.

by Bert Ghezzi

Reflect

Little Things Mean a Lot

Ron, my neighbor, has a serious lung disease. His doctor cannot do anything more to make Ron get better, so he put him on oxygen and painkillers to keep him comfortable. Ron is strong-willed, fights for life, and tries to take care of himself. Early one morning not long ago, I walked outside and found him dragging a heavy oxygen tank and struggling to get into his car. "What are you doing, Ron?" I asked. "Taking short breaths," he said. "I'm going to try to go to the store to buy a light bulb." I persuaded him to get back into the house. And I went and bought him a light bulb.

That simple act triggered my decision to help Ron. I began dropping by regularly and offering to do things for him. He didn't like asking for help, but I persisted, and he finally let me serve him. So I began to shop for his favorite foods—spinach, black olives, and custard pie, which you might not like very much, but Ron craves. Every morning I pick up his newspaper from the driveway and put it on his doorstep. I take out his garbage for him. I'm not very handy, but I figured out how to reset the switches on his garage door opener and garbage disposal. Several evenings a week I visit him, and we share our day. And I always make the Sign of the Cross on Ron's forehead and ask the Lord to strengthen him, clear his lungs, and give him a good night's sleep.

Ron and I have become good friends. I know that if he were well, he would be offering to help me. My friendship with Ron has taught me an important lesson about living the Christian life. That is, I show my love for God by serving others. As Mother Teresa said, "The needs are great, and none of us, including me, ever do great things. But we can all do small things, with great love, and together we can do something wonderful."

BERT GHEZZI is a father, grandfather, and author of 20 books, including *Voices of the Saints.*

A Full Heart

Our actions show our love. Small choices, such as choosing to smile at someone who doesn't like you, express your faith. In the heart below, list small ways you can serve others as a way to show your love for God.

Session 5 > Celebrating Ordinary Time 41

IF TIME ALLOWS

Circles of Love

Draw five concentric circles on the board. Ask a volunteer to name one of the "small things" from the activity and write it in the center circle. Then have young people name several possible positive effects of this action and write them in the adjacent ring. Next, have young people name possible effects of those effects and write them in the third ring. Continue until the outermost ring is filled. Read aloud the original "small thing" and the possible effects recorded in the outermost ring. Point out that the great potential within every small act is what makes that act so powerful.

(1) Begin

Have a volunteer read aloud the introductory text. Ask young people to define *discipleship.* (Possible answer: sharing God's message with others, following Christ) Explain that discipleship is not just for people in the New Testament or people at church. Say: ***Being a disciple means choosing to act with gentleness and love many times a day. For example, if a salesperson is rude, you might return the rudeness, you might silently growl, or you might assume that the person is having a bad day and ask God to give him or her a hand.*** Ask: ***Which response is that of a disciple?*** (the last) Invite young people to tell about times when someone responded to them with unexpected generosity, or did the opposite, and to describe how this "little thing" affected them.

(2) Connect

Have volunteers take turns reading Little Things Mean a Lot. Say: ***The author of this article made a choice to help Ron, but he ended up receiving gifts too.*** Ask: ***What were they?*** (friendship, a deeper understanding of the Christian life, firsthand knowledge of the power of "small acts of love")

Ask a volunteer to read aloud Matthew 25:40–45. Have young people work with a partner to complete the A Full Heart activity. Afterward, have volunteers share examples of "small things" that show love.

(3) Close

Tell young people about Saint Thérèse of Lisieux, the Little Flower. Discuss her ideas about being a disciple and why she is known for her "Little Way." Encourage young people to choose one of the "small things" they wrote or heard while completing the activity to put into action today.

① Begin

What's What? Have a volunteer read aloud the directions. Depending on time, have young people complete the page at home or in class. Invite young people to meet in groups to discuss their ideas.

② Connect

Say What? Ask volunteers to read aloud and define the terms. Review each term in the Glossary if necessary.

Now What? Invite a volunteer to read aloud the section. Encourage young people to close their eyes and take a moment to consider their responses. Then ask them to write their ideas.

③ Go in Peace

Collect materials and return them to their appropriate places. Encourage young people to follow through with their Now What? ideas during the week. Say: *Remember that all Works of Mercy address people's needs, but some provide for material needs and others are a response to emotional or spiritual needs. Set a goal of performing at least one Corporal and one Spiritual Work of Mercy.*

3-Minute Retreat
Give young people an opportunity for quiet meditation at **www.loyolapress.com/retreat**.

Respond

What's What?

Use each phrase in a brief paragraph that tells what the idea means to you and how you can think, speak, and act as a young Catholic. Answers will vary.

1 take up your cross (PAGE 35)

_____
_____
_____
_____
_____

2 everyday disciple (PAGES 36–37)

_____
_____
_____
_____
_____

3 responding to the Gospel (PAGES 38–39)

_____
_____
_____
_____
_____

4 caring for those who are sick (PAGE 40)

_____
_____
_____
_____
_____
_____

Say What?

Know the definitions of these terms.

convocation
Corporal Works of Mercy
Great Commission
Ordinary Time
Spiritual Works of Mercy

Now What?

Saint Thérèse of Lisieux and Saint Vincent de Paul answered Jesus' call to be disciples. They dedicated their lives to performing Works of Mercy. Jesus is calling you today. How will you answer him? How will you find courage and strength to share the gifts God gave you with others? Write your ideas below.

Answers will vary.

_____
_____
_____
_____
_____
_____
_____
_____

42   *Unit 1 • One True Faith*

IF TIME ALLOWS

Service: Random Acts of Mercy

Work with your catechetical leader to organize a Random Acts of Mercy event for your parish. Schedule a day when young people and their families assist parishioners who need help with simple tasks such as yard work or visiting the homebound. After the event, host a reception and share experiences of serving others by doing God's work.

✝ *Family and Community*

Session Assessment Option

An assessment for this session can be found at www.findinggod.com.

Unit Assessment Option

If you wish, photocopy the Unit Assessment on pages T-354–T-356. Administer the assessment during the session or send it home.

PLAN AHEAD: Get Ready for Session 6

Consult the catechist preparation pages to prepare for Session 6 and determine any materials you will need.

Faith in ACTION
Unit 1

Faith is alive when we put it into action every day of our lives. Faith is expressed in our attitudes and values and in the way we relate to people and the world around us. Taking action to make a more just world is an essential part of living the Gospel. Jesus preached not only with words but also with actions. We are called to do the same.

In this unit we explored important beliefs of our Catholic faith—the Trinity, God's Revelation, and our response to God. We were also introduced to the Church's rich tradition of Catholic Social Teaching. The Church calls us to put the needs of people who are poor and vulnerable first. Here are some ideas for how you can do this.

> "It is an eternal obligation toward the human being not to let him suffer from hunger when one has a chance of coming to his assistance."
>
> —Simone Weil, French philosopher

Become Gleaners

Purpose
Learn about the practice of gleaning as a way for people who are poor and hungry to get food; become a gleaner by collecting food and distributing it to those in need.

Background
The Gleaners is a famous painting by the French artist Jean-François Millet. Painted in 1857, it portrays peasants scavenging a harvested wheat field. Life was rough for people at the time, and they often resorted to gleaning, which is the collecting of crops left over in farmers' fields after harvesting. Today mechanical harvesting often leaves behind crops that would normally go to waste. With the farmers' permission, humanitarian groups practice gleaning in these fields so that they can distribute the food to those who are poor and hungry.

Steps
1. Read Leviticus 23:22. What do you learn about God from this passage? What is God's message to you in this passage?

2. Initiate monthly food drives and drop-off locations to collect nonperishable food to share with people who are in need.

3. Ask volunteers to coordinate the pickup of donated food each month, sort it into bags or boxes, and store it.

4. Form a partnership with local churches, food pantries, shelters, and soup kitchens that could use the food. Ask adults in your school or parish to help you deliver the food.

Detail from *The Gleaners*, Jean-François Millet.

Unit 1 > Faith in Action **43**

Act

IF TIME ALLOWS

Become Gleaners: Ruth and Naomi

✝ Scripture provides an example of the practice of gleaning in Chapter 2 of Ruth. Tell young people that Ruth was the great-grandmother of David and that she shares in the ancestry of Jesus. Have young people read the Book of Ruth. Discuss the story and the theme of showing commitment to others and keeping promises.

MATERIALS: Get Ready for Faith in Action

For these projects, you will need resource materials and computers with Internet access, Bibles, the prayer service planning guide and prayer service planning tips, art supplies, and writing supplies. Also see the project steps.

FAITH IN ACTION

Complete one of the suggested Faith in Action projects as a class, or organize young people into two groups, having each group complete a different project. Note that directions continue on the next page.

① Prepare

Discuss the project ideas with young people and involve them in the decision-making process to determine a project. Discuss the project in terms of faith and being a "person for others." Ask: ***What do you hope for from this project? What are you concerned about? Whom will you serve, and how will your service be beneficial to them and to you? Are you prepared to recognize the humanity in those you will meet? How does this project help you put your faith into action? What theme or themes of Catholic Social Teaching will you be experiencing in the project?***

② Implement

Have young people follow the directions to complete Become Gleaners on page 43 or Living Faith on page 44. Be sure young people do research before taking action. For example, searchable keywords for Become Gleaners include the following: *hunger and poverty, food waste, food drive,* and *gleaners.* Searchable keywords for Living Faith include the following: *homeless, right to shelter,* and *out of the cold.*

Be sure young people are supervised during their project as appropriate. Consider asking for parent volunteers to be Faith in Action facilitators for the entire year.

✝ *Family and Community*
The Poor and Vulnerable
Solidarity

③ Close

Bring closure to the project by leading young people in completing one of the following:

Prayer Service Download and print out the prayer service planning guide and prayer service planning tips at www.findinggod.com. Have young people plan and implement a prayer service that expresses both gratitude to God for the opportunity to serve and hope for the people whom they served.

Pass It On Have young people meet with younger children to share their experiences and inspire them to get involved. If photos or videos are available, have young people display them and use them as part of their presentation.

✝ *The Poor and Vulnerable*

Living Faith

Purpose

Identify areas in your community where people who are homeless live; work with your community to provide basic necessities to people in need.

Background

Many communities provide shelter and services for people who are homeless. Although these services are helpful, the need for basic necessities and continued assistance is an ongoing problem. Some people in need of assistance are reluctant to seek help in shelters, soup kitchens, or other places where services are provided. They may be afraid. Others worry about losing their dignity. Some suffer from physical or mental illnesses that make them unable to seek help, and others have simply lost hope. Whether or not they seek help from service providers, people who are homeless need help and protection.

Steps

1. Mobilize a group to collect basic necessities for people who are homeless, such as combs, soap, toothbrushes, and toothpaste. Determine the best way to collect the items. Your group may sponsor a drive, collect financial donations and then purchase items, or get businesses to donate items.

2. Contact local organizations that provide services to those who are homeless. Schedule a date and time for dropping off donations.

3. Organize a group to assemble and package the collected items. Ask adult volunteers to help distribute the packages to the organizations of your choice.

4. Consider sharing your project with others in the school or parish by videotaping the assembly and distribution of packages. Show the videotape at an open house, parent meeting, or other assembly to increase awareness and encourage greater participation in helping those who are homeless.

> "To take away the goods of another is nothing, in comparison to taking away their dignity and honor. In taking away our neighbors' dignity and honor, they lose all."
>
> —Saint Vincent de Paul

Act

IF TIME ALLOWS

Living Faith: Advocating for Those Without Shelter

Discuss stereotypes associated with those who are homeless, such as a belief that all who are homeless must be lazy or uneducated. Then acknowledge a variety of reasons why some people find themselves without shelter.

Invite a community leader or an advocate for those who are homeless to be a guest speaker, and ask him or her to provide both statistics and real-life stories about the issue. Use the information to raise your school's or parish's awareness of those who are homeless. Develop a campaign that protects the dignity of those in need and works to meet their material needs. Young people may publish articles, make and display posters, sponsor a collection drive, or work with a local community group.

✝ *The Poor and Vulnerable*

Unit 2

Catechist Preparation pages open each unit and session.

UNIT 2

The Early Life of Jesus

Unit 2 focuses on the mystery of the union of the divine and human natures of Jesus, Son of God. In this unit, young people will learn the following concepts.

SESSION 6 Jesus Became One of Us

Young people learn that Jesus Christ is true God and true man in the unity of his divine Person. This understanding of Jesus Christ's identity is a core belief of the Catholic faith. Because of the Incarnation, we know Jesus is our model of humanity. Jesus taught us how to pray to the Father.

SESSION 7 Jesus Is God with Us

Names for Jesus are connected to the history of Salvation. *Jesus* means "God saves." One title for Jesus, *Emmanuel*, reminds us that Jesus himself represents the New Covenant. The name *Christ* is also important to our faith. God knows our names and speaks to us in many ways—through his Law, Scripture, other people, dreams, and our deepest longings.

SESSION 8 Jesus Is for All People

Luke's Infancy Narrative tells us about Jesus' humble birth. Jesus is our divine king who humbly serves us all. Luke helps us understand that Jesus came to save all people in every state of life. Jesus and his family faced many hardships, which is a reminder that God exalts unexpected people. The Infancy Narratives reveal truths about Jesus' divinity. Jesus is the fulfillment of prophecies about the Messiah.

SESSION 9 Jesus Grew in Wisdom, Age, and Grace

Mary and Joseph find Jesus in the Temple with the teachers. Jesus begins to understand the mission to which God his Father calls him. He remains faithful to the Fourth Commandment, obeying Joseph and Mary by returning home with them. Family life binds us together, but we still want to follow our own paths and form our own identities just as Jesus and his parents learned. Jesus is present in our families. Our families become a domestic church and help us learn values, virtues, and service to others.

SESSION 10 Celebrating Advent and Christmas

Young people learn how to prepare to receive the Light of the World, Jesus Christ, during Advent. Young people explore how the one true gift of Christmas is Jesus. We welcome Jesus by celebrating feast days and holy days during Advent and Christmas.

UNIT SAINT

Blessed Marie of the Incarnation

Blessed Marie of the Incarnation lived humbly among the people she served. In this way, she became like Jesus, who was truly God and truly man and our model of humanity. Blessed Marie of the Incarnation immersed herself in the language and customs of the Algonquin and Iroquois peoples. By doing this, she was able to teach and spread Jesus' Good News. Her missionary work brought the one true faith to a foreign land.

Prayer in Unit 2

In each session of Unit 2, establish the pattern and tone for prayer. Young people use the prayer form *lectio divina* and pray verses of Psalm 34 that speak of God's justice. Young people pray guided reflections. They also pray the Daily Examen, a form of Ignatian prayer.

✝ Catholic Social Teaching in Unit 2

The following themes of Catholic Social Teaching are integrated into this unit.

Call to Family, Community, and Participation Participation in family and community is central to our faith and to a healthy society. Family and communities must be supported and strengthened through active participation.

Life and Dignity of the Human Person The Catholic Church teaches us that all human life is sacred and that all people must be treated with dignity. As Catholics, we strive to respect and value people more than material goods. The foundation of our moral vision is our belief in the life and the dignity of the human person.

Rights and Responsibilities The Catholic Church teaches that every person has a right to live as well as the right to things required for human decency. As Catholics, it is our responsibility to protect fundamental human rights.

Solidarity Solidarity is the attitude that leads Christians to share spiritual and material goods. Solidarity unites rich and poor, weak and strong, and helps create a society that recognizes that we live in an interdependent world.

Faith in Action

In Unit 2, young people are invited to take a stand against violence by planning a project that raises awareness of the effects of domestic violence on families and society. Another project invites young people to promote peace in their families and communities by increasing their awareness of exposure to violence and rediscovering peaceful activities. Alternative service-project ideas also appear on the last page of each session in this guide.

TOGETHER *as One Parish*

Religious Education with the Parochial School

To nurture parish unity, organize joint school/RE events. You may want to sponsor mother/daughter or father/son events. For example, plan a community fashion show, dance class, or a board-game night. Assemble participants before the event to plan activities, develop committees, socialize, and get to know one another.

📖 **Literature Opportunity**
Keeping the Night Watch
by Hope Anita Smith
You might wish to have young people read this collection of poems about the healing process of a family and 13-year-old C.J., who is having trouble forgiving his father for leaving the family, even after he has returned to them.

✝ *Family and Community*

Jesus Became One of Us

 ## 3-Minute Retreat

Before you prepare the session, pause and be still. Take three deep breaths and be aware of the loving presence of God, who is with you on this journey.

Mark 1:9–11

It happened in those days that Jesus came from Nazareth of Galilee and was baptized in the Jordan by John. On coming up out of the water he saw the heavens being torn open and the Spirit, like a dove, descending upon him. And a voice came from the heavens, "You are my beloved Son; with you I am well pleased."

Reflection

The voice coming from the Heavens leaves no doubt that Jesus is God's beloved Son. Many people before him had performed this same ritual. Yet this baptism was like no other. Jesus, the Son of God, was standing in the River Jordan and humbly submitting to baptism by John. Why? Jesus was both human and divine. He showed us what it meant to be God's beloved child and to obey the Father. The baptism of Jesus invites us to become beloved children of God in the Sacrament of Baptism.

Questions

What difference does my belief that I am God's beloved child make in how I see myself and the world around me? What challenges do I face when I acknowledge that others are also God's beloved children?

 Concluding Prayer

Speak to God, using the words of this prayer or your own.

Jesus, in your humanity you teach me how to live the life of God's beloved child. Help me see myself and others as you see us.

Knowing and Sharing Your Faith in Session 6

Consider how Scripture and Tradition can deepen your understanding of session content.

Scripture

John 1:14 reveals a core belief of our Christian faith—the Incarnation is the Word of God taking on human form in the Person of Jesus.

Luke 11:2–4 tells us that Jesus taught us how to pray to God the Father.

Tradition

The Incarnation is the mystery of the union of the divine and human natures in one Person of the Trinity, the Son of God. Jesus was born in a humble stable. He was raised in the Jewish faith by Mary and Joseph. Jesus was born with a human soul and with limited human knowledge. He had to learn about the human condition from experience, just as we learn. He lived a daily life much as we do. He had to work for a living. He was a Jew and lived his life with obedience to the Law. He knew happiness, and he also knew pain and suffering.

Catholic Social Teaching

In this session the integrated Catholic Social Teaching theme is **Life and Dignity of the Human Person**. See page 45b for an explanation of this theme.

Window on the Catechism

Jesus as fully God and fully man is discussed in *CCC* 456–478.

General Directory for Catechesis

Catechesis as a means of bringing us into communion with God and Jesus is found in *GDC* 143.

One-Hour Session Planner

SESSION 6 Jesus Became One of Us

Session Theme: *The Incarnation is God's supreme act of love for humanity. Jesus Christ, the Son of God, is God made flesh. Jesus is our model of humanity.*

Before This Session

▶ Display the *Finding God* poster Prologue of the Gospel of John.

▶ Bookmark your Bible to Mark 2:1–12, Mark 8:27, Mark 12:28–34, Mark 14:36, Matthew 5:13–14, Matthew 11:25, Matthew 14:22–33, Matthew 26:36–46, John 1:1–5, John 1:14, John 2:13–16, John 3:16, John 10:30, John 11:34–35, John 11:41–44, John 14:6–7, John 15:12–17, Luke 5:5–11, Luke 8:1–3, Luke 11:2–4, and Philippians 2:6–7. Place the open Bible in your prayer space.

▶ Read the Guide for this session, choose any additional If Time Allows activities that you might have time to complete, and gather the listed materials.

STEPS	APPROXIMATE TIME
Engage *Unit Saint:* Blessed Marie of the Incarnation PAGES 45–46 *Daily Examen* PAGE 45 *Jesus Became One of Us* PAGE 47	10–20 minutes
Explore *The Word Became Flesh* PAGES 48–49 *Pray as Jesus Taught Us* PAGES 50–51	30–40 minutes
Reflect *Prayer:* Enter Fully into Prayer PAGE 52 *Where Do I Fit In?* PAGE 53	10–15 minutes
Respond *What's What?* PAGE 54	10–15 minutes

Prayer in Session 6

Continue the pattern and tone for prayer in the program. Pray the short opening prayer that relates to a key concept. Young people are also invited to experience an online 3-Minute Retreat at the end of the session. Session 6 gives young people the experience of *lectio divina,* a form of prayer in which young people use their imaginations while reading Scripture. Follow the Prepare directions on the Catechist Guide page before sharing with young people.

TAKE IT HOME

Homework options:

Defenders of the Incarnation	PAGE 49
Model of Humanity	PAGE 51

Materials

REQUIRED

▶ Pictures from different stages of your life (page 48)

▶ *Finding God* poster: Prologue of the Gospel of John (page 48)

▶ Bibles (pages 48, 51, 52)

▶ Writing supplies (pages 49, 51, 53, 54)

▶ Tape measure, small classroom object (page 50)

▶ Computers with Internet access (page 54)

OPTIONAL

▶ Gym mats (page 46)

▶ Bibles (pages 47, 50, 52)

▶ Session 6 BLM, T-357 (page 48)

▶ Writing supplies (pages 50, 53, 54)

▶ Voice recorder (page 52)

▶ Art supplies, computers with Internet access (page 54)

▶ Session 6 Assessment, www.findinggod.com (page 54)

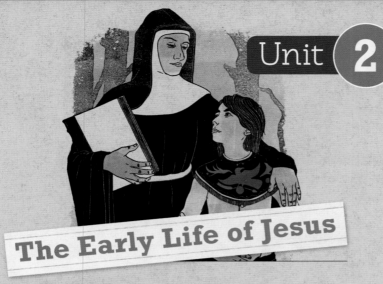

Unit 2

The Early Life of Jesus

Blessed Marie Guyart (1599–1672), wife, mother, missionary, and mystic, was born in Tours, France. In the 1600s, it was traditional for parents to arrange marriages. Marie wanted to become a nun, but her parents arranged for her to marry a silk manufacturer named Claude Martin. After two years of marriage and the birth of a child, Claude died. At age 19, Marie was a widow. Her desire to enter the religious life had never left. At the age of 30, she joined the Ursuline nuns in Tours and began her work for God as Sister Marie of the Incarnation. Eventually this work took her far from her homeland.

How the Saint Relates { Sister Marie of the Incarnation imitated the life of Jesus, who lived humbly among the people. She sought to serve him by immersing herself in the culture of the native people she served, learning their language and customs as a way to teach and spread Jesus' message.

45

OPENING PRAYER

Daily Examen

Suggest that young people frequently pray the Daily Examen on page 279 in Prayers and Practices. Guide them through the steps of this powerful prayer.

- Still your mind and relax. Take a few deep breaths. Ask for the grace to see the day through God's eyes. Thank him for his many gifts.

- Review your day in your mind. Go hour-by-hour. Ask yourself, "When did I feel peaceful, secure, and hopeful? When did I feel restless, dejected, or anxious?" Reflect on one strong feeling. Ask yourself, "Did I move toward God in those moments, or did I move away from him?"

- Ask the Holy Spirit to help you answer some questions: "What was God saying to me? How did he say it? How did God want me to respond?" Ask God's forgiveness for any time you failed to love.

- Now ask yourself what you are supposed to do today. Ask God to help you respond to the day's challenges in a way that reflects Jesus' teachings.

- Pray the Lord's Prayer silently when you are ready. Now bring your attention back to this room.

UNIT OPENER

OUTCOMES

▶ Identify Blessed Marie of the Incarnation as a missionary to the New World.

▶ Define *Incarnation, missionary,* and *novices.*

① Begin

Read aloud the unit title. Explain that in this unit, young people will explore Jesus, the Son of God, and the mystery of the union of his divine and human natures.

Invite young people to discuss which foreign country they would choose to visit. Ask volunteers to share their reasons. Say: ***Today you will read about a woman who made a choice to travel far away from home to serve God's people. In a way she was like an ambassador for God.*** Discuss the work that an ambassador might do. Ask: ***How could you represent God among others even without traveling to some distant country?*** (Possible answers: by living peacefully with others, by following the Ten Commandments)

② Introduce the Saint

Ask a volunteer to read the paragraph on page 45. Say: ***You probably count on your family and other important adults to help you make important decisions. Marie's dream might have surprised her family.*** Ask: ***How do you know if your life's work is what God planned for you?*** (Possible answers: You feel called. You feel fulfilled.) ***What lesson can we learn from Blessed Marie?*** (Possible answers: Be patient. Trust in God. Ask for God's guidance.)

How the Saint Relates

Read aloud the feature. Explain that we are like Blessed Marie of the Incarnation when we encounter God in those we serve.

③ Connect

Have a volunteer read aloud the first paragraph. Say: **The belief that Jesus has two natures, divine and human, united in one Person is distinct to our Christian faith.** Say: **Every time we pray the Nicene Creed, we reaffirm our belief in the Incarnation.**

Have volunteers read the remaining two paragraphs on the page. Ask: **In what ways was Marie suited to work with novices?** (She enjoyed instructing and felt enthusiasm for proclaiming Jesus.) Ask: **What challenges did she face as a missionary?** (She had to overcome cultural and language barriers.)

Past Meets Present

Read aloud the feature. Explain that the truth of Jesus Christ is intended for all nations. Jesus called the Apostles to preach the Gospel. We hear the Gospel in the spoken word and in the written word. Point out that Saint Paul changed the hearts of others by acknowledging both their human and spiritual needs. Saint Damien of Molokai spread God's Word by tending to and living with those who were very sick.

④ Close

Say: **Blessed Marie of the Incarnation took different paths throughout her life. She set aside her dreams for a while, but every path was a courageous yes to God's call. Marie made a difference in the world. She gave herself to people selflessly and experienced God's love in her work.**

Invite young people to reflect on how they can say yes to God. Invite volunteers to share their thoughts. Invite them to ask God for guidance as they choose paths in life.

Blessed Marie of the Incarnation

Why would Marie Guyart choose to name herself after the **Incarnation?** God's supreme act of love for humanity is the Incarnation. The Incarnation means that Jesus Christ, the Son of God, is God made flesh. Jesus is fully God and fully man in one Person. In Jesus, God became one of us and gave his life for us to save us from sin. The humanity of Jesus is made known in his human joys, sorrows, and emotions. Because Jesus has a divine nature, we know God's faithful love. And since Jesus also has a human nature, in him we see the best example of humanity we could ever know. Perhaps Jesus was the inspiration for Marie's work. Jesus showed her how to live a life full of love for God and others.

In the city of Tours, Sister Marie cared for **novices,** young women who entered the convent but had not yet taken vows. She enjoyed instructing and felt a great enthusiasm for proclaiming Jesus. Marie answered a calling to leave her homeland and spread the Gospel to North America as a **missionary.** A missionary is a person sent by Church authority to spread the Gospel through evangelization and catechesis. Sometimes a missionary goes to a country where few people have heard about Jesus. Other times a missionary is sent abroad to serve the spiritual needs of the faithful who live in isolated or underserved regions.

Marie eventually made the four-month journey to Canada, arriving in a French colony in Quebec in 1639. Immediately upon her arrival, she learned the Algonquin and Iroquois languages to be able to explain the Good News of Jesus. Because there were no materials about the Catholic faith in those languages, she took up the task herself, writing dictionaries for the people with whom she worked. For the next 30 years, she dedicated herself to the Algonquin and Iroquois peoples while learning about their culture. Marie served God well as a missionary because she became one of the people.

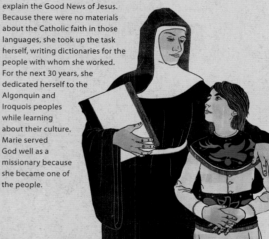

Past Meets Present

PAST: Saint Paul, like Sister Marie, traveled to other countries. He preached the Gospel while enduring hardships and imprisonments. He established churches and wrote letters that became part of the Bible. Saint Paul wrote, "To the weak I became weak, to win over the weak. I have become all things to all, to save at least some. All this I do for the sake of the gospel, so that I too may have a share in it." (1 Corinthians 9:22–23)

PRESENT: Five Catholic missionaries, each notable to his or her state's history, are honored today in the National Statuary Hall Collection in the U.S. Capitol. One statue honors Saint Damien of Molokai, who traveled with a shipload of parishioners suffering from leprosy and devoted the rest of his life to the settlement on Molokai, Hawaii. Father Damien cared for their physical and spiritual needs until he himself died of the disease in 1889.

 46 *Unit 2 • The Early Life of Jesus*

🔥 *ADVENTURES IN FAITH*

Push and Pull

Remind young people that similar to Marie, we all have important choices to make and can feel pushed and pulled as we listen to God, ourselves, and others while we consider what to do. Then have young people perform this demonstration. Have partners sit on the floor facing each other. Ask partners to put the bottoms of their feet together and grip hands tightly. At the count of three, ask partners to pull and push, using the tension to get to their feet. Remind them that it is their responsibility not to let go of their partner's hands. Bring the group together.

Explain that it is hard to know what God wants us to do. We may feel pushes and pulls. We may question ourselves or others. We may find it difficult to share our deepest dreams or desires. Invite young people to ask for God's guidance with life choices. Remind them that God will always help them get to their feet.

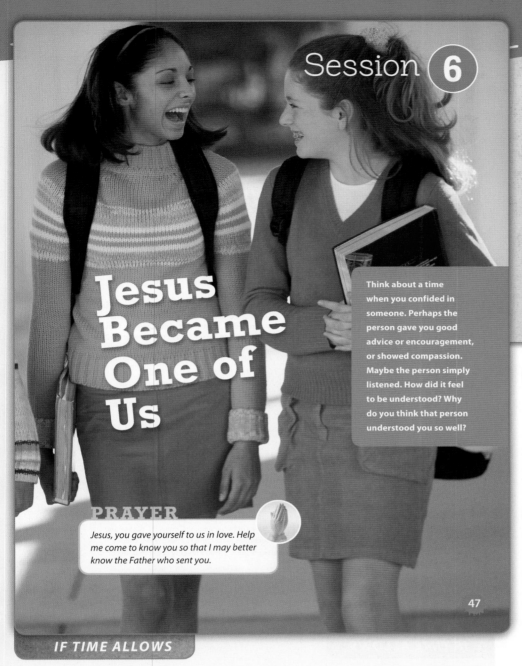

Session 6

Jesus Became One of Us

Think about a time when you confided in someone. Perhaps the person gave you good advice or encouragement, or showed compassion. Maybe the person simply listened. How did it feel to be understood? Why do you think that person understood you so well?

PRAYER

Jesus, you gave yourself to us in love. Help me come to know you so that I may better know the Father who sent you.

47

IF TIME ALLOWS

Who Is This Man?

The disciples had a hard time understanding what it meant to follow Jesus. Read aloud Mark 8:27. Ask: **What did Jesus ask?** ("Who do people say that I am?") Ask: **How did the disciples respond?** (John the Baptist, Elijah, one of the prophets) Read aloud Mark 8:29. Ask: **How did Peter respond?** (the Messiah) Explain that the disciples likely thought that following Jesus would lead to recognition and power in the world. Ask volunteers to read aloud Mark 8:31–38. Ask: **What is the message of discipleship?** (Being a disciple means serving the kingdom. People will reject them and they will suffer, but Jesus will be with them, sharing the load of the cross.)

Ask young people to find metaphors in Matthew 5:13–14 that Jesus used to describe the disciples. (the salt of the earth, the light of the world) Have them give reasons why these are good descriptions and write their ideas in a paragraph. Ask volunteers to share their paragraphs with the group.

 Go to **www.findinggod.com/sessionextenders** for an article about Jesus, the Son of God. You may wish to share this with the group.

OUTCOMES

▶ Explain that Jesus Christ is true God and true man in the unity of his divine Person.

▶ Describe ways that Jesus reflects and models a deeply personal relationship between people and God.

▶ Pray *lectio divina*.

▶ Define *catholic, consubstantial, dignity of the human person, Great Commandment, heresy, lectio divina,* and *miracle*.

① Set the Stage

Read aloud the text and questions in the box on page 47. Give young people time to reflect or ask them to record their ideas. Ask volunteers to share their thoughts with the group.

② Get Started

Pose these riddles to young people:

▶ If you have it, you want to share it. If you share it, you don't have it. What is it? (a secret)

▶ The more you have of it, the less you see. What is it? (darkness)

Point out that some riddles are easier than others to solve. Even when given the answer, we still might not "get it." Read aloud the session title and say: **When the disciples were learning who Jesus was, they often didn't "get it." Human beings can never fully comprehend the mystery of Jesus' divine and human natures. Though divine, Jesus understands our human concerns and experiences.**

Prayer

Say: **Ask God the Son to help you draw closer to God the Father as we pray together.** Pray aloud the prayer. Conclude by praying the Sign of the Cross.

① Begin

Bring in pictures from different stages in your life. Tell stories that demonstrate your various reactions to situations or events at different times in your life. Ask: **What are some human emotions?** (Possible answers: happiness, jealousy, love, anger, joy, despair, hopefulness, gratitude) Write responses on the board. Invite volunteers to share times when they've displayed their own humanity—for good or bad. Say: **As members of the human race, we have much in common.**

② Connect

✝ Display the *Finding God* poster Prologue of the Gospel of John. Read aloud the title and page. Say: **Jesus was always divine. God's plan for our Salvation was to send his Son.** Have young people read John 3:16 in their Bibles. Connect the reading to the Incarnation, the Word became flesh. Jesus was to be, and still is, our model of holiness. Ask a volunteer to read aloud John 14:6–7 in their Bibles.

To emphasize Catholic belief in the Incarnation, have the group turn to page 276 in Prayers and Practices and pray together the Nicene Creed. Remind young people that reflecting on the meaning of the words in a prayer is how to take a prayer to heart.

Our Catholic Character

Ask a volunteer to read aloud the feature. Read aloud the definition of *catholic* in the Glossary. Explain that today the Catholic Church has a clear structure of hierarchy with the pope as the leader of the worldwide Church. The pope is assisted by cardinals, bishops, priests, and other Church leaders. Because the earliest Christian communities had no centralized authority, their expression of faith sometimes varied.

The Word Became Flesh

Martha and Mary mosaic, Franciscan Church, Israel.

AS Catholics, who do we believe God is? How can we understand him? How can we understand the relationship between God the Father and God the Son? Each time we pray the Creed, we proclaim our beliefs.

In the Gospel of John, we learn that the Son of God, the Word, existed from the beginning of time with the Father. Divine in nature, the Son of God brings the light of life to the human race.

> In the beginning was the Word,
>   and the Word was with God,
>   and the Word was God.
> He was in the beginning with God.
> All things came to be through him,
>   and without him nothing came to be.
> What came to be through him was life,
>   and this life was the light of the human race;
> the light shines in the darkness,
>   and the darkness has not overcome it.
>
> *John 1:1–5*

The Word of God taking on human form in the Person of Jesus is called the Incarnation (literally "in flesh"), a core belief of our Christian faith. In the Incarnation we see God's great love for us. By God's great sacrifice, we are saved and reconciled to God. We know that God is our loving and caring father.

> And the Word became flesh
>   and made his dwelling among us,
>   and we saw his glory,
>   the glory as of the Father's only Son,
>   full of grace and truth.
>
> *John 1:14*

Our Catholic Character

As Christianity steadily grew and spread around A.D. 100, the distance and differences in beliefs, customs, cultures, philosophies, and other factors threatened the unity of various Christian communities. Those who believed in a united and worldwide, or **catholic,** expression of faith wanted to distinguish their beliefs and traditions from other communities of believers. As Jesus' identity as both God and man was disputed over the years, the decisions of two ecumenical councils, Nicaea and Chalcedon, formulated the basic Catholic doctrine that identifies Jesus Christ as having two natures, divine and human, that exist together. This understanding of Jesus Christ's identity is a core belief of our faith that lasts to this day.

48 *Unit 2 • The Early Life of Jesus*

IF TIME ALLOWS

Session 6 BLM

✝ **John the Evangelist—The Eagle** Explain that John's Prologue tells us that the Word became flesh. The union of Jesus' divine nature and human nature is one that we cannot completely grasp. However, our faith assures us that Jesus was both truly God and truly man. Provide each young person with the Session 6 Blackline Master [T-357]. As they use the Blackline Master, ask them to reflect on John's Prologue and their capacity to embrace their faith in the mystery of the Incarnation.

SACRED ART

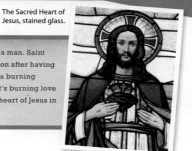

The Sacred Heart of Jesus, stained glass.

Catholic devotion to the Sacred Heart reminds us that Jesus was a man. Saint Margaret Mary Alacoque, a 17th-century nun, spread the devotion after having visions of Christ, who told her about his loving heart. Images of a burning heart, either pierced or surrounded by thorns, symbolize Christ's burning love for humanity, even though pierced by our sins. By imitating the heart of Jesus in its limitless love, we best reflect the image of God.

Fully God, Fully Man

Jesus was not part man and part God. As the Son of God, Jesus is at the same time both fully God and fully man. He is not one or the other; his divine nature and his human nature are distinct but inseparable. Without ceasing to be God, Jesus assumed human form and became our brother.

Jesus lived among us, as a man at a specific time and place in history (A.D. 1, Palestine). He was human in every way except sin. Born to a Jewish woman, the Virgin Mary, he grew up in the town of Nazareth and learned the trade of carpentry. He had intellect, will, and a body that was susceptible to suffering and death. Jesus knew what it was like to be loved and befriended, as well as abandoned and misunderstood. Throughout his life Jesus expressed human qualities.

In the raising of Lazarus, we read about the human and the divine natures of Jesus. When Jesus arrived in Judea, his friend Lazarus, the brother of Martha and Mary, had been dead for four days. Jesus was overcome with grief at Lazarus's tomb. (John 11:34–35) Later in this account, Jesus performed a **miracle** of truly divine nature—he raised Lazarus from the dead. (John 11:41–44)

In the early days, the Church defended the true divine and true human natures of Jesus Christ against any **heresy**, or false teaching. In 325 the first ecumenical council in Nicaea composed a Creed to clarify that the Son of God is of the same substance as the Father. We affirm this belief when we pray that Jesus is "true God from true God, begotten, not made, **consubstantial** with the Father." We believe that today Jesus sits at the right hand of God and intercedes for us.

As we think about Jesus in Heaven, we must remember that Jesus was truly man, with eyes and hands and a voice and a heart. In his ever-present spirit, Jesus asks us to be his hands and his voice in the world today.

God and Man

Read and categorize these Scripture passages as the Revelation of either Jesus' divine or human nature. Put an *X* in the correct column.

	Divine	Human
Luke 8:1–3		X
Mark 2:1–12	X	
Luke 5:5–11	X	
John 2:13–16		X
Matthew 14:22–33	X	
Matthew 26:36–46		X

Study Corner

DEFINE

catholic
miracle
heresy
consubstantial

REMEMBER

Jesus is the Son of God. Without losing his divine nature, he assumed human nature. Jesus Christ is true God and true man in the unity of his Divine Person.

TAKE IT HOME

Defenders of the Incarnation

Explain that the early Church found it necessary to clarify and defend the mystery of the Incarnation. Have them research and summarize the beliefs of one false teaching—or heresy—in the early Church: gnosticism, arianism, or nestorianism. They should also tell about the teachings of the early councils: Nicea [A.D. 325], Ephesus [A.D. 431], Chalcedon [A.D. 451], and Second Constantinople [A.D. 553]. Provide a time frame for young people to prepare posters to display. If some young people prefer, they may organize a slide-show presentation that highlights the heresy and the Church's response.

Sacred Art

Read aloud the Sacred Art feature. Discuss the heart as a symbol of Jesus' love for us. Say: *When we imitate the heart of Jesus in the things we say and do, we best reflect Jesus' divine nature.*

Read aloud the first paragraph under Fully God, Fully Man. Write the headings *Divine* and *Human* on the board. Say: *As we read, let's identify details that belong in each column.*

Have young people read the next two paragraphs. Read the meaning of *miracle* in the Glossary. Ask: *What details would you write beneath the heading Divine? the heading Human?* Write their ideas on the board. Say: *Because Jesus performed miracles, some early Christians decided that Jesus was God and not a man—seeming to have the physical appearance of a man but not actually being human.*

Read aloud the last two paragraphs. Read aloud the definition of *heresy* in the Glossary. Ask: *What is the Church's teaching about the two natures of Jesus?* (In 325 the first ecumenical council of Nicaea decreed Jesus as having a divine and human nature.) Read the meaning of *consubstantial* in the Glossary. Ask volunteers to find lines in the Nicene Creed that relate to this teaching. Ask: *How is the council's teaching upheld?* (Jesus maintained the same divine nature as the Father.)

Have young people complete the God and Man activity with a partner.

③ Close

Invite young people to record answers to these questions:

▶ When you contemplate Jesus as man, what is your favorite thought?

▶ What do you think of first when you contemplate Jesus' divine nature?

1 Begin

Bring in a tape measure and invite a volunteer to place a small object on the floor exactly four feet away from a wall. Ask a second volunteer to move that object half the distance [two feet] to the wall. Repeat a third time [one foot]. Say: *We could continue to move this object half the distance to the wall, but theoretically it would never reach it—there would always be some distance, however miniscule.* Ask young people to think about this demonstration as they read the page.

2 Connect

 Invite volunteers to read the title of the article and the opening paragraphs. Refer young people to the definition of the *Great Commandment* in the Glossary. Ask: *How does Jesus show his care for others?* (Answers will vary.)

Invite a volunteer to read aloud the first paragraph in Jesus Prays to Abba. Discuss the boldness of Jesus' choice to call God "Abba." Remind young people about the demonstration from the Begin step. Say: *In our demonstration about distance, we got close but never touched the wall. In contrast, Jesus doesn't just bring us closer to the Father. Jesus puts us directly in contact with God the Father, removing all distance between us.*

Have young people follow in their Bibles as you read aloud John 10:30. Ask: *How can knowing Jesus mean knowing the Father?* (The Father and Son are actually one.)

Invite young people to discuss affectionate or endearing nicknames they have for family members or friends, or nicknames that others have for them. Encourage them to tell the stories behind the names. Ask: *Do you feel closer to people you address this way? Do they feel closer to you?* (Answers will vary.)

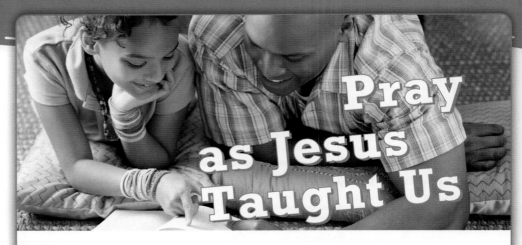

Pray as Jesus Taught Us

WHY is the Incarnation meaningful in our daily lives? God's deep love for us and his desire to share divine life is revealed. In Jesus, God became man, and because of Jesus, our Salvation was won.

Jesus' last days gave witness to his true humanity. He experienced joy at a triumphant entry into Jerusalem, anger at money changers in the Temple, and betrayal at the hands of one of his own Apostles. His Passion and Death are stark reminders of his human suffering. "For God so loved the world that he gave his only Son, so that everyone who believes in him might not perish but might have eternal life." (John 3:16) In such great sacrifice, we come to know the pure love of a caring God.

Jesus became one of us and is our model of humanity. He experienced life with others. He was present at weddings, at dinners, in the gatherings of friends and of strangers, in a room in a house where a small girl lay dead from illness, and among people so ill, poor, and disabled that others wanted to stay far away.

Jesus, the Son of God, was fully God but humbled himself to share in our humanity. Jesus did not come to be served but to serve.

Who, though he was in the form of God,
[Jesus] did not regard equality with God
something to be grasped.
Rather, he emptied himself,
taking the form of a slave,
coming in human likeness; . . .

Philippians 2:6–7

Jesus is a model of holiness, and we look at his life on earth as the greatest example of how to live. Following Jesus' example is a way to come to know God and a way to become closer to him. After all, Jesus gave his disciples the **Great Commandment**, "This is my commandment: love one another as I love you." (John 15:12)

Jesus Prays to Abba

Jesus modeled a deeply personal and intimate relationship with people and with God the Father. When Jesus addressed God in prayer, he used the Aramaic word *Abba*, meaning "father" but more like "Papa" or "Daddy." (Mark 14:36) This informal way of addressing the Almighty was unprecedented in Hebrew culture.

> **Jesus became one of us and is our model of humanity.**

50 *Unit 2 • The Early Life of Jesus*

IF TIME ALLOWS

Nicodemus, Friend of Jesus

 Explain that Jesus showed us ways of relating to people and to God the Father. We want to maintain a close relationship with Jesus. Jesus had many friends. Some special friends were Peter, John, Lazarus, Lazarus's sisters Martha and Mary, and Mary Magdalene. Another friend was Nicodemus, a Pharisee. Have volunteers read aloud John 3:1–17, 7:50–52, and 19:39–40. Discuss the friendship between Nicodemus and Jesus. Discuss how Jesus' human nature helped Nicodemus understand divine truth. Have them share their responses with a partner or write them on paper.

When Jesus tells us to call on God in Heaven as our Father, he shows us the kind of relationship we are called to seek with God. We approach God as our own parent—a parent who is near, who requires no formal language, and to whom we can turn for daily matters, both large and small. We approach God in this way when we have gratitude in our hearts for the abundant love he has shown us. We can trust in God's wisdom, express sorrow for our sins, make amends, and surrender to his plan for us. God, as parent, is always inviting us.

Relationship with God

Belief in the Incarnation changes the way we see everything. A window to God opens, inviting us to find him in all things. We know that God is with us, and we seek him in everything that surrounds us. We know that God is not far away. Our God is close to us, he is concerned for us, and he recognizes our human triumphs, sorrows, friendships, and pain.

Jesus opened up a new way of relating to God, our Father. In the Gospel of Luke, one of Jesus' disciples said, "Lord, teach us to pray." He said to them, "When you pray, say:

> Father, hallowed be your name,
>   your kingdom come.
> Give us each day our daily bread
>   and forgive us our sins . . .''
>
> *Luke 11:2–4*

In addition to relating to God through prayer, Saint Ignatius of Loyola believed that we invite God to speak to us through life's experience and the use of our senses. Jesus taught us that God is the best of fathers. He understands our human imperfections and frailties and welcomes us back over and over when we stray. Jesus' personhood, prayer, and example tell us that our relationship to God is and can be deeper and far more personal. Jesus' wisdom, guidance, and holy counsel apply to our identity today, what we face, and what we need.

Jesus reminded us that we could find God everywhere. He tells his disciples, "In my Father's house there are many dwelling places." (John 14:2) Jesus says he prepares a place for us there. He invites us to be in his presence.

Explore

SACRED ART

The artwork of painter Michael O'Brien expresses the holiness of existence and the **dignity of the human person.** Because of the Incarnation, the guiding principle of Catholic Social Teaching is the dignity of the human person. In their pastoral letter *Economic Justice for All,* the U.S. bishops insisted that every economic decision and institution must be judged in light of whether they protect or destroy the dignity of the human person. "We believe the person is sacred—the clearest reflection of God among us. Human dignity comes from God, not from nationality, race, sex, economic status, or any human accomplishment. We judge any economic system by what it does for and to people and by how it permits all to participate in it. The economy should serve people, not the other way around."

Jesus and the Children,
Michael O'Brien, 1998.

Session 6 > Jesus Became One of Us **51**

Model of Humanity

Jesus is our model of humanity. Have young people think about the qualities that Jesus taught and modeled in the Great Commandment. Have young people write, illustrate, and present a poem or short story about some ways to live the Great Commandment in their everyday lives. As an option, some young people may prefer to present their poem or story in a slide-show presentation.

INCLUSION
Hearing

Participation Someone with a hearing impairment might find group discussions difficult. Try to seat young people in a circle or facing as many group members as possible. When you are leading a discussion, position yourself directly in front. Encourage young people to request information to be repeated by signaling with a raised hand.

Continue reading the section Jesus Prays to Abba. Emphasize that Jesus taught that God loves us as a Father. The Father is concerned about us and cares for us the way a father cares for his children. Have young people open their Bibles and read Hosea 11:4. Ask: *What image reminds us of God's love for us?* (raising an infant to his cheeks)

Have volunteers take turns reading the section Relationship with God. Ask: *How can you invite Jesus into your life?* (prayer and loving actions) Explain that we often meet new friends through introductions. Explain that Ignatius of Loyola and Francis Xavier met while students at the University of Paris. With a lot of patience, time, and prayer, Ignatius awakened Francis to his empty lifestyle and introduced him to Jesus Christ. Saint Francis Xavier became a great missionary. Say: *Inviting God into our daily lives is contagious. We have a choice to pray and live in relationship with God, inviting new friends along the way.*

Ask volunteers to discuss why the Incarnation changes the way we see the world. Say: *Jesus was not off-limits, unattainable, or distant. Jesus is God living among us, and our God walks and talks with us. He knows our thoughts and feelings because the Son had human thoughts and feelings.*

Sacred Art

Read aloud the Sacred Art feature. Ask a volunteer to read the meaning of *dignity of the human person* in the Glossary. Remind young people that God created man in his own image. The *Catechism of the Catholic Church* tells us every person possesses dignity because God made us in his image.

③ Close

Invite young people to read John 15:12–17. Have them respond to the Scripture's meaning and write about their responsibilities to God and others.

Prayer

Follow the steps to guide young people through the prayer on page 52.

Young People's Page

Prepare Pray the prayer in advance to become familiar with it.

Pray Read aloud the title. Ask volunteers to read aloud the paragraphs in the left column. Discuss the form of prayer *lectio divina*, and deepen young people's understanding by comparing it to the way we read personal mail—we savor it, often rereading parts of it.

 Have young people bring their Bibles to the prayer space and sit quietly. Prompt them to get ready to pray by getting into a comfortable position. Encourage them to breathe slowly in and out and let go of any distracting thoughts. Pause briefly and say: *As I proclaim the Scripture, let the words sink in.* Read slowly and expressively Mark 12:28–34. Then guide young people through the first meditation step, prayerfully reciting aloud.

Pause and say: *Open your heart to receive the Word of God as I read the Scripture passage a second time.* Prayerfully read the Scripture again. Read the second step of the meditation, inviting young people to draw or take notes as they listen.

Following a brief time of reflection, lead young people through the Pray and Contemplate parts. After a prayerful silence, say: *Together let's pray aloud the words of the closing part of the prayer.* Conclude the prayer. Say: *As we continue the session, recall your conversation with God. Thank him for always being present to you today and in the future.*

Prayer

Enter Fully into Prayer

Jesus taught us to enter fully into prayer by engaging our whole being, including all our sorrows, joys, fears, and loves.

Jesus expressed joy to his Father for revealing the kingdom not only to the educated and the leaders of the time but to everyone. (Matthew 11:25) In the garden of Gethsemane before his Crucifixion, Jesus prayed with great anguish. (Matthew 26:38–39) No matter which form of prayer you enter into, you can feel comfortable bringing all that you are to the experience.

Lectio divina, Latin for "sacred reading," is an ancient form of Christian prayer in which you use your imagination while reading Scripture. It is a way of spending time with the Word of God and having a prayerful conversation with him. To get ready for *lectio divina,* quiet your thoughts. The first step is to read a Scripture passage slowly. The second step is meditation—letting the words sink in and echo within you while you reflect on what God might be saying to you. The third step is prayer. God speaks to you, and you respond with your own words. The final step is contemplation, sitting quietly with God, beyond words and feelings.

Lectio Divina
Jesus and the Scribe

Read: Mark 12:28–34 (The Great Commandment)

Meditate: In your imagination, place yourself with Jesus and the scribe. What do you see? Who is gathered? Listen to the conversation. Picture the clothing, mannerisms, reactions, and facial expressions. How do you think the scribe feels at the beginning of the conversation? At the end?

Read a second time: Mark 12:28–34 (The Great Commandment)

Meditate: Now imagine yourself as the scribe. Ask Jesus the same question: "Which is the first of all the commandments?" Listen as Jesus answers. Think about what Jesus' words mean in your life right now. If you wish, draw your ideas or take notes.

Pray: Share your reflections with God. Ask him if there is anything else he wants you to notice. Thank God for his presence and this time of prayer.

Contemplate: Spend a few moments in prayerful silence with God.

All: Jesus, through your life you showed your deep love of God and your limitless love of all people. Help us love God with our whole heart, our whole mind, and our whole strength. Help us love others with a heart like yours. Amen.

52   *Unit 2 • The Early Life of Jesus*

IF TIME ALLOWS

Pray the Psalms

 Remind young people that Jesus prayed the psalms, which describe the whole range of human emotions. We pray best when we engage both our will and our heart in our prayer. Invite young people to find a psalm in the Bible that they like. Give them time to pray it to a partner before praying it aloud into a voice recorder. Keep the recorded prayers in the prayer space, and encourage young people to listen to them during free time.

FYI

Coaching Young People to Pray

Remind young people that no matter what form they use to pray, they are in the holy presence of God. He always hears them and invites them into a deeper conversation. Encourage young people to pray in any way that brings them closer to God.

WHERE Do I Fit In?

Because Jesus became one of us, we know we are never alone. Not only is God present with us every step of the way, but as members of a faith community, we also help and support one another.

by Annie Azrak

I Am Not Alone

Last summer my parents packed their bags and left for a two-week vacation. This was the first time that I was left alone to watch over my sister, who is an adult with special needs. On the very night my parents left for their vacation, a tremendous rainstorm engulfed our area. I found myself driving through deep, fast-moving water. I had to stop the car. When I called my sister at her apartment, she spoke through panicked sobs. "My apartment is flooding, and I don't know what to do!" she cried. "I am so scared!"

I was overcome with worry and questions. I thought, "How do I get to my sister?" I was stranded in my car, miles from her, and I knew that she needed my help and assurance. I felt completely helpless and alone. I closed my eyes and asked, "God, what do you want me to do?" Just then my phone rang. The caller was my good friend, and she volunteered to take my sister to her home until I could arrive. I felt relieved.

I remembered a joke about a man caught in a flood. As the water lapped at his knees, a boat came by. "Get in!" the crew shouted. "No, thanks," said the man. "God will save me." As the water reached his waist, a helicopter hovered overhead and threw him a rope. "Don't bother," the man shouted. "God will save me any minute now." Finally, the water swallowed him, and he drowned. At the gates of Heaven, he asked Saint Peter, "Why didn't God save me?" Saint Peter replied, "He sent you a boat and a helicopter! Were you expecting a chariot of fire?" Help had been there the whole time—the man just didn't take it.

ANNIE AZRAK is a premedical student who hopes to treat those who do not have access to medical care.

I used to think that it was up to either me or God to fix problems. But when I reflect on that rainstorm, I see that God does not want me to face every challenge alone. Neither does he want me to wait around, expecting a miracle. God answered my prayer when the phone rang. My experience taught me that God wants us to turn to him for help, but he wants us to turn to one another too.

Reflect

Living for Others

The writer understood her experience when she remembered a joke about a man in a flood. Tell a short anecdote or make up a joke of your own that illustrates how God provides people to turn to for help. Write your notes on the lines below. Then write your anecdote or joke on another sheet of paper.

_____
_____
_____
_____
_____
_____
_____
_____
_____
_____

Session 6 > Jesus Became One of Us   53

IF TIME ALLOWS

God, Our Help

Have young people spend a few minutes recollecting all the ways, large and small, that others have helped them in the past 24 hours. Ask them to list the names and actions of the helpers on a sheet of paper.

When they are finished, have them write a prayer of gratitude, using the following form and personalizing it with the items on their list. Write on the board: *Ever-present God, thank you for [helping action] through the hands and heart of [name].*

Invite volunteers to take turns praying aloud their completed expression of gratitude, possibly in the prayer space or during an organized prayer session.

1 Begin

Read aloud the title and the introductory text. Point out that an important way to "fit in" as a member of any community is to offer help to others. Another important way to "fit in" is to accept the help we are offered. Ask: *Do you find it harder to offer help or to receive help? Why?* Discuss how this changes from person to person. Say: *Some may find it easy to offer help around the house, for example, but grow shy in a classroom setting and not volunteer to help.* Remind young people that both offering and receiving help are ways of growing closer to God.

2 Connect

Ask young people what they think the title means. Have a volunteer read aloud the first paragraph of I Am Not Alone. Ask: *What would you do in this situation?* (Answers will vary.) After several young people offer suggestions, have volunteers read the remaining paragraphs. Ask: *What did the author learn about important responsibilities?* (They must often be shared.) Ask: *What did she learn about the workings of God?* (He often works through the love and support of others.) Return young people's attention to the joke in the third paragraph. Have young people think about times they were thrown a lifeline at the last minute and recognized it—or didn't.

Read aloud the directions for the Living for Others activity. Have young people complete the activity independently.

3 Close

Invite young people to share the article with a family member and then ask him or her to tell a story about receiving God's help through the actions of others.

① Begin

What's What? Read the directions aloud and ask a volunteer to rephrase them in his or her own words. Point out the extra step they will take to find the secret phrase. Have young people complete the page independently.

② Connect

Say What? Ask volunteers to read aloud and define the terms. Review each term in the Glossary if necessary.

Now What? Ask a volunteer to read aloud the question. Invite each young person to make a two-column chart and jot down strengths in one column and weaknesses in the other before answering the question independently.

③ Go in Peace

Collect materials and return them to their appropriate places. Encourage young people to look again at the two-column chart they made before writing their response in Now What? Say: *Review your responses. Think of other ways you can grow closer to Jesus by embracing your humanity, both the good and the bad, in the same loving way that God embraces you.* Ask: *Why is it so hard for many people to accept their weaknesses? How might people rely too heavily on their strengths alone?*

3-Minute Retreat
Give young people an opportunity for quiet meditation at **www.loyolapress.com/retreat**.

What's What?

Respond

Fill in the letter blanks to complete each sentence. Use the circled letters to discover the secret phrase.

1. Jesus is like us in all things but S I N. (PAGE 49)

2. Jesus had two N A T U R E S, human and divine. (PAGE 46)

3. Blessed Marie of the Incarnation spread the Gospel to native peoples in C A N A D A. (PAGE 46)

4. I N C A R N A T I O N refers to the belief that God was made flesh in Jesus. (PAGES 46, 48–49)

5. The pastoral letter E C O N O M I C *Justice for All* teaches about the dignity of people. (PAGE 51)

6. The Son of God, the W O R D, existed from the beginning of time with the Father. (PAGE 48)

7. Jesus is fully H U M A N and fully divine. (PAGE 49)

8. All of us can be the hands and V O I C E of Jesus on earth. (PAGE 49)

9. Jesus was made flesh and gave his life for us to S A V E us from sin. (PAGE 46)

10. A M I S S I O N A R Y leaves a homeland to spread the Gospel. (PAGE 46)

11. A prayer in which you use your imagination while reading Scripture is called L E C T I O D I V I N A. (PAGE 52)

Secret Phrase:

S A C R E D H E A R T

Say What?
Know the definitions of these terms.

catholic	Incarnation
consubstantial	*lectio divina*
dignity of the human person	miracle
Great Commandment	missionary
heresy	novices

Now What?
What can you do this week to embrace both your human strengths and weaknesses while you grow closer to Jesus?

Answers will vary.

54 *Unit 2 • The Early Life of Jesus*

IF TIME ALLOWS

Service: Be a Peacemaker
Remind young people that the Church calls on nations to find ways to prevent conflicts and protect human life. Tie the discussion to conflict resolution within a school community. Ask young people to identify common sources of conflict at school. Work with volunteers to form a peer-mediation group dedicated to the goal of defusing and settling peer conflicts. Have members post visible reminders that promote peaceful resolutions, such as posters, blogs, or a classroom Web site. Guide effective prevention and management strategies.

✝ *Life and Dignity*

Session Assessment Option
An assessment for this session can be found at www.findinggod.com.

PLAN AHEAD: Get Ready for Session 7

Consult the catechist preparation pages to prepare for Session 7 and determine any materials you will need.

Jesus Is God with Us

 3-Minute Retreat

Before you prepare the session, pause and be still. Take three deep breaths and be aware of the loving presence of God, who is with you on this journey.

Matthew 1:23

"Behold, the virgin shall be with child
        and bear a son,
    and they shall name him Emmanuel,"
which means "God is with us."

Reflection

An angel appeared in a dream to Joseph to proclaim the Good News. The long wait of the people of Israel is over, the promised Messiah is coming, born of a virgin, and named Emmanuel, "God with us." This is celebrated in the most beloved of our Christian feasts when we celebrate the birth of new hope for ourselves and for the world. As the Son of God, Jesus incarnates God's love for the world. As one of us, Jesus reconciles us to the Father. The coming of Emmanuel means the new birth of hope in our hearts.

Questions

How can I express the new hope promised by the presence of Emmanuel, "God with us"? How can I share that new hope with others?

 Concluding Prayer

Speak to God, using the words of this prayer or your own.

Jesus, help me be truly aware of what it means to have you ever present in my life.

Knowing and Sharing Your Faith in Session 7

Consider how Scripture and Tradition can deepen your understanding of session content.

Scripture

Matthew 1:23 connects Jesus' birth to the fulfillment of prophecies. *Emmanuel* means "God is with us."

Isaiah 43:1 teaches us that God calls us by name.

Tradition

The word *Incarnation* refers to the fact that the Second Person of the Trinity became man. Jesus is God made flesh. The Incarnation means that between God and us there is now a mediator, who is Emmanuel, "God with us." As the Son of God, Jesus can speak for God. As man, Jesus can speak for us. Jesus became man so that he could live among us and be our Savior. In doing so, he taught us what it means to be truly human. Jesus is the great educator in humanity. From him we can learn the most important things we need to know in order to be truly alive.

Catholic Social Teaching

In this session the integrated Catholic Social Teaching themes are **Call to Family, Community, and Participation** and **Life and Dignity of the Human Person.** See page 45b for an explanation of these themes.

Window on the Catechism

The titles given to Jesus in the New Testament are discussed in *CCC* 430–451.

General Directory for Catechesis

Jesus as mediator and fullness of Revelation is discussed in *GDC* 41.

One-Hour Session Planner

SESSION 7 Jesus Is God with Us

Session Theme: *The names for Jesus are connected to Salvation History. God calls us by name and speaks to us in many ways.*

Before This Session

▶ Bookmark your Bible to Matthew 1:18–21, Matthew 1:23, Matthew 18:20, Matthew 28:20, Isaiah 7:13–14, Isaiah 9:5–6, Isaiah 11:1–2, Isaiah 43:1, Genesis 15:1, and Psalm 77. Place the open Bible in your prayer space.

▶ Read the Guide for this session, choose any additional If Time Allows activities that you might have time to complete, and gather the listed materials.

STEPS	APPROXIMATE TIME
Engage *Jesus Is God with Us* PAGE 55	10 minutes
Explore *Explore Names for Jesus* PAGES 56–57 *How Does God Speak to Us?* PAGES 58–59	30–40 minutes
Reflect *Prayer:* Called by Name PAGE 60 *Where Do I Fit In?* PAGE 61	10–15 minutes
Respond *What's What?* PAGE 62	10–15 minutes

Prayer in Session 7

Pray aloud the prayer at the beginning of the session and invite young people to reflection with an online 3-Minute Retreat at the end of the session. Session 7 includes a guided reflection with an option either to listen to a recorded version or lead using a script. Follow the Prepare directions on the Catechist Guide page before sharing with young people.

TAKE IT HOME

Homework options:

Describing God	PAGE 57
Dreams in the Scriptures	PAGE 59

Materials

REQUIRED

▶ Writing supplies (pages 55, 57, 60, 61, 62)

▶ Bible (pages 56, 57, 59)

▶ CD player (page 60)

▶ CD 2, Track 3: "Called by Name" (11:38) (page 60)

▶ Computers with Internet access (page 62)

OPTIONAL

▶ Clean jars or cans, art supplies, slips of paper, small objects that symbolize young people (page 55)

▶ Bibles (pages 56, 61)

▶ Session 7 BLM, T-358 (page 56)

▶ Computers with Internet access (page 57)

▶ Large glass jars, questions taped to jars, water, basket, small pebbles (page 58)

▶ Art supplies, white cloth, sewing materials (page 62)

▶ Session 7 Assessment, www.findinggod.com (page 62)

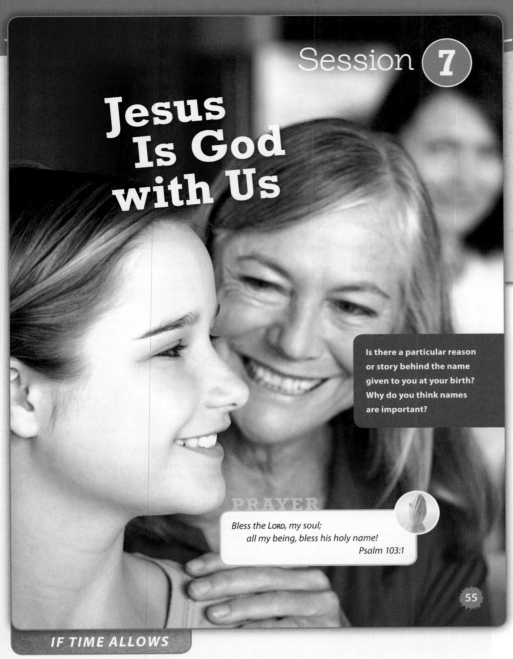

Session **7**

Jesus Is God with Us

Is there a particular reason or story behind the name given to you at your birth? Why do you think names are important?

PRAYER

Bless the LORD, my soul;
all my being, bless his holy name!
Psalm 103:1

55

IF TIME ALLOWS

What's Inside?

Point out that labels on cans in grocery stores set the products apart and describe contents to the buyer. Suggest that a person's name, particularly a nickname, works in a similar way because it gives a clue as to what's inside. Tell young people to wash out and use a clean jar or can. Have them decorate the outside with their name and add slips of paper with words or phrases that describe their personality or tell ways they are unique individuals. Display the cans in class and invite young people to explore the contents of one another's cans.

✝ *Life and Dignity*

↗ Go to **www.findinggod.com/sessionextenders** for information about the Gospel of Matthew. You may wish to share this with the group.

SESSION 7
OUTCOMES

▶ Describe how names for Jesus are connected to Salvation history.

▶ Explain the many different ways that God speaks to us.

▶ Meditate as a way to move toward God in prayer.

▶ Define *adoration, Christ, Emmanuel, Infancy Narrative,* and *monstrance.*

① Set the Stage

Read aloud the questions in the box on page 55. Give young people a few minutes to discuss with a partner or record their ideas before asking volunteers to share with the group.

② Get Started

Point out that a nickname might be related to a person's personality, abilities, or character traits. Say: *In the early 1900s, "Shoeless" Joe Jackson played baseball for the Chicago White Sox. Wearing a new pair of spikes during a game caused blisters on his feet. The team was short of players so he played wearing only socks. When he hit a triple, he got the nickname, and it stuck throughout his career.*

Organize young people into small groups. Ask them to think of an adjective that describes themselves or others in a distinct way. Caution young people to reject hurtful or negative nicknames. Invite volunteers to share the nicknames and explain their significance. Read aloud the session title. Explain that they will learn about the significance of Jesus' name in this session.

 Prayer

Say: *Remember that when we pray, we call God by name.* Pray aloud the prayer. Conclude by praying the Sign of the Cross.

① Begin

Write the letters *A.K.A.* on the board. Ask: *Do you know what this means?* (also known as) Point out that some people are better known by other names. Say: *A writer might take a pen name.* Ask: *What is the pen name of Samuel Clemens?* (Mark Twain) *Mary Ann Evans?* (George Eliot) Say: *An entertainer might change a name for self-expression, flair, or other reasons.* Write birth names of entertainers on the board and have young people guess who they are. For example, rock star Bono's birth name is Paul Hewson. Say: *Jesus' names have significant meanings. They are not just for flair.*

② Connect

✝ Read aloud the article title, the opening paragraph, and the first two sections. Read aloud the meaning of the term *Infancy Narrative* in the Glossary. Ask: *In the Gospel of Matthew, when is Jesus proclaimed divine?* (Matthew 1:20) Ask a volunteer to read aloud the verse. Ask: *Why is it significant that the angel addresses Joseph as "son of David"?* (It fulfills the prophecy that the Messiah will rise from the House of David.)

Have volunteers read aloud the section Name Him Jesus. Say: *Your name is important to you. In the Sacrament of Baptism, it's the very first question posed to your parents or god-parents. "What name do you give this child?" With that name, your parents and godparents make a promise that you will belong to Christ, and the priest or deacon traces the Sign of the Cross on your forehead.*

Ask a volunteer to explain what the expression "living up to your name" means. (Answers will vary.) Ask: *How does Jesus live up to the meaning of "God saves"?* (Jesus won Salvation for our sins through his Death and Resurrection.)

Explore Names for Jesus

Annunciation mosaic, St. Thomas the Apostle Church, Phoenix, Arizona.

WHEN the angel Gabriel announces to Mary that she has been chosen to be the Mother of God, Mary accepts with joy. Joseph also receives a message from an angel. The visit to Joseph proclaims Jesus as divine.

Matthew's Infancy Narrative

An **Infancy Narrative**, an account of the infancy and childhood of Jesus, appears in the first two chapters of Matthew's and Luke' Gospels. In the Gospel of Matthew, we learn that Joseph was troubled by the news of Mary's pregnancy. Joseph and Mary were not married and hadn't had sexual relations. Who was the father? Joseph, a kind and just man, was unwilling to expose Mary to public disgrace. Instead, he planned to leave her quietly. (Matthew 1:18–19)

Before Joseph could do this, an angel of the Lord appeared to him in a dream. "Joseph, son of David, do not be afraid to take Mary your wife into your home. For it is through the holy Spirit that this child has been conceived in her." (Matthew 1:20) This is when Jesus was proclaimed divine.

Son of David

In Matthew's narrative, the angel addresses Joseph with the title "son of David." The angel is saying that Mary's child is the fulfillment of the covenant of old. As the foster father of Jesus, Joseph passes on this title to Jesus, showing that Jesus fulfills the covenants with Abraham and David. The prophecy that the Messiah will rise from the House of David is fulfilled.

Name Him Jesus

The angel tells Joseph, as he told Mary, that the child will be named Jesus. "She will bear a son and you are to name him Jesus, because he will save his people from their sins." (Matthew 1:21) This is the first time that the words *sin* and *save* appear in the New Testament in a meaningful way.

The name *Jesus* is an English (or anglicized) version of the Greek for the Hebrew name *Yeshua*. Yeshua was not an uncommon name in Jesus' time and place. In Aramaic the name *Yeshua* means "God saves." Joseph would have understood the meaning of the name. He did not understand how Jesus would save his people, but he believed the angel's words. In response to the visit from the angel, Joseph accepted Mary into his household and cared for the child Jesus as his own son.

God Is with Us

Matthew's narrative gives new meaning to events in the Old Testament by shedding light on the birth of Jesus. Matthew connects Jesus' birth to the fulfillment of the prophet Isaiah, who foretold a child born to a virgin and named **Emmanuel.** (Matthew 1:23) *Emmanuel,* Matthew writes, means "God is with us." Joseph and Mary, as faithful Jews, would have known the meaning of the word. They would have understood that Jesus would be God's presence among us. The name Emmanuel expresses the terms of the covenant. God promises to be with us, and we promise to have faith in Jesus and to follow him.

56 *Unit 2 • The Early Life of Jesus*

IF TIME ALLOWS

Session 7 BLM

✝ **Matthew the Evangelist—The Man** Explain that sometimes we refer to people as being "down to earth." Matthew refers to Jesus as Emmanuel to show that through Jesus, God became one of us. For this reason, the symbol of Matthew's Gospel has traditionally been a man to represent how "down to earth" God chose to become. Provide each young person with the Session 7 Blackline Master [T-358]. Ask them to use the Blackline Master to learn more about Matthew.

The name Emmanuel is a key statement of faith—God is with us. Matthew emphasizes this idea at the start of his Gospel and again in the middle when Jesus tells his followers, "For where two or three are gathered together in my name, there am I in the midst of them." (Matthew 18:20) And he mentions it at the end of his Gospel when Jesus says, "I am with you always, until the end of the age." (Matthew 28:20) When Matthew wrote about Jesus being Emmanuel, God with us, he was telling about the presence of Jesus to all of humankind.

Matthew's Infancy Narrative includes additional events in the story of Jesus' birth. It tells of the star leading the Magi to Jesus' stable, King Herod's plot, the massacre of the infants, and the flight into Egypt. Matthew's Infancy Narrative reveals Jesus as the fulfillment of prophecies and hopes throughout the ages. Matthew's audience would recognize that Jesus retraced the steps of Moses's journey when Mary and Joseph took the infant Jesus to Egypt to escape the murderous rage of King Herod. Jesus himself is the New Covenant.

Jesus the Christ

Another name for Jesus is **Christ.** The word *Christ* is the Greek version of the Hebrew word for *Messiah.* In Jesus' time, and for a long time afterward, people did not have surnames. People with the same first name distinguished themselves by adding where they came from, who their father was, or what they did for a living. The Jews of Jesus' time would have addressed him as either Yeshua Ben Yosef or Yeshua Bar Yosef (both meaning "Jesus, son of Joseph") or Yeshua Ha-Nozri ("Jesus of Nazareth").

In Latin the letter *J* is rendered as *I*, so when Pontius Pilate ordered that the inscription "Jesus of Nazareth, King of the Jews" be placed on Jesus' cross, it was abbreviated *INRI: Iesus Nazarenus Rex Iudaeorum.* Even on the cross, the name Jesus, "God saves," is written for all to see.

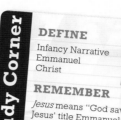

Study Corner

DEFINE
Infancy Narrative
Emmanuel
Christ

REMEMBER
Jesus means "God saves." Jesus' title Emmanuel reminds us that Jesus himself represents the New Covenant.

SACRED ART

George Adamson was a 20th-century author, illustrator, and cartoonist. In this artwork, how does the artist draw attention to the figure of Jesus? Who are the other people? The Son of God chose to live in the common world of our human experiences. Therefore, when we are looking for the presence of God, we don't have to look "out there." God became man so that we would be able to discover the presence of God in one like us in all things but sin. Jesus Christ continues to dwell in and among us each day, in our ordinary lives. Jesus is Emmanuel.

Nativity Scene, George Adamson, 1973.

Session 7 > Jesus Is God with Us 57

TAKE IT HOME

Describing God

Write the following names to describe God on the board: *The Mighty, The Protector, The Compassionate, The Powerful, The Responder, The Forgiver, The Provider.*

Have each young person choose one name and answer these questions on a note card: "What does the name reveal about God?" "What does it call you to do or be?"

Write the names on a paper banner in colorful letters, and have young people tape their note cards to it. Display the banner.

INCLUSION

Gifted

Build a Web Site If you work with gifted or talented young people, encourage them to build a Web site to use with the group throughout the year. Allow development time and encourage adult volunteers who are adept with technology to provide resources or assistance. Young people may choose to incorporate discussions and Take It Home assignments into the site.

Have volunteers take turns reading aloud God Is with Us. Ask: *What does Emmanuel mean?* (God is with us.) Ask: *How does Matthew's Infancy Narrative show that Jesus is the New Covenant?* (In the events surrounding Jesus' birth, many prophesies were fulfilled. Events in Matthew's narrative parallel events in the Old Testament, such as Jesus retracing Moses' journey when the Holy Family escapes to Egypt.)

Further discuss Jesus as the promised Messiah by organizing small groups to read the following passages from the Old Testament, and then have them explain how each was fulfilled by Jesus: Isaiah 7:13–14, Isaiah 9:5–6, Isaiah 11:1–2.

Have young people read and discuss the section Jesus the Christ. Ask: *What does the word Christ mean?* (It is the Greek version of the Hebrew word for *Messiah.*) Explain that *Messiah* means "anointed one." Say: *The name Christ is important to our faith and one of many titles assigned to Jesus.*

Sacred Art

Read aloud the feature. Have volunteers share their answers to the questions posed. Ask young people to discuss how the artist's portrayal of the Nativity brings them closer to understanding "God is with us."

③ Close

To close this discussion, say: *Jesus' birth gives new meaning to events in the Old Testament. Jesus is God with us.* Ask: *At what times in your life has God been with you as your closest and most reliable friend?* Invite young people to reflect on or write their answers. Encourage volunteers to share their responses.

① Begin

Take an informal survey. Ask young people to vote for their favorite way to talk to a friend, such as face-to-face, on the telephone, via e-mail, tweeting, text messaging, or video calling. Ask: *How do you talk to Jesus?* (Possible answers: praying, singing, listening)

② Connect

Read aloud the article title and ask a volunteer to read aloud the opening paragraphs. Discuss how we use names during communication. Say: *God knows each of us by name.* Explain that God is always listening and always inviting you to respond. He truly has "called you by name." Say: *When you think that God isn't listening to you, there might be something else going on. Maybe you're simply not listening to God.* Encourage discussion of this idea by using the story of Jonah in the Bible. Explain that Jonah, full of pride, tries to leave God behind. Say: *Jonah's suffering in the belly of a fish was not a just punishment from God; rather, it had a transformative effect on him. He finally heard God.* Ask: *Have you ever experienced a turning point in your own life? What was it? Could God have been speaking to you during this time? What was he telling you?* (Answers will vary.)

Read aloud the section Through Mystery and in Word. Ask: *What are some ways God speaks to you?* (Possible answers: in nature, family, the sacraments, through other people)

Our Catholic Character

Read aloud the feature. Explain that we encounter God through the inspired words of Scripture in the Mass. We celebrate Jesus' institution of the Sacrament of the Eucharist and the sending forth of the disciples to serve Christ.

How Does God Speak to Us?

IF you know someone by name, you probably find it easier to talk to him or her than if the person is a stranger. We know God by name. The prophet Isaiah teaches us that God certainly knows our names.

> But now, thus says the LORD,
>   who created you, Jacob, and formed you, Israel:
> Do not fear, for I have redeemed you;
>   I have called you by name: you are mine.
>
> *Isaiah 43:1*

Our Catholic Character

The Mass is the "source and summit" of our spiritual life—the perfect environment to communicate with God. Our Lord is present through the priest, the Scriptures, the Holy Eucharist, and in the people gathered. You are with God, and he is with you as you listen, pray, and sing.

Your name is personal; it belongs to you. Your name is a reminder that no one else is exactly like you. God calls you by name. You belong to God, and he wants you to grow closer to him. Just as finding ways to communicate keeps people closely connected, in a similar way, God seeks a loving communication with each of us. Jesus showed us a warm, caring relationship with the Father when he prayed to Abba.

How can you know when God is speaking to you? God is always present, talking to you often and at length. God's voice may be hard to recognize if you aren't listening or haven't figured out that God speaks to you in more than words. Sometimes you need to listen for God speaking through your thoughts, ideas, feelings, memories, and desires. It is important to listen with your heart.

Through Mystery and in Word

The Bible shows different ways that God speaks to people. It offers clues that tell how we might hear God's voice.

When Moses first encounters God, God's voice seems to come from a burning bush. Then on Mount Sinai, God gives Moses the Ten Commandments. These stories show that God speaks in miracles—in the wonderful, the unlikely, the mysterious. God also speaks to us through his Law and through Scripture, the Word of God.

58   *Unit 2 • The Early Life of Jesus*

ADVENTURES IN FAITH

Called by Name

Explain that it is our Christian challenge to live out our lives the way God intended. The Gospel of Jesus Christ and his life, Death, Resurrection, and Ascension hold challenges and answers. Place large glass jars in a quiet part of the room or in the prayer space. Add a few inches of water and affix one question to the outside of each jar, such as the following: *Are you a peacemaker? Do you turn the other cheek? Do you pray for your enemies? Do you respect all kinds of people? Do you forgive easily? Do you do what is asked gladly? Are you a minister of Christ, even when it is difficult?* Provide a basket of small pebbles next to the jars. At any time during the month, tell young people to add a pebble to any jar if they can answer yes to the question. Encourage them to reflect on the ripple the pebble makes as a visual reminder that small acts of goodness can lead to greater effects. As the days go by, encourage young people to participate in these challenges by asking: *What would it take for you to add a pebble to a jar?*

Through People

God has always used people to speak to us. Remember that God spoke through the prophets, and Jesus chose the Apostles to make disciples of all nations. God may speak to you through people who love you and who want to help you in your spiritual growth. Think about a person who has your best interests at heart, a person who tries to keep you safe, healthy, and moving in the right direction. How might God be speaking to you through this person?

In Dreams and Other Ways

In the Bible, God speaks through the power of dreams. God spoke to Abraham in dreams, as he spoke to Jacob and his son Joseph. He spoke to Joseph when he was betrothed to Mary, and even, in the time of Moses, he spoke to Pharaoh in Egypt. There is no one way by which God speaks to people. The prophet Elijah sensed God's presence in a quiet whisper, and God spoke to Job in a mighty whirlwind.

Ask God to help you listen for God's voice, from wherever it might come. Every dream or prompting may not be a message from God, but he may be heightening your awareness about something in your life that needs your attention.

Through Your Own Deepest Longings

It's natural to reflect on your own hopes and desires. However, God's plan for you may not match yours. You will sense that God's voice is present when your desires are at one with God's values and how God wants you to live.

In Memories, Thoughts, and Feelings

When you enjoy pleasant memories of family, friendship, holiness, or service to others, you may feel a sense of peace or a call to action. In ways such as these, you might hear God's voice because you feel God's presence. God is with you every moment of your life. He is with you in times of great happiness, and he is with you in moments of utter despair. God never abandons you. If you keep your heart open, you will hear his voice.

Through Scripture

Every time we read the Gospels, we discover that the words of Jesus are as relevant today as when he first spoke them. Jesus' central message is forgiveness. Jesus gave his disciples his example of forgiveness and healing over and over again. You follow Jesus every time you forgive a friend, ease a burden, or act as a peacemaker.

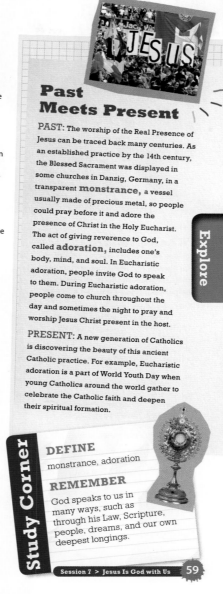

Past Meets Present

PAST: The worship of the Real Presence of Jesus can be traced back many centuries. As an established practice by the 14th century, the Blessed Sacrament was displayed in some churches in Danzig, Germany, in a transparent **monstrance**, a vessel usually made of precious metal, so people could pray before it and adore the presence of Christ in the Holy Eucharist. The act of giving reverence to God, called **adoration**, includes one's body, mind, and soul. In Eucharistic adoration, people invite God to speak to them. During Eucharistic adoration, people come to church throughout the day and sometimes the night to pray and worship Jesus Christ present in the host.

PRESENT: A new generation of Catholics is discovering the beauty of this ancient Catholic practice. For example, Eucharistic adoration is a part of World Youth Day when young Catholics around the world gather to celebrate the Catholic faith and deepen their spiritual formation.

Explore

Study Corner

DEFINE
monstrance, adoration

REMEMBER
God speaks to us in many ways, such as through his Law, Scripture, people, dreams, and our own deepest longings.

Session 7 > Jesus Is God with Us **59**

TAKE IT HOME

Dreams in the Scriptures

📖 Have young people find and read the following Scripture stories. Have them identify to whom God is speaking. Ask them to write a brief summary of each account and add an illustration. Bind the summaries together into a book and keep it in the prayer space for young people to read.

- Genesis 28:10–17 and Genesis 31:10–16 (Jacob)
- Genesis 37:5–8 and Genesis 37:9–11 (Joseph)
- Genesis 41 (Pharoah)
- 1 Kings 3:5–14 (Solomon)
- Daniel 4:2–27 (Nebuchadnezzar)
- Matthew 2:13 and Matthew 2:19 (Joseph, Jesus' foster father)
- Acts of the Apostles 16:9–10 (Paul)
- Matthew 2:1–12 (the Magi)

Ask a volunteer to read Through People. Invite discussion about modern prophets or disciples. Ask: **Whom does God speak through?** (Possible answers: those called to religious life, family members, teachers, those who have our best interests in mind)

Read aloud the next section. Say: **Recall the advice "Follow your dreams." God certainly had that in mind when he spoke to people in dreams.** Read aloud Genesis 15:1 as young people follow along in their Bibles, and repeat "the word of the Lord came to Abram in a vision." Say: **Abraham experienced God in the stillness and quiet of his sleep.** Ask: **How might technology, media, and computers separate us from an experience with God?** (They may distract us from God's presence.)

Ask a volunteer to read aloud the third section. Explain that some things we desire may not be part of God's plan. Say: **Focus on what God wants, and listen with your mind and heart in a prayerful, reflective way.**

Read the last two sections and invite volunteers to summarize.

Past Meets Present

Read aloud the feature. Explain that Pope Benedict XVI began an important new tradition at the celebration of World Youth Day in 2005 when he ended the vigil with silent Eucharistic adoration instead of a loud musical finale. The 2011 World Youth Day featured a monstrance set into a towering 16th-century silver-and-gold structure because the pope wished to proclaim Jesus Christ as the central person of World Youth Day.

③ Close

Invite young people to answer these questions:

▶ How has God spoken to you?

▶ How did you recognize his voice?

Prayer

Choose an approach and pray with young people.

APPROACH 1

Guided Reflection

Prepare Listen in advance to the recorded guided reflection "Called by Name" [CD 2, Track 3]. Decide if you will play the recording or pray aloud the reflection yourself. If you choose to lead, listen to the recording a second time, following the script [pages T-341–T-342] and noting pauses and tone. You can then follow the script exactly or adapt it as you wish.

Pray During the session, have volunteers read aloud the text in the left column. Explain that through prayer we can make a change in our lives that directs us toward God. Encourage young people to think of prayer as a movement toward God. Play the recording or lead using the script, joining the young people in reflective prayer. If you pray aloud the script, play reflective music softly.

APPROACH 2

Young People's Page

Prepare Pray the prayer in advance to become familiar with it.

Pray Invite young people to prepare for prayer. Slowly pray aloud the guided reflection, or have young people silently pray the text. Say: ***Respond to questions in the silence of your hearts or write responses on paper.***

After allowing time for reflection, pray aloud the concluding prayer while young people reflect in silence. Say: ***Jesus showed us how to live. Ask God to give you courage to make good choices every day of your life.***

Prayer

Called by Name

When God created human beings, he created within us a desire for himself. Just like a stomach hungers to be satisfied with food, our whole being hungers to be satisfied with God.

God's deepest desire is for you to turn to him. Everyone is created with this hunger for God. Even when you stray from God, he doesn't abandon you. Instead, God tirelessly calls you by name, urging you to a change of heart and a conversion back toward him.

God created you to be unique. No two people are exactly the same. You do not have to become like someone else to serve God. You will serve God with the special talents, personality, and characteristics that make you unique.

God calls you into relationship with him, and he calls you by name, meaning he calls you to take what is best and what is good about yourself and be his voice and his hands in this world in some way that perhaps only you can best accomplish.

Guided Reflection: Am I Who I Say?

Imagine yourself in a quiet place with Jesus. Jesus asks you to describe yourself. Think about it for a moment. What is your personality? What makes you special? What is important to you?

Now Jesus asks you a question. If you could call yourself by any name in your everyday life, what would it be? What name really describes who you are in your heart? Is it a conventional name like John or Emily? Is it a symbolic name like Sun? Is it a descriptive name like Dances with Joy? Share the name with Jesus and tell why you chose it.

Hear Jesus ask you one more question. If someone observed you for 24 hours, would that person be able to tell what you value the most? How does the way you live your life reveal your values—the choices you make, the friends you have, the things you do? Do your choices reflect what you say you value? Share your thoughts with Jesus and listen to whatever he wants to share with you.

All: Jesus, we want to be your disciples. Grant us the strength and courage to let our lives be signs of your kingdom by the choices we make. We ask this in your name. Amen.

60 · *Unit 2 • The Early Life of Jesus*

IF TIME ALLOWS

Pray Again

If you used the recorded guided reflection, you might conclude the session by praying the Sign of the Cross.

FYI

Coaching Young People to Pray

Before praying, remind young people that God never gives up on them, even when they feel like giving up. Encourage young people to ask God for the grace to turn to him. Ask them to recognize God's love and desire for them so they might acknowledge their built-in desire for God.

WHERE Do I Fit In?

by Jim Cruise

We are all created by God with a distinct and wonderful purpose, ultimately to live with him forever. But because of the effects of Original Sin, we can be easily distracted from this goal and follow the temptations that lead us away from God and others. Through the Church and the sacraments, God continually offers us the grace to reorient our lives to him and to a loving relationship with others in our lives. This is the true path he calls us to.

Answered Prayers

When I was in seventh grade, I wanted to make the basketball team in the worst way. All of my friends were trying out, and I wanted to be with them. For months I begged my dad for a basketball hoop. He finally gave in, and I practiced hard on the lopsided cement driveway. Almost every day I was dribbling, shooting, and passing the ball with friends.

Team tryouts lasted for three days. I missed the first two days because I was sick in bed with a fever. I had only one more chance to make the team, but I wasn't the only one. A kid named Benny also missed the first two days.

I did my best in the tryout, but Benny was a much better player than I was. Afterward, I walked home because I wanted time to pray. I begged God to let me make the team. I said Our Fathers and Hail Marys all the way home. When I reached home, I went to my bedroom and started reading the Bible. I had never read the Bible on my own before. I was hoping for a miracle.

The next day we gathered in the gym to hear Coach Wagner announce who had made the team. My friends whooped and cheered as each of their names was called. Benny's name was called. Mine wasn't. I didn't make the team. I was devastated. I didn't understand. I had prayed so hard.

Coach Wagner took me aside afterward and encouraged me. He urged me to consider another

sport and suggested the swim team. I took his advice and discovered I really liked swimming. I also made a good friend named Bill who became my best friend. Many years later I was the best man at his wedding.

In retrospect, not making the basketball team wasn't the catastrophe I thought it was. My prayers *were* answered—just not in the way I wanted them to be. Instead, God led me to a lifelong friend and the discovery of a new talent.

JIM CRUISE, the "Spoon Man," is a Catholic evangelist who performs his musical interactive comedy routine all over the country.

Becoming You

Describe how God answered a prayer in either an expected or unexpected way. Copy the boxes below on a separate sheet of paper. Then add your ideas to each one.

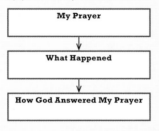

My Prayer
↓
What Happened
↓
How God Answered My Prayer

Session 7 > Jesus Is God with Us   61

Reflect

IF TIME ALLOWS

It's Not Just You

Explain that the pattern of prayer, silence, and unexpected answers shows up not only in our own lives but in Scripture too. Arrange young people in pairs and have them read Psalm 77, Parts I and II, including the footnotes describing the historical context. Then have them summarize each part. Ask: **How are the conclusions drawn by the speaker in Parts I and II different?** (Possible answer: Part I— God has forgotten us; Part II—God is powerful and moves in mysterious ways.) Discuss what must have happened in the life of the speaker after he or she wrote Part I but before he or she wrote Part II. (Possible answers: quiet prayer; deep listening; a decision to trust)

---

① Begin

Ask young people to name things they have prayed for in the past, including materialistic requests, such as a new phone or a trip to Disney World. Record their responses on the board. Ask which prayers came true in exactly the way they had hoped. Discuss these, if any. Say: **Fortunately, praying is not like online shopping.** Ask: **What would happen if we did get everything we asked for?** (Possible answer: We might become self-absorbed or greedy.) Say: **To discover how God does answer our prayers, we can pay attention and listen closely for what God wants us to know during the events of our lives.** Ask a volunteer to read aloud the introductory text.

② Connect

Invite volunteers to take turns reading aloud Answered Prayers. Have young people share similar experiences of their own. Then direct their attention to the fifth paragraph, and ask: **What was Coach Wagner's advice?** (Try another sport.) Ask: **How might a person who does not trust God respond to this advice?** (He or she might take it as an insult or be offended.) Ask: **How does the author respond to it?** (He follows it.) Ask: **What is the outcome?** (He discovers a new talent and the person who would become his best friend.) Have young people look again at the prayers recorded on the board from the Begin step, and encourage them to ask themselves, "How was this prayer answered after all?" Then have them complete the Becoming You activity independently.

③ Close

Invite volunteers to share their responses to the Becoming You activity. Say: **If you couldn't figure out what to write in the third box, that's okay. Keep looking and listening in a spirit of trust for God's answer.**

① Begin

What's What? Read aloud the directions. Explain there is only one best answer. Encourage young people to refer to the pages shown to find the answers. Have young people complete the activity independently.

② Connect

Say What? Ask volunteers to read aloud and define the terms. Review each term in the Glossary if necessary.

Now What? Read aloud the directions. Invite partners to discuss their ideas before writing. Invite them to continue writing on a separate sheet of paper if needed.

③ Go in Peace

Ask volunteers to collect materials and return them to their appropriate places. Encourage young people to continue strengthening their relationship with God during the week. Ask: ***How might you better listen for God speaking to you at home or in school? How do you think God wants you to respond?***

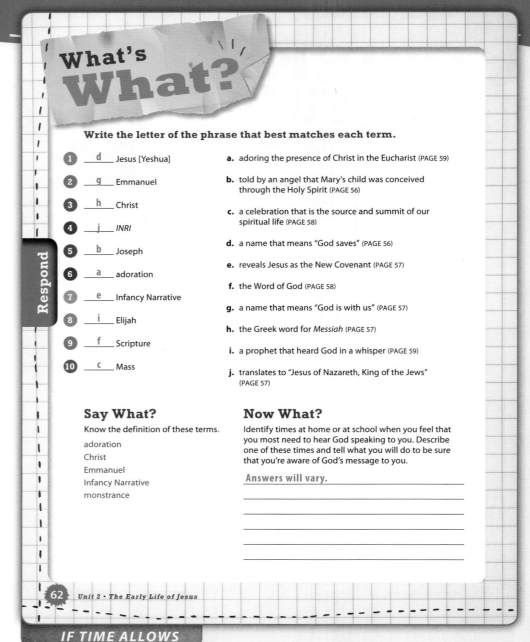

What's What?

Write the letter of the phrase that best matches each term.

1. __d__ Jesus [Yeshua]
2. __g__ Emmanuel
3. __h__ Christ
4. __j__ *INRI*
5. __b__ Joseph
6. __a__ adoration
7. __e__ Infancy Narrative
8. __i__ Elijah
9. __f__ Scripture
10. __c__ Mass

a. adoring the presence of Christ in the Eucharist (PAGE 59)

b. told by an angel that Mary's child was conceived through the Holy Spirit (PAGE 56)

c. a celebration that is the source and summit of our spiritual life (PAGE 58)

d. a name that means "God saves" (PAGE 56)

e. reveals Jesus as the New Covenant (PAGE 57)

f. the Word of God (PAGE 58)

g. a name that means "God is with us" (PAGE 57)

h. the Greek word for *Messiah* (PAGE 57)

i. a prophet that heard God in a whisper (PAGE 59)

j. translates to "Jesus of Nazareth, King of the Jews" (PAGE 57)

Say What?

Know the definition of these terms.

adoration
Christ
Emmanuel
Infancy Narrative
monstrance

Now What?

Identify times at home or at school when you feel that you most need to hear God speaking to you. Describe one of these times and tell what you will do to be sure that you're aware of God's message to you.

Answers will vary.

62   *Unit 2 • The Early Life of Jesus*

IF TIME ALLOWS

Service: Live Your Baptismal Promises

Tell young people that they became part of the Church at their Baptism. Clothed in Christ, they carry a name that God knows by heart. Because they are no longer infants, it is their responsibility to live up to their baptismal promises and make a more conscious effort to live as Christ. Ask young people to volunteer for the parish ministry that supports the baptismal program. They may volunteer to assist in making items such as programs, small white baptismal bibs, or parish-related baptismal keepsakes.

✝ *Family and Community*

Session Assessment Option

An assessment for this session can be found at www.findinggod.com.

3-Minute Retreat
Give young people an opportunity for quiet meditation at **www.loyolapress.com/retreat**.

PLAN AHEAD: Get Ready for Session 8

Consult the catechist preparation pages to prepare for Session 8 and determine any materials you will need.

Jesus Is for All People

 ## 3-Minute Retreat

Before you prepare the session, pause and be still. Take three deep breaths and be aware of the loving presence of God, who is with you on this journey.

Luke 2:26–28

It had been revealed to [Simeon] by the holy Spirit that he should not see death before he had seen the Messiah of the Lord. He came in the Spirit into the temple; and when the parents brought in the child Jesus to perform the custom of the law in regard to him, he took him into his arms and blessed God. . . .

Reflection

When Joseph and Mary came into the Temple with the infant Jesus, there was nothing that would show that they were in any way special. They carried two doves to sacrifice—the sign of the poor. They would be mostly ignored by anyone of importance. But Simeon, inspired by the Holy Spirit, saw through their poverty to the infinite blessing that they were to the world. In a world where it is easy to stereotype others by their physical appearance, clothes, or ethnic origin, we can remember Simeon. The same Holy Spirit that inspired Simeon gives us the grace to see through stereotypes and discover the person God loves beyond outward appearances.

Questions

How easy do I find it to stereotype people and take them for granted? What grace can I pray for to help me see others as God sees them?

 ### Concluding Prayer

Speak to God, using the words of this prayer or your own.

Jesus, help me see others through the eyes of Simeon as the blessed persons you have created them to be.

Knowing and Sharing Your Faith in Session 8

Consider how Scripture and Tradition can deepen your understanding of session content.

Scripture

Luke 2:7 reminds us that Jesus' birth reveals a humble king for all, laid in a manger and wrapped in swaddling clothes.

1 Corinthians 1:27–29 connects the early hardships in Jesus' life to the idea that God exalts the lowly.

Tradition

Beginning with Jesus' birth, Luke, the writer of the Infancy Narrative, wants us to understand that Jesus is our Savior—the one who brings Salvation. Salvation is the full and final restoration of our relationship with God, which has been damaged by sin. Grace is a gift to us accomplished through the life, Death, Resurrection, and Ascension of Jesus Christ. It is to be sought, not in the unknowable future, but by living in the immeasurable and ever-present love of God.

Catholic Social Teaching

In this session the integrated Catholic Social Teaching theme is **Solidarity.** See page 45b for an explanation of this theme.

Window on the Catechism

The mystery of Jesus' infancy and his hidden life are discussed in *CCC* 522–524.

General Directory for Catechesis

Jesus as mediator and fullness of Revelation is found in *GDC* 40.

One-Hour Session Planner

SESSION 8 Jesus Is for All People

Session Theme: *The hardships in Jesus' early life fulfilled prophecies and served as a reminder that the Savior came to save everyone.*

Before This Session

▶ Bookmark your Bible to Luke 1:33, Luke 2:1, Luke 2:4–5, Luke 2:7, Luke 2:13–14, Luke 17:21, Wisdom 7:4–6, John 10:11, 1 Corinthians 1:27–29, Matthew 2:6, Matthew 2:15, Matthew 2:18, Matthew 2:23, Psalm 22, and Psalm 34:4–8. Place the open Bible in your prayer space.

▶ Read the Guide for this session, choose any additional If Time Allows activities that you might have time to complete, and gather the listed materials.

 Prayer in Session 8

Pray aloud the short opening prayer that relates to central session concepts. Young people are also invited to experience an online 3-Minute Retreat at the end of the session. In Session 8, young people pray lines of a psalm and recognize a prayer in the form of a poem. Follow the Prepare directions on the Catechist Guide page before sharing with young people.

STEPS	APPROXIMATE TIME
Engage *Jesus Is for All People* PAGE 63	10 minutes
Explore *The Birth of Jesus* PAGES 64–65 *Hardship in Jesus' Life* PAGES 66–67	30–40 minutes
Reflect *Prayer:* God Delivers the Just PAGE 68 *Where Do I Fit In?* PAGE 69	10–15 minutes
Respond *What's What?* PAGE 70	10–15 minutes

TAKE IT HOME

Homework options:

A World in Need of Swaddling   PAGE 64

Solidarity Presentations   PAGE 67

Materials

REQUIRED

▶ Writing supplies (pages 63, 64, 65, 67, 69, 70)

▶ Globe or world map (page 64)

▶ Bibles (page 64)

▶ Computers with Internet access (page 70)

OPTIONAL

▶ Butcher paper for a banner, writing supplies (page 63)

▶ Large indoor or outdoor area (page 65)

▶ Session 8 BLM, T-359 (page 66)

▶ Bibles (pages 66, 68, 69)

▶ Writing supplies (page 69)

▶ Visual and audio components, such as slide-show presentation software and digital recorders (page 69)

▶ Session 8 Assessment, www.findinggod.com (page 70)

Session 8
Jesus Is for All People

What do you think goes through the minds of people who have lost their homes because of natural disasters, political unrest, or financial instability? What might they fear? For what might they hope?

Lord, I am grateful for shelter. Please come to the aid of all those who are living as refugees, separated from their homes.

63

IF TIME ALLOWS

Gratitude Banner

Have young people think about places that provide shelter or make them feel safe. Remind them that many places can be called home. Families might live in houses or apartments, others may live in relatives' houses, and some may live in community shelters. Emphasize that "home is where the heart is." Ask them to reflect on the goodness of God and then write messages or poems of gratitude on a paper banner labeled *Gratitude* that you display in class.

Go to **www.findinggod.com/sessionextenders** for the biblical image of the shepherd. You may wish to share this with the group.

Go to **www.findinggod.com/sessionextenders**

SESSION 8
OUTCOMES

▶ Describe Jesus' humble beginnings in Luke's Infancy Narrative, recognizing that Jesus came to save all people in every state of life.

▶ Identify the challenges and hardships that Jesus' family faced.

▶ Pray a psalm of thanksgiving for God's justice.

▶ Define *census, Magi, novena, prophecy, refugees, solidarity,* and *swaddling.*

1 Set the Stage

Read aloud the questions in the box on page 63. Give young people time to reflect on or record their ideas. Invite volunteers to share their responses.

2 Get Started

Ask young people to accompany you outdoors to an open area. Find places to sit comfortably, and ask the group to quiet themselves. Say: *Imagine that it is impossible to return to the room we just left, or any shelter, for an entire week. What would be different? What would be a hardship? What conveniences would you miss?* Allow young people to suggest challenges, such as lack of shelter from the weather or living without electricity, running water, desks, or chairs. Say: *When you face hardships in life, it doesn't mean that God has left you. He is with you every step of the way.* Read aloud the session title and say: *Jesus didn't come to lead only the rich or powerful; Jesus was a king for all people.*

Prayer

Say: *As we pray aloud, remember those who suffer without shelter.* Pray aloud the prayer. Conclude by praying the Sign of the Cross.

① Begin

Say: ***The Kingdom of God is unlike any earthly kingdom.*** Use a globe or world map to point out countries that still have, or have had in the past, some form of monarchy or one-leader rule. (Possible answers: Cuba, Syria, North Korea, Great Britain, The Netherlands, Spain, Saudi Arabia) Invite young people to imagine the Kingdom of God. Say: ***When you recognize God's rule, you use your imagination to see people, life, and the world in new ways. When people asked Jesus where they could find the Kingdom of God, the Gospel of Luke tells us that he replied, "[T]he kingdom of God is among you."*** [Luke 17:21]

② Connect

Read aloud the article title and invite volunteers to read the opening paragraphs and the section Luke's Infancy Narrative. Ask: ***Who is the Roman emperor at this time in history?*** (Caesar Augustus) Say: ***Caesar Augustus was a symbol of Roman power because he defeated all his enemies and unified the Roman empire. Luke wants his readers to see Jesus as a bringer of peace in a completely different way.***

Ask volunteers to read the remaining sections on the page. Ask: ***What prophecy is fulfilled?*** (The Messiah will come from the House of David.) Discuss Jesus' humble birth. Tell young people that in Jesus' time, swaddling clothes were long strips of cloth wrapped snugly and horizontally around the child. Ask: ***What does the detail about swaddling reveal?*** (Mary and Joseph gave Jesus care, and Jesus depended on his earthly parents.)

Read aloud the directions in the Birth Announcement activity. Point out that a tagline is memorable and recalls a big idea. Words must carry a big message in a small space.

The Birth of Jesus

Modern icon of the Nativity, Israel, 1980.

ON the surface, countries run by dictators might appear unified and peaceful. The truth is that what seems like unity and peace on the surface is actually brought about by force, brutality, or fear tactics. This kind of "peace," defined as a fearful, silent population, is only temporary.

In Jesus' time the Roman emperor Caesar Augustus was a dictator in this regard, vanquishing his enemies and expanding the Roman Empire. The citizens he ruled called him not only a man of peace but also, in Latin, *divi filius*—the son of god.

Luke's Infancy Narrative

The Gospel of Luke introduces the story of the birth of Jesus, citing Caesar Augustus by name. (Luke 2:1) Jesus too is a bringer of peace but not a peace as Caesar made it—by violence and fear. Luke's narrative helps us understand that Jesus' peace is the Salvation of God for the entire world, a kingdom not limited to the Roman Empire. Jesus alone is the true Son of God.

Son of David

In Luke's time it was common for people to think that great and powerful people were born into privilege. But Jesus was born to Mary in Bethlehem, a small city near Jerusalem. This city, according to Scripture, is where David was born and crowned king. Joseph, as a descendant of David's, traveled to the city with Mary to register for the **census,** the count of citizens. (Luke 2:4–5) So the place of Jesus' birth contributes to his identity as the Messiah and as the Son of David.

Firstborn Son

Luke records that Mary gave birth to her "firstborn son." (Luke 2:7) Jesus is the firstborn of many brothers and sisters in a spiritual family. He is the first of the always-growing community of people who work together to serve God's kingdom on earth. Mary is the spiritual mother of all Jesus came to save.

Swaddling Clothes

Luke's Gospel helps us understand that while Jesus is a king, he is a humble king who serves all. Mary wrapped Jesus in **swaddling** clothes, symbolizing the poverty and humility of Jesus' birth in a stable among animals. The act of swaddling, or wrapping the infant with strips of cloth, also reminds us that King Solomon was wrapped in swaddling clothes as a baby. (Wisdom 7:4–6)

Birth Announcement

Imagine that an advertiser hires you to write a billboard message for teens about the meaning of Jesus' birth. Write your tagline, an effective slogan that identifies your purpose.

_____

_____

_____

_____

64   *Unit 2 • The Early Life of Jesus*

TAKE IT HOME

A World in Need of Swaddling

Point out that just as Jesus' swaddling as an infant was a sign of Mary and Joseph's care for him, many people in the world are vulnerable to pain and suffering and are in need of care and compassion. Have groups brainstorm situations that cause people to be in need of care and compassion, such as unemployment, natural disasters, sickness, and divorce, and then name ways they might help.

Encourage young people to deepen their reflection by researching news accounts that give details of people who care for those in need during times of trouble. Ask them to write down possible solutions to the problems. Have young people prepare a brief presentation to share with the group.

✝ *Solidarity*

Manger

Mary placed the infant Jesus in a manger. Mangers were troughs used by shepherds and farmers to feed the animals. Luke tells us that because there was no room for Joseph and Mary at the inn, Jesus, the "Son of the Most High," (Luke 1:33) started life in a stable with simple accommodations. Placing the swaddled Jesus in the manger can remind us that Jesus himself will be food for the world.

Shepherds

Jesus' birth announcement was significant because it was made to shepherds, the humblest members of society. Shepherds were usually poor and dismissed by society as uneducated and unable to keep Jewish Law. Because shepherds lived outdoors in pastures with their sheep, many people considered them undesirable company.

Jesus is "the good shepherd" who "lays down his life for the sheep." (John 10:11) Because the proclamation of Jesus' arrival came first to shepherds, Luke showed that Jesus came to save everyone, not just a privileged few.

Savior

Jesus came from humble beginnings and demonstrated humility throughout his life. He brought a message of love to everyone, from simple fishermen to tax collectors. He is our example for living in a way that brings God's love to the world.

Jesus is our Savior, not a worldly leader. He comes to restore us to wholeness, to rescue us from sin, and to make it possible for us to be reconciled with others and with God.

In Luke's Infancy Narrative, Jesus is proclaimed the Son of God who came to save the world. Those who first recognized him were those who recognized their own need and dependence on God. Like Mary, they reflected in their hearts on the true meaning of Salvation. Today we are still called to reflect on how Jesus comes into the world, where he is recognized, and where society neglects its obligation to help those in need. Every time we open ourselves to the concerns of others, we discover the birth of Jesus in our own hearts.

Past Meets Present

PAST: Saint Francis of Assisi (1181–1226) wanted people to share his devotion to the Christ Child. In 1223 he made a living image of the scene of Jesus' birth. Francis built a small stable out of wood and gathered farm animals. At midnight Mass he placed a baby in a manger and gathered people around a scene of the Holy Family. Francis spoke of Christmas as a time of gentleness and generosity, and he reminded people of Jesus' humble beginning.

PRESENT: A **novena,** a Catholic prayer tradition, is prayed for nine days in a row. The Mexican celebration of *Las Posadas* is a Christmas novena that reenacts Mary's and Joseph's search for shelter. The celebration lasts for nine days from December 16–24. Some Spanish-speaking Catholics celebrate *Las Posadas* in various ways, depending on their culture. Often people dressed as members of the Nativity go house-to-house, singing a song that asks if there is room at the inn. The hosts of the home sing a reply. Christmas carols are sung, and food is sometimes served.

Explore

Study Corner

DEFINE

census
swaddling
novena

REMEMBER

Jesus came from humble beginnings. Jesus is the Savior who came to save everyone, not just a privileged few.

Session 8 > Jesus Is for All People **65**

🔥 ADVENTURES IN FAITH

Circle Tag

Have young people choose a partner. Organize the group into a circle in a large indoor or outdoor area, such as a gym or a park. Have partners interlock elbows. Choose one pair to leave the circle. Name one person in the pair a "chaser" and the other a "runner." At your signal, the partners run around the outside of the circle while the others remain still. If the chaser catches the runner, they switch roles. The runner has an option to stop anywhere along the circle and lock elbows with someone to avoid being caught. If this happens, the person who was "bumped" from the circle now becomes the runner. Continue playing for a reasonable period of time. Use the game to connect to the idea of inclusion and exclusion in school or the community. Ask: ***In life, whom do we take into our circle, and whom do we often leave out?*** Invite discussion about how young people relate with those who are challenged in some way [such as financially or physically] or those who are different from them [such as age or ethnicity]. Ask: ***What would Jesus say about inclusion and exclusion?***

Read aloud the section Manger. Ask: ***What does the detail about the manger reveal?*** (Jesus will be food for the flock.)

Ask a volunteer to read aloud the section Shepherds. Explain that the image of a shepherd was often used to describe the kings of the Old Testament because the kings were to care for God's people with the same responsibility as a shepherd would care for his flock. Say: ***Jesus is often shown as a shepherd because of his care for God's people.***

Ask a volunteer to read the section Savior. Say: ***Jesus calls us to realize that we all stand in need before God. Jesus welcomed sinners and outcasts out of social exile.*** Ask: ***Who are social exiles today?*** (Possible answers: those who are homeless, those who are suffering from physical or mental illnesses) Ask: ***How can we invite them into society?*** (Possible answers: by acting with care and compassion or by speaking up for the weak)

Past Meets Present

Read aloud the feature. Read aloud the meaning of *novena* in the Glossary. Explain that the Christmas crèche is a popular Catholic sacramental. Point out that the songs in *Las Posadas* ask for *posada*, or shelter. The nine days of the procession correspond to the nine months Jesus was in Mary's womb.

③ Close

Invite young people to reflect on or record answers to this question: ***How can I follow Jesus' example and bring a message of love to all?***

① Begin

Discuss how easy it is to access news on the Internet, social-networking sites, smartphones, or newspapers. Ask volunteers to help categorize the news as triumph stories or hardship stories. Have a volunteer read aloud the article title. Say: **Luke's Infancy Narrative introduces us to a Savior who is rooted in God's promises to Israel but destined for the Salvation of the world.**

② Connect

✝ Read aloud the first two paragraphs and the definition of the word *refugees* in the Glossary. Remind young people that no person's life is complete bliss or total misery. Say: **The hardships in Jesus' early life reflect his humanity.**

Ask volunteers to read aloud the sections The Magi and Out of Egypt. Ask: **Who accepts the Good News?** (the Magi) **Who rejects it?** (Herod) Point out that, similar to Jesus' flight to Egypt, many refugees are building new lives in the United States and other nations. Cite examples, such as musician Wyclef Jean, who fled Haiti when he was nine years old, and scientist Albert Einstein, who fled anti-Semitic Germany in the 1930s.

Say: **The Infancy Narrative is the whole Gospel in miniature. The underlying meaning is far more important than the details of the stories.** Ask: **What important meanings have you read about so far?** (Possible answers: Jesus' birth fulfills the prophecy of the Messiah; Jesus was a refugee, so we advocate for those less fortunate.)

Our Catholic Character

Read the feature. Have young people read the definition of *solidarity* in the Glossary. You might also refer them to page 300 in Prayers and Practices. Discuss solidarity as a call to action that dismisses the notion of a world intended to benefit those who "have" versus those who "have not."

Hardship in Jesus' Life

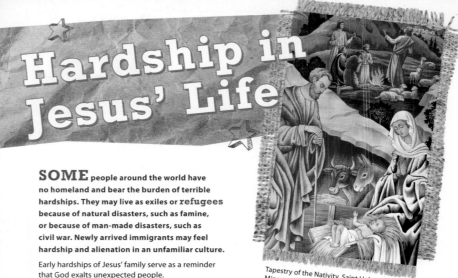

Tapestry of the Nativity, Saint Helena's Church, Minneapolis, Minnesota.

SOME people around the world have no homeland and bear the burden of terrible hardships. They may live as exiles or **refugees** because of natural disasters, such as famine, or because of man-made disasters, such as civil war. Newly arrived immigrants may feel hardship and alienation in an unfamiliar culture.

Early hardships of Jesus' family serve as a reminder that God exalts unexpected people.

"Rather, God chose the foolish of the world to shame the wise, and God chose the weak of the world to shame the strong, and God chose the lowly and despised of the world, those who count for nothing, to reduce to nothing those who are something, so that no human being might boast before God."

1 Corinthians 1:27–29

Our Catholic Character

Catholic Social Teaching tells us that as we grow in faith in God, we grow in **solidarity** with people all over the world. Faith, instead of isolating or dividing us, makes us more aware of the interdependence among individuals and nations. We are affected personally by the human suffering following natural or man-made disasters in distant countries. Pope John Paul II, in his encyclical letter *On Social Concern*, says, "Solidarity helps us to see the 'other'—whether a person, people or nation . . . as our 'neighbor,' a 'helper,' to be made a sharer on a par with ourselves, in the banquet of life to which all are equally invited by God."

The Magi

Even though the heavens opened up and angels sang of Jesus' birth, (Luke 2:13–14) Jesus was born into very dangerous circumstances. Matthew's Infancy Narrative tells how King Herod, greatly troubled by the prophecy of the Messiah's birth, wants the **Magi** to locate Jesus, supposedly so he may do Jesus homage. The word *Magi* refers to the men who came from the East by following a star, the first Gentiles to believe that Jesus was the Messiah. After finding Jesus, the Magi, who were warned in a dream not to return to Herod, depart for their own country.

Out of Egypt

An angel of God appeared to Joseph in a dream, telling him to flee with Mary and Jesus to Egypt. Joseph listened, and they stayed in Egypt until the death of Herod.

In a similar way, people all over the world pick up their families and flee persecution, fearing for their lives. Jesus, in Egypt, is a refugee. Throughout his ministry, he continues to advocate for those who are poor, outcast, and unwanted.

66 *Unit 2 • The Early Life of Jesus*

IF TIME ALLOWS

Session 8 BLM

✝ **Luke the Evangelist—The Ox** Explain that Luke's Gospel relates the mystery of who Jesus is by having readers follow the journey of the Church from its roots in Judaism to a Christian religion that became well-established in the cities of the Roman empire. Luke's Gospel begins with the announcement of the birth of John the Baptist in the small place called Judea. In contrast, Luke tells that Jesus, born during the reign of Caesar Augustus, will have a far-reaching impact. Provide each young person with the Session 8 Blackline Master [T-359]. Have them work independently to learn more about the Gospel of Luke.

SACRED ART

This African artwork, a painting from the Jesus Mafa Collection, is a visual response to an event in the life of Jesus Christ. Originating with a group in Northern Cameroon in Africa, this painting portrays the Holy Family's flight into Egypt. To make the painting, group members dramatically interpret a reading from the Bible, photograph the dramatization, and paint from the photos.

The Flight into Egypt, Mafa Collection.

Massacre of the Infants

Matthew described how Herod gave orders for the death of every male child under the age of two in the vicinity of Bethlehem to ensure that the Messiah would not reach adulthood. Herod, a ruthless dictator, tried to hold on to power through violence. The bloodshed of the massacre of the infants surrounds the beginning of Jesus' life, and bloodshed surrounds it again with his Death on the cross. Herod attempted to rob Jesus of life, and on Calvary, Jesus' Death and Resurrection secured eternal life for humanity.

Prophecy

Jesus' early hardships fulfilled many prophecies about the Messiah. A **prophecy** is a divine communication that comes through a human being. When Herod asked the Magi where the Messiah was to be born, they recited the words of the prophet:

"And you, Bethlehem, land of Judah,
 are by no means least among the rulers
 of Judah;
since from you shall come a ruler,
 who is to shepherd my people Israel."

Matthew 2:6

Another prophecy said that the Messiah, similar to Moses, would come out of Egypt:

"Out of Egypt I called my son."

Matthew 2:15

When Herod ordered the massacre of the infants, Jeremiah's prophecy was fulfilled:

"A voice was heard in Ramah,
 sobbing and loud lamentation;
Rachel weeping for her children,
 and she would not be consoled,
 since they were no more."

Matthew 2:18

After the angel told Joseph to return to the land of Israel, his concern over Herod's son Archelaus, who was ruling over Judea, prompted Joseph to take the family to Nazareth, fulfilling the words of the prophet:

"He shall be called a Nazorean."

Matthew 2:23

Jesus' Life, Our Lives

We see God's prophecy fulfilled in moments of hardship as well as moments of blessedness. We know that Jesus' love for us leads to his Crucifixion and that through his saving act, Jesus comes into glory, and we are saved from sin. Jesus' Incarnation is to share in human suffering so that we may know Jesus is with us and that through Jesus we can bring God's love to others.

Our compassion and solidarity with refugees, immigrants, and persecuted people around the world are our recognition and response to hardships endured by Jesus' family and his saving actions on the Cross.

Study Corner

DEFINE

refugees
solidarity
Magi
prophecy

REMEMBER

Mary and Joseph fled into Egypt to save Jesus' life. King Herod inflicted violence to maintain his power, but Jesus willingly submitted to violence; through his Death and Resurrection, he triumphs over sin and death.

Session 8 > Jesus Is for All People **67**

> Explore

TAKE IT HOME

Solidarity Presentations

Have partners discuss times when they had great joys and times when they suffered hardships. Have them answer the question: **How did Jesus walk with me every step during these times?**

Share examples of news stories that tell about the plight of refugees, exiles, immigrants, or others who find themselves without a homeland, and discuss them with the group. Bring newspapers to the group or ask young people to research safe and approved Web sites. After learning about an issue, ask young people to design a thought-provoking meditation about the plight of a group suffering hardship, possibly using a slide-show presentation to get the message across to others. Encourage creativity as they select images and reflective music to accompany their presentations.

 Solidarity

Sacred Art

Read aloud the feature. Point out the unusual and painstaking method taken to make the painting. Ask: *What effect might you suppose the artist is seeking with an audience?* (realism, connection to the event, art as a way of experiencing or feeling) Relate the plight of the Holy Family fleeing to Egypt with the Catholic Social Teaching of solidarity and how we view refugees or displaced people.

Have a volunteer read the section Massacre of the Infants. Ask: *How did Jesus conquer the bloodshed that surrounded his human life?* (His Death and Resurrection secured our eternal life.)

Read aloud the section Prophecy. Ask a volunteer to read aloud the definition of the word *prophecy* in the Glossary. Explain that the Infancy Narratives reveal truths concerning Jesus' divinity. Say: *When Jesus was in his hometown, people wondered where he got his knowledge. They only saw a man, a carpenter's son, and struggled with the idea that Jesus was divine.* Explain that the Infancy Narratives reveal the fulfillment of prophecies that the early Church gained over a period of time following Jesus' Resurrection.

Ask a volunteer to read Jesus' Life, Our Lives. Explain that Jesus shared in our humanity. Our faith life parallels the path of our human life with its celebrations, heartaches, doubts, and faith-filled responses along the way.

③ Close

To conclude the discussion, invite young people to reflect on or write their responses to these questions:

► When in my life have I fled from carrying the message of God's love to all people?

► What can I do to follow Jesus' example of acceptance of all people?

Prayer

Follow the steps to guide young people through the prayer on page 68.

Young People's Page

Prepare Pray the prayer in advance to become familiar with it.

Pray Read the title God Delivers the Just and the paragraphs that precede the prayer service. Ask: **How would you describe a psalm?** (a prayer in the form of a poem, intended to be sung, with the intent of expressing deep human emotion)

Then have young people bring their books to the prayer space. Invite them to prepare for prayer by getting into a comfortable position and quieting themselves. Arrange them into two groups and draw their attention to their parts as Side 1 or Side 2. Say: **When groups pray the psalms, it is typical to take turns praying. Reflect on the words you pray, listening closely for God's response in your heart.** Read aloud the Response. Point out the symbol that follows each Side, explaining that it is a signal to repeat the Response. Invite everyone to pray these parts.

Pause briefly and then pray aloud the Leader part, followed by the Response by all. Have each Side pray aloud its assigned part slowly and reverently, pausing briefly in between verses for the recitation of the Response. At the conclusion say: **Think about the greatness of God and our hope in his justice. As we continue the session, ask God to show you how to be his eyes and hands as you work for justice in the world.**

Prayer

God Delivers the Just

Psalms, prayers in the form of poems that were written to be sung in public worship, express some aspect of the depth of human prayer.

Jesus knew the psalms and even prayed part of Psalm 22 on the cross. The psalms express a variety of human emotions, desires, and needs. They reflect real-life situations and problems. Although the style of language may be unfamiliar, their poetry draws us in and helps us express our human emotions in prayer.

Psalm 34 is a prayer of thanksgiving that speaks of God's justice. This prayer makes reference to fearing God. In this case, synonyms for the Hebrew word *fear* are *awe* or *respect*. This fear acknowledges the greatness of God, not the condition of being afraid of him. Even though hardships are part of human life, God is greater than these hardships. Injustice, poverty, disappointment, misfortune, hunger, and cruelty are part of our world. Prayer touches on all these things while reaffirming our hope in the Lord at the same time.

God Delivers the Just

Leader: Let us pray together the Response and become aware of God's justice.

Response: Magnify the LORD with me;
and let us exalt his name together.

Side 1: I sought the LORD, and he answered me,
delivered me from all my fears. ℟.

Side 2: Look to him and be radiant,
and your faces may not blush for shame. ℟.

Side 1: This poor one cried out and the LORD heard,
and from all his distress he saved him. ℟.

Side 2: The angel of the LORD encamps
around those who fear him, and he saves them. ℟.

Psalm 34:4–8

68 *Unit 2 • The Early Life of Jesus*

IF TIME ALLOWS

A Psalm a Day

Encourage young people to keep their hearts "soft," even during troubling times when they might wish to harden them. By keeping their hearts soft, they will be better able to hear God speak to them. Plan to begin with a psalm from the Bible each time the group meets. Invite young people to suggest favorite verses and rotate readers who will pray aloud.

FYI

Coaching Young People to Pray

Assure young people that even though suffering is part of our human experience, we have the example of Jesus to help us meet the challenges as well as celebrate the joys in our lives. To get young people ready to pray, ask them to reflect on times when their faith has given them strength during times of hardship.

WHERE Do I Fit In ?

It can be hard to make a place for yourself in the world. You may not always be welcomed, and sometimes you might be altogether rejected. A sense of belonging can make all the difference. God always makes a welcoming place for you.

by Cara Mia Cicciarelli

Reflect

I Belong Wherever I Am

Every summer our family spent a vacation at Pennellwood, a 100-year-old family camp in the woods of southwestern Michigan. The camp was a hot, sticky, mosquito-filled place—and wonderful. Pennellwood consisted of 20 screened-in cabins, a lodge for meals, a few activity centers, and a "lake" that was really a dammed-up river. Pennellwood was closed off from the outside world, a little nook of unchanging charm from decade to decade. We would trade in our cell phones and video games for fishing poles and outdoor games of Capture the Flag. We forgot about TV shows that went unwatched and text messages that went unanswered. Young people wandered freely without causing parents any concern because once the dinner bell rang, we would surely appear, ready to heap our plates with comfort food. At the end of each season, we gathered to sing and tell stories around a bonfire. The sense of community was very strong, and I never felt more comforted than I was at those campfires.

After Pennellwood's final season of operation, our close summer community disbanded. That first summer without the campground, the weeks dragged on and on for me. I felt hollow without the familiarity of lazy days full of camp activities and the cool lake waters. I felt as if a part of me was auctioned off along with our beloved cabin.

I began looking for other places where I could feel the acceptance, love, comfort, and freedom that I had found at Pennellwood and now missed. I discovered that if I looked for God's presence in my ordinary life at school, while doing chores, or while spending time with friends, I could reclaim those feelings.

When I paused to notice the beauty of nature, the goodness in myself or others, or the bonds of my community, I knew that Pennellwood lived on in my heart. God lets me know that I belong wherever I am, and that he is present with me—anywhere.

Always Welcome

On a separate sheet of paper, write an e-mail message to a friend that either describes a time when you felt God's welcoming presence or a time when you needed to respond in a certain way to rediscover God's presence and love.

To:	Becca
Cc:	Mary
Subject:	My Trip to Pennellwood

CARA MIA CICCIARELLI is a high school student who enjoys the fine arts, including vocal and dance studies.

Session 8 > Jesus Is for All People 69

Making It Happen

Have group members work together to write a skit that includes a situation that requires a community-building response as a way to recognize God's welcoming presence. Encourage young people to reach consensus on an appropriate response to the situation before they begin writing the skit. When all groups are ready, have them take turns performing. Invite audience members to provide positive feedback after each skit.

INCLUSION
Gifted

Design a Prayer Service
If you have young people who are gifted learners, ask them to further develop the discussion of belonging and being welcomed in God's presence. Invite them to write a prayer service that includes readers, petitions, or Bible verses. Encourage them to embellish the service with visual and audio components, such as a slide-show presentation and musical accompaniment. Have the group participate in the prayer service.

---

① Begin

Read aloud the introductory text. Ask volunteers to tell about times when they felt as if they were exactly where they were supposed to be. Ask: *What does it take to feel as if you belong?* (Answers will vary.)

② Connect

Ask young people to explain what they think the title means. Then have volunteers take turns reading aloud I Belong Wherever I Am. Invite young people to share similar stories of loss or change. Say: *The author experienced God in the community of Pennellwood. When the community disbanded, she felt homesick for that sense of holy togetherness.* Ask: *How did she rediscover it?* (She began recognizing God's presence in other places and in her ordinary life.) Say: *God called the author to actively seek the experience of community. As we grow and our lives change, we have to do the same thing. Instead of merely existing within a community, we have to make community happen. Since God is always with us, and we always belong to him, we always belong—no matter where we are.* Encourage young people to recall this critical point when they experience the loss of a sense of belonging. Have young people brainstorm ways they can transform situations such as these into ones of belonging.

Read aloud the directions in the Always Welcome activity. Have young people complete the activity independently.

③ Close

During the next group meeting, invite young people to share the e-mail messages that they wrote in the activity. Remind them that any action that brings them closer to others also brings them closer to God.

① Begin

What's What? Read aloud the directions. Suggest that young people use the page reference and the process of elimination to narrow choices to the best answer. Have young people complete the page independently or with a partner.

② Connect

Say What? Ask volunteers to read aloud and define the words. Review each word in the Glossary if necessary.

Now What? Ask a volunteer to read aloud the section. Invite each young person to respond independently. Encourage them to continue on another sheet of paper.

③ Go in Peace

Collect materials and return them to their appropriate places. Encourage young people to assess the success of their actions on a daily basis. Ask: **Did you extend yourself to someone who is suffering, or do you need to recommit yourself or refine your ideas?**

3-Minute Retreat
Give young people an opportunity for quiet meditation at **www.loyolapress.com/retreat**.

What's What?

Respond

Circle the letter of the choice that best completes each sentence.

1 _____ was the Roman emperor at the time of the birth of Jesus. (PAGE 64)
- **a.** Julius Caesar
- **c.** Caesar Augustus ✓
- **b.** Nero
- **d.** Pontius Pilate

2 Jesus, Son of God, starts out life among _____. (PAGES 64–65)
- **a.** those who are poor
- **b.** those who are lowly
- **c.** animals
- **d.** all of the above ✓

3 After his birth, Jesus was laid in a manger, which is _____. (PAGE 64)
- **a.** a feeding trough for animals ✓
- **b.** a typical crib
- **c.** a loft in a barn
- **d.** a vehicle for travel

4 Jesus was wrapped in swaddling clothes just like _____. (PAGE 64)
- **a.** King Herod
- **c.** King Tut
- **b.** King Julius
- **d.** King Solomon ✓

5 Jesus, the Savior, comes for _____. (PAGE 65)
- **a.** religious people
- **b.** smart people
- **c.** all people ✓
- **d.** good people

6 In 1223 _____ built a scene of the birth of Jesus with a stable and animals. (PAGE 65)
- **a.** Saint Patrick
- **c.** Saint Matthew
- **b.** Saint Francis of Assisi ✓
- **d.** Saint Stephen

7 The massacre of the infants refers to an order by _____ to kill every male under the age of two years. (PAGE 66)
- **a.** Herod ✓
- **c.** Pontius Pilate
- **b.** Caesar Augustus
- **d.** Romans

8 An angel of the Lord appeared to Joseph in a dream and told him to take Mary and Jesus and flee to _____ until the danger had passed. (PAGE 66)
- **a.** Bethlehem
- **c.** Egypt ✓
- **b.** Nazareth
- **d.** Galilee

9 After Herod's death, the Holy Family leaves Egypt and settles in _____. (PAGE 67)
- **a.** Bethlehem
- **c.** Jordan
- **b.** Nazareth ✓
- **d.** Galilee

Say What?
Know the definitions of these terms.

census	refugees
Magi	solidarity
novena	swaddling
prophecy	

Now What?
Jesus' message is for everyone. Describe ways you can help someone who is excluded, experiencing rejection, or in need of help.

Answers will vary.

_____
_____
_____

70 *Unit 2 • The Early Life of Jesus*

IF TIME ALLOWS

Service: English as a Second Language

In our ever-shrinking world, the call for solidarity becomes more valuable as we work for justice and peace. Assess the school or parish need to provide services to those newly arrived to the United States. Organize volunteers to address those needs. For example, young people may volunteer their time to work with English language learners, providing tutoring and friendship. Another idea is to organize a culture fair to celebrate and embrace their new parishioners traditions.

✝ *Solidarity*

Session Assessment Option

An assessment for this session can be found at www.findinggod.com.

PLAN AHEAD: Get Ready for Session 9

Consult the catechist preparation pages to prepare for Session 9 and determine any materials you will need.

Jesus Grew in Wisdom, Age, and Grace

 ### 3-Minute Retreat

Before you prepare the session, pause and be still. Take three deep breaths and be aware of the loving presence of God, who is with you on this journey.

Acts of the Apostles 2:17

"It will come to pass in the last days," God says,
   "that I will pour out a portion of my spirit
      upon all flesh.
Your sons and your daughters shall prophesy,
   your young men shall see visions,
   your old men shall dream dreams."

Reflection

Many people who heard Peter's speech at Pentecost thought that the visions and dreams he spoke of were the result of too much wine. He reminded the people of the words of Joel. When we allow the Spirit to move in us, we become dreamers too. The "portion of the spirit" that falls on us is needed by the rest of the world. When we trust our visions and dreams of love and service to others and join them with the visions and dreams of others, God's dream for the world becomes a reality.

Questions

How would I describe God's plan for the world? How do I participate in making that plan come true?

 Concluding Prayer

Speak to God, using the words of this prayer or your own.

God of all Creation, your Spirit fills the earth. Walk with me as I boldly proclaim your dream for the world.

Knowing and Sharing Your Faith in Session 9

Consider how Scripture and Tradition can deepen your understanding of session content.

Scripture

Luke 2:49 gives a glimpse into the young Jesus' recognition of his Father's sending him into the world on his mission as the Messiah.

Mark 3:34–35 tells us how Jesus defines a family.

Tradition

Luke's story of Jesus as a boy in the Temple highlights some of the ingredients of good family life. Joseph and Mary were doing their best to raise their son in their Jewish faith, involving him in their worship of God. After losing and finding Jesus, they talked to him in order to better understand the situation. Jesus was at the cusp of adulthood in his culture, and he had ventured forth on his own, taking a step toward becoming the person God was calling him to be. In the end, he returned home and was obedient to Mary and Joseph.

Catholic Social Teaching

In this session the integrated Catholic Social Teaching theme is **Call to Family, Community, and Participation.** See page 45b for an explanation of this theme.

Window on the Catechism

The mystery of Jesus' infancy and his hidden life are discussed in *CCC* 532–534.

General Directory for Catechesis

Jesus as mediator and fullness of Revelation is found in *GDC* 40.

One-Hour Session Planner

SESSION 9 Jesus Grew in Wisdom, Age, and Grace

Session Theme: *Jesus begins to understand that God, his Father, is calling him to a special mission.*

Before This Session

▶ Bookmark your Bible to Luke 2:41–52, Mark 3:21, Mark 3:31–35, Matthew 10:7–8, and Ephesians 4:25. Place the open Bible in your prayer space.

▶ Read the Guide for this session, choose any additional If Time Allows activities that you might have time to complete, and gather the listed materials.

STEPS	APPROXIMATE TIME
Engage *Jesus Grew in Wisdom, Age, and Grace* PAGE 71	10 minutes
Explore *Jesus in the Temple* PAGES 72–73 *Finding God in Family* PAGES 74–75	30–40 minutes
Reflect *Prayer:* Gifts Received, Gifts Given PAGE 76 *Where Do I Fit In?* PAGE 77	10–15 minutes
Respond *What's What?* PAGE 78	10–15 minutes

Prayer in Session 9

Pray together the prayer at the beginning of the session and invite young people to access an online 3-Minute Retreat at the end of the session. Session 9 includes a guided reflection, a meditative prayer in which young people use their imaginations, about using God-given gifts to serve others. Follow the Prepare directions on the Catechist Guide page before sharing with young people.

TAKE IT HOME

Homework options:

Letters of Love   PAGE 73

Map of Your Life   PAGE 74

Materials

REQUIRED

▶ Bibles (pages 72, 75)

▶ Writing supplies (pages 72, 73, 75, 78)

▶ CD player (page 76)

▶ CD 1, Track 7: Reflective Music (page 76)

▶ Poster board, magazines, photographs, art supplies (page 77)

▶ Computers with Internet access (page 78)

OPTIONAL

▶ Session 9 BLM, T-360 (page 71)

▶ Media player (page 72)

▶ Movie *Whale Rider* (page 72)

▶ Parish bulletins (page 75)

▶ Writing supplies, stationery (page 77)

▶ Writing supplies, album or notebook, photos (page 78)

▶ Session 9 Assessment, www.findinggod.com (page 78)

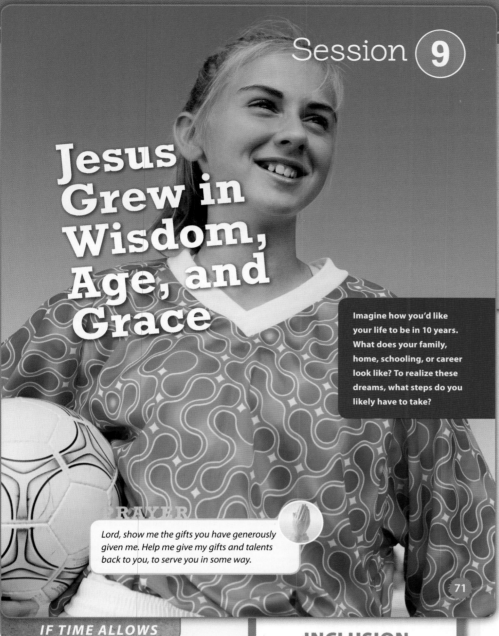

Session 9

Jesus Grew in Wisdom, Age, and Grace

Imagine how you'd like your life to be in 10 years. What does your family, home, schooling, or career look like? To realize these dreams, what steps do you likely have to take?

PRAYER

Lord, show me the gifts you have generously given me. Help me give my gifts and talents back to you, to serve you in some way.

71

Session 9 BLM

Big Dreams Dreams are a way of seeing. Dreams influenced many people in the Bible and led them to certain actions. Explain that their personal dreams influence their lives as well. Provide each young person with the Session 9 Blackline Master [T-360]. Have them work independently to describe the future they imagine for themselves and the steps they can take to build that future.

INCLUSION

Chronic Illness

Tips for Success Encourage young people with chronic health conditions to participate in session activities as much as possible without becoming fatigued. If they become frustrated with completing a task, ask a volunteer to help them, offer extra time to complete the task, or customize the tasks to encourage achievement.

Go to **www.findinggod.com/sessionextenders** for perspective about Jesus in the Temple. You may wish to share this with the group.

SESSION 9
OUTCOMES

▶ Identify the ways that Jesus begins to understand that God the Father is calling him to a mission.

▶ Describe how we learn to pray and use experiences in the family to reach out in service to others.

▶ Pray a guided reflection to recall gifts received from God.

▶ Define *Cardinal Virtues, domestic church,* and *synagogue.*

① Set the Stage

Read aloud the text in the box on page 71. Give time for young people to reflect upon the questions or write responses. Then ask volunteers to share their ideas in small groups.

② Get Started

Ask: ***What do you want to do or be when you are an adult?*** Assure young people that some of them may already know what they want to do in the future while others may not. In either case, suggest that it helps to talk their ideas over with people they trust or admire and ask for guidance. Remind them that they should take opportunities to develop their skills and interests, which may give them direction. Say: ***As you envision a direction for your life, letting yourself imagine future scenarios is a way to "try on" your ideas.*** Read aloud the session title. Say: ***When Jesus was your age, he began to dream about how he wanted to spend the rest of his life.***

Prayer

Say: ***As we pray together, ask for the Holy Spirit's help to know God's will for us as we dream about today and the future.*** Pray aloud the prayer. Conclude by praying the Sign of the Cross.

① Begin

Tell young people that *coming of age* means "the attainment of respectability or maturity." Say: **This is an impressive milestone.** Ask: **Do you think everyone comes of age at the same time? Why or why not?** (No, everyone's life journey is different.)

Read aloud the article title and ask a volunteer to read the first two paragraphs. Assign partners to read Luke 2:41–52 to hear about Jesus' own coming of age. Encourage young people to ask God to help them stay alert to God's plan for them as they stretch their wings and chase their dreams.

② Connect

Invite volunteers to read aloud the sections Lost and Jesus in the Temple. Say: **When Jesus stayed behind, he sat among the rabbis.** Ask: **Why is Jesus a good model of behavior?** (He listened to the Jewish teachers and asked questions.) Ask: **How does this reflect wisdom?** (Possible answers: Jesus was more interested in following his Father's will than proving his knowledge; Jesus respected the accumulated knowledge his elders had gathered over a lifetime.) Ask: **Why were the elders surprised by Jesus' words?** (Possible answer: They were amazed that one so young could be so wise. They were impressed by Jesus' ideas.)

Our Catholic Character

Ask a volunteer to read the feature. Discuss the definition of the *Cardinal Virtues* in the Glossary. Say: **Like our physical health, our spiritual health also has requirements. These virtues are essential if we want to live close to God and others.** Refer young people to page 269 in Prayers and Practices. Discuss possible ways to live according to each Cardinal Virtue.

Jesus in the Temple

IN Jesus' time there were no Bar or Bat Mitzvahs, the Jewish ritual in which young people read the Torah in the synagogue and become "children of commandment."

Today a Jewish male has a Bar Mitzvah when he turns 13 years old. Luke's story, commonly referred to as the Finding in the Temple (Luke 2:41–52), takes place during Passover when Jesus is 12 years old and represents an important time in his life.

Lost

Passover, the Jewish festival celebrated every spring, recalls how the Lord delivered the Hebrews from slavery in Egypt. In Jesus' time the Temple in Jerusalem would have been crowded at Passover with men and women, families, pilgrims, and holy people preparing for the great celebration. It is not that surprising that Jesus got separated from Mary and Joseph or even that his absence wasn't noticed until Mary and Joseph were on their way back home. They may have assumed that Jesus was somewhere else in the huge caravan.

Jesus in the Temple

Mary and Joseph returned to Jerusalem to look for Jesus. After searching for three days, they discovered him in the Temple among rabbis. Jesus was not lecturing or preaching to the Jewish elders. Rather, he was "listening to them and asking them questions." (Luke 2:46) His ability to understand and speak about the Jewish faith at such a young age impressed the teachers who had studied the faith and the Law their entire lives. Luke 2:47 says that "all who heard him were astounded at his understanding and his answers."

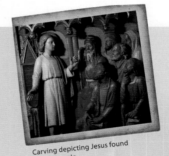

Carving depicting Jesus found in the Temple.

Our Catholic Character

In Luke 2:51–52 we learn that while Jesus was living with his parents in Nazareth, he advanced in wisdom, age, and favor before God and others. He did so by practicing the virtues that lead a person to live in relationship with God and others. These four virtues—prudence, justice, fortitude, and temperance—are called the **Cardinal Virtues.** Jesus learned to be prudent, choosing the right course of action. He learned to be just, giving God and his neighbors what was due them. He learned to be strong, determined to do what was right in the face of obstacles. He learned to practice temperance, being moderate both in seeking pleasure and in using his possessions.

72 *Unit 2 • The Early Life of Jesus*

IF TIME ALLOWS

Coming of Age

Expand discussion about family, respect, dignity, unexpected wisdom, and coming of age by viewing with young people the movie *Whale Rider*, based on a novel of the same name by Witi Ihimaera. The story, set in modern-day New Zealand, tells about Maori people who believe their ancestor Paikea was saved from drowning by riding home on the back of a whale. Only Paikea's descendants, firstborn sons, are given the title of chief, but a young girl has a daring dream to become chief. Her road to recognition and maturity includes hardships as well as inspiring and mystical events occurring along the way. You may wish to visit the U.S. Conference of Catholic Bishops Web site for other movie reviews at http://usccb.org.

Why Have You Done This to Us?

Mary and Joseph were astonished to see Jesus in the midst of the teachers. But why? Were they astonished that he wasn't afraid? That he wasn't looking for them? That he was so comfortable with adults—important adults? That he knew so much about Scripture despite being so young?

Mary and Joseph must have experienced a variety of thoughts and feelings, including immense relief that Jesus was safe. Mary might have wondered how her son could disregard the worry she would feel as a parent. Mary has a question of her own: "Son, why have you done this to us?" (Luke 2:48)

My Father's Business

By way of reply, Jesus asks a question of his mother: "Why were you looking for me? Did you not know that I must be in my Father's house?" (Luke 2:49) For Jesus, the calling to be near the Father is obvious. Perhaps Jesus is surprised that he has even caused them worry. He might be wondering why his parents would look for him anywhere else. The story is not one of Jesus' disobedience to his parents but of an awakening that the Father is calling him to a special mission. Jesus has a sense about his future. He is beginning to know and understand his special relationship with God, his Father.

But Luke writes that Mary and Joseph do not understand the meaning of Jesus' words. Even so, seeing Jesus in the Temple among the teachers must have planted the seed of understanding about the work the Father was calling Jesus to do.

This is an extraordinary time for both Jesus and his parents. Jesus is obedient to them and returns to Nazareth. He knows the commandments, and the Fourth Commandment instructs him to respect and obey his parents. The commandment applies to parents, as well, calling them to help their children live full, healthy lives and to prepare them for the work that God wants them to do. Scripture tells us that "his mother kept all these things in her heart." (Luke 2:51) Mary would think about Jesus' words later on, knowing that her Son loved her but was answering his Father's call.

Mutual Respect

For families to live in harmony, it's important for parents and children to respect one another and understand their respective roles. Think about a time when you and a family member showed each other mutual respect. Record your ideas on the lines.

_____

_____

_____

_____

_____

_____

_____

_____

_____

_____

Explore

Study Corner

DEFINE
synagogue
Cardinal Virtues

REMEMBER
Mary and Joseph found Jesus in the Temple with Jewish teachers, who were astounded at his understanding and answers.

Jesus begins to understand that God, his Father, is calling him to a special mission.

Session 9 > Jesus Grew in Wisdom, Age, and Grace 73

TAKE IT HOME

Letters of Love

Assign young people to write letters of love to their parents or caregivers. They should speak from the heart, letting parents know why they honor, respect, and are grateful for them. If some young people feel as if they haven't been doing a good job following the Fourth Commandment, ask them to write about how they can do better in the future. Ensure each young person has written a letter. Collect and store each letter in an envelope identified with a name.

Send a formal request home to parents or caregivers, telling them about the assignment and requesting that they return the gesture by writing a letter to their child. Ask them to place their letter in an envelope identified with the name of its recipient.

Invite parents to an informal open house for an exchange of letters. To ensure no young person goes without a letter, monitor the return of parent letters and ask other adults, such as teachers or relatives, to fill in so everyone receives a letter and knows that he or she is loved, respected, and appreciated.

✝ *Family and Community*

Have young people read the two sections on the page. Say: *Family life binds us together, but we still want to follow our own paths and form our own identifies. This tension can interfere with harmony in a family.* Say: *Think about what Mary asks Jesus and how he answers her.* Ask: *What had Mary probably expected from Jesus?* (that he would have known she would worry) Ask: *What did Mary not understand?* (Jesus was responding to a special calling from his Father.)

Explain that Jesus would have been familiar with the Fourth Commandment because Mary and Joseph were raising him in their religious tradition. Say: *Jesus was in the Temple because in some way he was preparing to follow the mission God his Father called him to follow. Even so, he respected and obeyed his parents by returning with them to Nazareth.*

Point out that the Fourth Commandment isn't intended only for children; it applies to parents as well. Ask: *What are some ways parents keep the Fourth Commandment?* (Possible answers: Parents have a sacred duty to teach their children about prayer and to lead them in growing in their faith. They are called to respect their children, provide for them, and educate them.) Ask: *How do Mary and Joseph keep the Fourth Commandment?* (They begin to recognize their responsibility to prepare Jesus for the work that God wants him to do.)

Read aloud the directions for the Mutual Respect activity. Invite young people to complete the activity and share their ideas with the group.

③ Close

Ask: *How can you come of age and still show respect and obedience to your parents or caregivers?* Invite discussion, encouraging young people to share and defend their opinions.

1 Begin

Ask young people to describe how they learned to play a sport or game. Comment on the importance of learning from others who have played longer than they have. Say: **The same is true of prayer. The best way to learn to pray is by praying with someone who can teach us how to pray. We learn to pray with our families.** Have a volunteer read aloud the article title Finding God in Family and the first paragraph.

2 Connect

Read aloud the section A Domestic Church. Say: **When we pray, we take prayers to heart. We think about what the words mean and experience the prayer in a deep and meaningful way.** Ask a volunteer to read aloud the definition of the term *domestic church* in the Glossary.

Arrange groups to discuss some realities of family life. Invite volunteers to share aloud examples of happy and difficult times a family can experience. Point out that because all families are different, they might respond in different ways to situations. Reread the quotation from Pope John Paul II and ask volunteers to explain what it means to them.

✝ *Family and Community*

Past Meets Present

Ask volunteers to read the feature. Mention that children are reminders of the potential that exists in God's Kingdom and that some children, through no fault of their own, need help when their own family structure is broken. Explain that Saint John Bosco reminds us that other people, whether biological relatives or not, can be our family, and we are all members of God's family. God is our Father.

Past Meets Present

PAST: Saint John Bosco (1815–1888) took care of poor and forgotten youth in need. He was ordained a priest in 1841 and sent to Turin, Italy. John inspired young people who lived on the streets by the way he taught and by his life of prayer. Soon he was running a boarding house with the help of his mother, Margaret. Many more young people came to him for faith instruction and boarding, and he founded the first Salesian Home to care for their needs.

PRESENT: Today the Salesians number in the tens of thousands and are found in over 100 nations. Offering more than just food and shelter, the ministry rebuilds lives and helps young people learn a trade that will lead to employment. Other work includes assistance for women, food programs, youth clubs, health services, and emergency relief. Salesians also staff many third-world mission foundations. Today the Salesians of Don Bosco are the third-largest order in the Catholic Church.

Finding God in Family

JESUS grew up in Nazareth. Like his foster father Joseph, Jesus was known as a carpenter. Raised a Jew, he learned Scripture, the commandments, hard work, respect, and obedience. It is in family life that we live out our full human experience just as Jesus did.

A Domestic Church

The family is the first place of education about faith and prayer. When a Christian family of faith worships and prays together, they become a **domestic church** where children learn to pray. But learning to pray is far more than memorizing words to particular prayers. When the words prompt a response to God, we recognize God's presence, follow Jesus' example, grow in faith, serve others, and receive God's grace.

Living the realities of Christian life daily means experiencing good times and challenging times. Faithful family life strengthens the Church and God's presence in the world. Consider what Pope John Paul II wrote about families in *On the Role of the Christian Family in the Modern World*: "Joys and sorrows, hopes and disappointments, births and birthday celebrations, wedding anniversaries of the parents, departures, separations and homecomings, important and far-reaching decisions, the death of those who are dear, etc.—all of these mark God's loving intervention in the family's history."

74 *Unit 2 • The Early Life of Jesus*

TAKE IT HOME

Map of Your Life

Tell young people that when John Bosco was nine years old, he had the first of many dreams that characterized his life. In this dream he was playing with his friends outside his house. The boys began to quarrel and curse, and John tried to break it up, swinging his fists. A figure, who appeared to be Jesus, told him that this was the wrong way to accomplish anything. Jesus told John to be kind, strong, and humble. There was more to the dream, and John followed it, even though he didn't fully understand what he was supposed to be doing. By observing traveling performers, John taught himself how to walk on a tightrope and juggle. He would engage an eager audience, but first, he would lead them in a little prayer.

Tell young people that their dreams, or goals, help them map out their life's path. Have them make their life map on poster board, adding labels that tell where they have already been and where they hope to be one day. Encourage them to add visual meaning by incorporating appropriate cues, such as road signs [stop, one-way, yield, detour, do not enter, and so on] and forks in the road to show times of decisions. Ask volunteers to display and explain their life maps to the group.

Who Is Family?

In Chapter 3 of Mark's Gospel, Jesus makes a radical attempt to change people's minds about how they define family. When the crowd tells Jesus that his family is outside asking for him, Jesus replies, "Who are my mother and [my] brothers?" (Mark 3:33) Referring to the faithful gathered around him, Jesus says, "Here are my mother and my brothers. [For] whoever does the will of God is my brother and sister and mother." (Mark 3:34–35)

Jesus tells us that gathering must come first. Jesus' presence depends on it. If we are to depend on Jesus to help us in a time of need, Jesus depends on us to realize that other people—whether we are related to them by blood or by law or by simple human biology—are our family. With one another, we abide in love.

Family's Role in Society

The family is the first place we learn tolerance, respect, patience, acceptance, forgiveness, and love. If we cannot live these virtues within our own family, how well can we live them for other people, those who are our brothers and sisters in Christ? Pope John Paul II pointed out that the family is an essential school for social life that teaches a true and mature way of expressing unity with others. The role of the family does not stop with educating children but extends to their service in society as they grow. In the 1987 encyclical *On Social Concern*, Pope John Paul II writes "Today perhaps more than in the past, people are realizing that they are linked together by a common destiny, which is to be constructed together, if catastrophe for all is to be avoided. . . ." We can grow and become a full person only through our relationships and participation in society.

Social Roles

Describe your roles in your family and in social service. Write your ideas below or on another sheet of paper.

_____

_____

_____

_____

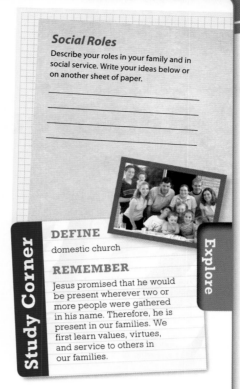

Study Corner

DEFINE

domestic church

REMEMBER

Jesus promised that he would be present wherever two or more people were gathered in his name. Therefore, he is present in our families. We first learn values, virtues, and service to others in our families.

Explore

SACRED ART

Marijan Detoni, a Croatian artist, wants his art to reflect social reality. This oil painting of needy people sharing a meal reminds us that the family is a foundation for building broader community relationships. Family life can increase awareness of and responsibility to the needs of others. Pope John Paul II wrote "note must be taken of the ever greater importance in our society of hospitality in all its forms, from opening the doors of one's home and still more of one's heart to the pleas of one's brothers and sisters." (*On the Role of the Christian Family in the Modern World*)

Meal, Marijan Detoni, 1935.

Session 9 > Jesus Grew in Wisdom, Age, and Grace   **75**

ADVENTURES IN FAITH

Two or More in My Name

Enlist the help of adult chaperones and organize young people into small groups. Ask each group to review your parish bulletin and choose an upcoming parish or diocesan event to attend together. Provide time for groups to attend.

Arrange a group discussion at the end of the experience to report on what happened. Have groups comment on how they felt God's presence during the event. Ask them if anything surprised them during the experience. Finally, ask groups to suggest how they can continue to encounter God's presence in their day-to-day lives.

✝ *Family and Community*

Ask a volunteer to read aloud Who Is Family? Then read aloud Mark 3:21 from the Bible. Ask: **What did Jesus' relatives fear?** (that Jesus was out of his mind) Ask: **Why?** (Jesus' healing was creating a stir, and even some relatives disbelieved.) Have partners read more verses in Mark 3:31–35. Say: **Although it sounds as if Jesus is rejecting his own mother and relatives, he is not. Jesus is showing that doing God's will, not family ties, is what matters to achieve the Kingdom of God.**

Ask a volunteer to read aloud Family's Role in Society. Say: **Often our world is not a very peaceful place.** Ask: **How can a peaceful family help build a peaceful world?** (Possible answer: Each family is a small part of society at large. More peaceful families contribute to greater peace in society.) Ask: **What are ways that families can overcome differences?** (Answers will vary.) Ask: **How can we experience God's presence in the world?** (Possible answer: When people, whether related or not, practice virtuous living and act with love, God is present.)

Read aloud the directions for the Social Roles activity. Ask young people to discuss ideas with a partner before writing a response. Ask volunteers to share their ideas.

Sacred Art

After reading the feature, reflect on Blessed John Paul II's words by telling young people stories about modern good samaritans in the news. Ask young people to share stories that illustrate hospitality by opening either the doors of one's home or opening one's heart to others.

③ Close

Invite young people to write responses to this question. Ask: **What can you do at home this week to help strengthen your relationship with someone in your family?**

Prayer

Follow the steps to guide young people through the prayer on page 76.

Young People's Page

Prepare Pray the prayer in advance to become familiar with it.

Pray Ask volunteers to read the paragraphs and Bible verse in the left column. Invite young people to comment about ways they can use their gifts as a disciple of Jesus. Ask volunteers to discuss the words of Blessed Teresa of Calcutta and suggest other people who exemplify those who use God-given gifts to serve others.

Have young people bring their books to the prayer space. Invite them to prepare for prayer by getting into a comfortable position and quieting themselves. Encourage them to become aware of God's presence with them. You may wish to play reflective music [CD 1, Track 7] quietly. Say: **Take a few deep breaths. Rest in Jesus' presence. Thank him for the gifts you have received. Remember that he is inviting you to conversation.** Pause for a few moments. Slowly pray aloud the guided reflection, or have young people silently pray the text. Allow time for young people to meditate following each idea presented. Following the last meditation, invite them to pray aloud the All part. To conclude, say: **As we continue the session, ask God to show you how you can use your gifts in a way that allows the world to know him better.**

Prayer

Gifts Received, Gifts Given

Ever since he called his first disciples, Jesus has been calling people to follow him. Followers of Jesus show their love for God by serving others.

Jesus instructed his first disciples:

> As you go, make this proclamation: "The kingdom of heaven is at hand." Cure the sick, raise the dead, cleanse lepers, drive out demons. Without cost you have received; without cost you are to give.
>
> *Matthew 10:7–8*

God gives us gifts and talents to accomplish his holy will. These gifts originate with God. We are not so independent that our gifts and talents come from ourselves. We foster and develop our gifts, but we realize that we are in a partnership with our Lord. We do our best to use our gifts, mindful that God the Father, God the Son, and God the Holy Spirit is the power in our lives that makes all things possible.

Blessed Teresa of Calcutta echoes these ideas in her words about her service to those who are poor in India:

> "I do this because I believe I am doing it for Jesus. I am very sure that this is his work. I am very sure. I am very sure that it is he and not me."

76   *Unit 2 • The Early Life of Jesus*

Guided Reflection

What are some things you have received freely from God? It might be a talent or an ability, or something you just enjoy doing. Maybe it's a supportive family or a friend who cares. Share your thoughts with Jesus.

Jesus reminds you that these gifts are meant to be shared. We are called to serve others by using our gifts, such as by spending time with an elderly relative or neighbor or befriending a new classmate. Talk over with Jesus some ways you might use your gifts to serve.

Jesus reminds you that serving others has hidden costs, like less free time or allowance, or maybe being teased. You will face challenges in living out your faith. But Jesus also reminds you that he is with you to help and encourage you in your service. Spend a moment just resting in Jesus' presence. Then thank him for your gifts and this time of sharing.

All: Lord Jesus, make us aware of the gifts we've received from your Father's hands. Encourage us to develop them. Inspire us to be open to the ways you call us to share our gifts. May we please you and help make the world a better place. We ask this with confidence in your name. Amen.

IF TIME ALLOWS

Another Family

Encourage young people to remember that when they are together as a group, they are a kind of family. Ask them to join hands and form a circle. Go around the circle and have young people suggest things that they can do individually and as a group to live together in love and service to one another.

FYI

Coaching Young People to Pray

Before praying, encourage young people to imagine Jesus is right beside them. Have them use their senses to imagine his voice, his touch, and his face. Ask them to think about what Jesus would do in service of others.

WHERE Do I Fit In?

Even small experiences that seem insignificant at the time can shape the person you are becoming. Who or what helps you to discover the person God intends you to be?

by Claire Colombo

How Do I Discover My Real Identity?

Reflect

Therefore, putting away falsehood,
speak the truth, each one to his neighbor,
for we are members one of another.

Ephesians 4:25

It happened when I was in the first grade. Winter was over, spring was on its way, and Sister Theresa Margaret wanted us to take down the snowflakes we'd taped to the windows back in December. She was very clear. "Children, when I say 'Go,' I want you to get up, find your snowflake, remove it, and return to your seat. No talking, no running, no grabbing."

Sister's orders threw me into a panic. December was ages ago! I had no idea where I'd taped my snowflake. The class sprang into action at Sister's "Go!" Everyone found their snowflakes easily because each one had its artist's name printed on the front. But mine was nowhere to be found. My heart thumped wildly. Where was my snowflake?

Then I remembered what happened on snowflake-hanging day. I had been unable to find a spot on the glass so Sister helped me. We taped my artwork to the window—with my name against the pane!

I looked around. Everyone was back in his or her seat—except me. I had not followed Sister's directions. I had not retrieved my snowflake. "Claire *Miller*!" she snapped. "Come *here*!" I was about to receive a consequence. I was paralyzed with fear.

Suddenly, though, I heard myself speaking—shy, awkward me, speaking with confidence, explaining the mix-up. "You helped me hang my snowflake," I was saying, "and my name ended up facing the pane." I tried to put it delicately, without blame. After several moments, Sister walked to the window and dislodged the single remaining paper snowflake. Sure enough, there was my name, facing the wrong way. Nevertheless, I did receive a consequence—a good one! Sister handed me the snowflake and gave my shoulders a little squeeze. "Thanks for telling the truth," she said.

To this day, I consider myself a truth-teller. I write for a living, which is all about telling the truth—even when it's hard to tell. At those moments, I feel Sister Theresa Margaret's arm around my shoulders. "Go on, Claire," she says. "It's who you are."

CLAIRE COLOMBO is a freelance writer and educator who lives in Austin, Texas, where snowflakes are never a problem.

Who Are You Meant to Be?

Who are you becoming? Use your own photographs or pictures from magazines to make a collage on poster board that represents you. Cut out words or phrases that help explain your ideas and add them to your collage.

Session 9 > Jesus Grew in Wisdom, Age, and Grace   77

IF TIME ALLOWS

BTW—Thanks!

Have young people imagine that Sister Theresa Margaret, years after the events in this story, received a note of gratitude from the author. Discuss how this would make Sister Theresa Margaret feel. Point out that we are often completely unaware of the impact we make on others' lives—and that if we only knew, we might see our own lives differently.

Have young people think about their response to the question in the introductory text and write a note of gratitude to that person for helping God shape their lives.

✝ *Family and Community*

---

1) Begin

Have young people think of something they have made and of which they are proud—an artwork, a video, a poem, or a playlist, for example. Ask them to describe the process of making it. Ask: *Where did you get the idea? How was the final product different from the first idea?* (Answers will vary.) Discuss that the creative process is made up of a series of decisions, actions, and adjustments that seem partly controlled by us and partly controlled by something greater than us. Say: *This is also true for us as God's creations. God created you at conception but continues to shape you every day, granting you his grace and inviting the experiences and actions of your life to bring you closer to him.* Read aloud the introductory text. Have young people respond to the question.

2) Connect

Invite volunteers to take turns reading aloud How Do I Discover My Real Identity? Have young people describe times they found themselves doing something courageous, loving, or impressive when they least expected to. Say: *At these times, God was moving in your life, shaping you into something that you weren't before.* Discuss this idea in relation to their examples of acting with courage. Ask: *What does your "surprise action" say about who you really are, or who God wants you to be?* (Answers will vary.) Invite young people to complete the Who Are You Meant to Be? activity independently.

3) Close

Invite volunteers to share their completed collages. Ask viewers of each collage to describe the person reflected in it. Then revisit the question in the introductory text and have young people amend their earlier responses.

① Begin

What's What? Read aloud the directions. Remind young people to refer to the page shown to find the details that answer each question. Have young people complete the page in small groups.

② Connect

Say What? Ask volunteers to read aloud and define the terms. Review each term in the Glossary if necessary.

Now What? Ask a volunteer to read aloud the section. Invite each young person to answer independently.

③ Go in Peace

Collect materials and return them to their appropriate places. Encourage young people to initiate conversations about prayer at home with their family members, remembering to pray before meals and to go to Mass on Sundays. Say: **Thank your family members for sharing their faith.**

3-Minute Retreat
Give young people an opportunity for quiet meditation at **www.loyolapress.com/retreat**.

What's What?

Respond

Write answers using details from the text.

1 Where did Mary and Joseph find Jesus as a boy when he was lost? What was he doing there? (PAGE 72)

They found him in the Temple. He was listening and asking questions of the teachers.

2 How does Jesus surprise the Jewish elders? (PAGE 72)

They are astounded by his answers and knowledge about Scriptures at such a young age.

3 What are the four Cardinal Virtues? Why are they important to your faith? (PAGE 72)

They are prudence, justice, fortitude, and temperance. They help a person be close to God and to others.

4 What does Jesus begin to understand when he is 12 years old? (PAGES 72–73)

God the Father has a mission for him. This is a coming-of-age time for Jesus.

5 How does Jesus follow the Fourth Commandment? How do Mary and Joseph follow the Fourth Commandment? (PAGE 73)

Jesus respects and obeys his parents. He returns to Nazareth with them. Mary and Joseph help Jesus prepare for the work God has in mind.

6 Why is the family called a domestic church? (PAGE 74)

It is the first place that children learn to pray and live as Christians.

7 What does Jesus teach about family in the Gospel of Mark? (PAGE 75)

Whoever does God's will is family. We are called to gather in his name, and we care for one another.

Say What?
Know the definitions of these terms.

Cardinal Virtues
domestic church
synagogue

Now What?
Describe one way your family demonstrates that it is a domestic church. Thank a family member for providing this way.

Answers will vary.

IF TIME ALLOWS

Service: Families Unplugged

Take a survey to assess how much family time is spent "plugged in" to TV, the Internet, music, and so on. Brainstorm ways for families to spend more time together "unplugged." Encourage simple and free activities, such as hiking, community sports, or board games. Emphasize connecting regularly through a common activity or experience. Have volunteers develop and write a contract for families to sign as a pledge. Ask young people to add comments in a group album, post photos, or tell what their families did together "unplugged."

✝ *Family and Community*

Session Assessment Option

An assessment for this session can be found at www.findinggod.com.

PLAN AHEAD: Get Ready for Session 10

Consult the catechist preparation pages to prepare for Session 10 and determine any materials you will need.

Celebrating Advent and Christmas

 ## 3-Minute Retreat

Before you prepare the session, pause and be still. Take three deep breaths and be aware of the loving presence of God, who is with you on this journey.

Luke 1:54–55

"He has helped Israel his servant,
    remembering his mercy,
according to his promise to our fathers,
    to Abraham and to his descendants forever."

Reflection

In her prayer to God, the *Magnificat,* Mary tells us that God continues to remember his promises. Remembering the Scriptures is not simply recalling a past event but acknowledging that just as God had acted on behalf of the people in the past, he is acting in the same way in our lives today. The same mercy that God has offered to the people in the past, he continues to offer to us today.

Questions

How ready am I to receive the mercy God offers to me? What can I do to prepare myself to be a faithful child of God as Abraham was?

 Concluding Prayer

Speak to God, using the words of this prayer or your own.

Faithful God, you have kept your promise to Mary, and through her you remind me of your faithfulness to me. Help me be open to receiving your mercy today.

Knowing and Sharing Your Faith in Session 10

Consider how Scripture and Tradition can deepen your understanding of session content.

Scripture

Isaiah 42:16 recalls the prophet Isaiah's words that promised a Messiah who would be their guide.

Matthew 2:11 shows the Magi's gifts as signs that they had come to serve Jesus, their divine king.

Tradition

In his Gospel, Luke wants to show that Jesus came to save everyone. Luke calls attention to the role of those who are poor and lowly, outcast, and afflicted. He calls attention to those who recognize their dependence on God in the ministry of Jesus. In Matthew's Gospel, Jesus' first visitors were the Magi, people who had access to leaders in high places. In Luke's Gospel, Jesus is seen first by shepherds, people who spent their lives in the fields with animals. That scene from Luke's Gospel is the first of many in which Luke reverses expectations in order to show that God uses everyone to hear and proclaim his Word.

Catholic Social Teaching

In this session the integrated Catholic Social Teaching themes are **Call to Family, Community, and Participation** and **Life and Dignity of the Human Person.** See page 45b for an explanation of these themes.

Window on the Catechism

The mystery of Jesus' infancy and hidden life is discussed in *CCC* 522–534.

General Directory for Catechesis

Jesus as mediator and fulfillment of Revelation is found in *GDC* 40 and 41.

One-Hour Session Planner

SESSION 10 Celebrating Advent and Christmas

Session Theme: *We prepare our hearts during the season of Advent to celebrate the birth of Jesus at Christmas.*

Before This Session

▶ Display the *Finding God* poster The Liturgical Year.

▶ Determine whether you will use the Unit Assessment option listed on page 86.

▶ Determine whether you will also discuss the Advent and Christmas seasonal pages in the back of the Young People's Book.

▶ Bookmark your Bible to Isaiah 42:16, John 8:12, 1 Timothy 6:11–16, 2 Samuel 22:29, Job 12:22, Romans 13:11–12, Luke 2:1–7,11,19, Psalm 96:1–2,7–8,11–13, and Revelation 21:23. Place the open Bible in your prayer space.

▶ Read the Guide for this session, choose any additional If Time Allows activities that you might have time to complete, and gather the listed materials.

STEPS	APPROXIMATE TIME
Engage *Celebrating Advent and Christmas* PAGE 79	10 minutes
Explore *Living in the Light of Advent* PAGES 80–81 *The Gift of Christmas* PAGES 82–83	30–40 minutes
Reflect *Prayer:* Welcome Jesus! PAGE 84 *Where Do I Fit In?* PAGE 85	10–15 minutes
Respond *What's What?* PAGE 86	10–15 minutes

Prayer in Session 10

Continue the pattern and tone for prayer throughout the program. Young people pray a short opening prayer that relates to a key session concept and are invited to access an online 3-Minute Retreat at the end of the session. Session 10 shows young people how to welcome Jesus and glorify him by listening to Scripture and praying verses from the Psalms. Follow the Prepare directions on the Catechist Guide page before sharing with young people.

TAKE IT HOME

Homework options:

Picture It Collages PAGE 80

Holiday Family Time PAGE 83

Materials

REQUIRED

▶ Signs with labels (page 79)

▶ *Finding God* poster: The Liturgical Year (page 79)

▶ Writing supplies (pages 79, 81, 83, 85, 86)

▶ Scarf to use as a blindfold (page 80)

▶ Bibles (page 80)

▶ Baby pictures (page 82)

▶ Flashlights, small mirror (page 85)

▶ Computer with Internet access (page 86)

OPTIONAL

▶ Reference materials (page 79)

▶ Black and white poster board, blue painter's tape (page 81)

▶ Session 10 BLM, T-361 (page 82)

▶ Art supplies, colored pencils, writing supplies, software for slide-show presentations (page 84)

▶ Art supplies (page 85)

▶ Toys to donate, stationery (page 86)

▶ Session 10 Assessment, www.findinggod.com (page 86)

▶ Unit 2 Assessment, T-362–T-364 (page 86)

Session 10

Celebrating Advent and Christmas

WE prepare our hearts during the season of **Advent** to celebrate the birth of Jesus at **Christmas.** Advent begins four Sundays before Christmas and marks the start of the Church's liturgical year. When Advent ends, the season of Christmas begins. The Feast of the Baptism of the Lord, celebrated on the first Sunday after the Epiphany (January 6), closes the Christmas season.

Advent is a time for preparing ourselves to celebrate the coming of Jesus. It is a time for us to develop an attitude of hopefulness and joyful anticipation for the coming of Jesus. We can grow in this way as we celebrate liturgy and as we live our everyday lives. We remember the Jewish people who lived in hope awaiting the birth of the Messiah, and we joyfully anticipate the day when Christ will return in glory.

At Christmas we joyfully celebrate that Jesus' birth in Bethlehem brought God's promise of peace and Salvation to the world. We respond to the miracle of the season by acknowledging that the one and only true gift we need to receive is Jesus. God's greatest gift to his people over 2,000 years ago is the greatest gift we receive today—his Son, our Savior Jesus Christ.

Explain what this sentence means to you: *God's gift of Jesus is the greatest gift we'll ever receive.* What life experiences help you know this is true?

PRAYER

Jesus, be with us as we prepare our hearts to celebrate your coming at Christmas. Help us experience and share the joy of your birth.

79

IF TIME ALLOWS

Christmas Customs

Have young people work with a partner, group, or independently to research Christmas customs or traditions that represent various cultures. Have them choose a format to present their information. For example, they may choose a play, an interactive activity, a slide show presentation, or a demonstration. Arrange a day for presentations and allow time for discussion and exploration.

INCLUSION
Specific Learning

Audio Recordings If you work with young people with specific learning issues related to reading, record yourself reading aloud the session and burn the recording onto a CD for young people to use at home.

SESSION 10
OUTCOMES

▶ Describe how to best prepare to receive the Light of the World, Jesus Christ.

▶ Explain that the one true gift of Christmas is Jesus.

▶ Glorify Jesus in prayer.

▶ Define *Advent, Christmas, feast days, Feast of Our Lady of Guadalupe, Holy Day of Obligation, Nativity,* and *sanctuary.*

① Set the Stage

Display signs labeled *The Mass and Parish Life, Home Decorations, Music or Performances, Special Food and Meals.* Organize young people into four groups and assign one category to each group. Ask each group to list ways their families and communities prepare for Christmas based on their category. Have groups rotate to each sign and repeat the process. Read aloud the session title and boxed text.

② Get Started

Display the *Finding God* poster The Liturgical Year and have young people turn to page 222 and read the paragraphs about Advent and Christmas.

Invite young people to write responses to the text in the box on page 79. Then read aloud the page. Say: **Look around the room at the signs. How can we remember why we're celebrating?** (Possible answers: We can pray special prayers. We can notice God at work in friends and family. We can attend Mass regularly.)

 Prayer

Say: **Let's pray together asking Jesus to be with us as we joyfully anticipate the celebration of his birth.** Pray the prayer together. Conclude by praying the Sign of the Cross.

↗ Go to **www.findinggod.com/sessionextenders** for interactive Advent retreat ideas. You may wish to share this with the group.

① Begin

Bring in a soft cotton scarf to use as a blindfold. Clear an area of obstacles. Ask a volunteer to wear the blindfold and find his or her way to the door. Ask: **What was it like to walk around in darkness?** Ask volunteers to tell about a time when they got lost in the dark and how they felt. Say: **We're about to read about darkness and light and its connection to Advent.**

② Connect

Read aloud the article title. Have pairs of young people read the page. Bring the group back together and ask: **In Scripture, what does darkness represent?** (evil, sin, living without guidance from God, turning away from God) Ask: **What does light represent?** (goodness, Jesus Christ, Salvation, following God the Father and Jesus Christ, being in relationship with God)

To illustrate the ideas of darkness and light in Scripture, arrange young people in four groups. Assign each group one passage to read and discuss:

▶ John 8:12
▶ 1 Timothy 6:11–16
▶ 2 Samuel 22:29
▶ Job 12:22

Say: **With your group, read aloud your passage and discuss how the images of light and dark are used and what they mean.** As time allows, ask a member of each group to share their ideas.

Our Catholic Character

Read aloud the feature. Ask a volunteer to read aloud the definition of *Feast of Our Lady of Guadalupe* in the Glossary. Remind young people that the Catholic Church is worldwide and honors the same saints. The Feast of Our Lady of Guadalupe is important for all Catholics but also reflects the cultural tradition of Mexican Catholics.

Living in the Light of Advent

ASSOCIATING ideas with darkness or light as a way to express a point that is important to our faith is found in both the Old and New Testaments.

Look at some common associations that follow:

➡ Darkness: evil, sin, living without following guidance from God, turning away from God

➡ Light: goodness, Jesus Christ, Salvation, following God the Father and Jesus Christ, being in relationship with God

On various occasions, the prophet Isaiah used the contrast of darkness and light to speak to the Israelites about the promise of a Messiah, a Savior for humankind:

> I will lead the blind on a way they do not know;
> by paths they do not know I will guide them.
> I will turn darkness into light before them,
> and make crooked ways straight.
> These are my promises:
> I made them, I will not forsake them.
>
> *Isaiah 42:16*

Jesus, who was promised to the Israelites and remains with us today, is the one true Light. The Israelites waited and prayed generation after generation for this light to come. Blessed with the gift of faith, they trusted that God would send them a Savior. Just as the Israelites believed and prepared, so do we. Advent is our time to ready our hearts and minds. Jesus, the Light of the World, has come to show us the way, and we look forward to the day he will return so that we can be with him forever.

Through Jesus Christ, our crooked ways are made straight. That's a comforting thought and a reason for great joy and hope. The promise of Christ's Light is why we celebrate Advent—why we get ready in our churches, in our homes, and in our hearts.

Our Catholic Character

During Advent we celebrate the Feast of the Immaculate Conception on December 8, which reminds us that Mary was born without Original Sin. Even before she was born, Mary was chosen by God to be the mother of Jesus. Several important celebrations occur during Advent. Many celebrations reflect ethnic and cultural traditions and recall saints or our Catholic Tradition. For example, the **Feast of Our Lady of Guadalupe** is an important Mexican celebration of Mary's appearance to Juan Diego. In the United States, it's celebrated on December 12. December 13 is the Feast of Saint Lucy, also known as Saint Lucia, whose name means "light." It is celebrated during the time of the longest nights of winter.

80 *Unit 2 • The Early Life of Jesus*

TAKE IT HOME

Picture It Collages

Have each young person choose one of the following themes:

• living in the light of Christ

• throwing off works of darkness

• putting on the armor of light

• awakening from sleep

Invite young people to gather photos or illustrations, their own or from media sources, and use them to make a collage showcasing the theme. Each collage should include a phrase from Scripture as its title. Display completed collages and invite volunteers to explain their ideas to the group.

SEASONAL SESSIONS

Advent and Christmas
Work through pages 223–230 together with young people to learn more about Advent and Christmas. These special sessions can each take up to one hour to complete.

Awake from Sleep

The New Testament proclaims that the Messiah has come and that Jesus is in fact the Light of the World. This is good news—news to be happy about. And to prepare for Christ's coming again, Scripture tells us to examine our thoughts, words, and actions and check ourselves to be sure that we're ready. Consider this Scripture passage from Paul's Letter to the Romans:

> And do this because you know the time; it is the hour now for you to awake from sleep. For our salvation is nearer now than when we first believed; the night is advanced, the day is at hand. Let us then throw off the works of darkness [and] put on the armor of light; . . .
>
> *Romans 13:11–12*

"Awake from sleep" is our call to action—to be happy, present, and engaged in anticipating the coming of the Savior. Advent is our time of preparation, a time to awaken our faith. We don't want to go through the motions without consciously considering the coming of our Savior.

In History, Grace, and Glory

In History Jesus Christ came to us in history, born in a humble stable in the little town of Bethlehem. For centuries, God's Chosen People were promised a Messiah who would come to save the world. During Advent the Scripture readings at Mass remind us of how our ancestors in faith prepared for the Messiah. We can listen to the Word of God and take these messages to heart.

In Grace During Advent we reflect on the mystery of the Incarnation, our belief that the Son of God, Jesus Christ, became flesh in the womb of Mary and was born fully human, without loss of his divinity. Christ, the Light, comes to us today in grace through the people and events in our daily lives. He also comes to us through the sacraments, especially the Holy Eucharist, and in prayer.

In Glory Christ's final coming will be in glory to judge the living and the dead. He will come to take us to our eternal reward, revealed as "The city [that] had no need of sun or moon to shine on it, for the glory of God gave it light, and its lamp was the Lamb." (Revelation 21:23) To share his life in Heaven, we prepare for his coming by loving and living as Jesus did.

Your Advent

You can celebrate Advent in your own unique way, in a way that gives you personal joy. If you like to spend time alone or reading, you might set aside five extra minutes before you go to bed to pray or read Scripture. You might also record reflections during Advent, perhaps thoughts from Scripture readings and the homilies from Mass or the Feast of the Immaculate Conception. How you prepare is up to you.

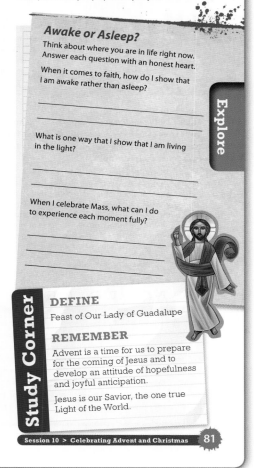

Awake or Asleep?

Think about where you are in life right now. Answer each question with an honest heart.

When it comes to faith, how do I show that I am awake rather than asleep?

_____
_____
_____

What is one way that I show that I am living in the light?

_____
_____
_____

When I celebrate Mass, what can I do to experience each moment fully?

_____
_____
_____

Explore

Study Corner

DEFINE

Feast of Our Lady of Guadalupe

REMEMBER

Advent is a time for us to prepare for the coming of Jesus and to develop an attitude of hopefulness and joyful anticipation.

Jesus is our Savior, the one true Light of the World.

Session 10 > Celebrating Advent and Christmas 81

🔥 **ADVENTURES IN FAITH**

Dark or Light

Divide the room into two sections with a long piece of blue painter's tape. Then tape up a black poster board on one side of the room and a white poster board on the other side. Tell young people that the "dark side" of the room represents fear and despair and that the "light side" of the room represents security and hope. Present typical middle-school scenarios and ask young people to stand on the side that most likely represents how they imagine themselves reacting. Ask young people on the "light side" to explain how they came to a position of security and hope. Invite each person on the light side to reach out a hand to a person on the dark side and pull them over to the light.

For example, ask: *How do you react when friends don't invite you to an important event?* Say: *Stand on the light side if you react with security or hope. Stand on the dark side if you react with fear or hopelessness.* Afterward, you might ask: *Can a volunteer on the light side share his or her thoughts?* He or she can then lead a person standing on the other side over to the light side.

Have a volunteer read aloud Awake from Sleep. Ask: *What are some ways that you can be "awake" in your daily life?* (Possible answer: You can pray before meals and bed; you can notice goodness in others; you can pause to give thanks for blessings throughout the day.)

Read aloud the section In History, Grace, and Glory. Ask: *How do we experience Jesus' coming in history?* (by listening to Scripture) Ask: *How do we experience Jesus' coming in grace?* (through people, events, prayer, and the sacraments) Ask: *Who will experience Jesus' final coming?* (everyone) Explain that in Christ's Second Coming, he will gather all those who have lived according to the Spirit of love to share in his eternal life.

Read aloud the section Your Advent. Invite young people to think about what they might do to personalize their Advent experience.

Have young people read the directions and complete the Awake or Asleep? activity. Have them continue writing on a separate sheet of paper if needed.

③ Close

Have young people arrange their seats in a circle. Ask them to name items or events that they anxiously await. Ask: *What do you do during your wait? What might cause your hope to fade or weaken as you wait? What do you do to keep hope alive?* (Answers will vary.)

Say: *Advent helps us keep our hope alive in the coming of Jesus. We all share one another's anticipation and excitement as we wait together. Let's each share one hope or wish that we have during this season of Advent.* Begin the sharing with an idea. For example, say: *My hope for Advent is to remember to use my words and actions to honor Jesus.*

① Begin

In advance ask young people to bring in a picture of themselves as a baby. Have young people pass around their pictures. Talk about how much a family is blessed when a child is born. Invite volunteers to tell the story of where and when they were born and any interesting circumstances surrounding their birth. Tell young people that just as their families passed along stories of their births, the Christian community told the story of Jesus' birth so the world would know of the coming of the promised Savior.

② Connect

✝ Ask volunteers to read aloud the paragraphs on the page. Read the meaning of the word *Nativity* in the Glossary. Ask: **Which two Gospel writers tell us about Jesus' birth?** (Matthew and Luke) Ask: **What is unique about Luke's account?** (He stresses a different kind of king and kingdom. He points out that Jesus came to save everyone, including the poor and outcast. He highlights Mary's role in Salvation History.) Ask: **Why do you think it's important for us to hear the story of Jesus' birth?** (Answers will vary.) Say: **By hearing the story of Jesus' birth, we learn more about his true identity as our Savior.**

Sacred Art

Ask a volunteer to read aloud the feature. Take some time to discuss the questions, guiding young people to recognize the difficult journey to Bethlehem for Mary and Joseph. If time is available, invite young people to share stories of long journeys.

The Gift of Christmas

MORE than 2,000 years ago, Jesus was born in the town of Bethlehem. Many of us can retell the story by heart. Only the Gospels of Matthew and Luke describe Jesus' birth.

Each writer of the **Nativity** story includes specific details. The Gospel of Luke begins with the announcement and birth of John the Baptist, tells about the Annunciation (the angel's announcement of Jesus' birth to Mary), and the Visitation (Mary's visit to her cousin Elizabeth). Luke explains Jesus' birth as an important world event by telling us that Caesar Augustus was the Roman emperor and that Mary and Joseph went to Bethlehem for the census. In Luke's story we read the Good News that Jesus' birth brings Salvation to those who are poor and lowly. Born quietly in humble surroundings and first received by poor shepherds, Jesus comes into the world not as an earthly king but as a divine king. He has come as a light to shine on all people, especially those who are overlooked or forgotten: those who are poor, sinners, lepers, outcasts, and foreigners.

The Gospel of Luke highlights Mary's role and her response of yes to Jesus' birth. After the visit from the shepherds, Luke's Gospel tells us "And Mary kept all these things, reflecting on them in her heart." (Luke 2:19) In Luke's Nativity story, Jesus' birth is good news because Jesus brings Salvation to the whole world.

SACRED ART

Journey to Bethlehem, Cathy Baxter, 20th century.

This watercolor-and-pastel artwork shows Joseph leading a pregnant Mary out of Galilee. Joseph had to return to his hometown of Bethlehem for a census and to pay taxes being collected by the Roman government. Imagine taking a long journey on foot, with no paved roads, technology, or protection from the elements or other dangers. Now imagine taking this journey with a woman who is expecting a baby. Do you think that you would be motivated to reach your destination as soon as possible? Would your anticipation be one of joy, worry, or a mixture of both?

82   *Unit 2 • The Early Life of Jesus*

IF TIME ALLOWS

Session 10 BLM

✝ **The Gospels Tell the Story** Organize young people into pairs and provide each with the Session 10 Blackline Master [T-361] and a copy of the Bible. Invite pairs to read the directions and complete the activity.

Covert Christmas Operations

Explain that a covert operation is an action undertaken in secret. Invite young people to participate in a covert Christmas operation by performing secret acts of kindness for a family member or member of the group. Brainstorm and write on the board a list of simple acts of kindness that can be performed without attracting attention or giving one's identify away. Have young people copy the list. Invite them to perform a different act of kindness in secret each day from Christmas Day until Epiphany. Then ask young people to reveal their identity to the recipient of their actions on Epiphany.

✝ *Family and Community*

First Gifts

Only Matthew's Gospel records the visit from the Magi—astronomers from the East—who joyfully follow the star in the sky until they find Jesus. They are overcome at finding him, falling to their knees and offering him gifts. "Then they opened their treasures and offered him gifts of gold, frankincense, and myrrh." (Matthew 2:11) These gifts were signs that the Magi had come to serve a king. They recognized Jesus as their divine king and dedicated themselves to his will.

The Magi's gifts were symbolic of divine kingship. Gold is a precious metal, the currency of royalty and those who are wealthy. Frankincense was an incense that, when mixed with flour and oil, was offered on the outer altar of a **sanctuary.** A sanctuary is a holy place to worship God, such as a church or temple. The third gift, myrrh, was one of the most important perfumes in biblical times—it was used to perfume the oil with which kings were anointed and was also used in burials.

One True Gift

Today the season of Christmas has become a commercialized industry where shopping and gift exchanges overshadow the real reason we celebrate. Many people are tempted to focus on material gifts instead of the gift of Jesus, who is the only gift that we really need.

Think about a gift that you wanted for Christmas, but shortly after you got it, the excitement wore off, and you put it aside and forgot it. That's not what Christmas is about. Christmas is a lasting celebration of the Light of Christ entering the world, a precious gift for whom we await excitedly. Jesus is the gift we want and need—a gift to hold dear and never forget.

God blesses all of us with the gift of Jesus Christ. We are given a Savior who showed us how to live according to God's will. Through his Death and Resurrection, we are given the gift of forgiveness of sins so that we can walk with God now and be with him in Heaven for all eternity. Jesus, the Light of the World, never disappoints us.

Past Meets Present

PAST: Why does the Church celebrate the Nativity on December 25? Many biblical scholars believe the choice of date is connected to the celebration of a pre-Christian feast. At the same time that Christianity was spreading, December 25 marked the Roman pagan custom of celebrating *Natalis Sol Invicti*, the rebirth of the sun at the winter solstice. Around A.D. 354 the Bishop of Rome called all Christians to celebrate the birth of Christ on that day. Early Christians would understand that Jesus is the Light of the World, brighter than the brightest light they knew, the sun.

PRESENT: Many Filipino Catholics participate in the Christmas novena known as *Simbang Gabi*, meaning "night worship." This predawn celebration of Mass lasts for nine days and is sometimes called *Misa de Gallo*, meaning "Mass of the Rooster." Beginning December 16 and leading up to Christmas Day, people awaken to the sound of church bells around 3:00 or 3:30 A.M., calling them to worship at Mass. Although the origin of this custom is obscure, most agree that the devotion requires a sacrifice of love to hear the Word of God so early in the morning before beginning daily duties. Ringing bells break the predawn silence with a message of hope and peace on earth.

Explore

Study Corner

DEFINE

Nativity
sanctuary

REMEMBER

Only the Gospels of Matthew and Luke describe Jesus' birth. Each includes unique details.

Jesus Christ is the one true gift of Christmas.

Holiday Family Time

Invite young people to organize an activity to be shared with their family during Advent or Christmas. This activity should be designed to take the focus away from material things and the busyness of the season. For example, the family might read a book together, such as *The Best Christmas Pageant Ever.*

Have young people bring in a step-by-step plan that includes materials, an activity description, and dates for completion. Have young people follow up with a report that describes the activity's success.

✝ *Family and Community*

Have volunteers read aloud First Gifts. Read the definition of *sanctuary* in the Glossary. Tell young people that on August 20, 2005, Pope Benedict XVI gave an address on World Youth Day that talked about the Magi and the lessons we can learn from them. Of the Magi, he said, "They had to change their ideas about power, about God and about man, and in so doing, they also had to change themselves. . . ." Ask: **How is God's power unlike any other power?** (Possible answers: God's power is in service to others, not in service to self. God's power is shared, not hoarded.)

Ask volunteers to read aloud One True Gift. Ask: **Has anyone ever heard the sayings, "Jesus is the reason for the season" or "Put Christ back in Christmas"? What do you think these sayings mean?** (Answers will vary.) Encourage young people to try to live out these ideas.

Past Meets Present

Read aloud the feature. Explain that Roman paganism represented a variety of religions whose followers believed in many gods. In the early days of Christianity, Christians made up only about 10 percent of the population, and they were routinely persecuted for their beliefs.

③ Close

To close the discussion, say: **Think of a new Christmas tradition that will help you stay focused on Jesus.** Invite young people to jot a list of ideas. For example, suggest that each day during Advent or Christmas, they reflect on a Scripture verse and write their reflections. Each year they could add to their book of reflections. If time allows, have them share their ideas for a new tradition with a partner, and ask them to continue to add other ideas to their lists.

Prayer

Follow the steps to guide young people through the prayer on page 84.

Young People's Page

Prepare Pray the prayer in advance to become familiar with it.

 Pray Read aloud the title and the paragraphs in the left column. Read aloud the definition of *Holy Days of Obligation* in the Glossary. Point out things that distinguish these days from national holidays. Explain that there are six Holy Days of Obligation and refer young people to page 291 of Prayers and Practices for more information about these days. Ask a volunteer to read aloud the definition of *feast days* in the Glossary. Remind young people that we celebrate the saints throughout the year on their feast days.

Have young people bring their books to the prayer space. Assign a Reader and provide him or her a Bible. Point out the parts in the prayer. Organize young people into two groups to pray Side 1 or Side 2. Encourage everyone to pray the All parts.

Invite young people to prepare themselves for prayer, quietly centering themselves, avoiding distractions, and becoming relaxed. Pause for a brief time and pray aloud the Leader part. After the Reader prays the Scripture reading from Luke, pause to allow young people time to meditate on the reading. Pray aloud the All part. Continue with the next Leader and All parts. Then have Side 1 and Side 2 pray aloud their verses. Pause after each Side prays to allow time for meditation. Pray aloud the final All part and Leader part. Conclude the prayer by praying the Sign of the Cross together.

Prayer

Welcome Jesus!

We welcome Jesus by celebrating feast days and holy days during Advent and Christmas.

A day when Catholics participate in the Eucharist to celebrate the great things that God has done through Jesus and the saints is called a **Holy Day of Obligation.** In the United States, December 8 honors the Solemnity of the Immaculate Conception. We also celebrate Christmas on December 25 and Mary, Mother of God on January 1 during these two Church seasons.

In addition, Catholics celebrate these **feast days:** the Feast of the Holy Family on the Sunday after Christmas, the Epiphany on January 6, and the Baptism of the Lord on the first Sunday after the Epiphany.

Give Glory to the Lord

Leader: Let us begin our prayer with the Sign of the Cross.

Reader: A reading from the holy Gospel according to Luke. [Luke 2:1–7] The Gospel of the Lord.

All: Praise to you, Lord Jesus Christ.

Leader: Let us offer our praise to God.

All: Glory to God in the highest.

Side 1: Sing to the LORD a new song;
　　sing to the LORD, all the earth.
　　Sing to the LORD, bless his name;
　　　proclaim his salvation day after day.

Psalm 96:1–2

Side 2: Give to the LORD, you families of nations,
　　give to the LORD glory and might;
　　give to the LORD the glory due his name!
　　Bring gifts and enter his courts;
　　　bow down to the LORD, splendid in holiness.

Psalm 96:7–8

Side 1: Let the heavens be glad and the earth rejoice;
　　let the sea and what fills it resound;
　　let the plains be joyful and all that is in them.

Psalm 96:11–12

Side 2: Then let all the trees of the forest rejoice
　　before the LORD who comes,
　　who comes to govern the earth,
　　To govern the world with justice
　　　and the peoples with faithfulness.

Psalm 96:12–13

All: Glory to God in the highest.

Leader: Let us pray together the Glory Be to the Father.

84 *Unit 2 • The Early Life of Jesus*

IF TIME ALLOWS

Psalm Illustrations

Have each young person choose verses from the prayer session. Ask young people to illustrate the verses using crayons, markers, colored pencils, or art materials of their choice. Have them attach a neatly written copy of the verses and the source to their illustrations. Display the illustrations, or if possible, have groups work together to share the verses in pictures, words, and music by making a slide-show presentation.

FYI

Coaching Young People to Pray

To prompt reflection after the verses, encourage young people to ask the Holy Spirit to help them be mindful of the ways they reflect the light of Christ and to help them grow in the ability to share their light with others.

WHERE Do I Fit In?

It's not always easy to find your way. You may struggle to do or say the right things. At times you may feel as if you don't know the way to go. Or you may take a wrong turn and lose your way. At these times, it is important to cultivate an attitude of hope and try to be a light to others, as Jesus is for us.

by Regina Kazanjian

Reflect

Being a Light to Others

Many people I respect and love have a passion for apologetics, which is the art of forming solid arguments for faith. I am not scornful of this—it's a worthy pursuit. But one of my greatest personal pitfalls is striving to be good enough on my own. I'm ashamed to face God until I've pulled everything together, until I look worthy, until I've cleared this or that problem out of my life. It's a bottomless hole because I never can be perfect on my own. I begin to believe that if I know all the right facts, I can craft a flawless argument and convince everyone to join my side. Ironically, this makes me hesitate to even bring up subjects of faith with my friends because I tell myself that my arguments just aren't "right" yet.

I have an even greater problem in my discussions with those who don't share my faith. I concentrate on making myself a "perfect witness." If I've been talking about the joy of Christ, I mistakenly feel that now I have to be happy all the time. I think that my listeners may be watching me now, and I can't let myself slip up and undermine my own argument!

Thankfully, I've come to realize that the key to being a light to others is to humbly accept that the light is not mine—it is just a reflection of God's own light. A reflecting object must be oriented toward its light source. The goodness I know, the truth I see, or the love that's changed me is constantly streaming from God, the source of all goodness and beauty. It's impossible for me to figure out God and be perfect. However, he has called me to keep my eyes fixed on him, to never hide my love for him, and to be open about his work in my life.

Lighting a Way

A single flame casts a dim light. Dozens of flames may illuminate an entire space. God doesn't expect you to be a perfect person, but he invites you to share his light with others.

Show how you share your light with the world. Hold a flashlight and stand in a circle with your group in a darkened room. Think of one way in which you have been a reflection of God's love and care to others. After sharing your idea, turn on your flashlight. Notice the growing brightness in the room as each person speaks and then adds his or her light.

REGINA KAZANJIAN is an undergraduate student at the University of Cincinnati.

Session 10 > Celebrating Advent and Christmas 85

IF TIME ALLOWS

Reflections of God

Make art supplies available and have young people make works of art that represent themselves as reflections of God's light. Explain that their work of art can be either symbolic or realistic, and that in keeping with the theme of the article, it is OK if the final product is far from perfect. When all young people are finished, encourage volunteers to share their work with the group and explain its meaning.

① Begin

Bring to class a flashlight and a small mirror. Lower the lights and then have a volunteer shine the light toward you as you use the mirror to reflect the light onto other young people in the group. Then read aloud the introductory text. Ask: *Based on our flashlight demonstration and the introduction, what do you think the main message of this article will be?* (Possible answer: We are called to reflect God's light to others.) Say: *In times of darkness, the light we offer others shines more brightly.*

② Connect

Have volunteers read aloud the title and the first two paragraphs of Being a Light to Others. Then discuss with young people areas of their lives in which they feel the need to be "perfect." If necessary, start the discussion with an example of your own. For example, say: *I am usually pretty relaxed, but when I give a formal presentation, I get extremely nervous and tend to over-prepare.* Next, ask whether young people feel a similar pressure to be perfect, or at least highly knowledgeable, when discussing their faith with others. Ask: *How can such an attitude keep us from doing God's work?* (Possible answer: It prevents us from saying anything at all.) Have a volunteer read aloud the concluding paragraph. Say: *We do not have to be the flashlight. We just have to be the mirror, angled toward God. Remembering this can relieve some of the pressure we feel.*

Read aloud the Lighting a Way activity. Encourage participation in the demonstration.

③ Close

Ask: *How do you light the way? How do faith communities? Which is more important?* (Answers will vary.)

① Begin

What's What? Have volunteers take turns reading aloud the directions and each main idea. Remind them that a supporting detail would relate to each big idea. Invite young people to complete the page. Have volunteers share their responses.

② Connect

Say What? Ask volunteers to read aloud and define the terms. Review each term in the Glossary if necessary.

Now What? Read aloud the section. Invite young people to brainstorm ideas and then respond independently.

③ Go in Peace

Collect materials and return them to their appropriate places. Encourage young people to monitor their progress in regard to the Now What? challenge throughout the week. Point out that the values of society may make it seem that wealth is a prerequisite for dignity, but this is not so. Catholic Social Teaching tells us that all human life is valued over material goods. Say: ***Jesus taught us that all people deserve to be treated with dignity. Consider being friendly to someone who has few friends, standing up for someone who is being bullied, or recognizing the talents or accomplishments of others, despite what they wear or how much money they have.***

3-Minute Retreat Give young people an opportunity for quiet meditation at **www.loyolapress.com/retreat**.

What's What?

Respond

After each topic sentence, write one supporting detail from the text.

1 Catholics celebrate Advent and Christmas during the Church's liturgical year for different reasons. (PAGE 79)

Possible answer: During Advent we prepare ourselves for Jesus' birth. At Christmas we welcome Jesus as the Savior of the world.

2 Themes of light and darkness appear in the Bible. (PAGES 80–81)

Possible answer: Isaiah 42:16 says "I will turn darkness into light before them, and make crooked ways straight."

3 Advent is a good time for us to "awake from sleep." (PAGE 81)

Possible answer: "Awake from sleep" is our call to action—to be happy, present, and engaged in anticipating the coming of our Savior.

4 Born quietly in humble surroundings and first received by poor shepherds, Jesus comes to us not as an earthly king but as a divine king. (PAGES 82–83)

Possible answer: Jesus has come as a light to shine on all people, especially those who are often overlooked or forgotten.

5 The Light of Jesus is the one true gift of Christmas. (PAGE 83)

Possible answer: Jesus is all we need for true happiness in this world.

6 Catholics celebrate feast and holy days during Advent and Christmas. (PAGE 84)

Possible answer: Catholics celebrate Mary, Mother of God on January 1 and the Epiphany on January 6.

Say What?

Know the definitions of these terms.

Advent
Christmas
feast days
Feast of Our Lady of Guadalupe
Holy Day of Obligation
Nativity
sanctuary

Now What?

Jesus was born as one of us. His humble beginnings tell us that every person has dignity in the eyes of God. What is one thing you can do this week to promote the dignity of others?

Answers will vary.

IF TIME ALLOWS

Service: Hope for Children with Cancer

Invite young people to recall some examples of ways to be a light in the world. Explain that one way is to help people who are sick. Encourage young people to collect toys to donate to a pediatric cancer wing at a local hospital. Ask them to write notes of encouragement and hope to the children who are going through treatment.

✝ *Life and Dignity*

Session Assessment Option

An assessment for this session can be found at www.findinggod.com.

Unit Assessment Option

If you wish, photocopy the Unit Assessment on pages T-362–T-364. Administer the assessment during the session or send it home.

PLAN AHEAD: Get Ready for Session 11

Consult the catechist preparation pages to prepare for Session 11 and determine any materials you will need.

Unit 2

Faith in ACTION

Part of the mission of the Catholic Church is to help shape the world. We are called to be part of the fabric of society, participating in social tasks and responsibilities. As members of society, Catholics take part in making the world a better place. Our families are the starting place for learning about justice.

In this unit we learned that Jesus, who is fully divine and fully man, expressed his humanity in profound ways, experiencing great joys as well as hardships and suffering. Jesus is "God with us," who is for all people. Our relationship with Jesus calls us to live in justice. One way that we can answer this call is to work for peace in the world. Here are some ideas to help you take a stand against violence and promote peace.

Act

A Shelter from Violence

Purpose

Plan a project that raises awareness of the effects of domestic violence on families and society. Plan to provide assistance to people affected by domestic violence.

Background

Domestic violence is physical or mental abuse that is used to gain or maintain power and control over a partner or family member. Domestic violence can happen to anyone—children, teens, or adults. Although it is often inflicted by a family member, domestic violence can also occur in a dating situation.

Steps

1. Find organizations in your area that serve the needs of people who suffer from domestic violence.

2. Use these or other suggestions for ways to help:
   - Have the group write letters to government officials in support of legislation against domestic violence and to provide funding for agencies that deal with domestic violence.

(continued on page 88)

"Peace is not just the absence of war. Like a cathedral, peace must be constructed patiently and with unshakable faith."

—Pope John Paul II

IF TIME ALLOWS

Promote Awareness and Action

Point out that many young people experience violence in their relationships. Some studies show that one in three teens reports knowing someone who has been punched, slapped, choked, or physically hurt by a friend. Explore with young people ways that they can deal with peer violence. To extend this activity, ask young people to work in pairs to locate other facts about peer or domestic violence and to share their findings with the group at a later meeting.

MATERIALS: Get Ready for Faith in Action

For these projects, you will need print and online resources on domestic violence, computers with Internet access, the prayer service planning guide and prayer service planning tips, and supplies for a Peaceful Encounters rally. Also see the project steps.

FAITH IN ACTION

Complete one of the suggested Faith in Action projects as a class, or organize young people into two groups, having each group complete a different project. Note that directions continue on the next page.

① Prepare

Discuss the project ideas with young people and involve them in the decision-making process to determine a project. Discuss the project in terms of faith and being a "person for others." Ask: ***What do you hope to learn from this project? What interests you about it? What concerns do you have about it? Whom will you serve, and how will your service be beneficial to them and to you? Are you prepared to recognize the humanity in those you encounter? How does this project help you put your faith into action? What theme or themes of Catholic Social Teaching will you be experiencing in the project?***

② Implement

Have young people follow the directions to complete A Shelter from Violence on page 87 or Toys Against Violence on page 88. Be sure young people do research before taking action. Consider inviting an expert on domestic violence to speak with the group. Also provide print and online resources and organize young people in small groups. Ask groups to present a brief report on their findings.

Be sure young people are supervised during their project as appropriate. Consider asking for parent volunteers to be Faith in Action facilitators for the entire year.

✝ *Rights and Responsibilities*

③ Close

Bring closure to the project by leading young people in completing one or both of the following:

Prayer Service Download and print out the prayer service planning guide and prayer service planning tips on www.findinggod.com. Have young people plan and implement a prayer service that expresses both gratitude to God for the opportunity to serve and hope for the people whom they served.

Pass It On Help young people organize a Peaceful Encounters rally for the school or parish. Help young people arrange activities for the event to promote awareness of domestic violence. An advertising committee might promote the event through the school newspaper, parish bulletin, or posters. Choose volunteers who participated in either service project to share their stories about the experience, what they learned, and how others can get involved. Organize young people to write and perform skits. Ask them to demonstrate ways to respond to situations in a peaceful, nonviolent manner that encourages others to use gentle words and actions when confronted with an emotional situation. Ask a local business to donate colorful plastic bracelets to distribute as daily reminders to act as peacemakers.

✝ *Life and Dignity*

Act

- Collect materials for arts-and-crafts projects that volunteers can use to teach children in shelters. Organize a time and date to visit a local shelter, and ask parents to chaperone.
- Educate your community by inviting experts to speak at a public forum, publish articles on domestic violence, and make available printed or online information that tells where to get help.

Toys Against Violence

Purpose

Become aware of the amount of violence people are exposed to on a daily basis; take a stand against violence by rediscovering peaceful activities.

Background

Our culture surrounds us with images of violence. Even simulated images, such as computer games, can desensitize us and make violence seem ordinary and more acceptable. What we see, what we read, and how we play really does shape us for better or worse.

Steps

1. For one week, record every instance of your exposure to violence, either through your direct participation or witnessing someone else. For example, did you use toy weapons, view violence on TV, play violent video games, or engage in verbal violence, such as insults? At the end of the week, share your findings with the group. What insights did you gain from recording your observations?

2. Brainstorm ways that you can reduce the amount of violence around you.

3. Find ways to surround yourself with nonviolent, fun, and engaging things or activities.

4. Share your new insights with the group. For example, you could teach younger children a nonviolent game that encourages cooperation. Be creative and at the same time take a stand against violence.

> "Blessed are the peacemakers, for they will be called children of God."
> —Matthew 5:9

88 Unit 2 • The Early Life of Jesus

IF TIME ALLOWS

Living Faith: Defining Violence

Discuss different forms of violence with young people. For example, explain that physical violence may be recognized readily, but verbal abuse might not be as overt. Together, brainstorm a list of various forms of violence. Discuss why some behaviors, games, or activities may not seem violent in an obvious way but really are. Help young people discern the role that personal and societal attitudes, peer pressure, or desensitization plays in the display of different forms of violence. Challenge young people to recognize and change any personal behaviors or attitudes that may harm themselves or others.

✝ *Life and Dignity*

Unit 3

Catechist Preparation pages open each unit and session.

Unit Opener   89

UNIT 3

The Public Life of Jesus

Unit 3 focuses on the mysteries of Jesus' public ministry. In this unit, young people will learn the following concepts.

SESSION 11 **Jesus Prepares for His Ministry**

Young people learn that by taking on the sins of the world, Jesus accepts his mission as Messiah. Though Satan tempts Jesus with power, honor, and wealth, Jesus resists and commits himself to serving his Father. Because Jesus had a human nature, he understands the difficulties we face when we're confronted with temptations. Young people pray the Prayer of Saint Thomas Aquinas.

SESSION 12 **Jesus Performs Signs**

The Gospel of John refers to Jesus' miracles as signs. Jesus' signs reveal who he is and who the Father is. Young people learn about Jesus' first miracle at the wedding feast at Cana and explore sacramental rites as outward signs that signify a divine reality. The prayer form *lectio divina* uses the repetition of Scripture verses to help the Word of God sink into young people's minds and hearts.

SESSION 13 **Jesus Is Our Teacher**

Moses received the Ten Commandments from God and gave them to the people. Jesus presented the Beatitudes with his own authority. Both the Ten Commandments and the Beatitudes are guides to live the life God wants us to live. The Beatitudes describe the Kingdom of God, which begins here and now when we respond to God's love by loving him and others. Young people are reminded of God's limitless generosity and love for them.

SESSION 14 **Jesus Heals and Forgives**

Jesus healed in mind, body, and spirit. Forgiveness was Jesus' central message throughout his ministry. Jesus gave us the Sacrament of Penance and Reconciliation as a way to reconcile our sins. God's care for those who are elderly or seriously ill is shown through the Sacrament of the Anointing of the Sick. The sacraments of healing bring us grace, helping us grow in our trust of God that we are not alone.

SESSION 15 **Celebrating Lent**

During Lent young people learn how to follow more closely the way of Jesus by imitating the way he lived. Lent is a time for us to repent and recall our baptismal promises. We can prepare for Easter by following Lenten practices of prayer, fasting, and almsgiving.

UNIT SAINTS

Matthew, Mark, Luke, and John

Matthew, Mark, Luke, and John are the authors of the Gospels, the first four books of the New Testament. Inspired by the Holy Spirit, the Evangelists recorded the life of Jesus and his role as our Savior. Although the accounts have much in common, they are not identical. Written at different times and for different audiences, each Gospel brings a unique perspective about the life of Jesus and the faith of the early Church.

Prayer in Unit 3

In each session of Unit 3, establish the pattern and tone for prayer. Young people pray *lectio divina*, a prayer by Saint Thomas Aquinas, a prayer to understand values of the Beatitudes, prayers of renewal, and a guided reflection. Young people also pray the Daily Examen, a form of Ignatian prayer.

✝ Catholic Social Teaching in Unit 3

The following themes of Catholic Social Teaching are integrated into this unit.

Call to Family, Community, and Participation   Participation in family and community is central to our faith and to a healthy society. Family and communities must be supported and strengthened through active participation.

Care for God's Creation   We have a responsibility to care for God's creation. We are called to make moral and ethical choices that protect the ecological balance of creation both locally and worldwide.

The Dignity of Work and the Rights of Workers   The Catholic Church teaches us to respect basic rights of workers: the right to productive work, to fair wages, to private property, to organize and join unions, and to pursue economic opportunity. Catholics believe that the economy is meant to serve people.

Life and Dignity of the Human Person   The Catholic Church teaches us that all human life is sacred and that all people must be treated with dignity. As Catholics, we strive to respect and value people more than material goods. The foundation of our moral vision is our belief in the life and the dignity of the human person.

Option for the Poor and Vulnerable   As Catholics, we are called to follow Jesus' example by making a specific effort to defend and promote the dignity of the poor and vulnerable and meet their immediate needs.

Rights and Responsibilities   The Catholic Church teaches that every person has a right to live as well as the right to things required for human decency. As Catholics, it is our responsibility to protect fundamental human rights.

Solidarity   Solidarity is the attitude that leads Christians to share spiritual and material goods. Solidarity unites rich and poor, weak and strong, and helps create a society that recognizes that we live in an interdependent world.

Faith in Action

In Unit 3, young people are invited to explore the protection of fundamental human rights, treating others with dignity and respect, and basic rights for workers. Service projects include showing appreciation for behind-the-scenes workers and raising awareness about child-labor abuse and poverty around the world. Alternative service-project ideas also appear on the last page of each session in this guide.

TOGETHER *as One Parish*

Religious Education with the Parochial School

To nurture parish unity, organize a school/RE family service exchange. Ask family members to determine either goods or services they are able to trade, such as painting, odd jobs, baby clothing, or cooking. By trading services and goods, members serve others without spending money. Working together builds relationships and community within the parish.

📖 Literature Opportunity
***Blessing's Bead* by Debby Dahl Edwardson**
You might wish to suggest that young people read this novel that contains two memorable narratives, one from the past and one from the present. A young Iñupiaq girl named Blessing learns the importance of home and family when she discovers information about the life of her great-grandmother, Nutaaq.

✝ *Family and Community*

Jesus Prepares for His Ministry

 ## 3-Minute Retreat

Before you prepare the session, pause and be still. Take three deep breaths and be aware of the loving presence of God, who is with you on this journey.

Matthew 2:13–14

When they had departed, behold, the angel of the Lord appeared to Joseph in a dream and said, "Rise, take the child and his mother, flee to Egypt, and stay there until I tell you. Herod is going to search for the child to destroy him." Joseph rose and took the child and his mother by night and departed for Egypt.

Reflection

Mary and Joseph had hardly bid farewell to the Magi when the threat of violence interrupted their lives. Heeding the angel's warning, Joseph took his family out of danger. This atmosphere of violence and danger did not end as Jesus grew up. It is no wonder that when Jesus began his public ministry, his message of love of one's enemies, justice, and respect for others sounded so revolutionary. His message continues to be revolutionary today. As Jesus' disciples, we are called to proclaim the same message today in the way we live.

Questions

What message from God have I heard and acted upon recently? How do my words and actions today reflect the call of Jesus to love and respect others?

 Concluding Prayer

Speak to God, using the words of this prayer or your own.

Loving God, your Son Jesus responded to hatred and violence with justice and love. Help me be his true disciple by following his words and actions.

Knowing and Sharing Your Faith in Session 11

Consider how Scripture and Tradition can deepen your understanding of session content.

Scripture

Luke 4:1–13 confirms Jesus' identity as the Messiah. Jesus renounces Satan's temptations and their false sources of security.

Matthew 13:1–23 recounts Jesus' parable of the sower, instructing us to allow God's Word to flourish and to be at work in our lives.

Tradition

The grace of Baptism has freed us from sin but not from temptation, the attraction we feel to act in ways we know are wrong. The attraction sometimes comes from outside us. At other times it arises from within. The attraction itself is not sinful. Dealing with temptation can be an occasion for moral growth as we strengthen our ability to follow our conscience. Only God knows all the good of which we are capable. Resisting temptation brings us closer to knowing God's grace and that goodness within us.

Catholic Social Teaching

In this session the integrated Catholic Social Teaching themes are **Rights and Responsibilities** and **Care for God's Creation.** See page 89b for an explanation of these themes.

Window on the Catechism

The Cardinal Virtues, grace, and facing temptation are discussed in *CCC* 1803–1811.

General Directory for Catechesis

The parable of the sower is discussed in *GDC* 15.

One-Hour Session Planner

SESSION 11 Jesus Prepares for His Ministry

Session Theme: *Jesus accepted his mission as Messiah and renounced Satan's temptations. Jesus prepared us to hear God's Word by teaching the parable of the sower.*

Before This Session

▶ Display the *Finding God* posters The Time Line of the New Testament and The Four Evangelists.

▶ Bookmark your Bible to Luke 3:11, Luke 3:13–14, Luke 3:16, Luke 3:21–22, Luke 4:1–13, Hebrews 4:15, Matthew 4:1–11, Matthew 13:3–9, Matthew 13:18–23, and Romans 13:1. Place the open Bible in your prayer space.

▶ Read the Guide for this session, choose any additional If Time Allows activities that you might have time to complete, and gather the listed materials.

Prayer in Session 11

Pray the prayer on the session opener page. Young people are invited to pray at the end of the session by accessing an online 3-Minute Retreat that encourages reflection on Scripture. Session 11 asks young people to look to the saints for guidance and includes a prayer by Saint Thomas Aquinas. Follow the Prepare directions on the Catechist Guide page before sharing with young people.

STEPS	APPROXIMATE TIME
Engage *Unit Saints:* Matthew, Mark, Luke, and John PAGES 89–90 *Daily Examen* PAGE 89 *Jesus Prepares for His Ministry* PAGE 91	10–20 minutes
Explore *Jesus, Son of God* PAGES 92–93 *Facing Temptation* PAGES 94–95	30–40 minutes
Reflect *Prayer:* Praying with the Saints PAGE 96 *Where Do I Fit In?* PAGE 97	10–15 minutes
Respond *What's What?* PAGE 98	10–15 minutes

TAKE IT HOME

Homework options:

Temptation Survival Kit	PAGE 93
Temptation Skits	PAGE 94

Materials

REQUIRED

▶ *Finding God* poster: The Time Line of the New Testament (page 89)

▶ *Finding God* poster: The Four Evangelists (page 90)

▶ Prepared messages inside an empty glass bottle (page 91)

▶ Bibles (page 93)

▶ Writing supplies (pages 93, 95, 97, 98)

▶ Computer with Internet access (page 98)

OPTIONAL

▶ Bibles, writing supplies, bottles, slips of paper for messages (page 91)

▶ Session 11 BLM, T-365 (page 92)

▶ Computers with Internet access (page 93)

▶ Chalk or tape, costumes (page 95)

▶ Reference materials, slide-show presentation software (page 96)

▶ Pop song, CD player (page 97)

▶ Interest inventory (page 98)

▶ Session 11 Assessment, www.findinggod.com (page 98)

Unit 3

The Public Life of Jesus

Matthew, Mark, Luke, and **John** are the authors of the Gospels, the first four books in the New Testament. The Gospels tell us about the life of Jesus and his role as our Savior and Redeemer. If you look closely, you'll discover that although the Gospels are all true and have a great deal in common, they are not identical. Each one is written in a different time for a different audience or community. None of the authors of the four Gospels wrote a biography, telling absolutely everything they knew about Jesus. Instead, inspired by the Holy Spirit, they recorded the faith of the early Church, a faith that has been passed down to us.

How the Saints Relate { Jesus performed signs and miracles, taught, healed, loved, and forgave. The words of Matthew, Mark, Luke, and John can help answer the questions, "Who is Jesus?" and "What does he teach?"

89

UNIT OPENER
OUTCOMES

▶ Explain that the four Gospels are the source of all truth and understanding about Jesus Christ.

▶ Define *bishops, Evangelists, ministry,* and *pope.*

① Begin

Read aloud the unit title. Explain that in this unit, young people will explore the mysteries of Jesus' public ministry.

Write the names of four national sports teams on the board. Ask volunteers to share their viewpoints. Say: ***Notice the different perspectives on, or ways of looking at, the teams. Because we have four Gospels, we have more than one perspective on Jesus in the Bible. Each Gospel tells the Good News from its own perspective. Together, they tell everything we need to know about Jesus, our Savior and Redeemer.***

② Introduce the Saints

Have a volunteer read the paragraph on page 89. Display the *Finding God* poster The Time Line of the New Testament. Explain that the dates of the written records are approximate: Mark, A.D. 65–70; Matthew and Luke, A.D. 70s–80s; John, A.D. 90s. Say: ***Jesus had already been crucified and had risen from the dead about 40 years before Mark wrote his Gospel account. Imagine how much the faith had grown during that time. Imagine how daily life, politics, and the audience influenced each writer. It is no wonder the accounts are not identical.***

How the Saints Relate

Read aloud the feature. Have young people discuss their understanding of the meaning of a reliable source. Say: ***The four Evangelists help us understand the public life of Jesus. Through their Gospels, the true identity of Jesus is revealed.***

Daily Examen

Suggest that young people frequently pray the Daily Examen on page 279 in Prayers and Practices. Guide them through these steps, pausing after each one.

• Rest, take some deep breaths, and clear your mind. Become aware of God's presence all around you. Thank God for giving us Jesus, his only Son, who came to save us and show us how to live. Think about a Gospel story about Jesus that showed the choices he made.

• Go through the events of the day, hour by hour, in chronological order. Think about your thoughts or feelings, what you said [or what you didn't say but should have], and what you did. Think about the choices you made through your actions and words.

• Focus on one or two choices you made. Ask yourself, "What would Jesus have said or done in my situation? How did I respond?" Ask God's forgiveness for any time you failed to love.

• Now look toward the rest of today and tomorrow. Ask yourself, "What do I need to do to follow the way of Jesus?" Ask Jesus to help you be aware of his presence.

• Pray *Amen* silently when you are ready.

③ Connect

Display the *Finding God* poster The Four Evangelists. Have a volunteer read aloud the title and paragraph. Ask a volunteer to read the definition of *Evangelists* in the Glossary. Ask: **Why were the Gospels written?** (to preserve the teachings of Jesus and to ensure that future generations would know his importance to our Salvation)

Have young people read Formation of the Gospels. Review the meanings of the vocabulary words in the Glossary. Ask volunteers to summarize the main ideas in the section. Draw three columns on the board and add the headings *First Stage*, *Second Stage*, and *Third Stage*. Write important details into each column.

Ask a volunteer to read the section Inspired by the Holy Spirit. Point out the second bullet and explain the idea of an authentic Christian community. Say: **For example, in the year A.D. 180, Saint Irenaeus wrote that he accepted the writings found in the New Testament because he had received them from the Church in Rome, which was founded by Saint Peter.** Explain that it took centuries for the Church to determine the official list of books that make up the Bible. Point out that this official list is called the *canon*. Say: **The writings contained within the Bible are our rule of faith.**

④ Close

Ask young people to explain what perspective means to them in light of what they have read about the four Gospel writers. Remind them that everything they need to know about Jesus is found in the Gospels. Say: **The Gospels are our source of truth. When we read them, we learn about Jesus and how he wants us to live.**

To learn more about the Evangelists, refer young people to pages 258–262 in Prayers and Practices.

Four Gospels, One Lord

The Gospels are at the center of our faith because Jesus Christ is the center of the Gospels. The four Gospel writers, called the **Evangelists,** wanted to preserve the teachings of Jesus so that future generations would recognize his importance to our Salvation. Each author tells us in a unique way what is important to know about Jesus and provides a point of view that is shaped by culture and historical time. The Gospels are the source of truth and understanding about how we are to live our lives.

Formation of the Gospels

The Gospels were not written simultaneously. They formed over a period of time. The first stage was the life and teachings of Jesus, including his birth and life in Nazareth, his public **ministry,** and finally his Death, Resurrection, and Ascension. When Jesus entered public life, he was accompanied by disciples, some of whom he chose to be Apostles. They saw the way Jesus lived and how he cared for others. They listened to his teachings. They spoke to Jesus after his Resurrection.

The second stage in the formation of the Gospels was the preaching of the Good News of the Salvation of Jesus Christ by the Apostles. This passing on by word of mouth of what they received from Jesus' teaching and example and what they learned from the Holy Spirit is our Catholic Tradition. The Good News is passed on to us today by the Apostles' successors, the **bishops** and the **pope.**

The final stage was the actual writing of the Gospels. The writers recorded the words and stories about Jesus that they remembered or had been told. Each Gospel writer composed his own account to show what Jesus meant to him and to others living in his community.

Inspired by the Holy Spirit

Early leaders in the Church established some rules to help them choose which writings were inspired by the Holy Spirit and told the truth about Jesus Christ.

➡ Did the writing link to the teachings of one of the Apostles?

➡ Did the writing come from an authentic Christian community?

➡ Did the writing conform to the "rule of faith"; that is, did the writing reflect the authentic faith that had been learned from the Apostles?

The four Gospels we have today do all these things and are the only Gospels accepted by the Church as truly inspired by the Holy Spirit as teaching the truth about Jesus Christ.

90 *Unit 3 • The Public Life of Jesus*

IF TIME ALLOWS

Gospel Alive

Explain that each Evangelist presented a portrait of Jesus to a specific audience and helped them meet the challenges of the time. Have young people select from any of the four Gospels some words or deeds of Jesus that are particularly meaningful to them today. Ask them to look for situations, lessons, or examples of paths to follow that seem to apply especially well to modern time.

In a small group, have young people discuss the following questions. Ask: **What challenges does your community face? What is your greatest personal challenge? Which examples of Jesus help you meet these challenges?** Ask volunteers to share aloud their ideas with the entire group.

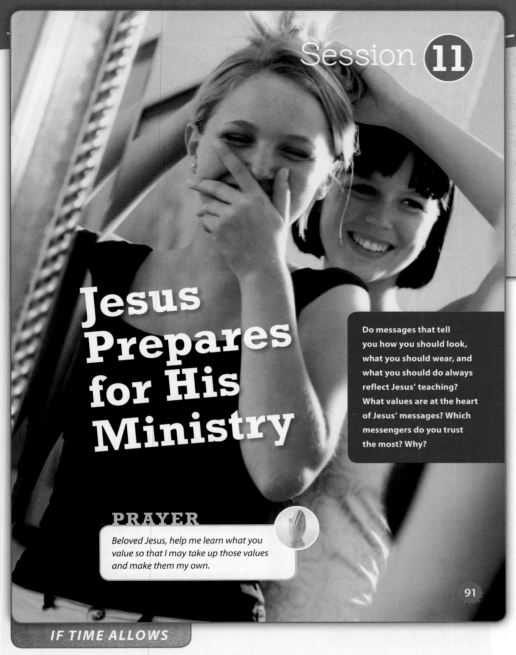

Session **11**

Jesus Prepares for His Ministry

Do messages that tell you how you should look, what you should wear, and what you should do always reflect Jesus' teaching? What values are at the heart of Jesus' messages? Which messengers do you trust the most? Why?

PRAYER

Beloved Jesus, help me learn what you value so that I may take up those values and make them my own.

91

IF TIME ALLOWS

Messages of Love

Organize the class into four groups and assign a different Gospel writer to each group. Invite groups to read and choose favorite teachings of Jesus' from their assigned Gospel. Have them record key words, verses, or ideas and decide what Jesus' message was in each case. Ask groups to share their ideas.

Provide bottles for each group. Ask group members to write Jesus' messages on slips of paper and have them put the messages inside the bottles. Keep the bottles in the prayer space or on display for young people to read and remember Jesus' messages of love.

Go to **www.findinggod.com/sessionextenders** for ways to discern between good and evil. You may wish to share this with the group.

OUTCOMES

▶ Explain Jesus' acceptance of his mission as Messiah.

▶ Explain that Jesus understands our temptations and shows us how to respond to them.

▶ Pray a prayer by Saint Thomas Aquinas.

▶ Define *epiphany, parable, Satan,* and *temptation.*

① Set the Stage

Have young people read aloud the questions on page 91. Ask volunteers to share aloud their responses.

② Get Started

Prepare a message-in-a-bottle prop. Display it and briefly discuss its purpose and who might write and send such a message. Beforehand, prepare several sample messages. Ask: ***Can you guess who wrote these messages?*** For example, "I don't always do my chores, but I'm working on it." (a child to a parent) "I'll be there for you next year. High school will be the best!" (a friend) "Nothing works better on stains than Blast-It!" (television ad) "Put your talents to use and join one of our parish groups." (a church) "Learning how to write an essay will help you succeed in life." (a teacher) Say: ***A message may deliver a big idea with few words. If you discover the values at the heart of the message, then you can decide whether you want to listen to it.*** Read aloud the session title. Say: ***Jesus, a master teacher, has a big message for us.***

 Prayer

Ask: ***How can we better understand Jesus' message?*** Pray aloud the prayer. Conclude by praying the Sign of the Cross.

① Begin

Ask volunteers to discuss times when they were sent to do something. Ask: **When you were sent to do something, how did you feel?** (Possible answers: proud to be trusted, happy to have the responsibility, annoyed to be distracted) Say: **Jesus was sent to do something by the Father.** Read aloud the article title and the first paragraph. Ask: **Why did people ask John to baptize them?** (to repent publicly for their sinfulness)

② Connect

 Have volunteers read aloud Holy Spirit and Fire. Say: **John's baptism made it clear that there was no single right way to repent. The act of repenting was for everyone, but the reason to repent was unique for each person. Our Baptism is also a public statement. We become part of a faith community. We admit we need help—from God and other people—in order to follow the life of Jesus.**

Read aloud the section Anointed for the Mission. Ask a volunteer to summarize. Explain that although each Gospel is unique in its portrayal of Jesus' life, three of the four—Matthew, Mark, and Luke—have striking similarities. Because of this, these three Gospels are called *synoptic*, from the Greek word for "a seeing together." In the opening chapters of each Synoptic Gospel, God identifies Jesus as his "beloved Son" and Jesus receives the Holy Spirit.

Ask a volunteer to read aloud the section Manifestation of God and the meaning of *epiphany* in the Glossary. Discuss how Jesus' baptism is the Revelation of the Trinity.

Our Catholic Character

Ask a volunteer to read aloud the feature. Point out that the Feast of the Epiphany, which we celebrate during the Christmas season, is only one of the four epiphanies, but it is the best known.

Jesus, Son of God

JESUS' identity as the Son of God is revealed at his baptism by John the Baptist in the Jordan River. People were going to John for baptism as a public statement of their sinfulness and their repentance before the community.

Holy Spirit and Fire

When the crowds asked John what they must do to repent, he told them, "Whoever has two tunics should share with the person who has none. And whoever has food should do likewise." (Luke 3:11) To tax collectors, he said, "Stop collecting more than what is prescribed." (Luke 3:13) To soldiers, Luke instructed, "Do not practice extortion, do not falsely accuse anyone, and be satisfied with your wages." (Luke 3:14) Because John spoke this way, many in the crowd thought that he might be the long-awaited Messiah, an idea John dismissed. John told the people that he was baptizing with water, whereas the one to come after him would baptize "with the holy Spirit and fire." (Luke 3:16)

Our Catholic Character

The word *epiphany* takes its name from the Greek *epiphaneia*, meaning "manifestation, striking appearance." The Gospel writers used this term to describe events in the life of Christ when Jesus' divinity revealed itself. The Church recognizes four epiphanies of Christ when his divinity shines through his humanity: the Nativity, the adoration of the Magi, Jesus' baptism in the Jordan River, and Jesus' first sign at the wedding feast at Cana.

Anointed for the Mission

Jesus' coming to be baptized identified him as the Messiah that John had been talking about. By his baptism, Jesus submits entirely to the will of the Father. Jesus, who is without sin, takes the sins of the entire world upon himself so that we might have Salvation. In his baptism, Jesus accepts his mission as Messiah. Jesus' immersion in the water symbolizes that he will redeem the world by being submerged in Death and then rise into new life. God the Father, delighting in his Son, voices his pleasure and reveals Jesus' identity. "[H]eaven was opened and the holy Spirit descended upon him in bodily form like a dove. And a voice came from heaven, 'You are my beloved Son; with you I am well pleased.'" (Luke 3:21–22)

Manifestation of God

Jesus' baptism is an **epiphany,** the revelation of Jesus as the Son of God. The Father's voice, the Holy Spirit like a dove descending upon Jesus, and Jesus the Son are The Revelation of the Trinity—Three Persons in one God. The Father strengthened Jesus for his mission, and the Spirit anointed him.

The Messiah's Test

Jesus, at around 30 years old, accepts his mission at his baptism by John. Immediately following his baptism, the Spirit leads Jesus into the desert for a time of solitude so that he can prepare for his mission.

92 *Unit 3 • The Public Life of Jesus*

IF TIME ALLOWS

Session 11 BLM

Jesus' Baptism Explain to young people that in his treatise *On Baptism,* written around A.D. 200, Tertullian said that if people really understood what Baptism asked of them, they would "have more fear of obtaining it than of postponing it." Help young people understand this rather unusual quotation by telling them that Baptism commits them to follow Jesus Christ—no easy task. Explain that God doesn't leave them alone to fend for themselves but gives them his grace and protection in their service of him.

Provide each young person with the Session 11 Blackline Master [T-365]. As they use the Blackline Master to explore each Gospel account of Jesus' baptism, ask them to think about their own acceptance in the Sacrament of Baptism to follow the life of Christ.

For 40 days, Jesus remains in the harsh wilderness of the desert, living among wild animals. At the end of this time, when Jesus is tired and weak, **Satan** entices him with **temptation** three times, urging him to compromise his relationship with the Father or to live by values that would be completely different from those of the Father. (Luke 4:1–13)

Tempted in the Desert

Because Jesus has not eaten for 40 days, he is very hungry. Luke's Gospel tells us that the devil's first test of the Son of God takes advantage of Jesus' need for nourishment. "If you are the Son of God, command this stone to become bread." (Luke 4:3) Jesus rejects the suggestion because the Son of God is fed by God, not by bread alone. Satan persists and takes Jesus up to a very high mountain and shows him all the kingdoms of the world. He offers Jesus all the wealth and power of the world if only Jesus will worship him. Jesus replies that God alone is to be worshiped and served. (Luke 4:5–8) Then the devil takes Jesus to the top of the Temple and tells him to jump, for surely God will keep him safe from harm by sending angels to support him. Jesus replies that the Son of God does not put the Father to such foolish tests. Finally the devil leaves Jesus for a time. (Luke 4:9–13)

Jesus Is the Messiah

Satan tempts Jesus with power, honor, and wealth, which are all temporary and false sources of security. Satan tempts Jesus to be a different kind of Messiah, a Messiah with a material kingdom instead of a spiritual one. Because Jesus renounces the temptations, his true identity as the Messiah, the Son of God, is confirmed.

Jesus is the "new Adam" because he remains faithful, whereas Adam found temptation too hard to resist. Jesus' 40 days in the desert mirror the 40 years the Israelites spent wandering in the desert. While the Israelites lost faith in God over and over as they faced temptations, Jesus remains obedient and faithful to the will of God the Father. Jesus conquers Satan and his hollow promises, not for himself, but for love of humanity and the Father. "For we do not have a high priest who is unable to sympathize with our weaknesses, but one who has similarly been tested in every way, yet without sin." (Hebrews 4:15)

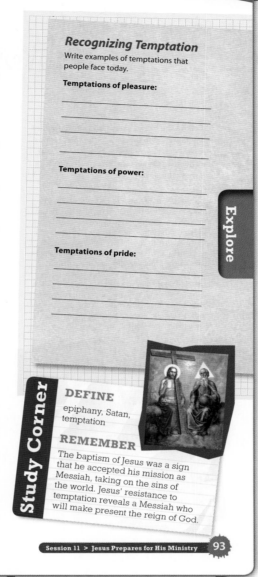

Recognizing Temptation

Write examples of temptations that people face today.

Temptations of pleasure:

_____

_____

_____

_____

Temptations of power:

_____

_____

_____

_____

Temptations of pride:

_____

_____

_____

_____

Explore

Study Corner

DEFINE

epiphany, Satan, temptation

REMEMBER

The baptism of Jesus was a sign that he accepted his mission as Messiah, taking on the sins of the world. Jesus' resistance to temptation reveals a Messiah who will make present the reign of God.

Session 11 > Jesus Prepares for His Ministry **93**

TAKE IT HOME

Temptation Survival Kit

Emphasize that temptation is part of every Christian's life. Remind young people that they can prepare themselves in case of emergency by assembling survival kits. Have young people assemble a survival kit to help them avoid temptations. Have them make and decorate a shoebox and then fill it with objects, photos, or labeled drawings that help them focus their lives in a good direction. Examples of contents include prayers, the Bible, sports activities, and sacramentals. Ask volunteers to share their survival kits with the whole group, explaining why they chose its contents.

INCLUSION
Autism Spectrum

Support Learning with Technology For the activity Recognizing Temptation, provide visual support by giving young people with autism-spectrum disorder the option to find images on an approved Web site instead of writing their responses.

Ask a volunteer to read the section The Messiah's Test. Refer young people to the Glossary and read the definitions of *Satan* and *temptation*. Say: ***Even the Son of God underwent tests and trials in obedience to the Father's will. Think about times when you've been tempted.*** Ask: ***How long was Jesus in the desert?*** (40 days) Say: ***The number 40 appears in the Bible more than 80 times. This repetition is significant. The number represents a period of time in which someone's faithfulness is tested and determined.***

Read aloud Tempted in the Desert and discuss Jesus' three temptations. Ask: ***What modern-day examples could parallel each temptation?*** (Possible answers: first—seeking fulfillment in pleasure and things rather than in God; putting our needs first; second—making things more important than God; seeking power and wealth; third—doing flashy things to get noticed; trying to convince God to do things your way)

Have the group read the section Jesus Is the Messiah. Ask: ***How is Jesus' identity as the Messiah confirmed?*** (He renounces Satan and a material kingdom. He is the new Adam. He spends 40 days in the desert and remains faithful to God.) Have young people read Matthew 4:1–11 to learn how Jesus responds to Satan at each temptation. Say: ***Jesus commits himself to serving his Father and is protected by grace in his service.***

Read aloud the directions for the Recognizing Temptation activity and ask the group to brainstorm ideas. Then ask young people to complete the activity independently.

③ Close

Invite young people to write answers to these questions:

▶ What temptations are most difficult for you to resist?

▶ How can you take steps to avoid them?

① Begin

Brainstorm possible temptations that teens face. Draw a two-column chart on the board and record young people's ideas in the first column. Then discuss what Jesus would have done had he faced each temptation and record their answers in the second column. Read aloud the article title. Say: *Just like you, Jesus had real temptations. He shows us how to respond to them by relying on his relationship with the Father.*

② Connect

Ask a volunteer to read the first paragraph. Say: *The struggle to avoid temptation and sin is a struggle that all people share.* Caution young people against making excuses for giving into temptation by thinking or saying, "You just don't understand." Point out that Jesus understands. He faced real temptations. We are called by his life and example to ask for God's help in resisting temptations.

Have young people read the next two paragraphs. Ask: *Why is temptation dangerous for a Christian?* (It turns our attention away from God's truth and can lead to sin.) Ask: *What guidance does Jesus provide regarding temptation?* (Jesus gave the example of his own life and helped the disciples understand his mission so they could carry on his teaching.) Ask: *What did Jesus often use to make the meaning of his teaching more understandable?* (He often taught with parables.) Have a volunteer read aloud the definition of *parable* in the Glossary. Ask: *Who succeeds the Apostles and continues to safeguard Jesus' teaching?* (the pope and the bishops) As a group, discuss how temptations are false promises. Encourage young people to be alert for them and to think before they act. Invite them to keep watch for one another, encouraging one another to make good choices.

Facing Temptation

JESUS, like us except in sin, experienced real temptation in the desert. The temptations were ones all human beings face—things that look good on the surface but actually diminish our true calling.

The story of Jesus' temptation in the desert shows us how the Word of God is rooted in Jesus, how it helps him, and how it can help us. Temptation is an attraction that can lead us to disregard God's loving invitation. If the temptation starts with a person, he or she might try to convince you that you should have something or do something. The person might lie or make an attractive offer. Instead of giving you a lasting gift, the tempter really wants to take something away from you, such as your safety, your independence, your self-control, or your reliance on God and your obedience to him. Everyone is tempted, but the Holy Spirit helps us resist temptation and choose to do what God intends for us.

Christ in the Wilderness, Laura James, 20th century.

Jesus followed God perfectly and without sin, a grace shared with his mother, Mary. Even so, he still faced temptations. Because of this, Jesus understands how difficult it is for us when we face temptations. He did not leave us alone without guidance. Jesus gave the disciples the example of his own life and helped them understand his mission. When Jesus taught, he was also preparing his disciples to carry on his Word and lead his Church. Jesus often used a **parable** to give added explanations and to answer questions. At one point in the Gospel of Matthew, Jesus asked his disciples if they understood the meaning of his parables, and they answered yes. This is an important point because they would not have been able to pass along Jesus' teachings without this understanding. Jesus' teachings, safeguarded by the Apostles and by their successors, the pope and the bishops, are alive today in the Word of God.

Parable of the Sower

In Jesus' time, farmers understood the struggles of growing food on Israel's rocky land. Jesus used this knowledge to teach about hearing the Word of God, a tool for resisting temptation. In Jesus' telling of the parable of the sower, he uses familiar images. A sower drops seeds that fall in different places on the ground. Some seeds fall on the path, and birds eat it.

Study Corner

DEFINE
parable

REMEMBER
Jesus understands how difficult it is for us when we face temptations because he faced temptations too. Jesus is like us, but he alone follows God perfectly and without sin.

94   *Unit 3 • The Public Life of Jesus*

TAKE IT HOME

Temptation Skits

Ensure that young people understand that temptation is an enticement to desire something, but sin is the actual choosing to do what is wrong instead of right. Ask young people to write a short skit that shows how temptation can lead to sin. Encourage them to write an ending that shows a way to resist temptation successfully. When the group meets next time, young people may want to work with volunteers to read aloud or act out their skits for the group.

Some seeds fall on rocky ground. Because there is not enough soil to support them, they wither for lack of roots. Some seeds fall among thorns, and they are choked. But some seeds fall on rich soil, and much fruit is produced. (Matthew 13:3–9)

The seed, Jesus explained, is God's Word. Some of it falls in places where it can live and flourish, and some of it falls in places where it cannot sprout and grow. We are like the ground in the parable. The seed sown on the path is like the person who hears the Word without understanding it, allowing evil to come and steal it away. The seed sown on rocky ground is like a person who receives the Word joyously, but when faced with a test, falls away. The seed sown among thorns is the Word choked from someone's heart by worldly worries and desire for riches. Only the seed sown in rich soil flourishes and bears much fruit because God is at work in someone's life. (Matthew 13:18–23)

We Are Tested

As a young person, you face many temptations that get in the way of being faithful to the Word of God. Giving in to temptation makes you like stony ground where seeds can't take root and grow. Good intentions to avoid temptation can blow away like seeds in the wind if they are not rooted in prayer and perseverance. When you experience temptation, remember that Jesus faced temptation too. God wants you to live the best life you can. Moments of temptation can be overcome if you root yourself in determination to follow God.

Expect temptation so that you can prepare for it. Rely on the example of the saints who have gone before you. Put your energy into healthy activities, such as sports, the arts, music, and volunteer work. Remember Jesus' parable about the farmer. The Church is like the rich soil that will help the seed of faith grow in you. Turn to Jesus often in prayer. Receive the sacraments, listen to Scripture, and be determined to live a good life.

SACRED ART

Vincent Van Gogh's oil on canvas was inspired by an 1850 painting called *Sower* by Jean-François Millet. Van Gogh believed Millet's artwork brought the spirit of Christ to life on the canvas. Van Gogh, who had studied theology, regarded his art as a way to bring spiritual comfort and peace. Elements in this oil painting contain images from Jesus' parable of the sower, such as a path, the sun, and blackbirds eating some of the seed the sower is scattering. In the background, vertical stalks of grain show the seed that has taken root and grown.

Past Meets Present

PAST: Saint Thomas Becket (1118–1179) resisted temptation and held strong to faith and to the Church. Becket, a priest, had a friendship with King Henry II of England. Eventually, the king elevated Thomas to the highest position in the Catholic Church in England, the Archbishop of Canterbury. When the king wanted to use his power to control the Church, Thomas stood against him. As a result, the king had Thomas killed.

PRESENT: Although the Church recognizes the need for authority to govern people, Catholic Social Teaching insists that authority must be exercised for the common good of society, using morally acceptable means. "[T]here is no authority except from God, and those that exist have been instituted by God." (Romans 13:1)

Sower with the Setting Sun, Vincent Van Gogh, 1888.

Session 11 > Jesus Prepares for His Ministry 95

ADVENTURES IN FAITH

Temptation Circles

Use chalk or tape to mark off three large, interlocking circles on the ground. Label these circles *Temptations*. Inside the first circle write *nourishment*; inside the second circle, write *wealth and power*; inside the third circle, write *save yourself*. Explain the label *nourishment* as meaning to put oneself first or to seek fulfillment in pleasure, such as playing video-games for hours or sleeping excessively. Explain the label *save yourself* as meaning to cut corners or to show off.

Say: *We face temptations every day, just as Jesus did in the desert. Temptations are hard to resist.* Ask: *If you had to choose, which one of these temptations is the hardest?* Invite young people to step up and stand inside that circle. To ease reluctant participants, be sure to take a place inside a circle too.

After all young people are in place, tell them they will work together during the week to write and perform a temptation skit. The skit should demonstrate both the enticement and the tools they can use to resist temptation. Encourage creativity by suggesting costumes related to the theme of their skits. For example, someone might dress as a king for the wealth-and-power skit.

Ask a volunteer to read the section Parable of the Sower. With the group, look carefully at each part of Jesus' explanation. Ask volunteers to give modern examples that parallel Jesus' teaching.

Read aloud the section We Are Tested. Ask volunteers to describe additional ideas for resisting temptations that occur in everyday life. Write their ideas on the board or ask them to copy them on paper. Remind them to use the list of suggestions often. Say: *Just as an athlete prepares for an event, you need to prepare for inevitable times of temptation so you aren't caught off-guard.*

Point out that Jesus quoted Scripture when he rebuked Satan in Matthew 4:1–11. Say: *Every time you conquer temptation, the seed, God's Word, takes root in your life. You grow in a healthy way toward adulthood because God is at work in your life.*

Past Meets Present

Invite a volunteer to read aloud the feature. Discuss examples of human laws that don't correspond with the spiritual teachings of the Church.

✝ *Rights and Responsibilities*

Sacred Art

Read aloud the feature. Have young people find the images from Jesus' parable in Van Gogh's art. Ask volunteers to suggest how a visual representation in a work of art can help gain insight into a religious teaching.

③ Close

Invite young people to respond to these questions on a sheet of paper:

► What can you do every day to arm yourself against temptation?

► How can you help others resist temptation?

Prayer

Follow the steps to guide young people through the prayer on page 96.

Young People's Page

Prepare Pray the prayer in advance to become familiar with it.

Pray Read aloud the title. Ask volunteers to read aloud the paragraphs in the left column. Explain that Pedro Arrupe, fondly known as Don Pedro, was Superior General of the Jesuits between 1965 and 1983. Although not a saint, he worked for the common good and promoted social justice during a remarkable life as a "contemplative in action." Remind young people that saints and people like Arrupe are inspiring because, although imperfect, they seek the greater glory of God and the betterment of their fellow humans. Say: ***Today we will pray together a prayer by Saint Thomas Aquinas, a great theologian and Doctor of the Church. Explain that Saint Thomas Aquinas was a brilliant scholar who showed that faith and reason could coexist.***

Then have young people bring their books to the prayer space and sit quietly. Say: ***Relax and take a few deep breaths. Open your hearts and minds.*** Pray the Sign of the Cross. Then invite young people to pray Saint Thomas Aquinas's prayer. Together, pray aloud slowly and reverently, pausing briefly after each phrase of the prayer. Say: ***Let's continue to pray together.*** Then pray the All part. At the end, say: ***Meditate on the words we just prayed and listen for God's response.*** After a brief silence, say: ***As we continue the session, ask God to help you recognize the goodness in yourself and others and to show you how to follow the example of the saints and other holy people.***

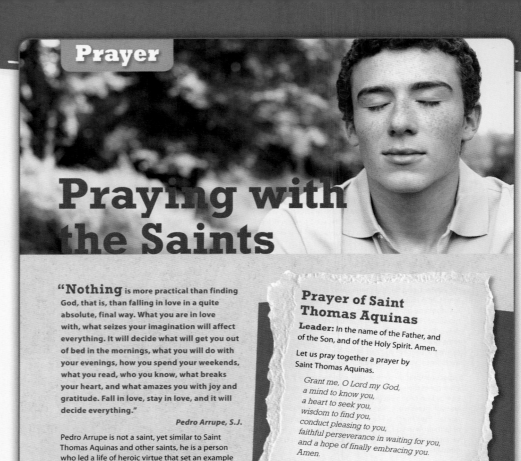

Prayer

Praying with the Saints

"**Nothing** is more practical than finding God, that is, than falling in love in a quite absolute, final way. What you are in love with, what seizes your imagination will affect everything. It will decide what will get you out of bed in the mornings, what you will do with your evenings, how you spend your weekends, what you read, who you know, what breaks your heart, and what amazes you with joy and gratitude. Fall in love, stay in love, and it will decide everything."

Pedro Arrupe, S.J.

Pedro Arrupe is not a saint, yet similar to Saint Thomas Aquinas and other saints, he is a person who led a life of heroic virtue that set an example for all Christians.

Saints have witnessed to their faith in ordinary and extraordinary ways. The saints' love of God prompted them to know the heart of Jesus, taking what Jesus valued, and making it their own so that their hearts would be similar to Jesus'. This does not mean that the saints were perfect. Instead, it means that they trusted in God's love and mercy. God was able to work through them in powerful ways. Many saints wrote prayers that enrich the spiritual lives of all believers. Through their prayers we can see what they valued and try to follow their ways in our own lives.

Prayer of Saint Thomas Aquinas

Leader: In the name of the Father, and of the Son, and of the Holy Spirit. Amen.

Let us pray together a prayer by Saint Thomas Aquinas.

*Grant me, O Lord my God,
a mind to know you,
a heart to seek you,
wisdom to find you,
conduct pleasing to you,
faithful perseverance in waiting for you,
and a hope of finally embracing you.
Amen.*

All: Oh Lord, may we use our minds to comprehend the Catholic faith and to come to know what Jesus taught. May we come to know you through our love of others. May we treasure the grace of finding God in all things. May we act so that our behavior shows that we are disciples of your Son, Jesus. May we persevere in faith, overcoming all obstacles. May we keep in our imaginations the vision of ourselves embracing Jesus at the end of our lives. May we all live in eternal happiness in Heaven with God. Amen.

96 *Unit 3 • The Public Life of Jesus*

IF TIME ALLOWS

Saint Thomas Aquinas

Tell young people that Saint Thomas Aquinas is the patron saint of students. Encourage them to work in a group to research and learn more about his life as a Dominican. Then, ask them to research their own patron saints independently and present their findings in a slide-show presentation or a poster.

FYI

Coaching Young People to Pray

Before praying, ask young people to consider what brings them closer to God. Invite them to pay attention to their senses, feelings, and thoughts about the words to the prayer.

WHERE Do I Fit In?

If you accept all messages blindly, you might fail to recognize God's invitation to live with integrity. Seeking deeper truths frees you to resist false trappings and allows you to live your life authentically as a follower of Christ.

by Jennon Bell

Seeking Real Truth

Once a week I meet a group of friends to play a trivia game. We win prizes or bragging rights, but primarily we get together for the good company and to flex our brain muscles. Usually, something interesting happens.

The announcer asks the question, and we stare blankly at one another, hoping the answer will magically come to us. Then as the clock clicks down and the tension rises, a nugget of information bursts into my brain. I blurt out the correct answer, right at the buzzer. My friends ask, "How did you know that?" I respond, "I'm not sure. I just *knew it.*"

Some things I know because I've learned them, whether through study, experiments, or experience. But then there are things I just "know." I'm not sure how that information got there. I like to think that the mind is like a sponge, constantly absorbing data and tidbits that permeate our everyday lives. We're bombarded by information from the Internet, television, newspapers and magazines, lyrics, text messages, conversations, and advertisements. How can I know that the messages I'm hearing are trustworthy, worthwhile, and most importantly, a reflection of what I believe?

As Catholics, we have a multitude of resources to help us weigh the messages we receive. The Beatitudes, a Daily Examen, the Commandments,

a parish priest or church group, Scripture readings, family, or a quiet meditation can provide the support and guidance I need to focus my attention on what is influencing my daily choices. I like to think of these faith tools as a filter for my mind's inbox. And above all else, I trust the conscience I have cultivated as a Catholic so that when someone asks, "How do you know that?" I can say with confidence, "I just know it."

JENNON BELL is a curriculum editor from Illinois who loves to read, bake, and perform improvisation.

Reflect

Unlocking the Message

What kind of media message is contrary to your Catholic values? What kind of media message supports your Catholic values? Write examples on the lines. If needed, continue on another sheet of paper.

False Message

_____

_____

_____

True Value

_____

_____

_____

_____

Session 11 > Jesus Prepares for His Ministry · 97

Active Listening

Explain that preparing for the "media marathon" doesn't mean completely unplugging from media but learning to have internal conversations about the messages we hear. To illustrate, play a pop song that you have previewed for appropriate content. As young people listen, invite them to think about the lyrics. Ask: *What ideas go against their values? What ideas match their values?* Have young people jot down key words or phrases from the song. Afterward, invite young people to share their thoughts with the group. Encourage them to practice this kind of active listening in their daily lives.

① Begin

Have a volunteer read aloud the introductory text. Write the word *integrity* on the board and ask what it means. (firmly maintaining moral values, honesty; doing what's right) Say: **Integrity *means all these things. Literally, it means being integrated— always matching actions with what is known to be true.*** Next, ask how young people can know whether something is true. Say: ***Distinguishing the truth can be hard. This article gives pointers on how we might go about it.***

② Connect

Have volunteers take turns reading aloud Seeking Real Truth. Ask young people to speculate about the consequences of running a marathon without training for it. Say: ***A person must train for a marathon by building muscle and endurance. The same is true for the "media marathon" we face every day. We have to train ourselves to filter out the junk from the messages we receive.*** Ask: ***How does the author suggest we do this?*** (by praying the Beatitudes or a Daily Examen, talking with people of faith, reading the Bible, or meditating) Say: ***If we traded in one-quarter of our total media time to spend on these activities, our truth-knowing muscles would grow strong.***

Have young people complete the Unlocking the Message activity independently. When everyone is finished, invite volunteers to share their ideas with the group.

③ Close

Have young people share strategies that either they or their families already use to process or minimize media messages. Invite young people to implement one additional strategy to put into practice.

1 Begin

What's What? Read the directions aloud and have young people complete the puzzle independently.

2 Connect

Say What? Ask volunteers to read aloud and define the words. Review each word in the Glossary if necessary.

Now What? Ask a volunteer to read aloud the section. Give time for quiet reflection before young people write their responses. Distribute slips of paper so they can write their reminder.

3 Go in Peace

Collect materials and return them to their appropriate places. Encourage young people to use one of the strategies they learned in this session to avoid temptations. Say: *As we go through our week, may we remember the values at the heart of Jesus' messages and resist any temptations that might lead us away from him.*

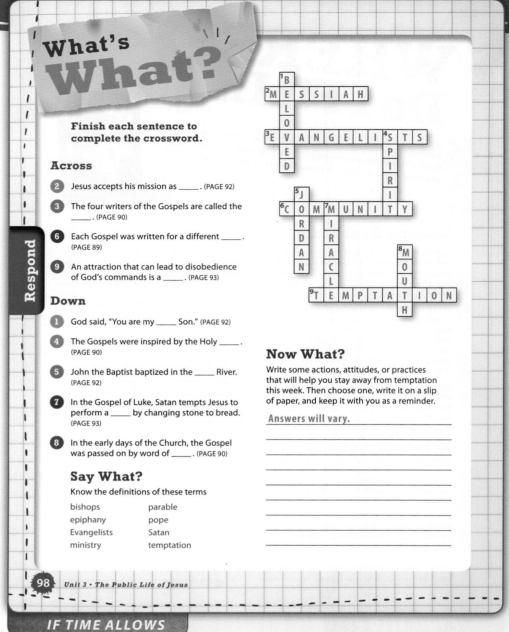

What's What?

Respond

Finish each sentence to complete the crossword.

Across

2 Jesus accepts his mission as _____. (PAGE 92)

3 The four writers of the Gospels are called the _____. (PAGE 90)

6 Each Gospel was written for a different _____. (PAGE 89)

9 An attraction that can lead to disobedience of God's commands is a _____. (PAGE 93)

Down

1 God said, "You are my _____ Son." (PAGE 92)

4 The Gospels were inspired by the Holy _____. (PAGE 90)

5 John the Baptist baptized in the _____ River. (PAGE 92)

7 In the Gospel of Luke, Satan tempts Jesus to perform a _____ by changing stone to bread. (PAGE 93)

8 In the early days of the Church, the Gospel was passed on by word of _____. (PAGE 90)

Say What?

Know the definitions of these terms

bishops   parable
epiphany   pope
Evangelists   Satan
ministry   temptation

Now What?

Write some actions, attitudes, or practices that will help you stay away from temptation this week. Then choose one, write it on a slip of paper, and keep it with you as a reminder.

Answers will vary.

_____
_____
_____
_____
_____
_____
_____
_____
_____

98 *Unit 3 • The Public Life of Jesus*

IF TIME ALLOWS

Service: God's Handiwork

Have young people organize a "get up and out in the world" campaign for teens that encourages outdoor programs as a way to direct physical energy positively and to experience God in nature. Begin with an interest inventory or a classroom fair that includes educational materials and speakers. Enlist adult guides and chaperones to supervise activities such as bike rides, camping, track events, nature walks, baseball games, canoeing trips, and so on.

✝ *God's Creation*

Session Assessment Option

An assessment for this session can be found at www.findinggod.com.

3-Minute Retreat

Give young people an opportunity for quiet meditation at **www.loyolapress.com/retreat**.

PLAN AHEAD: Get Ready for Session 12

Consult the catechist preparation pages to prepare for Session 12 and determine any materials you will need.

Jesus Performs Signs

3-Minute Retreat

Before you prepare the session, pause and be still. Take three deep breaths and be aware of the loving presence of God, who is with you on this journey.

John 2:9–11

And when the headwaiter tasted the water that had become wine, without knowing where it came from (although the servers who had drawn the water knew), the headwaiter called the bridegroom and said to him, "Everyone serves good wine first, and then when people have drunk freely, an inferior one; but you have kept the good wine until now." Jesus did this as the beginning of his signs in Cana in Galilee and so revealed his glory, and his disciples began to believe in him.

Reflection

One thing we learn from Jesus in the Gospels is that abundance is a sign of God's kingdom. Scarcity does not exist in God's vocabulary. God is so much bigger than anything we can imagine. Jesus demonstrated that fact over and over again throughout his public ministry. The closer we draw to Jesus, the more we will notice that Christian life is abundant with God's grace for ourselves and others.

Questions

In what ways have you experienced the abundance of God? What about your life has changed as you have drawn closer to Jesus?

Concluding Prayer

Speak to God, using the words of this prayer or your own.

Jesus, you reveal the Kingdom of God in signs of abundance. May your signs and wonders lead me ever closer to you.

Knowing and Sharing Your Faith in Session 12

Consider how Scripture and Tradition can deepen your understanding of session content.

Scripture

John 6:9–13 describes another of Jesus' miracles of abundance in the multiplication of the loaves.

Matthew 28:16 tells us the words of Jesus' Great Commission. Jesus instituted the sacraments so we may encounter him on our faith journey.

Tradition

The Catholic Church is a sacramental Church, recognizing seven sacraments. The sacraments tell us what God's love is doing in our lives. The sacraments are effective signs that bring about what they signify. The sacraments represent God's action at peak moments of our spiritual journey, giving us strength to live our Christian vocation in our everyday lives. They signify God's blessing at birth, adolescence, adult life, old age, and death. The sacraments are part of the public worship of the Church; that is, the entire Church participates in every celebration of a sacrament.

Catholic Social Teaching

In this session the integrated Catholic Social Teaching themes are **Call to Family, Community, and Participation** and **Rights and Responsibilities.** See page 89b for an explanation of these themes.

Window on the Catechism

The signs and symbols of the liturgy and the sacraments are discussed in *CCC* 1145–1162.

General Directory for Catechesis

The tasks of catechesis to know the faith, celebrate it, live it, and bring it to prayer are described in *GDC* 84 and 85.

One-Hour Session Planner

SESSION 12 Jesus Performs Signs

Session Theme: *Jesus' signs reveal that he is the one who fulfills the Father's promise to us with abundance.*

Before This Session

▶ Bookmark your Bible to John 2:1–12, John 6:9–13, John 10:10, John 20:23, Genesis 2:24, Genesis 41:55, Matthew 18:21–35, Matthew 19:8, Matthew 28:19, and Luke 22:19. Place the open Bible in your prayer space.

▶ Read the Guide for this session, choose any additional If Time Allows activities that you might have time to complete, and gather the listed materials.

STEPS	APPROXIMATE TIME
Engage *Jesus Performs Signs* PAGE 99	10 minutes
Explore *Miracle at Cana* PAGES 100–101 *Sacraments as Signs* PAGES 102–103	30–40 minutes
Reflect *Prayer:* Filling Our Water Jars PAGE 104 *Where Do I Fit In?* PAGE 105	10–15 minutes
Respond *What's What?* PAGE 106	10–15 minutes

Prayer in Session 12

Pray the short opening prayer at the beginning of the session and encourage young people to reflect on Scripture by accessing an online 3-Minute Retreat at the end of the session. In Session 12 young people will use the prayer form *lectio divina* to meditate about the Word of God and draw them into deeper conversation with God. Follow the Prepare directions on the Catechist Guide page before sharing with young people.

TAKE IT HOME

Homework options:

Who, Me?	PAGE 100
Sacraments Game	PAGE 103

Materials

REQUIRED

▶ Backpack, small objects (page 99)

▶ Photographs or drawings of different kinds of signs (page 100)

▶ CD player (page 101)

▶ CD 1, Track 4: "The Feeding of the 5,000" (4:07) (page 101)

▶ Birthday candle, wedding ring (page 102)

▶ Bible (page 103)

▶ Writing supplies (pages 104, 105, 106)

▶ Computers with Internet access (page 106)

OPTIONAL

▶ Sign-up sheet for projects (page 99)

▶ Empty box or container (page 101)

▶ Session 12 BLM, T-366 (page 102)

▶ Mural paper, marker, slips of paper, tape (page 104)

▶ Writing supplies (page 104)

▶ Art supplies, writing supplies for anti-bullying campaign (page 106)

▶ Session 12 Assessment, www.findinggod.com (page 106)

Session 12

Jesus Performs Signs

To what are you committed? Even though you might be tempted to give up on commitments, relationships, or responsibilities when things get difficult, with courage and determination, you can see them through. When have you put in some extra effort to stick with a commitment?

PRAYER

Lord Jesus, bless my efforts to stay committed to you. Let me know the abundance of your love and grant me your Salvation.

99

IF TIME ALLOWS

Make a Commitment

Organize the class into small groups and have them brainstorm a practical list of volunteer activities they could perform for a period of time this year. The activities might be group-, family-, school-, parish-, or community-related projects. Post a sign-up sheet and request a commitment for the specified period of time.

✝ *Family and Community*

➜ Go to **www.findinggod.com/sessionextenders** for a discussion about Jesus' signs. You may wish to share this with the group.

OUTCOMES

► Describe Jesus' first miracle that took place during the wedding feast at Cana.

► Explain your understanding of sacramental rites as outward signs that signify a divine reality.

► Meditate on the Word of God.

► Define *penance, repentance, rite, sacraments,* and *signs*.

① Set the Stage

Read aloud the text and questions in the box. Give young people time to think and then write their responses.

② Get Started

Ask for a volunteer to participate in a demonstration that requires some strength. Place an empty backpack on the volunteer's back. Say: **Please carry this across the room and back.** When the volunteer accomplishes the task, add a small weight, such as a book, to the backpack. Have the volunteer repeat the same walk. Do the same thing again one more time. Ask the volunteer to describe which trip was the easiest. Ask: **How committed do you have to be to see something difficult all the way through until the end?**

Have a volunteer read aloud the session title. Ask: **How do you think the idea of commitment and the session title might be related?** (Possible answer: Jesus committed himself to his mission as the Messiah. Jesus performed signs to reveal God's commitment.)

 Prayer

Ask: **Let's pray together to ask God for courage and strength in our commitment to him.** Pray aloud the prayer. Conclude by praying the Sign of the Cross.

① Begin

Find and display photographs, or draw simple signs on the board, such as a road sign, a Chi-Rho, someone using sign language, and a mathematical sign used in an equation. Ask: **What do all these signs have in common?** (They express a thought, an idea, a belief, or a command.) Say: **Signs are useless unless you learn their meaning.**

② Connect

Ask a volunteer to read the article title and the first three paragraphs. Point out that John's Gospel is unlike the other Gospels in several ways. It includes a Prologue, a Book of Signs, and a Book of Glory. John uses the word *signs* instead of *miracles* to reveal Jesus as the One sent by God. Ask a volunteer to read aloud the definition of *signs* in the Glossary. Refer young people to read more about the Gospel of John on pages 261–262 in Prayers and Practices. Ask: **What do the signs in the Gospel of John reveal?** (the glory of God and a glimpse of what the Kingdom of God is like)

Ask volunteers to read the section "Do Whatever He Tells You." Ask: **How does Mary show faith?** (Mary sets the stage for Jesus' glory to be revealed to his disciples.) Explain that Jesus often used a wedding feast in his parables. Say: **Abundant wine was a sign of God's kingdom.** Explain that the jars that Jesus used had been set aside for the ritualistic washings that were important to the Pharisees. Say: **When Jesus brought new wine from these jars, he replaced human, rigid rules with God's bountiful love, mercy, and compassion.**

Our Catholic Character

Discuss the idea that Christian marriage is more than a civil union. Matrimony is a sacrament, and the fidelity of the union signifies the fidelity of Christ and the Church.

Miracle at Cana

Wedding Feast at Cana, Latin Rite Wedding Church, Cana, Israel.

IN John 2:1–12, Jesus performs his first miracle, an act of power or wonder that is attributed to God. The first half of John's Gospel contains seven **signs**, each revealing the glory of God and giving us a glimpse of what the Kingdom of God is like. The wedding at Cana shows the significant role of Mary in Jesus' ministry.

Jesus, his mother, and the disciples are invited to a wedding in the town of Cana in Galilee. Although he has disciples, Jesus has not yet begun his public ministry. It was common for wedding feasts to last a long time, even days. At this wedding feast, the wine runs out, an embarrassment for the family, who will have to send everyone home.

In the midst of the celebration, Jesus' mother hears about the wine. When Mary tells Jesus the wine has run out, an interesting exchange between mother and Son takes place. Jesus says, "Woman, how does your concern affect me? My hour has not yet come." (John 2:4) Jesus is asking his mother how this fact involves him.

Our Catholic Character

The couple at the wedding feast at Cana made a promise, a personal covenant, with God and each other. In Jesus' time, religious authorities accepted divorce. Jesus refused to be drawn into the argument between sides that argued the grounds for divorce. Instead, he reminded them what God said at the beginning. "That is why a man leaves his father and mother and clings to his wife, and the two of them become one body." (Genesis 2:24) "Therefore, what God has joined together, no human being must separate." (Matthew 19:6)

100 *Unit 3 • The Public Life of Jesus*

"Do Whatever He Tells You"

Mary directs the servers, "Do whatever he [Jesus] tells you." (John 2:5) John reveals Mary as an ever-faithful model of faith. She places her belief in Jesus. Interestingly, these are the last words we hear Mary speak in the Gospel of John.

Mary's words echo an occasion of famine when the Pharaoh of Egypt told the Israelites to go to Joseph, the son of Jacob, and do whatever he said to do. (Genesis 41:55) Pharaoh had entrusted Joseph with tremendous authority in Egypt, and Joseph fed the starving people to relieve the famine. In a similar way, the wine had run out at the wedding feast, and Jesus, to whom God had given authority, rewarded Mary's trust and faith by providing in abundance.

Jesus had not expected to perform any "sign" this day. Upon Jesus' direction the servers filled six water jars, each holding 20 to 30 gallons, and Jesus transformed the water into wine. The wine was very good; in fact, it was so good that the headwaiter was amazed it had been saved for last. (John 2:6–10)

Similarly, God provides for us in great abundance, and the world has been given all it needs through the coming of Jesus Christ. Mary's faith-filled words at the wedding feast set the stage for Jesus' glory to be revealed to his disciples. "Jesus did this as the beginning of his signs in Cana in Galilee and so revealed his glory, and his disciples began to believe in him." (John 2:11) The disciples' faith, then, followed from Mary's faith.

TAKE IT HOME

Who, Me?

Opportunities to serve others sometimes come at unexpected or inopportune times. Have partners read John 2:1–12. Ask them to discuss times when they weren't planning on doing something but didn't want to disappoint someone. Ask them to describe how they felt and what happened during their unexpected moment of "How does this involve me?"

Following discussion with a partner, assign each young person to write about his or her ideas, including the choice that was made, the result of the choice, and how the decision made a positive difference. Encourage them to illustrate their stories with pictures or photos. Have volunteers share their stories with the group.

Miracles of Abundance

The first 12 chapters of John's Gospel are referred to as the Book of Signs because Jesus performs many miracles that reveal God's glory. In different ways these signs, or miracles, show us God's abundant love for us. In John's Gospel, Jesus multiplies five barley loaves and two fish so that about 5,000 people can eat. Jesus takes the food, gives thanks, and distributes it, and the people eat as much as they want. When the disciples gather what is left, they are able to fill 12 wicker baskets. (John 6:9–13) Just as at Cana, Jesus performs a sign to reveal that God's promises are fulfilled with abundance.

The stories of signs in the Gospel of John reveal not only who Jesus is but also who the Father is. In Cana, Jesus shows that he is the one who fulfills the Father's promise to humankind with abundance. He says, "I came so that they might have life and have it more abundantly." (John 10:10) Jesus' love, mercy, and compassion are as abundant as food and drink multiplied for all people.

Jesus' greatest sign of his abundant love for us is his Crucifixion when he died for the sake of our Salvation. Jesus calls us to follow his example and be a channel for God's abundant love and mercy—not distributing love or compassion with an eyedropper but acting in a way that reflects the divine love that has no limit.

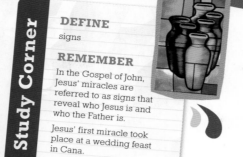

Study Corner

DEFINE

signs

REMEMBER

In the Gospel of John, Jesus' miracles are referred to as signs that reveal who Jesus is and who the Father is.

Jesus' first miracle took place at a wedding feast in Cana.

Living Abundantly

God's abundant grace flows through us. We may not be able to turn water into wine, but God's grace enables us to do the good that we can do, such as

→ turning a negative outcome into a positive one by changing our outlook and our attitude.

→ turning a stranger or an outcast into a friend.

→ turning an enemy into someone we love and for whom we pray.

While it is commendable to plan to do things of service for other people, Jesus' first miracle reminds us that opportunities to do good may come when we don't expect them. As Jesus did, we may initially ask, "What does this have to do with me?" Because we have Jesus' example, his words, his guidance, and the abiding Spirit of God within us, we *can* make a difference.

SACRED ART

Mosaic from the apse of Santi Maria e Donato, 12th century.

The Italian city of Murano is a miniature Venice, built on several islands and divided by canals. Famous for its glass-making, the city is home to the cathedral Santi Maria e Donato. Legend credits Emperor Otto I for the church's devotion to the Virgin Mary. When Otto's ship was caught in a terrible storm in the Adriatic, he promised to build and dedicate a church to Mary wherever she directed. When the storm ended, an apparition directed him to Murano. The cathedral includes a mosaic of the Virgin Mary set in an apse (a semicircular recess) of gold and overlooking a marble altar.

Session 12 > Jesus Performs Signs **101**

Explore

Have volunteers read aloud the section Miracles of Abundance.

If desired, play the recorded Scripture story "The Feeding of the 5,000" [CD 1, Track 4]. Then continue discussing examples of the abundance of God's kingdom.

Ask a volunteer to read the section Living Abundantly. Review the meaning of God's grace—a gift from God that helps them live their lives the way God would want them to live. Ask volunteers to tell of times when their life has been touched by the grace of God.

Encourage young people to notice times during the week when they think to themselves, "What does this have to do with me?" Say: ***Think about ways God is present during little acts of goodness.*** Ask: ***What might God's grace enable you to do this week?***

Sacred Art

Read aloud the Sacred Art feature. Discuss Mary's last recorded words in Scripture, "Do whatever he tells you," and how they reveal faith worthy of imitation. Have volunteers identify popular devotions to Mary, such as the Rosary. Encourage young people to set aside time to pray to Mary every day.

③ Close

Say: ***God's promises are filled with abundance.*** Ask: ***How can we imitate God's generous love and mercy in practical ways? How often do we respond to Mary's command, "Do whatever he tells you"?*** Invite open discussion, encouraging young people to express their views.

ADVENTURES IN FAITH

Small Miracles

Hold up an empty box or container. Discuss how surprised they would be if all of a sudden it was overflowing with things they value. Say: **We can't perform miracles in the way that Jesus did, but we can do good in the world, such as performing small acts of kindness.** Remind them that the world is full of small miracles.

Have young people sit in a large circle. Give the empty box to the first person. Have that person open the box and speak about one of the following: miracles that happen in the world, a personal miracle story they would like to share, natural phenomena they consider a miracle, or how they can do some good in the world this week. When the first speaker finishes, have him or her close the lid and pass the box to the next person in the circle. Invite young people to continue and follow the same process, passing the box around the circle until everyone has contributed ideas.

① Begin

Hold up a birthday candle and a wedding ring. Ask: *What occasions do you associate with these?* (a birthday party and a wedding) Ask: *What traditions might you see performed at a wedding banquet?* (Possible answer: a toast) *at a birthday party?* (Possible answer: blowing out birthday candles) Say: *Traditions identify and set special occasions apart.*

② Connect

Read aloud the article title and the first two paragraphs. Ask a volunteer to read aloud the definitions of *sacraments* and *rite* in the Glossary. Say: *Sacraments are part of the liturgy, or the public worship of the Church. When we celebrate the sacraments, we use objects and actions to make present the sacred.* Explain that a rite is a religious act and unlike a popular tradition in a culture.

 Have young people read the section Instituted by Christ. Say: *Christ is made present in the sacraments. The sacraments were given to us by Jesus Christ; they are rooted in Scripture in his words and actions. They are signs of what God is doing in our lives.*

Invite volunteers to read aloud Sacraments of Initiation. Say: *These sacraments bring us into the Church and help us grow as members. The grace we receive through the Holy Spirit allows us to be Jesus' disciples in the world.* Say: *Of the three Sacraments of Initiation, only the Eucharist is received more than once.* Explain that we join together as a faith community to celebrate the sacraments. In this way we become part of the Body of Christ.

Sacraments as Signs

WE encounter Jesus at key times during our faith journey when we receive the **sacraments.** Sacraments are holy, visible signs that signify a divine reality. Through the sacraments, Christ acts in us to save us. The grace received through the Holy Spirit enables us to carry out our mission as disciples.

The seven sacraments are Baptism, Confirmation, Eucharist, Penance and Reconciliation, Anointing of the Sick, Matrimony, and Holy Orders. A sacrament is a sacred **rite,** a ceremonial religious act that is a sign of God's love and presence in our lives.

Instituted by Christ

Jesus gave us the sacraments so that we may encounter him on our journey of faith. Jesus' Great Commission to his disciples was to "Go, therefore, and make disciples of all nations, baptizing them in the name of the Father, and of the Son, and of the holy Spirit, . . ." (Matthew 28:19) At the Last Supper, Jesus offered his body and blood and then told his disciples, "[D]o this in memory of me." (Luke 22:19) Jesus told his disciples, "Whose sins you forgive are forgiven them, and whose sins you retain are retained." (John 20:23) Each sacrament was given to us by Jesus so that God's life and love could fill our lives.

The sacraments are Christ's actions in our lives. When you were baptized, Christ cleansed you of Original Sin and brought you into his Church. In Confirmation you are filled with the Holy Spirit. When you confess your sins to a priest, Christ acts through the priest to free you from the guilt and burden of your sinfulness. If you get married at some point in your life, it will be Christ who joins you and your spouse together, filling you with the love and grace you will need to live together to form a family. Sacraments help us remain healthy in body, mind, and soul. They strengthen the Church community and reinforce commitments among people and between people and the Church.

Signs and symbols taken from everyday life are present in the sacramental rites. For example, washing with water, breaking bread, or sharing a cup express the sanctifying presence of God in Baptism and the Holy Eucharist. Sacramentals, such as the oil used in Confirmation and the Anointing of the Sick, as well as the prayers and blessings, are important in the rites of the sacraments.

Sacraments of Initiation

Baptism In Baptism we are born into new life with Christ. Baptism takes away Original Sin and makes us members of the Church. Its sign is the pouring of water.

Confirmation Confirmation fills us with the Holy Spirit and seals our life of faith in Jesus. Its signs are the laying on of hands on a person's head, most often by a bishop, and the anointing with oil. Like Baptism this sacrament is received only once.

Eucharist The Eucharist nourishes our life of faith. We receive the Body and Blood of Christ. Its signs are bread and wine. Through the power of the Holy Spirit, the priest consecrates the bread and wine, which becomes the Body and Blood of Christ. This is a sign of Jesus' Death for our Salvation.

102 *Unit 3 • The Public Life of Jesus*

IF TIME ALLOWS

Session 12 BLM
Sacramentals Word Search
Provide each young person with the Session 12 Blackline Master [T-366]. Ask young people to use the Blackline Master to better understand the use of sacramentals as an expression of our Catholic beliefs. Encourage them to point out the sacramentals used during the rites of the sacraments.

INCLUSION

Cognitive Differences

Connecting Concepts
Encourage young people to associate daily routines with frequent reception of the Eucharist. Have them list ordinary routines at home or school. Invite discussion of the Eucharist as a good routine to follow.

Sacraments of Healing

Penance and Reconciliation In this sacrament we receive forgiveness and Jesus' healing grace. Forgiveness requires being sorry for our sins. The signs of this sacrament are our confession of sins to a priest, a **penance** to perform, our **repentance,** or sorrow for sins, and the words of absolution.

Anointing of the Sick This sacrament unites a sick person's sufferings with those of Jesus'. Oil, a symbol of strength, is the sign of this sacrament. A person is anointed with oil and receives the laying on of hands from a priest. This sacrament is a source of grace, helping people who are seriously ill or who are elderly to grow in faith and to trust in God that they are not alone. If God wills, the anointed person may experience physical healing. Jesus Christ is present, healing the person in a fundamental way and sharing his victory over sin and death.

Sacraments at the Service of Communion

Matrimony In Matrimony a baptized man and woman are united with each other as a sign of the unity between Jesus and his Church. Matrimony requires consent, as expressed in the marriage promises. The couple is the sign of this sacrament.

Holy Orders In Holy Orders, men are ordained priests to be leaders of the community or deacons to be reminders of our baptismal call to serve others. The signs of this sacrament are the laying on of hands and the prayer by the bishop asking God for the outpouring of the Holy Spirit.

Those who receive the Sacraments at the Service of Communion carry out the Church's mission by committing themselves to the Salvation of others. Marriage partners help each other grow in holiness. Priests and deacons serve God's people. "[I]f they contribute as well to personal salvation, it is through service to others that they do so. . . . " (CCC 1534) Through their vocations, priests and married people give special witness to Christ's presence in the world.

In summary, God gave signs of his love by becoming one of us and giving us the Church as our home. All through our lives, he gives the special signs of his love that we call the seven sacraments.

Past Meets Present

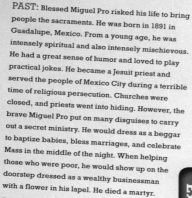

PAST: Blessed Miguel Pro risked his life to bring people the sacraments. He was born in 1891 in Guadalupe, Mexico. From a young age, he was intensely spiritual and also intensely mischievous. He had a great sense of humor and loved to play practical jokes. He became a Jesuit priest and served the people of Mexico City during a terrible time of religious persecution. Churches were closed, and priests went into hiding. However, the brave Miguel Pro put on many disguises to carry out a secret ministry. He would dress as a beggar to baptize babies, bless marriages, and celebrate Mass in the middle of the night. When helping those who were poor, he would show up on the doorstep dressed as a wealthy businessman with a flower in his lapel. He died a martyr.

PRESENT: Today Catholic missionaries often put their lives at risk to bring the sacraments and God's Word to people around the world. In its year-end report for 2011, the Congregation for the Evangelization of Peoples listed 26 pastoral workers killed. Those who sacrificed their lives included priests, women religious, and lay missionaries in Latin America, Africa, Asia, and Europe. At one time Pope John Paul II called missionaries who lost their lives "unknown soldiers, as it were, of God's great cause."

Explore

Study Corner

DEFINE

sacraments, rite, penance, repentance

REMEMBER

Sacraments are sacred rites that are signs of God's love and presence in our lives.

The seven sacraments were given to us by Jesus so that God's life and love can fill our lives.

Session 12 > Jesus Performs Signs **103**

TAKE IT HOME

Sacraments Game

Have young people make a board game that helps someone meet the sacraments. Their game may focus on a single sacrament or on all seven sacraments. Young people are responsible for conceptualizing the idea, although they may want to adapt their game to a known product. Explain that they will make and provide all parts required to play the game, such as a game board, directions, questions, game pieces, and so on. Some young people may prefer to develop an online game. Have young people explain and demonstrate to the group how to play their games. Following the demonstrations, allow time for the group to play them. Arrange to make the games accessible for future use.

Ask a volunteer to read Sacraments of Healing. Explain that these sacraments strengthen or restore us physically or spiritually and remind us of God's love and mercy. Through the Sacrament of Penance and Reconciliation, Christ acts through the priest to free us from the burden of sinfulness. Review the terms *penance* and *repentance* in the Glossary.

Ask volunteers to read aloud Matthew 18:21–35. Ask: *What is Jesus teaching?* (We are called to forgive others in the same way that the Father forgives us.) Discuss how forgiveness benefits not only the person being forgiven but also the one offering forgiveness. Ask: *How is it beneficial to offer forgiveness?* (Possible answer: It frees you from carrying a grudge.)

Explain that the Sacrament of the Anointing of the Sick used to be called *extreme unction*, meaning "last rites," but today it is not reserved solely for one's deathbed.

Read aloud Sacraments at the Service of Communion. Say: *Through commitment to others, people grow in holiness themselves.* Ask: *What does the union of marriage symbolize?* (unity between Jesus and the Church) Ask: *What does a priest's leadership represent?* (Christ at work in the Church community) Say: *All seven sacraments are Christ's actions in our lives.*

Past Meets Present

Read aloud the feature. Discuss traits needed to do Christ's work in the world, such as commitment, courage, and perseverance. Ask volunteers to describe times when they have acted as witnesses to their faith.

③ Close

Say: *The sacraments confer grace.* Invite young people to respond to the following with a partner or small group. Ask: *What is our responsibility to ensure the sacraments are fruitful in our lives?*

Prayer

Follow the steps to guide young people through the prayer on page 104.

Young People's Page

Prepare Pray the prayer in advance to become familiar with it.

Pray Read aloud the title of the page. Ask volunteers to read aloud the paragraphs in the left column. Remind young people that *lectio divina* is a special way to read the Word of God that involves four steps: listening to Scripture, meditating, praying, and contemplating. Say: **The prayer form lectio divina uses the repetition of Scripture verses to help the Word of God sink into our minds and hearts.**

Then have young people bring their books to the prayer space and sit quietly. Say: **Calm your mind, rest, and become aware of God's presence with us.** After a brief pause, slowly and prayerfully pray aloud the words of John 2:1–12. Say: **Let the words echo within you.** Then guide young people through the meditation step, prayerfully reading aloud the directions. Allow young people time to meditate. Ask: **What might God be saying to you?** Pause again.

Pray aloud the Scripture passage a second time and lead the second meditation, allowing time for young people to write their responses.

Pause briefly before leading young people through the invitation to pray and contemplate, allowing an appropriate amount of time. At the conclusion, say: **Sit quietly with God, beyond words and feelings.** Allow time for prayerful silence and then invite them to pray aloud the words of the closing prayer.

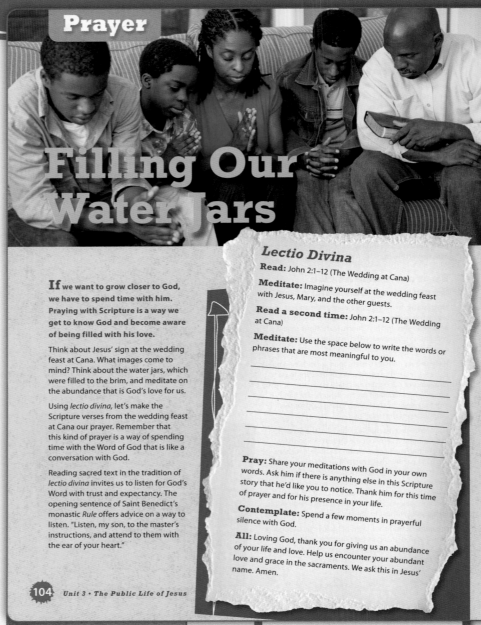

Prayer

Filling Our Water Jars

If we want to grow closer to God, we have to spend time with him. Praying with Scripture is a way we get to know God and become aware of being filled with his love.

Think about Jesus' sign at the wedding feast at Cana. What images come to mind? Think about the water jars, which were filled to the brim, and meditate on the abundance that is God's love for us.

Using *lectio divina*, let's make the Scripture verses from the wedding feast at Cana our prayer. Remember that this kind of prayer is a way of spending time with the Word of God that is like a conversation with God.

Reading sacred text in the tradition of *lectio divina* invites us to listen for God's Word with trust and expectancy. The opening sentence of Saint Benedict's monastic *Rule* offers advice on a way to listen. "Listen, my son, to the master's instructions, and attend to them with the ear of your heart."

104 *Unit 3 • The Public Life of Jesus*

Lectio Divina

Read: John 2:1–12 (The Wedding at Cana)

Meditate: Imagine yourself at the wedding feast with Jesus, Mary, and the other guests.

Read a second time: John 2:1–12 (The Wedding at Cana)

Meditate: Use the space below to write the words or phrases that are most meaningful to you.

_____

_____

_____

_____

_____

Pray: Share your meditations with God in your own words. Ask him if there is anything else in this Scripture story that he'd like you to notice. Thank him for this time of prayer and for his presence in your life.

Contemplate: Spend a few moments in prayerful silence with God.

All: Loving God, thank you for giving us an abundance of your life and love. Help us encounter your abundant love and grace in the sacraments. We ask this in Jesus' name. Amen.

IF TIME ALLOWS

Living Water Jar

Remind young people that Jesus did not simply provide more wine at Cana—he provided an abundance of wine. Say: **Think about times when you have done just enough to get by and when you have gone above and beyond the call of duty.** Draw a large water jar on mural paper and display it. Ask young people to write on slips of paper ways they can show love, mercy, or compassion in abundance. Have them tape their ideas to the water jar as reminders to commit themselves to Christlike actions.

FYI

Coaching Young People to Pray

Invite young people to visualize the image of a jar overflowing, and remind them that the water is God's love for them. Invite them to think about the many small ways their lives are blessed. Encourage young people to imagine themselves overflowing with God's abundant blessings.

WHERE Do I Fit In?

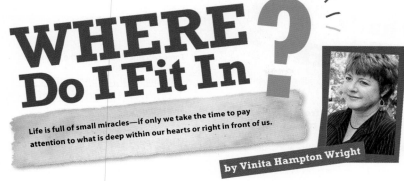

Life is full of small miracles—if only we take the time to pay attention to what is deep within our hearts or right in front of us.

by Vinita Hampton Wright

Miracles, Really

We don't know much about Jesus' life before the wedding feast at Cana. But it's interesting that his mother went right to him when a problem came up—as if she already knew he could perform a miracle. A person doesn't just suddenly develop a full-blown talent for miracles. You have to wonder: had Mary seen him develop as a miracle worker as he was growing up and discovering who he was? In the same way, we don't learn how to listen to the Holy Spirit in a few days or even a few years. The spiritual life is a daily thing, and as people who are part of God's miraculous family, we progress gradually, not all at once.

Since early childhood I was afraid of the dark—dark rooms, nighttime, any place where I couldn't see well. I was so embarrassed by my fear that I didn't talk about it to anyone until I was past 30 years old. One day I mentioned it to a friend, and we talked about patterns of fearful thinking that I had learned from people in my family. After that talk, I discovered that this fear had simply left me. It was a miracle! I wasn't paralyzed by fear of the dark anymore.

That "miracle" was part of a long process. I had spent a lot of time reflecting on my problem, praying for help, and developing a friendship with the person in whom I confided. Finally, I reached the point where I could admit to my friend, "I'm afraid of the dark." Then the miracle happened.

Jesus turned water into wine, performed healings, and multiplied food so that crowds could eat supper, be made whole, and be set free. Such miracles were evidence of his divine nature. It seems for us, though, that the miracles that matter most are the interior changes that bring us freedom—from fear, anger, sorrow, and alienation. Those miracles take place in us day by day as we pay attention to what's really going on, within us and around us. Then we bring God, and people who love us, into the conversation.

VINITA HAMPTON WRIGHT is the author of *Days of Deepening Friendship* and *Simple Acts of Moving Forward.*

Making Miracles Happen

Making a change for the better takes time, deeper spiritual awareness, and prayer. On the lines below, write the steps that the author took to overcome her fear of the dark. Then think of a "miracle" you'd like to happen in your own life. Write some steps you can take to make your miracle come true.

1. reflected on her problem
2. prayed for help
3. developed a friendship
4. admitted her fear to her friend

Making My Miracle Come True

1. _____
2. _____
3. _____
4. _____

Session 12 > Jesus Performs Signs 105

Reflect

IF TIME ALLOWS

Jar Full of Miracles

Suggest that calling a needed change to mind and imagining a solution is an important part of paying attention to possible ways we can shed burdens that prevent us from responding fully to God and others.

Bring an empty glass jar and marbles to class. Display the jar in a prominent place. Start to fill the "miracle jar" by offering a story of your own interior change. Describe the change you hoped to make and the steps you took until it happened. Then drop a marble into the jar. Invite young people to add a marble to the jar after telling their own story. If possible, keep the jar displayed throughout the year and allow young people to continue sharing their stories until the jar is full.

---

① Begin

Have a volunteer read aloud the introductory text. Say: ***There are many healings and events in the natural world described in the Scriptures and in Christian history that cannot be explained through human understanding. The events that support our faith can only be accounted for by the action of God in human history.*** Ask young people to discuss Jesus' miracles. Explain that when we see God's hand at work in the world, everyday objects and events take on added beauty.

② Connect

Have volunteers take turns reading aloud Miracles, Really. Invite young people to share their own experiences of miracles. Guide young people to trace the events leading up to the miracle. After discussing several examples, ask: ***How would you describe the difference between a miracle and plain old good luck?*** (Possible answer: A miracle brings you closer to God or to others or makes you a better version of yourself, while good luck merely increases your fortune, pleasure, or leisure.) Guide young people to reach consensus on a definition for a *miracle* and *good luck*, and then encourage them to keep the distinctions in mind as they complete the Making Miracles Happen activity independently.

③ Close

Point out that the word *miracle* comes from an Old French verb meaning "to look at." Encourage young people to practice looking at the world with "miracle eyes"—eyes that see God everywhere.

① Begin

What's What? Ask a volunteer to read aloud the directions. Encourage young people to work with a partner to locate supporting details for each main idea.

② Connect

Say What? Ask volunteers to read aloud and define the words. Review each word in the Glossary if necessary.

Now What? Ask a volunteer to read aloud the section. Encourage young people to think about the sacraments, sacramental rites, and their understanding of grace before they write their responses.

③ Go in Peace

Collect materials and return them to their appropriate places. Explain that receiving a sacrament is just the beginning of a faith journey. Say: **The sacraments are gifts, and God invites us to put them into action in our lives.** Invite young people to "unwrap" the gift of the sacrament they write about and use it. If they have yet to receive the sacrament, encourage them to imagine how they could use it in their lives in the future.

Minute Retreat
Give young people an opportunity for quiet meditation at **www.loyolapress.com/retreat**.

Respond

What's What?

Write a detail from the text that supports each main idea.

① Jesus' first sign took place at a wedding feast at Cana. (PAGE 100)

Possible answer: Jesus changes water into wine.

② Mary, the mother of Jesus, plays a significant role in Jesus' ministry. (PAGES 100–101)

Mary is a model of faith and trust in Jesus when she directs the servers to do whatever Jesus tells them.

③ In the Gospel of John, Jesus' signs reveal who Jesus is and who the Father is. (PAGES 100–101)

Jesus shows that he is the one who fulfills the Father's promise to humankind with abundance.

④ Signs and symbols from everyday life are used during sacramental rites. (PAGE 102)

Possible answer: The water used in Baptism expresses God's sanctifying presence.

⑤ The sacraments were instituted by Christ. (PAGE 102)

Jesus gave us each sacrament so that God's life and love could be part of our journey of faith.

⑥ Three sacraments are called the Sacraments of Initiation. (PAGE 103)

Baptism, Confirmation, and the Eucharist are the Sacraments of Initiation.

⑦ Two sacraments are called the Sacraments of Healing. (PAGE 103)

The Sacraments of Penance and Reconciliation and the Anointing of the Sick are the Sacraments of Healing.

⑧ Two sacraments are called the Sacraments at the Service of Communion. (PAGE 103)

Matrimony and Holy Orders are the Sacraments at the Service of Communion.

Say What?

Know the definitions of these terms.

penance	sacraments
repentance	signs
rite	

Now What?

Write key ideas about one particular sacrament. As you look forward to the days ahead, describe how the grace of this sacrament can help you follow Jesus more closely.

Answers will vary.

IF TIME ALLOWS

Service: Anti-Bullying Campaign

Remind young people of Jesus' initial response to Mary in John 2:4, "Woman, how does your concern affect me?" But Jesus didn't ignore the request—he stepped in, revealing God's glory. Point out that bullying peaks in middle school, and victims of cyberbullying [Internet, e-mails, text messaging, instant messages, or cell phones] can be harassed virtually 24 hours a day. Encourage young people to work with school or parish leaders to put an anti-bullying program into practice that makes a safe environment for all young people.

✝ *Rights and Responsibilities*

Session Assessment Option

An assessment for this session can be found at www.findinggod.com.

PLAN AHEAD: Get Ready for Session 13

Consult the catechist preparation pages to prepare for Session 13 and determine any materials you will need.

Jesus Is Our Teacher

 ### *3-Minute Retreat*

Before you prepare the session, pause and be still. Take three deep breaths and be aware of the loving presence of God, who is with you on this journey.

Matthew 5:23–24

"Therefore, if you bring your gift to the altar, and there recall that your brother has anything against you, leave your gift there at the altar, go first and be reconciled with your brother, and then come and offer your gift."

Reflection

You have probably heard the expression "first things first" many times. That's what Jesus is telling his listeners. He wants them, and us, to get our priorities straight. Worship and daily life are not separate from each other. When we truly separate worship from our daily lives, we risk becoming hypocrites, saying one thing and doing another. Jesus tells us to take care of broken relationships before offering our gifts to God. In this way, we can live according to the Kingdom of God described in the Beatitudes.

Questions

What steps can I take today to help bring my inner life into harmony with my outer life? With whom could I be reconciled before I leave my gift at the altar?

 #### Concluding Prayer

Speak to God, using the words of this prayer or your own.

Jesus, Prince of Peace, you call me to be reconciled with those with whom I am in conflict. Open my heart to show my love for you by the way I treat others.

Knowing and Sharing Your Faith in Session 13

Consider how Scripture and Tradition can deepen your understanding of session content.

Scripture

Matthew 5:3–10 reveals the Beatitudes, Jesus' description of the Kingdom of God.

Luke 15:3–7 helps us understand the importance of every person in the Kingdom of God with the parable of the shepherd and the 100 sheep.

Tradition

Matthew's Gospel places the Beatitudes at the heart of Jesus' Sermon on the Mount. They confront us with decisive moral choices. They invite us to purify our hearts and to seek the love of God above all else. The Beatitudes reveal the goal of human existence— God's invitation to share his own blessedness. They are addressed to each of us personally and also to the Church as a whole—the new people made up of those who accepted the promise and live in faith.

Catholic Social Teaching

In this session the integrated Catholic Social Teaching themes are **Life and Dignity of the Human Person** and **Call to Family, Community, and Participation.** See page 89b for an explanation of these themes.

Window on the Catechism

The Beatitudes are discussed in *CCC* 1716–1724.

General Directory for Catechesis

The Beatitudes as a message of liberation are discussed in *GDC* 103 and 104.

One-Hour Session Planner

SESSION 13 Jesus Is Our Teacher

Session Theme: *In the Beatitudes, Jesus invites everyone to happiness in this life and eternal joy in the next.*

Before This Session

▶ Display the *Finding God* poster The Beatitudes.

▶ Bookmark your Bible to Matthew 5:3–10, Matthew 5:23–24, Matthew 6:32, Matthew 13:18–23, Matthew 13:24–30, Matthew 13:31–33, Matthew 13:36–43, Matthew 13:44–50, Matthew 23:27, John 14:6, Luke 8:10, Luke 15:3–7, Luke 17:21, Mark 4:30–32, and 1 Corinthians 2:6–16. Place the open Bible in your prayer space.

▶ Read the Guide for this session, choose any additional If Time Allows activities that you might have time to complete, and gather the listed materials.

 Prayer in Session 13

Pray the short opening prayer at the start of the session. Encourage young people to access an online 3-Minute Retreat at the end of the session. Session 13 includes an extended guided reflection, giving young people a special experience in meditative prayer. Follow the Prepare directions on the Catechist Guide page before sharing with young people.

STEPS	APPROXIMATE TIME
Engage *Jesus Is Our Teacher* PAGE 107	10 minutes
Explore *Sermon on the Mount* PAGES 108–109 *The Kingdom of God* PAGES 110–111	30–40 minutes
Reflect *Prayer:* 20/20 Vision PAGE 112 *Where Do I Fit In?* PAGE 113	10–15 minutes
Respond *What's What?* PAGE 114	10–15 minutes

TAKE IT HOME

Homework options:

Take a Poll	PAGE 109
Kingdom of Heaven	PAGE 111

Materials

REQUIRED

▶ Large photo of a lighthouse (page 108)

▶ *Finding God* poster: The Beatitudes. (page 108)

▶ Writing supplies, art supplies (page 109)

▶ Bibles (pages 110, 111)

▶ CD player (page 112)

▶ CD 1, Track 5: "Paying the Price" (14:00) (page 112)

▶ Construction paper, art supplies (page 113)

▶ Computers with Internet access (page 114)

OPTIONAL

▶ Newspapers, magazines (page 107)

▶ Art supplies, photos (page 108)

▶ Bibles (page 110)

▶ Session 13 BLM, T-367 (page 112)

▶ Writing supplies (page 113)

▶ Paint, painting supplies (page 114)

▶ Session 13 Assessment, www.findinggod.com (page 114)

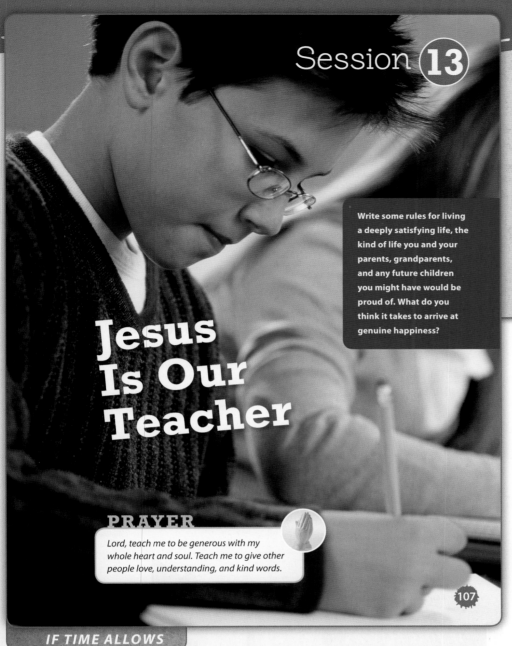

Session **13**

Write some rules for living a deeply satisfying life, the kind of life you and your parents, grandparents, and any future children you might have would be proud of. What do you think it takes to arrive at genuine happiness?

Jesus Is Our Teacher

PRAYER

Lord, teach me to be generous with my whole heart and soul. Teach me to give other people love, understanding, and kind words.

107

IF TIME ALLOWS

Happiness Rules

Be aware that young people will need guidance to reflect more deeply about the concept of true happiness. Explain that our culture often supports values that run contrary to Jesus' teachings. Organize young people into small groups and distribute copies of newspapers and magazines. Invite groups to find stories and pictures that deal with the topic of happiness. Tell them to be ready to discuss whether their examples illustrate true happiness or reflect the shallow values or popular culture. Use the whole-group discussion as an opportunity to spark gentle debate, encouraging respect for all ideas while providing guidance that supports moral character, strong values, and Catholic Social Teaching.

Go to **www.findinggod.com/sessionextenders** for an article about social justice. You may wish to share this with the group.

► Explain how the Ten Commandments and the Beatitudes tell us how to live the way God wants us to live.

► Explain how Jesus invites everyone into the Kingdom of God.

► Pray to follow the Beatitudes as a way to follow the will of God.

► Define *Beatitudes, Kingdom of God, Kingdom of Heaven, Magisterium,* and *Sermon on the Mount.*

① Set the Stage

Read aloud the text in the box. Give young people time to reflect and discuss their responses with a partner.

② Get Started

Write on the board examples of rules commonly found at home, at school, in sports, in a board game, and in the community. Ask: *How do you feel about rules? How do they make life better? When can they become intrusive?* (Answers will vary.) Ask: *What is their purpose?* (Possible answers: to establish order, to achieve goals, to provide safety) Say: *Most rules help us conduct our outer lives.* Ask: *What rules help us conduct our inner lives?* (Possible answers: the Ten Commandments, the Greatest Commandment, the Beatitudes)

Have a volunteer read aloud the session title. Ask: *How might the idea of rules and the session title be related?* (Possible answer: Jesus, the master teacher, gave humankind rules so people could gain Salvation.)

 Prayer

Ask: *Let's pray together, remembering that Jesus invites us to dream about and build a better world.* Pray aloud the prayer. Conclude by praying the Sign of the Cross.

① Begin

Display a large photo of a lighthouse and have a volunteer explain its purpose. Ask: **Why is a lighthouse set up high?** (so its light can be seen from far away) Say: **A lighthouse guides a ship to safety. It doesn't steer or take over the ship; it simply gives light to guide its safe passage.** Have a volunteer read the article title. Say: **Throughout the ages, God continues to provide light and guidance for humankind.**

② Connect

Have a volunteer read aloud the introductory paragraphs. Ask: **How is Jesus the new Moses?** (He taught a new way to live.) Say: **Jesus is like the lighthouse. He gives the light that guides, but it is up to us to respond.** Discuss the terms, using the Glossary as needed.

Display the *Finding God* poster The Beatitudes. Read aloud The Beatitudes. Say: **The Beatitudes answer, "How can I be happy?"** Help young people understand the "blessed" in each beatitude by relating Christian attitudes. For example, *poor in spirit*—showing gratitude, remembering that everything you have comes from God; *those who mourn*—sharing in others' pain, turning to God for help; *the meek*—being kind or suffering for love of others. Do the same thing for the remaining "blessed" descriptions.

Point out that Matthew's version of the Beatitudes differs from Luke's. Encourage young people to read more about the Gospel of Matthew on pages 259–260 in Prayers and Practices.

Our Catholic Character

Read aloud the feature. Discuss the just war doctrine. Ask: **What is the meaning of the phrase, "If you want peace, work for justice"?**

✝ *Life and Dignity*

Sermon on the Mount

WHEN Moses encountered God on Mount Sinai, he received the Ten Commandments, a covenant of faith between God and the Israelites.

Matthew shows Jesus as the new Moses, the divine teacher of a new way to live. Similar to Moses, Jesus went up a mountain. We call Jesus' instructions the **Sermon on the Mount.** The centerpiece of Jesus' teaching in Matthew 5:3–10 has become known as the **Beatitudes,** eight guidelines for Christlike living that lead to happiness in this life and eternal joy in the next. The Beatitudes describe life the way it is lived in the **Kingdom of God,** on earth as it is in Heaven.

Sermon on the Mount, Laura James, 2010.

Our Catholic Character

In the *Pastoral Constitution on the Church in the Modern World* in 1965, the bishops called the accumulation of nuclear weapons "one of the greatest curses on the human race." An arms race at the cost of helping the poor is an injustice that leads to excessive economic or social inequalities.

The just war doctrine outlines four conditions that must be met for a war to be considered just:

* The damage inflicted by the aggressor must be very serious.

* All ways to end the violence must have been shown not to work.

* A genuine chance of ending the violence through war must be indicated.

* The use of war must not produce evils and disorders worse than the evil that caused it.

The Church reminds us that even in a just war, combatants must follow the moral law. Acting in ways contrary to the law of nations is a crime.

The Beatitudes

Blessed are the poor in spirit,
    for theirs is the kingdom of heaven.
Blessed are they who mourn,
    for they will be comforted.
Blessed are the meek,
    for they will inherit the land.
Blessed are they who hunger and thirst
    for righteousness,
    for they will be satisfied.
Blessed are the merciful,
    for they will be shown mercy.
Blessed are the clean of heart,
    for they will see God.
Blessed are the peacemakers,
    for they will be called children of God.
Blessed are they who are persecuted
    for the sake of righteousness,
    for theirs is the kingdom of heaven.

Matthew 5:3–10

108 *Unit 3 • The Public Life of Jesus*

IF TIME ALLOWS

Wanted: Beatitude People

Have young people choose a person from the past or present who exemplifies the Christian attitudes taught in the Beatitudes. Have them make and decorate a wanted poster like the kind that was common in the American West in the 1800s, except their posters are seeking good guys, not bad guys. [Leave off the "dead or alive" wording]. Encourage young people to include a photo or illustration of the person and information telling why or how the person lives or lived according to the values of Jesus. For example—*Wanted: Martin Luther King Jr. for hungering and thirsting for righteousness. Reward: Priceless.* Display the posters in class.

INCLUSION

Cognitive

Living the Beatitudes If you have young people with cognitive differences, write the key Beatitude descriptors [e.g. *poor in spirit*] on the board. Brainstorm examples of people who live according to each Christian attitude. Write their ideas on the board.

The Kingdom of God

The eight Beatitudes describe the "blessed" as those who meet the challenge of living according to the values of Jesus. Living the Beatitudes helps us enter the **Kingdom of Heaven,** Matthew's term for the Kingdom of God. The Beatitudes are easily misunderstood. "Blessed are those who mourn" does not mean that Jesus wants you to suffer, but he does want you to comfort others during mournful times, just as he comforts you. The Beatitudes are not easy to accept. "Blessed are the poor in spirit" challenges you to detach yourself from craving wealth and comfort. Instead of watching out for your own good, the Beatitudes encourage you to be concerned for justice and to look out for the good of others. It takes courage to live the Beatitudes. It is not easy to be a peacemaker or to be merciful to those considered enemies. The Beatitudes challenge you to live in ways that society often discourages.

The Kingdom of God is the gathering by Jesus of those on earth who begin to live the divine life the Father calls us to live. The more you live the Beatitudes, the closer you come to the Kingdom of God. God intends us to be part of his Kingdom right now. The happiness promised to us in the Beatitudes asks us to make difficult moral choices, but the reward is eternal happiness with God.

The Commandments and the Beatitudes

Both the Ten Commandments, also called the Decalogue, and the Beatitudes are directives on how to live the life that God wants us to live. Like the Ten Commandments, the Beatitudes place great value on human life, the purity of spirit, and on respectful, loving relationships among people. Both offer the wisdom to live a good life in relationship with God and others.

But there are differences. Whereas Moses gave the instruction he received from God, Jesus spoke with his own authority as the Son of God. While Moses held up the two tablets of the Law as ideals of life, Jesus embodied the ideal. Jesus lived the ideal. "I am the way and the truth and the life. No one comes to the Father except through me." (John 14:6) While Moses was a messenger, Jesus was the message.

The Ten Commandments give God's law while the Beatitudes are reflections of attitudes and actions characteristic of Christian life. The Ten Commandments are concerned with what we shall and shall not do while the Beatitudes are concerned with what it takes to live a blessed life. The Beatitudes do not replace the Ten Commandments, nor are they "better." Both are necessary to understand the life to which God calls us.

The Ten Commandments and the Beatitudes each point the way to wisdom, peace, and eternal life. They represent two signposts, each beginning in God, and each leading to the same destination: sharing eternal life with God.

The Beatitudes

Choose a beatitude, and explain to a partner how you can live it in today's world. Draw a symbol to represent the beatitude, using the space below or another sheet of paper, and explain your idea.

Explore

Study Corner

DEFINE
Sermon on the Mount
Beatitudes
Kingdom of God
Kingdom of Heaven

REMEMBER
The Beatitudes are the centerpiece of Jesus' Sermon on the Mount. The Beatitudes describe the Kingdom of God.

Session 13 > Jesus Is Our Teacher   **109**

TAKE IT HOME

Take a Poll

Ask young people to survey at least 10 people, including group members, family members, parishioners, and members of the community, asking the following question: *What is the biggest issue that needs to be solved in the world today?*

If a camcorder is available, young people may want to make a video of the responses. Other alternatives include using voice recorders, or they may write responses on paper. Ask young people to present the results of their polls. Then help them associate the results of the surveys to particular beatitudes.

Have volunteers read the section The Kingdom of God. As a group, discuss reasons why the Beatitudes are often misunderstood and why they can be hard to follow. (Answers will vary.) Discuss the meaning of the word *Kingdom of Heaven*, using the Glossary if needed.

Ask young people to read The Commandments and the Beatitudes. Ask: *What is another name for the Ten Commandments?* (Decalogue) Ask: *How are the Beatitudes and the Ten Commandments alike?* (They show how to live in relationship with God and others.) Say: *Obeying God's laws is not piling up good deeds so that God will be impressed and think well of you. He already loves you immeasurably.* Explain that we try to follow the Ten Commandments and the Beatitudes as ways to respond to that abundant love. Say: *These rules from God are a gift, not a dreary task, and they are worthy of a joyful response.*

Ask: *What kinds of things might Jesus challenge today?* (Possible answers: false cultural values, greed, war, racism) Explain that the word *hypocrite* comes from a Greek word meaning "stage actor, pretender." Say: *Jesus often pointed out hypocrites. We live in a different time from Jesus but can see the need to challenge "actors" and "pretenders" in society today who promote teachings that run contrary to the Kingdom of God.*

Read the directions for The Beatitudes activity and have young people complete it independently. Ask volunteers to display and explain their symbols to the group.

(3) Close

Ask: *Why does it take courage to live the Beatitudes?* Invite open discussion, encouraging young people to express their views freely while showing respect for others' opinions.

① Begin

Demonstrate the complexity of explaining difficult ideas by giving the following directions for raising a mainsail on a sailboat. Ask two volunteers to pantomime the actions. Say: *Attach the halyard and sheet. Put the main halyard on a winch. Open jammers. Turn into the wind. Have one person sweat the halyard while another takes in the slack on the winch. Insert a winch handle and crank. Cleat the halyard.* Say: *Unlike this technical language, Jesus used familiar associations that spoke to people's hearts when he taught about the Kingdom of God.*

② Connect

Have a volunteer read the title and first two paragraphs. Ask: *How do parables help us understand Jesus' Word?* (They help us compare divine reality to ordinary experiences.) Ask a volunteer to read aloud Matthew 13:31–33. Ask: *What words does Jesus begin with?* ("The kingdom of heaven is like . . .") *To what does he compare the kingdom?* (a mustard seed and yeast)

Read aloud the section The Mustard Seed. Discuss the emphasis on small beginnings that produce abundant results. Say: *The Kingdom of God that Jesus spoke about is meant to be understood as our present and our future. When we pray the Lord's Prayer, we pray "thy kingdom come," but Jesus' parables alert us to the presence of God's kingdom right now.* Continue a discussion about the present kingdom by reading Luke 17:21, when Jesus tells the Pharisees, "The kingdom of God is among you."

Sacred Art

Have volunteers read aloud the feature. Discuss how we know that each one of us is precious to God. Invite a volunteer to read aloud Luke 15:3–7.

The Kingdom of God

COMMUNICATING an

unfamiliar idea or experience can be difficult. Jesus brought important meaning to his lessons by helping his listeners understand big ideas.

Jesus knew the value of comparisons when describing the Kingdom of God, which is God's rule of love, justice, and peace in our hearts and in the world. Jesus spoke in parables—stories that compare an ordinary, everyday experience with a reality of God's truth. Jesus compared the Kingdom of God to ordinary objects such as a grain of wheat, a mustard seed, yeast, wheat and weeds, treasure, pearls, and a net cast into the sea.

The Mustard Seed

Jesus invited everyone into the Kingdom of God. The key to the Kingdom of God is acceptance of Jesus' Word. Jesus' audience had firsthand experience with farming, fishing, and making bread, so Jesus used language and analogies drawn from their daily lives. Jesus used ordinary objects and ideas to help people understand what it meant to belong to the Kingdom.

Mark 4:30–32 relates Jesus' parable of the mustard seed. "To what shall we compare the kingdom of God, or what parable can we use for it? It is like a mustard seed that, when it is sown in the ground, is the smallest of all the seeds on the earth. But once it is sown, it springs up and becomes the largest of plants and puts forth large branches, so that the birds of the sky can dwell in its shade." Through this parable, Jesus teaches that our faith takes root in small ways. God's grace grows and reaches far beyond what we are capable of doing on our own. It also teaches that our small, kind deeds in everyday life further the Kingdom of God. The kingdom shelters everyone and grows surprisingly beyond its small beginnings.

SACRED ART

Philippe de Champaigne, born in Brussels, painted in the Baroque style. Baroque art is a term that describes an artistic style that originated in Rome at the beginning of the 17th century. Baroque style reflects a preference for pictorial clarity and narrative relevance in religious art. Jesus is often shown as a shepherd because of his care for God's people. In Philippe de Champaigne's painting, Jesus is carrying the stray sheep he has found. Jesus, the Good Shepherd who proclaims the Kingdom of God, cares for every need.

The Good Shepherd, Philippe de Champaigne, ca. 1650–1660.

ADVENTURES IN FAITH

You Are the Kingdom

 Remind young people that they enter the Kingdom of God by living the way of the Beatitudes. God wants them to be part of the kingdom in the present. The Beatitudes are challenges to live with courage in a way that brings their inner and outer lives into balance. Explain that when they say one thing and live another, they become like the hypocrites that Jesus criticized so readily. "You are like white-washed tombs, which appear beautiful on the outside, but inside are full of dead men's bones and every kind of filth." [Matthew 23:27]

Have young people read Matthew 5:23–24. Discuss how Jesus is telling them to forgive and mend broken relationships before they offer gifts to God. Tell young people that they can live their faith by applying this principle to their lives. Invite them to identify someone with whom they need to be reconciled. Then encourage them to take steps to mend this relationship. After time has passed, invite volunteers to share their reconciliation stories in small groups.

The Lost Sheep

Jesus made it clear that every person is important in the Kingdom of God. In Luke 15:3–7, Jesus tells the parable of a shepherd who had 100 sheep. When one strayed, the shepherd left behind 99 sheep to look for the one that was lost. When the lost sheep was found, the shepherd asked his friends to share with him in his joy. Jesus said, "I tell you, in just the same way there will be more joy in heaven over one sinner who repents than over ninety-nine righteous people who have no need of repentance." (Luke 15:7)

The Kingdom Is Now

So, what is the Kingdom of God? It's not a geographical place like the kingdoms of earthly kings. It is the reality that occurs when God's will is done on earth as it is in Heaven. Taking Jesus' teachings to heart leads to action and change.

Jesus' parables teach that the Kingdom of God is among us. Parables challenge us to think in new ways. We wonder how the Kingdom of God really is like a wedding feast or a hidden treasure. We reflect on the nature of the tiny mustard seed and better understand what Jesus is saying about faith and small beginnings. While worldly kingdoms fade away, the values of the Kingdom of God are timeless.

Taking Jesus' words to heart, particularly the Beatitudes, can help you come to know more deeply the Kingdom of God. Living the words and putting their values into actions in daily life brings you closer to the kingdom. Jesus teaches that we do not have to wait until we die to enter the kingdom. He wants us to build the kingdom here and now.

If Only . . .

Our ability to imagine enables us to think about how things could be better for us, our community, or our world. You might think "If only there was no war . . ." "If only I hadn't lost my temper . . ." or "If only my teacher understood me better . . ." Paul tells us to put on "the mind of Christ." (1 Corinthians 2:16) Then our imagination can move us past how things are to how things could be. Our imagination is a gift from God and a tool for our enjoyment, but it is also for our growth in holiness. Our imagination, combined with Jesus' guidance and God's laws, can help us build the Kingdom of God as Jesus intended.

Past Meets Present

PAST: Jesus taught and prepared his disciples to lead his Church. He gave explanations and answered the Apostles' questions. "He answered, 'Knowledge of the mysteries of the kingdom of God has been granted to you; but to the rest, they are made known through parables so that they may look but not see, and hear but not understand.'" (Luke 8:10) With understanding, the Apostles were able to pass down Jesus' teachings to us.

PRESENT: The **Magisterium** is the office of the pope and bishops in communion with him, who are the authoritative teachers in the Church. The pope, who is the successor of Peter, joins with the assembly of bishops from all over the world, called the college of bishops, to govern the whole Church. Acting in the name of Christ, the Magisterium has full authority to preach the Catholic faith, which is to be believed and applied to moral life.

Explore

Study Corner

DEFINE

Magisterium

REMEMBER

Jesus invited everyone into the Kingdom of God.

The Kingdom of God begins here and now when we respond to God's love by loving him and others.

Jesus taught by using parables.

SOME YIELDED FRUIT

Session 13 > Jesus Is Our Teacher **111**

TAKE IT HOME

Kingdom of Heaven

Write on the board the words from Matthew's Gospel: *The kingdom of heaven is like . . .* Ask young people to complete the simile by thinking of ordinary objects that people would recognize in today's world. Encourage comparisons that reflect the true meaning of the Kingdom of God. Have them add their reasoning in a sentence or two. For example, "The kingdom of heaven is like a global positioning system [GPS]. Living the values of the kingdom guides me to my destination." Have them make and decorate Kingdom of Heaven banners to display around the room.

Read aloud The Lost Sheep. Ask: **How is a repentant sinner like a lost sheep?** (God joyously welcomes the return of the sinner.)

Read aloud The Kingdom Is Now. Ask volunteers to take turns reading aloud the parable of the sower in Matthew 13:18–23; the parable of the weeds among wheat in Matthew 13:24–30; the parable of the weeds in Matthew 13:36–43; and Jesus' comparisons of the Kingdom of God to buried treasure, fine pearls, and a fishing net in Matthew 13:44–50. Say: **Jesus invites us to live his Word today, even in the small way of the mustard seed, yeast, or hidden treasure.**

Ask a volunteer to read aloud the section If Only . . . Read aloud and discuss Paul's letter in 1 Corinthians 2:6–16. Explain that Jesus' teaching about the Kingdom of God is important in the Gospels. Point out that Matthew, writing to a Jewish audience, uses the term *Kingdom of Heaven* 32 times. Mark and Luke use the term *Kingdom of God*, and John uses the term *eternal life* in place of the word *kingdom*. Ask: **Why is it so hard for some people to imagine the Kingdom of God?** (Answers will vary.) Ask: **Why did Jesus remind the disciples that they would have to become more like children to enter the Kingdom of God?** (Possible answers: Children are open, innocent, and guileless. They ask for help.)

Past Meets Present

Read aloud the feature. Discuss the role of teaching in the formation of our faith. Use the Glossary to discuss the term *Magisterium*.

(3) Close

In light of Jesus' instruction to be like children, ask: **What is the difference between a childlike attitude and a childish attitude?** (*Childlike* implies innocence. *Childish* implies immaturity.)

Prayer

Choose an approach and pray with young people.

Guided Reflection

 Prepare Listen in advance to the recorded guided reflection "Paying the Price" [CD 1, Track 5]. Decide if you will play the recording or pray aloud the reflection yourself. If you choose to lead, listen to the recording a second time, following the script [pages T-343–T-344] and noting pauses and tone. You can then follow the script exactly or adapt it as you wish.

Pray During the session, have volunteers read aloud the paragraphs in the left column. Discuss ways to see people the way God wants us to see them. Either play the recording or pray aloud using the script, joining young people in meditative prayer. If you pray aloud the script, play reflective music softly in the background [CD 1, Track 7].

Young People's Page

Prepare Pray the prayer in advance to become familiar with it.

Pray Have volunteers read aloud the title and paragraphs in the left column. Invite young people to the prayer space. Assign readers for Side 1 and Side 2. Invite young people to quiet their minds. When you are ready to begin, slowly pray aloud the Leader part. Pause and invite young people to pray aloud reverently the All section. Pause. Have the Side 1 and Side 2 readers pray aloud their sections. Pray the next Leader part, and after a brief pause, invite everyone to pray aloud the All section.

Prayer

20/20 Vision

Seeing as God Sees

When Jesus gave us the Beatitudes, he showed us how to see with different eyes.

When we understand the values of the Beatitudes and translate them into action, the love of God illuminates the world. In this way we help build the Kingdom of God today on earth.

In the Beatitudes, Jesus teaches us to respect other people and to treat their lives as sacred. Jesus teaches us to love our enemies. Following the Beatitudes is a way to follow the will of God.

The Beatitudes teach us how to give. Instead of depleting us, we become richer. Matthew 6:32 assures us that the Father knows what we need before we ask him. God answers prayers, and if we ask, it will be given to us; if we seek, we will find; and if we knock, the door will be opened for us. As parents care and provide for their children's needs, so God the Father will provide for us and give good things to us if we ask.

Leader: God made us in his own image and likeness. It can be easy to think about ourselves or those we love as made in God's image. But what about other people? Sometimes we have to search for that likeness to God. We need a different kind of vision to help us see beyond the surface so that we can begin building the Kingdom of God right here, right now.

Let us pray together.

All: God of All Creation, each of us is created in your image and likeness. We are a reflection of you that the world needs to see. We want to show others your face and to see you clearly in our brothers and sisters.

Side 1: Jesus, Light of the World, you are always with us to guide us. Sometimes our vision gets blurred by values that are different from the ones you teach us. We need courage to revere and respect your divine life in all creation. We want to let our light shine.

Side 2: Spirit of Life, you live in us and remind us that we are never alone. When we have difficult choices to make, send your light and truth to guide us. May your wisdom lead us to love others as the Father loves them. We want others to see your life in us. Help us see the divine life in others.

Leader: Let us pray the following blessing with and for one another and remember how important it is to support one another in living our life of faith.

All: May God bless you and be with you. May the holiness of God shine forth from you. May God grant you the vision to see his divine life in everyone you meet. Amen.

112 · *Unit 3 • The Public Life of Jesus*

Pray Again

If you used the recorded guided reflection, you might conclude the session by praying the Sign of the Cross.

Session 13 BLM

Entering the Kingdom of God
Provide each young person with the Session 13 Blackline Master [T-367]. Ask them to use the Blackline Master to help them better understand qualities to incorporate into their everyday lives as Christians as they wait for the fulfillment of the Kingdom of God.

Coaching Young People to Pray

Before praying, invite young people to ponder God's limitless generosity. Remind them that they can live the Kingdom of God in the present world if they trust in his love and care.

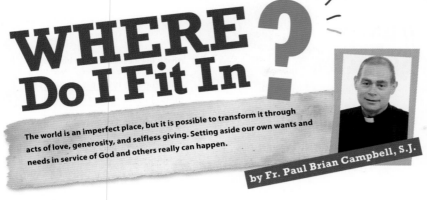

WHERE Do I Fit In?

The world is an imperfect place, but it is possible to transform it through acts of love, generosity, and selfless giving. Setting aside our own wants and needs in service of God and others really can happen.

by Fr. Paul Brian Campbell, S.J.

Reflect

The Kingdom of God Is Like . . .

I was lucky enough to study in Paris for a couple of years. As my time there was ending, someone suggested that I should go and visit Lourdes in southwestern France. I knew that about 150 years ago, Our Lady appeared to Saint Bernadette at Lourdes and pointed her to a spring of healing water.

Over the years, many miracles are said to have occurred, but I was less than eager to visit. Friends had told me it was a total tourist trap, full of cheap souvenir stores and over-the-top pilgrims. It didn't sound like a good time could be had there. In the end, however, I decided to go and see it for myself.

The town was just as cheap and touristy as I had been told, with endless rows of stalls selling plastic statues, gaudy rosary beads, and all sorts of religious souvenirs. It made my flesh crawl, and I was reminded of Jesus throwing the money changers out of the Temple in Jerusalem.

What I was not prepared for, however, was the profound atmosphere of serenity and loveliness I witnessed the moment I entered the Shrine. It took me a little time to understand what was happening, but I slowly came to recognize that in this place the Reign of God was being made visible. Inside the Shrine, those who were sick, poor, and vulnerable took priority, and everyone cared for them. It was a place especially for them, and God was very present. Hundreds of volunteers, including lots of teenagers,

assisted those who were sick with a tenderness and joy that made them shine. It was such a holy place that everyone seemed to radiate peace and serenity. It is how every place on earth should be all the time.

It was a rare privilege to witness such goodness, and it is definitely the closest I've ever been to the Reign of God. I came away from Lourdes a better person or, at least, much less cynical than before.

Building the Kingdom

What can we do to build places of grace in our homes, communities, and world? Write your ideas on separate rectangles of construction paper. Cut out these "bricks." As a group, assemble and tape the bricks in the form of a structure on mural paper.

- Donate my allowance to charity.
- Volunteer time at the animal shelter.
- Participate in park cleanup.
- Help an elderly neighbor.

FR. PAUL BRIAN CAMPBELL, S.J., is a Jesuit priest and the Publisher at Loyola Press in Chicago, Illinois.

Session 13 > Jesus Is Our Teacher **113**

IF TIME ALLOWS

So, What *Is* It Like?

Remind young people that a simile uses the word *like* or *as* to compare two different things that have something in common. For example, "The feather drifted to the ground like an autumn leaf." Next, arrange young people in groups, and have them brainstorm images to complete the simile "The Kingdom of God is like . . ." Instruct groups to come up with at least five creative comparisons between the Kingdom of God and everyday events or experiences. As groups present their similes, challenge them to name the shared quality or qualities on which each simile rests.

① Begin

Ask young people to describe a barn using all their senses. Say: **Barns are sometimes unpleasant or messy. But God chose to be born as man in a stable.** Ask: **What does this tell us about the unpleasant places in our own world?** (God dwells in those places.) Invite a young person to read aloud the introductory text. Say: **God's work often begins with an invitation to go where we'd rather not.** Read aloud the title of the article. Point out that the title is formatted as a simile. The Kingdom of God is going to be compared to the ideas within the article.

② Connect

Have volunteers take turns reading aloud the article. Ask: **Did the story end the way you expected it to? Why or why not?** (Answers will vary.) Then ask whether young people have had similar experiences at religious sites that are popular with tourists, and if so, to describe them. Ask: **What brings God's presence to such places, regardless of the noise, greed, and tacky souvenirs that are sometimes present?** (Possible answers: the faith of the people who visit; the willingness of God to love us, despite our flaws) Have young people complete the Building the Kingdom activity. When each person has completed at least one paper brick, ask the group to work together to shape them into a structure.

③ Close

Invite young people to choose one of the paper bricks from their structure that draws their attention most strongly. Have them resolve to bring that brick to life in the coming days or weeks.

1 Begin

What's What? Read aloud the directions. Encourage young people to work in small groups to answer each question.

2 Connect

Say What? Ask volunteers to read aloud and define the terms. Review each term in the Glossary if necessary.

Now What? Ask a volunteer to read aloud the section. Give time for reflection. Invite each young person to answer the question independently.

3 Go in Peace

Collect materials and return them to their appropriate places. Invite young people to follow through with their Now What? idea during the week. Say: *Sometimes the best way to form a good habit is to practice and apply it in a small way. Choose a small way to live out the spirit of the beatitude you chose. Challenge yourselves to build on your actions as you do more and more to welcome the Kingdom of God.*

3-Minute Retreat
Give young people an opportunity for quiet meditation at **www.loyolapress.com/retreat**.

Respond

What's What?

Answer each question, using details from the text.

1 What is the centerpiece of Jesus' teaching on the Sermon on the Mount? (PAGE 108)
the Beatitudes

2 What do the Beatitudes describe? (PAGE 108)
life the way it is lived in the Kingdom of God, on earth as it is in Heaven

3 What do the Beatitudes value? (PAGES 108–109)
Possible answers: human life, purity of spirit, loving relationships, compassion, mercy, and peace

4 Why do we follow both the Beatitudes and the Ten Commandments? (PAGE 109)
Both are necessary to understand the life to which God calls us.

5 How did Jesus explain the Kingdom of God? (PAGE 110)
He taught with parables.

6 To what does Jesus compare the Kingdom of God? (PAGE 110)
a grain of wheat, a mustard seed, yeast, wheat and weeds, treasure, pearls, and a net cast into the sea

7 What is the meaning of the parable of the shepherd and the lost sheep? (PAGE 111)
The kingdom is for everyone, even sinners. God rejoices over each person who repents.

8 How do the Beatitudes ask you to live the Kingdom of God right now? (PAGE 111)
Jesus invites you to take action and live the values that reflect his love in the world.

Say What?

Know the definitions of these terms:

Beatitudes
Kingdom of God
Kingdom of Heaven

Magisterium
Sermon on the Mount

Now What?

What can you do to welcome the Kingdom of God in the coming week? Reread the Beatitudes and notice which one speaks to you most. Imagine Jesus speaking it directly to you. Think of one thing you can do in your life this week to live out the spirit of that beatitude.

Answers will vary.

114   Unit 3 • The Public Life of Jesus

IF TIME ALLOWS

Service: Murals of Love

Explain that building community spirit is one way to show our love for the world. Accompany the group on a walk in the business district of your community and around the school grounds. Ask volunteers to work with city officials or school administrators to plan and paint a mural on a designated wall as a beautification project. Invite young people to develop inspiring artwork suggestions. Encourage interested parents or local artists to join in planning. Upon approval, help volunteers organize painting teams and adult supervision.

✝ *Family and Community*

Session Assessment Option

An assessment for this session can be found at www.findinggod.com.

PLAN AHEAD: Get Ready for Session 14

Consult the catechist preparation pages to prepare for Session 14 and determine any materials you will need.

Jesus Heals and Forgives

3-Minute Retreat

Before you prepare the session, pause and be still. Take three deep breaths and be aware of the loving presence of God, who is with you on this journey.

Mark 2:9–12

"Which is easier, to say to the paralytic, 'Your sins are forgiven,' or to say, 'Rise, pick up your mat and walk'? But that you may know that the Son of Man has authority to forgive sins on earth"—he said to the paralytic, "I say to you, rise, pick up your mat, and go home." He rose, picked up his mat at once, and went away in the sight of everyone. They were all astounded and glorified God, saying, "We have never seen anything like this."

Reflection

Everyone listening to Jesus that day knew that only God had the authority to forgive sins. Suspicion and judgment filled their minds and hearts. Who was this man? Jesus not only healed the man physically, but he forgave his sins. The man left healed in both mind and heart. His faith and trust, and that of his friends, led to his personal healing. When we approach Jesus in faith, we give him the opportunity to surprise us with so much more.

Questions

Is there something about me that I desire to ask Jesus to hear and heal? When have I encountered God's forgiveness? How did that experience change me?

 Concluding Prayer

Speak to God, using the words of this prayer or your own.

Jesus, you forgave the sins of the man who was paralyzed, and all who saw glorified God. Grant me the grace to give glory to you by witnessing to your forgiving love.

Knowing and Sharing Your Faith in Session 14

Consider how Scripture and Tradition can deepen your understanding of session content.

Scripture

Matthew 18:22 makes clear Jesus' central message of forgiveness throughout his ministry.

James 5:14–15 tells us about Jesus' appointed mission to the Apostles to anoint and heal those who were sick.

Tradition

Every book of the Bible challenges us to change our lives. The entire Old Testament can be read as the story of a journey made by people who are constantly struggling against sin. The prophets continuously challenged the Jewish people to change their ways. In the New Testament, Jesus based his entire message on repentance. As he began his public ministry, Jesus proclaimed that all people should repent and believe in the Gospel. In this context, *repent* means more than being sorry for one's sins; it means to turn one's life around. In the Catholic Tradition, repentance and conversion are viewed as lifelong processes.

Catholic Social Teaching

In this session the integrated Catholic Social Teaching theme is **Life and Dignity of the Human Person.** See page 89b for an explanation of this theme.

Window on the Catechism

The Sacraments of Healing are discussed in *CCC* 1420–1532.

General Directory for Catechesis

Catechesis and the message of Salvation through the forgiveness of sins are described in *GDC* 101–102.

One-Hour Session Planner

SESSION 14 # Jesus Heals and Forgives

Session Theme: *Forgiveness, a key message of Jesus' ministry, is given to us in the Sacrament of Penance and Reconciliation as a way to reconcile our sins.*

Before This Session

▶ Bookmark your Bible to Mark 1:29–31, Mark 2:1–12, Mark 5:35–43, Mark 6:6–13, Mark 9:27–31, Matthew 18:22, John 9:1–41, John 20:22–23, Numbers 21:8, and James 5:14–15. Place the open Bible in your prayer space.

▶ Read the Guide for this session, choose any additional If Time Allows activities that you might have time to complete, and gather the listed materials.

STEPS	APPROXIMATE TIME
Engage *Jesus Heals and Forgives* PAGE 115	10 minutes
Explore *Jesus Heals* PAGES 116–117 *The Gift of Healing* PAGES 118–119	30–40 minutes
Reflect *Prayer:* Asking Forgiveness PAGE 120 *Where Do I Fit In?* PAGE 121	10–15 minutes
Respond *What's What?* PAGE 122	10–15 minutes

Prayer in Session 14

Pray aloud the short opening prayer and encourage young people to experience an online 3-Minute Retreat at the end of the session. In Session 14 young people will use a special form of prayer, *lectio divina*, where they listen to Scripture, meditate, respond with their own prayer, and contemplate. Follow the Prepare directions on the Catechist Guide page before sharing with young people.

TAKE IT HOME

Homework options:

Symbols of Healing	PAGE 117
Healing Presence	PAGE 118

Materials

REQUIRED

▶ Writing supplies (pages 115, 119, 121, 122)

▶ CD player (pages 116, 120)

▶ CD 1, Track 2: "The Man Born Blind" (5:03) (page 116)

▶ Bible (pages 118, 119)

▶ CD 1, Track 7: Reflective Music (page 120)

▶ Computers with Internet access (page 122)

OPTIONAL

▶ Writing supplies (pages 115, 121, 122)

▶ Session 14 BLM, T-368 (page 116)

▶ Video-conference software (page 118)

▶ Plastic glasses covered with yellow tape, cotton balls or ear plugs, latex gloves, adhesive wraps, elastic wraps, kernels of corn, straws, shirt with buttons, phone book, cell phone, coins in a zippered pouch (page 119)

▶ Voice recorders, photos of senior citizens, art supplies (page 122)

▶ Session 14 Assessment, www.findinggod.com (page 122)

Session 14

Jesus Heals and Forgives

Sometimes on the road of life we encounter difficulties—bumps in the road. Occasionally when life throws something unexpected at us, we might have to slow down or even change direction. What "bumps" have you encountered recently?

PRAYER

Dear Jesus, help me remember that no matter what I face, you are with me. Give me courage, hope, and strength when I encounter difficulty.

115

IF TIME ALLOWS

New Directions

Assign partners to brainstorm a list of serious challenges that people face that can cause their lives to change direction, such as unemployment, injury, illness, or divorce. Encourage them to list at least two directions a person might take if faced with the challenge. Then have them brainstorm a list of people or organizations who offer help to face challenges, such as family members, priests, counselors, doctors, social workers, lawyers, or the Church. Have partners share their ideas with the whole group.

➤ Go to **www.findinggod.com/sessionextenders** for Gospel stories of Jesus' healing. You may wish to share this with the group.

SESSION 14
OUTCOMES

▸ Give examples of Jesus' physical and spiritual healing that made forgiveness his central message.

▸ Describe the Sacrament of Penance and Reconciliation and the Anointing of the Sick as Sacraments of Healing.

▸ Pray *lectio divina*.

▸ Define *Anointing of the Sick, blasphemy, capital sins, contrition, imperfect contrition, mortal sins, perfect contrition, sacramental seal, Second Vatican Council,* and *venial sins.*

① Set the Stage

Read aloud the text in the box. Give young people time to respond to the questions in small groups.

② Get Started

Ask young people to rank the following problems on a scale from 1–10 with 1 meaning "not at all serious" and 10 meaning "extremely serious": missing the bus; dead cell phone; losing wallet; getting grounded; forgetting permission slip; out of money; wearing two different socks; lousy lunch; bad hair day. Have small groups discuss their ideas and draw conclusions about bumps in the road. Ask: *What makes you want to push your way through a problem? What makes you feel like giving up?* Discuss how problems can be frustrating but may actually lead them to see things in a new and different way. Say: *In this unit you will learn how even illness can lead to a new experience of God's presence.*

 Prayer

Ask: *As we pray together, be glad in knowing that God never deserts us, even in our most difficult times.* Pray aloud the prayer. Conclude by praying the Sign of the Cross.

① Begin

Explain that certain insects and snakes use toxins released in their bite to paralyze their prey. Say: **The paralysis renders their prey helpless.** Ask: **How can sin paralyze you?** (Possible answer: It can prevent a loving relationship with God.) Read aloud the title.

② Connect

 Ask volunteers to read aloud the opening four paragraphs. Remind young people that it was easy to see that the paralyzed man had need of physical healing. Ask: **What did Jesus say that caused a stir?** ("Child, your sins are forgiven.") Ask: **Why did Jesus' opponents become upset by his words?** (They questioned his authority.) Say: **Jesus' visible miracle makes the healing of the man's sins, an invisible miracle, more believable to the witnesses.** Read aloud the definition of *blasphemy* in the Glossary. Encourage young people to read more about the Gospel of Mark on pages 258–259 in Prayers and Practices.

Have a volunteer read Jesus Cures the Man Born Blind. Point out how confused the man must have been, expecting everyone to rejoice over his cure instead of becoming angered. Invite young people to summarize what the man's healing by Jesus teaches about faith. Play the Scripture story "The Man Born Blind" [CD 1, Track 2].

Read aloud Jesus Empowers the Apostles to Forgive. Say: **Jesus understood the need for healing. His healing shows compassion, mercy, and the deeper need to be restored to a state of wholeness.** Ask: **How did Jesus prepare his Apostles to heal spiritual ills?** (He gave them the authority to forgive sin.) Say: **In the Sacrament of Reconciliation, we ask for God's forgiveness and for the healing that takes place when we return to a state of grace.**

Jesus Heals

DURING his public ministry, Jesus healed many people. Perhaps the paralyzed man represents the most unusual way someone came to Jesus for healing.

The house where Jesus was preaching was jammed with people. Four men who were carrying a paralyzed man couldn't make their way through the crowd, but they had an idea. Like many of the small homes in Palestine, the house had a thatched roof. The men lifted the paralyzed man onto the roof, pulled apart the thatching, and lowered him down on a mat into the room.

Jesus was moved by the faith shown by the man and those who carried him. He saw not only the man's physical paralysis but also his need for spiritual healing. Jesus saw how the man's sins had been getting in the way of his well-being. Jesus' words surprised everyone. "Child, your sins are forgiven." (Mark 2:5) These words, considered **blasphemy** by the scribes, caused a stir. Didn't this man, Jesus, know that only God could forgive sins?

Jesus knew what they were thinking and said, "Why are you thinking such things in your hearts? Which is easier, to say to the paralytic, 'Your sins are forgiven,' or to say, 'Rise, pick up your mat and walk'? But that you may know that the Son of Man has authority to forgive sins on earth"—he said to the paralytic, "I say to you, rise, pick up your mat, and go home." (Mark 2:8–11) Jesus healed the man in body and soul with authority, telling him that he had been forgiven and healed. Jesus speaks, and it is so.

Jesus Cures the Man Born Blind

John 9:1–41 tells how Jesus cured a man born blind. Jesus put clay on the man's eyes and told him to wash in the pool of Siloam. When the man did so, he could see for the first time in his life. The religious authorities questioned him sharply, inquiring who had done this for him. The man claimed that Jesus, who must be a prophet and one sent from God, cured him. Unhappy with the explanation, the authorities questioned the man's parents and

then returned again to challenge his faith. The man continued to proclaim Jesus' miraculous healing until he was thrown out of the Temple. Jesus sought out the man and asked him if he believed. Recognizing Jesus with eyes of faith, he worshiped him. The religious authorities, who could see with their own eyes, were spiritually blind while those who receive the gift of faith from God are the ones who see.

Jesus Empowers the Apostles to Forgive

Forgiveness is a central message throughout Jesus' ministry. When Peter asked Jesus how often he must forgive, Jesus responded, "I say to you, not seven times but seventy-seven times." (Matthew 18:22) Jesus prepared his Apostles for their ministry by giving them the authority to forgive sins. After his Resurrection, Jesus appeared to his disciples and said, "Receive the holy Spirit. Whose sins you forgive are forgiven them, and whose sins you retain are retained." (John 20:22–23)

Sacrament of Healing

Ordained priests have the same authority as the Apostles to forgive sins through the Sacrament of Penance and Reconciliation. This powerful sacrament invites us to draw closer to God. The Holy Spirit

116 Unit 3 • The Public Life of Jesus

The Palsied Man Let Down Through the Roof, James Jacques Joseph Tissot, ca. 1886–1894.

IF TIME ALLOWS

Session 14 BLM

The Deadly Seven Remind young people that sin weakens their relationship with God. Recognizing the capital sins, which can lead someone down the wrong path, is one preparatory step to avoid them. Provide each young person with the Session 14 Blackline Master [T-368]. Ask them to use the Blackline Master to help them better understand how to seek forgiveness and return to God.

works through this sacrament to turn us away from sin and toward God the Father. When we say, do, or desire something that is contrary to God's will, we commit sin. Sin goes against reason and harms our relationship with God and others.

Even though Original Sin is washed away in the Sacrament of Baptism, human beings struggle against sin throughout their lifetimes. When sin becomes a habit, even **venial sins,** our less serious sins, can lead a person farther away from a close relationship with God and others. **Capital sins** can lead someone to commit more serious sins. The capital sins are pride, covetousness, envy, anger, gluttony, lust, and sloth. **Mortal sins** are serious decisions to turn away from God by doing something known to be wrong. During confession, we receive God's merciful forgiveness for sin. After receiving the sacrament, we are reconciled with God, with others, and with all of creation.

Repentance

God does not give up on us when we sin. The Holy Spirit works within us and calls us to repentance to experience real sorrow for what we have done and to decide that we will stay away from sinning in the future. Repentance is also called **contrition.** When our sorrow is based on love of God above all else, we call it **perfect contrition.** When our sorrow is based more on the fear of punishment and other consequences we might receive for our sins, we call it **imperfect contrition.** The Sacrament of Reconciliation is a gift from Jesus to the Church that helps us recognize and remove the obstacles that sin puts in our way and gives us the grace we need to avoid sin in the future.

In the Sacrament of Reconciliation, we ask ourselves, "What direction am I heading? Am I moving toward God and my true self, or am I moving away from God and toward selfishness and sin?"

Seeking Forgiveness

Forgiveness of sins is important in order to have a healthy relationship with God, other people, and ourselves. After we take the first step of repentance, we go to a priest to confess our sins; express sorrow for them, usually by reciting the Act of Contrition; state our intention to avoid these sins in the future; and promise to repair any damage our sins may have

done to others. We confess all grave, or mortal, sins, as well as any venial sins that come to mind.

The ordained priest, who represents Jesus and the Church, gives an appropriate penance. Penance consists of prayers or actions that repair the damage caused by our sins and will help us turn away from sin and live closer to God. The priest then speaks the words of absolution through which we experience Jesus' forgiveness.

The Church encourages us to receive the sacrament regularly. In this way, we are reconciled with God and are filled with his life and love. We are reconciled with the Church and with the people we may have hurt. If we confessed a mortal sin, we are saved from eternal punishment. Our conscience is cleared, and we are at peace with God, others, and ourselves. We receive grace for future struggles with temptation and to avoid sin in the future.

Explore

Our Catholic Character

The practices of the modern Church for the Sacrament of Reconciliation focus on the need for reconciliation with God and with the community instead of an individual's private confession. People can now celebrate the sacrament in a confessional or talk with a priest face-to-face. In either practice the dignity of the person is most important. The priest is bound to absolute secrecy, called the **sacramental seal,** regarding the sins confessed to him.

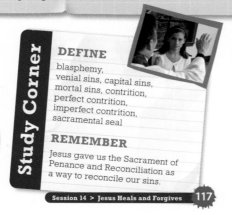

Study Corner

DEFINE
blasphemy,
venial sins, capital sins,
mortal sins, contrition,
perfect contrition,
imperfect contrition,
sacramental seal

REMEMBER
Jesus gave us the Sacrament of Penance and Reconciliation as a way to reconcile our sins.

Session 14 > Jesus Heals and Forgives   117

TAKE IT HOME

Symbols of Healing

Explain that the symbol of a snake entwined around a staff is an ancient symbol of healing. Even today the medical profession uses this symbol. Show young people this image, easily available on the Internet. Point out the contradiction of the image, as a serpent has often been looked upon as a source of death, not healing. Refer young people to Numbers 21:8. The Lord told Moses to make a serpent out of bronze and mount it on a pole. When people who had been bitten by a serpent looked upon it, they were healed. Have young people make their own symbol of the physical, spiritual, or emotional healing they receive from Jesus and the Church. Ask them to reflect on the ideas of contrition, forgiveness, and conversion as they make their design on large sheets of construction paper. Display their work in the room.

Read aloud the section Sacrament of Healing. Discuss the terms, using the Glossary as needed. Ask: **What is sin?** (doing or desiring something that is contrary to God's will) Ask: **What happens during confession?** (We receive God's merciful forgiveness for sins. We are reconciled with God and others.)

Have volunteers read aloud the section Repentance. Say: **When you are truly sorry, you decide to do better.** Explain that a call to conversion is a call to change. Say: **Conversion is not a command but an opportunity to break bad habits and become more like Christ.** Discuss *contrition*, using the Glossary to clarify each term further.

Read aloud the section Seeking Forgiveness. Remind young people that the Church continues the healing work begun with Jesus in the Sacrament of Penance and Reconciliation. Explain that asking and receiving forgiveness is crucial, but it is equally important to rebuild trust, heal hurts, and strengthen relationships by turning away from sin.

Review the steps taken when seeking forgiveness. Ask young people to refer to pages 296–297 in Prayers and Practices. Then pray together the Act of Contrition, using page 275 in Prayers and Practices. Have young people look in the Glossary and define these key elements: *confession, penance, contrition,* and *absolution.* (confession—telling your sins; penance—prayer, act of denial, or a work of charity; contrition—true sorrow for sins; absolution—pardon of sin)

Our Catholic Character

Read the feature and discuss the meaning of the *sacramental seal.*

③ Close

Ask: **How does the Sacrament of Penance and Reconciliation heal your relationship both with God and the Church?** Invite open discussion, encouraging young people to express their opinions.

1 Begin

Ask volunteers to perform impromptu skits that demonstrate acts of hospitality. Suggest different hospitality relationships, such as restaurants to customers, you to friends, or families to out-of-town guests.

 Read aloud Mark 1:29–31. Say: **Notice how the woman responds to her healing. She receives Jesus' healing touch, and her immediate response is to serve others.**

2 Connect

Read aloud the article title The Gift of Healing. Ask volunteers to take turns reading the paragraphs in the first column. Say: **Jesus knew that the leper was isolated and cut off from the community.** Ask: **What people today live on the fringe of society because others fear them?** (Possible answers: those with mental illness, physical disabilities or deformities, disease) Ask: **What is Jesus' message in curing the leper?** (Society, groups, and individuals are called to recognize attitudes that result in the exclusion of others. It is our responsibility to accept the call to reach out to those who are excluded.) Say: **Jesus' healing shows his limitless compassion and opens the Kingdom of God to everyone.**

 Have volunteers read aloud Apostolic Mission. Ask: **Whom do you turn to when you are hurting?** (Answers will vary.) Say: **Jesus wants you to turn to him in faith when you are suffering. He also wants us to reach out with compassion to heal one another.** Explain that while they may not be capable of healing someone physically, they can work miracles of love in their everyday lives by treating others with compassion and kindness. Say: **Jesus healed the whole person. He calls each of us to bring his healing presence to those who are lonely, isolated, or discriminated against.**

The Gift of Healing

JESUS came to heal spiritual and physical affliction. His words and touch freed and transformed hearts and bodies. With every healing, God's kingdom was manifested.

The Gospel of Mark reveals Jesus as a powerful healer. After Jesus healed the mother-in-law of Simon (later to be called Peter), the townspeople brought all who were sick to Jesus so that they might be healed. Among the people he cured were people thought to have unclean spirits within them and those with a terrible disease called leprosy. At that time people with such conditions were shunned by society. Lepers could not live with their families, and many wandered from town to town, begging in order to stay alive. They had to announce their condition as they walked to warn those who were near to stay away so as not to catch the contagious disease. But Jesus didn't stay away. He drew closer to those who needed healing, and they were healed.

When Jesus healed, he made it possible for people to return to a life with their families and society. In the Gospel accounts, much of Jesus' interaction with people involves healing them and welcoming them back to full acceptance in the community.

Apostolic Mission

Jesus sent his disciples on a mission to proclaim the Kingdom of God and to continue the care and concern he showed during his teaching. (Mark 6:6–13) Jesus told them to travel with few possessions, to trust in God to provide for them, and to preach repentance to the people. In Jesus' name, "[t]hey drove out many demons, and they anointed with oil many who were sick and cured them." (Mark 6:13)

The disciples were Jesus' ambassadors on a mission to tell the people that they were not alone, that the healing touch of God was in their midst. We know from the Letter of James that Jesus' appointed mission to his disciples—to anoint and heal those who were sick—continued in the early Church.

"Is anyone among you sick? He should summon the presbyters of the church, and they should pray over him and anoint [him] with oil in the name of the Lord, and the prayer of faith will save the sick person, and the Lord will raise him up. If he has committed any sins, he will be forgiven."

James 5:14–15

118 *Unit 3 • The Public Life of Jesus*

Healing Presence

Ask young people to find pictures in newspapers or magazines that show how the world today needs healing. Have them arrange the pictures into a collage. Ask them to write several paragraphs with the heading "A Healing Presence." Ask them to describe ways people can bring healing to their families, schools, or neighborhoods.

INCLUSION

Chronic Health Conditions

Self-Expression Young people with chronic health conditions may be particularly sensitive to the topic of healing. Encourage them to express their feelings in their writing. If health reasons keep them away from the class for a period of time, arrange a video conference so members of the group can share friendship and extend get-well wishes.

Sacrament of the Anointing of the Sick

The Church brings God's care and concern to those who are seriously ill by celebrating with them the **Anointing of the Sick.** This sacrament is meant for those who are suffering the difficulties of illness or old age. The sacrament brings healing on the spiritual level and, if it is God's will, on the physical level. The Anointing of the Sick is a source of grace, helping the person grow in faith and trust in God that he or she is not alone. The sacrament also provides forgiveness of sins, both venial and mortal, if the person is truly sorry but unable to make a confession. Jesus Christ is present, healing the person in a fundamental way and sharing his victory over sin and death.

Celebrating the Sacrament

When the priest approaches the person, who may be conscious or unconscious, he places his hands over the suffering person and prays. With the Sign of the Cross, he then anoints the forehead and hands of the person with oil that has been blessed by the bishop during Holy Week.

Before the **Second Vatican Council,** reception of the Anointing of the Sick took place only on a person's deathbed. Today the sacrament can be administered any time there is a danger of death, so it does not have to be a one-time occurrence. The Church wants to stay with the person throughout his or her journey of suffering and death. The anointing of a sick person is an action of the entire Church, and it must be administered by a priest or bishop.

Healing Has Many Faces

Write one way that you have experienced healing from others through these forms.

Presence _____

Physical care _____

Encouragement _____

Prayers _____

Study Corner

DEFINE

Anointing of the Sick
Second Vatican Council

REMEMBER

God's care for those who are elderly or seriously ill is shown through the Sacrament of the Anointing of the Sick.

Jesus heals not only physical sickness, but also the whole person.

SACRED ART

Little Girl Arise,
Laura James, 20th century.

Artist Laura James, born in Brooklyn, New York, is a self-taught painter. She made this painting, rendered in the Ethiopian art style, for one of the most sacred books in the Church, *The Book of the Gospels,* a lectionary published in 2000. The artist conveys the biblical theme of healing by blending colors, patterns, and imagery in an appealing, multicultural way. The painting reflects the Bible account of Jesus healing Jairus's daughter in the Gospel of Mark. (Mark 5:35–43)

Session 14 > Jesus Heals and Forgives **119**

ADVENTURES IN FAITH

Simulation of Old Age

Help young people examine their degree of empathy towards sickness and the elderly. Ask them to respond to these survey questions written on the board: *Do you feel uncomfortable around the elderly? Do you enjoy their wisdom? Do you ever think about growing old? Do you find joy in visiting someone who is elderly? Do you pray for them?*

Arrange a simulation of what it is like for many elderly people who have physical limitations. Organize young people in small groups. Have them wear plastic glasses covered with yellow tape to mimic deteriorating eyesight or cataracts; cotton balls or ear plugs to limit hearing; latex gloves with adhesive wraps around knuckles to limit dexterity; elastic wraps around knees to limit movement; kernels of corn in shoes to replicate aches and pains; and straws to breathe through to imitate shortness of breath. Have young people perform a variety of ordinary activities: button a shirt, find a phone number in a telephone book, dial a cell phone, take coins from a zippered pouch, recognize an approaching person, and other tasks of your choice. At the end of the experiment, have group members describe their experiences and express any changes in their empathy for the elderly.

Have a volunteer read the section Sacrament of the Anointing of the Sick. Use the Glossary to read the definition of *Anointing of the Sick.* Ask: **How might someone with a serious illness feel? How might an elderly person feel?** (Possible answers: lonely, frustrated, isolated, afraid, discouraged) Say: **It is easy to understand how very sick or elderly people may long for health, envy it in others, and fear for their loss of independence. They may search for God because they feel he has forgotten them.** Explain that the sacrament is administered to those who are struggling, either physically or spiritually, with their illness or with old age.

Read the last section Celebrating the Sacrament. Tell young people that the forehead and hands are anointed during the rite, and the priest prays, "The Lord in his love and mercy [may] help you with the grace of the Holy Spirit." Say: **Just as Christ suffered, the anointed are reminded to persevere in their faith and trust in God. They are strengthened and comforted.** Use the Glossary to discuss the meaning of *Second Vatican Council.* Explain that the Second Vatican Council ushered in a time of great change in the Church.

Have a volunteer read aloud the directions for the Healing Has Many Faces activity. Ask young people to complete it independently.

Sacred Art

 Read aloud the feature. Then have a volunteer read aloud Mark 5:35–43. Explain that works of service or prayer for the seriously ill help those who are suffering know that they are not alone.

③ Close

Invite young people to respond to the following question on a separate sheet of paper. Ask: **When have I needed physical or spiritual healing?**

Prayer

Follow the steps to guide young people through the prayer on page 120.

Young People's Page

Prepare Pray the prayer in advance to become familiar with it. Tell young people that you are going to lead them through a form of prayer, *lectio divina*, using the story of Jesus healing the man who was paralyzed.

Pray Read aloud the title and ask a volunteer to read the paragraphs in the left column. Explain that as followers of Jesus, we forgive others, not so they will forgive us in return, but because God has forgiven us. Point out that the more readily we can forgive others, the more we can experience the forgiveness of Jesus in our own lives.

Assign a volunteer to read Mark 2:1–12 the first time. Assign a different volunteer to read it the second time. Review the prayer form *lectio divina*, reminding young people that they will listen to Scripture, meditate, respond with their own prayer, and contemplate. Have young people bring their books to the prayer space. Quietly play reflective music [CD 1, Track 7]. Say: **Clear your mind of distractions. Relax and know that God is present.** Pause for a few moments.

Have the first reader pray aloud the words of Scripture from the Bible. Pause briefly. Reverently, take young people through the Meditate part. Pause and allow time for meditation. Have the second reader pray aloud the Scripture passage a second time. Pause for meditation. Lead young people through their prayerful response and contemplation, pausing briefly after each one. Then invite young people to pray aloud the All part as the conclusion. Together pray the Sign of the Cross.

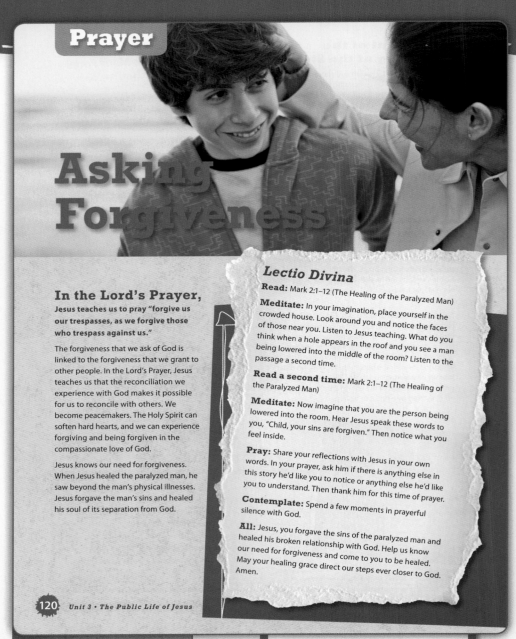

Prayer

Asking Forgiveness

In the Lord's Prayer,

Jesus teaches us to pray "forgive us our trespasses, as we forgive those who trespass against us."

The forgiveness that we ask of God is linked to the forgiveness that we grant to other people. In the Lord's Prayer, Jesus teaches us that the reconciliation we experience with God makes it possible for us to reconcile with others. We become peacemakers. The Holy Spirit can soften hard hearts, and we can experience forgiving and being forgiven in the compassionate love of God.

Jesus knows our need for forgiveness. When Jesus healed the paralyzed man, he saw beyond the man's physical illnesses. Jesus forgave the man's sins and healed his soul of its separation from God.

Lectio Divina

Read: Mark 2:1–12 (The Healing of the Paralyzed Man)

Meditate: In your imagination, place yourself in the crowded house. Look around you and notice the faces of those near you. Listen to Jesus teaching. What do you think when a hole appears in the roof and you see a man being lowered into the middle of the room? Listen to the passage a second time.

Read a second time: Mark 2:1–12 (The Healing of the Paralyzed Man)

Meditate: Now imagine that you are the person being lowered into the room. Hear Jesus speak these words to you, "Child, your sins are forgiven." Then notice what you feel inside.

Pray: Share your reflections with Jesus in your own words. In your prayer, ask him if there is anything else in this story he'd like you to notice or anything else he'd like you to understand. Then thank him for this time of prayer.

Contemplate: Spend a few moments in prayerful silence with God.

All: Jesus, you forgave the sins of the paralyzed man and healed his broken relationship with God. Help us know our need for forgiveness and come to you to be healed. May your healing grace direct our steps ever closer to God. Amen.

120   Unit 3 • The Public Life of Jesus

IF TIME ALLOWS

Guest Visit

Arrange to have a parish priest come to class to explain the Sacrament of Penance and Reconciliation to young people, answer questions they may have, and encourage their participation in the sacrament.

FYI

Coaching Young People to Pray

Before praying, encourage young people to use their imaginations. Ask them to thank Jesus for granting them forgiveness for their sins. Invite them to ask for help in forgiving others in the same way they have been forgiven by God.

WHERE Do I Fit In?

When drivers get behind the wheel, they adjust their rearview mirrors in an effort to eliminate any blind spots. Sometimes it is hard to see beyond our own human weaknesses. We suffer spiritual "blind spots" when we struggle to act or see with eyes of faith.

by Carl Reed

Reflect

Two Wrongs Don't Make a Right

You never forget the day you get your face punched in by the school bully. I haven't. I remember the anger, the pain, and the humiliation as if it were only yesterday. I was walking home from school that mild spring day and carrying a couple of library books under my arm. I was daydreaming about the new *Star Trek* paperbacks and about the WWII *Spitfire* fighter plane I was assembling. Suddenly, someone jolted my arm, and the books catapulted out of my hand. I turned and there was Mike, the school bully, sneering at me. I yelled, and we went at each other. I got the worst of it—a black eye, bloodied nose, and torn lip. Mike was a year older, almost a hundred pounds heavier, and a foot taller.

I vowed revenge. I dreamed about it. I plotted it. Even though I prayed every night before getting into bed, this plot for revenge was one thing I didn't discuss with God. That was between Mike and me. A week later I got together with a couple of close friends who had also been bullied by Mike. We ambushed him in the alley behind his house and knocked him down. I had a baseball bat. I stood over him, ready to use it. My friends urged me on. But then I heard a voice in my head saying, "Whatsoever you do to the least of my brothers . . ."

Surely those words didn't apply to bullies! Besides, I'd already told God (by my silence) to stay out of this. I poked Mike in the chest with the bat, raised it, and had the thought, "Those who live by the sword, die by the sword." Part of me wanted to see Mike

hurt. But the other part of me knew that beating him up would be abject moral and spiritual failure. It would mean that I had become as monstrous, violent, and evil as the bully himself. I turned away. We left Mike there. He never bothered us again.

I learned something life-altering that day about the power of mercy. In the years that followed, I've prayed the Lord's Prayer many times: "[F]orgive us our trespasses, as we forgive those who trespass against us . . ." The words take on deeper, richer, truer shades of meaning with every passing decade of life. As a boy, I had told God to stay out of it. Thank God—O merciful God, O loving God—he didn't listen.

A Different Way to See

Stories of physical blindness in the Bible remind us that spiritual blindness afflicts all of us. Read Matthew 9:27–31. On the lines below, make a list of personal blind spots. Choose one, and on another sheet of paper, write ways to respond to it with eyes of faith.

_____
_____
_____
_____
_____
_____

CARL REED has spent over thirty years in sales.

Session 14 > Jesus Heals and Forgives **121**

IF TIME ALLOWS

Director's Cut

Arrange young people in groups. Have each group write a humorous skit featuring a young person who is on the brink of making a bad choice when he or she hears the voice of God. Explain that the "voice of God" can take a variety of forms—and that it might not be a literal voice at all. Instruct groups to make two different endings for the skit. In one ending, the main character heeds the voice of God, choosing restraint and forgiveness. In the other ending, he or she doesn't. Have groups perform both of their skits for the whole group. Discuss responses that recognized and overcame human weaknesses.

---

① Begin

Have a volunteer read aloud the title and the introductory text. Ask young people to explain what the title means to them. Suggest that when you respond to a wrong with another wrong, you don't solve the problem; instead, you make it worse. Say: *It is easy to understand this idea in the abstract. In real life, it's not so easy. Our ideas about fairness get in the way. If someone hurts me, it is "only fair" that he or she gets hurt in return—right?* Have young people share anecdotes about small acts of vengeance that backfired. Say: *Our desire for justice can blind us unless we practice seeing with eyes of faith.*

② Connect

Have volunteers take turns reading aloud Two Wrongs Don't Make a Right. Ask: *Why do you think Mike never bothered the author again?* (Possible answer: He was shaken by the experience; he was impressed by the author's refusal to hurt him.) Ask: *How do you think Mike would have responded if the author had hurt him?* (Possible answer: Violence might escalate.) Say: *In the heat of the moment, it is difficult to remember how powerful forgiveness is. We might not hear Scripture verses when we are feeling vengeful—or prideful, or selfish—but if we stop and listen, God will speak to us in some form or another.*

Read aloud the directions and Scripture passage in the activity. Have young people work independently to complete it.

③ Close

Explain that while "two wrongs don't make a right," just walking away from a situation may not solve the problem, either. Encourage young people to discuss with you or another trusted adult possible responses to unfair treatment they may be experiencing.

1 Begin

What's What? Ask a volunteer to read aloud the directions. Have young people work with partners to match each clue to the appropriate word or phrase.

2 Connect

Say What? Ask volunteers to read aloud and define the terms. Review each term in the Glossary if necessary.

Now What? Ask a volunteer to read aloud the section. Before writing, invite young people to recall that although they may not be able to heal someone physically, they can perform good deeds that help heal a person. Ask volunteers to share their ideas with the group.

3 Go in Peace

Collect materials and return them to their appropriate places. Invite young people to continue bringing Christ's healing presence to additional people in different ways. Say: ***Jesus had a limitless capacity for love, mercy, and compassion.*** Ask: ***How can you imitate Jesus' healing presence with others?*** Say: ***Remember that people can suffer in mind and body. Emotional pain, such as loneliness, despair, or sadness, can accompany physical illnesses too.*** Ask: ***How can you act on the Corporal or Spiritual Works of Mercy to bring healing to others?***

3-Minute Retreat
Give young people an opportunity for quiet meditation at **www.loyolapress.com/retreat**.

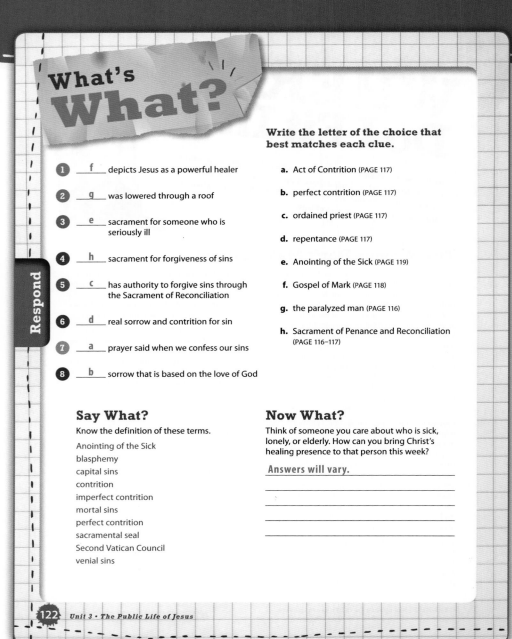

What's What?

Write the letter of the choice that best matches each clue.

1. __f__ depicts Jesus as a powerful healer
2. __g__ was lowered through a roof
3. __e__ sacrament for someone who is seriously ill
4. __h__ sacrament for forgiveness of sins
5. __c__ has authority to forgive sins through the Sacrament of Reconciliation
6. __d__ real sorrow and contrition for sin
7. __a__ prayer said when we confess our sins
8. __b__ sorrow that is based on the love of God

a. Act of Contrition (PAGE 117)
b. perfect contrition (PAGE 117)
c. ordained priest (PAGE 117)
d. repentance (PAGE 117)
e. Anointing of the Sick (PAGE 119)
f. Gospel of Mark (PAGE 118)
g. the paralyzed man (PAGE 116)
h. Sacrament of Penance and Reconciliation (PAGE 116–117)

Say What?
Know the definition of these terms.
Anointing of the Sick
blasphemy
capital sins
contrition
imperfect contrition
mortal sins
perfect contrition
sacramental seal
Second Vatican Council
venial sins

Now What?
Think of someone you care about who is sick, lonely, or elderly. How can you bring Christ's healing presence to that person this week?

Answers will vary.
_____
_____
_____
_____

122   *Unit 3 • The Public Life of Jesus*

IF TIME ALLOWS

Service: Honoring the Past
Remind young people that one of the Catholic Social Teaching themes explains that all human life is sacred and that every person deserves to be treated with respect and dignity. Organize a partnership with a local senior citizen center as a service project. Explain that young people will interview and record a senior citizen's oral history during scheduled visits. Help small groups develop a starter list of key questions to ask. Have them incorporate audiotapes and photos into a display. Invite seniors and their guests to listen to the tapes and share time together.

✝ *Life and Dignity*

Session Assessment Option
An assessment for this session can be found at www.findinggod.com.

PLAN AHEAD: Get Ready for Session 15

Consult the catechist preparation pages to prepare for Session 15 and determine any materials you will need.

Celebrating Lent

 3-Minute Retreat

Before you prepare the session, pause and be still. Take three deep breaths and be aware of the loving presence of God, who is with you on this journey.

Mark 1:29–31

On leaving the synagogue he entered the house of Simon and Andrew with James and John. Simon's mother-in-law lay sick with a fever. They immediately told him about her. He approached, grasped her hand, and helped her up. Then the fever left her and she waited on them.

Reflection

Jesus shows himself to be a man of compassion the minute he enters the home of Simon and Andrew. Simon's mother-in-law is ill. Jesus' compassionate presence and the healing touch of his hand cure her. She responds by rising and offering hospitality to Jesus and the other guests. We can also participate in the healing of the world through our participation in the work of Catholic Relief Services or our local Saint Vincent de Paul Society.

Questions

How can I reach out today to someone in need? How might I become more conscious of the help I can bring to others by simply being present to them?

 Concluding Prayer

Speak to God, using the words of this prayer or your own.

Compassionate Jesus, you sent your disciples to teach and to heal, showing others how close God is to those in need. Gift me with the grace of being your healing presence to those who are in need.

Knowing and Sharing Your Faith in Session 15

Consider how Scripture and Tradition can deepen your understanding of session content.

Scripture

Matthew 20:34 tells us that Jesus, moved with pity, restored the sight of two blind men.

Mark 1:15 marks the first recorded words of Jesus in his public ministry, words that remind us to repent and believe in the Gospel.

Tradition

When we read Gospel stories that deal with suffering, Jesus does not explain it, but he teaches us how to respond to it. Jesus showed compassion toward those who were suffering, healing those who were sick. Jesus rejected the notion that suffering is a punishment for sin in his healing of the man born blind [John 9:1–41]. Jesus taught us to trust that God, the compassionate one, is present at all times. Finally, Jesus taught us through his Passion that suffering is redemptive. Through faith, our suffering can be transformed because we know that God is with us even in our darkest moments.

Catholic Social Teaching

In this session the integrated Catholic Social Teaching themes are **Option for the Poor and Vulnerable, Solidarity,** and **Call to Family, Community, and Participation**. See page 89b for an explanation of these themes.

Window on the Catechism

The proclamation of the Kingdom of God in the compassionate life of Jesus is found in *CCC* 541–553.

General Directory for Catechesis

Catechesis, or its mission to proclaim the Kingdom of God, is described in *CDC* 101–102.

One-Hour Session Planner

SESSION 15 **Celebrating Lent**

Session Theme: *We imitate the life of Christ by performing Lenten practices of prayer, fasting, and almsgiving.*

Before This Session

▶ Display the *Finding God* poster The Liturgical Year.

▶ Determine whether you will use the Unit Assessment option listed on page 130.

▶ Determine whether you will also discuss the Lent seasonal pages in the back of the Young People's Book.

▶ Bookmark your Bible to Philippians 2:5, Matthew 20:34, Matthew 26:39, Matthew 28:20, Luke 22:25–26, John 13:15, John 14:18, Mark 1:15, Mark 8:37, and Joel 2:12–17. Place the open Bible in your prayer space.

▶ Read the Guide for this session, choose any additional If Time Allows activities that you might have time to complete, and gather the listed materials.

STEPS	APPROXIMATE TIME
Engage *Celebrating Lent* PAGE 123	10 minutes
Explore *More Like Christ* PAGES 124–125 *Preparing the Way of the Lord* PAGES 126–127	30–40 minutes
Reflect *Prayer:* Renew Our Hearts PAGE 128 *Where Do I Fit In?* PAGE 129	10–15 minutes
Respond *What's What?* PAGE 130	10–15 minutes

Materials

REQUIRED

▶ *Finding God* poster: The Liturgical Year (page 123)

▶ Bibles (page 125)

▶ Earbuds (page 126)

▶ Slide-show presentation software (page 129)

▶ Writing supplies (page 130)

▶ Computers with Internet access (page 130)

OPTIONAL

▶ Writing supplies (pages 123, 125, 126, 128, 129, 130)

▶ Note cards (page 125)

▶ Session 15 BLM, T-369 (page 126)

▶ Session 15 Assessment, www.findinggod.com (page 130)

▶ Unit 3 Assessment, T-370–T-372 (page 130)

Prayer in Session 15

Young people pray aloud the short prayer on the session opener page and are invited to access an online 3-Minute Retreat that guides them through a reflection about a Scripture verse at the end of the session. In Session 15 young people offer prayers of renewal. Follow the Prepare directions on the Catechist Guide page before sharing with young people.

TAKE IT HOME

Homework options:

Global Family Bumper Sticker PAGE 124

The Glamorous Life PAGE 127

Session 15

Celebrating Lent

CATHOLICS celebrate a time in the Church when they follow more closely the ways of Jesus. We take up spiritual practices and disciplines that help us identify with Jesus more closely as we prepare to celebrate Easter.

During **Lent** we come to a greater recognition of Jesus' dying and rising throughout our lives. To follow Jesus means that we must empty ourselves—our egos, fear, selfishness, and any attachments that threaten to become false gods so that we might rise to the new life of joy, courage, generosity, and freedom that Jesus won for us on the cross and in his Resurrection.

The liturgical season of Lent begins on **Ash Wednesday.** Marked by ashes traced in the Sign of the Cross on our foreheads as a sign of our dependence on God, the whole community is led by the Holy Spirit to prepare the way of the Lord and welcome him into our lives. Just as Jesus fasted in the desert for 40 days before beginning his ministry, we spend the 40 days of Lent with fasting, prayer, and charitable deeds done for others. Lent is a season of preparation for Jesus Christ's Resurrection at Easter and the promise of eternal life.

> **What is getting in my way of growing closer to God? What habits, beliefs, fears, or attachments stand between me and following Jesus? What would you like your Lenten journey to be?**

PRAYER

Jesus, help me spend the season of Lent learning to live as you did so that I will be ready to celebrate your Death and Resurrection during Holy Week and Easter.

123

SESSION 15
OUTCOMES

▶ **Choose to imitate the life of Christ during Lent.**

▶ **Perform practices of prayer, fasting, and almsgiving during Lent.**

▶ **Meditate about personal renewal.**

▶ **Define** *abstain, Advocate, almsgiving, Ash Wednesday, conversion, fasting, Lent,* **and** *Pentecost.*

① Set the Stage

Say: *Light and activity are gifts. So are darkness and rest. We wouldn't be able to enjoy one without the other. The season of Lent reminds us that to experience Christ's light, we must also follow him through the dark.*

Read aloud the text in the box and allow time for quiet reflection. Display the *Finding God* poster The Liturgical Year. Ask a volunteer to read the paragraph about Lent on page 222.

② Get Started

Have volunteers read aloud the page. Ask what the word *attachments* might mean. (Answers will vary.) Say: *Uncontrolled attachments are habits of the heart that put the object of our attachment ahead of our willingness to respond freely to God's love and his desire for our well-being.* Provide an example, such as excessive social networking, and ask how such an attachment might interfere with a person's relationship with God. (Possible answer: It might discourage face-to-face connections.) Review the terms *Lent* and *Ash Wednesday*, using the Glossary as needed.

 Prayer

Say: *Let's ask Jesus to help us follow his example during Lent.* As a group, pray aloud the prayer. Conclude by praying the Sign of the Cross.

IF TIME ALLOWS

Letting Go

Invite young people to imagine a day without an attachment they've identified as hurtful to their relationship with God. Ask them to write a short list of spiritually nourishing activities they could follow instead. When young people are done with their lists, have them share with a partner the attachment that they identified and their list of alternative activities that allow them to grow closer to God.

INCLUSION
Emotional

Small Steps If you have young people with emotional disorders, the idea of giving up an attachment might make them feel anxious and unsafe. Remind them of the peace and safety they can find in prayer. Teach them ways to relax using breathing exercises or music. Encourage them to take small steps to break an unhealthy attachment.

Go to **www.findinggod.com/sessionextenders** for a Lenten video reflection. You may wish to share this with the group.

1 Begin

Ask two volunteers to model the game of peek-a-boo. Then ask: **Why do you think very young children find this game so amusing?** (Answers will vary.) Say: **According to scientists, babies are born hard-wired to recognize other human faces. In other words, we are born craving face-to-face experiences. Our deepest desire is to be truly seen.**

2 Connect

Read aloud the title. Have a volunteer read aloud the introductory paragraphs and the section A Man of Compassion. Ask the group to discuss times when they have seen others suffer and have been moved to help, as well as times when they have ignored suffering. Say: **The hearts of all human beings are connected. We can choose to strengthen this connection, or we can choose to ignore it.** Have young people name some dangers of ignoring it. (Possible answers: We become selfish, isolated, or lonely.)

Say: **Sometimes we feel pressured to act in less than compassionate ways. This might give a temporary sense of security, power, or popularity. But over time, ignoring others' suffering can separate us from the human family and cause us pain.**

Past Meets Present

Have young people read the feature. Discuss the idea of a "global family." Ask if technology encourages or discourages action on behalf of those who suffer through-out the world.

✝ *The Poor and Vulnerable*

More Like Christ

Past Meets Present

PAST: All four Gospels include the story of the crowds who gathered to see Jesus. He recognized they would be hungry. Though the Apostles worried that there wasn't enough for everyone to eat, Jesus told them, "Give them some food yourselves." (Mark 6:37) That day everyone had enough to eat.

PRESENT: Catholic Relief Services (CRS) was founded by the Catholic bishops of the United States on the principle that each person possesses a basic dignity that comes directly from God. Its mission is to assist those who are poor and disadvantaged, alleviate the suffering of all people, promote the development of communities and individuals, and work for peace and justice throughout the world. CRS believes that we are all part of the global family; no matter where we come from, we are brothers and sisters to one another. CRS also provides ways that individuals and parishes can participate in this mission to help people in need.

124 *Unit 3 • The Public Life of Jesus*

BECAUSE Lent is a time for new beginnings, it is an appropriate time to consider the beginning of your own faith—your Baptism. Saint Paul says the best way to embrace your Baptism is to imitate Christ.

In the Letter to the Philippians, Paul pleads that we regard ourselves humbly. "Have among yourselves the same attitude that is also yours in Christ Jesus." (Philippians 2:5) Who is better for us to imitate than Christ? It is important for our spiritual life to think about who Jesus was and what he did so that we might recommit ourselves to following him.

A Man of Compassion

The writers of the Gospels tell many stories in which Jesus heals, forgives, or reconciles. "Moved with pity, Jesus touched their eyes. Immediately they received their sight, and followed him." (Matthew 20:34) They tell us that Jesus' motivation is always compassion for those who are suffering. Instead of seeing a crowd, he sees individuals who have their own stories, their own pain, and their own desire to be healed and reconciled. He sees a man who has leprosy, a woman beset by demons, and the father whose child is deathly ill. He not only sees their pain, but he also feels it and responds to it.

The word *compassion* means to "suffer with" another person, and that is the central message of the Gospel. Jesus became a man with a nature like ours who took on the pain of our sins so that we might have life.

TAKE IT HOME

Global Family Bumper Sticker

Before assigning the homework, talk about phrases that can be found on bumper stickers, such as "God Bless the U.S.A." Invite discussion of this statement, pointing out that asking for God's blessing is fine but reminding them that God does not favor the United States over other nations or Americans over other people.

Have young people design a "global family" bumper sticker that expresses the idea that all humans are connected or that encourages compassion in the face of world suffering. Allow them to share their completed designs with the group.

✝ *Solidarity*

SEASONAL SESSION

Lent

Work with young people through pages 231–234 to learn more about Lent. This special session can take up to one hour to complete.

A Man of Courage

Jesus showed courage in the way he lived and died. Even as a boy, Jesus entered into discussion with the elders in the Temple. Many times Jesus upset crowds because he spoke with the authority of God. When storms raged on the Sea of Galilee, Jesus courageously stood and calmed the waters. He confronted evil. When he saw money changers conducting business in the Temple where true sacrifice was supposed to take place, he cast them out of the Temple. Knowing that he was likely to be put to death when he reached Jerusalem, Jesus set out for Jerusalem. His complete trust in the Father and obedience to him led Jesus to pray, "[N]ot as I will, but as you will" during his agony in the garden. (Matthew 26:39) During Lent we pray for the courage to live our faith.

A Man of Service

"He said to them, 'The kings of the Gentiles lord it over them and those in authority over them are addressed as 'Benefactors'; but among you it shall not be so. Rather, let the greatest among you be as the youngest, and the leader as the servant." (Luke 22:25–26) During Jesus' temptation in the desert following his baptism, Satan offered Jesus power over all the kingdoms of the earth. Jesus, who knew his Father's heart, refused Satan because he understood that power was meant for service.

The night before he died, Jesus gave a great lesson in service. John's Gospel describes how Jesus washed the feet of his disciples. When Peter objected that the teacher should not put himself into a servant's role, Jesus told him that washing the feet of others was key to gaining a share in the kingdom. Jesus told his disciples, and he tells us, "[A]s I have done for you, you should also do." (John 13:15)

A Man of Promises

Jesus is the fulfillment of God's promise to send a Redeemer. He is our model of faithfulness to promises. Jesus told his disciples, "I will not leave you orphans." (John 14:18) He promised to send the Holy Spirit as an **Advocate** and guide; on **Pentecost** that promise was fulfilled. Jesus gave the disciples the Eucharist so that they might be strengthened and nourished every time they gathered to break bread. He taught them how to pray.

As we strive to imitate the life of Jesus during Lent and throughout the year, connecting with him is as easy as whispering the prayer, "Lord Jesus Christ, Son of God, have mercy on me, a sinner."

Study Corner

DEFINE
Advocate, Pentecost

REMEMBER
During Lent we follow more closely the way of Jesus by imitating the way he lived.

SACRED ART

Mosaics are pieces of marble, glass, or other material pressed into a design or picture. This mosaic of Jesus washing Peter's feet is in the Cathedral of Monreale, near Palermo, Sicily, which is home to a spectacular display of mosaics representative of Byzantine influence. A total of 130 mosaic scenes, all made on a background of yellow-gold tiles, show religious events that represent the Old and New Testaments. In this mosaic, Jesus leads as a humble servant to others.

Jesus and Saint Peter, detail from Jesus washing the feet of the Apostles, 12th century, mosaic.

Session 15 > Celebrating Lent **125**

ADVENTURES IN FAITH

Responding Like Christ

Write the following situations on note cards, arrange young people in small groups, and give one card to each group.

- A friend makes fun of someone who is a little clumsy.
- A person who is homeless stands on a street corner.
- A kindergartener looks lost in the hallway.
- Your friend chooses a movie you know you are not allowed to watch.
- Your teacher asks for volunteers to help clean out a storage closet.
- A friend says he or she feels completely alone.

Have group members discuss their given situation and decide which Christlike traits they would need in order to respond to the person or situation: compassion, courage, service, or faithfulness to his promise. Then have young people come up with a brief skit that demonstrates a Christlike response in one or more ways. Have groups perform their skits for the class. After each, invite the audience to identify the Christlike qualities illustrated in the skit.

✝ *Family and Community*

Read aloud A Man of Courage. Say: **The word courageous means "acting in spite of one's fear," not "lacking fear."** Have young people give examples of courageous acts. Ask them to read Luke 22:42. Say: **Jesus felt the entire range of human emotions, including fear. He expressed his fear but surrendered himself to his Father's will. Jesus is a good model for prayer. First, tell God how you feel, and then surrender yourself to his will.**

Invite volunteers to read aloud A Man of Service. Explain that Jesus reversed many of the accepted ideas about authority and worldly power. Say: **In Jesus' time, the idea of leaders serving the people was a radically new and shocking idea.** Have young people name leaders they know who use their power to help others. Say: **Leaders who serve do not aim to control others.**

Have young people read A Man of Promises. Have young people find the terms *Advocate* and *Pentecost* in the Glossary and discuss their meanings. Explain that the prayer at the end of the section is called the Jesus Prayer. Guide young people to page 278 of Prayers and Practices and encourage them to pray it often.

Sacred Art

Read aloud the feature and discuss the art. Ask: **What details communicate Jesus' attitude of humility? What does the expression on Peter's face tell you?** (Answers will vary.)

③ **Close**

✝ Ask a volunteer to read aloud Matthew 28:20. Ask: **How do Jesus' words make you feel?** (Possible answers: comforted, reassured, joyful) Say: **These are amazing words. We are never alone. Jesus is always with us. What promise does Jesus want from us in return?** (to be present to others; to care for others)

① Begin

Ask a young person to tell about a time when he or she felt close to God. When the volunteer begins to speak, pantomime being distracted by putting in earbuds to listen to music. Say: *God is always trying to tell us something important, just as [Name] was. But if we distract ourselves excessively with TV, the Internet, or other attachments, we ignore God. We block him out, just as I rudely blocked out [Name].* Respectfully ask the young person to share once again. Afterward, thank him or her. Say: *We hear God best when we are quiet and open to listening.*

② Connect

Have volunteers take turns reading aloud the introductory paragraphs and both sections on the page. Discuss young people's experiences of being "unplugged." Point out that God is always calling each of us his "beloved child," and we are invited by God to listen and reflect on this calling. Say: *Lent is a time for being honest with ourselves. It is a time to own up to our shortcomings and to honor our identity as children of God.*

In the last section, recall with young people the story of the prodigal son. Invite young people to share lost-and-found stories. Discuss common emotions, such as fear or worry when something is lost and joy and relief when it is found. Say: *Repentance brings us a similar sense of relief. It can be hard to admit that we are lost, but as soon as we do, God sweeps us up in a loving embrace.*

Our Catholic Character

Read aloud the feature. Say aloud the words of the *Kyrie,* as shown, with young people, first in English and then in Greek. Ask young people which version they prefer and why.

Preparing the Way of the Lord

WHEN was the last time you were totally unplugged? In other words, you had no phone, no music, no TV or video, no e-mail, texts, tweets, or distractions.

Did you get bored? Anxious? Confused? What did you think about? Did it become uncomfortable for you after 40 minutes? Or maybe 40 seconds?

Each year on the first Sunday of Lent, the Gospel reading at Mass tells how Jesus was led out to the desert for 40 days and 40 nights. Jesus removed himself from his daily activities and took the time to reflect and pray. He had plenty to contemplate. Just prior to his trip to the desert, during his baptism in the Jordan River, Jesus heard a voice from Heaven, revealing that he was God's "beloved Son." Now, in the desert, he thought about what he had just experienced. He fasted and prayed in preparation for his public ministry of preaching, healing, and proclaiming the Good News of God's love and mercy.

Christ in the Desert, Maria Laughlin, 2006.

Get Unplugged

Lent is a time for us to follow Jesus' lead and get unplugged from distractions of all sorts. We might be distracted by unhealthy eating habits, ways we spend our free time, or ways we treat family and friends. The Church encourages us to use the time-honored spiritual practices of Lent, including fasting, prayer, and almsgiving, as ways to loosen the grip that habits and attachments have on us so that we can focus instead on being embraced by and embracing God. Lent calls us to repentance and recalling (or preparing for) our Baptism.

Our Catholic Character

When we pray the *Kyrie, Eleison* at Mass, we echo the voices of millions of Catholics throughout the centuries. The *Kyrie,* one of the oldest prayers we pray at Mass, is Greek for "Lord, have mercy." Even when the Mass was spoken in Latin, the words were retained in Greek. Now this part of the Mass can be said in either English or the original Greek. Responding to the celebrant's lead, we say three times, *Kyrie, eleison. Christe, eleison. Kyrie, eleison.* (Lord, have mercy. Christ, have mercy. Lord, have mercy.) During Lent, these words take on special meaning as we repent and seek mercy from God.

Repent, the Kingdom of God Is Near

The first recorded words of Jesus in his public ministry were "This is the time of fulfillment. The kingdom of God is at hand. Repent, and believe in the gospel." (Mark 1:15) Repentance, turning away from sin and changing your life to live as God wants you to live, is the doorway to the Kingdom of God. Taking the actions—both in your heart and in your behavior—to reconcile your life with God is at the heart of Lent.

126 Unit 3 • The Public Life of Jesus

IF TIME ALLOWS

Session 15 BLM

Lost and Found Provide each young person with the Session 15 Blackline Master [T-369]. Read aloud the introductory paragraph and the directions. Then have young people complete the activity with a partner. Remind them that God invites us to find surprising meanings in his words, and encourage pairs to be as creative as possible when thinking of ways they are like the "lost" in each parable. When partners finish completing the chart, have young people complete the bottom section independently. Then invite partners to share with the group the contents of their chart and their responses to the final section.

The father's welcoming of his runaway son in the parable of the prodigal son conveys a truth that makes repentance not only possible but also appealing. We can rely on the promise of God's forgiveness and mercy.

Recall Your Baptism

Remember that in Baptism you were cleansed of Original Sin, joined to the Church, and received the Holy Spirit. With the help of these graces, you can live a new life, trusting in God and following the guidance of the Holy Spirit. By being plunged into the waters of Baptism, we connect to Jesus' dying as well as his rising.

Jesus calls us to **conversion,** which is the movement of a contrite heart away from sin and toward love of God and neighbor. Baptism celebrates our desire for conversion and our commitment to it. At Lent we renew our baptismal promises.

➔ Do you reject sin,
   so as to live in the freedom of God's children?

➔ Do you reject the glamour of evil,
   and refuse to be mastered by sin?

➔ Do you reject Satan,
   father of sin and prince of darkness?

➔ Do you believe in God, the Father almighty,
   creator of heaven and earth?

Practice of Prayer

During the season of Lent, you are asked to renew your commitment to prayer, the central action of your spiritual life. You might choose to read Scripture daily, pray the Rosary, or pray the Stations of the Cross. In addition to daily prayer, the Church encourages you to celebrate the Sacrament of Reconciliation.

Practice of Fasting

Another important spiritual practice to observe during Lent is fasting. **Fasting** is limiting the amount of food you eat for a period of time. When you fast, you do so to express sorrow for your sins and to become more aware of your dependence on God. Catholics between the ages of 18 and 59 are asked to fast on Ash Wednesday and Good Friday.

Another part of fasting is to choose to **abstain,** or not eat a particular food. Catholics 14 years and older are asked to abstain from meat on Ash Wednesday, Good Friday, and all the Fridays of Lent.

Some people choose to add their own personal fast or abstinence during Lent by choosing to give up a favorite food, such as pizza, as a reminder that God comes first in our lives and that we are dependent on God for everything.

Practice of Almsgiving

During Lent the Church asks you to practice **almsgiving.** To give alms is to offer money, possessions, time, or talent to those in need. Some people combine this practice with their fasting. For example, they might give up one meal each week and donate the money they would have spent on this food to those who are needy. By practicing prayer, fasting, and almsgiving, you can make Lent your own retreat to the desert, getting ready to rejoice in the Good News of Jesus' Resurrection on Easter.

Our Lenten Journey

During Lent we recognize our need to repent and recall our Baptism. We prepare ourselves through prayer, fasting, and almsgiving. When we receive ashes at the start of Lent, one of two prayers is prayed: "Turn away from sin and be faithful to the Gospel" or "Remember, man, you are dust and to dust you will return." Our Lenten journey, then, is a time to turn away from our sinfulness and recommit ourselves to following Jesus.

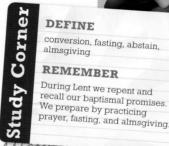

Study Corner

DEFINE
conversion, fasting, abstain, almsgiving

REMEMBER
During Lent we repent and recall our baptismal promises. We prepare by practicing prayer, fasting, and almsgiving.

Session 15 > Celebrating Lent **127**

TAKE IT HOME

The Glamorous Life

Point out that the language used to describe evil in the baptismal promises may not seem directly related to our everyday lives; however, we don't have to look far to find examples of the "glamour of evil" or the darkness of Satan. Show young people some magazine advertisements that glamorize excess. Point out that virtually every form of media is saturated with similar ads. Discuss the values that each ad is tempting the viewer to adopt and whether young people consider each value Christlike. Invite young people to be aware of the ads they view over the coming week. Challenge them to find examples of an ad that strikes them as particularly insidious or sinister and one that seems to promote Christlike behavior. During the next group meeting, discuss young people's examples.

Have volunteers read aloud Recall Your Baptism. Say: ***Repentance and conversion are closely related. The first is about healing, and the second is about using our spiritual health to do God's work. Recalling our baptismal promises is one way to renew our commitment to God.*** Ask: ***Which prayer is recalled by the last baptismal promise?*** (the Apostles' Creed or Nicene Creed)

Have the group read the remaining sections on the page and discuss each section. Ask: ***Which three spiritual practices are discussed?*** (prayer, fasting, almsgiving) Ask: ***How is prayer helpful during our preparation of the way of the Lord?*** (It is the central action of spiritual life.) Explain that the U.S. bishops explain fasting as eating one full meal. Smaller amounts of food are permitted at the other two meals of the day, but neither should equal a full meal. Explain that abstaining from meat is a way to identify with those who are poor or subsist on simple diets. Avoiding meat but eating huge quantities of other food defeats the purpose of this traditional Lenten practice. Mention that giving money may be the most obvious way to give alms, but encourage young people to think of how they can offer their time or talent in other meaningful ways.

Discuss the section Our Lenten Journey. Ask: ***Why is a journey a good way to describe what we do during Lent?*** (Lent is a process, a trip with a beginning and a destination in mind, unique to each person. It unfolds over a period of 40 days.)

③ Close

Explain that each person is required to prepare the way of the Lord. Ask: ***What can you do without as a way to follow Jesus' lead? What can you add to your daily life to recommit to Jesus?*** Discuss young people's ideas as a group.

Prayer

Follow the steps to guide young people through the prayer on page 128.

Young People's Page

Prepare Pray the prayer in advance to become familiar with it.

 Pray Read the title and have a volunteer read aloud the paragraphs at the top of the page. Say: ***Every godly "no" contains a bigger "yes."*** Invite young people to give examples of what this means. For example, "When I say 'no' to junk food, I say 'yes' to physical health." Discuss the idea of renewal. Ask: ***What are common things that renew?*** (Possible answers: subscriptions, licenses, seasons) Connect this idea of renewing things to a different kind of renewal—spiritual renewal of heart and the renewal of their baptismal promises.

Next, have young people bring their books to the prayer space and prepare to pray. Give them time to get comfortable and ask them to quiet their minds. Assign a Reader. Prepare to read the Leader parts. Encourage everyone to respond to the All parts. Remember to pray parts slowly and reverently and to allow sufficient time for meditation. Lead young people in praying together the Lord's Prayer. Continue with praying each part, pausing briefly between each one. Be sure to give sufficient time for young people to reflect after each bulleted question.

Say: ***As we continue the session, listen closely for God's voice asking you to take certain actions this Lent. Then ask him to help you take those actions faithfully and lovingly.***

Prayer

Renew Our Hearts

Lent is a season of self-denial. This self-denial can be a time of self-discovery, where we realize our true identity and desires.

We say no to certain things to say a bigger yes to what matters more—our own relationship with God. We ask Jesus to be with us and renew our hearts as we undertake this journey of Lent.

Prayer of Renewal

Together pray the Lord's Prayer.

Leader: The grace of Lord Jesus be with us now and forever.

All: Amen.

Leader: During Lent we follow the model of Jesus in the desert. In our prayers and fasting, we remind ourselves of our need for God in our lives. In our almsgiving we show our commitment to those who are poor. As we begin Lent, let us ask God to renew our hearts and help us follow God's ways.

Reader: A reading from the Book of Joel. [Joel 2:12–17]
The Word of the Lord.

All: Thanks be to God.

Leader: Let us pray silently as we consider how we will renew our lives this Lent through prayer, fasting, and almsgiving. Reflect silently on these questions.

- What can I do to renew my prayer life?
- How can fasting help me recognize what I really need from God?
- What can I do to help those in need this Lent?

Ask God what he wants you to do this Lent as you turn away from sin and grow more faithful to the Gospel.

Leader: We pray that God will accept our Lenten sacrifices and give us the strength to persevere in our promises. We ask this through Christ our Lord.

All: Amen.

128 Unit 3 • The Public Life of Jesus

IF TIME ALLOWS

The Yes Inside the No

Have young people work with a partner to brainstorm things they might say no to during the season of Lent. Then have them share their lists with the group. Write young people's lists on the board. Then consider each item, asking young people what yes is contained inside it. List these in a second column. Conclude by suggesting that self-denial is a relative term and that seen from a different perspective, each act of self-denial is also a precious gift.

FYI

Coaching Young People to Pray

Before praying, suggest that young people write a short petition to pray when they feel tempted to violate a Lenten promise. Recommend that, when possible, they distance themselves physically from a temptation, sit quietly for one minute, and pray the petition before returning to what they were doing.

WHERE Do I Fit In?

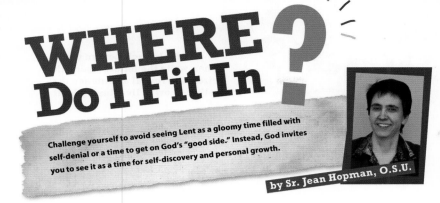

Challenge yourself to avoid seeing Lent as a gloomy time filled with self-denial or a time to get on God's "good side." Instead, God invites you to see it as a time for self-discovery and personal growth.

by Sr. Jean Hopman, O.S.U.

Saying Yes to What Matters

When I was in junior high, I was a challenger. If I didn't see the meaning of a rule or tradition, I was the first to challenge it. If something didn't make sense to me, I wasn't going to do it. A rule in my house was to eat what was served. My mother fixed our plates, and we were expected to finish them or face the consequences, which in my home was to remain at the table until the plate was clean. To motivate us, my mother would say, "Think of the starving children in China." My flippant response would be to offer to send them the food.

One day at school I was talking with friends about what to give up for Lent—candy, soda, movies. I wondered, "How does giving up something for 40 days bring me closer to Jesus? Is that really what God wants?"

My questions challenged me to think of Lent in a new way. My religion class took on a Lenten project of making bag lunches once a week and distributing them with a local organization who fed the hungry. Seeing those who came for food— individuals, families, kids my own age—touched me. I decided to fast from lunch on our weekly food distribution day as a way to be in solidarity with other people's suffering—people I had actually met. These people didn't have hot food each evening or the ability to give up luxuries like candy.

Fasting from lunch one day a week in solidarity with the hungry of my town had more meaning to me than giving up candy. By fasting, I could offer a small sacrifice with great meaning. When I started to feel hungry on those days, I could thank God for what I had and pray for God's continued help for those in need. That Lent, my eyes were opened to the needs of people around me, and I learned the meaning of sacrifice.

SR. JEAN HOPMAN, O.S.U., is vocation director for the Ursulines of the Roman Union, U.S.A.

Making Lent Meaningful

Solidarity is a theme of Catholic Social Teaching. See pages 298–300 in Prayers and Practices for information about the other themes. What is something you can do throughout Lent to follow a theme of Catholic Social Teaching?

Form an action plan of ways to return to God during Lent. Prepare a slide-show presentation of your ideas and share it with the group as a way to encourage one another on your Lenten journeys.

Reflect

Session 15 > Celebrating Lent 129

IF TIME ALLOWS

Lenten Giving

Explain that anonymous giving is an especially powerful way to practice solidarity because it relieves the recipient of any feelings of debt while allowing the giver to give without the hope of payment in kind. Have young people jot down several ways they could give anonymously to someone in need during Lent. Explain that the gift need not be monetary. Young people could, for example, place an elderly neighbor's morning paper on his or her doorstep, or they could do stealth chores around the house. After young people have recorded several possibilities, have them choose one recipient who is most truly in need and encourage their resolve to give anonymously to this person throughout Lent and the entire year.

✝ *Family and Community*

① Begin

Have a volunteer read aloud the introductory text. Discuss young people's attitudes toward Lent, encouraging them to be honest about their ideas regarding sacrifice and self-denial. Ask: **What do you find hard? Why?** (Answers will vary.) Explain that when we connect our Lenten actions to people in the real world, the reasons for the actions become more meaningful. In turn, they make us eager to stay connected to those people at all times, not just during Lent.

② Connect

Have volunteers read aloud the title and first two paragraphs of Saying Yes to What Matters. Ask young people if they ever have similar thoughts about Lenten or other religious practices. Assure them that questioning is both normal and good, especially as they enter adolescence and grow more independent. Say: **Our questions about God lead us to seek answers that make sense. This rhythm of questioning and answering is what the spiritual life is all about.** Have volunteers read aloud the remaining paragraphs in the article. Ask: **How did the author's questions lead her to an answer that made sense?** (Her questions took her beyond a superficial understanding of Lent. They helped her find a Lenten practice that connected her to an authentic reason for following the practice.)

Read aloud the activity. Have young people complete the activity at home. Later, have volunteers share their presentations with the group.

③ Close

Encourage young people to share their slide-show presentations with their family as the starting point of a Lenten plan for the family.

① Begin

What's What? Read aloud the directions. Then have young people complete the activity at home or with a partner.

② Connect

Say What? Ask volunteers to read aloud and define the terms. Review each term in the Glossary if necessary.

Now What? Read aloud the section. Invite each young person to write a prayer independently. Encourage young people to continue writing on a separate sheet of paper.

③ Go in Peace

Have young people collect their materials and return them to their appropriate places. Encourage young people to mark a calendar each time they pray their prayer. Invite them to write a new prayer for the next week. Say: **Recall that Lent is a time to prepare for Easter. Pray for help to grow closer to the light of Christ.**

3-Minute Retreat Give young people an opportunity for quiet meditation at **www.loyolapress.com/retreat**.

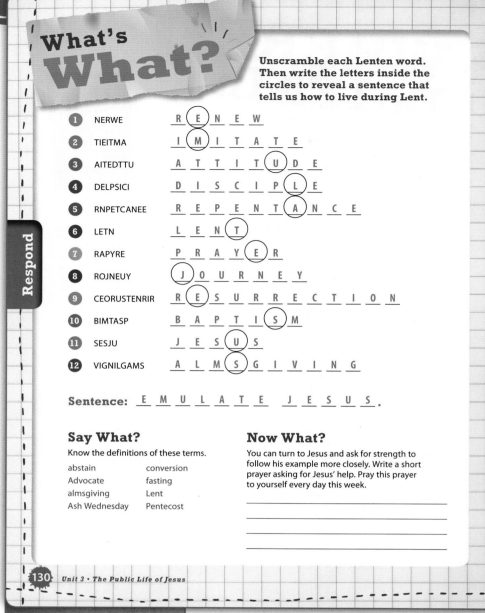

What's What?

Respond

Unscramble each Lenten word. Then write the letters inside the circles to reveal a sentence that tells us how to live during Lent.

1. NERWE — R E N E W
2. TIEITMA — I M I T A T E
3. AITEDTTU — A T T I T U D E
4. DELPSICI — D I S C I P L E
5. RNPETCANEE — R E P E N T A N C E
6. LETN — L E N T
7. RAPYRE — P R A Y E R
8. ROJNEUY — J O U R N E Y
9. CEORUSTENRIR — R E S U R R E C T I O N
10. BIMTASP — B A P T I S M
11. SESJU — J E S U S
12. VIGNILGAMS — A L M S G I V I N G

Sentence: E M U L A T E   J E S U S.

Say What?
Know the definitions of these terms.

abstain · conversion
Advocate · fasting
almsgiving · Lent
Ash Wednesday · Pentecost

Now What?
You can turn to Jesus and ask for strength to follow his example more closely. Write a short prayer asking for Jesus' help. Pray this prayer to yourself every day this week.

130 · *Unit 3 • The Public Life of Jesus*

IF TIME ALLOWS

Service: A Change of Heart

Explain that almsgiving is one way to experience conversion during Lent. Tell young people that according to U.S. Treasury estimates, Americans have $1.5 million in the form of change around their houses. Challenge young people to gather loose change from their backpacks, coat pockets, or desk drawers and donate it to charity.

✝ *The Poor and Vulnerable*

Session Assessment Option

An assessment for this session can be found at www.findinggod.com.

Unit Assessment Option

If you wish, photocopy the Unit Assessment on pages T-370–T-372. Administer the assessment during the session or send it home.

PLAN AHEAD: Get Ready for Session 16

Consult the catechist preparation pages to prepare for Session 16 and determine any materials you will need.

Faith in ACTION

As workers provide for the needs of their families at their jobs, they are also commissioned to promote workplace justice. Workplace justice includes the right to dignified work and acting in a way that supports the common good. We have the responsibility to contribute to a just environment by making moral decisions and living by the values that Jesus taught.

In this unit we explored the public life of Jesus. The signs Jesus performed were testaments of service to others. They showed us God's desire to care for and heal humanity. Jesus taught us that the true path to happiness is found in the Beatitudes and in the parables of the Kingdom of God. We are coworkers with God to build his kingdom on earth. Any good work that we do is valuable, no matter how small or seemingly insignificant. The following ideas show how you can value workers and promote workers' rights in today's world.

> "The human contribution is the essential ingredient. It is only in the giving of oneself to others that we truly live."
>
> —Ethel Percy Andrus, founder of American Association of Retired Persons (AARP)

Act

Behind the Scenes

Purpose
Recognize the people in your life whose helpful work often goes without recognition; show your appreciation for these people and how much you value their work.

Background
Many ordinary people work hard in support of others because it is the right thing to do. Selfless people who work behind the scenes may not get the appreciation they deserve. It is important to recognize and appreciate the contributions of workers who deserve part of the credit for success.

Steps
1. Look around your parish, school, or community. Who are the people who do behind-the-scenes work? Whose contributions make things work better and are vital to success? Who deserves a thank you?

2. Think of creative ways that you can show your appreciation for workers who are often taken for granted.

Unit 3 > Faith in Action **131**

IF TIME ALLOWS

Catholic Social Teaching
Provide information about the Church's teaching on the dignity of work and the rights of workers. The United States Conference of Catholic Bishops provides resources on this teaching. Encourage young people to visit their Web site at www.usccb.org.

Wage Law in Jesus' Parable
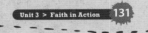 Have a volunteer read aloud Matthew 20:1–16. Ask small groups to discuss the meaning of the parable and what it implies about the dignity of work and the right to fair wages.

MATERIALS: Get Ready for Faith in Action

For these projects, you will need writing supplies, print and online resources on the abuse of child labor, computers with Internet access, Bibles, the prayer service planning guide and prayer service planning tips, stationery, envelopes, and stamps. Also see the project steps.

FAITH IN ACTION

Complete one of the suggested Faith in Action projects as a class, or organize young people into two groups, having each group complete a different project. Note that directions continue on the next page.

① Prepare
Discuss the project ideas with young people and involve them in the decision-making process to determine a project. Discuss the project they choose in terms of faith and being a "person for others." Ask: ***What do you hope to learn from this project? What interests you about it? What concerns do you have about it? Whom will you serve, and how will your service be beneficial to them and to you? Are you prepared to recognize the humanity in those you encounter? How does this project help you put your faith into action? What theme or themes of Catholic Social Teaching will you be experiencing in the project?***

② Implement
Have young people follow the directions to complete Behind the Scenes on page 131 or A Labor of Love on page 132. Be sure young people do research before taking action. Have them brainstorm a list of people whom they would like to honor in the first activity. Organize small groups to research and report on the abuse of child labor for the second activity.

Be sure young people are supervised during their project as appropriate. Consider asking for parent volunteers to be Faith in Action facilitators for the rest of the year.

✝ *Work and Workers*
Life and Dignity
Rights and Responsibilities

3 Close

Bring closure to the project by leading young people in completing one or both of the following:

Prayer Service Download and print out the prayer service planning guide and prayer service planning tips at www.findinggod.com. Have young people plan and implement a prayer service that expresses both gratitude to God for the opportunity to serve and hope for the people whom they served.

Pass It On Have young people share their experiences as a way to inspire others to get involved in each cause. Encourage them to post information about the projects on the school or parish Web site. For the first project, have young people identify whom they selected, the reasons why they selected those workers, and what they did to show their appreciation for them. For the second project, have young people tell what they did to protest the abuse of child labor. Young people might include blogs about what they did, what they learned, and how they feel about this cause. Invite them to add photos that show them in action on the projects. Ask young people to suggest further initiatives or ways to involve others in their work. Encourage viewers of the Web site to respond with comments or feedback for young people.

✝ *Work and Workers*
  Solidarity

A Labor of Love

Act

Purpose

Learn about the rights of workers and about child-labor abuse around the world; find out what you can do to raise awareness about child labor and poverty.

Background

The rights of workers are sometimes ignored and trampled on. Always a serious injustice, it is especially shocking when the workers are children. In 1995, 12-year-old Craig Kielburger decided to do something about the issue. Along with 11 school friends, Craig founded the group Free the Children to fight the abuse of child labor. The goal of the foundation is "to free children from abuse, exploitation, and the idea that they are not old enough or smart enough or capable enough to change the world."

Steps

1. Research child labor and learn its causes, effects, and what can be done to erase it.
2. Work with local or national organizations that seek solutions to this issue.
3. Take a stand and speak out. Raise awareness about child-labor abuse by writing to government officials. Protest child-labor abuse by refusing to buy goods that are made by child workers.
4. Consider ways that you can promote fair and just working conditions for young people in your community.

> "It does not require many words to speak the truth."
>
> –Chief Joseph, leader of the Nez Percé tribe

132 *Unit 3 • The Public Life of Jesus*

IF TIME ALLOWS

Living Faith: Sweatshops

Talk with young people about sweatshops, which are workplaces where workers are subjected to a harsh environment, unsafe conditions, long hours, and extremely low pay. Have young people research sweatshops. Explain that sweatshop conditions have been and continue to be exploited by companies in this country and internationally. Their research should include an exploration of the severe poverty families experience that helps explain workers' compliance with unjust working conditions. When young people have completed their research, challenge them to take action by boycotting any local businesses that exploit workers and organizing a letter-writing campaign in protest to companies who exploit their workers.

✝ *Work and Workers*

Unit 4

Catechist Preparation pages open each unit and session.

Unit Opener   133

UNIT 4

Jesus the Christ

Unit 4 focuses on Jesus' true identity and how he brings us life. In this unit young people will learn the following concepts.

UNIT SAINT

Saint Teresa Benedicta of the Cross

Saint Teresa Benedicta of the Cross became a teacher, writer, and social critic. Born into the Jewish faith, she later converted to Catholicism and became a Carmelite nun. Her faith sustained her until her death in a concentration camp during World War II. Like Jesus, she remained true to herself and her faith throughout suffering and persecution.

SESSION 16 ## Jesus Gives Us Himself

Young people learn that the Eucharist is at the center of the life of the Church. We experience the Real Presence of Jesus Christ at the consecration when the bread and wine become the Body and Blood of Jesus Christ. We go forth from the Eucharist at Mass to continue God's work in the world.

SESSION 17 ## Jesus Makes a Choice

In his Agony in the Garden, Jesus was tempted to avoid his suffering and Death, but he remained faithful to the mission to which the Father sent him. Jesus ensured our Salvation. Like Jesus, we are called to remain faithful sons and daughters of God. With the guidance of our family, the sacraments, and Church teachings, we can develop a fully formed conscience that helps us make good moral choices when we are tempted.

SESSION 18 ## Jesus Redeems Us

The Paschal Mystery is at the heart of our Catholic lives. We are called to reflect on, understand, and articulate who Jesus is and to live in a way that shows we know, understand, and follow him. Jesus' Passion and Death help us understand the victory he secured for us through his sacrifice on the Cross. We better understand our response as Jesus' disciples in the world.

SESSION 19 ## Jesus Brings Us New Life

As members of the Church, we are called to share Jesus' mission of building the Kingdom of God. The Holy Spirit assists us to find the presence of God in all things. Christ is present with us in prayer, in the Christian community, and in the sacraments. The Sacraments of Initiation mark our entry into the community of the Church, which was born as a result of the Resurrection.

SESSION 20 ## Celebrating Holy Week and Easter

During Holy Week and Easter, we commemorate the events that led to Jesus' Passion and Death on the Cross for our sins. We take time during Holy Week and Easter to become more aware of God's infinite love for us and to deepen our commitment to live as disciples. Jesus' Resurrection opens the promise of eternal life with him.

Prayer in Unit 4

In each session of Unit 4, establish the pattern and tone for prayer. Young people pray prayers of petition to thank God for the gift of food and to remind us to share our abundance, participate in a guided reflection about our response to suffering, and ask God for help in taking responsibility for living their faith. Young people also pray the Daily Examen, a form of Ignatian prayer.

✝ Catholic Social Teaching in Unit 4

The following themes of Catholic Social Teaching are integrated into this unit.

Call to Family, Community, and Participation   Participation in family and community is central to our faith and to a healthy society. Families and communities must be supported and strengthened through active participation.

Care for God's Creation   We have a responsibility to care for God's creation. We are called to make moral and ethical choices that protect the ecological balance of creation both locally and worldwide.

Life and Dignity of the Human Person   The Catholic Church teaches us that all human life is sacred and that all people must be treated with dignity. As Catholics we strive to respect and value people over material goods. The foundation of our moral vision is our belief in the life and the dignity of the human person.

Rights and Responsibilities   The Catholic Church teaches that every person has a right to live as well as the right to things required for human decency. As Catholics, it is our responsibility to protect fundamental human rights.

Solidarity   Solidarity is the attitude that leads Christians to share spiritual and material goods. Solidarity unites rich and poor, weak and strong, and helps create a society that recognizes our interdependence.

Faith in Action

In Unit 4, young people are invited to engage in social and political issues that address the life and dignity of others by implementing the following service projects: researching and sharing information about witnesses of Catholic social reform and designing a project that allows young people to express their faith in a public forum. Alternative service-project ideas also appear on the last page of each session in this guide.

TOGETHER *as One Parish*

Religious Education with the Parochial School

To nurture parish unity, organize a school/RE family prayer hike. Ask for adult volunteers to lead small groups along selected paths, stopping periodically to enjoy nature, engage in team-building activities, and read Scripture. End the prayer hike in a central area where the groups can reunite over a picnic.

📖 Literature Opportunity
Drums, Girls, and Dangerous Pie
by Jordan Sonnenblick
You might wish to have young people read about how the life of 13-year-old Steven Alper changes when his family learns that his younger brother, Jeffrey, has been diagnosed with leukemia. Steven's everyday problems become unimportant as the family scrambles to regroup, love one another, and maintain hope for the future.

✝ *Solidarity*

Jesus Gives Us Himself

3-Minute Retreat

Before you prepare the session, pause and be still. Take three deep breaths and be aware of the loving presence of God, who is with you on this journey.

Luke 24:30–31

And it happened that, while he was with them at table, he took bread, said the blessing, broke it, and gave it to them. With that their eyes were opened and they recognized him, but he vanished from their sight.

Reflection

In an instant, everything made sense to them. The discouragement and confusion of just a short while ago gave way to excitement and clarity. Jesus was alive! Their act of hospitality in welcoming the stranger to share a meal with them led to their discovery of the living Christ in the breaking of the bread. We know Jesus in the same way through our Eucharistic celebrations. We gather as one community to listen to Scripture and to receive the Body and Blood of Christ. Just as the disciples were strengthened by their encounter with Jesus, our sharing in word and sacrament strengthens us to go forth and put our faith into action.

Questions

In what way have I discovered that in being hospitable with others, I am welcoming Jesus into my life? What difference does participating in the Eucharist make in my life?

 Concluding Prayer

Speak to God, using the words of this prayer or your own.

Jesus, you reveal yourself in the breaking of the bread. May my heart burn with the joy of your presence among us.

Knowing and Sharing Your Faith in Session 16

Consider how Scripture and Tradition can deepen your understanding of session content.

Scripture

Luke 22:7–20 tells us about the Last Supper that Jesus shared with his Apostles.

Luke 9:11–17 recounts Jesus' miracle of feeding the crowd of 5,000 with five loaves and two fish.

Tradition

The Eucharist is the heart and summit of Christian life. In the Eucharist the Church and its members are united with the sacrifice of praise and thanksgiving that Jesus offered to all on the Cross. Christ himself, through the ministry of the priest, offers the Eucharistic sacrifice. And the same Christ, who is truly present under the form of bread and wine, is offered in the Eucharistic sacrifice. Sunday, the Lord's Day, is the principal day for the celebration of the Eucharist because it is the day of the Resurrection. It is the day we gather for Mass, the day to spend time with our family, and the day of joy and rest from work.

Catholic Social Teaching

In this session the integrated Catholic Social Teaching themes are **Call to Family, Community, and Participation** and **Solidarity.** See page 133b for an explanation of these themes.

Window on the Catechism

Eucharist as sacrifice, thanksgiving, memorial, and presence of the risen Lord is discussed in *CCC* 1356–1381.

General Directory for Catechesis

The role of the twofold table of the Word and of the Body of Christ in Christian formation is discussed in *GDC* 70.

One-Hour Session Planner

SESSION 16 Jesus Gives Us Himself

Session Theme: *In the Eucharist we recognize the Real Presence of Jesus Christ at the consecration.*

Before This Session

▸ Bookmark your Bible to Luke 9:11–17, Luke 14:12–14, Luke 22:7–20, Matthew 25:31–46, Acts of the Apostles 2:42, and Psalm 46:11. Place the open Bible in your prayer space.

▸ Read the Guide for this session, choose any additional If Time Allows activities that you might have time to complete, and gather the listed materials.

STEPS	APPROXIMATE TIME
Engage *Unit Saint:* Saint Teresa Benedicta of the Cross PAGES 133–134 *Daily Examen* PAGE 133 *Jesus Gives Us Himself* PAGE 135	10–20 minutes
Explore *A New Passover* PAGES 136–137 *Jesus and the Eucharist* PAGES 138–139	30–40 minutes
Reflect *Prayer:* Jesus Feeds Hungry Hearts PAGE 140 *Where Do I Fit In?* PAGE 141	10–15 minutes
Respond *What's What?* PAGE 142	10–15 minutes

Prayer in Session 16

Continue the pattern and tone for prayer throughout the program. The session opens and closes with an opportunity for prayer, including an online 3-Minute Retreat. Session 16 includes prayers of petition that remind us to share our abundance with others in the same way that God has shared his abundance with us. Follow the Prepare directions on the Catechist Guide page before sharing with young people.

TAKE IT HOME

Homework options:

Dear Diary	PAGE 136
Kindness Coupons	PAGE 138

Materials

REQUIRED

▸ Media player (page 133)

▸ Clip from *Superman* (page 133)

▸ Celebration items, such as healthy treats, small gifts, beverages (page 136)

▸ Paper bag from a fast-food restaurant, slips of paper (page 138)

▸ Bibles (page 139)

▸ Writing supplies (pages 141, 142)

▸ Computers with Internet access (page 142)

OPTIONAL

▸ Reference materials about Edith Stein, writing supplies, paper (page 134)

▸ Material appropriate for chosen medium (page 135)

▸ Session 16 BLM, T-373 (page 137)

▸ Bibles (page 139)

▸ Writing supplies (page 139)

▸ Transparency, overhead projector (page 140)

▸ Reference materials about a nonprofit international organization or computers with Internet access, poster board, art supplies (page 142)

▸ Session 16 Assessment, www.findingod.com (page 142)

Unit 4

Jesus the Christ

Saint Teresa Benedicta of the Cross was born Edith Stein in Breslau, Poland, the youngest child in a large Jewish family. Her seemingly ordinary start in life would turn out to be anything but ordinary. Edith grew up to be a philosopher, teacher, writer, and social critic. She became interested in Catholicism and was baptized into the Church in 1922. Eventually she became a Carmelite nun, taking the name Sister Teresa Benedicta of the Cross. When the Nazis invaded the Netherlands, she was sent to a concentration camp, where her faith sustained her until her death.

How the Saint Relates { Saint Teresa Benedicta of the Cross accepted persecution and suffering with the strength that came from her faith and her belief in eternal life. She did not avoid the danger that living faithfully required and accepted death in her service of Jesus.

133

OPENING PRAYER

Daily Examen

Suggest that young people frequently pray the Daily Examen on page 279 in Prayers and Practices. Guide young people through the steps.

• Relax and clear your mind. Become aware of God's presence.

• Replay the last 24 hours in your mind. Review your day hour by hour. Ask yourself, "What has made me happy today? What was I doing? Was I alone or with other people?"

• Ask the Holy Spirit to help you focus on one or two joyful moments. Don't think too hard about it; just let the experience of pure joy wash over you again. Ask yourself, "What does God want me to know about this occasion of joy?"

• Ask the Holy Spirit to guide you through a negative moment when you felt impatience, despair, or irritation. Listen for what God wants you to know. Ask yourself, "What would God say about my response? What does he want me to know?"

• Take a moment to thank God for your moments of joy and to ask for his grace in moments of difficulty.

• Pray *Amen* silently when you are ready. Now bring your attention back to this room.

OUTCOMES

▶ Explain Edith Stein's path to conversion and the Catholic faith.

▶ Describe how the faith of Saint Teresa Benedicta of the Cross sustained her throughout difficult times.

① Begin

Read aloud the unit title Jesus the Christ. Explain to young people that in this unit they will learn who Jesus is and how he brings us life. Play a brief clip from *Superman*. Have young people summarize the relationship between Clark Kent and Superman. Explain that even though the man Clark Kent becomes the superhero, he remains true to himself, his mission, and his identity.

Talk about the importance and difficulties in remaining true to our own identity. Ask: ***When is it easy to be yourself? What situations might tempt you to try to be someone else?*** (Answers will vary.)

② Introduce the Saint

Have a volunteer read about Saint Teresa Benedicta of the Cross. Ask: ***How did she remain true to her identity?*** (She stayed true to her identity by accepting death in her service of Jesus.) Ask: ***What kinds of struggles do you think she endured in a concentration camp?*** (Possible answers: religious persecution, separation from family and friends, harsh living conditions)

How the Saint Relates

Read aloud How the Saint Relates. Point out that, like Jesus, Sister Teresa Benedicta of the Cross did not take an easy path, which would have allowed her to avoid suffering. She remained true to herself and her faith.

③ Connect

Have a volunteer read aloud the title and first paragraph. Ask young people if they have ever witnessed or been affected by discrimination. Invite volunteers to tell how they felt.

Have a volunteer read The Path to Baptism. Ask: **What prompted Edith to become interested in the Catholic faith?** (seeing a woman taking time out of her day to talk to God in an intimate way; witnessing the faith of a war widow) Say: **Sometimes seeing other people live their true identities inspires and challenges us to do the same.**

Have a volunteer read The Nazi Terror. Provide some background information about World War II and the Nazis. Begin a discussion about the courage of Sister Teresa Benedicta of the Cross at this time in history, emphasizing that she was born a Jew but converted to the Catholic faith. Ask: **What emotions might she have felt during the Nazi persecution?** (Possible answers: disbelief at the inhumanity of the persecution, fear for her Jewish family and friends, determination to live as a witness to her Catholic faith) Say: **Sister Teresa Benedicta of the Cross endured unimaginable suffering yet remained true to herself.**

④ Close

Close by rereading Pope John Paul II's quotation from Sister Teresa's beatification ceremony in 1987. Discuss the meaning of his words. Then ask young people to reflect on some aspect of her life that affects them most powerfully. Have volunteers share their thoughts.

Strengthened by Faith

Edith Stein was an outstanding student in high school who enrolled at the University of Breslau in 1911 to study German and history. She had a special interest in philosophy and women's issues and transferred to Gottengen University in 1913 to study under the philosopher Edmund Husserl. This decision ended up affecting the path of her life. Edith wanted to be a professor, but because she was a woman and a Jew, she was refused. Years later she would teach at a school run by the Dominican Sisters. She would eventually earn the highest academic degree, a doctorate.

The Path to Baptism

As a young adult, Edith did not practice her Jewish faith. Looking back on her teen years, she said, "I consciously decided, of my own volition, to give up praying." Around 1917 she went to Frankfurt Cathedral and saw a woman stop in to pray. It made an impression on the future saint because this woman was clearly taking time out of her day to talk to God in an intimate way, instead of simply attending a scheduled service. That same year an associate and good friend died in World War I, and Edith went to console his widow. At first fearful of seeing how the widow would handle her loss, Edith was surprised by her faith. Later Edith said, "This was my first encounter with the Cross and the divine power it imparts to those who bear it. . . . It was the moment when my unbelief collapsed and Christ began to shine his light on me—Christ in the mystery of the Cross." In the summer of 1921, Edith read the autobiography of Saint Teresa of Ávila, a Carmelite nun. Edith later wrote, "When I had finished the book, I said to myself: 'This is the truth.'" She was baptized in 1922, and in 1934 she joined a Carmelite convent in Cologne, Germany, taking the name Sister Teresa Benedicta of the Cross. Sister Teresa, a convert, believed it was her vocation to intercede to God for everyone, in particular for Jewish people.

The Nazi Terror

By 1938 the German chancellor Adolf Hitler had begun persecuting the Jewish people. Although a devout member of the Carmelite Order, Sister Teresa's heritage as a Jew put her in danger. On New Year's Eve the prioress helped smuggle her to a convent in the Netherlands, where she submitted herself to God's will and began to prepare herself for death. Her sister Rosa, also a convert to Catholicism, was with her when the Gestapo arrested them in 1942. Her words to her sister were, "Come, we are going for our people." The two were among others who were transferred in August of that year to the infamous concentration camp Auschwitz. She and Rosa were killed by poison gas in a gas chamber probably two days later.

Sister Teresa Benedicta of the Cross was declared a saint on October 11, 1998. At her beatification ceremony in 1987, Pope John Paul II called her "an outstanding daughter of Israel and at the same time a daughter of the Carmelite Order. . . ." Her feast is celebrated on August 9.

134 Unit 4 · Jesus the Christ

Fact or Fiction?

Provide resources and have teams of three or four young people work together to research more facts about Edith Stein to use in a game. Have group members jot facts on paper. As they work, have them make up false statements about Edith Stein to include in their lists. Be sure they keep track of which statements are true and which are false. Have groups challenge one another to a contest, reading their lists aloud while members of the other groups determine which statements are fact and which are fiction.

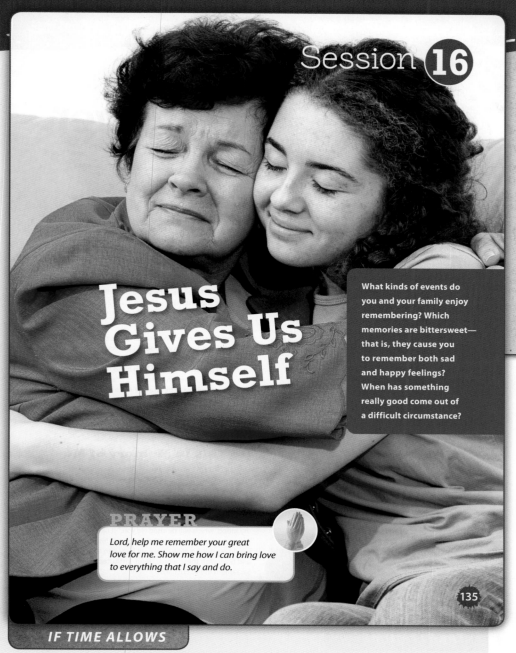

Session 16

Jesus Gives Us Himself

What kinds of events do you and your family enjoy remembering? Which memories are bittersweet—that is, they cause you to remember both sad and happy feelings? When has something really good come out of a difficult circumstance?

PRAYER

Lord, help me remember your great love for me. Show me how I can bring love to everything that I say and do.

135

IF TIME ALLOWS

True Nourishment

Arrange young people into small groups. Invite them to show how Jesus nourishes us by gathering images that show Jesus' comfort, love, teaching, healing, and so on. Encourage them to choose a medium for their presentation, such as a short video, a slide-show presentation, or a photo essay. Depending on the format they choose, they may incorporate narration, music, text, and interviews. Arrange for groups to show their projects. Challenge viewers to explain the images of nourishment they see in the presentations.

➡ Go to **www.findinggod.com/sessionextenders** for an article about Jesus, the Bread of Life. You may wish to share this with the group.

OUTCOMES

▶ Explain ways that the Eucharist is the high point of the life of the Church.

▶ Explain that we experience the Real Presence of Jesus Christ at the consecration in the Eucharistic prayer, when the bread and wine become Christ's Body and Blood.

▶ Pray prayers of petition.

▶ Define *Institution Narrative, Last Supper, liturgy, Mystical Body of Christ, Pharisees, Real Presence,* and *transubstantiation.*

① Set the Stage

Read aloud the questions in the box on page 135. Give young people time to reflect on or write responses. Ask volunteers to share their ideas.

② Get Started

List on the board some situations:

▶ *Your grandparent is seriously ill.*
▶ *You don't get invited to a party.*
▶ *Your dog has run away.*
▶ *Your parents have been arguing.*
▶ *A close friend moves away.*

For each situation, have young people identify what they might need most. (Possible answers: advice, love, someone to listen, time, help) Say: ***When we are in need, we often turn to friends and family for love and support. They give of themselves in many ways.***

Read aloud the session title. Say: ***Jesus sacrificed himself so that he may always be with us. He is present with us and nourishes us through the Eucharist.***

 Prayer

Say: ***Let's take a moment to pray together and tell Jesus that we'll turn to him for all our needs.*** Pray aloud the prayer. Conclude by praying the Sign of the Cross.

① Begin

Bring in various items that could be part of a celebration, such as healthy treats, small gifts, beverages, and so on. Have young people sit in a circle. Say: **Today we're having a celebration: we're going to celebrate ourselves.** Distribute the items you brought in. Discuss young people's experiences with celebrations. Ask: **What kinds of things might be part of a celebration?** (Possible answers: food, conversations, decorations, laughter, storytelling, singing, sharing, traditions)

② Connect

Say: **When we share a meal with others, we satisfy more than just physical hunger.** Read aloud the article title and the first two paragraphs. Say: **We celebrate for many reasons and in many ways, but ultimately, a celebration is a time to share and commemorate something important.**

Have volunteers take turns reading the section Jesus' Last Meal. Reinforce that Jesus knew he was going to be put to death. He gave traditional Passover items a new and special meaning. Use the Glossary to discuss the meaning of *Last Supper*.

Have a volunteer read the section Do This in Memory of Me. Explain that Jesus' words revealed his sacrifice. He was giving himself to us. Reinforce that the word *memory* is usually used to refer to a recollection of something from the past. Say: **By remembering Jesus' words when he instituted the Eucharist, we acknowledge his action in our lives today.**

Past Meets Present

Read aloud the feature. Help young people conclude that God has always made his presence known throughout the ages. Ask a volunteer to explain the connection between the Institution Narrative we hear at Mass and Jesus' institution of the Eucharist at the Last Supper.

A New Passover

THINK of a festive holiday meal you enjoy with your family. Gathering with family and friends in celebration is a way to lift our spirits, even when times are difficult.

The same was true when Jesus and his disciples gathered to celebrate the Passover in Jerusalem. Passover was a happy and celebratory occasion at which the Jewish people recalled the liberation of the Israelites from captivity in Egypt, as chronicled in the Book of Exodus. Passover was their story, and it was one of the holiest and most joyous celebrations of the year. Jesus and his disciples were celebrating just as their ancestors had celebrated for centuries before them. It was a time for the people to remember God's Salvation—past, present, and future.

Past Meets Present

PAST: God made his presence known to the Chosen People in a burning bush, a column of smoke, a pillar of fire, the Ark of the Covenant, and in quail, manna, and water from a rock in the desert.

PRESENT: God's presence is most perfectly realized in the Eucharist at the **Institution Narrative**—when the priest recalls Jesus' words and actions at the Last Supper—and the bread and wine become the Body and Blood of Jesus Christ.

136 *Unit 4 • Jesus the Christ*

Jesus' Last Meal

What made this celebration of the Passover meal different was that Jesus knew something his friends did not. He knew that Judas Iscariot was plotting to betray him. He knew that Peter would deny him three times, and he knew that he was going to be arrested, tortured, and put to death on a cross. And so on this night, when Jesus gathered with his friends to eat the Passover meal, he wanted his disciples to remember this last meal with him. Luke 22:7–20 tells how Jesus gave his friends, the disciples, something of great importance.

The Passover meal follows a ritual that is outlined in Scripture. It includes a ceremony in which the family shares unleavened bread and a cup of wine. This sharing of bread and wine calls to mind the actual Passover event, when the people of Israel hurriedly ate unleavened bread before fleeing the slavery of Egypt. During the **Last Supper,** as Jesus and his disciples shared the bread and wine of Passover, Jesus gave these traditional items a completely different meaning.

Do This in Memory of Me

Luke tells us that as Jesus broke the bread and gave it to his disciples, he said a blessing. "This is my body, which will be given for you; do this in memory of me." (Luke 22:19) Jesus was giving himself to his disciples; he himself was the sacrifice. He gave the disciples the wine and said, "This cup is the new covenant in my blood, which will be shed for you." (Luke 22:20) Jesus was going to die on the Cross, and his sacrifice would establish a New Covenant between the people and God. With these words, Jesus instituted the Sacrament of the Eucharist.

TAKE IT HOME

Dear Diary

Ask young people to write a diary entry about the Last Supper from the point of view of one of the Apostles. Ask: **What might have been his thoughts? What might have been his feelings? How would his understanding of what he was witnessing be different from Jesus' understanding of the events?** Volunteers may wish to share their writing when they meet again with the group.

Food for the World

In the Eucharist we remember Jesus' gift of himself to the disciples and the entire Church at the Last Supper. As the celebration of Jesus' supreme sacrifice, the Eucharist is the heart and the high point of the life of the Church. We call the unique change of the bread and wine into the Body and Blood of the risen Jesus Christ **transubstantiation.** Jesus himself is food for the world.

The Eucharist is a celebration of Christ's Passover, his journey through life, Death, Resurrection, and Ascension that freed us from the slavery of sin and brought about our Salvation. The Eucharist as a memorial means far more than a simple memory of past events.

The Eucharist makes Jesus' gift of himself real for us here and now. It is a proclamation of how God is working in our lives today. In celebrating his memorial, what Jesus did for us through his suffering and Death becomes present to us in our lives. The sacrifice of the Eucharist is offered by Christ himself, the high priest of the New Covenant, acting through the priest presiding at every Mass in every Catholic community worldwide.

Sunday and Beyond

The principal day for celebrating the Eucharist is Sunday, which is the Lord's Day, the day of the Resurrection. This is the day of the Christian family, the day on which we rest from work and come together as God's people to worship God. Our coming together echoes what Jesus and the Apostles did long ago and shows that we are his followers. Just as Jesus gave himself as a sacrifice for others and continues to give himself to us in the Eucharist, we are to give ourselves to others. With the help of the grace of the Sacrament of the Eucharist, we serve others in Jesus' name.

Study Corner

DEFINE
Institution Narrative
Last Supper
transubstantiation

REMEMBER
The Eucharist is the heart of the life of the Church. With the grace we receive in the Eucharist, we serve others in Jesus' name.

SACRED ART

Judy McGrath, an artist living in Saint Louis, Missouri, is active in the community-arts movement. She is also an art therapist who has studied and taught in Central and South America. Her painting, *Last Supper*, is a reflection on the Eucharist as a meal with family and friends. At the table of the Lord, we seek spiritual nourishment given to us in the Eucharist. We long to be fed at the table of fellowship as we become what we receive, the Body of Christ. Jesus makes us one, just as he and the Father are one. We show reverence for the Body of Christ in the Eucharist and also in one another. Gathering at the table, we reveal our true nature as members of Christ's Body.

Last Supper, Judy McGrath, 2004.

Session 16 > Jesus Gives Us Himself **137**

IF TIME ALLOWS

Session 16 BLM

Jesus Teaches at Meals Explain that the Gospel of Luke includes many passages about Jesus sharing meals with others. Provide young people with the Session 16 Blackline Master [T-373] and have them complete it to find Jesus' teachings.

Nourishing Body and Soul

Arrange young people in small groups and have them imagine that they are going on a long camping trip and must plan their meals for the journey. Point out that they would need to bring along the right types of food to sustain them along the way.

Explain that we often use the word *journey* to describe our spiritual life and that the kind of food we need for a spiritual journey is different from the kind that provides only physical nourishment. Ask them whom or what they would like to have with them on their spiritual journey. Invite them to include a "spiritual meal plan." When groups are finished, have them report to the entire group.

Ask volunteers to read Food for the World. Reinforce that at the consecration, the bread and wine truly become the Body and Blood of Jesus Christ. This change is called transubstantiation. Have young people read the definition in the Glossary. Say: *We celebrate Jesus' supreme sacrifice. The Eucharist is the heart and high point of the life of the Church.* Ask: *How is the Eucharist a celebration of Christ's Passover?* (It recalls his life, Death, Resurrection, and Ascension, which brought us Salvation.) Ask: *How is the Eucharist more than a simple recollection of the Last Supper?* (We receive Christ in the Eucharist. We give thanks and go out into the world as his humble servants.)

Have a volunteer read Sunday and Beyond. Ask: *Why do we celebrate the Eucharist at Mass on the Lord's Day?* (Possible answers: We recall Jesus' Resurrection. We gather our family in prayer and rest from work. We echo the actions of Jesus and the Apostles.)

Sacred Art

Read aloud the feature. Have young people discuss the meaning of these two ideas:

▶ We bring all our hungers to the table of the Lord.

▶ All our longings can be fed at the table of fellowship.

Guide young people to understand that we look to our faith for love, support, and guidance and that we receive all that we need.

③ Close

Close the discussion by saying: *After receiving the Eucharist and leaving church, we offer ourselves to others.* Ask young people to think of one way they can bring God's love to others. Have volunteers share their ideas with the group.

1 Begin

Show a paper bag from a local fast-food restaurant. Say: *We often go to fast-food restaurants because we're in a hurry and want to have a quick, inexpensive meal.* Ask: *What are some of the problems with fast food?* (Possible answers: high fat content, high salt content, low nutritional value) Write responses on slips of paper and put them into the bag. Shake out the bag and explain that even if our appetites feel satisfied, we still lack something.

2 Connect

Have a volunteer read the article title and the first two paragraphs. Say: *Hunger refers to something beyond food in this context.* Ask: *What is it?* (something yearned for or needed spiritually) Ask: *What are some things that one might hunger for other than food?* (Possible answers: love, acceptance, companionship, understanding, forgiveness, happiness)

Read aloud Food to Celebrate. Explain that when we celebrate Mass, we remember what happened at the Last Supper. Say: *We gather at Mass to give thanks and praise to God the Father. Our celebration is not about going through the motions of the Last Supper once a week. We believe in the Real Presence of Jesus Christ in the Eucharist, meaning that the bread and wine truly become Christ's Body and Blood at the consecration.*

Ask a volunteer to read Food to Share. Then refer to pages 298–300 in Prayers and Practices to review Catholic Social Teaching. Ensure that young people make the connection between the reception of the Eucharist and their service to others. Say: *We live the Eucharist each day by caring for and serving others.* Discuss the meaning of the quotation from Pope John Paul II in 2004 regarding the authenticity of our Eucharistic celebrations.

Jesus and the Eucharist

JESUS satisfied people's hungers. In Luke 9:11–17, Jesus was healing and preaching to a large crowd. Late in the day, his disciples encouraged him to send the crowd away so they could find food and lodging. Jesus blessed the small amount of food that was available, and his disciples distributed it. The crowd had plenty to eat, and the surplus filled several baskets.

Jesus came to satisfy more than physical hunger. He also satisfies our spiritual hunger. In the story of Jesus' birth in the Gospel of Luke, Mary laid the baby Jesus in a manger, a trough used to feed animals. Luke used this image to symbolize that Jesus had come to be food for the world. At the Last Supper, Jesus instituted the Sacrament of the Eucharist. The Eucharist is Jesus feeding his people with his Body and Blood. In receiving the Eucharist, our spiritual hungers are blessed and satisfied. We receive the love of God in Christ Jesus.

Food to Celebrate

Just as the disciples gathered with Jesus around a table where Jesus gave them his Body and Blood, the Last Supper continues today at the Eucharist with the altar as our gathering table. At the Eucharist our minds and hearts remember Jesus' life, Death, Resurrection, and Ascension. We experience anew the **Real Presence** of Jesus Christ because the glorified Christ who died for our sins and rose from the dead is truly present—body, blood, soul, and divinity—at the consecration, when the bread and wine become the Body and Blood of Jesus Christ. The risen Christ's presence in the Eucharist is a mystery of God that we can never fully comprehend. In the Eucharist, Jesus' final gathering with his disciples continues around the world. The Eucharist is our celebration and reminder of Jesus' continued presence in our lives.

Food to Share

In every celebration of the Eucharist, Christ truly gives himself to us, and we are united with him. Catholic Social Teaching reminds us that we cannot gather at the Eucharist if Jesus' concern for those in need is not consistently reflected in our liturgical celebrations. Many people have no food to put on their table or even a table to gather around. Pope John Paul II wrote the following in preparation for the year of the Eucharist in 2004: "By our mutual love and, in particular, by our concern for those in need we will be recognized as true followers of Christ. This will be the criterion by which the authenticity of our Eucharistic celebrations is judged."

138 · *Unit 4 · Jesus the Christ*

TAKE IT HOME

Kindness Coupons

Ask young people to think of ways they can serve others. Brainstorm ideas with the group, such a mowing the lawn, cooking a meal for the family, babysitting, volunteering with a charitable organization, and so on. Using a drawing or design program, have young people make a gift certificate that they can give to someone, redeemable for that deed or service. Allow time throughout the year for young people to describe their experiences to the group.

✝ *Family and Community*

Together at the Table

In the Eucharist, Jesus Christ shows us how to be his followers. Just as he gave himself as a sacrifice for others and continues to give himself to us in the Eucharist, we are to give ourselves to others. When you receive Holy Communion with the words "The Body of Christ" or "The Blood of Christ," it is as if Jesus is saying, "Here I am," the same words God wants us to say to others. With the help of the grace of the Sacrament of the Eucharist, we serve others in Jesus' name.

Frequent reception of Holy Communion helps us better recognize the Real Presence of Jesus Christ in the Eucharist. We celebrate the Eucharist over and over because we constantly need spiritual nourishment as we go through life. However, we must be in a state of grace, free of mortal sin, to receive the Body and Blood of Christ in Holy Communion. Because sin damages our relationship with Christ, we need the Sacrament of Reconciliation to restore that relationship before we receive Holy Communion again.

Divorced Catholics may still receive Holy Communion. However, when divorced Catholics remarry without an annulment, they may not receive Holy Communion because the Church still considers them married to their original spouse. Catholics who seek an annulment, which is a finding by a Church tribunal that an essential element for a sacramental marriage was missing, are free to marry and receive Holy Communion. Either way, divorced Catholics still belong to the Church and can participate in the life of the Church.

Celebrating the Eucharist regularly is our way of renewing the commitments we made in Baptism and Confirmation to belong to God's people and to serve God's kingdom. In response to this gift of Christ's Real Presence, we are encouraged to engage ourselves fully at Mass, demonstrated by gathering with the community, listening with open hearts, singing, participating, and offering honest prayers to the God who welcomes us.

Reverencing the Body of Christ

The word *liturgy* means "the work of the people." We leave the church to go forth and put into practice our baptismal promises and to do the work of discipleship. When we receive the Body and Blood of Jesus Christ at the Eucharist, we become the Body of Christ. We show reverence for the risen Jesus who gives himself in the Blessed Sacrament. And we also show reverence toward the Church gathered in his name.

Saint John Chrysostom (A.D. 347–407) preached about our sending forth, our acceptance of mission, after we receive the risen Lord at the Eucharist. While preaching on the parable of the sheep and the goats (Matthew 25:31–46), he told his congregation, "Do you wish to honor the body of Christ? Do not ignore him when he is naked. Do not pay him homage in the temple [here at Mass] clad in silk, only then to neglect him outside where he is cold and ill-clad. He who said, 'This is my body,' is the same who said: 'You saw me hungry and you gave me no food,' and 'Whatever you did to the least of my brothers you did also to me. . . .'"

Jesus comes to us in Holy Eucharist and unites us with himself and to one another as members of the **Mystical Body of Christ.** Even those physically separated from the Liturgy of the Eucharist, such as those who are in a hospital or nursing home, remain united with the entire Catholic community when they receive the Eucharist from a priest, deacon, or extraordinary minister of Holy Communion.

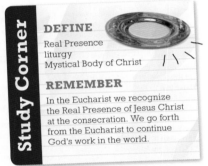

Study Corner

DEFINE
Real Presence
liturgy
Mystical Body of Christ

REMEMBER
In the Eucharist we recognize the Real Presence of Jesus Christ at the consecration. We go forth from the Eucharist to continue God's work in the world.

Session 16 > Jesus Gives Us Himself **139**

Explore

ADVENTURES IN FAITH

For You Were Hungry

Have young people look for ways to serve those around them. Ask them to think about their families, school, or neighborhood. Have partners read Matthew 25:31–46. Invite them to complete these lines adapted from the Gospel of Matthew, filling in the blanks with a need that they observed and what they did as a response to meet the need.

> For you were _____ and I _____.
>
> For you were _____ and I _____.
>
> For you were _____ and I _____.

Encourage volunteers to share the needs that they witnessed and their responses to these needs.

✝ *Family and Community*

Have volunteers take turns reading Together at the Table. Ask: **Why do we receive Holy Communion often?** (It is spiritual nourishment.) Ask: **What is required of us before we receive the Eucharist?** (We must be in a state of grace, free of mortal sin.)

Be mindful of young people whose parents are divorced. Say: **The Church encourages divorced Catholics to continue full participation in the life of the Church, including the Eucharist, but there are requirements.** Clarify the requirement of an annulment for a Catholic who remarries. Point out that Matrimony is a sacrament of the Church, not only a civil union. A remarriage cannot be recognized in the Church's eyes unless an essential element was found to be missing from the original marriage during the formal process of annulment.

Ask volunteers to read the section Reverencing the Body of Christ. Have young people read Matthew 25:31–46 in their Bibles. Ask them to work in small groups to summarize what Saint John Chrysostom means in relation to the Gospel of Matthew. Ask volunteers to explain how this teaching applies to their lives. Refer young people to the Glossary and read aloud the definition of *Mystical Body of Christ*.

③ Close

Invite young people to write answers to these questions:

▶ How has Jesus Christ nourished my spiritual hunger?

▶ What are some ways I can give of myself to others?

▶ How can I better recognize the needs of others and respond to them as a follower of Jesus?

▶ How do I best honor Jesus' command to "Do this in memory of me"?

Prayer

Follow the steps to guide young people through the prayer on page 140.

Young People's Page

Prepare Pray the prayer in advance to become familiar with it.

 Pray Read aloud the title. Have volunteers read aloud the paragraphs in the left column. Ask a volunteer to read aloud the definition of *Pharisees* in the Glossary. Explain that Jesus often disagreed with the Pharisees because of their strict observance to the letter of the law even when it disregarded the spirit of the law.

Say: *Jesus taught his followers to share.* Tell young people that even though much of the world has an abundance of food, many people die from starvation or go to sleep hungry every night. Explain that as Catholics, we pray at meals to thank God for the gift of food and to remind ourselves to share this abundance with others. Say: *In addition to asking his followers to share food, Jesus asks them to feed other kinds of hungers that people have by giving comfort, care, and love.*

Invite young people to bring their books to the prayer space. Say: *Focus your attention on God's presence right now, among us in this space.* Assign the Scripture reading. Pause briefly and together pray the Sign of the Cross. Have the Reader read the verses from Luke. Invite the entire group to pray the All part. Pray each Leader part slowly and reverently, pausing before the response is prayed. Allow a brief time for meditation following each response. At the conclusion, pray together the Lord's Prayer. Say: *Let's ask God to help us always share our abundance with others.*

Prayer

Jesus Feeds Hungry Hearts

Jesus placed great emphasis on sharing meals with others. He ate with sinners and tax collectors, with crowds of people, and with the disciples.

Jesus also ate with **Pharisees**, a sect in Judaism that believed in strict observance of the Law and with whom he shared a mutually contentious relationship. Some of the parables of Jesus center on meals as a way to teach about the Kingdom of God. In one parable, Jesus instructs hosts to invite those who are poor and outcast to a fancy banquet instead of inviting the rich. (Luke 14:12–14)

Jesus' parables concerning meals give a deeper meaning to the Eucharist at the Last Supper, the most important meal Jesus shared with his disciples, and to the Emmaus story, when two disciples recognize the risen Christ in the breaking of the bread. In the Acts of the Apostles, Luke tells us that after Jesus' Death and Resurrection and following Pentecost, "They [the followers of Jesus] devoted themselves to the teaching of the apostles and to the communal life, to the breaking of the bread and to the prayers." (Acts of the Apostles 2:42)

140 Unit 4 • Jesus the Christ

Petitions: Jesus Fills Us

Pray the Sign of the Cross together.

Reader: A reading from the holy Gospel according to Luke. [Luke 22:14–20]
The Gospel of the Lord.

All: Praise to you, Lord Jesus Christ.

Leader: Bring to mind all those who are hungry. (Pause.) For those who are hungry for food and drink, . . .
All: May we do all we can to provide for them. Let us do this in memory of you, Jesus.

Leader: For those who are hungry for friendship, . . .
All: May we reach out in kindness and generosity. Let us do this in memory of you, Jesus.

Leader: For those who are hungry for understanding, . . .
All: May we truly listen to their words. Let us do this in memory of you, Jesus.

Leader: For those who are hungry for forgiveness, . . .
All: May we forgive as God forgives us. Let us do this in memory of you, Jesus.

Leader: For all those who are hungry for joy, . . .
All: May we give them a smile and lift their spirits. Let us do this in memory of you, Jesus.

Leader: Lord, you sacrificed yourself for us. May we sacrifice for others. We believe in the Eucharist. Inspire us to celebrate the Eucharist and live the Eucharist. Amen.
Pray the Lord's Prayer together.

IF TIME ALLOWS

Serving God's People

Have partners compose an additional petition for the prayer. Write the petitions on the board or on a slide to be projected, and pray the new petitions as a group at a future prayer service. Use the same Response or invite suggestions for a different one.

FYI

Coaching Young People to Pray

Remind young people that there is no one right way to pray. God listens to all prayers that come from the heart, regardless of where a person is or what words he or she uses. Encourage young people to speak to God in whatever way they are comfortable, with full knowledge that God hears them.

WHERE Do I Fit In?

Jesus has not left us alone. He nourishes us in the Eucharist and the other sacraments. He invites you to recognize his presence in others.

by Steve Connor

Lifting Burdens

"Be still and know that I am God!"

Psalm 46:11

She lived in the neighborhood. All day she walked around with her shopping cart full of bags. If it was a sunny and warm day, she might remove one of her four coats. If it was a cold and wet day, you could hardly see her beneath the hats and scarves. People brought her food. Most times she didn't speak. Sometimes you heard a muffled, "Thanks." When you gave her a cup of coffee, though, she would look out from her layers, look you straight in the eye, and say, "Thanks. I need that."

One drizzly, cool fall day I found out that my best friend had died. He had been sick with cancer, so the news was not totally unexpected, but it jolted me. I went for a walk. In a nearby park, I found a dry bench and sat down to pray. Closing my eyes, I asked God to help me and to be with me as I remembered my friend. As I prayed, I heard a noise. I opened my eyes, and there she was, wrapped in her layers, and pushing her cart. She came to the bench and sat down.

I wanted to be alone. As I stood to leave, she said, "How are you today?" I wasn't sure I heard her, but I responded, "OK." She looked up at me and said, "You seem a little sad." For someone who barely said anything, she had a lot to say! I sat back down and told her, "I am sad. My best friend just died." As I spoke the words, I started to cry. She moved closer to me, and from under her coats came a gloved hand.

She gently reached over and placed her hand on mine. The tears flowed. We sat like that for about ten minutes. No words were spoken, but my prayer had been answered. Just when I needed it, God sent me someone to help me grieve. I thanked her and got up to leave. Maybe remembering her own needs, she looked up and said, "I could really use a cup of coffee."

> **Mystical Body of Christ**
>
> How can you help someone in a time of trouble? Complete each phrase with your ideas.
>
> When someone is bullied, I can . . .
>
> _____
> _____.
>
> When someone looks lonely, I can . . .
>
> _____
> _____.
>
> When someone suffers a disappointment, I can . . .
>
> _____
> _____.
>
> When someone is suffering physically, I can . . .
>
> _____
> _____.

STEVE CONNOR has worked in pastoral ministry for over 25 years and is Director for Adult Spirituality Resources at Loyola Press.

Session 16 > Jesus Gives Us Himself **141**

Reflect

IF TIME ALLOWS

Benchwarmer

Point out that the most important setting in the article is a public bench. Ask: **How does a public bench function differently from a sofa or an easy chair?** (People often sit on public benches to enjoy nature, rest, or when they are waiting for someone.) Invite young people to find a bench in the coming week and to sit on it for 10 minutes or so, "waiting" for God. Ask them to spend some of the time in silent prayer and some of it watching, listening, and engaging their senses. Afterward, have volunteers share their experiences—in particular, small or unexpected ways they recognized God's presence.

INCLUSION

Vision

Customized Design Young people with vision challenges may benefit from large and neat writing. Consider making personal posters or assignment sheets that match the content found on the board or in their book.

---

① Begin

Ask: **When someone orders you to do something, how do you feel about that task?** (Possible answers: resistant, nervous, afraid, angry) Ask: **When you order someone to do something, what kind of results do you get?** (Possible answers: insincere, half-hearted, careless) Say: **A quiet, gentle request often gets better results. Thankfully, God speaks to us in quiet, gentle ways. He invites us rather than orders us to notice him.** Ask a volunteer to read aloud the introductory text.

② Connect

Invite volunteers to take turns reading aloud Lifting Burdens. Ask: **What makes this a good story?** (Possible answers: Something unexpected happens. The person who usually needs help is the person who gives help.) Say: **Events like this happen every day all around us. But sometimes we don't realize they are Christ-filled moments until we stop long enough to think about them.** Draw young people's attention to the last line of the article. Ask: **What important lesson in faith do we find in the woman's words?** (Possible answers: The woman found something to give even when she had nothing—her consoling presence was a Spiritual Work of Mercy; we can give even when we feel poor and empty; we are invited to accept and give help.)

Invite young people to complete the Mystical Body of Christ activity with a partner. Challenge them to discuss at least two possible responses for each scenario, continuing on another sheet of paper if needed.

③ Close

Have partners share their ideas with the group. Invite young people to notice occasions throughout the day when they give or receive help.

① Begin

What's What? Ask a volunteer to read the directions aloud. You may choose to have young people complete the page independently at home or with a partner in class.

② Connect

Say What? Ask volunteers to read aloud and define the terms. Review each term in the Glossary if necessary.

Now What? Ask a volunteer to read aloud the section. Invite each young person to answer the question independently.

③ Go in Peace

Collect materials and return them to their appropriate places. Encourage young people to assess themselves on a daily basis to see if they have met their goals. Ask: *What else can you do to share Christ's presence with others?* Say: *If you feel discouraged, ask God for the grace and strength to recommit yourself and try again.* Encourage young people to receive the Eucharist often.

3-Minute Retreat
Give young people an opportunity for quiet meditation at **www.loyolapress.com/retreat**.

What's What?

Respond

Complete each sentence using details from the text. Use the circled letters to discover the secret word.

1. The celebration that recalls the liberation of the Israelites from slavery in Egypt is _____ . (PAGE 136)

2. Jesus instituted the Eucharist at the Last _____ . (PAGE 136)

3. In the Eucharist we celebrate Jesus' supreme _____ . (PAGE 137)

4. Eucharist is the heart and the _____ of the life of the Church. (PAGE 137)

5. On the road to Emmaus, two disciples recognize the risen Christ in the breaking of the _____ . (PAGE 140)

6. Jesus knew that _____ would deny him three times. (PAGE 136)

7. Jesus Christ becomes truly present at the consecration, when the bread and _____ become the Body and Blood of Jesus Christ. (PAGE 138)

8. _____ is spiritual nourishment for the world. (PAGE 137)

9. In every celebration of the Eucharist, Christ _____ us with himself and with one another. (PAGE 138)

```
¹ P A S S O V E R
    ² S U P P E R
  ³ S A C R I F I C E
⁴ H I G H   P O I N T
    ⁵ B R E A D
    ⁶ P E T E R
        ⁷ W I N E
    ⁸ J E S U S
  ⁹ U N I T E S
```

Secret Word:
E U C H A R I S T

Say What?
Know the definitions of these terms.

Institution Narrative
Last Supper
liturgy
Mystical Body of Christ

Pharisees
Real Presence
transubstantiation

Now What?
When we celebrate the Eucharist, we recognize Jesus Christ as present in our lives. What can you do this week to receive Christ's presence and share it with others?

Answers will vary.
_____
_____
_____
_____
_____

142 Unit 4 • Jesus the Christ

IF TIME ALLOWS

Service: International Help
Have young people research a nonprofit international organization that alleviates hunger. Allow them to decide whether to volunteer their time or to make posters to promote awareness of the organization's work. If they make posters, have them develop a plan for implementation, getting permission to place them around the school or parish.

✝ *Solidarity*

Session Assessment Option
An assessment for this session can be found at www.findinggod.com.

PLAN AHEAD: Get Ready for Session 17

Consult the catechist preparation pages to prepare for Session 17 and determine any materials you will need.

Jesus Makes a Choice

 ## 3-Minute Retreat

Before you prepare the session, pause and be still. Take three deep breaths and be aware of the loving presence of God, who is with you on this journey.

1 Corinthians 6:19–20

Do you not know that your body is a temple of the holy Spirit within you, whom you have from God, and that you are not your own? For you have been purchased at a price. Therefore, glorify God in your body.

Reflection

Saint Paul uses the metaphor of a temple to remind the Christian Church in Corinth that their bodies are sacred. For Jewish people of that time, the Temple in Jerusalem was the holiest place on earth. Through Baptism the Holy Spirit lived in them, so they were the dwelling places of God and were to treat themselves and others with respect. We, too, are temples of the Holy Spirit, so the moral choices we make can either show respect for ourselves or lead us on the path of destruction. We are called to treat ourselves and others with dignity, making sure that our moral choices glorify God.

Questions

How do my actions reflect an understanding that my body is a temple of the Holy Spirit? How can I glorify God by the way I treat my body?

 ### Concluding Prayer

Speak to God, using the words of this prayer or your own.

Loving God, your Spirit fills me and makes me holy. Help me treat myself and others with the reverence we deserve as temples of the Holy Spirit.

Knowing and Sharing Your Faith in Session 17

Consider how Scripture and Tradition can deepen your understanding of session content.

Scripture

Mark 14:36 reminds us of Jesus' great love for us and his obedience to his Father's will in spite of deep anguish at Gethsemane.

1 Corinthians 8:11–12 tells us Paul's instruction for acting as support for one another concerning moral decisions.

Tradition

The *Catechism of the Catholic Church* (1750) teaches us that there are three sources for determining the morality of a human act: the object chosen (What am I choosing to do?), the intention (Why am I choosing this action?) and the circumstances of the action (When, how, and where am I performing the action?). If the object is an evil action, the act as a whole is wrong no matter how good the intention. A good intention never justifies an evil action. If the object of the action is good, but the motive for doing it is wrong, it is not a moral action. Circumstances can modify the choice of an evil act if the person making the choice is being coerced into performing it.

Catholic Social Teaching

In this session the integrated Catholic Social Teaching theme is **Rights and Responsibilities.** See page 133b for an explanation of this theme.

Window on the Catechism

The morality of human acts is discussed in *CCC* 1750–1754.

General Directory for Catechesis

Moral formation as one of the fundamental tasks of catechesis is discussed in *GDC* 85–87.

One-Hour Session Planner

SESSION 17 Jesus Makes a Choice

Session Theme: *Just as Jesus stayed true to his identity as the Son of God, we are called to stay true to our identities as sons and daughters of God.*

Before This Session

▶ Bookmark your Bible to Genesis 2:18, Mark 14:34, Mark 14:36, Luke 22:44–46, Matthew 26:38–39, 1 Corinthians 8, Romans 12:9–12, and Numbers 6:24–26. Place the open Bible in your prayer space.

▶ Read the Guide for this session, choose any additional If Time Allows activities that you might have time to complete, and gather the listed materials.

STEPS	APPROXIMATE TIME
Engage *Jesus Makes a Choice* PAGE 143	10 minutes
Explore *Jesus' Night of Sorrow* PAGES 144–145 *Making Moral Choices* PAGES 146–147	30–40 minutes
Reflect *Prayer:* Acting in Good Conscience PAGE 148 *Where Do I Fit In?* PAGE 149	10–15 minutes
Respond *What's What?* PAGE 150	10–15 minutes

Materials

REQUIRED

▶ Writing supplies (pages 145, 149, 150)

▶ Computers with Internet access (page 150)

OPTIONAL

▶ Writing supplies (pages 143, 144, 149)

▶ Session 17 BLM, T-374 (page 146)

▶ Digital recorder (page 149)

▶ Session 17 Assessment, www.findinggod.com (page 150)

 Prayer in Session 17

A short prayer relating to a key concept begins the session, and an invitation to experience an online 3-Minute Retreat ends the session. In Session 17, young people take responsibility for developing a strong conscience and pray for help in making moral choices in their lives. Follow the Prepare directions on the Catechist Guide page before sharing with young people.

TAKE IT HOME

Homework options:

Who I Am   PAGE 145

In the News   PAGE 147

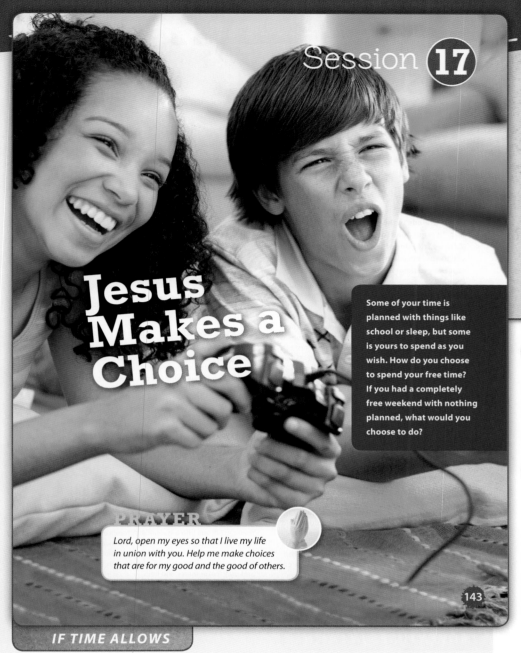

Session 17

Jesus Makes a Choice

Some of your time is planned with things like school or sleep, but some is yours to spend as you wish. How do you choose to spend your free time? If you had a completely free weekend with nothing planned, what would you choose to do?

PRAYER

Lord, open my eyes so that I live my life in union with you. Help me make choices that are for my good and the good of others.

143

IF TIME ALLOWS

1,440 Minutes

Ask young people to make a list of everything they did in the previous 24 hours, from the time they awoke until the time they went to sleep. Ask them to consider specific ways they lived in union with God. Then ask them to consider in what ways they overlooked chances or turned away from God. When they have finished, ask volunteers to share from their lists how they spent their minutes.

Go to **www.findinggod.com/sessionextenders** for an article about making moral choices. You may wish to share this with the group.

OUTCOMES

► Explain that just as Jesus remained faithful to his Father, we are called to remain faithful sons and daughters of God.

► Identify how to make moral decisions and how to develop a fully formed conscience.

► Pray for help to live our Catholic faith.

► Define *Agony in the Garden, conscience, moral choice,* and *social sin.*

① Set the Stage

Have young people read aloud the text in the box. Ask them to share ideas with a partner or write responses to the questions.

② Get Started

Ask: **By a show of hands, how would you spend your free time?**

► How many would sleep in late?
► How many would go to a mall?
► How many would spend time with friends?
► How many would spend time with God?

Guide young people to realize that they are faced with many decisions each day. But making the right decision is not always easy.

Have a volunteer read the session title. Ask: **How do you think the temptation to make a bad decision and a betrayal of one's true identity relate to the session title?** (Jesus had a human nature so he faced temptations, but he remained faithful to his identity.)

 Prayer

Say: **Let's take a moment to pray together that we may always remain faithful to God.** Pray aloud the prayer. Conclude by praying the Sign of the Cross.

1 Begin

Say: **Today we will have a test that will count for half of your final grade.** Pause for a few moments. Say: **You can choose to take the test alone, or you can take it with a partner.** Ask for a show of hands to indicate how many would prefer to take the test with a partner or alone. Ask young people who prefer to work with a partner to give reasons for their choice. (Possible answers: They are unprepared, lack confidence, need help, and so on.) Say: **Sometimes being alone frightens us. Friends often bring us comfort, joy, and help.** Tell young people they aren't really having a test today.

Ask a volunteer to read the article title and the first paragraph. Connect the quotation from Genesis to the previous discussion.

2 Connect

Have volunteers read the remaining three paragraphs in the first column. Explain that Jesus knew what was going to happen to him. Ask: **For what did Jesus pray to his Father?** (to take away what was about to happen to him) Ask: **What happened when Jesus asked the disciples to keep watch while he prayed?** (They fell asleep three different times.) Ask: **Why is it hard to stand by someone in hard times?** (Possible answers: fear, despair, grief, exhaustion)

Ask a volunteer to read Stay Awake. Say: **We, too, are called to be awake and aware in our lives, even when we are tempted to evade, avoid, and turn away from difficult tasks.** Ask volunteers to read aloud the meanings of *Agony in the Garden* and *social sin* in the Glossary. Have young people compare and contrast personal sin and social sin.

Ask: **When can media and other distractions become an escape or crutch?** (Possible answers: They can keep us from facing up to challenges or the plan that God wishes us to follow.)

Jesus' Night of Sorrow

Golgotha Chapel ceiling detail of Gethsemane, Church of the Holy Sepulcher, Jerusalem.

AS a prelude to the creation of Eve, God said, "It is not good for the man to be alone." (Genesis 2:18) One of the hardest parts of life and the human condition is being alone—especially in times of trial and trouble.

In Chapter 14 of the Gospel of Mark, we learn about the night Jesus' disciples abandoned him. After the Passover meal, Jesus and the disciples went to a small garden called Gethsemane located outside the east wall of the city of Jerusalem, on the Mount of Olives. Knowing his arrest was imminent, Jesus was troubled and distressed. He was about to face the greatest test of love someone could face, a test that would ask him to live in accordance with the Father's divine plan. Jesus asked the disciples to keep watch while he prayed. "My soul is sorrowful even to death. Remain here and keep watch." (Mark 14:34)

Jesus prayed to his Father, "Abba, Father, all things are possible to you. Take this cup away from me, but not what I will but what you will." (Mark 14:36) The disciples, meanwhile, had fallen asleep. Three times Jesus left them to pray, and three times he returned to find the disciples asleep. The disciples could not stay awake with Jesus through his time of trial.

By the third incident, Jesus told them to get up because his betrayer (Judas Iscariot) had arrived, accompanied by a crowd with swords and clubs. After Judas betrayed him with a kiss, his accusers laid hands on Jesus and arrested him. Soon afterward the disciples left him and fled. Jesus, the Son of God, was abandoned by his friends, the same men he had loved and with whom he had walked, taught, shared meals, laughed, and prayed.

Stay Awake

The Gospel of Luke tells us that Jesus' prayers during his **Agony in the Garden** were so fervent that his "sweat became like drops of blood falling on the ground," and Jesus found the disciples "sleeping from grief." (Luke 22:44–45) Finally he said to his disciples, "Why are you sleeping? Get up and pray that you may not undergo the test." (Luke 22:46)

Jesus was fully awake in every sense of the word. God invites you to stay awake, too, to be vigilant against both personal sin and **social sin,** such as racism, sexism, denial of health care, and destruction of the environment. For what does God invite you to stay awake to see? To know? To feel? To do? To be?

As young people, it is good to pay attention to how you use video games, the Internet, or other distractions that can numb you to the present reality. If used as ways to avoid facing something painful, they can lull you into a state of indifference. Escaping through distractions might hinder your awareness of the needs of others. Instead of escaping life around you, Jesus invites you to turn yourself over to his care and pray for his mercy and help.

144 *Unit 4 · Jesus the Christ*

 ADVENTURES IN FAITH

Stay Awake

Remind young people that Jesus asked his disciples to stay awake with him during his time of trial. Explain that bullying is aggressive, abusive behavior that can happen face-to-face or online. Invite young people to examine their own views on bullying. Write on the board statements concerning bullying such as the following and ask young people to respond yes or no to each on a sheet of paper.

- *Bullying is always a physical altercation.*
- *Victims of bullying ask for it.*
- *Teasing can be a way to bully.*
- *Only adults bully.*
- *Bullies want to feel powerful.*
- *Not joining in bullying will stop the behavior.*

Afterward, discuss ideas with the group. Invite them to stay awake to their own tendencies to bully. Discuss strategies to stand up for victims of bullying and to avoid becoming one.

✝ *Rights and Responsibilities*

Thy Will Be Done

Jesus' words in the Gospel of Matthew reveal his troubled heart in words very similar to Mark's account. (Matthew 26:38) Jesus does not want to die. When he prays, he expresses his sorrow, fear, and a longing for companionship. He prays deeply and fervently. In verse 39 of Chapter 26, he asks his Father for this cup—this difficult moment—to pass him by. At this most difficult time, Jesus gives himself over to the Father's will.

It is okay to tell God and loved ones when you are afraid or confused. Living a Christian life requires staying fully awake and facing adversity. By turning to God in times of human weakness, you give yourself to God, relying on his grace to be your strength.

Jesus stayed close with the Father in the Garden of Gethsemane. He trusted the Father and acted on that trust. Jesus remained faithful in spite of the temptation to escape what was to come. Following God's will is not always easy, and it is hard to let go of the desire to control your own destiny. But God never abandons you. You are never truly alone.

God Is with Us

Jesus stayed true to his identity as the Son of God. The risen Christ would be with his friends again, sitting with them and even sharing a meal with them. Despite Peter's denials of him, Jesus would make him the rock of his Church. Despite Jesus' Crucifixion and Death, he would ascend to God his Father.

If Jesus suffered so that he may share in your suffering, the hope, life, and victory that Jesus experiences is something in which you also may share. Even when you feel alone or filled with deep sorrow, Jesus is with you—always near and waiting to be your source of strength.

SACRED ART

Georges Henri Rouault, a French artist who also worked in stained glass, was an Expressionist painter who tried to portray inner reality rather than focusing only on the exterior appearance of a subject. In this painting, he makes use of color, line, and form to represent Jesus' emotions as he faced his impending Death on the Cross.

Are You Awake?

Where in the world today do you find human suffering, and how can you respond to lessen it?

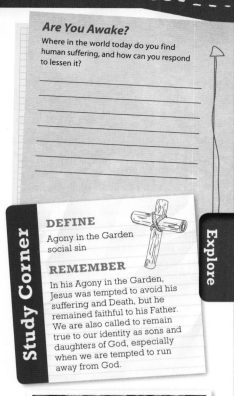

Study Corner

DEFINE
Agony in the Garden
social sin

REMEMBER
In his Agony in the Garden, Jesus was tempted to avoid his suffering and Death, but he remained faithful to his Father. We are also called to remain true to our identity as sons and daughters of God, especially when we are tempted to run away from God.

Explore

Nocturne (Gethsemane), Georges Henri Rouault, oil on canvas, 1915.

Session 17 > Jesus Makes a Choice   **145**

TAKE IT HOME

Who I Am

Have young people work with a partner to draw outlines of themselves on separate sheets of mural paper. Ask them to work independently to fill in their own outlines with words or phrases that describe their true identity. Tell them that the words or phrases they choose should provide insight into who they are and what they believe. The next time the group meets, ask volunteers to share their identity outlines with the group, adding explanations, stories, or descriptions. Have young people add the heading *Child of God* to their paper outlines and display them around the room.

Ask a volunteer to read Thy Will Be Done. Ask: **Why might it be difficult for people to admit that they do not want to face up to something difficult?** (Possible answers: They are afraid that it indicates defeat or a lack of confidence or strength.) Point out that following God's will is not always easy. Jesus modeled a trusting relationship with the Father to show us how to have faith. Say: **It is normal to experience moments of weakness or times of trouble. God does not promise that everything in your life will be easy, but he invites you to turn to him with confidence for his help.**

After a volunteer reads God Is with Us, remind them that they will face temptations to abandon their identities as children of God. Assure them that God is always with them, ready to help if only they trust in God's will. Say: **Jesus' victory is ours to share if we stay faithful to him.**

Ask a volunteer to read the directions in the Are You Awake? activity. Remind them that human suffering may affect an individual or an entire group. Invite volunteers to give examples of human suffering and ways to respond to it.

Sacred Art

Read aloud the Sacred Art feature. Ask: **Which emotions do you think the artist is trying to portray?** Ask volunteers to explain the effects of the colors, lines, and forms. Ask: **How does the painting make you feel?** (Answers will vary.)

③ Close

Close the discussion by having young people think about one area in their lives where they will make an extra effort to stay awake and aware. Point out that they may recognize this area because it tempts them to avoid, ignore, or turn away from God.

① Begin

Write these questions on the board:

▶ *If you could watch only one TV show, which would it be?*

▶ *If you could eat only one food, what would it be?*

Ask volunteers to suggest responses and discuss their ideas. Say: **Many of the choices we make are easy. They are clear, they don't affect others, and they don't interfere with our belief system.** Explain that other choices are not so easy because they involve serious issues or present conflicts with our belief system.

② Connect

Read aloud the title Making Moral Choices. Ask a volunteer to read the first two paragraphs. Refer young people to the Glossary and discuss the meaning of *moral choice*. Explain that we tend to think that moral choices are black and white—wrong or right. Say: **Unfortunately, moral choices are more complex than that. The Church helps us recognize different shades of moral right and wrong.**

Read aloud Two Schools of Thought. Ask young people to name the competing beliefs for the Corinthians. (eating unacceptable foods, worshiping other gods, eating in temples devoted to other gods) Explain that these may seem like strange choices to argue. Discuss modern moral choices that people make.

Our Catholic Character

Have a volunteer read aloud the feature. Read the definition of *conscience* in the Glossary. Point out that trusting an informed conscience requires a thoughtful response that may be contrary to popular societal attitudes. Encourage them to place themselves in God's gentle hands as they pray for guidance.

Making Moral Choices

SOME choices require little thinking, such as what to eat for breakfast or what to wear. Other choices are more difficult, especially when they force you to choose between competing values.

Making a **moral choice** means choosing to do what is right or choosing not to do what is wrong. Saint Paul addressed moral issues with the early Christian community in Corinth, a port city in Greece between Asia and Western Europe. Similar to modern American port cities such as New York and Miami, Corinth was ethnically diverse and had lots of people with competing cultures and ideas. The Corinthian Christians, influenced by their Jewish roots, believed certain foods were acceptable to eat while others were not. This was an important issue for the time because following a proper diet was considered a way of honoring God's law.

Two Schools of Thought

Some Christians in Corinth chose to eat meat that had been sacrificed to pagan gods earlier in the day. They were not troubled by this because they believed that meat, after all, was only meat. They understood that there was one God and that Jesus was the Son of God. Other Christians, though, objected to the practice and were uncomfortable eating meat that had been used in Temple sacrifice. The Christians who chose to eat the meat thought that they had greater insight into the freedom won by Jesus Christ.

Letter to the Corinthians

Paul teaches about moral decisions in relation to eating the meat in 1 Corinthians 8. Moral choices are made by people who are free and take responsibility for their actions. The morality of any act has three dimensions: the act chosen, the intention behind the act, and the circumstances behind the act.

Our Catholic Character

In order to make good moral decisions, you have to have a fully formed **conscience,** which is the inner voice that helps you judge the morality of your actions. The Church understands that you must always obey the certain judgment of your own conscience. How do you form your conscience? You follow the guidance of parents and teachers. You learn from your mistakes and those of others. You also pray for guidance, read and listen to Scripture, and learn about the teachings of the Church. You learn to consider the effects of your actions on others. Without a fully formed conscience, you are left to make decisions without a guide. The consequence of a poorly formed conscience is that it may lead to a life of self-delusion and self-destruction.

146 *Unit 4 • Jesus the Christ*

IF TIME ALLOWS

Session 17 BLM

Making Moral Choices Remind young people that we make all kinds of decisions each day, but only some of them involve moral choices. Provide each young person with the Session 17 Blackline Master [T-374]. Ask them to use the Blackline Master to better understand what is required of them when they make a moral choice.

The Act Chosen For the Corinthian Christians who decided to eat meat sacrificed to pagan gods, the act that was chosen was the good of feeding oneself and others. We need to eat to live, and offering hospitality to others is a Christian obligation. So those who served the meat or who were dining with friends in the Temple were acting in a morally good way because the meat helped fulfill their need for food.

The Intention Behind the Act If the intention was to serve themselves and their guests a good meal, this was a morally good thing to do. But suppose they knew that serving meat that had been part of a pagan sacrifice would make their guests uncomfortable, and they served it anyway to show off their superior understanding of Christian teaching? Then the act would be morally wrong because they did not have good intentions.

Circumstances Behind the Act Because food was scarce in Paul's time, people had to eat what was available. If meat from a pagan temple was all there was to eat, it would lessen the moral issue of whether the host was offending the conscience of his or her guest. Using similar reasoning, if a person is tricked or forced into committing an immoral act, his or her responsibility is lessened. It is never a good moral choice to do an immoral act for the sake of some imagined positive result.

Knowing How to Choose

Although Paul agreed in principle that meat was just meat, and the one group was correct in eating it, he believed their actions of superiority and their shaming of their fellow Christians were morally wrong. Paul wanted both groups of Christians in Corinth to support each other, not present situations in which one group built itself up at the expense of the other. "Thus through your knowledge, the weak person is brought to destruction, the brother for whom Christ died. When you sin in this way against your brothers and wound their consciences, weak as they are, you are sinning against Christ." (1 Corinthians 8:11–12)

How can you live a moral life? Gather for liturgical prayer with fellow Catholics on Sunday. The Lord's Day gives you the time for rest and leisure to help your family, cultural, social, and religious lives grow. Receive grace in the Eucharist and the other sacraments. Listen to your conscience. Follow the Ten Commandments, the Great Commandment, the New Commandment, and the Beatitudes. Know the teachings of the Church, live the Golden Rule, and follow the example of the saints to help you make good moral choices.

Past Meets Present

PAST: Katharine Drexel was born into a wealthy family but gave up a life of luxury. As a nun, she started a religious congregation called the Sisters of the Blessed Sacrament, who were dedicated to helping African Americans and Native Americans. Before her death, Saint Katharine Drexel established schools, missions, and Xavier University of Louisiana. Her decisions were unpopular with some people, but she knew that the right choice might not be the popular choice.

PRESENT: The Oblate Sisters of Providence, the first Catholic religious community for women of African descent, has been committed to the education of children and service to the poor for over 175 years. The order's ministry of providing a transitional place for neglected and abused girls continues at the Mary Elizabeth Lange Center in Baltimore, Maryland. The Sisters also provide eldercare, social services, and service to Hispanic ministry.

Study Corner

DEFINE
moral choice
conscience

REMEMBER
The morality of an act has three dimensions—the act chosen, the intention behind the act, and the circumstances behind the act. We develop a fully formed conscience through the guidance of parents and teachers, prayer, Scripture, Church teachings, and learning from our mistakes.

TAKE IT HOME

In the News

Ask young people to select a current moral dilemma facing the world. Organize them in small groups and have them scrutinize the issue in relation to the three dimensions discussed in this session: the act chosen, the intention of the act, and the circumstances that surround the act.

Invite groups to write a brief report that explains what they learned about the issue and what the Church teaches about it. Encourage them to give reasons why the issues stir up strong emotions and why some people avoid taking a moral stand. Remind young people that many of these issues are social justice concerns and Catholic Social Teaching invites us to take action to bring justice to the world.

✝ *Rights and Responsibilities*

Have volunteers read aloud Letter to the Corinthians. Ask: **What is the criteria for a moral choice?** (People are free and take responsibility for the choice.) Say: **Paul's letter to the Christians of Corinth taught the process of making a moral decision.** Ask: **How many dimensions are there in determining the morality of an act?** (three) Ask: **What are they?** (the act chosen, the intention behind the act, and the circumstances behind the act) Discuss the meaning behind each dimension in relation to the problem Paul was addressing with the Christians in Corinth.

Read the section Knowing How to Choose. Emphasize the role that an informed conscience plays in moral choices. Ask volunteers to summarize the meaning of Paul's letter. Point out that his instruction is clear, yet the thinking required for the moral decision is not simple or clear-cut.

Past Meets Present

After volunteers take turns reading the feature, ask young people to name a moral decision that Saint Katharine Drexel made. (She invested in the education and well-being of minority students when many people opposed this idea.) Invite young people to point out or comment on current social situations that require people to take a moral stand.

③ Close

To close the discussion, invite young people to reflect on the following questions:

▶ What is one moral decision you have made or still need to make?

▶ What do you need to consider when you make your decision?

▶ Who or what can help you make your decision?

Prayer

Follow the steps to guide young people through the prayer on page 148.

Young People's Page

Prepare Pray the prayer in advance to become familiar with it.

Pray Have a volunteer read aloud the title of the page and the paragraphs. Invite young people to suggest reasons that tell why prayer is an effective tool to use when they are trying to make a moral decision. (Possible answer: Prayer is an opportunity to reflect, seek guidance, and listen for God's response.) Then have young people bring their books to the prayer space and sit quietly. Say: **Take a few deep breaths and relax. Focus your attention on God's presence.**

Assign the part of Reader. Invite the entire group to pray the All parts. Pause briefly and pray aloud the Leader part slowly and reverently, praying the Sign of the Cross. Lead the All response so that young people pray in unison. Have the Reader read the passage from Romans. Follow with the All response. Continue with the remaining parts. Pause and allow time for meditation between the bulleted questions, maintaining a longer pause following the last one. Pray aloud the passage from Numbers. Invite young people to respond *Amen*.

As a conclusion to the prayer service, say: **Think about a situation in your life in which you will need to make an important decision.** Ask: **How might you use your conscience to follow the right path?** Say: **Let's ask God to help us take responsibility for living our faith and making good choices.**

Prayer

Acting in Good Conscience

Each one of us is called to take responsibility for living the Catholic faith and making good choices.

Prayer is an essential practice in developing a strong conscience. Praying helps us see the right path and gain the willingness to follow it. With the help of the Holy Spirit, we can consider how to make the correct choices in life.

Taking Responsibility

Leader: Let us begin this time of prayer together by praying the Sign of the Cross.

In the name of the Father, and of the Son, and of the Holy Spirit. Amen.

All: Loving God, we come before you with gratitude for all that you have given us. We ask for your help as we pause and take responsibility for our lives and the choices we make. We ask this through Christ, your Son and our Lord. Amen.

Reader: A reading from the Letter of Paul to the Romans.

Let love be sincere; hate what is evil, hold on to what is good; love one another with mutual affection; anticipate one another in showing honor. Do not grow slack in zeal, be fervent in spirit, serve the Lord. Rejoice in hope, endure in affliction, persevere in prayer.

Romans 12:9–12

The Word of the Lord.

All: Thanks be to God.

Leader: In light of the Word of God we've just heard, let's spend a few minutes in silence to reflect on how we take responsibility for living our faith. Think about these questions as I read them aloud.

- Do I make myself look good at the expense of others?
- Do I ever choose to do the right thing for the wrong reason?
- Do I learn from my mistakes as well as those of others?
- Do I consider what effect my actions may have on others?
- Do I show respect for my body and the bodies of others?

Pause and reflect.

Leader: The LORD bless you and keep you!
The LORD let his face shine upon you, and be gracious to you!
The LORD look upon you kindly and give you peace!

Numbers 6:24–26

All: Amen.

148 *Unit 4 · Jesus the Christ*

IF TIME ALLOWS

Instructing One Another

Arrange to share visits to another catechist's room so that young people can talk with others about their experiences making moral decisions. Encourage young people to hold a panel discussion as a way to point out situations that involve moral choices and to give one another tips for ways to strengthen their conscience.

✝ *Rights and Responsibilities*

FYI

Coaching Young People to Pray

Before praying, encourage young people to ask God for help in taking responsibility for living their faith. Have them think about the questions posed during the prayer service. Ask them to focus on one question over the next week.

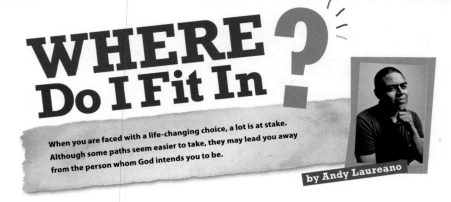

WHERE Do I Fit In?

When you are faced with a life-changing choice, a lot is at stake. Although some paths seem easier to take, they may lead you away from the person whom God intends you to be.

by Andy Laureano

Reflect

What Does Courage Look Like?

"The pack" was a group of four eighth graders who walked around together, bullied kids, and vandalized the park. We called them "the pack" because they resembled a wolf pack. They sat by the soccer bench and laughed at the kids playing soccer. We always avoided them.

My friend Francisco and I always skateboarded by the basketball courts. One day "the pack" approached us and took our skateboards away. They made fun of us and said the only way we could get the boards back was to join them. The shortest kid handed Francisco a can of paint and ordered him to paint on the walls. Francisco shook his head in fear. Then the tallest kid snatched the paint from him and painted our skateboards red. They threw our boards across the basketball court and shoved us to the ground.

This continued to happen for a few days. Every day they used a different color of paint. Francisco decided that the best way to stop them was to join "the pack." I remember going home every day and putting my hands together to pray before I went to sleep. At first I thought praying was childish. I was 12 years old. I could have just stood up to them. Or I could have done what Francisco did and started to paint walls and school property. All I prayed for was to be safe and to get good grades.

"The pack" eventually stopped bothering me. But Francisco stopped skateboarding. I stopped talking to him. Eventually he got kicked out of school. My mother asked me where Francisco had gone, and I told her the story about "the pack." She told me that I had done the right thing. I think that I did the right thing too.

True to Yourself

The writer stuck to his convictions. Many martyrs, such as Blessed Miguel Pro, Saint Thomas Becket, and Saint Isaac Jogues sacrificed everything for their convictions.

When have you needed to stick to a conviction because you knew it was the right thing to do? In a brief essay, write about the experience on a separate sheet of paper.

ANDY LAUREANO is the Associate Director of Alumni Tracking and Support at the Cristo Rey Network. On a typical weekend, you may find him skateboarding in downtown Chicago.

Session 17 > Jesus Makes a Choice   149

IF TIME ALLOWS

Back, Pack!

Have young people work in small groups to write lyrics for a pop song about resisting "the pack," which could be a situation similar to the author's or any situation that requires standing up for your convictions. Explain that they may write their own tune or use a melody they already know. Remind young people that many songs are narratives. Since a narrative tells a story, suggest that their songs do the same. Instruct groups to write at least two verses and one refrain for their song. Group members may prefer to record their songs. Invite each group to perform or play their song. Allow time for group discussion.

---

① Begin

Have a volunteer read aloud the introductory text and the article title. Ask: **What actions do you visualize when you hear the word courage?** (Possible answers: rescuing someone from a burning building, entering a dark cave) Say: **Sometimes an act of courage is heroic. Most times, though, an act of courage is small and quiet. It can even be mistaken as an act of weakness or cowardice by certain people.** Elicit examples or comments from young people.

② Connect

Have volunteers take turns reading What Does Courage Look Like? Say: **For the author, "the pack" was a very real and threatening group of people.** Ask: **In our own lives, who or what might "the pack" be?** (Possible answers: peers who pressure us to act in ways that do not match our values; media messages that tempt or misguide us) Ask: **What did the author do to resist "the pack"?** (He did not follow their orders. He prayed.) Ask: **How did God answer the author's prayer?** (by giving him the strength not to give into his fear and "the pack") Say: **The author's choice wasn't outwardly heroic. Members of "the pack" might have viewed his choice as cowardly. But it put the author on a very different life path than his friend Francisco, who allowed fear to win.** Have young people describe some effects of decisions on different life paths.

Read aloud the True to Yourself activity and have young people complete it independently.

③ Close

Invite volunteers to read aloud their essays from the activity. Commend them for making quiet, courageous choices. Display their writing with the heading *Real Heroes.*

① Begin

What's What? Ask a volunteer to read aloud the directions. Have young people complete the activity individually or with a partner.

② Connect

Say What? Ask volunteers to read aloud and define the terms. Review each term in the Glossary if necessary.

Now What? Ask a volunteer to read aloud the section. Invite young people to consider their responses carefully before writing. Point out that they probably turn to different people or resources in different circumstances. Encourage them to consider who or what would best be able to help them with the matter of their conscience. Ask: **Who will have your best interests at heart? Who will tell you the truth?** Remind young people that the best resource might not always tell them what they prefer to hear.

③ Go in Peace

Collect materials and return them to their appropriate places. Encourage young people to discuss a variety of people or resources to turn to for guidance. Say: **Being able to recognize a moral choice is an important step to living a Christian life.** Ask: **Why might the steps for developing an informed conscience vary from person to person?** Say: **You are making moral choices now, and they will continue to be part of your lives. Invite God into your decisions so you can live as his sons and daughters.**

3-Minute Retreat
Give young people an opportunity for quiet meditation at **www.loyolapress.com/retreat**.

What's What?

Use details from the text to answer the questions.

1 Use your own words to describe what happened in the Garden of Gethsemane. (PAGE 144)

Jesus prayed for his Father to take away the suffering to come. His disciples fell asleep three times. Jesus was arrested.

2 How did Jesus stay true to his identify as the Son of God? (PAGES 144–145)

Jesus trusted in the Father. He submitted to the Father's will, even though he was tempted.

3 Why did Paul write to the Christians in Corinth? (PAGES 146–147)

They disagreed whether to eat meat that had been offered in the Temple to pagan gods. One group felt superior and shamed the other.

4 How do we form our conscience? (PAGE 146)

We use the guidance of parents and teachers; we learn from our mistakes; we pray, read Scripture, and learn Church teachings.

5 What must be true of a person making a moral choice? (PAGE 147)

He or she must be free to make the choice and must accept the responsibility for his or her actions.

6 What are the three dimensions of a moral act? (PAGE 147)

the act chosen; the intention behind the act; the circumstances surrounding the act

Say What?
Know the definitions of these terms.

Agony in the Garden
conscience
moral choice
social sin

Now What?
If something was bothering your conscience, to whom or to what would you turn to for guidance? Why?

Answers will vary.

IF TIME ALLOWS

Service: Bulletin Article

Arrange for the group to contribute an article to your parish's bulletin as a service project to encourage moral decision making. Assign young people to write about the process of making a moral decision and how these decisions make them better members of the Church. Write the group's key points on the board and help them organize their ideas into an effective article. Ask group members to edit, proofread, and prepare the work before submitting the article for publication.

✝ *Rights and Responsibilities*

Session Assessment Option

An assessment for this session can be found at www.findinggod.com.

PLAN AHEAD: Get Ready for Session 18

Consult the catechist preparation pages to prepare for Session 18 and determine any materials you will need.

Jesus Redeems Us

 3-Minute Retreat

Before you prepare the session, pause and be still. Take three deep breaths and be aware of the loving presence of God, who is with you on this journey.

Mark 15:37–39

Jesus gave a loud cry and breathed his last. The veil of the sanctuary was torn in two from top to bottom. When the centurion who stood facing him saw how he breathed his last he said, "Truly this man was the Son of God!"

Reflection

At Jesus' most horrible and humiliating moment, his agony and Death, the centurion realizes that he is standing face-to-face with the Son of God. The true meaning of Jesus' kingship is revealed as he hangs lifeless on the Cross. The Death of Jesus puts his life, and ours, into a new perspective. His Death is all about love—love of God and love for us. For his followers then and now, the Death of Jesus is a call to reach out in love. It is a call to believe that love is stronger than death. It is a call to make God's kingdom of love a reality.

Questions

What do I see when I draw close to the Cross? How do my words and actions help make God's love real to those around me?

 Concluding Prayer

Speak to God, using the words of this prayer or your own.

Jesus, Redeemer, your Passion and Death brought us to life. Help me be a true disciple following you on the way to the Cross.

Knowing and Sharing Your Faith in Session 18

Consider how Scripture and Tradition can deepen your understanding of session content.

Scripture

Mark 8:34–35 tells us what it takes to follow Jesus as a true disciple.

Luke 23:34 reveals Jesus' message of forgiveness, the key message throughout his ministry, as he hung on the Cross.

Tradition

When we speak of Jesus' Death on the Cross, we say he died for our redemption. The word *redeem* means "to buy back." When we sin, we offer our allegiance to that which is not God. In essence, that which is not God takes possession of us. God loves us so much that he redeemed us by sending his only Son, Jesus. Through his life, Death, Resurrection, and glorious Ascension, Jesus delivers, or redeems, us from sin and evil, thus allowing us to once again be possessed solely by God. Jesus freely offered himself for our redemption, and by doing so, showed us that the way of redemption is to lay down one's life for others.

Catholic Social Teaching

In this session the integrated Catholic Social Teaching theme is **Call to Family, Community, and Participation.** See page 133b for an explanation of this theme.

Window on the Catechism

Jesus' Crucifixion, Death, and burial are discussed in *CCC* 572–635.

General Directory for Catechesis

The historical character of the mystery of Salvation is presented in *GDC* 108.

One-Hour Session Planner

SESSION 18 Jesus Redeems Us

Session Theme: *Jesus' glory is revealed through his suffering, Death, and Resurrection so we know how to live as his disciples in the world.*

Before This Session

▶ Bookmark your Bible to 1 Corinthians 5:7, Mark 8:29, Mark 8:33–35, Mark 9:7, Mark 15:33–39, Isaiah 53:11, Luke 23:34, and Matthew 25:31–46. Place the open Bible in your prayer space.

▶ Read the Guide for this session, choose any additional If Time Allows activities that you might have time to complete, and gather the listed materials.

STEPS	APPROXIMATE TIME
Engage *Jesus Redeems Us* PAGE 151	10 minutes
Explore *The Suffering Servant* PAGES 152–153 *The Moment of Truth* PAGES 154–155	30–40 minutes
Reflect *Prayer:* The Victory of the Cross PAGE 156 *Where Do I Fit In?* PAGE 157	10–15 minutes
Respond *What's What?* PAGE 158	10–15 minutes

Prayer in Session 18

Offer young people the prayer experiences at the beginning and end of the session. Session 18 includes an extended guided reflection, a special approach to meditative prayer that enables young people to consider Jesus' message to his disciples about suffering. Follow the Prepare directions on the Catechist Guide page before sharing with young people.

TAKE IT HOME

Homework options:

Picturing Jesus	PAGE 152
A Civilization of Love	PAGE 155

Materials

REQUIRED

▶ Media player (page 152)

▶ Movie or TV clip (page 152)

▶ Writing supplies (pages 153, 157, 158)

▶ CD player (pages 152, 156)

▶ CD 1, Track 6: "Transfiguration" (5:47) (page 152)

▶ CD 1, Track 3: "Face to Face" (9:53) (page 156)

▶ CD 2, Track 5: Reflective Music (page 156)

▶ Computers with Internet access (page 158)

OPTIONAL

▶ Blank identification cards or cardstock, art supplies (page 151)

▶ Session 18 BLM, T-375 (page 153)

▶ Bibles (page 153)

▶ Computers with Internet access, blog page or school Web site, digital camera, video camera, digital recorder (page 154)

▶ Writing supplies (pages 156, 157, 158)

▶ Art supplies (page 157)

▶ Cardstock (page 158)

▶ Session 18 Assessment www.findinggod.com (page 158)

Session 18

Jesus Redeems Us

When you go through security at an airport or apply for a library card, you are asked to show identification. People want to make sure you are who you say you are. So who are you? What's the truest thing you can say about yourself?

PRAYER

I am your servant, Lord. Draw me close to your heart and never let me be parted from you.

151

SESSION 18

OUTCOMES

- ► Explain how to live in a way that shows we know, understand, and follow Jesus.
- ► Explain the meaning of Jesus' Death and our Christian response to suffering.
- ► Pray a guided reflection concerning our response to suffering.
- ► Define *Apostles' Creed, Paschal Mystery, Passion,* and *Transfiguration*.

① Set the Stage

Have young people read the text in the box. Ask them to discuss it with a partner or write their responses.

② Get Started

Ask volunteers to share one true thing about themselves. Discuss the importance of having an identity. Ask: **How are identities formed?** (Possible answers: by our actions and experiences; by our thoughts; according to what others say about us) Ask: **How is it possible that someone may see you in a different way than you see yourself?** (Possible answers: They may not know you very well, or you may not see yourself as honestly as they do.)

Ask young people what Jesus might have said about his true self. Say: **Jesus' dying and rising is central to Christian life. Through his Death and Resurrection, we are saved.** Ask the group to consider how Jesus' true identity and the session title are related.

 Prayer

Say: **As we pray, ask God to teach you how to stay true to your Christian identity.** Pray aloud the prayer. Conclude by praying the Sign of the Cross.

IF TIME ALLOWS

My "Me" I.D.

Provide each young person with a blank identification card [available at craft stores or online] or a similar-sized piece of cardstock. Ask young people to fill their cards with words, phrases, or images that represent ideas of their true selves. Encourage them to represent themselves honestly. When they complete their I.D.s, ask volunteers to explain their cards to the group. Consider laminating the cards for durability.

INCLUSION

Emotional

Developing Self-Control
Young people with emotional challenges will benefit from having group rules and expectations posted clearly in the room. As necessary, point out the rules and their consequences. Consider seating young people who have emotional challenges close to you. Use positive words to reward good behavior.

➜ Go to **www.findinggod.com/sessionextenders** for meditations of Jesus' seven last words. You may wish to share this with the group.

① Begin

Play a clip from a TV show or movie that you have previewed and approved. List the main characters' names on the board. Ask volunteers to describe one of the characters and have others guess who it is. Ask: **Do you think that all labels are necessarily true and accurate? Why or why not?** Guide the group to understand that labels can be misleading and can prevent us from seeing a clear, complete, or accurate picture. Encourage them to work toward a deeper understanding of themselves or another person before they assume a label is true. Say: **Our identities consist of more than labels.** Read the article title and the first two paragraphs.

② Connect

Have volunteers take turns reading aloud the paragraphs in Who Is Jesus? Ask: **Why does Jesus instruct the disciples not to tell anyone about his miracles?** (His identity is not limited to healing.) Ask: **Who do people believe Jesus is?** (a prophet, Elijah, John the Baptist) Ask: **How is Jesus' identity revealed in the Transfiguration?** (Jesus' appearance changes, and he speaks with Elijah and Moses; a voice identifies him as the beloved Son.)

Play the Scripture story "The Transfiguration" [CD 1, Track 6]. Say: **Jesus asked his disciples, "Who do people say that I am?" He asks us that question every day. As Christians we are called to be open to the Holy Spirit, who helps us understand who Jesus is—God and man, Lord and Savior—and what he is calling us to do as his followers.**

Past Meets Present

Read aloud the feature. Have volunteers explain what the lamb symbolizes in 1 Corinthians 5:7 and why the image of Jesus as the Lamb of God is appropriate.

The Suffering Servant

WHO do people say you are? Do people know you by a role—as a son or daughter, a cousin, a niece or nephew, an altar server, an artist, or a soccer player? But who are you, really? Are you all those things? Or are you some, none, or far more than those things?

Jesus knew what it was like to be known by many roles and titles. At various times in the Gospels, Jesus was called prophet, teacher, the Christ, Messiah, son of Mary and Joseph, Son of God, Lord, rabbi, Elijah, the Nazarene, healer, King of the Jews, Master, and the Savior. Jesus—who is he?

Prince of Peace icon, Father Gabriel Chavez de la Mora, O.S.B., Prince of Peace Abbey, Oceanside, California.

Past Meets Present

PAST: In 1 Corinthians 5:7, Christ is called "our paschal lamb." The word *paschal* is associated with the Hebrew word *pesach*, or Passover. Celebrated every year, Passover recalls when the Jewish people sacrificed a lamb and sprinkled its blood on their door posts so that the Angel of Death would pass over their homes and spare the lives of their firstborn children. The lamb became a symbol of redemption.

PRESENT: The **Paschal Mystery,** which is the work of Salvation that Jesus Christ accomplished through his Passion, Death, Resurrection, and Ascension, is at the heart of our lives as Catholics. Jesus is the Lamb of God because by his Death he took away the sins of the world and redeemed us. We remember Jesus' saving Death when we celebrate the Eucharist in every Mass.

152 *Unit 4 • Jesus the Christ*

Who Is Jesus?

Although the very beginning of the Gospel of Mark proclaims that Jesus Christ is the Son of God, the revelation unfolds gradually throughout the entire Gospel. For example, when Jesus heals a number of people, he tells his disciples not to speak of it. Jesus is more than a miraculous healer.

When Jesus learned that people believed he was John the Baptist, Elijah, or one of the prophets, he asked his disciples, "Who do people say that I am?" (Mark 8:29) Peter answered for all of them, saying that Jesus was the Messiah. Jesus cautioned the disciples not to tell anyone. Why was Jesus reluctant to make himself known? Jesus knew that he was not the kind of Messiah the people expected. He was not an earthly king. He was the suffering servant who would endure physical and mental cruelty to redeem the world and make eternal life possible.

The apostles Peter, James, and John witnessed the **Transfiguration,** when Jesus' appearance changed—his face shining like the sun and his clothes white as light—and he spoke with Elijah and Moses on the mountain. Afraid and hardly able to speak, the men witnessed a cloud overshadow them and heard a voice proclaim, "This is my beloved Son. Listen to him." (Mark 9:7) Even after witnessing this event and the disclosure of Jesus' divine glory, the Apostles still did not fully understand Jesus' mission as Messiah nor their role as his disciples. They wanted to pitch tents to honor Jesus, Moses, and Elijah, but Jesus knew the Apostles would be commissioned to go forth to spread the Word.

TAKE IT HOME

Picturing Jesus

Have young people reflect on what they have learned so far about Jesus' identity. Provide them with magazines or newspapers. Ask them to make a collage that uses images and words to show who Jesus is to them. Display the collages and encourage a discussion that focuses on various ways to interpret Jesus' identity.

Who Is a Disciple?

The Gospel of Mark tells us how to be a disciple, a true follower of Jesus. The Apostles had a hard time understanding what it meant to follow Jesus. They thought that following Jesus would mean that they would have power and recognition in this world. But suffering was part of Jesus' life. Similarly, everyone has times of disappointment, sorrow, and suffering. In such times we recall the sufferings of Jesus and rely on our Christian faith to help us accept our hardships with trust in God.

The disciples had seen Jesus' miracles and heard his words when he taught to the crowds. It was hard for them to understand that Jesus would suffer on the cross. But Jesus knew that he would.

Words that describe the glory that will follow the Messiah's suffering are found in Isaiah 53:11.

> Because of his anguish he shall see the light;
>   because of his knowledge he shall be content;
> My servant, the just one, shall justify the many,
>   their iniquity he shall bear.

Jesus Predicts His Suffering

In the Gospels, Jesus tells the Apostles that the Son of Man will suffer greatly. He predicts his suffering and Death, or his **Passion,** and tells the Apostles about his rejection, Death, and rising after three days. Peter does not understand and is greatly disturbed by Jesus' words. Peter takes Jesus aside and rebukes him. In reply, Jesus scolds Peter. "Get behind me, Satan. You are thinking not as God does, but as human beings do." (Mark 8:33) Jesus refuses to avoid the suffering that lies ahead of him because that would be contrary to his obedience to his Father and to the fulfillment of God's plan for humankind.

Glory Through the Cross

Jesus' Crucifixion revealed the real meaning of who Jesus is. Looking at the bruised and battered Jesus on the Cross, the Roman centurion recognizes and exclaims, "Truly this man was the Son of God!" (Mark 15:39) It is at this point in Mark's Gospel that we too recognize that Jesus is the Messiah, the Anointed One, the Christ. Jesus' glory is revealed through his Death and Resurrection, and humankind is redeemed.

Jesus redeemed our sins on the Cross. His redemption helps us better understand our own times of suffering and how we are invited to respond as true disciples. Jesus told his disciples that along the way they would suffer. People would reject them and even be hostile toward them. In the midst of their journey, though, Jesus would be with them, helping them endure and follow him. (Mark 8:34–35)

God is with us in both happy and sorrowful times. He invites us to respond to our human suffering with a faith that makes us stronger, more resilient, and more able to follow the selfless example of Jesus.

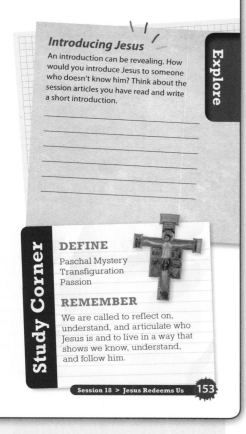

Introducing Jesus

An introduction can be revealing. How would you introduce Jesus to someone who doesn't know him? Think about the session articles you have read and write a short introduction.

Study Corner

DEFINE

Paschal Mystery
Transfiguration
Passion

REMEMBER

We are called to reflect on, understand, and articulate who Jesus is and to live in a way that shows we know, understand, and follow him.

Session 18 > Jesus Redeems Us   153

IF TIME ALLOWS

Session 18 BLM

Who Is Jesus? Distribute the Session 18 Blackline Master [T-375] to each young person. Have them think about the names and roles given to Jesus in the Bible as they complete the activity.

Isaiah's Servant Songs

Have young people read Isaiah 42:1–4. Arrange young people into small groups and ask them to summarize what the passage means. Then have them compare the passage to the meaning of Isaiah 53:11 on page 153.

Ask volunteers to read aloud Who Is a Disciple? Say: **Being a true disciple is not as easy as it may seem.** Ask volunteers to explain why the disciples had difficulty grasping a true understanding of what it meant to be a disciple. (After witnessing Jesus' miracles and hearing his teaching, it was incongruous to imagine that suffering would be part of Jesus' life, or theirs.) Discuss the verse from Isaiah and how it describes Jesus. Ask: **Why is Jesus described as the suffering servant?** (Jesus, innocent and without sin, suffered greatly to redeem the world.)

Ask a volunteer to read Jesus Predicts His Suffering. Young people may be confused about Jesus' rebuke of Peter. Say: **Jesus scolds Peter because Jesus knows what he must endure soon, and Peter is tempting him to avoid his mission.**

Read aloud Glory Through the Cross. Reinforce that Jesus' Crucifixion is central to our Catholic faith. Have young people discuss the Roman centurion's declaration. Ask: **How do we better understand the meaning of the Cross in our own times of suffering?** (Jesus invites us to live our lives with faith and trust in God, who is with us throughout every difficult moment. Being a disciple means that we, too, will suffer.)

Read aloud the directions in the Introducing Jesus activity. Then have young people complete the activity independently.

③ Close

Have young people reflect on or write responses to these questions:

▶ How does my life reflect an understanding of Jesus?

▶ How can I better follow Jesus, especially in times of suffering or trouble?

① Begin

Discuss examples of terrorism in today's world. Explain that terrorism uses fear to coerce people.

 Ask a volunteer to read the first two paragraphs on the page. Read aloud Mark 15:33–39.

② Connect

Ask young people to explain how the threat of crucifixion might have affected people during Jesus' time. (Possible answer: People may have been afraid to speak up for their beliefs or take a stand against the government.)

Read aloud the section Mark's Message. Say: **Contrary to the common belief that someone who experienced crucifixion must have been abandoned by God, Mark's Gospel tells us that in Jesus' ultimate sacrifice, the living God is revealed to us.** Ask volunteers to explain how Jesus' Death explains everything in light of Jesus' miracles, parables, words, or deeds. (Possible answer: Jesus instituted the Sacrament of the Eucharist at the Last Supper. His sacrifice on the Cross established a New Covenant between the people and God.)

Sacred Art

Have a volunteer read aloud the feature. Encourage young people to express what the sculpture means to them. Ask: **In what way does Mary's expression of serenity and faith reflect a Catholic view?** (Mary's gentle face displays her recognition of Jesus' great love and ultimate sacrifice. Jesus won for us the possibility of eternal life in Heaven.)

The Moment of Truth

WE only discover the depths of Jesus' love in his Death on the Cross. (Mark 15:33–39) In the Roman empire, crucifixion was not a punishment born of justice. It was a cruel and humiliating form of execution.

The Roman empire crafted crucifixion both to humiliate and degrade people perceived to be its "enemies." Most importantly, it was intended to put fear in the hearts of the people. Crucifixion was saved for rebels against Roman authority as a warning for anyone who would dare question their rule. After people saw or heard of Jesus' torture—his scourging, beating, mocking, and carrying of the instrument of his own death through the streets—no one would dare speak, act, or think in Jesus' name for fear of a similar punishment. Crucifixion was such a horrible death, in fact, that people believed it had to be a sign that the person had been abandoned by God.

Mark's Message

The Gospel of Mark tells us otherwise. This was the moment of truth. Jesus was alone on his Cross, despised by the Romans, ridiculed by his peers and countrymen, and abandoned by his disciples. Jesus was the suffering servant. If you want to know who Jesus really is, you have to look at the Cross. Once you understand its meaning, you can understand Jesus' miracles, parables, words, and deeds. Mark's Gospel tells us that Jesus' Death explains everything. He asks us to see the living God most clearly in Jesus' battered and bruised body.

Christian Suffering

Jesus was without sin and did not have to suffer. His love for humankind was so great and his obedience to the Father so strong that he freely chose to suffer.

SACRED ART

The *Pietà*, in Saint Peter's Basilica in Rome, is one of Michelangelo's most famous sculptures. The word *Pietà* means "pity" or "compassion." Carved from marble, the sculpture depicts the Blessed Mother holding the lifeless body of Jesus on her lap. This was a popular subject for northern European artists at the time, but Michelangelo's approach differs in his portrayal of Mary, which features a Catholic view of human suffering. Although Michelangelo shows a sorrowful Blessed Mother, she also has an attitude of serenity and faith.

The *Pietà*, Michelangelo, 1499.

154 Unit 4 • Jesus the Christ

 ADVENTURES IN FAITH

Let's Change This

Organize small groups and set up a blog page or dedicate a space on the school or parish Web site. Ask each group to show photographs that represent suffering in the world. Have them add writing to accompany the photos, along with their suggestions of ways to release love into the world. Remind young people that Jesus is present in all who suffer.

For example, young people may photograph and write about an empty storefront because it represents a loss of jobs in their community. They may suggest supporting local businesses as one way to relieve the suffering. Or they may photograph a wilted plant to represent the suffering caused by a lack of food to feed the hungry. They may suggest sponsoring a food drive as a way to relieve the suffering. Encourage young people to include interviews, videos, or other information that highlights the issue.

✝ *Family and Community*

Because of the Incarnation, Jesus' suffering was like ours. He understands our times of hopelessness, pain, and loneliness because he experienced them and shared our pain.

On the Cross, Jesus taught the most important lessons we have to learn in order to be his followers. Jesus' sacrifice shows us how much God loves us. Through his suffering, redeeming Death, Resurrection, and Ascension, Jesus saves all of God's creation. Jesus teaches us from the Cross to give our lives selflessly for others and to realize that doing God's work often involves sacrifice and suffering.

Mystery of Love

It may seem contradictory, but the instrument of execution used by the Romans, the cross, is a universal sign of hope for Christians. We pray the Sign of the Cross as a reminder that our whole life is lived under the sign that saved us, the Cross of Jesus. Jesus' Cross shows the depths of what it means to follow him. It reminds us of the conflict we often feel between our own will and submitting to the will of God the Father, and it proclaims that even senseless suffering can be redemptive if accepted with faith and love.

Forgiveness

Jesus taught us to love everyone, even our enemies, just as he offered his life for everyone, even those who hated him. As Jesus was crucified, he prayed "Father, forgive them, they know not what they do." (Luke 23:34) Even in the worst of circumstances, Jesus chose to forgive.

He invites us to respond with a similar decision to forgive others as an act of faith and as a response to his own selfless love and forgiveness.

Jesus Saves, Even in Death

When we pray the **Apostles' Creed,** we acknowledge with the words "he descended into hell" that after Jesus died, and before he had risen, he went to the realm of the dead to gather all the just people who had died before him. What we believe is that Jesus met them as their Savior, proclaiming the Good News to them. He gathered them and brought them to Heaven with him. This shows that Jesus' work of redemption is for the entire human family, of all times and in all places.

Our Response

When Jesus' followers saw him on the Cross, they must have thought, "This is the end." Everything changed for the disciples, including their notions of a Messiah, their hopes for the future with Jesus, and their role in Jesus' ministry. So often in our own lives, when things get difficult, we think, "This is the end." How does Jesus want us to respond to suffering in our own lives? Although we can never fully understand suffering, we can work to eliminate the evil that causes suffering. We can comfort others, and we can accept our suffering with strength and dignity to be a light to those around us. Through it all, Jesus is present, reassuring us that this is not the end as long as we place our faith in his Resurrection.

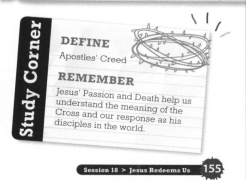

Our Catholic Character

When we see other people suffer, our response is to take action. In his encyclical letter *On the Christian Meaning of Human Suffering*, Pope John Paul II wrote, "Suffering is present in the world in order to release love, in order to give birth to works of love towards neighbor, in order to transform the whole of human civilization into a 'civilization of love.'" Jesus' words in the parable of the Last Judgment in Matthew 25:31–46 also help us understand how we find Jesus in acts of love and acts of assistance for those in need. Whenever we stop to feed the hungry, care for the sick, or visit the imprisoned, we do it to Jesus. He is present in everyone who suffers. All who suffer become sharers in Christ's suffering.

Explore

Study Corner

DEFINE
Apostles' Creed

REMEMBER
Jesus' Passion and Death help us understand the meaning of the Cross and our response as his disciples in the world.

Session 18 > Jesus Redeems Us **155**

TAKE IT HOME

A Civilization of Love

Pope John Paul II wrote about transforming civilization into a "civilization of love." What might that civilization look like? Ask young people to make two columns on a sheet of paper. In the first column, have them identify an unloving action. In the second column, have them identify what might be done to turn the unloving action into one of love.

Encourage them to consider the transformative effects that small, loving actions can have and our challenge to build a "civilization of love." Challenge young people to follow through on their loving actions. At a future time when the group meets, ask volunteers to share their experiences with the group.

✝ *Family and Community*

Read aloud the section Christian Suffering. Ask: **What does Jesus' Crucifixion tell Christians about suffering?** (Because Jesus was fully human, he knows and understands our own suffering.) Ask: **What is the lesson of the Cross?** (Possible answer: We are called to do God's work in the world, giving ourselves selflessly and even enduring hardships.) Explain that *redeem* means "to restore worth." Jesus' Death restored eternal life.

Have a volunteer read Mystery of Love. Ask: **Where have you seen an image of the cross?** (Possible answers: church, baptismal font, stained-glass windows, necklaces, priest's chasuble, chalice, Paschal Candle) Have young people summarize why the cross is a universal sign of hope for Christians.

Read aloud the section Forgiveness. Ask volunteers to explain why Jesus' teaching in Luke 23:34 is radical.

As a group, recite the Apostles' Creed, found on page 276 in Prayers and Practices. Then read aloud Jesus Saves, Even in Death. Ask: **In the Apostles' Creed, what belief do we acknowledge after Jesus died but before he had risen?** (Jesus went to the realm of the dead, gathered the just, and brought them to Heaven with him.)

Have volunteers read the section Our Response. Discuss the disciples' response to Jesus' Death and how the end was also a beginning.

Our Catholic Character

Read the feature and Bible verses aloud. Discuss Pope John Paul II's words. Relate acts of love to the Corporal Works of Mercy.

③ Close

Invite young people to write answers to the following questions:

▶ How do I respond to suffering?

▶ How do I live for others?

▶ How do people recognize me as one of Jesus' followers?

Prayer

Choose an approach and pray with young people.

APPROACH 1

Guided Reflection

Prepare Listen in advance to the recorded guided reflection "Face to Face" [CD 1, Track 3]. Decide if you will play the recording or pray aloud the reflection yourself. If you choose to lead, listen to the recording a second time, following the script [pages T-345–T-346] and noting pauses and tone. You can then follow the script exactly or adapt it as you wish.

Pray During the session, have volunteers read aloud the paragraphs in the left column. Explain that since ancient times, people have thought of the heart as the center of human emotion. Tell young people that Jesus teaches us to pray from the heart. Play the recording or lead using the script, joining young people in reflective prayer. If you pray aloud the script, play reflective music softly in the background [CD 2, Track 5].

APPROACH 2

Young People's Page

Prepare Pray the prayer in advance to become familiar with it.

Pray Invite young people to prepare for prayer. Say: *We all carry burdens. Think about a cross you bear. Remember that Jesus is always beside you, helping you carry it.* Slowly pray aloud the guided reflection, or have young people silently pray the text. Invite young people to pause and meditate after each part. Close by inviting young people to pray aloud the Lord's Prayer with you.

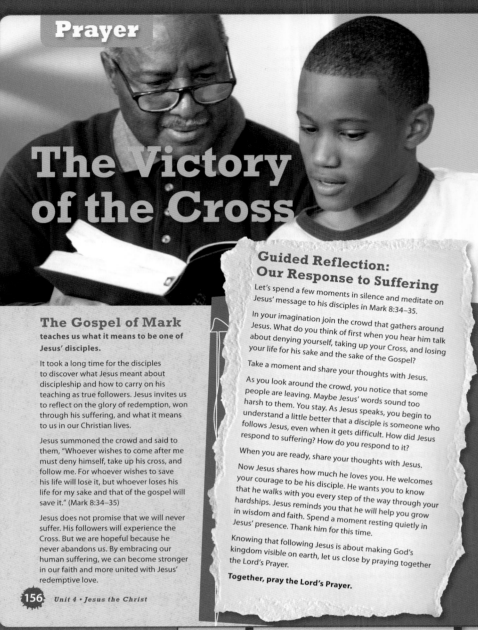

Prayer

The Victory of the Cross

The Gospel of Mark
teaches us what it means to be one of Jesus' disciples.

It took a long time for the disciples to discover what Jesus meant about discipleship and how to carry on his teaching as true followers. Jesus invites us to reflect on the glory of redemption, won through his suffering, and what it means to us in our Christian lives.

Jesus summoned the crowd and said to them, "Whoever wishes to come after me must deny himself, take up his cross, and follow me. For whoever wishes to save his life will lose it, but whoever loses his life for my sake and that of the gospel will save it." (Mark 8:34–35)

Jesus does not promise that we will never suffer. His followers will experience the Cross. But we are hopeful because he never abandons us. By embracing our human suffering, we can become stronger in our faith and more united with Jesus' redemptive love.

156 *Unit 4 • Jesus the Christ*

Guided Reflection: Our Response to Suffering

Let's spend a few moments in silence and meditate on Jesus' message to his disciples in Mark 8:34–35.

In your imagination join the crowd that gathers around Jesus. What do you think of first when you hear him talk about denying yourself, taking up your Cross, and losing your life for his sake and the sake of the Gospel?

Take a moment and share your thoughts with Jesus.

As you look around the crowd, you notice that some people are leaving. Maybe Jesus' words sound too harsh to them. You stay. As Jesus speaks, you begin to understand a little better that a disciple is someone who follows Jesus, even when it gets difficult. How did Jesus respond to suffering? How do you respond to it?

When you are ready, share your thoughts with Jesus.

Now Jesus shares how much he loves you. He welcomes your courage to be his disciple. He wants you to know that he walks with you every step of the way through your hardships. Jesus reminds you that he will help you grow in wisdom and faith. Spend a moment resting quietly in Jesus' presence. Thank him for this time.

Knowing that following Jesus is about making God's kingdom visible on earth, let us close by praying together the Lord's Prayer.

Together, pray the Lord's Prayer.

IF TIME ALLOWS

Writing Reflections
Have young people work with a partner or in a small group to write their own two-paragraph guided reflection based on Mark 8:34–35. Depending on how much time you have, incorporate the new reflections during a prayer session at a later date with the group.

FYI

Coaching Young People to Pray

Before praying, remind young people to use their imaginations to make prayer more meaningful. Encourage them to incorporate all their senses as they see themselves in the crowd with Jesus. Ask yourself, "What do I see, hear, touch, taste, or smell? How do I feel?"

WHERE Do I Fit In?

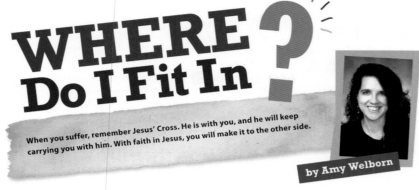

When you suffer, remember Jesus' Cross. He is with you, and he will keep carrying you with him. With faith in Jesus, you will make it to the other side.

by Amy Welborn

The Other Side of Suffering

In eighth grade, I was ruthlessly mocked by a bunch of truly mean girls.

I suffered.

During the years before and after eighth grade, things were weird and tense at home, and sometimes I was sure my world would fall apart completely.

I suffered.

Years later, I labored and gave birth.

Oh, I suffered.

And some years after that, one February morning, my husband had a heart attack and died.

My children and I suffered.

You've suffered, too, in all kinds of ways—some small, some great. Your times of suffering may be like mine, or they may be different. Your suffering may have been brought about by your own choices, the choices of others, or seemingly, no choices at all. The suffering just happened, and it *hurt*. Suffering, whether physical or emotional pain, means there's a huge distance between where we are and where we know we should be. God created us for love, truth, joy, wholeness, and life. When we suffer, we feel far away from all of these, and maybe even far away from God.

But here's the irony. When we live in Christ and let Christ live in us, that place of suffering is turned upside down. That place has a name—the Cross. For

Jesus was in that place—that place where he was mocked, where he hurt, where he was abandoned, where he seemed to have failed, where he asked God "Why?" and where his earthly life was stripped away.

Are you suffering? Jesus has been in the place where you are. He's there with you now, in whatever suffering you're enduring. He will always be with you. The Cross wasn't the end for Jesus, and if you live in faith, suffering won't be the end for you.

Reflect

The Victory of the Cross

Because Christ's Cross leads to Resurrection, we meet our human suffering with hope and encouragement. Read Luke 9:23.

Then explain how each example of renewed hope shown below is the other side of suffering. Write your ideas on another sheet of paper.

1. A woman loses her job and starts her own company.
2. You are cut from the team so you become the team manager.
3. The reflecting pools at Ground Zero in New York City become a national memorial.
4. A town rebuilds after a tornado.
5. After you lose your family pet, you help your elderly neighbor care for his dog.

AMY WELBORN is a mother of five and the author of *Wish You Were Here: Travels Through Loss and Hope*.

Session 18 > Jesus Redeems Us **157**

IF TIME ALLOWS

Cross Words

Have young people draw a cross with sections large enough to write in. Invite them to write key words on the horizontal part of the cross that reflect ways they suffer or have suffered. Explain that they can use "code words" understood only by them if they are reluctant to share sensitive or personal feelings. Next, have them write messages of hope from Jesus to themselves on the vertical bar; for example, *I am with you. You will get through this. Hold on to me.* Encourage young people to meditate prayerfully before writing these messages. When they are finished, invite them to keep their crosses and revisit them whenever they need help or support in times of trouble. Encourage any young person who is burdened with serious suffering to seek help from a family member, priest, teacher, or trusted adult.

---

① Begin

Have a volunteer read aloud the introductory text. Ask: **When you stub your toe, what might go through your mind?** (Possible answer: only thoughts about the pain) Say: **It's natural to focus only on ourselves when we are in pain. We want to draw into ourselves and protect ourselves like a wounded animal.** Remind young people that, as Christians, we are asked to remember Jesus' suffering in times of our own suffering. This can be hard since pain makes us self-centered, but if we practice, we will receive an amazing gift. Ask: **What is the gift?** (Possible answers: hope, the other side of pain, understanding of Christian life)

② Connect

Have volunteers take turns reading The Other Side of Suffering. Explain that when something is ironic, it is the opposite of what we expect. Ask: **Why does the author say that our feelings of being far away from God during suffering are ironic?** (because that is when Jesus is closest to us) Say: **To say "Jesus is with us" is not just a figure of speech. It is God's most basic message to humanity: You are not alone. I am with you. Your suffering is not the end of the story.** Invite young people to close their eyes, invite Jesus to join them, and spend a few moments sharing their suffering with him.

Have young people complete the activity The Victory of the Cross with a partner. Invite volunteers to share ideas with the group.

③ Close

Encourage young people to repeat the kind of meditation they did today whenever they are in pain. Remind them that one way that God helps us is through other people and that suffering can be shared with family or a trusted friend or adult.

① Begin

What's What? Read aloud the directions. Have young people complete the activity independently or with a partner. Remind them to use details from the text in their answers.

② Connect

Say What? Ask volunteers to read aloud and define the terms. Review each term in the Glossary if necessary.

Now What? Ask a volunteer to read aloud the question. Encourage young people to answer honestly, recognizing that they may still be working toward a Christian response to suffering. Invite them to answer the question independently.

③ Go in Peace

Have young people collect materials and return them to their appropriate places. Encourage them to find ways to respond to suffering this week, no matter how big or small their response. Remind them that a response to suffering is not necessarily a solution for it. Instead, it is an action or an attitude that best reflects what we've come to understand about Jesus, the Son of God, and his saving action on the Cross. Ask: **How would Jesus encourage you to respond as you deal with your own hardships? What small actions or words can help relieve the suffering of someone else?**

3-Minute Retreat
Give young people an opportunity for quiet meditation at **www.loyolapress.com/retreat**.

What's What?

Complete each sentence with details from the text.

1. The Gospel of Mark tells us _____. (PAGES 152–153)
   Possible answers: what it means to be a disciple of Jesus; how Jesus' divinity was revealed

2. Jesus is the suffering servant because _____. (PAGES 152–153)
   through the Messiah's suffering and Death, he redeems the world

3. After he predicts his own suffering, Jesus scolds Peter because Jesus _____. (PAGE 153)
   chooses to fulfill God's plan for all people to be saved rather than avoid his suffering

4. At his Crucifixion, Jesus is recognized as the Son of God by _____. (PAGE 153)
   the Roman centurion

5. Jesus' Crucifixion is the moment of truth for Christians because _____. (PAGES 154–155)
   to understand the meaning of the Cross is to understand Jesus' teaching, miracles, and deeds and what it means to be his follower

6. For Christians the cross is a universal sign of hope because _____. (PAGE 155)
   Possible answers: Jesus' Cross saved us; it reminds us to be true followers of Jesus; it reminds us of the conflict between our will and God's will

7. As Christians we can respond to our own suffering by _____. (PAGE 155)
   Possible answers: easing someone else's pain; praying for God's grace; gaining strength and greater love; remaining hopeful

Say What?
Know the definitions of these terms.

Apostles' Creed
Paschal Mystery
Passion
Transfiguration

Now What?
How will you respond this week when faced with your own suffering or with someone else's suffering?
Answers will vary.

158 · *Unit 4 • Jesus the Christ*

IF TIME ALLOWS

Service: Meals on Wheels
Select one or more local people who are in need, such as someone who is ill, someone who cannot cook for himself or herself, or someone who cannot afford to buy food. Arrange for young people to use a kitchen space, such as a parish kitchen. Then have young people work together with adult volunteers to plan, purchase, and prepare an entire nutritious meal. Deliver the meal, being sure to include a card with a list of the ingredients and the names of those who prepared it.

✝ *Family and Community*

Session Assessment Option
An assessment for this session can be found at www.findinggod.com.

PLAN AHEAD: Get Ready for Session 19
Consult the catechist preparation pages to prepare for Session 19 and determine any materials you will need.

Jesus Brings us New Life

 3-Minute Retreat

Before you prepare the session, pause and be still. Take three deep breaths and be aware of the loving presence of God, who is with you on this journey.

Luke 15:21–24

"His son said to him, 'Father, I have sinned against heaven and against you; I no longer deserve to be called your son.' But his father ordered his servants, 'Quickly bring the finest robe and put it on him; put a ring on his finger and sandals on his feet. Take the fattened calf and slaughter it. Then let us celebrate with a feast, because this son of mine was dead, and has come to life again; he was lost, and has been found.' Then the celebration began."

Reflection

A feast in his honor was the last thing the prodigal son expected when he returned home. After all, hadn't he caused his father great pain and disappointment? Unconditional love is like that. That is the quality of love God the Father extends to us when we celebrate the Sacraments of Initiation. We are all prodigals in need of forgiveness and in need of grace. The Sacraments of Initiation welcome us in. Let the celebration begin!

Questions

What surprises me most about the forgiving father's response? About the son's response? How does it feel to know that I am the prodigal one being welcomed in?

 Concluding Prayer

Speak to God, using the words of this prayer or your own.

Merciful God, seeker of the lost, you stand ready to receive me when I make my way back to you. Help me accept the grace of the sacraments to imitate your unconditional love in my relationships with others.

Knowing and Sharing Your Faith in Session 19

Consider how Scripture and Tradition can deepen your understanding of session content.

Scripture

Mark 16:6 is the angel's amazing revelation that Jesus had been raised.

Acts of the Apostles 8:14–17 reminds us that the Apostles administered the sacraments in Jesus' name.

Tradition

The Catholic Church is a sacramental Church, recognizing seven sacraments. Sacraments are signs—they tell us something. They tell us what God's love is doing in our lives. They bring about what they signify. The sacraments that welcome us into the Church are the Sacraments of Initiation: Baptism, Confirmation, and Eucharist. In the water of Baptism, we receive new life, have Original Sin taken away, and become members of the Church. In Confirmation, we are sealed and strengthened by the Holy Spirit. In the Eucharist, we receive Jesus Christ's Body and Blood in Holy Communion as spiritual food for the journey.

Catholic Social Teaching

In this session the integrated Catholic Social Teaching themes are **Call to Family, Community, and Participation** and **Solidarity.** See page 133b for an explanation of these themes.

Window on the Catechism

The Sacraments of Initiation are discussed in *CCC* 1210–1419.

General Directory for Catechesis

The tasks of catechesis—to know the faith, to celebrate it, to live it, and to grow in prayer—are described in *GDC* 84 and 85.

One-Hour Session Planner

SESSION 19 Jesus Brings Us New Life

Session Theme: *We find Christ's presence in prayer, in the Christian community, and in the sacraments.*

Before This Session

► Bookmark your Bible to Mark 8:34, Mark 10:45, Mark 16:1–7, 1 Corinthians 15:54–55, Luke 18:22, Luke 22:19–20, Luke 24:48–49, John 3:5, John 15:12–15, Acts of the Apostles 8:14–17, and Matthew 22:36–40. Place the open Bible in your prayer space.

► Read the Guide for this session, choose any additional If Time Allows activities that you might have time to complete, and gather the listed materials.

Prayer in Session 19

Pray together the short prayer on the session opener page. Encourage young people to access the online 3-Minute Retreat at the end of the session. In Session 19 young people will offer petitions as witnesses for Christ. Follow the Prepare directions on the Catechist Guide page before sharing with young people.

STEPS	APPROXIMATE TIME
Engage *Jesus Brings Us New Life* PAGE 159	10 minutes
Explore *An Empty Tomb* PAGES 160–161 *Sacraments of Initiation* PAGES 162–163	30–40 minutes
Reflect *Prayer:* Reflecting God's Love PAGE 164 *Where Do I Fit In?* PAGE 165	10–15 minutes
Respond *What's What?* PAGE 166	10–15 minutes

TAKE IT HOME

Homework options:

Social Justice Flyers   PAGE 160

What Will It Take?   PAGE 163

Materials

REQUIRED

► Writing supplies (pages 160, 165, 166)

► Bible (pages 160, 164)

► Signs of Baptism, such as water, a white garment, oil, and a symbol or picture of fire (page 162)

► Computers with Internet access (page 166)

OPTIONAL

► Portable radio (page 159)

► Session 19 BLM, T-376 (page 161)

► Video camera, digital recorder, or writing supplies (page 162)

► Bibles, markers, mural paper, art supplies, magazines (page 164)

► Video cameras, smartphones, or computers, art supplies, writing supplies (page 166)

► Session 19 Assessment, www.findinggod.com (page 166)

Jesus Brings Us New Life

Session 19

> **What do you hope to find when you join a group? Are you looking for fun, a sense of belonging, or something else? How can your affiliation with a group challenge, support, or enliven your life?**

PRAYER

Lord, I know that your life is within me. With all my brothers and sisters around the world, we are the family of God. Send your Holy Spirit to strengthen the Church.

159

IF TIME ALLOWS

Clarity in Jesus

Bring in a portable radio to use in a demonstration. Invite volunteers to take turns tuning in different stations until they find a clear signal. Point out that until you tune into a station's signal, the sound is fuzzy and unclear. Tell young people that they will learn that, in the Gospel of Mark, the full meaning of Jesus' kingship remains unclear until a certain moment of clarity occurs—what some people call an "aha moment."

➜ Go to **www.findinggod.com/sessionextenders** for an article about Jesus' Resurrection. You may wish to share this with the group.

SESSION 19
OUTCOMES

▶ Explain how the Holy Spirit assists us in finding Christ's presence in prayer, in community, in the sacraments, and in all things.

▶ Identify the Sacraments of Initiation as our initiation into the Body of Christ.

▶ Offer petitions as witnesses for Christ.

▶ Define *doxology, marginalized,* and *social justice.*

① Set the Stage

Have a volunteer read aloud the text in the box. Allow time for young people to reflect on or write responses to the questions. Invite volunteers to share their ideas with the group.

② Get Started

Write the following examples of tasks on the board: *do homework, mow the lawn, practice piano, babysit a sibling.* Discuss what it means to make a sacrifice. Ask volunteers to describe sacrifices they make routinely or sacrifices they have made in the past. Point out that one motivation for making a sacrifice is to gain something better later on. Ask: **For whom or what would you sacrifice? What makes it worth your sacrifice? What things, in your opinion, are not worth a sacrifice?** (Answers will vary.) Ask a volunteer to read the session title. Ask: **What might this title mean in light of our discussion? What sacrifice did Jesus make? Why did he make it?**

 Prayer

Say: **Let's pray together to ask God to remind us that we are his family.** Pray aloud the prayer. Conclude by praying the Sign of the Cross.

① Begin

Ask partners to make a list of choices for the top three movies of all time. Point out that many movies hinge on one scene that gives meaning to the rest of the story. Young people should describe what they consider to be the key scene in each movie listed. Invite them to share their lists with the entire group. Tell young people that they will learn about a key scene in the Gospel of Mark.

② Connect

 Read aloud Mark 16:1–7. Then ask a volunteer to read aloud the title and the first three paragraphs. Explain that in first-century Jewish society, women weren't allowed to serve as public witnesses. Imagine what it must have been like to be one of these women, receiving this message and then relaying it to an incredulous group of Jesus' disciples. Say: ***The message here is that the women had been looking for Jesus in the wrong place—he was not among the dead. In fact, he was among the people he served. The message was a challenge to the women, and it is a challenge to us as well.***

Have a volunteer read aloud the section The Resurrection. Ask: **How does the verse from First Corinthians reflect the beliefs of our faith?** (Death is the end of our human life, but Jesus conquered Death by his Resurrection. He gave us hope for eternal life with him.) Emphasize that the Resurrection is the central mystery of our faith.

Our Catholic Character

Have a volunteer read the feature. Ask a volunteer to read aloud the meaning of *social justice* in the Glossary. Explain that as members of the Church, we are called to share in Jesus' mission of building the Kingdom of God right now.

An Empty Tomb

Women at the tomb, Clayton and Bell, stained glass, St. Peter's Church, Albany, New York.

SOMETIMES we find what we're looking for when we join a group at school, in sports, or at church. Other times we might be surprised at what we find—or what we don't.

On the Sunday morning following Jesus' Death on the Cross, Mary Magdalene; Mary, the mother of James; and Salome were surprised when they went to the tomb to anoint Jesus' body. A young man clothed in a white robe said to them, "Do not be amazed! You seek Jesus of Nazareth, the crucified. He has been raised; he is not here." (Mark 16:6)

He told the women to bring a message to Peter and the disciples—that if they wanted to see Jesus, they would have to go to Galilee, as Jesus had told them. This was remarkable news, and the women fled the tomb, trembling and bewildered. They had received a message telling them where to find the risen Jesus.

The Resurrection

For Christians, Jesus' Resurrection is the central mystery of our faith. Every Easter we celebrate Jesus' Resurrection and our hope for eternal life.

"Death is swallowed up in victory.
Where, O death, is your victory?
Where, O death, is your sting?"

1 Corinthians 15:54–55

After Jesus' Death on the Cross, his disciples probably felt confused, disappointed, and heartbroken. They probably felt alone and afraid. But on the third day, the women found an open and empty tomb. Jesus had triumphed over Death. Jesus' Resurrection is God's promise that if we live our lives well and follow his plan as his disciples, we will share eternal life with him.

Our Catholic Character

The Church's strong emphasis on **social justice,** the fair and equal treatment of every member of society, keeps us faithful to the Kingdom of God. The Kingdom of God is revealed when we work to assure justice for those who are poor, when we relieve the suffering of the oppressed, when we console the sorrowful, and when we actively seek a new social order in which the dignity of all human beings is recognized and respected. With the help of God's grace, we are able to continue the work of Jesus in building the Kingdom of God.

TAKE IT HOME

Social Justice Flyers

Remind young people that social justice is central to Catholic Social Teaching. Have them refer to pages 298–300 in Prayers and Practices for more information about the role of social justice in Catholic Social Teaching. Encourage young people to consider what social justice means to them. Invite them to share personal experiences of when social justice has affected their families, friends, or community.

Ask each young person to make an advertising flyer that sheds light on a current social justice issue. Invite them to take a stand on the issue and include a call to action. Talk with your parish office about including replicas of the flyers in upcoming parish bulletins or providing space for a public display.

✝ *Solidarity*

Where Will I Find Jesus?

Today we find the risen Christ in his Church—the worldwide community of baptized believers who work together to serve the coming Kingdom of God under the leadership of the bishops, with the Bishop of Rome—the pope—at the head. We also find Jesus in church every time the community gathers to celebrate the sacrifice of the Mass on Sundays and Holy Days of Obligation.

We find Jesus in God's actions in the sacraments, especially in the Sacrament of the Eucharist, where we encounter the Real Presence of Jesus Christ in his Body and Blood, given to us as spiritual nourishment.

Today we do not see Jesus in his physical body, as he showed himself to his followers in Galilee. Instead, we have to look for Jesus in the types of places where he ministered. We find Jesus among the **marginalized,** those who are unimportant or powerless in society, such as victims of discrimination; those who are poor; or people who are mistreated in society because of their race, religion, or gender. We find Jesus among victims of war and among those who work for peace. We find him among those suffering from physical, mental, or emotional illness. When you help the elderly, make someone who is sick more comfortable, or assist those who are disabled, you are doing more than a nice act. As followers of Jesus Christ, you are blessed with opportunities to find Jesus in many people.

Jesus Is with Us

After Jesus was raised from the dead, he ascended to the Father in Heaven. Jesus and the Father sent the Holy Spirit to teach and guide us and to aid us in understanding all that Jesus had done in saving us. It is the Holy Spirit who assists us to find the presence of God in all things. As we accept and welcome the grace of the Holy Spirit, every day becomes a discovery of the presence of God—sometimes in places where we least expect it.

The Gospel of Mark assures us that Christ is present with us in prayer and worship, in Christian community, in situations of love and respect, and in peacemaking and working for justice. What does Jesus call us to do as his followers?

Serving the Kingdom

As Christians, Jesus calls us to go forward and be among those who are poor and in need. In Mark 8:34, Jesus says that to be a true disciple means to deny yourself, take up your cross, and follow him. This means that we unite human suffering to the suffering of Jesus and join him in serving the needs of others in the Kingdom of God. "For the Son of Man did not come to be served but to serve and to give his life as a ransom for many." (Mark 10:45)

What will you do? Will you seek Jesus? Jesus said, "Then come, follow me." (Luke 18:22) We follow him away from the empty tomb and into life with its challenges and promises of redemption.

Explore

Study Corner

DEFINE

social justice
marginalized

REMEMBER

The Holy Spirit assists us to find the presence of God in all things.

We find the risen Christ among the suffering. Christ is present with us in prayer, in the Christian community, and in the sacraments.

Session 19 > Jesus Brings Us New Life **161**

IF TIME ALLOWS

Session 19 BLM

Jesus Is Everywhere Plan a brief walk outdoors around the school, church, and neighborhood. Provide each young person with the Session 19 Blackline Master [T-376]. Organize teams of three or four young people. Challenge teams to identify where they found Jesus during their walks or where they have found him in the past. Have them write their ideas on the blackline master. Ask volunteers to share and explain their ideas with the group.

INCLUSION

Hearing

Circle Up If you have young people with hearing differences, some information during discussions might be lost. Consider arranging seats or desks in a circle so that group members can see one another. Encourage readers to speak loudly, slowly, and clearly. Also stand close by and face young people when speaking.

Have volunteers take turns reading Where Will I Find Jesus? Ask: **Where are some places we find Jesus Christ?** (in his Church worldwide, in the local church where we gather, in the reception of the sacraments, among the marginalized, among victims of war, among peacemakers, and among those who are sick and suffering)

Have a volunteer read Jesus Is with Us. Ask: **How are we guided in understanding all that Jesus has done in saving us?** (through the power of the Holy Spirit) Say: **As we accept and welcome the grace of the Holy Spirit, every day becomes a discovery of the presence of God in places where we least expect it.** Ask: **Where do we discover Jesus' presence?** (in prayer and worship, in Christian community, in situations of love and respect, in peacemaking and working for justice) Invite volunteers to identify other places where Jesus is present.

Read aloud Serving the Kingdom. Ask volunteers to talk about times when they have encountered Jesus in daily situations but failed to recognize him. Make the connection that Jesus is among us in many ordinary places and people. Say: **Jesus invites and challenges us to extend our hands in service not only to those who are easy to serve, like our family and friends, but to those who are powerless and forgotten.** Explain that we are challenged to seek Jesus. Ask: **Can you describe a time when you were looking for Jesus in the wrong places, like the women who found the empty tomb?** (Answers will vary.) Say: **Jesus is among the living.**

③ Close

Encourage young people to discuss their questions. Ask:

► How would Jesus minister to people who are ridiculed, left out, gossiped about, or ignored?

► What more can you do to recognize Jesus?

① Begin

Discuss clubs or groups to which young people belong and what they did to become members. Then say: **When we receive the Sacraments of Initiation, we become members of the Church. However, our membership is not the same as a club membership. We enter into the Body of Christ, marking a new beginning in our spiritual journey.**

② Connect

Have volunteers take turns reading the paragraphs in the first column. Explain that initiation into the life of the Church is part of our faith journey. Ask: **Which sacraments are not repeated?** (Baptism and Confirmation) Ask: **Why do we celebrate the Eucharist as often as possible?** (We are nourished with the Body and Blood of Jesus Christ. We renew the commitments we made in Baptism and Confirmation.) Emphasize that Baptism is always the first sacrament received, no matter the age of the recipient. Young people may have questions about adult Baptism, called Rite of Christian Initiation of Adults [RCIA]. If possible, invite a priest or catechumen to explain the process.

 Ask a volunteer to read aloud the section Baptism. Discuss the similarities and differences between Jesus' baptism by John the Baptist in the River Jordan and our Baptism. Ask: **How is knowing the meaning of the word Baptism helpful in understanding the sacrament?** (By entering into the waters of Baptism, we are cleansed of sin and enter a new life of grace.) In advance, arrange to display the outward signs of Baptism: water, a white garment, oil, and fire [for safety, provide a symbol or picture for fire].

Read aloud the verses in Acts of the Apostles 8:14–17. Ask: **How did Peter and John confer the Holy Spirit on the believers in Samaria?** (through prayer and laying on of hands)

Sacraments of Initiation

THE word *initiation* means "to make a beginning." Of the seven sacraments in the Catholic Church, three are designated as Sacraments of Initiation because they mark a new beginning in our journey of faith.

The first of these three is Baptism, in which Original Sin is washed away and we receive new life in the Holy Spirit. In the Sacrament of Confirmation, we are strengthened with the Holy Spirit and dedicate ourselves to serving the Kingdom of God on earth. In the Sacrament of the Eucharist, our bodies and souls are nourished with the Body and Blood of Jesus Christ.

The Sacraments of Baptism and Confirmation do not have to be repeated because they leave a permanent mark on our souls. We celebrate the Eucharist over and over again because we constantly need to remember who we are and what we are called to do as followers of Jesus Christ. Celebrating the Eucharist regularly is our way of renewing the commitments we made in Baptism and Confirmation.

Many Catholics are baptized as infants and later receive the Sacraments of the Eucharist and Confirmation. People of all ages can receive the Sacraments of Initiation, but Baptism is always the first sacrament received. Anyone who has reached the age of reason, which is seven years of age or older, and wishes to be baptized, can enter into a process called the Rite of Christian Initiation of Adults (RCIA), which prepares him or her to receive all three Sacraments of Initiation at the Easter Vigil on Holy Saturday.

Baptism

Our Baptism is not like the baptism of Jesus in the Jordan River by John the Baptist. Jesus' baptism was a way of showing his willingness to wade into the world of sin in order to save us and bring Salvation. It was also the Father's way of showing that Jesus was indeed his only Son, filled with the Holy Spirit.

The Greek root of the word *baptism* means "to immerse." In Baptism we enter into the waters, where we symbolically die to sin and emerge to a new life of grace. In John 3:5, Jesus tells Nicodemus that "no one can enter the kingdom of God without being born of water and Spirit." Baptism gives us birth into a new life in Jesus Christ. We receive forgiveness of Original Sin and all personal sins, and we become members of the Body of Christ, the Church. The visible symbols of Baptism include water, a white garment, oil, and fire.

Confirmation

To *confirm* means "to strengthen." When we receive the Sacrament of Confirmation, we are strengthened in the Holy Spirit. In Acts of the Apostles 8:14–17, the Apostles Peter and John travelled to Samaria and "laid hands" on people who had been baptized so that they could receive the Holy Spirit. The tradition

---

ADVENTURES IN FAITH

Interviews

Ask young people to interview another member of the group. Tell them that the interview can be videotaped, handwritten, or recorded. Recognize that seventh graders may be preparing to receive the Sacrament of Confirmation. In case some young people have not yet received Baptism, ask them to interview others but not answer the questions themselves. Write the following questions on the board, but young people may add to this list as desired:

- *What sacraments have you received?*
- *How did you prepare for the reception of the sacrament?*
- *What has receiving the sacrament meant to you?*
- *If you could give one piece of advice to a young person about receiving the sacraments, what would it be?*
- *In what ways are you entering more fully into the life of the Church?*
- *How are you living the values and ideas of the Church?*

Ask volunteers to share their interviews with the group.

of prayer and laying on of hands continues to this day in the Catholic Church. In the Sacrament of Confirmation, the bishop anoints the forehead with Chrism and says, "Be sealed with the gift of the Holy Spirit."

Strengthened by the Holy Spirit, the confirmed person participates more fully in the mission of the Church and continues the spiritual journey with renewed inspiration. When Jesus appears to the Apostles in Jerusalem after his Resurrection, he says, "You are witnesses of these things. And [behold] I am sending the promise of my Father upon you; but stay in the city until you are clothed with power from on high." (Luke 24:48–49)

Eucharist

Receiving the Body and Blood of Christ for the first time is referred to as First Holy Communion. The Eucharist initiates us into the community of the faithful who regularly partake of the Real Presence of Jesus Christ.

Jesus told the Apostles at the Last Supper, "This is my body, which will be given for you; do this in memory of me." (Luke 22:19) Jesus himself is the sacrifice. When Jesus gave his disciples the wine, he said, "This cup is the new covenant in my blood, which will be shed for you." (Luke 22:20)

Jesus' sacrifice on the Cross establishes a New Covenant between God and humankind, and so when we first receive the Eucharist, we enter into that covenant more fully. When we celebrate the Eucharist regularly, our Salvation in Jesus Christ is made present to us in the most profound way.

Initiated Into the Body of Christ

Through the Sacraments of Initiation, we are incorporated into the Church. The word *incorporate* is based on the Latin word for *body* (corpus), and so we enter into the Body of Christ and the people of God.

The Church is the people of God throughout the whole world. The Church is also the Body of Christ. When Jesus died and rose, he established a community of believers as his own body so that we form one family and one people of God. Christ is the head of his people, and his law is love of God and neighbor. The Church's mission is to make the light of Christ evident to the world and to be a seed of unity, hope, Salvation, and holiness for humankind.

When we receive the Sacraments of Initiation, we are not only initiated into the Church but are also called to initiate the Church's values and ideas into our own lives and the lives of people around us.

Study Corner

DEFINE

doxology

REMEMBER

The Sacraments of Initiation are Baptism, Confirmation, and Eucharist. They mark our entry into the community of the Church, which was born as a result of the Resurrection.

SACRED ART

Elizabeth Wang is a British artist who hopes her art will "encourage people to grow in holiness by believing and living the Catholic faith to its fullness." The title of this work of art reminds us of the words of the priest's prayer during the Concluding Doxology at the end of the Eucharistic Prayer. A **doxology** is a Christian prayer praising and giving glory to God, often referencing the three divine Persons of the Trinity. Through the Sacraments of Initiation, we enter into the life of the Church with Jesus Christ as its head. In Christ all people of the world are brought into unity.

Through Him, With Him, Elizabeth Wang, 2006.

Session 19 > Jesus Brings Us New Life **163**

TAKE IT HOME

What Will It Take?

Ask young people to think about some goals they have for themselves. Then assign them to make a list of steps in order to achieve each of these goals:

- obtain a driver's license
- earn acceptance into a good college
- play a musical instrument proficiently

The next time the group meets, discuss their lists. Point out that for many things in life, we need to accomplish something before we can achieve our goal.

Explain that to receive the Sacrament of Baptism, we do not have to achieve a level of proficiency in order to enter the Church. The grace we receive in Baptism is a gift from God that is freely given. However, it becomes our responsibility to enter fully into a Christian life by putting this gift into action in the way we live our lives as Jesus' disciples.

Read aloud the section Confirmation. Point out that the Confirmation rite uses the same signs that Peter and John used; in addition, the bishop anoints with Chrism. Ask: *What did Jesus mean by asking the disciples to wait until they were "clothed with power"?* (The Holy Spirit would come.)

Ask volunteers to take turns reading the section Eucharist. Ask: *What does the celebration of the Eucharist recognize?* (the Real Presence of Jesus Christ) Emphasize that the Liturgy of the Eucharist is more than a simple reenactment of Jesus' words at the Last Supper. Say: *After the consecration, we know that Jesus Christ is present, and we are spiritually nourished by his Body and Blood when we receive the Eucharist.*

Have volunteers take turns reading Initiated Into the Body of Christ. Discuss the meaning of Church, reinforcing that it does not refer to a physical building but to the worldwide community of believers. Ask: *After receiving the Sacraments of Initiation, what is your mission as a member of the Church?* (to make the light of Christ evident in the world)

Sacred Art

Invite young people to identify what they see in the fine art and to interpret its meaning. Read the feature aloud. Point out the artwork title *Through Him, With Him*. Relate the meaning of the art to the words prayed during the Eucharistic Prayer in the Concluding Doxology. "Through him, and with him, and in him, O God, almighty Father, in the unity of the Holy Spirit, all glory and honor is yours, for ever and ever."

③ Close

Ask volunteers to summarize the Sacraments of Initiation. Ask them to think about what these sacraments mean to them personally and encourage them to share their ideas.

Prayer

Follow the steps to guide young people through the prayer on page 164.

Young People's Page

Prepare Pray the prayer in advance to become familiar with it.

✝ ***Pray*** As young people listen, read aloud Matthew 22:36–40. Ask volunteers to take turns reading the paragraphs in the left column. Discuss the concept of love and its impact on what we say and do every day. Say: ***God's love for us is immeasurable. Every time we reflect his love in the world, we are living our faith.***

Have young people bring their books to the prayer space. Assign the five Reader parts and encourage them to read slowly and reverently. Remind young people that everyone prays aloud the All part and the Response that follows each petition. Point out the symbol for the Response.

Then invite young people to relax and recognize God's presence. Say: ***Let's focus our attention on God's deep and unending love for us.*** Have Reader 1 begin the prayer by reading aloud the passage from John. After everyone prays the All part, pause briefly. Have Reader 2 pray aloud, followed by the Response by all. Allow young people time to meditate. Have Readers 3, 4, and 5 take turns praying their petitions, allowing time for young people to meditate between each petition. Following the final petition and response, say: ***Let's take a few moments to think about the words we just prayed. Think about what it means to lay down one's life for a friend. Think about what it means to sacrifice.*** Pause. Say: ***Add your own personal petitions in the silence of your hearts.*** Allow time for silent prayer. Conclude by reading the Leader part. Pray together the Lord's Prayer.

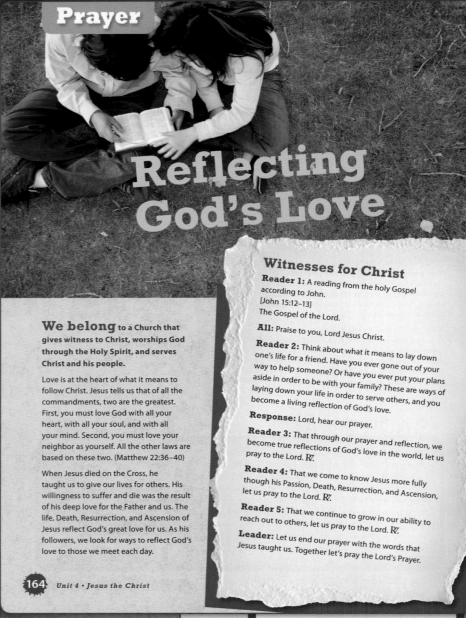

Prayer

Reflecting God's Love

We belong to a Church that gives witness to Christ, worships God through the Holy Spirit, and serves Christ and his people.

Love is at the heart of what it means to follow Christ. Jesus tells us that of all the commandments, two are the greatest. First, you must love God with all your heart, with all your soul, and with all your mind. Second, you must love your neighbor as yourself. All the other laws are based on these two. (Matthew 22:36–40)

When Jesus died on the Cross, he taught us to give our lives for others. His willingness to suffer and die was the result of his deep love for the Father and us. The life, Death, Resurrection, and Ascension of Jesus reflect God's great love for us. As his followers, we look for ways to reflect God's love to those we meet each day.

164 Unit 4 • Jesus the Christ

Witnesses for Christ

Reader 1: A reading from the holy Gospel according to John. [John 15:12–13] The Gospel of the Lord.

All: Praise to you, Lord Jesus Christ.

Reader 2: Think about what it means to lay down one's life for a friend. Have you ever gone out of your way to help someone? Or have you ever put your plans aside in order to be with your family? These are ways of laying down your life in order to serve others, and you become a living reflection of God's love.

Response: Lord, hear our prayer.

Reader 3: That through our prayer and reflection, we become true reflections of God's love in the world, let us pray to the Lord. ℟.

Reader 4: That we come to know Jesus more fully through his Passion, Death, Resurrection, and Ascension, let us pray to the Lord. ℟.

Reader 5: That we continue to grow in our ability to reach out to others, let us pray to the Lord. ℟.

Leader: Let us end our prayer with the words that Jesus taught us. Together let's pray the Lord's Prayer.

IF TIME ALLOWS

Lord, Hear Our Prayer

✝ Use colored markers to write the words from John 15:12–15 in large letters on a section of mural paper. Display the quotation and invite young people to use colored markers to write their ideas for ways to put these words into actions. They may also add drawings or cut out pictures from magazines to illustrate the words.

FYI

Coaching Young People to Pray

Explain that in prayers of petition, we express our needs as children of God. Tell young people that God gives us many things, but that he also wants us to ask him for what we want or need through prayer. Encourage young people to pray to God as a loving Father who knows our needs before we ask.

WHERE Do I Fit In?

Seeing something with new eyes can change everything. Sometimes a place, event, or situation stays exactly the same, but you change in a way that allows you to live more abundantly.

by Terri Lynch-Caris

The Day Everything Changed

When I went away to college, I could make my own decisions. I decided what I was going to do each day. I decided when to go to bed and when to wake up. I could skip class if I wanted. I could decide who to see and where to go. On Sunday I could choose whether or not to go to church.

This new freedom was exciting, but it was also uncomfortable. Sometimes I felt lost and alone. It seemed that everyone knew where he or she was going on campus except me. Sometimes I felt like people were looking at me and laughing because they had friends and I didn't. I felt overwhelmed with coursework. Sometimes I slept in late or did schoolwork on Sunday mornings instead of going to church.

I am a Catholic, but I decided to try out different Christian churches on campus. They felt strange to me. The Bible message was the same, but the services were different, and they didn't offer Holy Communion. One day, almost by chance, I found the Catholic Church on campus. I went to Mass and immediately felt at home. I grew more excited as Mass went on, and when I received the Eucharist, it almost felt like my First Communion.

On that day, everything changed for me. The church became my anchor in new surroundings. Catholic life gave me a framework to make good choices. I realized that, just like God, I could depend on the Church. I had made the most important decision of my life—to rediscover and choose my Catholic faith.

TERRI LYNCH-CARIS is associate professor of industrial engineering at Kettering University in Flint, Michigan.

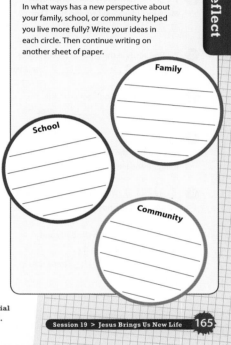

Eyes of Faith

In what ways has a new perspective about your family, school, or community helped you live more fully? Write your ideas in each circle. Then continue writing on another sheet of paper.

Family

School

Community

Reflect

Session 19 > Jesus Brings Us New Life   165

IF TIME ALLOWS

Cosmic Changes

Have young people think about times in their own lives when something happened that made their entire world seem better and brighter. Provide an example from your own life, if needed; then invite young people to share their own recollections. Point out that moments like these are gifts from God and experiences of God even if they are not obviously or directly related to the Church. Explain that although these moments cannot last forever, they foreshadow the elation we will feel when we are fully united with God.

---

① Begin

Have a volunteer read aloud the introductory text and the article title. Say: *This title sounds dramatic. Do you think the "everything" in this title will refer to something that happens on a global scale or within the author's heart?* (probably within the author's heart) Say: *When you have a change of heart, you see the entire world in a new way.*

② Connect

Have volunteers take turns reading The Day Everything Changed. Say: *The author says that she found the Catholic church "almost by chance."* Ask: *Why do you think she says "almost"?* (It seems as if God was guiding her—that it wasn't an accident at all.) Ask young people to describe their experiences attending Mass in other cities or countries. Point out that one of the most comforting things about being a Catholic is that a Catholic church and Sunday Mass can be found almost everywhere in the world—that we truly are a universal, or catholic, family. Encourage young people to remember this as their lives carry them to different places. Say: *Rediscovering the Church in her new home helped the author live life fully and wisely.*

Then have young people complete the Eyes of Faith activity independently. Point out that sometimes we are the ones who need to change or see things in a new way in order to grow closer to God.

③ Close

The next time young people attend Sunday Mass, encourage them to remember that Catholics all over the world are celebrating the same liturgy, just in a different place or language. Remind them that all of Christ's communities are bound together in the Holy Spirit.

1 Begin

What's What? Read aloud the directions and have young people complete the activity independently or in pairs.

2 Connect

Say What? Ask volunteers to read aloud and define the terms. Review the terms in the Glossary if necessary.

Now What? Ask a volunteer to read aloud the directions. Allow young people time to formulate a response. Invite them to write their responses independently.

3 Go in Peace

Collect materials and return them to their appropriate places. Encourage young people to realize God's presence at school this week. Say: **Remember that everyone needs God's love.** Ask: **Who are the people you might overlook or avoid? What habits or small changes in attitude can you practice to reflect God's love more frequently to each person you spend time with this week?**

What's What?

Fill in the letter blanks to complete each sentence. Use the circled letters to discover the secret word.

1. When the women arrived at the tomb of Jesus, they were told that he had R I S E N and gone to Galilee. (PAGE 160)

2. We find Jesus in every celebration of the Mass, including Sundays and Holy Days of O B L I G A T I O N. (PAGE 161)

3. We find Jesus in the types of places where he M I N I S T E R E D. (PAGE 161)

4. We find Jesus in God's action in the S A C R A M E N T S. (PAGE 161)

5. The H O L Y   S P I R I T helps us find the presence of God in all things. (PAGE 161)

6. B A P T I S M is the first sacrament we receive. (PAGE 162)

7. We are nourished with the Body and Blood of Jesus Christ in the E U C H A R I S T. (PAGE 163)

8. The Church is the Body of C H R I S T. (PAGE 163)

9. In the Sacrament of C O N F I R M A T I O N, the bishop says, "Be sealed with the gift of the Holy Spirit." (PAGE 163)

10. Jesus Christ is the head of the people of God who love God and love their N E I G H B O R. (PAGE 163)

Secret Word:

I N I T I A T I O N

Say What?
Know the definitions of these terms.
doxology
marginalized
social justice

Now What?
Write at least one thing you will do at school this week to reach out to someone in need of God's love.
Answers will vary.

_____
_____
_____
_____
_____
_____
_____
_____

166 *Unit 4 · Jesus the Christ*

Respond

IF TIME ALLOWS

Service: Finding God in All Things
Make arrangements with another catechist to have groups share videos with younger children. Arrange young people into small groups. Have groups produce a short video that shows how they have found God in all things. They may use camcorders, smartphones, or computers. Encourage groups to add music, narration, and interviews as they wish. If technology is unavailable, an alternative is to have groups make picture books to share.
✝ *Family and Community*

Session Assessment Option
An assessment for this session can be found at www.findinggod.com.

3-Minute Retreat
Give young people an opportunity for quiet meditation at **www.loyolapress.com/retreat**.

PLAN AHEAD: Get Ready for Session 20

Consult the catechist preparation pages to prepare for Session 20 and determine any materials you will need.

Celebrating Holy Week and Easter

3-Minute Retreat

Before you prepare the session, pause and be still. Take three deep breaths and be aware of the loving presence of God, who is with you on this journey.

Colossians 3:1–4

If then you were raised with Christ, seek what is above, where Christ is seated at the right hand of God. Think of what is above, not of what is on earth. For you have died, and your life is hidden with Christ in God. When Christ your life appears, then you too will appear with him in glory.

Reflection

Paul asks us to understand and accept what Christ has accomplished in his Resurrection. Jesus Christ now sits in his glorified humanity at the right hand of God, from where he sends the Spirit to bring us new life. In this new life of grace, our ultimate concerns are those of Heaven, not of earth. We are not to let any of the limited goals of the earth distract us from our ultimate destination. So we wait in joyful expectation of that final day of Christ's return.

Questions

How easily am I distracted by the limited goals of this world? What steps can I take to keep my eye on the joyful expectation of Christ's return?

Concluding Prayer

Speak to God, using the words of this prayer or your own.

Risen Lord, be patient with me while I await your return. Help me keep my eyes on what is truly important so I may live as you want me to live.

Knowing and Sharing Your Faith in Session 20

Consider how Scripture and Tradition can deepen your understanding of session content.

Scripture

John 13:15 reminds us that Jesus washed the feet of his disciples and called us to serve others.

1 Corinthians 2:9 reminds us of the mystery of eternity.

Tradition

Jesus' Resurrection was not a return to earthly life. In the Resurrection, Jesus passed from a state of death to another life beyond space and time. The entry of Christ's humanity into the glory of God remains a mystery that transcends and surpasses history. At our death, we will be judged by the risen Christ. At the end of time, the day of judgment, Christ will return to transform all of creation and establish the Kingdom of God in its fullness. Those who are saved will live in God's presence in Heaven. Those who rejected God's mercy will be eternally separated from God, a state that we call Hell.

Catholic Social Teaching

In this session the integrated Catholic Social Teaching themes are **Call to Family, Community, and Participation; Life and Dignity of the Human Person;** and **Option for the Poor and Vulnerable.** See page 133b for an explanation of these themes.

Window on the Catechism

The Resurrection and its significance are discussed in *CCC* 638–655. Our particular judgment of Heaven, Hell, or Purgatory and the Last Judgment are described in *CCC* 1020–1050.

General Directory for Catechesis

The historical character of the mystery of Salvation is presented in *GDC* 107 and 108.

One-Hour Session Planner

SESSION 20 Celebrating Holy Week and Easter

Session Theme: *We enter into the sacred mysteries at the heart of our faith during Holy Week. Jesus' Resurrection opens the promise of eternal life with him in Heaven.*

Before This Session

▶ Display the *Finding God* poster The Liturgical Year.

▶ Determine whether you will use the Unit Assessment option listed on page 174.

▶ Determine whether you will also discuss the Holy Week and Easter seasonal pages in the back of the Young People's Book.

▶ Bookmark your Bible to John 13:15 and 1 Corinthians 2:9. Place the open Bible in your prayer space.

▶ Read the Guide for this session, choose any additional If Time Allows activities that you might have time to complete, and gather the listed materials.

Prayer in Session 20

Pray aloud the short prayer on the session opening page while young people pray silently. Together pray the Sign of the Cross. Invite young people to access an online 3-Minute Retreat at the end of the session. In Session 20 young people pray to God for gifts of faith, hope, and love. Follow the Prepare directions on the Catechist Guide page before sharing with young people.

STEPS	APPROXIMATE TIME
Engage *Celebrating Holy Week and Easter* PAGE 167	10 minutes
Explore *Journey Through Holy Week* PAGES 168–169 *Promise of the Resurrection* PAGES 170–171	30–40 minutes
Reflect *Prayer:* Enter the Kingdom PAGE 172 *Where Do I Fit In?* PAGE 173	10–15 minutes
Respond *What's What?* PAGE 174	10–15 minutes

TAKE IT HOME

Homework options:

Stations of
the Cross   PAGE 169

Mosaics
and More   PAGE 170

Materials

REQUIRED

▶ *Finding God* poster: The Liturgical Year, yearbook pictures (page 167)

▶ Bible (pages 168, 171)

▶ Media player, recording or online video of the *Exsultet* (pages 169, 172)

▶ Computers with Internet access (page 174)

OPTIONAL

▶ Cloth, objects with special meanings (page 167)

▶ Session 20 BLM, T-377 (page 168)

▶ Bibles (page 168)

▶ Balloons (page 171)

▶ Writing supplies (page 173)

▶ Session 20 Assessment, www.findinggod.com (page 174)

▶ Unit 4 Assessment, T-378–T-380 (page 174)

Session 20

Celebrating Holy Week and Easter

OUR final preparations for Easter are made during Holy Week. We remember and commemorate the events that led to Jesus' acceptance of his Death on the Cross for our sins. We are hopeful because we know that Jesus will rise on Easter.

We often pray the **Stations of the Cross,** an important prayer through which we remember Jesus' Death for our Salvation. When we pray the Stations of the Cross, we walk from station to station and remember events from Jesus' Passion and Death. We remember these events with great hope because we know that death and evil do not triumph. Jesus will rise on Easter!

Holy Week, the week that precedes Easter, begins with Palm Sunday. We remember Jesus' triumphant entry into Jerusalem on Palm Sunday. On Holy Thursday we celebrate the gift that Jesus gave us in the Eucharist as we remember Jesus' Last Supper. On Good Friday we venerate the Cross and remember Jesus' Passion and Death. During the **Easter Vigil,** we wait to celebrate Christ's Resurrection, and we welcome new members into the Church in the Sacrament of Baptism. The **Triduum** represents the three days—Holy Thursday, Good Friday, Holy Saturday—during which we enter into the suffering, Death, and Resurrection of Jesus, leading up to Easter. On Easter Sunday, we celebrate Christ's Resurrection and the promise of new life in this world and the next.

> Where in your life do you experience sacredness and mystery? Name something in your life that you consider sacred. What do you do to honor and nurture your sense of God's sacred presence in your life?

PRAYER

Thank you God, for raising Jesus from the dead so that we might know the promise of eternal life. Help us share the Good News of Jesus' Resurrection with others.

167

IF TIME ALLOWS

Prayer Table

In advance ask young people to bring to class common objects that have a special meaning to them, such as photos of loved ones, gifts or mementos, or objects from nature. Prepare a prayer table by covering it with a cloth and placing a candle in the center. Ask young people to explain their objects and place them on the table. Invite prayers of thanksgiving for the people and things that bring us joy and for the eyes to see God in all things.

INCLUSION

Autism Spectrum

Visual Learners If you have young people with autism-spectrum disorder, point out the numbers next to each Station of the Cross on pages 284–285 in Prayers and Practices. Teach the prayer's sequence. Photocopy the pages, cut out each station, and glue to separate note cards so young people can practice using the cards to pray the stations in sequence.

Go to **www.findinggod.com/sessionextenders** for a Sunday Connection. You may wish to share this with the group.

▶ Identify the events of Jesus' life that we celebrate during Holy Week.

▶ Explain our beliefs in the promise of the Resurrection.

▶ Pray for gifts of faith, hope, and love.

▶ Define *Easter Vigil,* Exsultet, *indulgence, particular judgment, Purgatory, Stations of the Cross,* and *Triduum.*

① Set the Stage

Display the *Finding God* poster The Liturgical Year. Have young people turn to page 222 and read the paragraphs about Holy Week and Easter. Then read aloud the text in the box on page 167. Give young people time to reflect on or write responses.

② Get Started

Have young people read the paragraphs on the page. Display pictures from a yearbook. Ask: **Why do people take photos?** (Possible answer: to remember people and events) Explain that praying the Stations of the Cross helps us remember the events of Jesus' suffering and Death. Pray the Stations of the Cross together, using pages 284–285 in Prayers and Practices.

Ask: **What does the prefix tri- mean in Triduum?** (three) Ask: **Why does this make sense?** (The Triduum is the three days of remembrance before Easter—Holy Thursday, Good Friday, and Holy Saturday.) Point out Palm Sunday and the days of Triduum on the poster.

 Prayer

Say: **Let's thank God for the gift of life and the hope of eternal life with him.** Pray aloud the prayer. Conclude by praying the Sign of the Cross.

1 Begin

Ask young people to name favorite movies that they watch over and over. Ask: *If you know how the movie will end, why do you watch it again and again?* (Possible answers: It's a great story. The characters are compelling. I always see or hear something new.) Say: *Today we're going to read about the greatest story ever told and the most compelling character who ever lived. We know the outcome of this story, which is precisely why we love to tell it over and over again.*

2 Connect

Read aloud the opening two paragraphs. Draw a time line on the board with the heading Holy Week. Add Palm Sunday on one end and Easter Vigil on the other. Then add Holy Thursday and Good Friday. As sections are read, add brief descriptions to the time line. Say: *By traveling through this week with Jesus every year, we remind ourselves about our journey toward God—one that will involve the end of our human life and our hope for eternal life with him.*

Have volunteers read Entering Jerusalem. Explain that the people celebrating Jesus' arrival in Jerusalem—mostly Jews—hoped that he would establish a worldly kingdom by overthrowing the Roman government. Say: *Nervous Roman officials knew that the Jewish festival of Passover was a celebration of the Jews' liberation from Egypt, and they feared a similar rebellion.*

 Have a volunteer read aloud Receiving Jesus. Reread John 13:15. Review the meaning of *Paschal Mystery* in the Glossary. Ask: *What does Jesus want his disciples to do?* (serve others)

Read aloud At the Foot of the Cross. Explain that veneration of the Cross is not adoration of the actual object but what it represents—Christ's sacrifice for our Salvation.

Journey Through Holy Week

Christ Enters Jerusalem, 18th century, Ethiopian School.

DURING Holy Week we celebrate the most solemn liturgies of the Church year. The Church invites us to enter into the greatest mysteries at the heart of our faith—the suffering, Death, and Resurrection of Jesus.

Holy Week begins with Jesus' triumphant entry into Jerusalem on Palm Sunday and ends at the Easter Vigil on Holy Saturday. Through our participation in the sacred and ancient liturgies of Holy Week, we deepen our love for Jesus and come to better understand that he is the fulfillment of God's promise of Salvation.

Entering Jerusalem

Palm Sunday commemorates Jesus' triumphant entry into Jerusalem. Jesus arrived before the celebration of Passover, one of the biggest feasts in the Jewish calendar. Jews from many countries were gathering in Jerusalem, and Jesus was met by people waving palm branches, crying out "Hosanna," and laying their cloaks on the road before him. These were actions fit for a king. But despite this royal reception, Jesus knew that he was proceeding toward his own Death.

On Palm Sunday we are invited to enter into the events surrounding Jesus' Passion, Death, and Resurrection. In the Palm Sunday liturgy, we enact the initial warm welcome of the crowds that changes to shouts of, "Crucify him! Crucify him!" In Holy Week, we enter into our faith's sacred mysteries.

Receiving Jesus

On Holy Thursday we celebrate the Evening Mass of the Lord's Supper. The Scripture readings recall how on the night before he died, Jesus instituted the Sacrament of the Eucharist. We focus on actions that ritually and symbolically express the meaning underlying Jesus' Paschal Mystery—new life comes when we lovingly sacrifice for others.

The Mass on Holy Thursday includes a ritual washing of the feet, recalling how Jesus washed the feet of his disciples. "I have given you a model to follow, so that as I have done for you, you should also do." (John 13:15) We receive the Body and Blood of Jesus Christ in the Eucharist, and we receive Jesus' example of how to lead through loving service.

At the Foot of the Cross

The solemn mood of Good Friday is established as the priests and deacons lay facing downward in a profound gesture of reverence before the altar. The silence of the church invites us to think and pray about Jesus' ultimate sacrifice of dying on the Cross so our sins would be forgiven. We bear witness to Jesus' Passion and Death, even as we anticipate the celebration of his Resurrection.

A focal point of the Good Friday liturgy is the veneration of the Cross when the congregation is invited to offer a gesture of respect and devotion by

168 *Unit 4 • Jesus the Christ*

IF TIME ALLOWS

Session 20 BLM

Scenes from Holy Week Provide each young person with the Session 20 Blackline Master [T-377]. Read aloud the directions and invite young people to complete the activity over the coming week. Encourage them to share their drawings with the group.

Passover View

Have young people read Exodus 12 when God instructed the Israelites to sacrifice a lamb and sprinkle its blood on their doorposts so that the Angel of Death would pass over their homes. Extend the activity by having young people read John 1:29.

SEASONAL SESSIONS

Holy Week and Easter

Work with young people through pages 235–242 to learn more about Holy Week and Easter. These special sessions can each take up to one hour to complete.

touching or kissing the Cross. The prayerful service ends, again with no music and no procession. We experience the emptiness of waiting—waiting on God's promise.

From Darkness to Light

A vigil is a watch kept the evening before a celebration. On the evening before Easter Sunday, the faithful gather in a darkened church in anticipation of the celebration of Christ's Resurrection. The Service of Light begins with the priest and deacon lighting and blessing a new fire. From those flames, they light the Easter candle. The deacon or priest, holding the Easter candle aloft proclaims, "Light of Christ!" To which we respond, "Thanks be to God!" The Easter candle is processed to the sanctuary as the flame from this candle is spread to candles held by everyone in the assembly. As this is done, the *Exsultet,* a beautiful Easter hymn of praise, is sung. Soon the entire church is alive and lit with one light—the Light of Christ.

Liturgy of the Word

At the Easter Vigil, passages from the Old and New Testaments are read during the Liturgy of the Word. We hear the story of our Salvation—beginning with Creation and leading up to the discovery of Jesus' empty tomb. The readings help us understand God's tremendous love for us throughout thousands of years. We hear the struggles and challenges our ancestors faced waiting for the coming of a Savior. Jesus is the fulfillment of God's promises. Before the Gospel, we joyfully sing "Alleluia" for the first time since before Lent.

Study Corner

DEFINE
Exsultet

REMEMBER
The liturgies and rites of Holy Week help us enter into the sacred mysteries at the heart of our faith—Jesus' life, Death, and Resurrection, which have won our Salvation.

Liturgy of Baptism

After we listen to the readings, the Liturgy of Baptism is celebrated. This is the culmination of a journey that the participants in the Rite of Christian Initiation of Adults (RCIA) have made during the past year. The newly baptized are also confirmed and complete their initiation by receiving the Eucharist for the first time. As the congregation welcomes the new members of the Church, the members renew their baptismal promises.

Liturgy of the Eucharist

The Easter Vigil continues with the celebration of the Liturgy of the Eucharist. We hear the words "This is the Lamb of God" at every Mass. Hearing these words at the Easter Vigil reinforces the truth that Jesus, whose Good Friday sacrifice on the Cross gained our Salvation, is present for us at every Eucharist we celebrate. Mass concludes with a blessing that sends us forth into the world, ready to proclaim the risen Christ to the world: "Christ is Risen! Indeed he is Risen! Alleluia!"

Explore

Our Catholic Character

The Church believes that God is the Father of everyone. It is important to recognize our common roots and respect the Jewish faith, which is already a response to God's Revelation in the Old Covenant. It is wrong for Catholics to blame members of the Jewish faith for crimes committed during Christ's Passion or to believe that Scripture desires them to do so. Over the years the Church has worked to improve Catholic-Jewish relations. One example is a request from Pope John Paul II at a special Mass at Saint Peter's in 2000, asking forgiveness for Christians' sins against the Jewish people.

Session 20 > Celebrating Holy Week and Easter **169**

TAKE IT HOME

Stations of the Cross

Explain that praying the Stations of the Cross helps us experience who Jesus is and meditate on his suffering, Death, and Resurrection. Assign one of the stations to each young person. Ask him or her to draw the station on poster board and identify it by number and description. Invite young people to refer to pages 284–285 in Prayers and Practices. Encourage them to add a personal prayer to Jesus that coordinates with the specific station and thanks him for his selfless love. Display the stations in the room.

Invite a volunteer to read aloud From Darkness to Light. Point out that the Easter Vigil is a time of hopeful waiting. The darkness in the church soon gives way to light. Say: *As the Exsultet is sung, the participants light their candles from the Paschal Candle. The hymn proclaims how Jesus' Death freed us from sin. The hymn worships God for all his works and tells how Christ will live and reign forever.* Play a recording of the *Exsultet* or find an online video of an Easter Vigil service to show to young people.

Have volunteers read aloud Liturgy of the Word. Ask: *What is significant about the readings at the Easter Vigil?* (They trace our Salvation story.) Ask: *What do we sing for the first time since before Lent?* ("Alleluia")

Read the last two sections. If young people have attended an Easter Vigil Mass, invite them to share their recollections and impressions. Ask: *What rite is incorporated into the celebration of the Mass?* (the Liturgy of Baptism for new members of the Church) Ask: *Why are the words "This is the Lamb of God" meaningful at the Liturgy of the Eucharist?* (Jesus, innocent and without sin, died on the cross for our Salvation, rose, and is present in the Eucharist.)

Our Catholic Character

Read aloud the feature. Explain that tolerance and respect for other faiths leads to peace. Challenge young people to reject hatred and choose to love as Jesus did.

③ Close

Have young people thank Jesus in the silence of their hearts for the gift of his earthly journey, his great love for us, and for the liturgies we celebrate to commemorate that love.

1 Begin

Have young people imagine a story where the hero moves from success to success, easily surmounts every difficulty, and nothing gets in his or her way. Ask: *How believable would that story be? Can you identify with the hero?* (Answers will vary.) Explain that without difficulties to overcome, the story may not be realistic or easy to relate to. Jesus faced difficulties, suffering, and death. Suffering is part of the mystery of being human.

2 Connect

Have a volunteer read aloud the title and the first two paragraphs. Say: *Suffering is a mystery. Every human being experiences it. As Christians, we do not believe that God causes suffering, but we do believe that God is present with us in our suffering, as he was with Jesus. We also believe that we are called to relieve the suffering of others as Jesus did. The ultimate value of suffering is that it gives us opportunities to give and receive love.* Invite volunteers to tell about a time when someone they loved was suffering and how they helped relieve the pain. Ask: *How did the experience change the relationship?* (Possible answer: A bond of love was strengthened.)

Read aloud To Love Like Jesus. Say: *God gives you free will.* Discuss what makes love a choice.

Read aloud What Follows Death? Say: *It is easy to think only about right now, but we are really preparing for the reality of the four last things.* Remind young people that Jesus invites them to live a happy life that reflects his teachings. God is just.

Our Catholic Character

Have a volunteer read aloud the feature. Further explain that while we are forgiven, the effects of sin still remain. This is called temporal punishment.

Promise of the Resurrection

He Is Risen, He Qi, China.

CELEBRATING Holy Week and Jesus' Resurrection on Easter reveals God's response to some of the deepest issues that human beings ponder, such as how to make sense of suffering and what happens after death.

Jesus' Death teaches that suffering is a part of human life. Jesus modeled how to respond to suffering. Under the pressure of exhaustion, rejection, loneliness, and evil during his Passion and Death on the Cross, where did Jesus find the strength to endure violence and return only love? Jesus found strength in his union with his Father. Having experienced the depth of his Father's love, Jesus was filled with the love of the Holy Spirit. Through a life of prayer, he remained close to the Father through every trial.

Our Catholic Character

We continue to suffer the effects of our sins, even after we receive forgiveness; this is called temporal punishment. An **indulgence** is a lessening of temporal punishment gained through participation in prayer and works of charity. In addition to obtaining indulgences for ourselves, we can gain them for those in Purgatory, who benefit from the lessening of temporal punishment as they prepare to see the face of God.

170   *Unit 4 • Jesus the Christ*

To Love Like Jesus

Jesus found the strength to suffer on our behalf because he was grounded in the Father's love. The best response you can give is to love Jesus freely— not out of fear or because you are supposed to, but because he is good and worthy of your love. Pray for the grace to love Jesus because you *want* to love him.

In your daily life, you have many chances to love God and others. The choices you make in those situations make you who you are. If you offer actions of love toward others, you become more loving. If you do unkind and selfish things, you become less loving and may become insensitive to the needs of others. With each decision you make, you set a pattern for your life that shapes who you are becoming.

What Follows Death?

Jesus' Resurrection gives us a glimpse of what awaits us after our human lives are over. It is Jesus' promise of eternal life. Through Jesus' dying, rising, and ascending into Heaven, we realize that we have a place in Heaven with Jesus.

The Church invites us to reflect upon our beliefs in four last things: death, judgment, Heaven, and Hell. Everyone faces these four realities. Immediately following death is the judgment by Christ. The result of this judgment is Heaven, Hell, or Purgatory. The Church invites us to think about how we are living our lives. The choices we make each day matter. They have consequences now and into the future.

TAKE IT HOME

Mosaics and More

Explain that as Christians, we hope that all the pieces of our lives will "add up" to union with God in Heaven. Have young people tear sheets of colored construction paper into small pieces. Provide them with poster board and glue and have them use the construction-paper pieces to make a mosaic that represents their idea of Heaven, either abstractly or realistically. Allow young people to share their completed art with the group and display it in the room, if possible.

Death

At the moment of death, our hidden selves will be made plain to us, and we will realize whether the actions of our lives have brought us closer to or farther from Jesus. That moment is called the **particular judgment.** Have we followed Jesus or turned away? Our actions in life will determine whether we have a place with God in eternity.

Judgment

We all face God's judgment at the end of our mortal lives. God, in his tremendous compassion and love for us, will decide where we spend eternity based on how well we have loved others in this lifetime. Three possible outcomes accompany God's judgment.

➡ People who have followed Jesus perfectly in life can enter God's presence, which is the deepest goal of the human heart. They will see God face-to-face and experience complete and lasting joy. This is called Heaven.

➡ People may need to be purified of any selfishness that remains because only those totally transformed by love can enter the Kingdom of God. This temporary state of purification is called **Purgatory**—when every trace of a soul's sin is cleared away so the person may enjoy God's presence in Heaven.

➡ People who have freely refused in serious ways to follow God's command to love have put themselves in the state of mortal sin. Those who refuse to love cannot enter the Kingdom of God because God is love. They will be outside God's presence forever, and this eternal separation from God for whom we long is called Hell. It is the result of the free choice of a person to reject God's love and forgiveness once and for all.

Mystery of Eternity

The mystery of eternity with God is beyond all understanding. The Scriptures describe Heaven as life, light, peace, a wedding feast, wine of the kingdom, the Father's house, the heavenly Jerusalem, and paradise.

"What eye has not seen, and ear has not heard, and what has not entered the human heart, what God has prepared for those who love him, . . ."

1 Corinthians 2:9

We know that Heaven responds to our deepest longings. These images give us clues to understanding what Heaven will be like.

Study Corner

DEFINE

indulgence, particular judgment, Purgatory

REMEMBER

Jesus' Resurrection opens the promise of eternal life with him in Heaven. After death we will be judged by a loving and merciful God who will determine how we will spend eternity.

Explore

SACRED ART

This Russian mosaic of the Resurrection depicts Jesus breaking the doors of death and freeing Adam and Eve along with other men and women of the Old Testament. Mosaic art is made with small pieces of glass, stone, or other material. The subject of this art reminds us that God desires for every person to be saved in order to enjoy eternal life in Heaven with him. Jesus' Resurrection from the dead gives us hope of attaining that eternal life. Every Sunday when we celebrate the Eucharist, we celebrate Jesus' Resurrection from the dead and gain strength to follow him more faithfully.

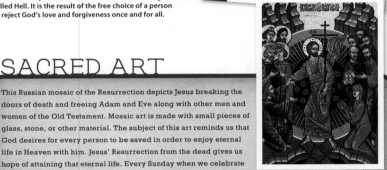

Mosaic of the Resurrection, Moscow, Russia.

Session 20 > Celebrating Holy Week and Easter **171**

ADVENTURES IN FAITH

Reaching Heaven

Push desks or tables aside and have young people stand in a circle. Give each young person an inflated balloon and have a supply of extra balloons near you. Tell young people that when you say "Go," they must hit the balloon into the air. Their challenge is to keep all the balloons in the air without holding them or allowing them to hit the ground, a desk, a person, or any surface. Explain that this is a timed activity, and that every five seconds, you will add another balloon. When a balloon hits a surface, one penalty point will be given, and when they have six penalties, the round will be over. Play five rounds, encouraging young people to strategize in order to maximize the amount of time they keep the balloons in the air.

When the game is over, point out that young people had to work together to improve their time. Explain that reaching Heaven is like this. When an individual becomes overly focused on getting himself or herself to Heaven, the effort becomes self-centered—the opposite of how God wants us to be—and that, paradoxically, our Salvation hinges on our efforts to build the Kingdom of God for all people on earth.

Have volunteers recall the four last things. (death, judgment, Heaven, and Hell) Then read aloud the section Death. Ask a volunteer to read the definition of *particular judgment* in the Glossary. Point out that our culture encourages us to value youth and to deny aging and death. Ask them to provide examples. (Possible answers: negative stereotypes of older people, admiration of movie stars, ads for beauty products) Say: **When the Church asks us to focus on the four last things, it is not trying to be gloomy. It is helping us stay focused on the things that really matter.** Ask what things really matter. (Possible answers: love of God, love of others, building God's kingdom)

Invite volunteers to read aloud Judgment. Say: **We know from experience that when we choose to love others, we experience joy. When we choose to hurt others, we also hurt ourselves. These experiences give us a small taste of Heaven and Hell during this life. They give us a clue that consistently choosing love will lead to the ultimate joy of Heaven and that consistently choosing hatred will lead to the ultimate pain of Hell.** Invite young people to share their thoughts. Emphasize that no person can know who will be saved and who won't and that we can never presume to make such judgments about others.

Read aloud Mystery of Eternity. Discuss the images that Scripture uses to describe Heaven. Invite young people to think of additional images.

Sacred Art

Read aloud the feature. Read Wisdom 1:13 and 2:24 to help explain that God did not make death, nor does he delight in it.

③ Close

Have young people write a prayer for a loved one who has died.

Prayer

Follow the steps to guide young people through the prayer on page 172.

Young People's Page

Prepare Pray the prayer in advance to become familiar with it.

Pray Ask volunteers to read aloud the title of the page and the paragraphs in the left column. If possible, play a recording of the *Exsultet* quietly.

Have young people bring their books to the prayer space and prepare themselves for prayer. Assign a volunteer the role of Leader and have him or her review the part before praying aloud. Encourage all young people to respond with the All part. Pause for a moment and then signal for the Leader to begin praying the Sign of the Cross, followed by reading the paragraph slowly and reverently. Have the group respond with the All part. Have the Leader continue through each part of the prayer as indicated, pausing briefly between each part to allow time for private meditation before all respond. At the conclusion, together pray the Sign of the Cross.

Say: *As you continue to move through the day, look for signs of the Kingdom of God all around you and for opportunities to give witness to it through acts of faith, hope, and love.*

Prayer

Enter the Kingdom

At Holy Saturday's

Easter Vigil liturgy, when the dark church is illuminated during the Service of Light, the people sing the *Exsultet*.

This beautiful Easter hymn of praise proclaims, "The power of this holy night dispels all evil, washes guilt away, restores lost innocence, brings mourners joy; it casts out hatred, brings us peace, and humbles earthly pride."

The hymn, a testimony to the light of Christ, gives us a vision of hope. It encourages us to walk in Christ's footsteps of forgiveness, reconciliation, and joy. Christ's light encourages us to become a guiding light for others as we do his work in the world.

People of Faith

Leader: In the name of the Father, and of the Son, and of the Holy Spirit. Amen.

Throughout his life, Jesus made it clear that in order to enter the kingdom, we have to recognize our need for God. We need God in a way that children need parents. Without God's help we could never enter the kingdom. If you want to enter the kingdom, you have to be a person of faith.

All: O God, we freely give ourselves to you. Help us nurture the gift of faith you have given us by following your Word, listening to what the Church teaches, and putting our faith into action.

Leader: If you want to enter the kingdom, you have to be a person of hope.

All: O God, without the gift of hope, our lives would have no meaning. Help us share our hope with others and look forward to the lasting joy and happiness of eternal life.

Leader: If you want to enter the kingdom, you have to be a person of love.

All: O God, when we look at your Son, Jesus, we learn what it means to love others. Help us love you above all things and show your love to all we meet.

Leader: Together let's pray.

All: Loving God, we want to enter eternal life with you. We know our need for you and count on your help. May we grow in our relationship with you during Holy Week and Easter as we prepare to accept the gift of your Son, Jesus Christ. We ask this in Jesus' name. Amen.

 172 *Unit 4 • Jesus the Christ*

IF TIME ALLOWS

The Kingdom, Here and Now

 Write the following passage from Luke on the board:

> The coming of the kingdom of God cannot be observed, and no one will announce, 'Look, here it is,' or 'There it is.' For behold, the kingdom of God is among you.
>
> *Luke 17:20–21*

Have partners discuss what they think Jesus' words mean. Then allow pairs to share their ideas with the group.

FYI

Coaching Young People to Pray

Before praying, tell young people that the Kingdom of God becomes more clear when we work to assure justice for those who are poor, aid the oppressed, console the sorrowful, and actively seek a new social order in which concrete steps are taken to address people's basic needs. Explain that actions such as these are prayer.

 The Poor and Vulnerable

WHERE Do I Fit In?

Baptism is a gift from God and a lifetime process of initiation into the family of God. As Tertullian claimed, "Christians are not born. They are made."

by Joellyn Cicciarelli

Faith and Hope

I answered the telephone in my college dorm room. It was Aunt Nadine—my young, cool aunt whom I saw only a few times a year. "What's wrong?" I said instinctively, thinking that a family disaster would be the only reason she might call.

"Oh, nothing," she laughed. "I just have a question. Would you like to be John's godmother?" I quickly said yes, and after we chatted for a while, I scribbled the date in my Roman History notebook.

After I hung up, I wondered if I had done the right thing. Who was I to be someone's godmother? Does Aunt Nadine know that she asked a kid who is broke and always late for class? Why did she think I was worthy? I thought about calling her back—about declining and telling her that I wasn't ready.

But then I stopped myself. I thought that maybe my aunt might see something in me that she admired—something good. I remember thinking, "If I'm mature enough to take my little cousin's Baptism so seriously, then maybe I *am* ready."

And so I did call her back, but it wasn't to decline. It was to get a ride to the church. In retrospect, I know I actually had the makings of a good godmother. I had love to give, and I had commitment to my family, to baby John, and to God, who blessed us all with the gift of faith.

JOELLYN CICCIARELLI is the Director of Curricula Development at Loyola Press and the proud godmother of four fine young men.

Commitment to Christ

How can parents or godparents help a newly baptized person on the road of Christian life? Why is Baptism a lifelong process for a Christian? Write your ideas on the lines.

_____
_____
_____
_____
_____
_____
_____
_____
_____
_____
_____
_____
_____
_____
_____
_____

Reflect

Session 20 > Celebrating Holy Week and Easter 173

IF TIME ALLOWS

Godparents in Training

Explain to young people that even though many of them may not be godparents, it's never too early to start practicing. Have them choose one of the ideas listed on the board [or one of their own activity responses] and write two or three sentences describing how they might put this idea into practice with a younger friend or relative in the weeks to come. Encourage young people to follow through with their idea and then to share their experiences—what they feel they gave and received—with the group.

✝ *Family and Community*

---

① Begin

Ask young people to recall learning to swim or ride a bike. Invite volunteers to describe who helped them and what teaching strategies they used. Then ask a volunteer to read aloud the introductory text. Say: ***We don't become Christians magically. We learn how to live as Christians in the same way that we learn how to swim or ride a bike—through the teaching and examples of others.*** Point out the title and remind young people that faith and hope are two of the three Theological Virtues.

② Connect

Invite volunteers to take turns reading aloud Faith and Hope. Have young people describe times when they made a commitment to do something and then had second thoughts. Ask what conclusion they eventually came to. Say: ***Times of second-guessing are important. They ask us to think carefully about a choice we've made. They tell us something about ourselves. Often, God speaks to us during these times—if we listen.*** Ask: ***What did the author realize as she debated her decision?*** (She realized that by taking the issue seriously, she was demonstrating her own readiness to be a godmother.) Ask: ***Why do you think the author will make a good godmother?*** (Answers will vary.)

Have young people complete the Commitment to Christ activity with a partner. Invite partners to share their ideas with the group.

③ Close

Invite young people to tell how their godparents enrich their lives. Then encourage them to thank God for the blessing of godparents and other people who guide them on the road of Christian life.

1 Begin

What's What? Read aloud the directions. Then have young people complete the activity independently or with a partner.

2 Connect

Say What? Ask volunteers to read aloud and define the terms. Review each term in the Glossary if necessary.

Now What? Read aloud the section. Invite each young person to answer the question independently.

3 Go in Peace

Have young people collect their materials and return them to their appropriate places. Encourage young people to remain mindful of the Now What? challenge during the week. Say: *Remember that emotional pain and suffering may not be as apparent as physical pain and suffering. Being attentive to people and mindful of their feelings helps you avoid inflicting pain and may help you recognize any suffering they are enduring.*

3-Minute Retreat
Give young people an opportunity for quiet meditation at **www.loyolapress.com/retreat**.

Respond

What's What?

Complete the puzzle using details from the text.

Across

2. At the end of our lives, we all face God's _____ . (PAGE 171)

5. The _____ candidates are welcomed into the Church at the Easter Vigil. (PAGE 169)

7. We celebrate Jesus' Resurrection on _____ Sunday. (PAGE 168)

8. Participants touch or kiss the cross in a rite called the _____ of the Cross during the Good Friday liturgy. (PAGE 168)

9. The idea of eternity is a _____ of our faith. (PAGE 171)

Down

1. We catch a glimpse of our own afterlife through Jesus' _____ . (PAGE 170)

3. We remember Christ's sacrifice for our Salvation every time we receive the _____ . (PAGE 169)

4. Holy Week begins on _____ . (PAGE 167)

6. One outcome of Christ's judgment, where one waits until the soul's sins can be cleansed, is _____ . (PAGE 171)

8. A _____ is a watch kept the evening before a celebration. (PAGE 169)

Say What?

Know the definitions of these terms.

Easter Vigil   Purgatory
Exsultet   Stations of the Cross
indulgence   Triduum
particular judgment

Now What?

In his suffering and Death, Jesus remained faithful to the Father and won our Salvation. What is one thing that you can do this week to help ease the pain and suffering of others?

Answers will vary.

174   *Unit 4 • Jesus the Christ*

IF TIME ALLOWS

Service: Care for Kids

Have young people brainstorm items that might comfort a critically ill child or teenager, such as warm socks, a soft blanket, or a simple game. Collect items and make care packages. Arrange for young people to deliver them to patients in a nearby children's hospital.

✝ *Life and Dignity*

Session Assessment Option

An assessment for this session can be found at www.findinggod.com.

Unit Assessment Option

If you wish, photocopy the Unit Assessment on pages T-378–T-380. Administer the assessment during the session or send it home.

PLAN AHEAD: Get Ready for Session 21

Consult the catechist preparation pages to prepare for Session 21 and determine any materials you will need.

Faith in ACTION
Unit 4

Acting as a disciple is to accept Jesus' message and to live as he did, sharing his mission, his suffering, and his joy. Jesus entrusted his disciples to continue his work in the world. As Catholics, working to build a just society that reflects the attitudes and values we believe as Jesus' followers is not optional.

In this unit we explored Jesus the Christ. Jesus sacrificed himself on the cross for our Salvation. We receive the Body and Blood of Christ in the Eucharist. Instead of being defeated by temptation, betrayal, and Death, Jesus' Resurrection tells us that God invites us to eternal life. These ideas engage your faith in social and political issues with the self-giving and love that Jesus demonstrated.

Faithful Citizenship

Purpose

Explore what it means to be a faithful citizen by learning about significant witnesses of the Catholic social movement.

Background

In 2003 the United States bishops issued a statement on how our faith calls us to be active citizens in our nation and in our world. This statement served as a reminder that each person is responsible for witnessing to the Church's commitment to human life and dignity. Young people, too, are called to this mission. "We must ensure that our nation's young people—especially the poor, those with disabilities, and the most vulnerable—are properly prepared to be good citizens, to lead productive lives, and to be socially and morally responsible in the complicated and technologically challenging world of the twenty-first century." (USCCB, *Faithful Citizenship: A Catholic Call to Political Responsibility*, 2003)

Steps

1. Choose from among a list of significant witnesses of the Catholic social movement in the last century, such as Dorothy Day, César Chávez, Archbishop Oscar Romero, Blessed Teresa of Calcutta, or Sister Helen Prejean. Research their lives and the stands they took in response to contemporary political thought in light of the call to social justice.

(continued on page 176)

> "There is plenty to do, for each one of us, working on our own hearts, changing our own attitudes, in our own neighborhoods."
>
> —Dorothy Day, social activist and founder of the Catholic Worker Movement

World Youth Day

Act

IF TIME ALLOWS

Faithful Citizenship Resources

The U.S. Catholic bishops publicize resources on faithful citizenship, including implementation ideas for families, religious education directors, teachers, and principals. Visit their Web site at www.usccb.org/faithfulcitizenship.

MATERIALS: Get Ready for Faith in Action

For these projects, you will need print and online resources about the Catholic Worker Movement, current newspapers, computers with Internet access, the prayer service planning guide and prayer service planning tips, supplies for a Social Justice Day, and writing supplies. Also see the project steps.

FAITH IN ACTION

Complete one of the suggested Faith in Action projects as a class, or organize young people into two groups, having each group complete a different project. Note that directions continue on the next page.

① Prepare

Discuss the project ideas with young people and involve them in the decision-making process to determine a project. Discuss the project they choose in terms of faith and being a "person for others." Ask: ***What do you hope to learn from this project? What interests you about it? What concerns do you have about it? Whom will you serve, and how will your service be beneficial to them and to you? Are you prepared to recognize the humanity in those you encounter? How does this project help you put your faith into action? What theme or themes of Catholic Social Teaching will you be experiencing in the project?***

② Implement

Have young people follow the directions to complete Faithful Citizenship on page 175 or Engaging in the Public Forum on page 176. Be sure young people do research before taking action. Provide print and online resources about the Catholic Worker Movement. Encourage young people to research current political issues in print or online newspapers and relate them to the common good.

Be sure young people are supervised during their project as appropriate. Consider asking for parent volunteers to be Faith in Action facilitators for this and the next unit.

✝ *Life and Dignity*
  Solidarity
  Family and Community

③ Close

Bring closure to the project by leading young people in completing one or both of the following:

Prayer Service Download and print out the prayer service planning guide and prayer service planning tips at www.findinggod.com. Have young people plan and implement a prayer service that expresses both gratitude to God for the opportunity to serve and hope for the people whom they served.

Pass It On Have young people share their experiences and inspire others to get involved. Help them organize a Social Justice Day for the school or parish. Encourage volunteers to dress in costume and take the parts of witnesses of the Catholic Worker Movement, such as Dorothy Day or Archbishop Oscar Romero. Ask these volunteers to write and deliver monologues to the audience that highlight the reformer's contributions to the cause of social justice. Other volunteers may organize themselves into two sides of a debate about a political issue they researched that requires a response for the common good. Encourage them to end with a call to action, such as a request to sign a petition, join a letter-writing campaign, or sign up as a volunteer for a program that promotes the common good.

✝ *Family and Community Solidarity*

2. Share your findings with one another and discuss ways that you can share the insights of people who have worked for justice in our world. Here are some ideas to jump-start your creativity.

- Make posters featuring the many people who have worked for justice. Include their pictures, vital statistics, contributions to justice, and compelling quotations. Display the posters in school, in the parish hall, or church.
- Invite a well-known local justice leader to talk with your parish, school, or community about what it means to be a faithful citizen.

Engaging in the Public Forum

Purpose

Design a project that allows you to express your faith publicly.

Background

Sometimes we might be reluctant to get involved in politics. However, we have a duty as citizens and as Catholics to engage with politics. "We are members of a community of faith with a long tradition of teaching and action on human life, and dignity, marriage and family, justice and peace, care for creation, and the common good. . . . Catholics have the same rights and duties as others to participate fully in public life. The Church through its institutions must be free to carry out its mission and contribute to the common good without being pressured to sacrifice fundamental teachings and moral principles." (USCCB, *Forming Consciences for Faithful Citizenship*, 2011)

Steps

1. Learn about the major public-policy issues in your community or state.

2. Choose one of the issues and research the topic. What are the different positions? What are the moral dimensions of the issue? How does Catholic Social Teaching address this issue?

3. Design a project that puts your faith into action. For example, your group can write letters to political leaders as a way to present your position. You might make a video or present a slideshow presentation to church or community leaders that raises awareness about the moral dimensions of the issue.

> "We do not exist for ourselves."
>
> —Thomas Merton, monk, social activist, poet, spiritual writer

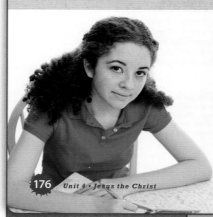

176   Unit 4 • Jesus the Christ

IF TIME ALLOWS

Living Faith: We Believe

Have young people familiarize themselves with the U.S. Catholic bishops' responses to major public policy issues, such as the death penalty, health care, and global climate change. Tell them to select one issue and raise awareness of it by writing an article for the parish bulletin or a letter to a member of Congress.

✝ *Life and Dignity God's Creation*

Unit 5

Catechist Preparation pages open each unit and session.

UNIT 5

Jesus Lives On

Unit 5 focuses on exploring God's presence in our lives and discovering our purpose and mission as disciples. In this unit young people will learn the following concepts.

SESSION 21 Jesus Opens Our Eyes

Young people recognize that Jesus' path through life, death, and eternal life is our path. We strive to find Jesus' presence in our lives. God creates us for a purpose. The work we do contributes to society and makes us coworkers with God. We discover our mission over time by listening for God's voice, meeting different people, and having many different experiences.

SESSION 22 Jesus Sends Us Forth with His Spirit

At Pentecost the Holy Spirit descended on the disciples, giving them the strength to embrace their mission to spread the Good News. Pentecost is the birthday of the Catholic Church. The Gifts of the Holy Spirit give Christians strength to lead moral lives. The Sacrament of Confirmation gives us the ability to share the dream of a better world and to serve God's kingdom. The Church's mission becomes our mission.

SESSION 23 We Are Called and Sent

Saint Paul was the greatest missionary of the early Church. His Epistles to early Christian communities provided guidance on moral choices and instructions about faith, virtue, and daily conduct that still apply today. We are called to conversion just as Saint Paul was called to conversion. God has given us ways to reconcile our relationship with him. When we pray, the Holy Spirit opens our hearts to love God more deeply and to serve him more fully.

SESSION 24 Jesus Calls Us to Eternal Life

The Book of Revelation relies on symbols and images and is not intended to be interpreted literally. In the Book of Revelation, God claims eternal victory over the forces of evil, which is the important message. Because of Mary, we know that if we serve God as faithfully as she did, we can anticipate Salvation and a life of happiness with God in Heaven.

SESSION 25 Celebrating Pentecost

During Pentecost, we celebrate the day that the Holy Spirit, sent by God, entered the Apostles' hearts and filled them with the strength and courage they needed to do God's work in the world. Today we celebrate the strength given to us by the Holy Spirit when we live faithfully as Jesus' followers.

UNIT SAINT

Saint Maximilian Mary Kolbe

Saint Maximilian Mary Kolbe wanted everyone to experience the happiness that comes from living in the presence of God. He founded a monastery in Japan. He also saved thousands of Jews from Nazi persecution but eventually lost his own life in a concentration camp. Like Jesus, the noble gift of his own life sends a message of love that resonates beyond his death.

Prayer in Unit 5

Young people offer prayers of gratitude, pray to the Holy Spirit, participate in a guided reflection about following God's call, and pray to practice the Theological Virtues of faith, hope, and charity. Young people also pray the Daily Examen, a form of Ignatian prayer.

✝ Catholic Social Teaching in Unit 5

The following themes of Catholic Social Teaching are integrated into this unit.

Call to Family, Community, and Participation Participation in family and community is central to our faith and to a healthy society. Families and communities must be supported and strengthened through active participation.

Care for God's Creation We have a responsibility to care for God's creation. We are called to make moral and ethical choices that protect the ecological balance of creation both locally and worldwide.

Rights and Responsibilities The Catholic Church teaches that every person has a right to live as well as the right to things required for human decency. As Catholics, it is our responsibility to protect fundamental human rights.

Solidarity Solidarity is the attitude that leads Christians to share spiritual and material goods. Solidarity unites rich and poor, weak and strong, and helps create a society that recognizes that we live in an interdependent world.

Faith in Action

In Unit 5 young people are invited to show Jesus' care for God's creation by implementing the following service projects: learning about seeds and planting them to make gifts for others and raising awareness about the importance of recycling as ways to honor God's Creation. Alternative service project ideas also appear on the last page of each session in this guide.

TOGETHER *as One Parish*

Religious Education with the Parochial School

To nurture parish unity, organize a school/RE family night that is devoted to Catholic trivia. Provide simple refreshments. Families may choose or draw names to determine teams. Ask questions that reflect information young people have studied throughout the year. Offer prizes to teams with the highest scores.

📖 Literature Opportunity
No Excuses
by Kyle Maynard

This inspirational autobiography is the story of Kyle Maynard, who was born without arms or legs below his elbows and knees yet overcame obstacles to become a champion athlete. The book shows what a positive attitude can give to someone whom others might see as disadvantaged. A devoted family, a strong faith, and personal determination help Maynard become a champion athlete.

✝ *Rights and Responsibilities*

Jesus Opens Our Eyes

 3-Minute Retreat

Before you prepare the session, pause and be still. Take three deep breaths and be aware of the loving presence of God, who is with you on this journey.

1 Corinthians 3:6–9

I planted, Apollos watered, but God caused the growth. Therefore, neither the one who plants nor the one who waters is anything, but only God, who causes the growth. The one who plants and the one who waters are equal, and each will receive wages in proportion to his labor. For we are God's co-workers; you are God's field, God's building.

Reflection

Paul reminds us that when we work in the Church or in the world, we are not loners who have only what we can personally bring to the task. The Church is the Body of Christ in which each person has a role. We complement one another in the skills and talents we bring to our vocations as Christians, and the wise person assesses and values the contribution made by others so that the work of God can flourish.

Questions

What skills and talents do I have that can contribute to the growth of the Kingdom of God? How can I best value the talents and skills that others bring to working in God's field?

 Concluding Prayer

Speak to God, using the words of this prayer or your own.

Lord Jesus, you call us all to be coworkers in the growth of your kingdom on earth. Help me be aware of all you have given me to share and to be open to the talents and services of others.

Knowing and Sharing Your Faith in Session 21

Consider how Scripture and Tradition can deepen your understanding of session content.

Scripture

Luke 24:13–16 tells us how the two disciples on the road to Emmaus failed to recognize Jesus.

1 Corinthians 12:4–6 is Paul's assurance that different spiritual gifts come from the same Spirit.

Tradition

This session draws our attention to the reality of work and its role in God's plan of Salvation. For working people, understanding the Kingdom of God is crucial because it is the place where the work of God and the work of people intersect. Serving the Kingdom of God is not simply a matter of getting people to Heaven but of transforming the earth according to God's will. The Second Vatican Council stated, "But the laity, by their very vocation, seek the kingdom of God by engaging in temporal affairs and by ordering them according to the plan of God." [*Dogmatic Constitution on the Church*, 31]

Catholic Social Teaching

In this session the integrated Catholic Social Teaching themes are **Call to Family, Community, and Participation** and **Care for God's Creation.** See page 177b for an explanation of these themes.

Window on the Catechism

Catechesis on creation is discussed in *CCC* 282–289. For the significance of human work, see *CCC* 378, 901, 1609, 1914, and 2427.

General Directory for Catechesis

Moral formation as one of the fundamental tasks of catechesis is discussed in *GDC* 85–87.

One-Hour Session Planner

SESSION 21 Jesus Opens Our Eyes

Session Theme: *Jesus' pathway through his life, Death, Resurrection, and Ascension is our path and our hope of being reunited with God.*

Before This Session

▶ Bookmark your Bible to John 3:18–19, 15:13, 20:16,26–28, 21:4–7, Luke 24:13–35, Acts of the Apostles 1:9–11, Ben Sira 14:3–19, Genesis 2:15, 1 Corinthians 3:9, 12:4–6, and Matthew 5:14–16. Place the open Bible in your prayer space.

▶ Read the Guide for this session, choose any additional If Time Allows activities that you might have time to complete, and gather the listed materials.

STEPS	APPROXIMATE TIME
Engage *Unit Saint:* Saint Maximilian Mary Kolbe PAGES 177–178 *Daily Examen* PAGE 177 *Jesus Opens Our Eyes* PAGE 179	🕐 10–20 minutes
Explore *Recognizing Jesus in Our Lives* PAGES 180–181 *Coworkers with God* PAGES 182–183	🕐 30–40 minutes
Reflect *Prayer:* Refreshing Our Memory PAGE 184 *Where Do I Fit In?* PAGE 185	🕐 10–15 minutes
Respond *What's What?* PAGE 186	🕐 10–15 minutes

🙏 Prayer in Session 21

Pray aloud the prayer that relates to the central session concepts on the opening page. Young people are also invited to reflect on Scripture by accessing an online 3-Minute Retreat at the end of the session. Session 21 includes a litany of gratitude for the gift of memory. Follow the Prepare directions on the Catechist Guide page before sharing with young people.

TAKE IT HOME

Homework options:

Recognizing Christ   PAGE 180

What Do You Do for a Living?   PAGE 182

Materials

REQUIRED

▶ Writing supplies (pages 179, 180, 181, 185, 186)

▶ Art supplies (page 179)

▶ CD Player (page 180)

▶ CD 2, Track 2: "On the Road to Emmaus" (5:16) (page 180)

▶ Beanbag (page 182)

▶ Bibles (pages 183, 185, 186)

▶ Computers with Internet access (page 186)

OPTIONAL

▶ Writing supplies (pages 179, 183, 184)

▶ Session 21 BLM, T-381 (page 181)

▶ Paper towel, water (page 181)

▶ Small boxes, slips of paper, wrapping paper, tape (page 183)

▶ Basket (page 184)

▶ Magazines, scissors, computers and printers with Internet access (page 185)

▶ Reference materials, poster board, art supplies (page 186)

▶ Session 21 Assessment, www.findinggod.com (page 186)

Unit 5

Jesus Lives On

Saint Maximilian Mary Kolbe grew up as a bright but mischievous boy. He was born Raymond Kolbe on January 8, 1894, in central Poland to a devout Polish Catholic family. When he was 10 years old, his mischievous ways tried his mother's patience. Exasperated, she asked him, "What is going to become of you?" Later, during prayer to the Virgin Mary, he asked himself this same question. Kolbe had a vision of Mary carrying two crowns: one white, for purity, and the other red, for martyrdom. When she asked him whether he would accept either of the crowns, he replied, "I choose both!" Kolbe, the mischievous boy, would live a life filled with passion for living out the example of Jesus Christ.

How the Saint Relates { Saint Maximilian Kolbe's life shows how one person who chooses to live for goodness and against evil can make a profound difference in the world. Kolbe spread Jesus' message of love and redemption wherever he was. His noble gift of his own life sends a message of love beyond his death.

OPENING PRAYER

Daily Examen

Suggest that young people frequently pray the Daily Examen on page 279 in Prayers and Practices. Remind them that this powerful prayer can help them become more aware of God's presence and strengthen their faith. Lead young people in praying these steps, pausing as appropriate:

• Relax and clear your mind. Ask God to help you become aware of his presence all around you.

• Replay the last 24 hours in your mind. Review your day in order hour by hour. Ask yourself, "What has made me happy today?" "Where did I encounter Jesus?" "When did I feel negative or empty?" "Where did I overlook Jesus in those moments?"

• Ask the Holy Spirit to help you focus on two or three moments to reflect on. Ask yourself, "What does God want me to know?" "What does he want me to do differently?"

• Take a moment to thank God for moments of joy and to ask for grace in difficult situations.

• Pray *Amen* silently when you are ready. Now bring your attention back to this room.

UNIT OPENER
OUTCOMES

▶ Give details that tell about Saint Maximilian Mary Kolbe's call to religious life.

▶ Explain ways that Saint Maximilian Mary Kolbe's life followed Jesus Christ's example.

① Begin

Read aloud the unit title. Tell young people that in this unit they will explore finding Jesus and learning their purpose and mission as disciples.

Arrange for two or three guest speakers to talk briefly to the group about their missions in life. Ask them to cover these topics:

▶ How do you describe your mission?

▶ How did you discover it?

▶ What inspiration guides you?

Discuss opportunities and challenges involved with living out missions.

② Introduce the Saint

Have a volunteer read about Saint Maximilian Mary Kolbe. Ask: ***What did young Kolbe ponder when he prayed to the Virgin Mary?*** ("What is going to become of me?") Ask: ***How would you describe his vision?*** (Mary was carrying two crowns: one white [purity] and one red [martyrdom].) Say: ***Because he accepted both crowns, how do you think Kolbe lived out the example of Jesus Christ?*** (Answers will vary.)

How the Saint Relates

Read aloud How the Saint Relates. Begin a discussion of missions that make a difference in the world. Ask: ***What are some real-life examples of people whose mission made a measurable difference in the world?*** (Answers will vary.)

③ Connect

Have a volunteer read aloud the title and the first two paragraphs. Ask young people what it means to be devoted to someone. (Possible answer: setting aside personal interests on behalf of someone else) Ask: **How did Kolbe win over enemies of the Church?** (through a religious movement that he organized called the Militia Immaculata)

Ask a volunteer to read the section Missionary Travels. Ask: **Why did Kolbe want to do missionary work?** (He wanted others to know the happiness that comes from experiencing the presence of God.) Ask: **How did Kolbe spread Jesus' teachings as a missionary?** (He founded a monastery in Japan.)

Ask volunteers to read aloud the section A Soldier for Christ. Point out Saint Maximilian Mary Kolbe's act of courage in hiding 2,000 Jews, explaining that fear probably prevented more people from taking the risks he did to help the Jews, risks that could have resulted in their arrest or death. Ask: **In what ways did he live Christ's example at Auschwitz?** (He offered himself to save another.)

Pray aloud, "No one has greater love than this, to lay down one's life for one's friends." [John 15:13] Say: **Kolbe stood up for what he believed as part of his mission to follow the example of Jesus Christ.**

④ Close

Close by asking young people to reflect on different aspects of Saint Maximilian Mary Kolbe's life. Ask: **What surprised you? What impressed you? What inspired you?** (Answers will vary.) Encourage volunteers to share their thoughts with the group.

Devoted to Mary

After his vision, Kolbe was especially devoted to Mary and pursued a life of prayer and service. In 1907 Kolbe and his brother Francis entered a Franciscan seminary in Lwów, the present-day city of Lviv, Ukraine. When he made his final vows in 1914, he chose the name Maximilian Mary in honor of the Blessed Virgin.

A gifted student, Kolbe earned doctorates in philosophy and theology. While he was a student in Rome, he witnessed demonstrations against the pope. In response, Kolbe organized a religious movement in 1917 called the Militia Immaculata to convert sinners and to win over enemies of the Catholic Church.

Missionary Travels

Kolbe wanted everyone to experience the happiness that comes from experiencing the presence of God. Between 1930 and 1936, he traveled to Japan, where he founded a monastery near Nagasaki. Kolbe chose to build the monastery on the side of the mountain, a site that many Japanese believed was not in harmony with nature. His decision later proved to be for the best. When the atomic bomb was dropped on Nagasaki in World War II, the monastery, shielded by the mountain, was unharmed.

A Soldier for Christ

In 1936, due to poor health, Kolbe returned to Poland. When the Nazis invaded Poland three years later, most people feared for their lives, but Kolbe spoke out against Nazi brutality. He hid 2,000 Jews from Nazi persecution, an undertaking that required great personal risks.

In 1941 Kolbe was arrested and sent to the concentration camp at Auschwitz. Later that year a man from his barracks escaped. In reprisal the camp commander chose 10 men to starve to death as a warning to the other prisoners. One of the men cried out, "My wife! My children!" Kolbe quietly stepped forward and asked to take the man's place. His request was granted, and the chosen 10 were placed together in a dark cell to die slowly from hunger and dehydration. During their time in the cell, Kolbe led the others in song and prayer to the Blessed Virgin. Finally, only Kolbe remained. The guards, impatient for the bunker to be emptied, executed him by lethal injection on August 14, the eve of the Feast of the Assumption. Saint Maximilian Mary Kolbe was a man who lived what he preached—total love for God and others. He was beatified in 1971 and canonized in 1982.

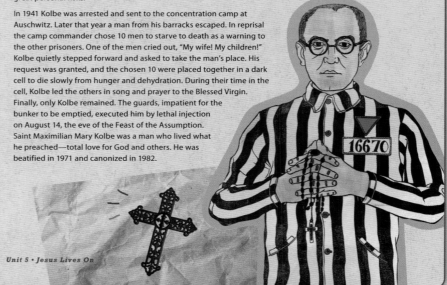

178   *Unit 5 • Jesus Lives On*

IF TIME ALLOWS

A Force for God

Remind young people that Kolbe's religious movement, Militia Immaculata, urged members to give their lives to Marian devotion while converting others and encouraging holiness. Point out that the word *militia* indicates an army of fighting forces.

Have young people think of a way to tell others about their faith. Ask them to choose a target group for their message. For example, they may want to appeal to young children, teens, adults, or the elderly. Or they may want to appeal to people in a particular line of work, such as nurses, sales professionals, or law enforcement officers. Ask them to give their movement a name and to make a charter that outlines their movement's purpose and some ways to achieve that purpose. Groups may want to make a poster, a short video, or start a blog that describes the purpose of their movement.

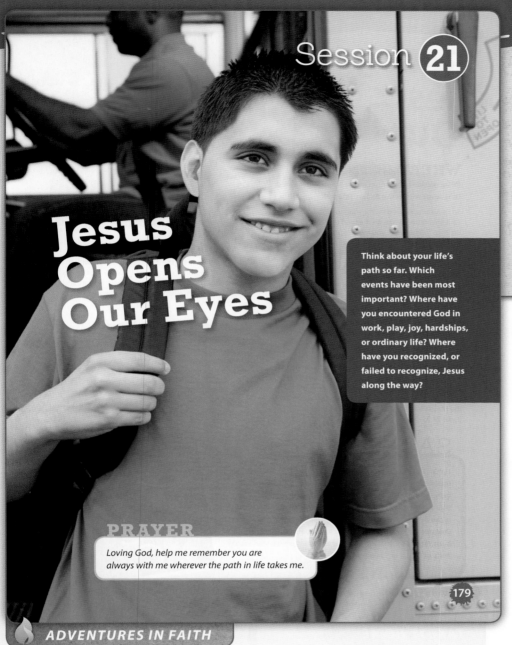

Session 21

Jesus Opens Our Eyes

Think about your life's path so far. Which events have been most important? Where have you encountered God in work, play, joy, hardships, or ordinary life? Where have you recognized, or failed to recognize, Jesus along the way?

PRAYER

Loving God, help me remember you are always with me wherever the path in life takes me.

179

ADVENTURES IN FAITH

Choosing Paths

Arrange to visit a maze at a local botanical garden or arboretum. Explain to young people that a maze can be a good place for solitude and quiet reflection about confusing paths in life. Ask them to walk the maze independently and prayerfully. At the completion of their maze walk, ask young people to write a short description about their experiences. Write some questions on the board as a guide:

- *How would you describe your time of reflection in the maze?*
- *When did God enter your thoughts?*
- *When did the maze's path reflect your own confusion about a path to follow? How did you respond to the challenge?*
- *What feelings, good or bad, were strongest during your walk? Why?*
- *Why is it important to take time to reflect on your purpose, mission, or work in the world?*

 Go to **www.findinggod.com/sessionextenders** for Gospel accounts about Jesus' appearances to the disciples after his Resurrection. You may wish to share this with the group.

OUTCOMES

▶ Explain that we follow the path of Jesus and live with the hope of being reunited with God.

▶ Explain the ways that our work expresses our vocation to be coworkers with God.

▶ Pray a litany of gratitude.

▶ Define *consumerism, dignity of work, Epistle,* and *the Way.*

① Set the Stage

Ask a volunteer to read aloud the text in the box. Give young people time to reflect on or write responses to the questions. Ask volunteers to share responses with the group.

② Get Started

Have young people take out a sheet of paper. Say: ***Draw your life's path. At the beginning of your life's path, draw a box and write your birth date and where you were born.*** Ask young people to add additional boxes and information along the path that represent important events in their lives. To get them started, suggest some events, such as starting school, moving to a different town, joining a team, getting an award, welcoming the birth of a sibling, or receiving a sacrament.

Have a volunteer read the session title Jesus Opens Our Eyes. Ask: ***How does drawing your life's path relate to the session title?*** (Possible answer: Jesus walks with us throughout all the events of our lives.)

Prayer

Say: ***Let's remember that God is always at our side.*** Pray aloud the prayer. Conclude by praying the Sign of the Cross.

① Begin

Allow young people time to reflect on the last 24 hours. Draw a two-column chart on the board with the headings *When?* and *Where?* Ask volunteers to describe when and where they have recognized Jesus and have them write their ideas on the chart.

② Connect

Ask a volunteer to read the title and opening paragraphs. Point to the board. Say: *As we demonstrated in the Begin step, Jesus is everywhere in our lives. He wants us to be open to seeing him. We're going to learn more about recognizing Jesus.*

Have a volunteer read the section Do I Know You? Ask: *Why didn't the disciples recognize Jesus?* (Possible answers: They were afraid. Their faith had been shaken because they had just witnessed Jesus' Death on the Cross.)
Ask: *When did they recognize Jesus?* (when he broke bread and prayed with them)

Ask young people to think about the disciples who did not recognize the risen Jesus. Play the recorded Scripture story "On the Road to Emmaus" [CD 2, Track 2]. Discuss the story. Ask volunteers to tell about times when they did not recognize the presence of God.

Ask a volunteer to read the section At God's Right Hand. Clarify the meaning of Jesus' Ascension. Explain that the Ascension is a great feast day for Catholics.

Draw a time line on the board and label these sections: Jesus' life, Death, Resurrection, and Ascension. Ask volunteers to add brief details to each section of the time line.

Sacred Art

Read aloud the feature. Ask volunteers to explain elements that are representative of the artist's culture as well as elements that express universal, or catholic, beliefs.

Recognizing Jesus in Our Lives

WHERE did Jesus go after his Resurrection? The angel at the tomb proclaimed that Jesus was going to Jerusalem.

Soon Jesus appeared on the road to Emmaus. Later Paul encountered him on the road to Damascus. In order to follow Jesus, you must recognize where to find him. Knowing this will help you clarify one of the key questions for your own life: "Where am I going?"

Do I Know You?

In the Gospel of Luke, two disciples are walking from Jerusalem to Emmaus on the morning of Jesus' Resurrection. Frightened and demoralized after witnessing the death of Jesus, they are no longer sure of their mission in life. Amazingly, the risen Christ appears and walks with them, but the two disciples don't recognize Jesus. (Luke 24:13–16)

The two disciples tell Jesus, "But we were hoping that he would be the one to redeem Israel." (Luke 24:21) Jesus challenges their interpretation of the role of the Messiah and speaks to them about seeing the Messiah in light of Moses and the prophets. (Luke 24:25–26)

When the risen Jesus breaks bread and prays with the disciples, they finally recognize him. With their hearts and minds burning, they recognize their mission, and they return to Jerusalem to announce their encounter with the risen Christ.

At God's Right Hand

After Jesus rose from the dead, he spent 40 days among his disciples before ascending to Heaven, where he is now and will be eternally present at the Father's right hand. Jesus' Ascension celebrates the entrance of his humanity into divine glory. This astounding event, described in Acts of the Apostles 1:9–11, tells how Jesus was lifted up in a cloud while the Apostles looked on. From Heaven,

SACRED ART

He Qi [Huh Chee], a Chinese artist, blends cultural traditions in this modernist work. Although the painting is rooted in Chinese culture, it is also universal because its subject is the Gospel, which rises above all cultures. In this painting, Christ is shown in the center, and the followers of Jesus are in the four corners. One interpretation suggests that Jesus' outstretched arms and body form a Eucharistic table for all his followers, who are the Body of Christ in the world.

The Risen Lord, He Qi, 1998.

TAKE IT HOME

Recognizing Christ
Invite young people to look for one significant situation during the day in which they recognize Jesus. Encourage them to look beyond the familiar and obvious. Ask them to write a paragraph detailing what they noticed and why it was significant to them. Encourage them to include a photograph, newspaper clipping, or illustration that connects to their ideas.

INCLUSION
Attention

In Motion For young people with attention differences, be sure they understand the directions in the Begin step by asking them to repeat what they are supposed to write. Encourage their use of energy in a productive way by inviting them to get up from their seats and add their ideas to the two columns on the board.

Jesus and the Father sent the Holy Spirit. From Heaven, Jesus will return again to gather all those who will join him and his mother, Mary, in the presence of God.

Jesus' life follows a pathway that leads through his life, Death, into Resurrection, and finally Ascension to Heaven. As followers of Jesus, then, this means that this is our path, too, as we live with the hope and anticipation of being reunited with God.

Remember Me

At times we can be like the two disciples on the road to Emmaus, walking along the path of life, uncertain about our mission and unable to recognize that Jesus is walking with us. What is the key to recognizing Jesus and knowing your mission in life?

In the Gospel of Luke, the two disciples listen to Jesus explain Scriptures. They see the bread being blessed, broken, and shared, and they recognize the risen Christ. They recognize their role of discipleship. That is why the Eucharist is close to the hearts of Catholics, who know it is the Real Presence of the risen Christ in their midst. Christ sends them forth with the mission to continue his teachings in the world. At Mass we, too, listen to Scripture as it is read and explained. Likewise, just as the two disciples gathered around a table and received bread from Jesus, we come forward to receive the Body and Blood of Jesus Christ in the Eucharist. The Gospel of Luke tells us that this is what Christians have been doing since the time of Jesus—worshiping God by listening to the living Word of God and receiving the Eucharist.

People on a journey choose paths. The early Christian community identified itself as **the Way.** The two disciples on the road to Emmaus were on a journey, and Jesus came to them in the Eucharist and gave them strength to complete their journey. That is what the Eucharist is—strength to make our way through life. In the Eucharist we are nourished to complete our own journey on the Way.

Your Road to Emmaus

We don't always know what our mission in life is. Even when we follow Jesus, we don't know exactly where that path will take us. A path may take us to a new school, to a different state or country, or into a new group of people whom we serve or befriend.

If Jesus appeared to you as he appeared to the disciples on the road to Emmaus and said, "Come with me," would you follow him? Would you follow him even without knowing where he was leading you? Don't be afraid to answer yes. Wherever your path leads, Jesus is walking with you. His Word and his presence are with you, to guide you and give you hope. Recognizing Jesus' presence is a way to recognize your own mission in life and what God calls you to be and do in the world.

On the Road

Think about the Emmaus story and how the two disciples felt before they recognized the risen Jesus. What can you do when you are afraid and unsure about your path in life?

_____

_____

_____

_____

_____

Study Corner

DEFINE
the Way

REMEMBER
We can be uncertain about our mission in life when we fail to recognize Jesus' presence. We encounter and recognize Jesus in the Eucharist. Jesus' life follows a path through life, Death, into Resurrection, and finally Ascension to Heaven. Following Jesus means that this is our path, too, as we live with the hope of being reunited with God.

Session 21 > Jesus Opens Our Eyes   181

IF TIME ALLOWS

Session 21 BLM

Patron Saint Search Provide young people with the Session 21 Blackline Master [T-381]. Read the introduction and the directions aloud. Encourage curiosity about vocations and missions by having young people complete the activity. Suggest suitable Catholic Web sites or other appropriate resources to aid their research.

Body of Christ

Demonstrate how a paper towel absorbs water. Remind young people that to absorb something is to take it in or to retain it. Point out that when we eat food, our bloodstream absorbs the nutrients from the food, such as vitamins, minerals, proteins, carbohydrates, and fat. Explain that the Eucharist is a spiritual food. When we consume it, we not only absorb or take in the Real Presence of Christ, but we ourselves are absorbed into the very life of God.

Ask a volunteer to read the first paragraph of Remember Me. Ask young people to discuss the question with a partner. Invite volunteers to share their ideas with the group. Ask: **What might prevent us from completing the mission God has for us?** (Possible answers: fear, uncertainty, contrary pressure from society) Explain that sometimes we all try to run away from Jesus, but at those times he meets us and walks beside us.

Have a volunteer read the second paragraph. Draw two columns on the board with the headings *Emmaus Story* and *Mass*. Ask volunteers to add details about recognizing Jesus. (Emmaus—when Jesus broke and blessed the bread, when Jesus prayed; Mass—in the Eucharist, which is Jesus' Real Presence; when we listen to the Word of God in Scripture)

Read aloud the last paragraph in the section. Ask: **What is significant about the name for the early Christian community?** (Jesus is the true path and the example to follow on our faith journey. He leads us. He shows the way to go.)

Invite volunteers to read aloud Your Road to Emmaus. Say: **Fear can paralyze you. Faith helps you keep moving. It helps you recognize what Jesus is actually calling you to do.**

Read aloud the directions in the On the Road activity. Have young people work independently to complete it before sharing responses.

③ Close

Say: **The Eucharist, the Body and Blood of Christ, is the spiritual food that helps us recognize our purpose.** Explain that in the Eucharist we recognize the Real Presence of Jesus and know that he is with us. During the week, encourage young people to recognize Jesus at other times and in other places.

1 Begin

Discuss different talents. Have young people sit in a circle and toss a beanbag to one another, naming one of their talents when they catch the bag. Be sure each young person has a turn. Point out that a talent might be a clue about the kind of work a person may find meaningful. Ask: **How do your dreams for your future match up with your talents?** (Answers will vary.)

2 Connect

Have a volunteer read aloud the session title and introductory paragraphs. Point out that from the beginning, God placed great value on meaningful work and having a mission.

Ask volunteers to take turns reading Jesus Understands Work. Point out the term *dignity of work*. Invite a volunteer to read aloud the definition in the Glossary. Explain that the Church is concerned about work issues because they have a direct connection to our spiritual well-being. Ask: **How are Jesus' views about work and workers often different from society's views?** (Jesus taught that simple, purposeful, and honest work is preferable to a society that applauds making money for its own sake, achieving at someone else's cost, and so on.) Point out that Jesus chose to associate with working people instead of people in high places of honor in society. Have young people suggest modern work-related issues that the Church speaks out against. (Possible answers: slavery, discrimination, physical and psychological oppression, long working hours, child labor, unfair wages)

Our Catholic Character

Read aloud the feature. Ask: **What current news events are related to dignity of work issues in this country and worldwide?** (Answers will vary.)

Coworkers with God

THE Book of Genesis tells us that Adam, the first man, was created with a purpose—to tend and cultivate the Garden of Eden. (Genesis 2:15)

From the very beginning, human beings have had a job and a mission. God knows the importance and value of work to the body and soul. As with Adam, God creates each of us with a purpose. As time goes on, you will begin to see more clearly what your purpose, or mission, in life will be and how work will play an important part of that mission.

Jesus Understands Work

Jesus understood the **dignity of work,** the sense of purpose and achievement that comes from doing work well. In work, people fulfill part of their potential given to them by God.

Our Catholic Character

Monsignor George Higgins (1916–2002), the son of a Chicago postal clerk, grew up during the Great Depression. Moved by the struggles of workers, he soon became known as the "labor priest" because he worked tirelessly for the rights and dignity of the working person. He stood up for workers on strike, ministered to people in labor unions, and tried to convince politicians to support legislation that ensures fairness to working people. He was awarded the Presidential Medal of Freedom with these words: "For more than 60 years now, [Higgins] has organized, marched, prayed, and bled for the social and economic justice of working Americans."

182 *Unit 5 • Jesus Lives On*

Work gives people a sense of purpose, dignity, and accomplishment, and it makes it possible for them to provide a dignified life for themselves and for their families. But when people are paid unfair wages that keep them in poverty, or when they work in harmful or inhumane conditions, it is difficult for them to achieve dignity and independence. Dignity of work is a basic principle of Catholic Social Teaching. All workers have a right to productive work, decent and fair wages, and safe working conditions.

Jesus knew work. He worked alongside Joseph to learn carpentry as a trade. He knew what it was like to make something with his bare hands. Many images in Jesus' parables involve workers. For example, a farmer goes out to sow his fields, workers toil in the vineyard, and the good shepherd cares for his sheep.

Jesus worked to bring the Good News of Salvation to all people. He didn't isolate himself, sit idly, or wait for the world to come to him. Instead, he traveled widely, preaching from place to place. The Gospels tell us that Jesus gathered disciples among fishermen. He ate with tax collectors. Jesus taught everyday people—working people leading ordinary lives. The Church looks to the example of Jesus as the model for issues related to work and workers.

Lure of Consumerism

One of the main reasons people work is to make money to meet their needs and the needs of those who depend on them. However, this reasonable goal can become blurred. At his opening address at World Youth Day in Australia in 2008,

TAKE IT HOME

What Do You Do for a Living?

Have young people select one person to interview about the work they do. Suggest that they ask questions such as the following, although they may add others:

- Which gifts or talents led you to this work choice?

- What other kinds of work interest you?

- How are you a coworker with God?

- In what ways do you honor the Seventh Commandment by doing an honest day's work?

- What does dignity of work mean to you?

Ask young people to summarize the key ideas from their interviews in a report to share aloud with the group.

Pope Benedict XVI warned young people against the lure of **consumerism** and "false idols." Consumerism is giving undue value to the acquisition of material goods. At its worst, consumerism puts things at the center of our lives, a place where only God should be. Speaking of the effects of consumerism, the pope said, "In our personal lives and in our communities, we encounter a hostility, something dangerous; a poison which threatens to corrode what is good, reshape who we are, and distort the purpose for which we have been created."

Material things are not sinful, but the misuse or hoarding of wealth and power is corrupt. We should not believe that life is all about the acquisition of material things and that the only point of work is to get a paycheck. Instead, we need to see that work is an important way to participate in God's creation. Jesus' example and teachings help give us perspective and direction when thinking about our own attitudes about work.

The Moral Use of Wealth

The Tenth Commandment teaches us not to desire more than we need or to desire what belongs to our neighbors. The *Pastoral Constitution on the Church in the Modern World,* a document from the Second Vatican Council, teaches that we should regard what we have as also meant for the benefit of others: ". . . people are bound to come to the aid of the poor and to do so not merely out of their superfluous goods."

Our Gifts, Our Calling

God has an active role in our lives, working in us to bring us to greater life and joy. When we take up his work, we are coworkers with God. God has given each of us gifts, talents, skills, and interests that are unique. Because these gifts come from God, they are spiritual gifts. Saint Paul speaks of these gifts in his first **Epistle,** or letter, to the Corinthians.

> There are different kinds of spiritual gifts but the same Spirit; there are different forms of service but the same Lord; there are different workings but the same God who produces all of them in everyone.
>
> *1 Corinthians 12:4–6*

When you think of your life's work, God encourages you to think about your mission or calling. Figuring out your calling often takes time and different experiences. Throughout this journey, Jesus is working with you, in you, and through you to guide the way.

Past Meets Present

PAST: The Wisdom of Ben Sira, also known by the title "Sirach," is a book of the Bible that was finished about A.D. 175. The writing covers topics such as law, poverty and wealth, and other matters, both religious and social. Recognized by the Catholic Church as canonical, the contents are divided into separate parts. Chapters 1–43 deal largely with moral instruction. Chapter 14 specifically instructs about the use of wealth.

PRESENT: All people have the right to the moral use of the earth's goods. Speaking to diplomats on June 16, 2005, Pope Benedict XVI reaffirmed that right. "The earth, in fact, can produce enough to nourish all its inhabitants, on the condition that the rich countries do not keep for themselves what belongs to all."

Study Corner

DEFINE

dignity of work
consumerism
Epistle

REMEMBER

Work gives people a sense of dignity and accomplishment. The work we do contributes to society and expresses our vocation to be cocreators with God. God creates us for a purpose. We discover our mission over time and with many experiences.

Session 21 > Jesus Opens Our Eyes 183

Explore

Talents as Gifts

Give each young person a small, empty box. Invite them to write at least one talent, trait, or skill on a slip of paper, put the slip in the box, and wrap the box. Challenge them to think of a person to whom they would like to give the box. It might be a family member, teacher, neighbor, classmate, or friend. Have them explain to that person that they have been thinking about vocations and missions and that they will try to use this talent in a helpful way for them this week. At a future gathering of the group, ask volunteers to share the results of their experiences.

 Family and Community

Have a volunteer read the section Lure of Consumerism. Ask: **What is consumerism?** (giving undue value to the acquisition of material goods) Ask: **When can material possessions be bad?** (when they become the center of life instead of God or when they lead to greed or hoarding of wealth and power)

Have a volunteer read The Moral Use of Wealth. Reread the quotation in the last sentence. Explain that *superfluous* means "extra." Say: **We should give even when we don't have anything extra to give. By sharing what we have, we nourish all.** Ask young people to name resources we can share and write their ideas on the board.

Ask volunteers to take turns reading the section Our Gifts, Our Calling. Ask: **Who are everyday or well-known people that use or have used their gifts in their work? What is or was their mission?** (Possible answers: teachers—education of youth; religious leaders—spiritual leadership of the Church; Blessed Mother Teresa—compassion in her mission to help those who are poor; Martin Luther King Jr.—orator and visionary for civil rights) Ask young people to identify other gifts that can help us be coworkers with God. (Answers will vary.)

Past Meets Present

Read aloud the feature. Have young people read Chapter 14, verses 3–19, in the Wisdom of Ben Sira. Compare the ideas about the use of wealth in Ben Sira to some common ideas about wealth today.

③ Close

Emphasize the importance of work in God's plan for us. Write 1 Corinthians 3:9 on the board: *"For we are God's co-workers; you are God's field, God's building."* Ask young people to discuss with a partner what the verse means. Encourage volunteers to share ideas.

Prayer

Follow the steps to guide young people through the prayer on page 184.

Young People's Page

Prepare Pray the prayer in advance to become familiar with it.

Pray Have young people read the title of the page and the paragraphs that follow. Ask volunteers to discuss times when their memories needed to be prodded in order to recall something that they already knew. Ask: **Why is memory a gift?** (Possible answers: Memory helps us learn from our experiences. Memory helps us appreciate.)

Assign the parts of Reader 1 and Reader 2. Remind young people that everyone prays the Responses and All part. Point out the symbol for the response that follows some parts. Then have young people bring their books to the prayer space and sit quietly. Say: **Take a few deep breaths and relax. Focus your attention on God's presence with us in this space.**

Begin reading aloud the Leader part slowly, pausing as indicated to allow time for young people to meditate on the ideas and questions in the silence of their hearts. Lead the Response. Have Reader 1 pray and pause before the Response. Have Reader 2 continue to pray and pause again before the Response. Pray aloud the Leader part, pausing long enough for petitions to be added by anyone who cares to do so. After the last petition, pray the Response, followed by the All part. Together pray *Amen* and the Sign of the Cross. Say: **We all experience times when we forget something important because we're distracted by worries or worldly concerns. Let's pray for the awareness to recognize Jesus in whatever situation we're in.**

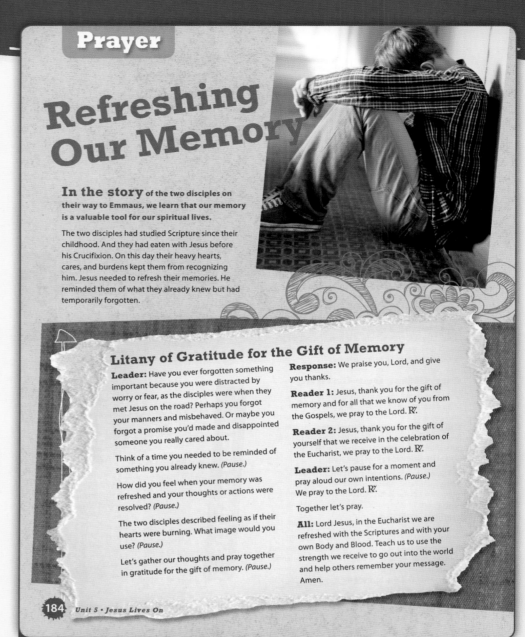

Prayer

Refreshing Our Memory

In the story of the two disciples on their way to Emmaus, we learn that our memory is a valuable tool for our spiritual lives.

The two disciples had studied Scripture since their childhood. And they had eaten with Jesus before his Crucifixion. On this day their heavy hearts, cares, and burdens kept them from recognizing him. Jesus needed to refresh their memories. He reminded them of what they already knew but had temporarily forgotten.

Litany of Gratitude for the Gift of Memory

Leader: Have you ever forgotten something important because you were distracted by worry or fear, as the disciples were when they met Jesus on the road? Perhaps you forgot your manners and misbehaved. Or maybe you forgot a promise you'd made and disappointed someone you really cared about.

Think of a time you needed to be reminded of something you already knew. *(Pause.)*

How did you feel when your memory was refreshed and your thoughts or actions were resolved? *(Pause.)*

The two disciples described feeling as if their hearts were burning. What image would you use? *(Pause.)*

Let's gather our thoughts and pray together in gratitude for the gift of memory. *(Pause.)*

Response: We praise you, Lord, and give you thanks.

Reader 1: Jesus, thank you for the gift of memory and for all that we know of you from the Gospels, we pray to the Lord. ℟.

Reader 2: Jesus, thank you for the gift of yourself that we receive in the celebration of the Eucharist, we pray to the Lord. ℟.

Leader: Let's pause for a moment and pray aloud our own intentions. *(Pause.)* We pray to the Lord. ℟.

Together let's pray.

All: Lord Jesus, in the Eucharist we are refreshed with the Scriptures and with your own Body and Blood. Teach us to use the strength we receive to go out into the world and help others remember your message. Amen.

184 · *Unit 5 • Jesus Lives On*

IF TIME ALLOWS

Gratitude

Have young people consider additional gifts from God for which they are grateful. Invite them to make a list of gifts that will help them discover the work that God intends for them to do. Provide a basket and ask young people to put their lists in it. Place the filled basket in the prayer space for future use.

FYI

Coaching Young People to Pray

Emphasize that praying is a way to keep in touch with God. Point out that praying to God each day can help guide them to future vocations. Before they pray, remind young people to focus on the words in the prayer and to rely on God to lead them in all they do. Emphasize that prayer is powerful and that God is always listening to them.

WHERE Do I Fit In?

When the women went to anoint Jesus' body, they found an empty tomb. Jesus Christ is as present today as he was more than 2,000 years ago. And if we take the time to notice, we can find him in the most unlikely people and in the most unexpected places.

by Keely Kriho

Meeting Jesus in a Surprising Way

I am a volunteer at a hospital during the school year (a volunteer called a "candy striper" because of my striped uniform). I help by wheeling patients around in gurneys and wheelchairs. I had a difficult time at first. I got very stressed out, especially when I had to wheel patients downstairs to be taken home after surgery. I wasn't sure what I was supposed to say to them, so most of the time, there was an uncomfortable silence between us. I felt very out of place, so much so that I was considering moving to a different department—until I was asked to bring down one very special patient.

Hesitantly, I approached this new patient, worried that she would either be too tired or too crabby to talk. As I neared her bed, I found a pleasant-looking, middle-aged woman who was chatting into a cell phone animatedly. She looked up at me, smiled, got off the phone, got out of bed, and placed herself in the wheelchair. "Hello!" she exclaimed merrily, getting settled in the chair. "Are you one of the candy stripers here?" "Yes," I replied. "I'm going to be taking you down to the parking garage today. Is that where you'll be picked up?" "Yes, honey," she replied kindly, smiling. I carefully wheeled her out, being careful not to disturb the bandages wrapped around her head and ears.

She chatted with me about school, jobs I wanted to look into, and why I had become a candy striper. She put me at ease, and we talked like old friends.

KEELY KRIHO is a sophomore at Lyons Township High School in LaGrange, Illinois.

Just before we got to the garage, we met the volunteer director, who recognized this lady. "How are you?" she asked. "Better," the patient replied. "They took out the brain tumor, but during the process my hearing was damaged. This surgery will hopefully help me hear better. In a while, they're going to try to fix my eye, but we don't know how that will go yet." She chatted calmly and matter-of-factly about the struggles she had gone through.

I thought to myself, "Who am I to complain when this seriously ill woman, perhaps dying, still manages to smile and meet life courageously?" I truly saw the risen Jesus in this woman. Out of the depths of sickness and despair, she met her unsure future with faith and showed that faith to me.

Build a Faith Community

We meet the risen Jesus in the Sacrament of the Eucharist, in Scripture, and in the faith community. Jesus opened his disciples' eyes to recognize him. Read John 20:16, Luke 24:30–35, John 20:26–28, and John 21:4–7. Discuss who recognized Jesus and tell how this happened.

Because the patient followed Jesus' example, the author recognized him. This patient encouraged the author in her own faith. On a separate sheet of paper, share a story about someone whose example deepened your love of Jesus.

Session 21 > Jesus Opens Our Eyes **185**

Reflect

IF TIME ALLOWS

The Faces of Christ

Have young people look through magazines or use the Internet to find images of people whose exemplary lives help open up our eyes when we feel tired or want to give up. Have them cut out or print these images and then use them to make a bulletin-board display titled "The Faces of Christ." Under each image, have young people affix a caption that reads *Christ*.

1 Begin

Have a volunteer read aloud the introductory text. Then read aloud 1 John 3:18–19 and discuss the verses.

Children, let us love not in word or speech but in deed and truth. [Now] this is how we shall know that we belong to the truth . . .

Say: *Children often copy behavior they see with their own eyes more than the words they hear someone say.* Invite young people to think of people they know who maintain faith, a positive attitude, and a giving spirit despite difficult or hopeless situations. Ask: *How do these people give an example that deepens love of Jesus?*

2 Connect

Have volunteers take turns reading aloud Meeting Jesus in a Surprising Way. Ask: *How did the author recognize Christ in the woman in the wheelchair?* (Possible answers: the woman's positive attitude and friendly demeanor; her interest in others; her hope in the face of suffering.) Ask: *How did the author's perspective change and convince her to remain a candy-striper?* (Her own concerns seemed very small in comparison.) Ask young people to pray silently as they ask God for the ability to be an example to others when they are struggling physically, socially, or emotionally.

Have them complete the Build a Faith Community activity independently. Invite volunteers to share what they wrote.

3 Close

Ask young people to demonstrate Christlike actions, especially when they are tempted to give up or walk away. Say: *As people of faith, Jesus entrusted us to encourage one another, carrying one another along our journeys of faith.*

① Begin

What's What? Read the directions aloud. Have young people complete the page independently.

② Connect

Say What? Ask volunteers to read aloud and define the terms. Review each term in the Glossary if necessary.

Now What? Ask a volunteer to read aloud the question. Invite young people to answer the question independently.

③ Go in Peace

Collect materials and return them to their appropriate places. Encourage young people to set aside distractions so that they can better recognize Jesus this week and think about how we might use our gifts in a positive way. Ask a volunteer to read aloud Matthew 5:14–16. Say:
Matthew tells us not to hide our light but to show it to the world. Using a gift from God now as a young person may help reveal the true mission that God intends for you.

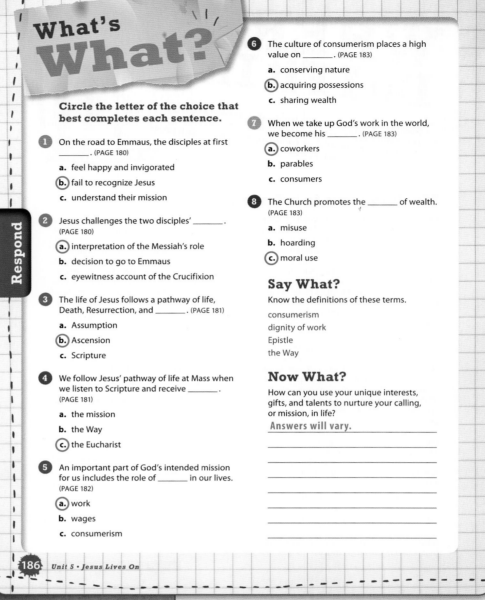

What's What?

Circle the letter of the choice that best completes each sentence.

1. On the road to Emmaus, the disciples at first _____ . (PAGE 180)
   a. feel happy and invigorated
   b. fail to recognize Jesus
   c. understand their mission

2. Jesus challenges the two disciples' _____ . (PAGE 180)
   a. interpretation of the Messiah's role
   b. decision to go to Emmaus
   c. eyewitness account of the Crucifixion

3. The life of Jesus follows a pathway of life, Death, Resurrection, and _____ . (PAGE 181)
   a. Assumption
   b. Ascension
   c. Scripture

4. We follow Jesus' pathway of life at Mass when we listen to Scripture and receive _____ . (PAGE 181)
   a. the mission
   b. the Way
   c. the Eucharist

5. An important part of God's intended mission for us includes the role of _____ in our lives. (PAGE 182)
   a. work
   b. wages
   c. consumerism

6. The culture of consumerism places a high value on _____ . (PAGE 183)
   a. conserving nature
   b. acquiring possessions
   c. sharing wealth

7. When we take up God's work in the world, we become his _____ . (PAGE 183)
   a. coworkers
   b. parables
   c. consumers

8. The Church promotes the _____ of wealth. (PAGE 183)
   a. misuse
   b. hoarding
   c. moral use

Say What?
Know the definitions of these terms.

consumerism
dignity of work
Epistle
the Way

Now What?
How can you use your unique interests, gifts, and talents to nurture your calling, or mission, in life?

Answers will vary.

186 *Unit 5 • Jesus Lives On*

Respond

IF TIME ALLOWS

Service: Caring for All of God's Creatures
Some people make it their mission to care for and protect cats and dogs. They volunteer at no-kill shelters, donate supplies or animal food, or take care of unwanted animals. Have young people research the problem of unwanted pets and suggest ways they can counter it. They may wish to increase awareness by making posters, submitting articles to the parish bulletin, or donating time at community pet-adoption events.

✝ *God's Creation*

Session Assessment Option
An assessment for this session can be found at www.findinggod.com.

3-Minute Retreat
Give young people an opportunity for quiet meditation at **www.loyolapress.com/retreat**.

PLAN AHEAD: Get Ready for Session 22

Consult the catechist preparation pages to prepare for Session 22 and determine any materials you will need.

Jesus Sends Us Forth with His Spirit

 3-Minute Retreat

Before you prepare the session, pause and be still. Take three deep breaths and be aware of the loving presence of God, who is with you on this journey.

John 14:15–17

"If you love me, you will keep my commandments. And I will ask the Father, and he will give you another Advocate to be with you always, the Spirit of truth, which the world cannot accept, because it neither sees nor knows it. But you know it, because it remains with you, and will be in you."

Reflection

The sending of the Holy Spirit was just one more sign of the Father's great love. Jesus longed for his disciples to know that even though he was leaving them physically, they would not be alone. Jesus wanted them to trust their own conversion process, which had been happening gradually over three years as he lived among them. Their transformation set them apart from "the world," that is, from those who could not accept the Spirit of truth. The Holy Spirit would continue to reveal the truth about God's kingdom to them and would strengthen them for the mission they were to carry out in Jesus' name.

Questions

What difference does the presence of the Holy Spirit make in your life? What difference does it make knowing that the Spirit is with you when Jesus sends you forth?

 Concluding Prayer

Speak to God, using the words of this prayer or your own.

Jesus, thank you for sending the Spirit to be with me and to guide me. Help me grow in confidence, knowing that the Spirit is with me as I go forth.

Knowing and Sharing Your Faith in Session 22

Consider how Scripture and Tradition can deepen your understanding of session content.

Scripture

Acts of the Apostles 1:8 tells us that Jesus sent the Apostles to be his witnesses in the world.

Matthew 5:16 instructs that our light, given by the Spirit, must shine before others for the glory of God.

Tradition

In liturgical prayers and works of art, we use symbols with biblical backgrounds to represent the Holy Spirit. Fire symbolizes the strength and force of the Holy Spirit. The wind symbolizes the Holy Spirit breathing life into the Church. Water represents the cleansing and life-giving action of the Holy Spirit in Baptism. The cloud is a symbol of the Holy Spirit because clouds provide life-giving water. Anointing with oil symbolizes the Holy Spirit's uniting us with Jesus the Messiah, the Anointed One. The image of the dove comes to us from the story of Jesus' baptism when Jesus saw "the Spirit, like a dove, descending upon him." [Mark 1:10]

Catholic Social Teaching

In this session the integrated Catholic Social Teaching theme is **Solidarity.** See page 177b for an explanation of this theme.

Window on the Catechism

The mission of Christ and the Holy Spirit brought together in the Church is described in *CCC* 737–747.

General Directory for Catechesis

The work of the Holy Spirit in the transmission of Revelation by the Church is described in *GDC* 42–45.

One-Hour Session Planner

SESSION 22 Jesus Sends Us Forth with His Spirit

Session Theme: *We celebrate the Holy Spirit's presence within us and within the Church.*

Before This Session

▶ Bookmark your Bible to Acts of the Apostles 1:8 and 2:3, Isaiah 11:2, Romans 8:14, and Matthew 5:16. Place the open Bible in your prayer space.

▶ Read the Guide for this session, choose any additional If Time Allows activities that you might have time to complete, and gather the listed materials.

STEPS	APPROXIMATE TIME
Engage *Jesus Sends Us Forth with His Spirit* PAGE 187	10 minutes
Explore *The Gift of Pentecost* PAGES 188–189 *The Seal of Confirmation* PAGES 190–191	30–40 minutes
Reflect *Prayer:* Stretching Our Wings PAGE 192 *Where Do I Fit In?* PAGE 193	10–15 minutes
Respond *What's What?* PAGE 194	10–15 minutes

Prayer in Session 22

Pray aloud a short opening prayer that relates to the session's key concept. Encourage young people to access an online 3-Minute Retreat that reflects on Scripture at the end of the session. In Session 22 young people will pray to the Holy Spirit for help to know God's will for them. Follow the Prepare directions on the Catechist Guide page before sharing with young people.

TAKE IT HOME

Homework options:

Happy Birthday	PAGE 188
Where We Belong	PAGE 190

Materials

REQUIRED

▶ Writing supplies (pages 187, 189, 193, 194)

▶ Bibles (page 188)

▶ CD player (page 192)

▶ CD 2, Track 1: "God's Dream for Us" (11:30) (page 192)

▶ CD 2, Track 5: Reflective Music (page 192)

▶ Computers with Internet access (pages 193, 194)

OPTIONAL

▶ Writing supplies (pages 189, 191, 192, 193, 194)

▶ Session 22 BLM, T-382 (page 189)

▶ Construction paper, slips of paper (page 189)

▶ Slips of paper, sealed basket or container (page 191)

▶ Session 22 Assessment, www.findinggod.com (page 194)

Session 22

Jesus Sends Us Forth with His Spirit

Recall a time when someone sent you to do something. Was your mission simple, such as an errand, or was it more difficult, such as delivering bad news? What did you need to take with you—talents, special skills, money, patience, courage, or something else?

PRAYER

Here I am Lord. I want to do your will. Doing your work in the world, Lord, is my deepest desire.

187

SESSION 22
OUTCOMES

► Explain why Pentecost is the birthday of the Catholic Church.

► Explain that because Confirmation ties us to the Body of Christ, the Church's mission becomes our mission.

► Pray to the Holy Spirit for help to answer God's call.

► Define *Chrism, Gifts of the Holy Spirit,* and *Good News.*

① Set the Stage

Have young people read aloud the text in the box. Give them time to reflect on or write responses. Invite volunteers to share their ideas.

② Get Started

Invite young people to discuss experiences of being sent on a mission. Ask volunteers to describe the events and what happened. Encourage comparisons among missions. For example, which missions were simple [walking the dog] and which were more challenging [helping your brother overcome his fear of public speaking]? Ask: **How do you feel when someone sends you to do something?** (Possible answers: privileged, responsible, nervous, excited) Lead young people to understand that they might feel apprehensive about the unknown but also excited about the responsibility or the chance to prove themselves.

Ask: **How do you think the idea of being asked to complete a task relates to the session title, Jesus Sends Us Forth with His Spirit?** (Answers will vary.)

Prayer

Say: **Let's take a moment to pray to God to help us do his work.** Pray aloud the prayer. Conclude by praying the Sign of the Cross.

IF TIME ALLOWS

A Life's Work
Arrange for your parish priest, a religious sister, a full-time volunteer, or a deacon to speak to your group about his or her personal experience with following a mission or answering a call to service. Ask young people to prepare questions in advance. Give the list to the guest speaker before he or she plans to visit.

INCLUSION
Emotional

Group Work Young people who have emotional differences may exhibit fear and anxiety in front of a group. Encourage but do not force participation. Arrange a simple signal, such as a thumbs up, so you can tell when these young people are prepared to be called on. Reinforce positive participation that complies with group rules.

 Go to **www.findinggod.com/sessionextenders** for an article about our Catholic mission. You may wish to share this with the group.

① Begin

Ask young people to think about a time when they were so enthusiastic about something that they could barely contain their excitement. Have young people tell about their experiences on a sheet of paper. Ask volunteers to share aloud. Say: **When we receive good news, look forward to something, or feel happy for another person, we often want to talk about it. It feels good to share our joy with others.**

Have a volunteer read the title and first paragraph. Say: **Pentecost is the day the Church was born.**

② Connect

Say: **The Holy Spirit is mentioned many times in the Bible**. Read aloud the second paragraph and the ideas next to the arrows. Write the heading *Luke* on the board. Ask young people to use their Bibles to find verses about the Holy Spirit in Luke's Gospel and write the specific chapter and verse or verses under the heading.

Ask a volunteer to read the remaining paragraphs beneath the arrows. Ask: **What other books in the Bible reference the Holy Spirit?** (the Gospel of John and the Acts of the Apostles) Tell young people that when the Holy Spirit descended on the disciples, they were so filled with God's love that they felt compelled to proclaim the works of God.

Ask volunteers to take turns reading the section The Holy Spirit Descends. Refer young people to the Glossary and read the meaning of *Good News.* Say: **The large gathering in Jerusalem at Pentecost included people from many countries.** Ask: **For whom is the Good News intended?** (everyone) Ask: **How do you know?** (The Apostles were given the ability to speak in tongues.)

The Gift of Pentecost

ARE you aware of how the Holy Spirit is at work in your life? Sometimes it's hard to notice. Prayer, a spirit of openness, and practice help us gain a steady awareness of the many ways the Holy Spirit is present every day.

The Third Person of the Trinity, the Holy Spirit, plays a prominent role in many parts of the Bible. The Gospel of Luke gives attention to the work of the Holy Spirit in the lives of Jesus, Mary, and the disciples.

➡ Luke tells how Mary is filled with the Spirit to conceive the Messiah.

➡ Inspired by the Holy Spirit, Elizabeth recognizes Mary as the mother of the Messiah.

➡ The Holy Spirit leads Jesus into the desert, and Jesus returns from the desert filled with the power of the Holy Spirit.

➡ Jesus proclaims in the synagogue that he is the one on whom the Spirit rests.

In Chapter 14 of the Gospel of John, Jesus tries to calm the Apostles' fears at the Last Supper. He promises not to leave them orphans, assuring them that the Father will send an Advocate, the Holy Spirit, in Jesus' name. The Holy Spirit will help and guide them. Through the Spirit, Jesus will remain with the whole Church. The gift of the Holy Spirit will be another sign of the Father's love for them, just as the gift of his Son had been a gift of love.

The Acts of the Apostles begins with Jesus ascending to Heaven. Jesus' last words to his disciples are a promise and a commission.

> "But you will receive power when the holy Spirit comes upon you; and you will be my witnesses in Jerusalem, throughout Judea and Samaria, and to the ends of the earth."
>
> *Acts of the Apostles 1:8*

What the Apostles received from the risen Jesus was more than assurance. It was a continuing and abiding gift of God's presence and strength.

The Holy Spirit Descends

Fifty days after the Ascension, Jesus' disciples fearfully huddled together behind locked doors. They wondered how they were going to carry on without Jesus. The Acts of the Apostles tells how the Jewish holy day of Pentecost arrived and, as Jesus promised, the Holy Spirit descended on the disciples, with "tongues as of fire." (Acts of the Apostles 2:3) The Spirit filled them with courage and empowered them to preach in many languages about the risen Christ to the crowds that represented many nations. The Apostles' ability to speak in different languages showed that the **Good News** transcended boundaries of language and culture, country and race. We celebrate Pentecost as the birthday of the Catholic Church because that is the day when the disciples took up Jesus' ministry and brought it to the entire world.

The Good News Proclaimed

On that first Pentecost, Peter boldly proclaimed to the crowd that Jesus, who was crucified, was Messiah and Lord. The early disciples called people to repentance and to Baptism in Jesus Christ, and they healed in Jesus' name.

188 *Unit 5 • Jesus Lives On*

TAKE IT HOME

Happy Birthday

Pentecost is considered the birthday of the Catholic Church. Have young people make birthday cards. Each card should include three facts from this article. Invite young people to be creative and use whatever materials they wish. Ask volunteers to present their cards to the group. Display them in a common area.

The Holy Spirit transformed the early Christian community and strengthened it for the task of witnessing to Jesus the Lord. This same Holy Spirit continues to strengthen the Church today. We are also called to faith by the Holy Spirit. We are initiated into the life of the Spirit in Baptism and Confirmation, and we are sustained in it through the Eucharist. Just as the Christians in Luke's time were called to live their values in the difficult Roman world, we recognize the Holy Spirit's guidance today. Each year on the Feast of Pentecost, we celebrate the Spirit's presence within us and within the Church.

Gifts of the Holy Spirit

We first receive the Holy Spirit in the Sacrament of Baptism. In the Sacrament of Confirmation, the grace of Baptism is strengthened, and we receive the **Gifts of the Holy Spirit.** Church Tradition has added the gift of piety to make a total of seven gifts.

"The spirit of the LORD shall rest upon him:
  a spirit of wisdom and of understanding,
A spirit of counsel and of strength,
  a spirit of knowledge and of fear of the LORD."
Isaiah 11:2

Study Corner

DEFINE
Good News
Gifts of the Holy Spirit

REMEMBER
At Pentecost the Holy Spirit descended on the disciples, giving them the strength to embrace their mission to spread the Good News. The seven Gifts of the Holy Spirit are wisdom, understanding, counsel, fortitude, knowledge, piety, and fear of the Lord.

The Gifts of the Holy Spirit listed in Isaiah 11:2, along with piety, give Christians the strength to lead moral lives. These gifts are permanent dispositions within us that help us heed the promptings of the Holy Spirit. Where we are morally strong, they make us stronger. Where we are weak, they give us strength. Saint Paul says, "For those who are led by the Spirit of God are children of God." (Romans 8:14)

Explore

Our Catholic Character

The Holy Spirit leads us to better understand God's will for us. We cooperate with the Spirit by developing habits of prayer that deepen our love and understanding of Jesus. One spiritual practice of prayerful reflection is called the "virtuous circle." It begins with reflection, which leads to gratitude, which leads to service. Service leads you back to reflection. When we practice the virtuous circle, we open ourselves to God's grace in a profound way.

Father Paul Brian Campbell explains how this process helped him. When he was teaching at Le Moyne College in Syracuse, New York, he loved the enthusiasm of his students but reflected that something was missing. "I had little pastoral contact with the elderly. This reflection led me to volunteer at a local hospice." At the hospice, Campbell cleaned the house or chatted with the residents and their families. "I quickly learned that I was getting far more than I was giving," says Campbell. "The quiet and cheerful professionalism of the hospice staff, the dignity accorded to the dying residents and the care and compassion that was evident made a profound impression on me."

Session 22 > Jesus Sends Us Forth with His Spirit 189

Have a volunteer read aloud The Good News Proclaimed. Tell young people that both Baptism and Confirmation are celebrations of the Holy Spirit. In many dioceses, Confirmation is celebrated during the Easter season. Say: *The Easter season is also a special time for Baptism and for recommitting ourselves to the promises our parents and godparents made at our Baptism.*

Ask a volunteer to read aloud Gifts of the Holy Spirit. Have young people find and underline the seven Gifts of the Holy Spirit in the section. (wisdom, understanding, counsel, strength, knowledge, fear of the Lord, and piety) Explain that in the Sacrament of Confirmation, we celebrate the strengthening of grace received at Baptism, and we celebrate the Gifts of the Holy Spirit in our lives.

Our Catholic Character

Have a volunteer read aloud the feature. Point out the words *reflection, gratitude,* and *service.* Discuss the meaning of the virtuous circle. You may want to guide the way to use the prayer by writing an example on the board. *Reflection: God has given me many talents; Gratitude: I am thankful for my love of music; Service: I sing in the church choir.* Remind young people that the Holy Spirit is in all of us and gives us help and guidance to live as Christ's disciples in the world.

③ Close

Close the discussion by saying: *We are empowered to be Christ's witnesses in the world today. At Pentecost we celebrate the Holy Spirit's presence within us.* Ask young people to practice praying the virtuous circle, focusing on reflection, gratitude, and service.

IF TIME ALLOWS

Session 22 BLM

Understanding God's Will Provide young people with the Session 22 Blackline Master [T-382]. Read the introduction and the directions aloud. Have them complete the activity as a way to practice prayerful reflection of God's will for them.

Living as Children of God

Cut out from construction paper the shapes of seven large tongues of fire. Label each shape with a gift of the Holy Spirit. Display the paper tongues of fire on a bulletin board. Distribute seven small slips of paper to each young person. Ask them to write a way that they can be led by each gift to lead a moral life. Then tell them to attach their slips to the particular paper tongue of fire.

1 Begin

Ask young people to identify words or phrases that come to mind in response to these two situations:

► a movie director ready to film a scene ("Lights! Camera! Action!")

► an announcer at the beginning of a race ("On your mark! Get set! Go!")

Point out that these phrases signal someone to begin an action.

2 Connect

Have volunteers read aloud the three introductory paragraphs. Discuss the ordinary meaning of *confirmation* and relate that meaning to the Sacrament of Confirmation. Say: **Jesus' directions to us are very clear; namely, to be his followers requires us to perform an action—proclaiming the Kingdom of God.** Explain that in the Sacrament of Confirmation, we are sent forth to do the work of the Gospel.

Have a volunteer read Sealed with the Spirit. Ask: **How many times is the Sacrament of Confirmation administered?** (once) **Why?** (because a spiritual mark is placed upon us that cannot be taken away) Ask young people what is required before receiving Confirmation and write their responses on the board. (state of grace, desire to receive, profession of belief in the Catholic faith, readiness to proclaim the Kingdom of God) Ask: **What does the bishop say as he places Chrism on the forehead of the person being confirmed?** ("Be sealed with the Gift of the Holy Spirit.") Read aloud the definition of *Chrism* in the Glossary.

Sacred Art

Read the feature. Ask: **Why might the artist have painted the figures different colors?** (to show universality, all races and nations) Say: **Although Picasso probably didn't paint this with Pentecost or Confirmation in mind, the figures and dove prompt us to think about the Sacrament of Confirmation.**

The Seal of Confirmation

PEOPLE often try to get confirmation for things such as facts, reservations, news, statistics, dates, and times of events.

We want to verify or prove what we seek to confirm. Once we confirm something, we don't need to confirm it again. It's done.

The word *confirmation*, whose Latin root means "to strengthen," is the name of a sacrament in the Catholic Church. The Sacrament of Confirmation places a spiritual mark on us that cannot be taken away, and so the sacrament is administered only once.

Sealed with the Spirit

The Sacraments of Baptism and Confirmation are closely tied together. Baptism welcomes us into the Church, and Confirmation strengthens us to live as full members of the Church. As with Baptism, there is no specified age when one can receive Confirmation, although many people are confirmed when they are young adults.

In order to receive the Sacrament of Confirmation, you must be in the state of grace. Additionally, you must want to receive the sacrament, profess your belief in the Catholic faith, and be ready to join with Jesus Christ in proclaiming the Kingdom of God.

As part of the Rite of Confirmation, the bishop places oil, called **Chrism,** on the forehead of the baptized person saying, "Be sealed with the Gift of the Holy Spirit." Confirmation ties us more closely to the Body of Christ. It helps us be witnesses to the Christian faith in the things we say and do. Confirmation involves us more closely in the Church's mission. In the Sacrament of Confirmation, the Holy Spirit fills us and charges us with helping the Church carry out its mission.

SACRED ART

Pablo Picasso, (1881–1973) a Spaniard, was one of the great artists of the 20th century. In 1952 while living in Vallauris, France, he painted the walls and ceiling of a 12th century chapel, which is now a museum. The full work is called *War and Peace*. The portion shown here is quite large and situated at the end of a room. For Picasso the dove was a symbol of peace. Notice the different colors of the figures and their positions in relation to the dove. At Pentecost the presence of the Holy Spirit is associated with fire and a dove. At Confirmation the Holy Spirit strengthens us to proclaim Christ to all the nations of the world.

The Four Corners of the World, Pablo Picasso, 1952–54.

 190 *Unit 5 • Jesus Lives On*

TAKE IT HOME

Where We Belong

Explain that in the early days of the Church, Jesus' followers were recognized in Antioch by the name *Christian*, and the name stuck. We still call ourselves Christians because Christ is central to our faith. Ask young people to learn about the name of the parish or another local parish. Have them consider why the name was chosen and what it means.

Ask young people to write a paragraph or two about what they learn. If you have a large group, you may wish to assign additional local parish names. Invite volunteers to read aloud their paragraphs when the group meets again.

Improved Vision

The Holy Spirit inspires us to see God's dream for us and for the world. We gain a vision of the kind of world God wants us to have. Jesus proclaimed the Kingdom of God in both word and deed.

➡ By curing the sick, he showed that the kingdom will be a place of health and wholeness.

➡ By raising the dead to life, he showed that it will be a place in which all life is respected.

➡ By caring for those in need and society's outcasts, he showed that in the kingdom, everyone will be respected and have what they need.

Guided by the Holy Spirit, we envision a better world and gain strength and inspiration to make the vision a reality.

Be Sent

When the disciples received the Holy Spirit, they embarked on a mission. Jesus sent them into the world to proclaim his message. We, too, are sent into the world at various times and in various ways. We are sent off to school or to camp. Later we may be sent off to college or into the world to find work. In addition to being sent in a literal sense, God invites us to grow spiritually, moving beyond our comfort zone into what we can become with God's help. The Holy Spirit inspires us to be the person God created us to be.

Be You

After you receive Confirmation, the Church's mission becomes your mission. As many people as there are in the Body of Christ reflects how many ways there are to fulfill that mission. God gives each of us unique spiritual gifts, and when we exercise those gifts—skills in helping people, talents for creativity, intelligence, or compassion—we honor God's gifts to us. Jesus tells us in the Sermon on the Mount, "Just so, your light must shine before others, that they may see your good deeds and glorify your heavenly Father." (Matthew 5:16)

Study Corner

DEFINE
Chrism

REMEMBER
Confirmation ties us more closely to the Body of Christ. Confirmation helps us be witnesses to the Christian faith in the things we say and do.

Past Meets Present

PAST: Saint Julie Billiart (1751–1816) served the Church's mission by using her talent for teaching to spread the Catholic faith. Because the French government suppressed the Catholic Church at this time in history, she could have been arrested. However, she did not let fear stop her from telling others about Christ. Eventually she founded the Sisters of Notre Dame to care for orphans, to educate poor girls, and to train Christian teachers.

PRESENT: The Sisters of Notre Dame are an international congregation of Catholic women religious who are committed to acting as witnesses to God's loving care and goodness. They use gifts and talents received from the Holy Spirit in various ministries. Some ways they serve include educating children and adults, assisting the poor, ministering to refugees, or working as doctors, nurses, social workers, artists, or musicians. Their work continues to spread. Their first mission in Central America began in 2008, and in 2010 they welcomed their first novices to missions in Mozambique and the Philippines.

Explore

Session 22 > Jesus Sends Us Forth with His Spirit **191**

🔥 **ADVENTURES IN FAITH**

Sent Into the World

After his Resurrection, Jesus continually greeted people with the phrase, "Be not afraid." Ask young people to reflect on their own fears. Ask: **Who or what might prevent you from carrying God's message to the world?**

Distribute slips of paper and have young people write things for which they are afraid and need God's help. Ensure their privacy by allowing them to write anonymously if they choose. Collect the folded slips and place them in a sealed basket or container.

Remind young people that Jesus assures us that he has not left us alone. Invite them to the prayer space and have them sit in a circle. Set the container in the middle. Encourage young people to close their eyes and pray silently to the Holy Spirit for help to conquer any fears that separate them from God.

Have young people read the section Improved Vision. Show a cause-and-effect relationship, using Jesus' words. Write the heading *Kingdom of God* on the board. Beneath the heading write *Cause: _____ Effect: _____* . Ask volunteers to share ideas. (Possible answer: *Cause*: Jesus cures the sick. *Effect*: The Kingdom of God will be perfect wholeness.)

✝ Have volunteers take turns reading the remaining sections Be Sent and Be You. Reiterate that through Confirmation, the Church's mission becomes our mission. Say: **Confirmation gives us the ability to share the dream of a better world and to serve God's Kingdom.** Ask young people to speculate about what can happen when people refuse to use their spiritual gifts to help others right now in the present. (Possible answers: God's vision for us will not be evident. For example, people might withhold solutions for social problems, or they might use their intellectual gifts for destructive purposes that cause evil. People may withhold compassion, refusing to relieve someone's suffering.)

Past Meets Present

Have volunteers read the feature. Point out that as we grow older, our ability to take care of others often grows too. Ask young people to share experiences of volunteer work they have done or would like to do in the future. Invite suggestions for practical ways to make these experiences possible.

③ Close

Close the discussion by having young people think about one area in which they can help build the Kingdom of God right now. Remind them that it is through the Holy Spirit that they are able to do this.

Prayer

Choose an approach and pray with young people.

APPROACH 1

Guided Reflection

Prepare Listen in advance to the recorded guided reflection "God's Dream for Us" [CD 2, Track 1]. Decide if you will play the recording or pray aloud the reflection yourself. If you choose to lead, listen to the recording a second time, following the script [pages T-347–T-348] and noting pauses and tone. You can then follow the script exactly or adapt it as you wish.

Pray Have volunteers read aloud the title for the page and the paragraphs. Discuss some ways in which young people are making their own decisions. Say: **Stretching your wings is important for real growth. But you must also remember your roots, which hold you firmly to the values you have learned.** Play the recording or lead using the script, joining young people in reflective prayer. If you pray aloud the script, play reflective music softly in the background [CD 2, Track 5].

APPROACH 2

Young People's Page

Prepare Pray the prayer in advance to become familiar with it.

Pray Read the opening paragraphs at the top of the page. Assign young people to read either Side 1 or Side 2. Invite young people to prepare for prayer. Read the Leader part and encourage everyone to respond to each All part. Prompt each side to pray their assigned parts slowly and reverently. Then invite everyone to respond with the All part. Close by inviting young people to pray together the Glory Be to the Father.

Prayer

Stretching Our Wings

Through prayer the Holy Spirit helps us stretch our wings, giving us the strength and grace to follow God's call.

At this time in your life, you take on greater responsibility. You embrace the positive values you've learned and begin to think for yourself. You begin to stretch your wings, try on new ways to think and act, and dream new dreams. During this time of great personal growth, ask the Holy Spirit to help you know God's will for you.

Prayer to the Holy Spirit

Leader: Let us pray to the Holy Spirit for help to know God's will for us. Let us pray that we follow God's will with a generous spirit.

All: Come, Holy Spirit, fill our hearts and kindle in us the fire of your love.

Side 1: Come, Holy Spirit, open our minds and hearts to hear God's voice and to know God's will for us.

Side 2: Come, Holy Spirit, help us know God's plan for the world and do our part to make it happen.

Side 1: Come, Holy Spirit, make us generous in using our gifts and talents to serve God's kingdom here on earth.

Side 2: Come, Holy Spirit, help us treat others with dignity and respect others as we begin to stretch our wings.

All: With faith and trust in the Holy Spirit, we ask God to hear and grant our prayers, which we make in Jesus' name. Amen.

192 *Unit 5 • Jesus Lives On*

IF TIME ALLOWS

Come, Holy Spirit

Have young people write their own prayers to the Holy Spirit, mirroring the language in today's prayer. Ask them to copy and then finish the phrase

Come, Holy Spirit, . . .

You may wish to collect young people's prayers and add them to the group prayer.

FYI

Coaching Young People to Pray

Remind young people that every time they pray, it is the Holy Spirit who teaches them the way. The Holy Spirit is present in their prayer and makes it not just human prayer but divine prayer. Through the power of the Holy Spirit, the People of God all over the world, although in diverse circumstances, persevere in the hope in which we have been saved.

WHERE Do I Fit In?

Confirmation is the sacrament that fulfills the grace we receive in Baptism. It seals, or confirms, this grace through the seven Gifts of the Holy Spirit. As confirmed members of the Catholic Church, we each accept our role as a disciple of Christ, fully participating in public worship, in the celebration of the sacraments, and in service to the Kingdom of God. In Confirmation we go forth to spread God's Word with others.

by Meredith Gould

Reflect

My Way to Confirmation

I grew up in the Jewish faith before becoming a Roman Catholic. I waited nearly a decade between my Baptism and my Confirmation. I was already an adult, but only if you added up years logged on the planet. I was hardly a grown-up—at least, not in the spiritual sense. More growing would have to happen before I'd want to be confirmed. I had to figure out some stuff.

For one thing, I questioned why Confirmation was considered a Sacrament of Initiation. Initiation into what? After all, I thought, Baptism is what "makes" us Christian. When I was a teen, I celebrated my *bat mitzvah*, the occasion when a young Jewish woman becomes a "daughter of the commandment," at Temple Sinai. The preparation included learning more about Jewish beliefs, values, ethics, and history. It also included service and social justice projects, something that has become a key feature of Catholic Confirmation preparation.

Although the Holy Spirit is never mentioned explicitly, I noticed that *bar* and *bat mitzvah* ceremonies are scheduled to coincide with Shavuot. One of five "appointed feasts of the Lord," Shavuot commemorates God giving the Law (Torah) to the Israelites on Mount Sinai—something I consider a big-time Holy Spirit event. And what Greek word for Shavuot appears in Christian Scripture? *Pentecost*!

MEREDITH GOULD, PhD, is an author, blogger, and communications strategist for faith-based organizations.

These are some dots I connected over 10 years. I welcomed the Holy Spirit to show up in my life. I spent the years between Baptism and Confirmation seeking and finding comfort in the Eucharist, support in my parish, and finding God in community service.

Once, after Reconciliation, a priest told me, "For your penance, keep praying 'Come, Holy Spirit.'" I did, and I managed to get "un-confused" to the point of seeking out my parish's deacon. "I believe my Easter is coming up this year," I told him. At age 51, I understood finally what God was offering in calling me to complete the Sacraments of Initiation and celebrate Confirmation. I had returned to the sacraments, regularly celebrating the Sacrament of Reconciliation and the Eucharist, and in that state of grace, finally received the Sacrament of Confirmation.

A Big Impact

The author states that she was ready to declare publicly her commitment to being a Roman Catholic much later in life. Even though Jesus told his disciples, "Be not afraid," she had some self-doubts until she received the gift of faith. On a separate sheet of paper, tell how you might use each Gift of the Holy Spirit following your Confirmation.

wisdom   piety   understanding   counsel
knowledge   fear of the Lord   fortitude

Session 22 > Jesus Sends Us Forth with His Spirit   193

IF TIME ALLOWS

Prayer to the Advocate

Have young people write a prayer to the Holy Spirit in which they ask specifically for guidance in their understanding and preparation for the Sacrament of Confirmation. Encourage them to include in their prayer a request for help overcoming any obstacles, such as doubt, fear, confusion, lack of interest, or lack of support. Invite young people to save the prayer and to pray it periodically as they move forward in their preparation for the sacrament.

① Begin

Have a volunteer read aloud the introductory text. Ask how God is calling young people to a more complete life of grace in the celebration of Confirmation. (Possible answer: Confirmation, like Baptism, is a Sacrament of Initiation, a call into a deeper relationship with God and others. It calls for a commitment to become a more active witness to Christ in the world.) Say: ***Even though your own celebration of Confirmation may be a few years away, it is not too early to think of how God is calling you to more active participation in the life of grace he offers. We prepare for Confirmation by regularly celebrating the Eucharist and the Sacrament of Reconciliation that keeps us in a state of grace.***

② Connect

Have volunteers take turns reading My Way to Confirmation. Ask: ***What do you think the title means?*** (Possible answer: The author took her own path to Confirmation.) Point out that the author "just knew" when she was ready to receive the sacrament. Say: ***The author took her time making the decision to be confirmed. She waited until it made sense to her—until the Spirit moved her toward her own personal Easter.*** Point out that the Spirit is always present and moving people.

Then have them complete the activity independently. Invite volunteers to read aloud their responses.

③ Close

Remind young people that the author's journey toward Confirmation began in doubt. Encourage them to e-mail their own questions about Confirmation to you or another Church leader in the coming weeks. Discuss questions in a future group meeting, possibly inviting a priest or deacon as a guest speaker.

① Begin

What's What? Read the directions aloud. Have young people complete the page independently at home or with a partner in class.

② Connect

Say What? Ask volunteers to read aloud and define the terms. Review each term in the Glossary if necessary.

Now What? Ask a volunteer to read aloud the section. Invite young people to answer the question independently and to share their responses with the group if they wish.

③ Go in Peace

Collect materials and return them to their appropriate places. Remind young people that because of the Holy Spirit, they can help build God's dream. Pray together the Prayer to the Holy Spirit on page 275 of Prayers and Practices. Encourage their participation in building the Kingdom of God throughout their lives. Say: ***Notice what God is telling you about your dreams, words, and actions. Ask yourself if your words and deeds align with the Kingdom of God.***

3-Minute Retreat
Give young people an opportunity for quiet meditation at **www.loyolapress.com/retreat**.

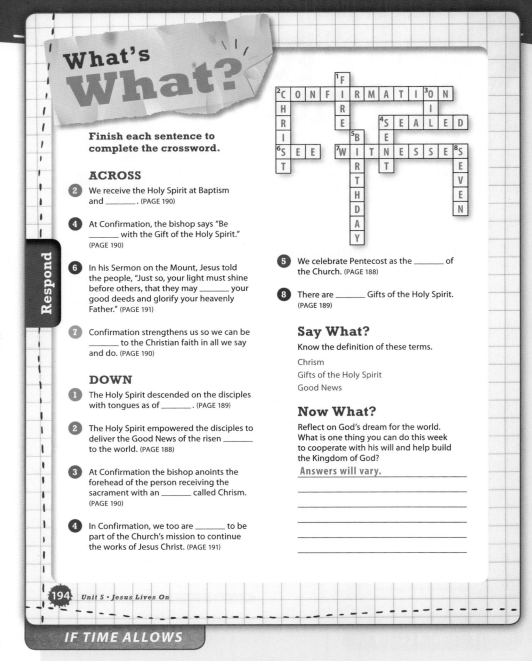

What's What?

Finish each sentence to complete the crossword.

ACROSS

2 We receive the Holy Spirit at Baptism and _____. (PAGE 190)

4 At Confirmation, the bishop says "Be _____ with the Gift of the Holy Spirit." (PAGE 190)

6 In his Sermon on the Mount, Jesus told the people, "Just so, your light must shine before others, that they may _____ your good deeds and glorify your heavenly Father." (PAGE 191)

7 Confirmation strengthens us so we can be _____ to the Christian faith in all we say and do. (PAGE 190)

DOWN

1 The Holy Spirit descended on the disciples with tongues as of _____. (PAGE 189)

2 The Holy Spirit empowered the disciples to deliver the Good News of the risen _____ to the world. (PAGE 188)

3 At Confirmation the bishop anoints the forehead of the person receiving the sacrament with an _____ called Chrism. (PAGE 190)

4 In Confirmation, we too are _____ to be part of the Church's mission to continue the works of Jesus Christ. (PAGE 191)

5 We celebrate Pentecost as the _____ of the Church. (PAGE 188)

8 There are _____ Gifts of the Holy Spirit. (PAGE 189)

Say What?
Know the definition of these terms.

Chrism
Gifts of the Holy Spirit
Good News

Now What?
Reflect on God's dream for the world. What is one thing you can do this week to cooperate with his will and help build the Kingdom of God?

Answers will vary.
_____
_____
_____
_____
_____

194 · Unit 5 · *Jesus Lives On*

Respond

IF TIME ALLOWS

Service: Prayers for Vocations

Ask young people to write prayers for vocations, whether religious or secular vocations. Suggest that they begin their prayers by thanking Church or community leaders. Ask them to reflect on the contributions that different people make to society. Encourage them to conclude their prayers by asking the Holy Spirit for guidance in their future vocations. Help young people organize a vocation day. They may invite guest speakers, including missionaries, doctors, volunteers in the community, or those in religious life.

✝ *Solidarity*

Session Assessment Option

An assessment for this session can be found at www.findinggod.com.

PLAN AHEAD: Get Ready for Session 23

Consult the catechist preparation pages to prepare for Session 23 and determine any materials you will need.

We Are Called and Sent

 ## 3-Minute Retreat

Before you prepare the session, pause and be still. Take three deep breaths and be aware of the loving presence of God, who is with you on this journey.

1 Corinthians 13:4–7

Love is patient, love is kind. It is not jealous, [love] is not pompous, it is not inflated, it is not rude, it does not seek its own interests, it is not quick-tempered, it does not brood over injury, it does not rejoice over wrongdoing but rejoices with the truth. It bears all things, believes all things, hopes all things, endures all things.

Reflection

This Scripture reflects what Saint Paul learned through his response to Jesus' call. We hear this reading most often during the Sacrament of Matrimony. But the qualities of love that Paul describes challenge each of us to examine our attitudes toward others, including family, friends, and strangers. Our attitude influences our actions. If we live each day with a loving outlook, then jealousy, envy, and anger disappear. We grow into people who seek the truth, and we rejoice when it is found. Love became the center of Saint Paul's life; it is also the foundation for the Sacraments at the Service of Communion.

Questions

What other quality of love could I add to Paul's list? What do I find most challenging about living life with a loving attitude?

 ### Concluding Prayer

Speak to God, using the words of this prayer or your own.

Gracious God, the world has great need of your love. Open my heart to receive your grace and the openness that I need to be a sign of your love to everyone I meet.

Knowing and Sharing Your Faith in Session 23

Consider how Scripture and Tradition can deepen your understanding of session content.

Scripture

Acts of the Apostles 9:4 recounts God's plea to Saul to conversion, which is also his plea to us.

Colossians 3:12–13 tells us Paul's fundamentals of Christian behavior and how to live as a follower of Christ.

Tradition

The Covenant between God and his people, Israel, is often described as a marriage covenant. The Covenant prepared the way for a new and everlasting covenant in which Jesus Christ unites himself with all humanity. The entire Christian life bears the mark of spousal love of Christ and the Church. Our Baptism prepares us to partake of the wedding feast that is the Eucharist. Catholic marriage is a sign of the covenant between Christ and the Church. The marriage between baptized persons is a sacrament of the New Covenant. To bind oneself for life to another human being may seem like a challenge. But the Good News we proclaim is that God loves us with an irrevocable love.

Catholic Social Teaching

In this session the integrated Catholic Social Teaching themes are **Call to Family, Community, and Participation** and **Rights and Responsibilities.** See page 177b for an explanation of these themes.

Window on the Catechism

The Sacraments at the Service of Communion are discussed in *CCC* 1533–1666.

General Directory for Catechesis

Catechesis in the family, the domestic Church, is discussed in *GDC* 226 and 227.

One-Hour Session Planner

SESSION 23 We Are Called and Sent

Session Theme: *Like Saint Paul, God calls us to conversion. Saint Paul's words are meant for us as much as for the early Christian communities.*

Before This Session

▶ Display the *Finding God* posters Saint Paul's Missionary Journeys and Time Line of the New Testament.

▶ Bookmark your Bible to Acts of the Apostles 9:4, Colossians 3:12–13, 1 Corinthians 13:13, and Ephesians 4:31–32. Place the open Bible in your prayer space.

▶ Read the Guide for this session, choose any additional If Time Allows activities that you might have time to complete, and gather the listed materials.

Prayer in Session 23

Pray aloud the opening prayer that asks Jesus to help us find the right way to go. Give young people an opportunity to experience an online 3-Minute Retreat at the end of the session. Session 23 includes a prayer that encourages young people to consider the role of a contrite heart in an authentic conversion to true discipleship. Follow the Prepare directions on the Catechist Guide page before sharing with young people.

STEPS	APPROXIMATE TIME
Engage *We Are Called and Sent* PAGE 195	10 minutes
Explore *Saint Paul Sees the Light* PAGES 196–197 *Letters of Saint Paul* PAGES 198–199	30–40 minutes
Reflect *Prayer:* Accepting the Challenge PAGE 200 *Where Do I Fit In?* PAGE 201	10–15 minutes
Respond *What's What?* PAGE 202	10–15 minutes

TAKE IT HOME

Homework options:

Breaking Free	PAGE 196
Real People, Real Writing	PAGE 198

Materials

REQUIRED

▶ Writing supplies (pages 195, 198, 201, 202)

▶ *Finding God* poster: Saint Paul's Missionary Journeys (page 198)

▶ *Finding God* poster: Time Line of the New Testament (page 198)

▶ CD player (page 198)

▶ CD 2, Track 4: "Paul Writes to Philemon" (5:59) (page 198)

▶ Computers with Internet access (page 202)

OPTIONAL

▶ Ice cubes, dish (page 195)

▶ Session 23 BLM, T-383 (page 197)

▶ Small milk cartons, pieces of string, nails, water, masking tape, basins (page 199)

▶ Computers with Internet access (page 200)

▶ Note cards, writing supplies (page 201)

▶ Age-appropriate books and tutoring materials (page 202)

▶ Session 23 Assessment, www.findinggod.com (page 202)

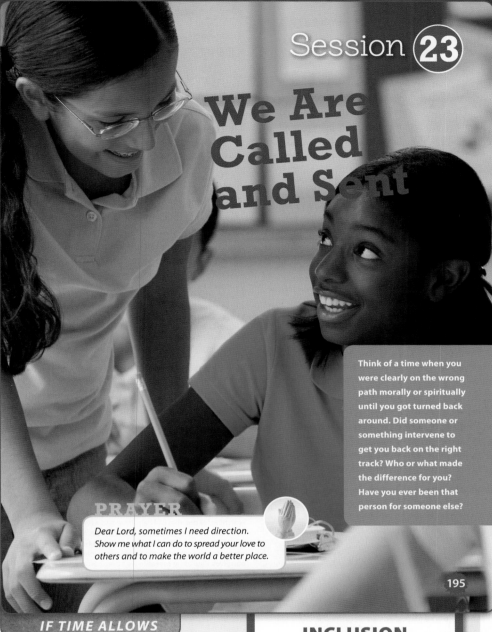

Session 23

We Are Called and Sent

Think of a time when you were clearly on the wrong path morally or spiritually until you got turned back around. Did someone or something intervene to get you back on the right track? Who or what made the difference for you? Have you ever been that person for someone else?

PRAYER

Dear Lord, sometimes I need direction. Show me what I can do to spread your love to others and to make the world a better place.

195

SESSION 23
OUTCOMES

▶ Explain the conversion of Saint Paul in relation to our own call to conversion.

▶ Explain the relevance of Paul's letters to early Christian communities in relation to modern challenges.

▶ Pray for a contrite heart.

▶ Define *chastity, deacons, Holy Orders, justification, Matrimony, obedience, poverty,* and *righteousness.*

① Set the Stage

Read aloud the text in the box. Give young people time to reflect on or write their responses. Ask volunteers to share their ideas with the group.

② Get Started

Copy the following on the board: *Yield—when one door closes, another one opens; Don't litter—stay alert because life is about to get more interesting; No Parking—let other people have their way; Detour—respect your neighborhood and the earth; Winding road—it's time to take some action.*

Say: ***Sometimes when trying to find an unfamiliar address, drivers head in the wrong direction. They might look for a road sign that points them in the right direction.*** Ask: ***What if road signs could be applied to life?*** Compare the directions of the road signs written on the board to life situations.

Say: ***With God's grace we can turn our lives back onto the right track.*** Ask: ***How do you think turning around on our spiritual path relates to the session title?*** (Answers will vary.)

🙏 Prayer

Say: ***Let's ask Jesus to help us find the right way to go.*** Pray aloud the prayer. Conclude by praying the Sign of the Cross.

IF TIME ALLOWS

Transformed by God's Grace

Bring in ice cubes and place them on a dish. Invite a volunteer to explain what will happen at room temperature. (The ice cubes will melt, changing from solid to liquid.) Point out that certain conditions cause a transformation in water, changing it from liquid to solid and vice versa. Use this physical transformation of matter, which is visible, to introduce the spiritual transformation that we undergo through God's grace.

INCLUSION
Vision

Readable Text Young people with vision impairments will benefit from enlarged print and pictures. Consider copying the text from the board onto a sheet of paper so that young people can easily see and fully participate. You might also consider writing the text on a transparency and using an LCD projector to improve readability.

➜ Go to **www.findinggod.com/sessionextenders** to learn about the teachings of Saint Paul. You may wish to share this with the group.

① Begin

Arrange young people in a circle. Brainstorm 10 inventions believed to have significantly changed the way people live. Discuss some ways that people react to new inventions. (Possible answers: excited, relieved, scared, apprehensive) Talk about possible reasons for these reactions.

② Connect

Explain that inventions can be difficult to accept because they involve letting go of old ways of doing things. Ask young people to think of friends or relatives who avoid or refuse to learn how to use modern technology. Say: ***Saint Paul learned to let go of his way of living in order to learn a new way of living in Jesus Christ.***

Have volunteers take turns reading the first three paragraphs. Ask: ***Why was Saul upset when a community of Jews believed that Jesus was the long-awaited Messiah?*** (Saul believed in strict observance of the Law; Jewish leaders denied that Jesus was the Messiah foretold by the prophets.)

 Have a volunteer read Saul Encounters the Risen Jesus. Discuss unit saints who experienced conversion. Ask: ***How did Paul's conversion begin?*** (He began to see the religious rules he had learned in a new light. He began to see how people need God's help.)

Ask a volunteer to read aloud the section Helpless to Help Ourselves. Say: ***The Jewish people, like the rest of the human family, longed for a way out of the pit of Original Sin. They wanted to be more than just conscious of sin—they wanted to be freed.***

Our Catholic Character

Read aloud the feature. Explain that living virtuous lives applies to all Christians, not only those in religious orders. Refer young people to pages 269 and 288 in Prayers and Practices for more information about virtues.

Saint Paul Sees the Light

HAVE you ever had an experience that changed how you look at your own life? Maybe you met a new group of friends, were inspired by a book or movie, celebrated a victory, or suffered a loss.

Saul, a young Jewish man who lived during the time of Jesus, faced a situation that made him look at himself with new eyes. Saul was a brilliant student who wanted to be a Jewish teacher. He studied the first five books of the Bible, which are known as the Torah, or "the Law." These revered books in the Jewish faith tell the story of Creation, of Abraham's faith, and of the liberation of the Hebrew people from slavery. They give the fundamental rules of how to follow God's will.

As a Jewish Pharisee, Saul believed in strict observance of the Law, both for himself and for all Jews. He was upset when a community of Jews believed that Jesus was the long-awaited Messiah. The Jewish leaders at the time denied that Jesus was the Messiah foretold by the prophets. To defend his religion, Saul led a persecution against those Jewish followers of Jesus in Jerusalem.

Our Catholic Character

As Catholics we are always being called to conversion. All baptized Christians, not only those who live in religious orders, are called to live holy lives by practicing the virtues of **poverty, chastity,** and **obedience.** Poverty requires living without an attachment to material goods. Chastity means respecting our bodies and the bodies of others. Obedience means respecting the authority of parents, teachers, and civil authorities.

Saul Encounters the Risen Jesus

As Saul continued his persecution of Jewish Christians throughout the land, he traveled to Damascus, where he encountered the risen Jesus Christ. "Saul, Saul, why are you persecuting me?" (Acts of the Apostles 9:4) Saul, shocked and blinded, had to be led by the hand to Damascus, where he fasted and prayed. This shattering experience led to Saul's conversion, his move from disbelief to belief. He began proclaiming that Salvation had been won through the life, Death, Resurrection, and Ascension of Jesus Christ. Saul became Paul the Apostle, the greatest missionary of the early Church. Paul began to see the rules that he had learned as a youth in a new light. He recognized that the human race inherited the consequences of the sin of Adam and Eve that we call Original Sin. Because of Original Sin, we are stuck in a tar pit, and try as we might, we cannot free ourselves.

Helpless to Help Ourselves

If we get stuck in a real tar pit, we might panic and thrash around wildly until we give up, exhausted. Or our mind might consider dozens of survival rules, searching for one that will help. If we had a lever, we could attempt to pry ourselves out of the pit. Yet all our knowledge and wishful thinking are useless because being so deeply mired in the tar, we are helpless to free ourselves. Paul came to realize we have another choice.

196   Unit 5 • Jesus Lives On

TAKE IT HOME

Breaking Free

Explain that the phrase "stuck in a tar pit" can be used to describe a bad situation from which it is difficult to get free. Have young people search the news for situations that could be considered modern-day tar pits, meaning bad situations that people find themselves stuck in. Give examples, such as unemployment, addictions, or sinful habits. Point out that a conversion of heart often begins with the realization that we are not greater than God. Instead, we rely on God for help.

Have them jot down three situations and bring in their lists to share with the entire group. Discuss possible ways out of these tar pits. Point out that Jesus' name means "God saves" and that whenever we find ourselves stuck in a tar pit, we can call on his name.

Salvation Through Jesus Christ

Paul discovered that God longs for the human family to be freed. God has freely given us Salvation through Jesus Christ by reaching out to us and reconciling us to himself. In Jesus, God provides us with the lever to pull ourselves out of the tar pit of sin. What we can't do for ourselves, God does for us. Through faith and Baptism, we receive the grace that we need to take away Original Sin and to live a new life in Jesus Christ. We also receive the daily graces we need to live as God wants.

God Makes Things Right

When we accept responsibility for hurting someone, we are willing to make the situation right. We may ask the person what we can do to heal the relationship—what we can do to make it right.

Paul says that the same thing happens in our relationship with God. Because of Original Sin, we can't make things right with God by ourselves. The good news is that God has provided a way to repair the relationship and reconcile us to himself. Paul calls this saving action of God **justification.** Justification is the action of the Holy Spirit in Baptism that cleanses us from sin and continually gives us the grace to walk in right relationship with God. Justification restores the right relationship between God and an individual. This right relationship between God and a person is called **righteousness.** Justification, then, is the act of God that gives us righteousness.

Study Corner

DEFINE

poverty, chastity, obedience, justification, righteousness

REMEMBER

Paul became the greatest missionary of the early Church. God also calls us to conversion. He has provided a way for us to repair and reconcile our relationship with him and invites us to live the Kingdom of God.

Called to Conversion

Like Saul, Jesus calls us to conversion because it is only through a change of heart that we can enter the Kingdom of God. It is by faith in the Gospel and through our Baptism that we gain Salvation, the forgiveness of sins, and the gift of new life.

Conversion is a lifelong pursuit. We can practice conversion daily by turning away from sin and choosing God. We can choose God by turning away from selfishness and choosing generosity. We can turn away from lies and choose to be honest. We can turn away from temptation and turn to prayer.

Conversion is a central theme of the Lord's Prayer. We recognize God as our loving Father and ask his help to do his will. We ask to be forgiven by him and promise to forgive others. When we pray, the Holy Spirit opens our hearts to love God more deeply and serve him more fully. In true conversion we find the strength to extend the love of God to others.

Explore

SACRED ART

Masaccio included this image of Saint Paul as part of a large altarpiece for a church in Pisa, Italy. It depicts the saint in noble robes while holding a sword, an indication of his martyrdom since he was executed with a sword during the reign of Nero. Paul is carrying a book, which represents the Epistles he wrote. The 13 Epistles credited to Saint Paul make up one-fourth of the New Testament.

Saint Paul, detail from altarpiece, Masaccio, 1426.

Session 23 > We Are Called and Sent **197**

IF TIME ALLOWS

Session 23 BLM

Then and Now Provide young people with the Session 23 Blackline Master [T-383]. Have them complete the activity to learn how some issues are timeless and have no generational bounds.

Right Relationship

Remind young people that a cause-and-effect statement shows a relationship between ideas that helps us understand something better. Tell young people that the cause represents what happened and the effect is the result of what happened. Write the following sentence from page 197 on the board, adding labels as shown to point out the cause-and-effect relationship:

> **[cause]** Through faith and Baptism, **[effect]** we receive the grace that we need to take away Original Sin and to live a new life in Jesus Christ.

Invite young people to complete the cause in this cause-and-effect relationship:

> **[cause]** Because of _____ (justification), **[effect]** the right relationship between God and an individual is restored.

Have a volunteer read aloud Salvation Through Jesus Christ. Reiterate that God gives us Salvation through Jesus Christ. But it is up to us to choose freely the reconciliation that God has provided for us through his Son.

Have a volunteer read aloud the section God Makes Things Right. Discuss the meaning of *justification* and *righteousness*, referring young people to their definitions in the Glossary. Emphasize that justification is the act of God and righteousness is the result.

Invite a volunteer to read Called to Conversion. Ask: ***From what is Jesus calling us to convert?*** (from sin to new life as his follower) Point out that the word *convert* means "to change from one use, purpose, or form to another." Say: ***Jesus asks us to change ourselves for the better.*** Explain that in Baptism, Jesus first calls us to conversion. This leads to a change of heart that leads us away from sin and toward God. Ask: ***How long does conversion take?*** (a lifetime)

Sacred Art

 Read aloud the feature. Explain that we can put together a picture of Saint Paul by reading the information about him in the New Testament. Refer to pages 262–263 in Prayers and Practices for more information about Saint Paul.

③ Close

Say: ***Saint Paul's experience of conversion was sudden and profound. We're all called to conversion and to a life of integrity and authenticity.*** Ask young people to look for opportunities to try something new or different and to be open to these opportunities.

① Begin

Arrange young people into teams of three or four. Tell them to jot down reasons for sending letters, e-mails, text messages, or tweets. Discuss possible reasons for sending, including to give information, to encourage a friend, to offer advice, to maintain a friendship, and so on.

② Connect

Say: *Saint Paul is an important figure in the Catholic faith and a fervent follower of Jesus. We'll learn more about how Paul provides us with insight and direction for following Jesus.*

Invite volunteers to take turns reading the first four paragraphs. Ask volunteers to summarize. Have young people compare Paul's reasons for writing his Epistles to the early Christian churches with the reasons they discussed at the start of the session in the Begin step.

Read aloud the section Sincerely Yours. Display the *Finding God* poster Saint Paul's Missionary Journeys and point out Paul's travels. Remind young people that travel in Paul's time was slow, dangerous, and difficult.

Display the *Finding God* poster Time Line of the New Testament. Point out Philemon on the time line and explain that this short letter is actually addressed to specific people. Explain that writing from prison, Paul addressed the issue of human slavery, arguing on behalf of Onesimus, a slave of Philemon's, whom Paul had converted to Christ. Play the recorded Scripture story "Paul Writes to Philemon." [CD 2, Track 4]

Have a volunteer begin reading aloud the section A Lasting Message. Ask: *Why are Paul's letters still valuable today?* (The doctrine and faith and the fundamentals of Christian behavior are the same.)

Letters of Saint Paul

SAINT PAUL was not a professor who wrote essays on theological topics. He was an apostle, one who preached the Gospel and taught the Christian community. Paul was a missionary and a pastor.

God called Paul to a life of faithfulness and commitment. Paul channeled his great yearning for God into a constructive, holy purpose. For the rest of his life, Saint Paul preached the living Word, guided growing Christian communities, and realized his life's true mission.

After Saint Paul had established a new church in a town or region, he would communicate with the new Christians with letters, the Epistles. He wrote Epistles in response to problems that had arisen mainly in the Christian communities that he himself had founded.

198

The New Testament contains many Epistles from Saint Paul. All together, 13 Epistles bear Paul's name, meaning that they were written personally by him or, in a few cases, by one of his followers. The Church accepts the Epistles as inspired by the Holy Spirit, and they are a wealth of counsel and wisdom that speak to us today.

Sincerely Yours

Paul, who experienced conversion and the Lord's forgiveness on the road to Damascus, never claimed to be perfect. He readily admitted his own faults to the people to whom he was writing, and he thanked friends and fellow believers who encouraged him. Paul possessed a humility and a humanity to which people could relate.

About the year A.D. 51, Paul wrote the first of two Epistles to the Christians in Thessalonica, which is currently the second largest city in Greece. Paul's letter to Thessalonica, the first Christian community he founded, was the first piece of New Testament literature written. Over the next 10 or more years, Paul traveled widely, preached, and wrote to other communities he had founded. During his many travels, Paul covered more than 14,000 miles.

A Lasting Message

Saint Paul's words are meant for us every bit as much as they were meant for the Christians of the first century. Why should we read letters that were written centuries ago? We face many of the same issues and struggles that Paul addressed almost 2,000 years ago. God's law and the principles of truth don't change.

TAKE IT HOME

Real People, Real Writing

Ask young people to find examples of writing that will likely be relevant to readers many years from now. In addition to informative writing, encourage them to consider the role of modern letters, e-mails, text messages, and blogs. Suggest that they look for writing that contains universal, timeless themes. To protect privacy, remind young people that any examples of personal writing that they select to bring to the group should be writing that they or their family members are willing to share with others.

While Paul wrote about doctrine and faith, he also wrote about fundamentals of Christian behavior, Christian virtue, and the best way to conduct oneself as a follower of Christ.

"Put on then, as God's chosen ones, holy and beloved, heartfelt compassion, kindness, humility, gentleness, and patience, bearing with one another and forgiving one another, if one has a grievance against another; as the Lord has forgiven you, so must you also do."

Colossians 3:12–13

Paul spoke with authority. His Epistles could be passionate and poetic, urgent, direct, and frank. The care and concern Paul had for his fellow Christians came through loud and clear in his letters.

It comes through to us today, too, as we read or listen to his letters in Scripture. We receive instruction, guidance, and support. Paul writes as one of us, in language that reflects the strength of his faith.

Called to Matrimony

Paul wrote that love was the preeminent gift from God. Many people who get married in the Church draw from Paul's first letter to the Corinthians as a reading in their wedding ceremony. "So faith, hope, love remain, these three; but the greatest of these is love." (1 Corinthians 13:13)

God created man and woman in his own image. As descendants of Adam and Eve, we are capable of entering into communion with other people through self-giving. This is most evident in the Sacrament of **Matrimony.** Love can call a man and a woman together for a shared mission in life. The selfless love and lifelong commitment between a man and a woman are signs of the enduring love that God has for us. The Sacrament of Matrimony, the lifelong union between husband and wife, is a sign of the union between Christ and the Church. This love is, in fact, the sign of the sacrament. The fidelity promised and kept between a wife and a husband reflects the faithfulness of God in his covenant with his people. This covenant was God's promise to always be with his people and care for them.

Called to Holy Orders

Men who receive **Holy Orders** continue the mission entrusted by Christ to his Apostles. Three degrees, or levels, of Holy Orders exist: **deacons,** priests, and bishops. Bishops, who enjoy the fullness

of the priesthood, are the successors of the Apostles. As Christ's representatives, they are ordained to teach, sanctify, and govern. A bishop is the head of a diocese and can preside at all seven sacraments. Assisting the bishops are priests who, by virtue of their ordination, act in the person of Christ. They preach the Gospel, shepherd the faithful, and celebrate the sacraments—except for ordination, which is exclusively reserved for bishops to celebrate. Married deacons are ordained to a ministry of service and are authorized to baptize, preach, and preside at weddings and funerals when there is no Mass. There are also unmarried deacons who have taken a vow of chastity and serve in this capacity as a step toward ordination to the priesthood.

Both clergy and the laity have vocations in life—that is, ways in which God calls them to serve, each according to his or her particular gifts. All sacraments lead us to Jesus and the love that God pours out to us through him. We can never lead a life of holiness on our own. We need the saving power of Christ. The Sacraments of Matrimony and Holy Orders are called Sacraments at the Service of Communion. Through vocations as clergy or laity, these witnesses to Christ's presence in the world discover a call to serve others.

Explore

Study Corner

DEFINE

Matrimony
Holy Orders
deacons

REMEMBER

Paul's Epistles to early Christian communities provided guidance on topics of faith, virtue, daily conduct, and issues that still apply today. The Sacrament of Matrimony is a sign of the union between Christ and his Church. Men who receive Holy Orders continue the mission entrusted by Christ to his Apostles.

Session 23 > We Are Called and Sent **199**

Conversion Reaction

Organize young people into small groups. Gather and distribute a small milk carton, a piece of string, a nail, water, masking tape, and a basin to each group. Have groups work together to follow these directions: Use the nail to punch a hole in the bottom right corner of each of the four sides of the milk carton. Cover each hole with masking tape. Open the top of the carton and punch another hole exactly in the middle of the top section of the carton. In your meeting space, thread the string through the hole, tie it, and hang it so that it swings freely above the basin. Fill the carton with water. Remove the tape from one corner, then off two opposite corners, and finally off the last corner. Have groups see that the carton spins.

Explain that the carton does not make itself spin. Associate this fact with conversion. Tell young people that in a similar way, the only reason we experience a conversion or turning around of our lives is in response to God's action. When we experience a conversion, it comes from God's grace and initiative.

📖 Have volunteers read the remaining paragraphs in A Lasting Message. Ask: *Why were Paul's Epistles effective?* (He spoke with authority, with passion, with poetic language.) Ask: *What gifts did Paul use in his answer to God's call?* (Possible answers: public speaking, writing skills, courage, perseverance)

Invite a volunteer to read aloud Called to Matrimony. Ask: *In Paul's first letter to the Corinthians, what are the three things that last?* (faith, hope, love) Have volunteers summarize the information about the Sacrament of Matrimony. Ask: *How are love and commitment signs in this sacrament?* (Lifelong love is a sign of God's enduring love for us.) Ask: *Why is fidelity important?* (Fidelity, or faithfulness, between a husband and wife reflects the faithfulness of God's covenant to be with and to care for his people.)

Ask a volunteer to read Called to Holy Orders. Have young people refer to page 288 of Prayers and Practices for more information on the Sacraments at the Service of Communion. Say: *Those who receive Holy Orders continue the mission begun by Christ.* Ask: *What are the three levels of Holy Orders?* (deacon, priest, bishop) Ask a volunteer to read aloud the definition of *deacon* in the Glossary. Discuss some ways that a deacon, priest, and bishop are the same and different.

③ Close

Say: *We've learned that we face many of the same struggles and challenges as people who belonged to the early Church long ago.* Reinforce that by reading Paul's letters, the Epistles, we're better able to understand our faith and ways to conduct our daily lives. Challenge young people to use ways of communicating with others in a responsible and affirming way.

Prayer

Follow the steps to guide young people through the prayer on page 200.

Young People's Page

Prepare Pray the prayer in advance to become familiar with it.

Pray Ask a volunteer to read aloud the title and paragraphs in the left column. Point out that true conversion requires a contrite heart. Discuss the meaning of *contrite* and its valuable role in conversion. Say: *Jesus invites us to conversion. Your Baptism is the beginning of conversion and a decision that your family made for you as a baby. Now that you are older, each step on your faith journey is a chance for you to choose conversion.*

Have young people bring their books to the prayer space. Assign young people as Side 1 or Side 2. Encourage them to sit quietly, relax, and open their hearts and minds to prayer. *Say: Breathe slowly and quiet your mind from distractions. Know that God is present.* Pause briefly and read the Leader part. Then pray together the Lord's Prayer. Prompt Side 1 and Side 2 to pray aloud their parts as shown, pausing for reflection between each part. At the conclusion, pray *Amen.* Invite young people to pray the Sign of the Cross. Say: *Let's ask God to help us accept life's challenges and welcome moments of conversion. We acknowledge that we are works in progress, and we pray for the grace to choose God as we move through life.*

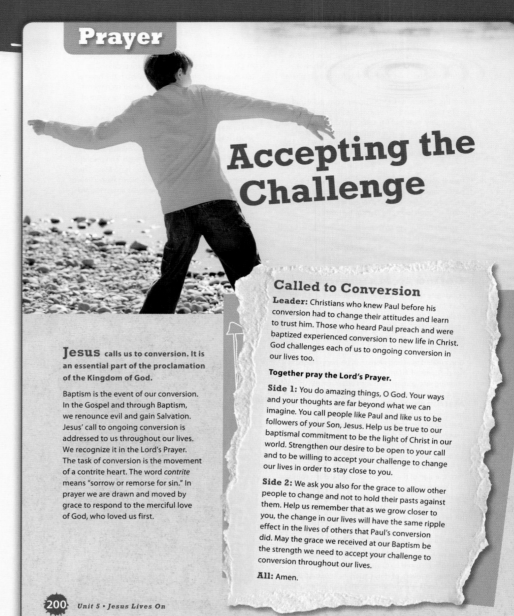

Prayer

Accepting the Challenge

Jesus calls us to conversion. It is an essential part of the proclamation of the Kingdom of God.

Baptism is the event of our conversion. In the Gospel and through Baptism, we renounce evil and gain Salvation. Jesus' call to ongoing conversion is addressed to us throughout our lives. We recognize it in the Lord's Prayer. The task of conversion is the movement of a contrite heart. The word *contrite* means "sorrow or remorse for sin." In prayer we are drawn and moved by grace to respond to the merciful love of God, who loved us first.

Called to Conversion

Leader: Christians who knew Paul before his conversion had to change their attitudes and learn to trust him. Those who heard Paul preach and were baptized experienced conversion to new life in Christ. God challenges each of us to ongoing conversion in our lives too.

Together pray the Lord's Prayer.

Side 1: You do amazing things, O God. Your ways and your thoughts are far beyond what we can imagine. You call people like Paul and like us to be followers of your Son, Jesus. Help us be true to our baptismal commitment to be the light of Christ in our world. Strengthen our desire to be open to your call and to be willing to accept your challenge to change our lives in order to stay close to you.

Side 2: We ask you also for the grace to allow other people to change and not to hold their pasts against them. Help us remember that as we grow closer to you, the change in our lives will have the same ripple effect in the lives of others that Paul's conversion did. May the grace we received at our Baptism be the strength we need to accept your challenge to conversion throughout our lives.

All: Amen.

200 **Unit 5 • Jesus Lives On**

IF TIME ALLOWS

Spreading Good Words

Discuss how Saint Paul used written communication to stir hearts to conversion. Challenge young people to review some of their recent communications, such as text messages, e-mails, and social media posts, and note how many of these messages are affirming, building others up and encouraging Christian beliefs. Invite young people to look at their written communication in a new way and recognize the power of the words that they send out into the world.

✝ *Rights and Responsibilities*

FYI

Coaching Young People to Pray

Tell young people that praying traditional prayers such as the Lord's Prayer helps them connect with their Catholic heritage. Compare traditional prayers to family heirlooms passed down through the generations. Encourage young people to take prayers to heart and to reflect sincerely on their words as they pray.

WHERE Do I Fit In?

Our communication says a lot about who we are, but more importantly, it can let people know *whose* we are—God's! Let's strive to communicate the way of Jesus with peace, kindness, generosity, humility, and forgiveness in all that we say and do.

by Bret Nicholaus

Of Faith and Phones

I took a course in college called Basic Communication. I most clearly remember the words that the professor wrote on the board the very first day. *You cannot not communicate. Everything you say, everything you do, everything you wear—all of it communicates something about you.* Even silence can send a powerful message. It can tell people that you're upset, focused, bored, or a dozen other things.

In today's world, much of our communication is based on technology. Only sleep stops many of us from endless tweets, texts, calls, and e-mails. As followers of Jesus, what should our communication "look" like? Should our typed or spoken messages communicate something different *because* we are Christians? Saint Paul, in his letter to the Ephesians, provides instructions for Christian living that can be easily applied to our communication.

> All bitterness, fury, anger, shouting, and reviling must be removed from you, along with all malice, [And] be kind to one another, compassionate, forgiving one another as God has forgiven you in Christ.
> *Ephesians 4:31–32*

Here are things I consider in my own daily communication: Am I using technology to lift people up or to bring them down? Do my texts and tweets reflect the fact that Jesus is Lord of my life? Do my phone calls and e-mails shine Christ's love into the hearts and minds of others?

BRET NICHOLAUS is the author of more than 25 books, including the national best seller *The Conversation Piece.*

The Best Text

Text messages generally consist of few words. Write a reply that reflects a Christian mind-set for each situation.

I can't believe Mike is wearing those ugly shoes!

_____
_____
_____

I have no intention of speaking to Leticia ever again.

_____
_____
_____

What can you do to help at the food pantry tonight?

_____
_____
_____

Reflect

Session 23 > We Are Called and Sent **201**

IF TIME ALLOWS

Ten Tech Commandments

Point out that our constant engagement with technological devices also communicates a message to the people around us. Have young people describe times they felt a person's use of a device in the presence of others was rude. Then work as a group to come up with "Ten Tech Commandments" that a Christian might follow in the company of others. For example, "You shall turn off your phone during dinner." Have young people record these commandments on a note card and share them with the group and with family members.

---

① Begin

Ask young people to recall a time when they sent a text or an e-mail that they later regretted. Discuss strategies people use to minimize regrettable communications. For example, suggest waiting 30 minutes before sending a sensitive e-mail or refraining from sending a text when your emotions are too high. Invite a young person to read the introductory text. Then ask how many young people think of texting and e-mailing as forms of discipleship. Say: ***Maybe starting today, we can all stretch our thinking about when and how we share the Good News.***

② Connect

Have volunteers read aloud Of Faith and Phones. Say: ***A text that reflects God's love does not necessarily mention God by name.*** Ask: ***What must it "look like" though?*** (Possible answers: It must be polite, gentle, generous, and patient. It must build the recipient up rather than tear him or her down.) Have young people recall a time when they received a hurtful text or e-mail. Ask: ***What do our instincts often tell us to do in such a situation?*** (Possible answer: Respond to it instantly and in an equally hurtful manner.) Ask: ***How and when might God want us to respond?*** (Possible answers: only after reflection and with forgiveness)

Have young people complete the activity The Best Text independently. Then invite volunteers to share their "texts" with the group.

③ Close

Remind young people that the speed with which we can transmit communications makes it important to think before hitting the Send button. Say: ***Words are powerful. Use them carefully.***

1 Begin

What's What? Read the directions aloud. Have young people complete the page independently. Ask volunteers to share their answers.

2 Connect

Say What? Ask volunteers to read aloud and define the terms. Review each term in the Glossary if necessary.

Now What? Ask a volunteer to read aloud the question. Invite each young person to answer the question independently. If volunteers wish to share their ideas, invite them to do so. Encourage them to continue their writing on another sheet of paper.

3 Go in Peace

Collect materials and return them to their appropriate places. Encourage young people to keep their hearts open to Jesus' call for conversion. Say: *True Salvation comes not through living perfectly, but through encountering Christ and living authentically.* Remind them that when they are truly sorry for offending God, forming a new habit that is pleasing to God is a way to prevent falling into sin again.

3-Minute Retreat
Give young people an opportunity for quiet meditation at **www.loyolapress.com/retreat**.

What's What?

Respond

Complete each sentence with details from the text.

1 Saul led a _____ against followers of Jesus in Jerusalem. (PAGE 196)

persecution

2 As he was traveling to Damascus, Saul encountered the risen _____ . (PAGE 196)

Jesus Christ

3 The experience of meeting Jesus led to Saul's _____ . (PAGE 196)

conversion

4 Saul became Paul the Apostle, the greatest _____ in the early Church. (PAGE 196)

missionary

5 Through faith and _____ , we receive the grace that we need to take away Original Sin. (PAGE 197)

Baptism

6 The action of the Holy Spirit in Baptism that cleanses us from sin is called _____ . (PAGE 197)

justification

7 We can read Paul's Epistles in the _____ . (PAGE 198)

New Testament

8 The Sacrament of _____ is a sign of the union between Christ and the Church. (PAGE 199)

Matrimony

9 The Sacrament of _____ continues the work begun by the Apostles. (PAGE 199)

Holy Orders

10 Three levels of Holy Orders are _____ , _____ , and _____ . (PAGE 199)

bishop

priest

deacon

Say What?
Know the definitions of these terms.

chastity	Matrimony
deacons	obedience
Holy Orders	poverty
justification	righteousness

Now What?
What is one habit you could change that would make you a better disciple of Christ?

Answers will vary.

202   *Unit 5 • Jesus Lives On*

IF TIME ALLOWS

Service: Tutoring

Discuss how tutoring is a way to bring good into the world. Arrange for the group to tutor younger children from the parish or community who need help with reading, math, or another subject. Arrange a time and place for the group to work with the children. Beforehand, gather age-appropriate books and other necessary materials.

✝ *Family and Community*

Session Assessment Option

An assessment for this session can be found at www.findinggod.com.

PLAN AHEAD: Get Ready for Session 24

Consult the catechist preparation pages to prepare for Session 24 and determine any materials you will need.

Jesus Calls Us to Eternal Life

 3-Minute Retreat

Before you prepare the session, pause and be still. Take three deep breaths and be aware of the loving presence of God, who is with you on this journey.

Revelation 12:1

A great sign appeared in the sky, a woman clothed with the sun, with the moon under her feet, and on her head a crown of twelve stars.

Reflection

While biblical scholars have given a number of explanations as to whom the woman "clothed in the sun" might be, for centuries Christians have identified the woman as Mary, the Mother of God. Being clothed in the sun recalls the glory in which God the Creator is clothed in Psalm 104:2, where God is clothed with majesty and splendor, robed in light like a cloak. The 12 stars indicate the 12 tribes of Israel. Through her Assumption, Mary sits with Jesus at the right hand of God. So we could not have a more apt image of the glory that God bestows on her. While on earth, Mary was like us in every way, but she was born without sin. She now lives with Jesus, praying for us, interceding for us.

Questions

How does knowing that Mary is interceding for me help me live a holy life? How do I need Mary and the saints to pray for me today?

 Concluding Prayer

Speak to God, using the words of this prayer or your own.

Loving Mary, in life you were the model disciple of Jesus, your Son. Pray for me that I may walk in his steps with the same fidelity that you displayed in your life on earth.

Knowing and Sharing Your Faith in Session 24

Consider how Scripture and Tradition can deepen your understanding of session content.

Scripture

Revelation 21:3–4 gives us a glimpse into a beautiful and hopeful future at the end of the world.

Matthew 25:31–32 tells us about the Last Judgment, describing a shepherd separating the sheep from the goats.

Tradition

Mary was called the Mother of the Church as early as the 12th century. In 1964, during the Mass at the end of the third session of the Second Vatican Council, Pope Paul VI officially proclaimed Mary as Mother of the Church. He said, "For the glory of the Blessed Virgin and our own consolation, we proclaim the Most Blessed Virgin Mary Mother of the Church, of the whole people of God, faithful and pastors, and we call her our most loving Mother." *The Dogmatic Constitution of the Church* [60–68] and the *Catechism of the Catholic Church* speaks of Mary not only as the Mother of Jesus, but also as the Mother of the People of God.

Catholic Social Teaching

In this session the integrated Catholic Social Teaching theme is **Rights and Responsibilities.** See page 177b for an explanation of this theme.

Window on the Catechism

Mary as Mother of Christ and Mother of the Church is presented in *CCC* 963–972.

General Directory for Catechesis

Devotion to Mary as Mother of God is discussed in *GDC* 196.

One-Hour Session Planner

SESSION 24 Jesus Calls Us to Eternal Life

Session Theme: *Mary's Assumption reflects her exalted place in the Communion of Saints and gives us hope of eternal life with God.*

Before This Session

▶ Bookmark your Bible to Revelation 21:3–4, Revelation 22:20, Matthew 25:31–32, Luke 4:18–19, Luke 24:50–53, and John 11:17–27. Place the open Bible in your prayer space.

▶ Read the Guide for this session, choose any additional If Time Allows activities that you might have time to complete, and gather the listed materials.

STEPS	APPROXIMATE TIME
Engage *Jesus Calls Us to Eternal Life* PAGE 203	10 minutes
Explore *The Struggle Between Good and Evil* PAGES 204–205 *Assumption of the Blessed Mother* PAGES 206–207	30–40 minutes
Reflect *Prayer:* Enter the Kingdom PAGE 208 *Where Do I Fit In?* PAGE 209	10–15 minutes
Respond *What's What?* PAGE 210	10–15 minutes

Prayer in Session 24

Join young people in praying the prayer on the opening page of the session. Invite young people to experience an online 3-Minute Retreat at the end of the session. In Session 24 young people will offer prayers for the virtues of faith, hope, and charity. Follow the Prepare directions on the Catechist Guide page before sharing with young people.

TAKE IT HOME

Homework options:

Recognizing
Literary Forms   PAGE 205

Marian
Feast Days   PAGE 207

Materials

REQUIRED

▶ Beanbag (page 203)

▶ Various types of writing, such as an instruction manual, cookbook, page from a social-networking site, or newspaper (page 204)

▶ Bible (page 206)

▶ Writing supplies (pages 209, 210)

▶ Computers with Internet access (page 210)

OPTIONAL

▶ Writing supplies (pages 203, 209, 210)

▶ Session 24 BLM, T-384 (page 206)

▶ Books about Haiti, computer with Internet access (page 209)

▶ Articles or resources about Catholic Relief Services (page 210)

▶ Session 24 Assessment, www.findinggod.com (page 210)

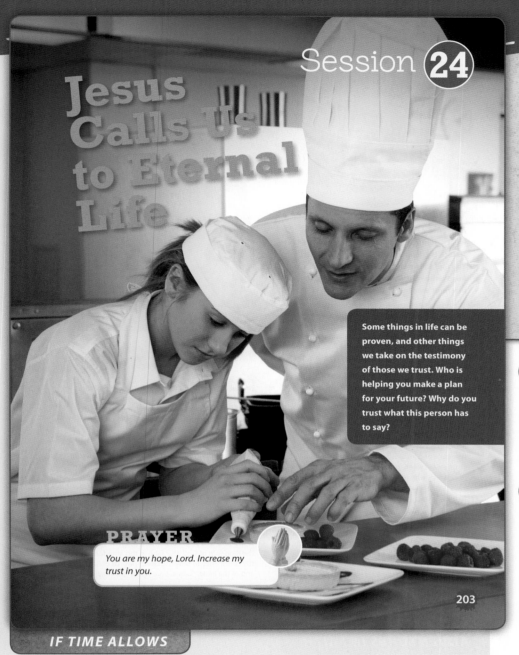

Session **24**

Jesus Calls Us to Eternal Life

Some things in life can be proven, and other things we take on the testimony of those we trust. Who is helping you make a plan for your future? Why do you trust what this person has to say?

PRAYER

You are my hope, Lord. Increase my trust in you.

203

IF TIME ALLOWS

In Style
Arrange young people into groups of three or four. Explain that the Book of Revelation is an example of a type of writing that was popular during the time it was written. Have young people copy the following category titles onto a sheet of paper: *Books, Movies, Music.* Challenge them to list three popular types under each category. When groups have finished, have them share their responses with the group. Explain that understanding the writer's purpose and audience helps us understand the Book of Revelation.

Go to **www.findinggod.com/sessionextenders** for information about the Assumption. You may wish to share this with the group.

SESSION 24
OUTCOMES

▶ Explain the use of symbolic language and imagery in the Book of Revelation.

▶ Explain that, like Mary, those who serve God will share eternal life with him.

▶ Offer prayers for the virtues of faith, hope, and charity.

▶ Define *apocalyptic literature, Assumption, Communion of Saints, infallible, Last Judgment, literary forms,* and *Theological Virtues.*

① Set the Stage
Read aloud the text in the box. Give young people time to reflect on the questions. Encourage volunteers to share their responses with the group.

② Get Started
Have young people stand in a circle. Say: *When we trust someone, we rely on their good judgment and wisdom.* Ask the group to brainstorm people who may be trustworthy, such as family members, neighbors, friends, teachers, or community leaders.

Toss a beanbag to one person. Ask him or her to name someone whose judgment and wisdom they rely on or have relied on in the past. Then ask that person to toss the beanbag to someone else in the circle. Prompt young people to continue tossing the beanbag until all have had a turn. Read aloud the session title. Say: *We place our trust in God to guide and save us. He sent us his Son, Jesus, to open the way to eternal life.*

 Prayer

Say: *Let's take a moment to pray together.* Pray aloud the prayer. Conclude by praying the Sign of the Cross.

1 Begin

Bring in various types of writing to share with the group. For example, you might use an instruction manual, a cookbook, a page from a social-networking site, and a newspaper. Display the examples or pass them around. Discuss how they are different and how they are the same. Say: **Writing comes in many different forms and styles and has different purposes.**

2 Connect

Read aloud the title and the first two paragraphs. Discuss the meaning of *persecute.* (to punish or harass) Ask young people to name groups that have been persecuted throughout history and the reasons for their persecution. Say: **The Book of Revelation was written to address a crisis. We'll learn more about the crisis that inspired this type of writing and what the writing means to us today.**

 Have volunteers take turns reading Good Versus Evil. Then ask young people to read silently as you read aloud Revelation 21:3–4 as shown at the end of the section. On the board write *Revelation is . . .* and *Revelation is not . . .* Ask volunteers to complete each sentence starter with information they learned in this section. (Revelation is apocalyptic literature, a symbolic interpretation of good versus evil, a vision of the promise of everlasting Salvation in Jesus, a message of hope; Revelation is not a factual account, a literal telling of the end of the world, a prediction of the future) Say: **Because the Book of Revelation is often misunderstood, it's important to learn about its writer, the time in which it was written, and the book's purpose if we are to appreciate the message it has for Christians.**

The Struggle Between Good and Evil

WHEN you want to make a point, you might use descriptive language to describe what's going on. "I have *tons* of homework!" "Coach is *killing* us with those wind sprints!" You intend to paint an image in someone's head although you don't expect the person to interpret your words literally.

The Book of Revelation is one of the most misunderstood books in the Bible because it contains language and descriptions that are not supposed to be taken literally. The Book of Revelation was written during a time of crisis. Domitian, the Roman emperor from A.D. 81 to 96, was persecuting Christians. The Book of Revelation was intended as a message of support, encouraging Christians who had doubts about their future to remain faithful and strong in the midst of threat and oppression.

Good Versus Evil

The Book of Revelation is **apocalyptic literature,** a form of writing that uses symbolic language and imagery to describe the eternal struggle between good and evil. The author of Revelation, who refers to himself as John, uses extravagant language to describe a vision revealed to him.

Revelation, when interpreted in a literal and factual way, can be seen as a prediction of the end of the world—something it was never intended to be. In fact, despite disturbing language and imagery, the conclusion of the Book of Revelation is uplifting, a declaration of the everlasting reign of God and his defeat of evil. It says the forces of good always will prevail. The author of Revelation is not describing literal events. Rather, we read the author's vision while keeping symbolism in mind, recognizing that our future, though uncertain, holds the promise of everlasting Salvation in Jesus.

As a message of encouragement and hope to Christians during a crisis, the Book of Revelation told them to endure suffering with the confidence that God would prevail. The central message of this book was that the victory had already been won in Jesus Christ. This message is meant for us today as well. We also experience times of conflict in our hearts between the forces of good and evil, and we sometimes have doubts about our future.

Jesus gave us a vision of eternity when he spoke about the Kingdom of God. Our faith in this kingdom gives us the confidence to pray the closing words of Revelation and of the Bible, "Come, Lord Jesus!" (Revelation 22:20)

204 *Unit 5 • Jesus Lives On*

🔥 **ADVENTURES IN FAITH**

Take a Poll

If possible, try to do this activity before the group has read the lesson. State that the Book of Revelation is an often misunderstood piece of writing. Ask young people to conduct a poll of 10 people in the group. They should ask each person to tell what they think the Book of Revelation is about and what images or words come to mind. After conducting their polls, ask young people to read aloud their results. Write responses on the board so that everyone sees the results.

The final chapter of Revelation points to a beautiful future to which we can pin our hopes.

> I heard a loud voice from the throne saying, "Behold, God's dwelling is with the human race. He will dwell with them and they will be his people and God himself will always be with them [as their God]. He will wipe every tear from their eyes, and there shall be no more death or mourning, wailing or pain, [for] the old order has passed away."
>
> *Revelation 21:3–4*

Understanding Symbolic Language

Catholics believe that in matters of religious truth, the Bible is free from error. Everything the Bible teaches about God and our relationship with God is true. At the same time, Catholics are not fundamentalists. We do not interpret every word or passage of the Bible literally. We recognize that the Bible contains many styles, or **literary forms,** of writing, such as history, proverbs, letters, parables, wisdom sayings, and poetry. At times stories and myth were seen as the vehicles through which the most essential and sacred truths of people were told and passed on. At other times apocalyptic literature, such as Revelation, was widely popular and seen as an appropriate way to reveal God's Word.

All forms of writing in the Bible have a sole purpose—to relay the truth found in God's Word.

Some forms work better than others to help listeners connect ordinary ideas or events in their lives in a way that reveals a deep spiritual truth or lesson in faith. For example, the story of Jonah and the whale is a divinely inspired parable that reveals what happens when a person tries to run away from God's call. When we run from God, as Jonah did, we encounter isolation. And even in our isolation, God can and will find us. The point of Jonah's story is not whether a man can factually survive in the belly of a large fish for three days. The greater truth is found in understanding our relationship with God.

Finding Truth

God speaks to us in sacred Scripture through the inspired writing of human authors. We need to study and seek what the authors intended to say and what God wants to show through their words. The writing of Scripture didn't happen by God dictating the message word by word as if to a scribe or secretary. The authors wrote while using their talents—and even their limitations—to convey God's message in the forms and language of their times, under the guidance and inspiration of the Holy Spirit.

We rely on the guidance of our pastors, teachers, catechists, and Scripture scholars to help us understand the meaning of Revelation and other books of the Bible. The pope and the bishops, known as the Magisterium, teach and guide the Church in matters of doctrine and morals, providing direction to the whole Church.

Study Corner

DEFINE

apocalyptic literature
literary forms

REMEMBER

To understand the Book of Revelation, we recognize that its literary form relies on symbols and images. It is not intended to be interpreted literally. In the Book of Revelation, God claims eternal victory over the forces of evil.

Revelation 14:14, The Reaper, Vision of Armageddon, German School, ca. 1530.

Session 24 > Jesus Calls Us to Eternal Life   205

Explore

TAKE IT HOME

Recognizing Literary Forms

Ask young people to use their Bibles to locate various literary forms. Ask them to mark passages or pages with sticky notes that identify each literary form. The next time the group gathers, ask volunteers to read aloud their examples without identifying the literary form. Have group members guess which literary form the reading exemplifies.

Have a volunteer read Understanding Symbolic Language. Say: **The Bible conveys God's message in different ways.** If needed, refer young people to the Glossary and read aloud the definition of *literary forms*. Ask: **What are some literary forms?** (Possible answers: myths, poetry, history, letters, parables, proverbs, Wisdom sayings) Say: **The Bible inspired writing that communicates God's truth in different ways.** Ask: **How do you know that the story of Jonah is not historical fact?** (It is a parable that teaches a lesson about what happens when we run away from God.) Ask: **Why does the Bible contain different literary forms?** (Some styles of writing connect with listeners better to relay God's Word or deliver a spiritual truth more effectively than others.)

Ask a volunteer to read aloud Finding Truth. Ask: **Where do we find guidance for our religious beliefs?** (Possible answers: pastors, teachers, catechists, Scripture scholars, the Magisterium) Ask young people to summarize what Catholics believe regarding the writing in the Bible. (The writing contains no religious error because it is divinely inspired. Everything the Bible teaches is true. The Bible contains different literary forms and is not always meant to be read literally.)

To continue the discussion about discovering the truth in the Bible, have young people read and discuss pages 254–255 in Prayers and Practices.

③ Close

Ask young people to explain how the phrase "judging a book by its cover" applies to the Book of Revelation. (The meaning of the book is not as it seems. The Book of Revelation shouldn't be taken literally.)

1 Begin

Encourage young people to share some ways that TV shows or movies have addressed the topic of life after death. Have them compare and contrast these depictions with their understanding of Catholic beliefs.

2 Connect

Encourage young people to look to the teachings of the Church, not popular media, to guide their understanding of life after death. Invite a volunteer to read the article title and the introductory paragraphs.

Ask a volunteer to read aloud Taken to Heaven. Ask another volunteer to read aloud the definitions of *Assumption* and *infallible* in the Glossary. Point out that we cannot comprehend fully some mysteries of our faith, but we know the teaching of Mary's Assumption is true because it was proclaimed infallibly.

Have a volunteer read Body and Soul. Point out that Mary did not ascend into Heaven but instead was assumed into Heaven. Ask a volunteer to read aloud the passage from Luke. Ask: **What do we know from Mary's Assumption?** (Mary had a special relationship with God. We have a share in eternal life if we are reconciled with God at the time of our death.)

Our Catholic Character

Invite a volunteer to read the feature. Explain that the Last Judgment is not a message of fear but a call to conversion, a reminder that everyone's life on earth comes to an end. Ask: **What do Catholics believe takes place immediately after death?** (Each person comes before God for an individual [particular] judgment and experiences Heaven, Purgatory, or Hell.) Have a volunteer read aloud Matthew 25:31–32 and discuss how Jesus describes the Last Judgment.

Assumption of the Blessed Mother

The Assumption, Saint Mary's of the Barrens Church, Perryville, Missouri.

WHAT happens to us after we die? The minds and imaginations of humankind have always pondered this question.

You have probably seen movies or TV shows that dramatize what the afterlife is like, and you may have read novels that deal with the subject. These are fictions, enjoyable in their own right as entertainment. To seriously consider and discuss what God has prepared for those who love him, we need to turn to the teachings of the Church, such as the Assumption of Mary, the mother of Jesus.

Our Catholic Character

In his encyclical *The Hope of Salvation (Spe Salvi)*, Pope Benedict XVI wrote that "The last Judgment is not primarily an image of terror, but an image of hope." Catholics believe that immediately after death, each person comes before God for an individual (particular) judgment and enters Heaven, Purgatory, or Hell. The **Last Judgment** refers to the end of time when Christ will return in glory and all will be raised from the dead to stand before God, at which time our relationship with him will be revealed to all. Jesus himself describes this last (general) judgment in Matthew 25:31–32, describing a shepherd separating the sheep from the goats. The message of the Last Judgment calls people to conversion so they are not separated from God forever.

Taken to Heaven

The root of the word *assume* means "to take," so when Mary was taken into Heaven, both body and soul, we refer to it as her **Assumption.** We celebrate the Feast of the Assumption on August 15. In 1950 Pope Pius XII declared the beliefs of our Catholic faith. "By the authority of our Lord Jesus Christ, of the Blessed Apostles Peter and Paul, and by our own authority, we pronounce, declare, and define it to be a divinely revealed dogma: that the Immaculate Mother of God, the ever Virgin Mary, having completed the course of her earthly life, was assumed body and soul into heavenly glory." This is an **infallible** declaration, meaning that the Church accepts the decree as truth informed and inspired by the Holy Spirit of God.

Body and Soul

The Bible offers no information on how, when, or where Mary's life on earth ended. Pope Pius XII's decree states that Mary had "completed the course of her earthly life," meaning that her holy mission on earth was complete. The decree also clarifies that Mary did not ascend into Heaven, as Jesus did; she was assumed, or taken, into Heaven. (Luke 24:50–53) Mary's Assumption reflects her unique relationship to Jesus as the Mother of God. It also is an indication that believers in Jesus and in his Resurrection can anticipate eternal, never-ending life after death with God, granted to those who die as God's friends.

206 *Unit 5 • Jesus Lives On*

IF TIME ALLOWS

Session 24 BLM
Assumption of Mary, the Blessed Mother Provide young people with the Session 24 Blackline Master [T-384]. Have them complete the activity to review ideas associated with Mary or the Assumption.

INCLUSION
Hearing

Group Work If some young people have hearing difficulties, make listening easier by eliminating excess background noise. During group work, have the young person face you. If young people tend to avoid speaking, encourage their effort and allow enough time for them to articulate their ideas. Offer plentiful praise to encourage their continued participation.

Communion of Saints

As the mother of Jesus, Mary holds an exalted place in the **Communion of Saints.** The Communion of Saints includes all who have been saved in Jesus Christ, whether living or dead. We are united in this union through our one faith and one Lord, whom we receive in the Eucharist.

A saint is not someone who is perfect. No one is perfect. Through God's grace, however, saints have received what we hope to receive one day after we complete the course of our earthly life—God's promised Salvation. A canonized or declared saint is a person whom the Church believes now lives with God in Heaven. By declaring a person a saint, the Church acknowledges God's grace at work in this person's life as an authentic witness to Christ. Because of the abundance of God's grace in their lives, the saints—just like Mary—can intercede before God on behalf of the living.

On November 1 we remember all these holy men and women recognized by the Church as saints. There are, however, many individuals who live now with God in Heaven who haven't been officially declared saints by the Church. On All Saints Day, we also honor and remember these undeclared saints, for their prayers benefit us too. When Saint Paul wrote to the early Christian communities, he sometimes addressed the people as saints. Saint Paul was acknowledging their holy lives and their destiny— Salvation through Christ.

What happens after we die? If we serve God as Mary did, faithfully and entirely, dedicating our lives to God, we anticipate Salvation and a life of happiness in Heaven. At death our life is changed, not ended. We know this by recalling Jesus' and Martha's conversation before the raising of Lazarus. Jesus assures Martha that her brother will rise again. Martha replies in faith, "I know he will rise, in the resurrection on the last day." Then Jesus identifies himself as the Resurrection and the Life. (John 11:17–27)

The soul is immortal, and we look forward to the final resurrection of the dead at the end of the world. In Heaven we become part of the Communion of Saints.

Past Meets Present

PAST: In 1531 Juan Diego, a native Mexican, was walking to Mass when the Blessed Mother, dressed as an Aztec princess, appeared to him. She spoke to Juan Diego in his native language and sent him to the bishop of Mexico with a request to build a church on the site. When Juan Diego told the bishop, he demanded a sign before he would believe the story. The Blessed Mother told Juan Diego to pick roses on the site. Although it was December and freezing, roses were in full bloom. Juan Diego gathered the roses in his tilma, a cactus-cloth cape. When he shook them out in front of the bishop, an image of Our Lady of Guadalupe was imprinted on Juan Diego's tilma.

PRESENT: Saint Juan Diego's tilma with the image of Our Lady hangs in the Basilica of Our Lady of Guadalupe at Tepeyac. Millions from around the world visit the site every year. Scientific investigations cannot explain the way in which the image is imprinted on the cloth or why the tilma has not decayed more than 480 years later. The Feast of Our Lady of Guadalupe is celebrated on December 12.

Study Corner

DEFINE
Last Judgment
Assumption
infallible
Communion of Saints

REMEMBER
Through Mary we know that those who serve God can look forward to eternal life with him. Mary holds an exalted place in the Communion of Saints.

TAKE IT HOME

Marian Feast Days

Point out that Mary is venerated by people all around the world. Ask young people to select a Marian feast day and either write a one-page report or make a brief video that details the feast. Have volunteers share their reports or videos with the group.

Ask: *What difference does it make to know that someone is sending you good wishes as you take a test, play a game, or do something stressful?* (Possible answer: It can help you do your best and give you confidence.) Have volunteers take turns reading the paragraphs in Communion of Saints. Emphasize that the Communion of Saints refers to all who have been saved, living or dead. Explain that saints are ordinary people who lived extraordinary lives. For canonization to occur, heroic virtue must be proved. Catholic saints are not mystified as godlike; instead their exemplary and holy lives as friends and servants of God make them worthy of his special love. Ask volunteers to tell the significance of November 1 and August 15. (All Saints Day and the Feast of the Assumption) Explain that the Communion of Saints intercedes for us, meaning works on our behalf. Say: *The holy men and women who have died continue to support us in our life of faith and through their intercession.*

Past Meets Present

Read the feature. Ask: *What sign validated Juan Diego's story for the bishop?* (Juan gathered roses that did not grow naturally in his cloak. An image of Our Lady of Guadalupe appeared on his cloak.) Ask: *Where is the cloak today?* (in the Basilica of Our Lady of Guadalupe at Tepeyac.) Point out that devotions to Mary remain popular Catholic practices as we seek her intercession on our behalf.

(3) Close

Say: *Just as Saint Paul called members of the early Christian communities saints, we too are called to be saints and to pray that people will see in us reflections of Jesus and evidence of God's grace.* Ask young people to pray to the saints, just as they would ask a very good friend to pray for them.

Prayer

Follow the steps to guide young people through the prayer on page 208.

Young People's Page

Prepare Pray the prayer in advance to become familiar with it.

Pray Read the title on the page. Ask volunteers to read the paragraphs in the left column. Remind young people that some virtues are gifts from God and others can be acquired by good actions. Refer young people to page 269 in Prayer and Practices and read more about virtues, if desired. Ask volunteers to give examples of situations that require a virtuous response.

Have young people bring their books to the prayer space and sit quietly. Say: *Take a few deep breaths and relax. Be still in God's presence.* Tell young people that you will read the Leader part. Invite the entire group to pray the All parts. Encourage them to reflect on the meaning of the words as they pray them aloud. Pause briefly and begin the prayer, speaking slowly and reverently. Continue to pray aloud, pausing briefly between each part as you alternate between the parts of Leader and All.

At the conclusion, say: *Let's ask God to remember his gifts to us of faith, hope, and love, and to help us acquire other virtues as we strive to grow closer to him.* End by praying together the Sign of the Cross.

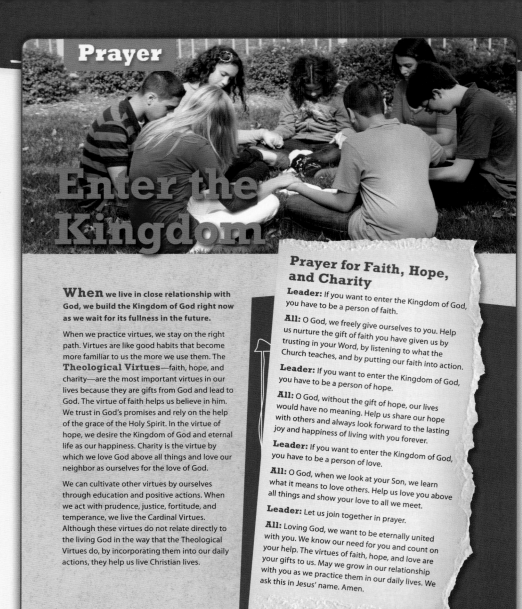

Prayer

Enter the Kingdom

When we live in close relationship with God, we build the Kingdom of God right now as we wait for its fullness in the future.

When we practice virtues, we stay on the right path. Virtues are like good habits that become more familiar to us the more we use them. The **Theological Virtues**—faith, hope, and charity—are the most important virtues in our lives because they are gifts from God and lead to God. The virtue of faith helps us believe in him. We trust in God's promises and rely on the help of the grace of the Holy Spirit. In the virtue of hope, we desire the Kingdom of God and eternal life as our happiness. Charity is the virtue by which we love God above all things and love our neighbor as ourselves for the love of God.

We can cultivate other virtues by ourselves through education and positive actions. When we act with prudence, justice, fortitude, and temperance, we live the Cardinal Virtues. Although these virtues do not relate directly to the living God in the way that the Theological Virtues do, by incorporating them into our daily actions, they help us live Christian lives.

208 *Unit 5 • Jesus Lives On*

Prayer for Faith, Hope, and Charity

Leader: If you want to enter the Kingdom of God, you have to be a person of faith.

All: O God, we freely give ourselves to you. Help us nurture the gift of faith you have given us by trusting in your Word, by listening to what the Church teaches, and by putting our faith into action.

Leader: If you want to enter the Kingdom of God, you have to be a person of hope.

All: O God, without the gift of hope, our lives would have no meaning. Help us share our hope with others and always look forward to the lasting joy and happiness of living with you forever.

Leader: If you want to enter the Kingdom of God, you have to be a person of love.

All: O God, when we look at your Son, we learn what it means to love others. Help us love you above all things and show your love to all we meet.

Leader: Let us join together in prayer.

All: Loving God, we want to be eternally united with you. We know our need for you and count on your help. The virtues of faith, hope, and love are your gifts to us. May we grow in our relationship with you as we practice them in our daily lives. We ask this in Jesus' name. Amen.

IF TIME ALLOWS

Responses

Invite each young person to compose an original response to each Leader part regarding faith, hope, and love. Ask them to follow the same format as the first three All parts, beginning with "O God, ..." At a later date, ask volunteers to write their responses on the board and pray the prayer again as a group, using the new responses.

FYI

Coaching Young People to Pray

Before praying, encourage young people to reflect on their understanding and feelings about faith, hope, and love. Ask them to remember their reflections as a way to make the words of the prayer more meaningful. Allow sufficient time for young people to reflect on the ideas in the prayer about the virtues.

WHERE Do I Fit In?

Jesus made powerful people nervous because he spoke truths that could be hard to hear. His teaching challenged people, institutions, and the status quo. When is it our Christian duty to take a stand against harmful policies?

by Anna Boekstegen

Reflect

Witness for Peace in Haiti

When I was in Haiti in 1993, I experienced how subversive it can be to really live the Gospel message. At that time the Haitian people suffered not only from extreme poverty but also because their hope for democracy had been squashed by a military coup in 1991 against the popular elected president Jean-Bertrand Aristide, a champion of the poor. Aristide was sent into exile, and his followers were persecuted, severely beaten, or killed. Many were no longer able to stay in their own homes for fear of being killed by the Macoutes and Zenglendos in the service of the military. I had learned a lot about Haiti from a friend who had worked in a rural parish in northern Haiti for more than 20 years. She had to leave Haiti when the military took over because of threats to her life.

I wanted to help the Haitian people. When I heard about the Witness for Peace volunteer program through Pax Christi, the national Catholic peace organization, I decided to go. Witness for Peace organized teams of human rights observers to document the abuses and let the world know about them. I was part of a team of three, stationed in Cap Haitien, the second largest city in northern Haiti. We met people who had been severely beaten or were afraid of being killed or abused. The pastors of local parishes told us about their parishioners who were literally hiding in the mountains because they were not safe in their own homes.

ANNA BOEKSTEGEN is a retired French, Latin, and German high school teacher.

One of these pastors was Father Rex. He himself had been threatened and was living in hiding. He saw his ministry in the footsteps of Jesus' teaching. He took seriously his ministry among his poor illiterate parishioners. Father Rex's actions were considered subversive by the military because people started to think for themselves and to organize.

"He has sent me to proclaim liberty to captives
and recovery of sight to the blind,
to let the oppressed go free,
and to proclaim a year acceptable to the Lord."
Luke 4:18–19

As it turns out, in 1994 the United States intervened, and President Aristide was able to return. Did our work of documenting abuses contribute to this outcome? We don't know. Perhaps it did.

Response to Injustice

Look through newspapers or magazines to find articles about social injustice around the world. Work with a partner to choose one situation. Think of a Christian response or solution that imitates the teachings of Jesus, and report your ideas to the group.

IF TIME ALLOWS

Haiti Today

Discuss what young people know about Haiti today. Invite small groups to research the post-1994 history of this small, beleaguered country and to report on current conditions. Encourage them to discover how Catholic Relief Services provides help to nations such as Haiti.

① Begin

Say: *Imagine this. Your parent has just explained that your family will be hosting an exchange student for six months. The student will be given your bedroom, and you will sleep on the couch.* Ask: *How do you feel?* (Answers will vary.) Ask a volunteer to read aloud the introductory text. Ask: *What does status quo mean?* (the way things are) Say: *Human beings like things to stay the same—even when others are in need. Jesus said the "same old same old" is not good enough. He asked us to change it into the Kingdom of God.*

② Connect

Read aloud the first sentence of Witness for Peace in Haiti. Explain that a subversive action or message challenges the status quo. People who subvert the system are often accused of being dangerous or even crazy. In times of fear and desperation, they are sometimes killed—as Jesus was.

Have volunteers take turns reading aloud the remainder of the article. Ask: *If people like the author or Father Rex knew for sure that the status quo would never change, do you think they would stop their efforts? Why?* (Possible answer: No, because individuals might still be helped or saved. They would maintain hope.) Say: *As Christians, it is our duty to continue working for justice even when—or especially when—things seem hopeless.* Invite young people to complete the Response to Injustice activity with a partner.

③ Close

Remind young people that it is our duty to challenge the status quo when people are being hurt or diminished, but that taking subversive actions for their own sake—to feel powerful or to express anger, for example—is never the right thing to do.

① Begin

What's What? Read the directions aloud. Have young people complete the page independently.

② Connect

Say What? Ask volunteers to read aloud and define the terms. Review the terms in the Glossary if necessary.

Now What? Ask a volunteer to read aloud the question. Invite young people to list their ideas independently. Invite volunteers to share their lists.

③ Go in Peace

Collect materials and return them to their appropriate places. Ask: *What are you doing today to prepare for experiencing the Kingdom of God in the future?* Invite young people to ponder this question for a moment and think of one thing they will do this week in response. Encourage them to follow the saints' example of holiness. Invite other ideas that they may use to put a Theological Virtue into practice.

Respond

What's What?

Write the letter of the choice that best matches each clue.

1. __e__ August 15
2. __g__ November 1
3. __h__ December 12
4. __a__ Revelation
5. __d__ the Blessed Mother
6. __b__ John
7. __f__ Communion of Saints
8. __c__ fundamentalists

a. book in the Bible that describes God's triumph over evil (PAGE 204)

b. the author, inspired by the Holy Spirit, of the Book of Revelation (PAGE 204)

c. people who interpret every word in the Bible literally (PAGE 205)

d. assumed into Heaven body and soul (PAGE 206)

e. Feast of the Assumption (PAGE 206)

f. includes all who have been saved in Jesus Christ (PAGE 207)

g. Feast of all Saints (PAGE 207)

h. Feast of Our Lady of Guadalupe (PAGE 207)

Say What?
Know the definitions of these terms.

apocalyptic literature
Assumption
Communion of Saints
infallible
Last Judgment
literary forms
Theological Virtues

Now What?
How can you put a Theological Virtue into practice this week? List your ideas.

Answers will vary.

_____
_____
_____
_____
_____
_____
_____

210 Unit 5 · Jesus Lives On

IF TIME ALLOWS

Service: Fight for Human Rights

In advance, locate articles or resources about Catholic Relief Services. Have young people select a cause about which they feel passionate. Invite them to write a letter that asks for basic human rights to be granted. They might include reasons why they believe a group's rights are being violated. Have young people share their letters with their parents and mail them from home.

✝ *Rights and Responsibilities*

Session Assessment Option

An assessment for this session can be found at www.findinggod.com.

3-Minute Retreat
Give young people an opportunity for quiet meditation at **www.loyolapress.com/retreat**.

PLAN AHEAD: Get Ready for Session 25

Consult the catechist preparation pages to prepare for Session 25 and determine any materials you will need.

Celebrating Pentecost

 3-Minute Retreat

Before you prepare the session, pause and be still. Take three deep breaths and be aware of the loving presence of God, who is with you on this journey.

Romans 8:26–27

In the same way, the Spirit too comes to the aid of our weakness; for we do not know how to pray as we ought, but the Spirit itself intercedes with inexpressible groanings. And the one who searches hearts knows what is the intention of the Spirit, because it intercedes for the holy ones according to God's will.

Reflection

Those who remember September 11, 2001, also remember the outpouring of prayer around the world. At that time, no one said that people did not know how to pray. But as we develop the habit of prayer on a regular basis, we can find ourselves hesitating, unsure what to say or do next. The apostle Paul understands these feelings of uncertainty and helplessness. And just as he assures the Church in Rome to whom he was writing, he assures us as well of the ongoing presence of the Holy Spirit, who knows our heart better than we do. So we place our trust in him, who will never lead us astray.

Questions

What steps can I take in prayer to rest in the Holy Spirit? What needs can I turn over to the Holy Spirit?

 Concluding Prayer

Speak to God, using the words of this prayer or your own.

God the Father, Son, and Holy Spirit, thank you for the life you share with me. Help me respond to your ever-present grace, that I may know, love, and serve you.

Knowing and Sharing Your Faith in Session 25

Consider how Scripture and Tradition can deepen your understanding of session content.

Scripture

John 14:26 records Jesus' comforting words to the Apostles, giving his assurance that the Holy Spirit would teach them and remind them of his Word.

1 John 5:6 tells us that the Spirit helps us bear witness: "The Spirit is the one that testifies, and the Spirit is truth."

Tradition

Realizing that prayer is not always easy, Saint Paul offered some advice in his Letter to the Romans, writing, "[T]he Spirit too comes to the aid of our weakness; for we do not know how to pray as we ought, but the Spirit itself intercedes with inexpressible groanings." [Romans 8:26] On the Feast of Pentecost, the Holy Spirit not only helped the disciples recall everything that Jesus said but also formed them in a life of prayer. Every time we pray, it is the Spirit who draws us on the way of prayer. The Holy Spirit, the artisan of God's works, is the master of prayer. [CCC 741] The Holy Spirit teaches us, the children of God, to pray in a manner in which the Church prays.

Catholic Social Teaching

In this session the integrated Catholic Social Teaching theme is **Call to Family, Community, and Participation.** See page 177b for an explanation of this theme.

Window on the Catechism

The role of the Holy Spirit in prayer is discussed in *CCC* 2623–2625 and 2670–2672.

General Directory for Catechesis

The role of the Holy Spirit in the work of Salvation is articulated in *GDC* 34, 37, and 42–45.

One-Hour Session Planner

SESSION 25 Celebrating Pentecost

Session Theme: *The Church began with the sending of the Holy Spirit on Pentecost. We serve the Kingdom of God when we use the Gifts of the Holy Spirit.*

Before This Session

▶ Display the *Finding God* poster The Liturgical Year.

▶ Determine whether you will use the Unit Assessment option listed on page 218.

▶ Determine whether you will also discuss the Pentecost seasonal pages in the back of the Young People's Book.

▶ Bookmark your Bible to John 14:18, John 14:26, Acts of the Apostles 2:2–3, Acts of the Apostles 17:28, and Galatians 5:22–23. Place the open Bible in your prayer space.

▶ Read the Guide for this session, choose any additional If Time Allows activities that you might have time to complete, and gather the listed materials.

STEPS	APPROXIMATE TIME
Engage *Celebrating Pentecost* PAGE 211	10 minutes
Explore *The Holy Spirit Guides the Church* PAGES 212–213 *The Holy Spirit Makes Us Holy* PAGES 214–215	30–40 minutes
Reflect *Prayer:* Gifts of the Spirit PAGE 216 *Where Do I Fit In?* PAGE 217	10–15 minutes
Respond *What's What?* PAGE 218	10–15 minutes

Materials

REQUIRED

▶ *Finding God* poster: The Liturgical Year (page 211)

▶ Compass, bowl of water, plastic lid, long magnet (page 212)

▶ Bible (page 213)

▶ Writing supplies (pages 213, 218)

▶ Computers with Internet access (page 218)

OPTIONAL

▶ Construction paper, glue, thick black marker, magazines (page 211)

▶ Session 25 BLM, T-385 (page 213)

▶ Writing supplies (pages 213, 217)

▶ Long pieces of rope, eye coverings, cards with the names of shapes (page 214)

▶ Art supplies (page 218)

▶ Session 25 Assessment, www.findinggod.com (page 218)

▶ Unit 5 Assessment, T-386–T-388 (page 218)

Prayer in Session 25

Join young people in praying a short opening prayer. Invite them to experience an online 3-Minute Retreat on a Scripture verse at the end of the session. In Session 25 young people offer prayers of petition to the Holy Spirit and pray Saint Augustine's Prayer to the Holy Spirit. Follow the Prepare directions on the Catechist Guide page before sharing with young people.

TAKE IT HOME

Homework options:

Ways to Be an Advocate PAGE 212

Hidden Meanings PAGE 215

Session 25

Celebrating Pentecost

THE feast of Pentecost is celebrated 50 days after Easter Sunday. It commemorates the day the Holy Spirit, sent by God, entered the Apostles' hearts and filled them with the strength and courage they needed to do God's work. We celebrate the gift of the Holy Spirit's presence among us on Pentecost.

In the Acts of the Apostles, we read that after Jesus ascended to Heaven, the Apostles gathered together in a house. Suddenly, what appeared to be tongues of fire touched each of them. Filled with the Holy Spirit, they began to speak, and a crowd gathered outside the house. Members of the crowd, who represented many different nations, heard the Apostles speaking in their own language.

The Apostles, inspired by the Holy Spirit, began doing the work of the Church, calling the whole world to faith in Jesus. It took great courage and perseverance to act as witnesses to Jesus Christ, but the Good News eventually spread throughout the Roman Empire. With guidance from the Holy Spirit, the first Christian community grew.

Today, the Holy Spirit continues to inspire us to live our faith and carry out the mission of the Apostles—to spread Christianity throughout the world. The Holy Spirit makes us holy and helps us grow more like Christ as we act as his witnesses in the world.

When have you faced a big challenge and felt hesitant or afraid to take action? Where did you find the strength and courage to do what you knew had to be done? How did you recognize the Holy Spirit's presence?

PRAYER

Thank you, Holy Spirit, for your gifts of courage and strength so I may live out my faith as a true witness of Christ.

211

SESSION 25

OUTCOMES

▶ Explain that God sent the Holy Spirit on Pentecost to fill the Apostles with the courage to spread the Good News.

▶ Identify the Gifts of the Holy Spirit as ways to grow in holiness.

▶ Offer prayers of petition to the Holy Spirit.

▶ Define *Paraclete*.

① Set the Stage

Read aloud the questions in the box. Have young people write their responses. Invite volunteers to share their experiences. Display the *Finding God* poster The Liturgical Year. Have young people turn to page 222 and read the paragraph about Pentecost.

② Get Started

Invite volunteers to share anything they know about sailing. Point out that a sailboat has no engine, so it relies on the force of the wind to move through water. Without wind, the sailboat would sit still in the water. Say: ***Today we're going to talk about a special kind of force that directs our lives and moves us in the right direction.*** Read aloud the session title and explain that the Holy Spirit moves through us and inspires us to do God's work.

Have volunteers read the page. Say: ***Just as the Holy Spirit filled the Apostles' hearts with the strength and courage needed to do God's work, so may our hearts be filled to live out our faith and carry out God's mission.***

 Prayer

Say: ***Let's join together in prayer to ask God to be with us during Pentecost.*** Pray the prayer together. Conclude by praying the Sign of the Cross.

IF TIME ALLOWS

Collage Action

Arrange young people into groups of four or five. Give each group a large sheet of construction paper, glue, and a thick black marker. Distribute magazines to each group. Have them name one way the Holy Spirit makes them holy and ask them to make a collage that illustrates the idea. Have them write a title on the collage as part of the design. Display the completed projects.

INCLUSION

Autism Spectrum

Picture This For young people with autism-spectrum disorders, take photos to illustrate key vocabulary words and concepts in this session. Introduce each word and concept. Explain each meaning and allow time for questions. Arrange the photos on poster board according to their order of appearance. Invite young people to refer to the board as needed.

 Go to **www.findinggod.com/sessionextenders** for symbols of the Holy Spirit. You may wish to share this with the group.

1 Begin

Bring in a compass to show young people. Encourage discussion about what a compass is and what it does. Then say: **A compass needle always points north because of the magnetic pull of the earth.** Explain that sailors used to make their own compasses before ones like these were developed in the 16th century. Say: **Sailors would float a small piece of wood in a bowl of water and place a magnetized metal object on top of the wood, so that the wood would always point north.** If possible, demonstrate by using a bowl of water, a plastic lid, in place of wood, and a long magnet. When finished, tell young people that to guide us in our spiritual lives, Jesus and the Father sent the Holy Spirit so that we wouldn't get lost.

2 Connect

Read aloud the title. Invite volunteers to read aloud the opening paragraphs. Ask: **Have you ever had the awful feeling that something bad was going to happen? About what were you worried?** (Answers will vary.) Say: **The Apostles had turned their lives over to Jesus. Suddenly they found themselves faced with the thought of losing him.** Explain that they were at a loss as to what to do. Ask: **What emotions do you think they were feeling?** (Answers will vary.) Write responses on the board. Discuss people who act as advocates and what they do. Relate the discussion to the Holy Spirit.

 Have a volunteer read the section The Spirit. Say: **God understood how the Apostles felt.** With an eraser, wipe away the responses you had written on the board as you say: **The Holy Spirit wiped away all their fears. He filled them with the courage and faith they needed to continue Jesus' work.** Ask: **Who continues the work of the Apostles today?** (the bishops)

The Holy Spirit Guides the Church

TIMES of change occur throughout your life, sometimes in rhythmic patterns just like the seasons. A school season begins, breaks, resumes, and ends. You may experience times of change in sports, entertainment, or family matters.

The Church celebrates seasons too. On the first Sunday of Advent, we celebrate the beginning of the Church year, remembering how God's people yearned for a Messiah. During the Christmas season, we celebrate the birth of Jesus, who is the fulfillment of God's promise to send a Savior. The Easter season is a 50-day celebration of the Resurrection of Jesus.

The Easter season comes to a close on the Feast of Pentecost, when we mark the beginning of the Church instituted by Jesus Christ. On this day we remember how a group of Jesus' followers, afraid and huddled together in a room, were filled with the Holy Spirit. The Spirit's coming fulfilled Jesus' promise that the Father would send them an Advocate, one who would be with them always.

On the night before he died, Jesus made a promise to the Apostles. Jesus knew they were worried about what would happen to them if he was arrested, or worse, put to death. The Apostles wondered what life would be like without Jesus there to lead them. Would he be completely gone from their lives after his Death and remain only as a mystery? They had followed Jesus and watched as he fed the hungry crowds, healed the sick, and walked on water. They listened as he spoke of his loving Father and described himself as the Good Shepherd. But now this life seemed to be coming to an end.

The Spirit

John's Gospel tells how Jesus spoke to the Apostles and calmed their worried hearts. He promised, "I will not leave you orphans; I will come to you. (John 14:18) Jesus explained, "The Advocate, the holy Spirit that the Father will send in my name—he will teach you everything and remind you of all that [I] told you." (John 14:26) This gift of the Holy Spirit would be another sign of the Father's love for them, just as the gift of the Son had been.

On the Jewish harvest feast of Pentecost, the Father sent the **Paraclete,** another name for the Holy Spirit. *Paraclete* is a Greek word that means "one who consoles or comforts, one who encourages or uplifts." Jesus kept his promise—the Spirit would remain with them and also with all of those who had come to believe, not just a chosen few.

The Holy Spirit would teach them everything, remind them of all that Jesus had said to them, and help them understand more fully Jesus Christ, the Messiah. With the inspiration of the Holy Spirit, the Apostles would continue Jesus' teaching through their preaching, writing, and actions. The successors of the Apostles, the bishops of the Church, continue this task for all generations until Jesus returns in glory. The mission of the bishops comes from the Holy Spirit in union with the Father and the Son.

212 *Unit 5 · Jesus Lives On*

TAKE IT HOME

Ways to Be an Advocate

Distribute sheets of paper to young people and tell them to write the phrase *Ways to Be an Advocate* at the top. Then instruct them to take the paper home and ask at least five friends and family members to each write one example of a way to be an advocate. Ask young people to decorate the paper and display it in a prominent spot in their homes. Encourage them to look at the paper every day to gain inspiration on new ways they can become Jesus' advocate.

SEASONAL SESSION

Pentecost

Work with young people through pages 243–246 to learn more about Pentecost. This special session can take up to one hour to complete.

Spirit Alive

The Holy Spirit is at the center of our lives, ready to motivate us at every moment to grow in holiness. When we allow ourselves to be led by the Holy Spirit, we are led by a God of strength and light. With this guidance, we will not go astray. The Holy Spirit helps us discern between good and evil and enlivens our lives of prayer. When we celebrate the sacraments, we are saved through the grace of the Holy Spirit.

In the Holy Spirit, we have a sure guide in our relationship with God and others. The Holy Spirit can help us live close to God and in loving relationship with those around us. We can pray the prayer of Saint John Vianney: "O God, send me thy Spirit to teach me what I am and what thou art."

Open Your Heart

To be open to the Holy Spirit means to allow him to enter into your life. Through prayer, the Holy Spirit teaches you to recognize and follow God's will. Whenever you pray the Lord's Prayer and say the words "thy will be done," you are practicing this openness. To be open to the Holy Spirit is to let go of your own willfulness. It means trusting in God's will, listening for what God wants you to do with your life, and learning how to make good choices.

What Is Truth?

Jesus promised to send the Spirit of truth. In Jesus' time there were two ways to talk about truth—the Hebrew way found in the Old Testament and the Greek way that would be reflected in the New Testament. The Hebrew view of truth was based on the reliability of the person speaking and that person's faithfulness to a relationship. This is what we mean when we say someone is true to his or her friends. The Greek view of truth was based on the reliability of the message. This is what we mean when we say that something is true or false.

The Holy Spirit is a spirit of truth in both senses. The Spirit represents God's faithfulness in love and what it means to live in a right relationship with God and others. Guided by the Holy Spirit, we are able to know the truth and be true to our calling.

Study Corner

DEFINE

Paraclete

REMEMBER

God fulfilled Jesus' promise to the Apostles by sending the Holy Spirit. They were filled with the faith and courage needed to spread his Word. Today we celebrate the strength given to us by the Holy Spirit when we live faithfully as Jesus' followers.

Explore

SACRED ART

The Holy Spirit is commonly portrayed in four ways: as fire, wind, water, and a dove. Fire represents the transforming strength and force of the Holy Spirit. Wind symbolizes the breath of God breathing new life into the Church. Water represents the cleansing and life-giving gift of Baptism. In this oil-on-copper artwork, Hans Rottenhammer shows the Holy Spirit, portrayed as a dove, descending on the Apostles.

The Descent of the Holy Spirit,
Hans Rottenhammer I, 1594–95.

Session 25 > Celebrating Pentecost **213**

IF TIME ALLOWS

Session 25 BLM

Symbols of the Holy Spirit Ask young people to work with a partner. Distribute Bibles and ask them to work together to complete the Session 25 Blackline Master [T-385].

Open Your Heart

Give one volunteer a folded sheet of paper with the sentence, "Today I want to open my heart and receive the Holy Spirit" written on it. Instruct the volunteer to whisper aloud the words when the group begins clapping. To the group, say: **When I say "go," clap your hands. Don't stop until I wave my hands over my head.** Pause and say: **Go!** After 30 seconds, wave your hands over your head, signaling young people to stop clapping. Ask: **Did anyone hear what [Name] read aloud?** Invite volunteers to respond. Explain how difficult it can be to concentrate on something when noise surrounds you. Say: **Something similar happens when we pray. The noise of the world can crowd our focus.** Point out that learning to meditate and contemplate can make our time in prayer more effective.

Have a volunteer read Spirit Alive. Ask: **How does the Holy Spirit help us when we allow him to lead us?** (The Holy Spirit helps us distinguish between good and evil, between what is true and what is false, and enlivens our lives.)

Invite a volunteer to read aloud Open Your Heart. Ask: **How can we be open to the Holy Spirit?** (praying the Lord's Prayer, letting go of what we want and trusting in God's will for us, celebrating the sacraments)

Have a volunteer read aloud What Is Truth? Say: **Let us keep our hearts open to the Holy Spirit in our lives so he may help us know the truth and be true to our calling.**

Sacred Art

Read aloud the feature. Discuss how helpful the use of symbols can be. Ask young people to close their eyes and picture the Holy Spirit. Then ask them to picture Jesus. Remark that they probably had an easier time picturing Jesus. Explain that because Jesus had a human nature, artists throughout the ages have portrayed his image in art.

Say: **The Holy Spirit did not take human form. Some people find it difficult to picture the Holy Spirit.** In Scripture, Mark 1:10 describes the Spirit coming like a dove to Jesus during his baptism. Acts of the Apostles 2:2–3 describes the Spirit as a wind and as tongues of fire.

(3) Close

Ask young people to consider how they can keep their hearts open to the Holy Spirit. Invite them to reflect on issues or concerns with which they want to pray to the Holy Spirit for guidance. Remind them that the Holy Spirit is always present. Invite them to write a short prayer to the Holy Spirit.

① Begin

Ask: *What do people mean when, referring to a favorite team, they say that their team "rules"?* (It is the best. It is dominant.) Arrange young people into groups of three or four and have them make a list of individuals or teams that they believe "rule" in categories such as TV drama, TV comedy, rock star, rock band, soft drink, and athlete. When they're finished, invite groups to share their lists. Then say: *When we pray, the Holy Spirit rules. He teaches us how to pray in many different ways.*

② Connect

Have a volunteer read aloud the title and the first two paragraphs. Say: *Pentecost is the birthday of the Church. We can continue the work begun by the Apostles when we develop our own relationship with God through prayer.*

Ask volunteers to read aloud the section The Spirit: Our Teacher in Prayer. Say: *There is no wrong way to pray. The Holy Spirit enables us to have a direct conversation with God.* Explain that it does not matter what words they use or where they happen to be at the moment. They are always able to pray to God and have their prayers heard. Discuss the key ideas that are in bold at the beginning of each paragraph.

Invite a volunteer to read aloud the section You Are Not Alone. Draw on the board a silhouette of an empty cup. Say: *We are like this empty cup.* Draw a shelf or ledge underneath the cup. Say: *The Holy Spirit is like this shelf. He is always there and ready to support us.* Then shade in the cup to show it completely full. Say: *God fills us with the Holy Spirit. He nourishes all our needs and lets us know we'll never be alone.*

The Holy Spirit Makes Us Holy

THE Church began with the sending of the Holy Spirit on Pentecost. The Apostles were given the courage to proclaim the Good News of Jesus and the strength to face the challenge of carrying that message throughout the world.

One central part of Jesus' message that the Apostles proclaimed was that God wants to be close to us. By guiding us in prayer, the Holy Spirit helps us grow closer to God. When we are open to the Spirit's promptings, we grow in holiness and become more like Christ.

The Spirit: Our Teacher in Prayer

A key element of holiness is to develop lifelong habits of prayer, and the Holy Spirit leads the way.

God started it. The first thing to know about prayer is that, whether we recognize it or not, our prayer is always a response to God's initiative. In our relationship with God, it is always God who makes the first move. God created us, and the Holy Spirit is always inviting us to a deeper relationship with him.

You've already got God's attention. We don't pray to get God's attention. In fact, God is actively seeking to get *our* attention. Praying will help us notice the many ways God is reaching out to us, inviting us into a lifelong conversation.

Prayer doesn't change God; prayer changes us. When we are young, a lot of our prayer may be an attempt to persuade God to give us something we want or to influence the outcome of a situation. As we grow in the Spirit, we realize that prayer helps us know God's will and gives us the strength and wisdom to align our lives with that will.

It's about relationship. The best reason to pray is simply because we love God, and the optimal outcome of our praying is to grow in that love. When we pray, the Holy Spirit fills our hearts with divine life and love. We lift our minds and hearts to God.

You Are Not Alone

We can quickly become discouraged if we think that we alone are responsible for our prayer. Prayer comes from the Holy Spirit, not just from us. In the Gospel of John, we learn that the Advocate will teach us what we need to know. Every time we pray, it is the Holy Spirit who teaches us the way. The Holy Spirit is present in our prayer and makes it not just human prayer but divine prayer.

We have an emptiness inside us that only God can fill. What fills us is the Holy Spirit. The Holy Spirit is the living breath of our prayer. The Spirit is given to the Church so that through his power, the whole community of the People of God, even though living in diverse circumstances all over the world, might persevere in the hope in which we have been saved.

214 *Unit 5 • Jesus Lives On*

 ADVENTURES IN FAITH

Hidden Polygon

Provide a large rope for every six to eight young people. A cotton clothesline will work. Also provide some type of eye coverings or blindfolds and cards with words that name different shapes [square, triangle, octagon, and so on]. Clear away desks and chairs. Tell group members to put on their eye coverings and keep at least on hand on the rope. Explain that the goal is to make a shape with the rope without looking at the rope or what they're doing. Instruct them that the first shape they need to make is a circle. Once they think they've made a circle, they can open their eyes and look. Then hand out the cards to each group. Groups are to make the shapes one at time at their own pace.

Once all groups have completed the task, ask: *How did you communicate while doing this exercise? What worked? What didn't?* Allow several responses. Explain to young people that doing things with their eyes closed can be very difficult. Point out that praying can be challenging sometimes—they may feel as if they're stumbling in the dark without any guidance. Explain that the Holy Spirit opens their eyes and guides them through prayer.

Gifts to Grow in Holiness

The Holy Spirit gives us seven gifts that prepare us to discover God's will for us and follow it throughout our lives. These Gifts of the Holy Spirit play an important role in all areas of our lives—at home, at school, in our worship, and even in our leisure activities. Think of how you experience these gifts in your own life. Ask the Holy Spirit to help you use the gifts to grow closer to God.

Wisdom

Wisdom helps us see as God sees. It helps us put God at the heart of our lives and love the things that God loves. Wisdom gives us the ability to know the real value of people and things.

Understanding

Understanding helps us open our eyes to the beauty, wisdom, and truth of our Catholic faith. Understanding helps us live our faith each day.

Counsel (Right Judgment)

Counsel helps us make good decisions in life. This gift helps us discern right from wrong and reminds us to seek good advice from others who are trustworthy guides. Counsel also helps us advise others.

Fortitude (Courage)

Fortitude is the courage to do what is right. Fortitude gives us the strength to follow God's will when we are tempted to take another path.

Knowledge

Knowledge is knowing the truth about God, about faith, and about the world.

Piety (Reverence)

Piety is also known as reverence. This gift of the Spirit helps us treat the people, places, and things in our life with reverence and respect because everything is a gift from God. Expressing our gratitude to God in prayer is a way of practicing piety.

Fear of the Lord
(Wonder and Awe in God's Presence)

This gift helps us appreciate the gift of life and God, the giver of life. It helps us remain aware that God is the Creator of everything that is.

Our Catholic Character

The Holy Spirit comes to us in Baptism and strengthens us in the Sacrament of Confirmation. Confirmation ties us more closely to the Body of Christ. It makes our link to the Church stronger and involves us more closely in the Church's mission. We become better witnesses to the Christian faith in the things we say and do.

In Confirmation we are charged with helping the Church carry out its mission. Jesus proclaimed the Kingdom of God and gave us a glimpse of that world by curing the sick, raising the dead to life, and caring for the poor. We gain the vision of the kind of world God wants us to have. The Holy Spirit inspires us to dream God's dream. Guided by the Holy Spirit, we work to bring about that dream by serving God's kingdom.

Study Corner

REMEMBER

The Holy Spirit is present in our prayers. We serve the Kingdom of God and grow in holiness when we use gifts received from the Holy Spirit.

Explore

Session 25 > Celebrating Pentecost **215**

TAKE IT HOME

Hidden Meanings

Write on the board this ancient proverb:

To know, but not to do, is not yet to know.

Ask young people to write the proverb on a sheet of paper and summarize what they think it means. (To truly know something means to act on it.) Invite young people to involve themselves more fully in prayer, always giving it 100 percent of their attention. Instruct young people to find and read Matthew 2:28–32. Ask them to explain the proverb and relate it in some way to Jesus' parable of the two sons. (Saying that you are a follower of Jesus without acting like one is pointless.)

Say: **The Holy Spirit gives us seven gifts that help us follow God and do what he asks of us. The Holy Spirit is our constant help.** Have volunteers take turns reading aloud Gifts to Grow in Holiness. Review the seven Gifts of the Holy Spirit and explain them as needed. Ask: **When might these gifts be necessary in life?** Have volunteers share their responses. As an extension, refer young people to the sections about the Gifts and the Fruits of the Holy Spirit in Prayers and Practices on page 269. Say: **The Gifts of the Holy Spirit help us become holy. The next time you are in need of the help of the Holy Spirit, you can pray for the grace of one of these gifts. Remember the Holy Spirit is always with us. We just need to open our hearts to accept his help in our lives.**

Our Catholic Character

Read the feature. Remind young people that many people receive the grace of Baptism as an infant; it is a decision made for them by someone else. Explain that as they grow older, they become more responsible for doing the work of the Body of Christ. The Sacrament of Confirmation gives them gifts to go into the world and make the vision of the Kingdom of God on earth a reality.

③ Close

Congratulate young people for participating in their own faith life by taking actions to grow closer to God. Explain that they're more aware of their relationship with God in prayer. With faith and practice, they will continue to grow in their ability to pray. Say: **Make prayer a habit and a priority in your life, asking the Holy Spirit to support and guide you.**

Prayer

Follow the steps to guide young people through the prayer on page 216.

Young People's Page

Prepare Pray the prayer in advance to become familiar with it.

Pray Ask a volunteer to read aloud the title of the page and the paragraphs. Explain that Saint John Vianney is the patron saint of priests. He had to overcome many challenges before becoming a priest, but he never gave up. Ask young people to reflect on or share aloud experiences when they felt like giving up. Ask: **Where did you get the strength to continue?** Ask volunteers to explain Saint John Vianney's quotation about private prayer and public prayer.

Invite young people to the prayer space. Ask them to quiet themselves and get into a comfortable position. Say: **No one goes through life without needing help. Let's pray to the Holy Spirit with humble hearts for guidance and help on our faith journeys.** Explain that petitions are prayerful requests. Point out that you will begin a petition, and they will complete it by praying aloud the words in each All part. Pray together the Lord's Prayer. Prompt young people to pray aloud the All part. Pray aloud the first petition, prompting everyone to complete the petition by praying aloud the All part. Pause briefly between each petition to allow time for meditation. When all petitions have been read, conclude by praying together Saint Augustine's Prayer to the Holy Spirit.

Prayer

Gifts of the Spirit

Saint John Vianney overcame many obstacles to become a priest. Guided by the Spirit, he had strength and vision to keep going.

Saint John Vianney encouraged liturgical prayer. He said, "Private prayer is like straw scattered here and there: If you set it on fire it makes a lot of little flames. But gather these straws into a bundle and light them, and you get a mighty fire, rising like a column into the sky; public prayer is like that."

Petitions to the Holy Spirit

Leader: Let us pray together the Lord's Prayer.

All: O God, send me your Spirit, to teach me what I am and who you are.

Leader: O God, send me your Spirit of Wisdom . . .

All: . . . to teach me to see the world as you see it and to know that you are the God who guides me.

Leader: O God, send me your Spirit of Understanding . . .

All: . . . to teach me to perceive your ways and to recognize that you are the God of Truth.

Leader: O God, send me your Spirit of Counsel . . .

All: . . . to teach me to seek advice and be open to our will and to believe that you are the God who calls me.

Leader: O God, send me your Spirit of Knowledge . . .

All: . . . to teach me to understand the truths of the universe and to know that you are the God who always stands ready to help me.

Leader: O God, send me your Spirit of Fortitude . . .

All: . . . to teach me what is right in the face of difficulties and to know that you are the God who strengthens me.

Leader: O God, send me your Spirit of Piety . . .

All: . . . to teach me to love and worship you and all that you created and to know that you are the God who is always present.

Leader: O God, send me your Spirit of Fear of the Lord . . .

All: . . . to teach me to recognize your glory and my dependence on you as the God of love.

Conclude with Saint Augustine's Prayer to the Holy Spirit.

Breathe in me, O Holy Spirit,
That my thoughts may all be holy.

Act in me, O Holy Spirit,
That my work, too, may all be holy.

Draw my heart, O Holy Spirit,
That I love but what is holy.

Strengthen me, O Holy Spirit,
To defend all that is holy.

Guard me, then, O Holy Spirit,
That I always may be holy.

216 *Unit 5 • Jesus Lives On*

IF TIME ALLOWS

I'll Have the . . .

Ask young people where they would go to lunch if they had an option. Discuss their responses. Point out that they have the option to make a choice. Explain that young people have a choice whether or not to accept the Gifts of the Holy Spirit. Remind them that these gifts are offered to them with love and are available to accept at any time.

FYI

Coaching Young People to Pray

Before praying, remind young people that no matter how they pray, they are in the presence of God. Encourage them to pay close attention to the meaning of the words in their prayers, as they are praying heart to heart with God who loves them.

WHERE Do I Fit In?

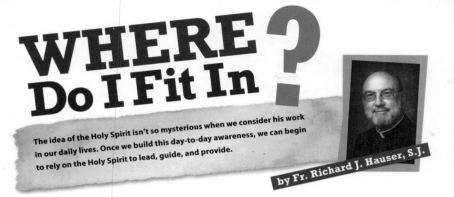

The idea of the Holy Spirit isn't so mysterious when we consider his work in our daily lives. Once we build this day-to-day awareness, we can begin to rely on the Holy Spirit to lead, guide, and provide.

by Fr. Richard J. Hauser, S.J.

Reflect

Counting on the Holy Spirit

All my life I said the words in the Creed each Sunday: "I believe in the Holy Spirit, the Lord, the giver of life." It wasn't until I was in my 30s that I had any idea of any specific effects of the Holy Spirit in my life. I could recite the seven Gifts of the Spirit: wisdom, understanding, counsel, knowledge, fortitude, piety, and fear of the Lord. But these were just words for me with no reference to my life.

So what happened? Very simply, I began taking seriously what the New Testament says about the Holy Spirit. I was struck by Saint Paul's assertion in his Letter to the Galatians: "[T]he fruit of the Spirit is love, joy, peace, patience, kindness, generosity, faithfulness, gentleness, self-control." (Galatians 5:22–23)

I realized that I was experiencing the "fruit of the Spirit" when I was loving, joyful, and peaceful. The realization was incredible. All my life I had mistakenly assumed the Spirit was present only during times I was praying. I assumed God had nothing to do with my other activities since they were merely "secular" and not "holy."

I began to realize that all the treasured relationships of my life are the "fruit of the Spirit." To my surprise, the richest experiences of my life turned out to be God moments!

And the special guidance and strength that gets me through tough times also comes from the Gifts of the Spirit—wisdom, understanding, knowledge, and fortitude!

Even my ability to love my neighbor as I love myself—especially my most needy neighbors— is a Gift of the Spirit!

And on and on.

Being a Christian means to live in God. "For 'In him we live and move and have our being.'" (Acts of the Apostles 17:28)

In short, I count on the Spirit every day of my life. I can't imagine my life without God's presence.

With Us and For Us

On a separate sheet of paper, make a list of the Fruits of the Holy Spirit, leaving space between each word. Challenge yourself to identify a situation in which you received each fruit in the last 24 hours. Write a brief description of each situation. Pray a silent prayer thanking the Holy Spirit for his presence in your life.

FR. RICHARD J. HAUSER, S.J., is a professor of theology and the director of graduate programs in theology, ministry, and spirituality as well as the rector of the Jesuit Community at Creighton University. He is the author of *In His Spirit* and *Moving in the Spirit*.

IF TIME ALLOWS

Acrostic Poem

Have young people create an acrostic poem by writing *HOLY SPIRIT* down the left side of a sheet of paper and then using each letter to begin a phrase that names an everyday object or experience through which the Holy Spirit can be experienced. Explain that the more "secular" their descriptions, the better, since God can be found even in a really good cup of hot chocolate.

1 Begin

Have a volunteer read aloud the introductory text. Invite young people to describe experiences they believe involved the workings of the Holy Spirit. Next, ask them to describe experiences in which they felt joy or received a perfect, unexpected gift. Say: **Once you start recognizing the Gifts of the Holy Spirit, these gifts will multiply. You'll be drawn ever closer to God.**

2 Connect

Read aloud the title and have volunteers take turns reading aloud the article. After the third paragraph, discuss the term *secular*. Explain that this word is normally used to describe activities and attitudes that are devoid of religious elements; for example, a secular wedding ceremony does not include prayers. Say: **As we know from experience, many people live their lives with a secular worldview with no reference to God or who believe that Christian life has nothing to offer them. As Catholics, we realize that they are depriving themselves of the grace God is offering them to live holy lives. We can take every opportunity to pray for them as they are loved by God.** After volunteers finish reading the article, direct their attention to the last line. Say: **An oxymoron is an idea that contradicts itself. Why is the idea of "life without God's presence" an oxymoron?** (Without God's presence, there would be no life at all.)

Have young people complete the With Us and For Us activity independently. Then ask them to share at least one situation.

3 Close

Point out that fruit contains seeds. When we experience the Fruits of the Holy Spirit in our daily lives, we are given seeds of God's love to plant in the lives of others.

① Begin

What's What? Have a volunteer read aloud the directions. Invite young people to complete the activity independently at home or with a partner in the group.

② Connect

Say What? Ask a volunteer to read aloud and define the word. Review the word in the Glossary if necessary.

Now What? Read aloud the section. Encourage young people to remember the Holy Spirit is with them. Ask them to recognize that God invites them to accept the challenges of living a Christian life. Encourage them to reflect on this idea before they write their prayers. Invite volunteers to share their prayers with the group.

③ Go in Peace

Collect materials and return them to their appropriate places. Encourage young people to read their prayers during the week. Ask: *How can you use your prayer to grow stronger in faith?* Invite young people to add new lines to their prayers and to pray them often. Say: *Making prayer a habit helps bring the Spirit alive in your life. Then you can be moved to take action to live out Christian values with courage and service to others.*

3-Minute Retreat
Give young people an opportunity for quiet meditation at **www.loyolapress.com/retreat**.

Respond

What's What?

Complete each sentence using details from the text.

1. On the Feast of Pentecost, we mark the beginning of the _____ . (PAGE 212)
   Church

2. Jesus promised that the Father would send an _____ , one who would be with them always. (PAGE 212)
   Advocate

3. With the inspiration of the _____ , the Apostles would continue Jesus' teaching through their preaching, writing, and actions. (PAGE 212)
   Holy Spirit

4. Four common symbols for the Holy Spirit are fire, wind, water, and _____ . (PAGE 213)
   a dove

5. Our _____ is always a response to God's initiative. (PAGE 214)
   prayer

6. The Holy Spirit is the _____ of our prayer. (PAGE 214)
   living breath

7. The Holy Spirit gives us _____ gifts that prepare us to discover God's will for us and follow it throughout our lives. (PAGE 215)
   seven

8. The gifts of the Holy Spirit are _____ . (PAGE 215)
   wisdom
   understanding
   counsel
   fortitude
   knowledge
   piety
   fear of the Lord

Say What?
Know the definition of this term.
Paraclete

Now What?
On the lines below, write your own prayer to the Holy Spirit. Ask for help and guidance to be Christ's witness in the world.

_____
_____
_____
_____
_____
_____
_____
_____
_____
_____
_____
_____
_____

218 Unit 5 • Jesus Lives On

IF TIME ALLOWS

Service: Thank-you Cards
Ask young people to design thank-you cards for someone in their community, such as a crossing guard, firefighter, coach, or school nurse. Encourage them to be specific when writing the reasons why they are thankful. Have young people mail or deliver the cards.

✝ *Family and Community*

Session Assessment Option
An assessment for this session can be found at www.findinggod.com.

Unit Assessment Option
If you wish, photocopy the Unit Assessment on pages T-386–T-388. Administer the assessment during the session or send it home.

Faith in ACTION
Unit 5

Many times the values of our Catholic faith clash with society's values. Discipleship requires that we apply Catholic Social Teaching to the issues of our time. These teachings guide our consciences and help us show our love for the world.

In this unit we explored how Jesus, who "came from the Father," returned to the Father in Ascension. After Jesus' Ascension, the Apostles, guided by the Holy Spirit, became witnesses of the Kingdom of God and spread Jesus' Word to the nations. We learned that the apostle Paul was the greatest of the early Christian missionaries, and we explored our call to eternal life. In his life and teaching, Jesus showed his care for humankind and all creation. Here are some ideas to get involved in nature as a way of proclaiming Jesus to the world.

"Judge each day not by the harvest you reap but by the seeds you plant."

—Robert Louis Stevenson, novelist, poet, and travel writer

Plant Seeds

Purpose
Learn about the process of a seed taking root. Plant seeds of flowers or herbs that can be given to others as gifts.

Background
Paul teaches us that we must be generous in sowing the seeds of God's message in our world. (2 Corinthians 9:6) One way to sow the seed of God's message is to plant flowers, fruits, grains, vegetables, and trees to show our care for the earth. Their provision of beauty, shade, nourishment, habitat, or joy shows God's endless love for us to the world.

Steps
1. Read the parable of the mustard seed in the Gospel of Mark 4:30–32. Reflect on the power of one little seed to do so much good. Share your reflections with one another.

2. Research the nature of a seed. What is inside? What makes it start growing? What are the conditions that help it take root and grow strong?

3. Choose flowers or herbs that you can grow from seeds. Research how to plant these particular seeds.

4. Collect the supplies you'll need for those seeds. Yogurt cups and egg cartons make good pots for the initial planting of seeds.

5. Decide what you are going to do with the plants. How can you use them in ways that sow God's message for someone else?

Act

IF TIME ALLOWS

Native Plants
Tell young people to consider using plants native to the area and to find out which can be grown indoors. Remind them to look for special planting instructions. Ask volunteers to plant and maintain flowerpots in the room.

✝ *God's Creation*

MATERIALS: Get Ready for Faith in Action

For these projects, you will need print and online resources about plants and environmental pollution, computers with Internet access, native plants and flowerpots, the prayer service planning guide and prayer service planning tips, supplies for a Nature Day, and art and writing supplies. Also see the project steps.

FAITH IN ACTION

Complete one of the suggested Faith in Action projects as a class, or organize young people into two groups, having each group complete a different project. Note that directions continue on the next page.

① Prepare
Discuss the project ideas with young people and involve them in the decision-making process to determine a project. Discuss the project they choose in terms of faith and being a "person for others." Ask: *What do you hope to learn from this project? What interests you about it? What concerns do you have about it? Whom will you serve, and how will your service be beneficial to them and to you? Are you prepared to recognize the humanity in those you encounter? How does this project help you put your faith into action? What theme or themes of Catholic Social Teaching will you be experiencing in the project?*

② Implement
Have young people follow the directions to complete Plant Seeds on page 219 or Recycle-Bin Bonanza on page 220. Be sure young people do research before taking action. Encourage them to find out what plants grow best in the climate where they live. Have them work in small groups to research the impact of non-biodegradable garbage on the environment.

Be sure young people are supervised during their project as appropriate. Consider asking for parent volunteers to be Faith in Action facilitators for this unit.

✝ *God's Creation*

③ Close

Bring closure to the project by leading young people in completing one or both of the following:

Prayer Service Download and print out the prayer service planning guide and prayer service planning tips at www.findinggod.com. Have young people plan and implement a prayer service that expresses both gratitude to God for the opportunity to serve and hope for the people whom they served.

Pass It On Have young people meet with younger children to share their experiences and inspire them to get involved in similar projects. Help young people organize a Nature Day. They may work with younger children to plant and care for an outdoor garden on parish grounds. As an alternative, they may plant and tend to indoor pots or containers.

As part of the day, include activities that encourage care for the environment and careful use of resources. For example, with adult supervision, have young people walk around parish grounds and pick up litter and recyclable objects. Young people can organize and prepare materials for a recycling pickup. Prepare and maintain a drop-off site on parish property for people in the community to join in the effort.

✝ *God's Creation*

Recycle-Bin Bonanza

Purpose
Establish or enhance recycling systems in your school or parish. Raise awareness about the importance of recycling.

Background
Almost everything that we use can be recycled and made into something new. When we throw things away, we add to landfills, and we unnecessarily take more of the earth's resources to make things that could have been made with recycled material.

Steps
1. Find out what recycling systems are already in place in your school or parish. If there are none, talk with school or parish leaders about how you can help.
2. Obtain recycling bins, or make them by reusing discarded containers and decorating them with fun colors, pictures, and words that remind people to recycle. Consult a local recycling facility to see how materials should be grouped. For example, you might have recycling bins for each of the following: mixed paper, glass, metal cans, batteries, printer cartridges, newspaper, and corrugated cardboard.
3. Place bins in high-trash zones.
4. Keep track of how much is recycled, and raise awareness by posting a chart online or in a printed publication that shows the impact of each month's recycling efforts.

> "Gather the fragments left over, so that nothing will be wasted."
> —John 6:12

Act

220 Unit 5 • Jesus Lives On

IF TIME ALLOWS

Living Faith: Making a Difference

Have young people keep track of their recycling efforts for one week. Encourage them to show their results in a line graph, bar graph, or pie graph and explain their results to the group.

They may discuss what is gained through each recycling effort. For example, explain that a 4-foot stack of newspapers is equivalent to a 40-foot fir tree.

✝ *God's Creation*

The Year in Our Church

Catechist Preparation pages open this unit.

SEASONAL SESSIONS

The Year in Our Church

Refer to the abbreviated Scope and Sequence below for themes, Scripture, *CCC* references, and saints and holy people found in the Seasonal Sessions. These sessions can be used independently or in conjunction with Celebrating Sessions 5, 10, 15, 20, and 25.

Season	Theme	Scripture	CCC References	Saints and Holy People
Advent PAGES 223–226	In the season of Advent, we prepare to celebrate Jesus' birth.	Luke 1:26–38 Luke 1:46–55	484–501	Mary Joseph Elizabeth
Christmas PAGES 227–230	During the Christmas season, we celebrate Jesus' birth.	Luke 2:1–14 Psalm 96:1–2,7–9,11–13	525–530	the Magi Zechariah Elizabeth Mary Joseph John the Baptist
Lent PAGES 231–234	The season of Lent is a time of conversion and preparation for the Feast of Easter.	Mark 1:11–13 Matthew 6:1–18 Joel 2:12–17 Jeremiah 6:26 Isaiah 58:5 Daniel 9:3 Jonah 3:6	538–540, 1095, 1438	John the Baptist Pope Urban II
Holy Week PAGES 235–238	During Holy Week, we remember that Jesus suffered and died for our Salvation.	Luke 19:28–48 Luke 23:33–46	134, 595–598, 1362–1366	disciples Peter Simon of Cyrene
Easter PAGES 239–242	During the Easter season, we celebrate the Resurrection and Ascension of Jesus Christ.	Luke 24:1–7 Luke 24:12 Luke 24:34	638–658, 1322–1344	the holy women Peter two Emmaus disciples the Apostles
Pentecost PAGES 243–246	At Pentecost we celebrate the coming of the Holy Spirit to bring life to the Church.	Acts of the Apostles 2:1–4,11,13,36 Isaiah 11:2	731–747	the Apostles women disciples Mary, the mother of Jesus Peter
All Saints Day PAGES 247–250	On All Saints Day, we celebrate all members of the Church, living and dead, united in Christ.	1 John 3:1–3	61, 946–962, 1331	Communion of Saints Saint Patrick Saint Joseph Our Lady of Guadalupe Saint Francis of Assisi Saint Frances Xavier Cabrini Mary, the Mother of God Saint Paul

Seasonal Sessions

Seasonal Sessions provide lessons for major feasts and seasons of the liturgical year. These sessions can be used independently or in conjunction with Celebrating Sessions 5, 10, 15, 20, and 25.

Session Steps

- ▶ **Engage**   a brief introduction that relates to young people's life experiences
- ▶ **Explore**   an exploration of Scripture and Catholic Tradition
- ▶ **Reflect**   a Prayer Service that relates to the session theme
- ▶ **Respond**   a culminating activity

As a Stand-Alone Session

If your program calls for more than 25 sessions, you can offer these seven sessions separately for as many as 32 sessions. To use them independently, consider the following options:

- ▶ Implement a session as each season or feast is approaching.
- ▶ Use all If Time Allows options.
- ▶ Incorporate the Blackline Master.
- ▶ Creatively enhance the Prayer Service with local customs and traditions. You may wish to have young people decorate your prayer space or sacred space for each season.

As a Supplement to a Celebrating Session

Each Seasonal Session can be used to further expand upon concepts taught in Sessions 5, 10, 15, 20, and 25. The following options integrate the Seasonal and Celebrating Sessions:

- ▶ In advance, review the coordinating sessions as you prepare.
- ▶ Based on the time you have with young people, decide which elements of the Seasonal Session can be easily incorporated into instruction of the Celebrating Session. For example, you might end the Celebrating Session with the Prayer Service from the Seasonal Session, or you might have young people complete the Seasonal Blackline Master after reading an Explore section in a Celebrating Session.
- ▶ Consider assigning a Seasonal Session as an at-home follow-up experience after you teach a Celebrating Session.

Assessment Options

- ▶ An assessment for each Seasonal Session can be found at **www.findinggod.com**.
- ▶ A unit assessment for The Year in Our Church can be found at **www.findinggod.com**.

The Year in Our Church

The Liturgical Calendar

The liturgical calendar shows us the feasts and seasons of the Church year.

The Liturgical Calendar

The liturgical calendar represents the celebration of the mystery of Christ, from the anticipation of his birth to the sending of the Holy Spirit. The Church marks the passage of time with a cycle of seasons and feasts that invites us, year after year, to deepen our commitment to Jesus. By inviting young people into these celebrations, you help them grow in the Catholic way of life.

① Set the Stage

Distribute copies of regular calendars to young people. Ask: *How is an ordinary calendar the same as and different from the liturgical calendar shown on page 221?* (Possible answers: same—both show special days; different—an ordinary calendar is divided into 12 months)

② Get Started

Point out that the first Sunday of Advent begins a new year in the Church. Say: *The Church keeps a calendar to mark special times in Jesus' life, Death, Resurrection, and Ascension.*

Explain that *Ordinary Time* means "that which is ordered." Point out that far from being of lesser importance to other times of the Church year, Ordinary Time plays an important role in our faith. During Ordinary Time, we find hope and joy in everyday events and in the readings that tell about Jesus' life. Say: *Ordinary Time follows the Baptism of our Lord [the first Sunday after the Epiphany] and continues until Ash Wednesday. A second period of Ordinary Time occurs from the Monday after Pentecost until Evening Prayer the night before Advent begins.*

Display the *Finding God* poster The Liturgical Year throughout the session and refer to it often.

IF TIME ALLOWS

The Liturgical Calendar BLM

Seasons and Feasts of the Church Year Distribute the Liturgical Calendar Blackline Master [T-389]. Have young people write the names of each season and feast in the appropriate section.

Organize small groups. Ask each group to use the *Lectionary for Mass* that you have provided to locate and read Scripture readings for each specific Church season. Before they begin, tell them the current year of the three-year cycle [Year A, Year B, or Year C] so they know which pages to reference when they begin looking for Scripture. As they read Scripture, encourage young people to write their favorite passages [book, chapter, verse or verses] on the calendar for each Church season.

The Liturgical Year

At the beginning of each seasonal session, direct young people to turn to page 222 and to read the paragraph about the season they will be celebrating. You may use the following summaries to provide additional information about each season.

Advent

Advent is a season of hope and joyful anticipation of the coming of Christ. While we prepare to celebrate the birth of Christ, we also anticipate his Second Coming during Advent.

Christmas

At Christmas we celebrate the birth of Jesus. This celebration lasts until the Sunday after Epiphany, the Baptism of the Lord. During this season we also celebrate the Epiphany, which is when Jesus was revealed to the whole world.

Lent

Lent is not a somber or sad season but one of joy, for we know that the happiness of Easter comes through the pain of the Cross. Throughout these 40 days, the Church prepares by praying, fasting, and giving alms.

Holy Week

Holy Week begins on Palm Sunday, marking Jesus' entrance into Jerusalem. We celebrate the culmination of the entire liturgical year by marking the Triduum—Holy Thursday, Good Friday, and Holy Saturday—our commemoration of Jesus' Death and our preparation for his Resurrection.

Easter

The Church sets aside 50 days to celebrate Jesus' Resurrection, the central feast of Christianity. These

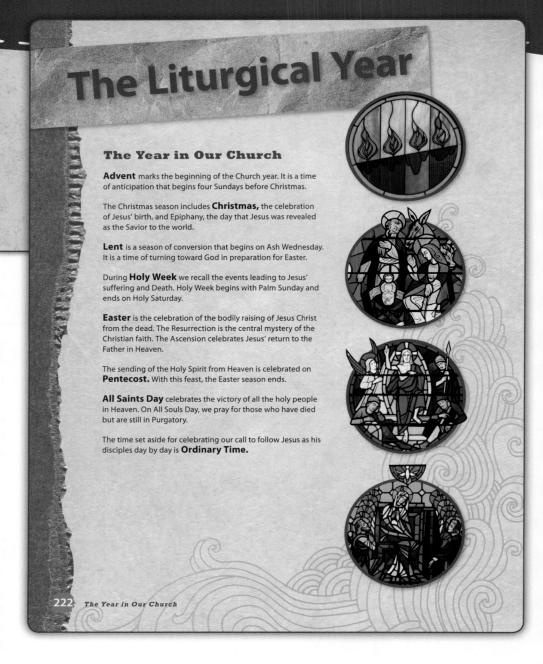

The Liturgical Year

The Year in Our Church

Advent marks the beginning of the Church year. It is a time of anticipation that begins four Sundays before Christmas.

The Christmas season includes **Christmas,** the celebration of Jesus' birth, and Epiphany, the day that Jesus was revealed as the Savior to the world.

Lent is a season of conversion that begins on Ash Wednesday. It is a time of turning toward God in preparation for Easter.

During **Holy Week** we recall the events leading to Jesus' suffering and Death. Holy Week begins with Palm Sunday and ends on Holy Saturday.

Easter is the celebration of the bodily raising of Jesus Christ from the dead. The Resurrection is the central mystery of the Christian faith. The Ascension celebrates Jesus' return to the Father in Heaven.

The sending of the Holy Spirit from Heaven is celebrated on **Pentecost.** With this feast, the Easter season ends.

All Saints Day celebrates the victory of all the holy people in Heaven. On All Souls Day, we pray for those who have died but are still in Purgatory.

The time set aside for celebrating our call to follow Jesus as his disciples day by day is **Ordinary Time.**

222 *The Year in Our Church*

50 days from Easter to Pentecost are celebrated as one feast day, sometimes called "the great Sunday." Easter is celebrated on the first Sunday after the first full moon of spring. In Luke's Gospel, Jesus instructs the disciples in Jerusalem for 40 days and then returns to the Father. We celebrate this return as the Feast of the Ascension.

Pentecost

At Pentecost we celebrate the descent of the Holy Spirit on the disciples, 50 days after Jesus' Resurrection. As such, Pentecost is our celebration of the birthday of the universal Church.

All Saints Day

The Communion of Saints, meaning those who are on earth, those who have died and are being purified, and the blessed in Heaven, is celebrated on All Saints Day [November 1] and All Souls Day [November 2].

Ordinary Time

Ordinary Time calls us to reflect on the Paschal Mystery and our call to discipleship throughout the year. Ordinary Time, typically 33 weeks, is a celebration that occurs twice a year, following the Christmas season and then again following Easter.

Advent

"May it be done to me according to your word."

Luke 1:38

Advent begins on the fourth Sunday before Christmas and marks the beginning of the Church's liturgical year. During Advent, we remember how the people of Israel awaited the Messiah. We also prepare ourselves to celebrate the birth of Jesus. Advent is a time of joyful anticipation for the day when Christ will return in glory.

PRAYER

Thank you, God, for this new year and the anticipation it brings. Open our ears to your guiding words and give us the courage to follow them.

Advent **223**

MATERIALS: Get Ready for the Session

For this session, you will need an Advent wreath and Bibles. Review any If Time Allows activities you intend to do for additional required materials.

OUTCOMES

▶ Tell the stories of the Annunciation and the Visitation.

▶ Explain that Advent is a time of joyful waiting for Jesus' birth.

① Set the Stage

Have young people recall a time when their family was preparing for a celebration. Ask them to explain what they did to get ready and to describe how they felt as they went about their preparations. Say: **Advent is also a time of preparation and excitement.**

② Get Started

Read aloud the Scripture verse in the box. Ask: **Who spoke these words?** (Mary) Then have a volunteer read aloud the paragraph. Say: **Advent takes place at the end of the calendar year, but it marks the beginning of the Church's liturgical year.** Using either the liturgical calendar on page 221 or the *Finding God* poster The Liturgical Year, have young people point out the season of Advent. Then say: **Advent is something like the New Year's celebration on an ordinary calendar but for the Church year.** Ask: **Why is Mary's prayer, "May it be done to me according to your word," a good one to use at the beginning of a new year?** (Possible answer: It asks God to open us up to the gifts and experiences of the coming months.)

 Prayer

Invite young people to pause and open their hearts and minds to prayer. Encourage them to close their eyes and listen to the prayer while you pray aloud. Together pray the Sign of the Cross.

① Begin

Ask young people to recall a time when they were chosen as a member of a club, sports team, academic team, or other selective group. Discuss how young people felt when they heard the news. (Possible answers: excited, nervous, proud) Say: *Mary was chosen by God to be the mother of Jesus. She probably experienced many different feelings in response to this news.*

② Connect

Have volunteers read aloud the title and the first three paragraphs. Ask young people to imagine this scenario happening today in their own home. Then ask: *What is so amazing about Mary's response to the angel?* (Possible answers: Being visited by an angel is not an everyday event. Mary may have felt amazed, confounded, or afraid. She demonstrated remarkable courage and trust.) Say: *Mary did not flee what she did not understand.* Ask: *What did she do instead?* (She stayed in the situation. She asked for clarification. She listened.) Say: *Mary stayed, asked a question, listened, and then said yes. She trusted God to lead her in the right direction.*

Invite a volunteer to read aloud the next paragraph. Say: *Mary is a great model of faith for us. When we are afraid or confused, her response teaches us that we can go to God, ask a question, listen, and then respond by saying yes. We can trust God to lead us where we need to go.*

Ask volunteers to take turns reading the last two paragraphs on the page. Ask: *What is the Feast of the Immaculate Conception?* (a celebration of Mary's freedom from sin from the moment of her conception) Ask: *What is the Annunciation?* (the angel Gabriel's announcement of Jesus' birth to Mary and her acceptance to be the mother of God)

Mary Accepts God's Promise

Annunciation, from the *Hastings Hours*, ca. 1475–83, vellum, Flemish School.

WE celebrate Mary during Advent. Luke 1:26–38 tells us how Mary was chosen by God to be the mother of Jesus and how she responded in faith. The angel's announcement of the birth of Jesus is called the Annunciation.

Mary was from a small town in Galilee called Nazareth. She was engaged to marry a man named Joseph. An angel of God visited Mary and announced that she had been chosen by God to bear a son, who was to be named Jesus. The angel Gabriel told her that this child would be the Son of God.

Mary wondered aloud how this could be, since she was a virgin. The angel told her that she would conceive by the power of the Holy Spirit. He also told Mary that her relative, Elizabeth, long believed to be unable to have children, was pregnant. Mary accepted the message of the angel with the words, "Behold, I am the handmaid of the Lord. May it be done to me according to your word." (Luke 1:38) Then the angel left her.

After the visit from the angel, Mary traveled to see her relative Elizabeth and found her with child, just as the angel had said. We call this special event in Mary's life the Visitation. Elizabeth and Mary greeted each other joyfully because they recognized the wonderful things that God was doing for them. We're reminded to spend time during Advent remembering the great things God has done throughout history and in our own lives.

Mary is a model of discipleship for us. She responded to God's messenger with a resounding yes. Her words to the angel are sometimes called Mary's *fiat*, a Latin word that means "let it be done." During Advent, we reflect on Mary's acceptance of God's call to be the mother of Jesus. We pray that we'll be as open to God's call as Mary was and that we'll respond with our own *fiat*.

God had chosen Mary to be the mother of Jesus from the moment of her conception. We celebrate that Mary was born without Original Sin on December 8, the Feast of the Immaculate Conception, which is a Holy Day of Obligation for Catholics.

224 *The Year in Our Church*

IF TIME ALLOWS

Stay, Ask, Listen, Respond

Remind young people that when Mary was visited by God's messenger, she stayed, asked a question, listened, and responded. Mary is a good model of discipleship for us when we are "visited" by confusing and challenging circumstances in our own lives.

Have young people think of a situation in their own lives that they would rather ignore or flee. Invite them to close their eyes and take this situation to God. Have them think of a question about the situation to ask God. Then encourage them to listen for God's guidance before responding with a yes, if possible, at this time. If they cannot honestly respond yes at this time, challenge them to reflect on what it would take for them to say yes. Encourage them to continue to face confusing or challenging events with courage and faith, asking God questions, listening, and responding yes.

The Visitation,
Bartholomaeus Bruyn,
ca. 16th century.

Advent

Advent Prayer: The Advent Wreath

The Church provides us with special prayers and devotions during Advent. The Advent wreath decorates the church or home during Advent. Some people place an Advent wreath on their dinner table.

An Advent wreath consists of a circle of evergreens and four candles that represent each of the four Sundays of Advent. The greenery in the wreath reminds us of the new life that Jesus will bring to us. The circle of the wreath represents God's unending love. The candles on the wreath are usually purple, the liturgical color for Advent, or white. A pink candle ordinarily is used for the third Sunday of Advent. This color reminds us to rejoice because the Lord is near. The light from the candles represents the light that came into the world at Jesus' birth. A new candle is lit each week.

Our Catholic Character

A number of Catholic prayers recognize Mary's special role in the mystery of Christ and the Incarnation of the Word. The words of the Hail Mary echo Luke's account of the Annunciation. (Luke 1:26–38) When Mary visits Elizabeth, her response to Elizabeth's greeting gives praise to God for the wonders he has done throughout the history of Israel. We find Mary's prayer, the *Magnificat*, in Luke 1:46–55. The *Magnificat* is prayed during Evening Prayer (Vespers), which is part of the Liturgy of the Hours.

 Advent **225**

IF TIME ALLOWS

Advent BLM

Circle of Life Provide each young person with the Advent Blackline Master [T-390] and read aloud the introductory text and the directions. Have young people complete the activity independently. Invite volunteers to share what they wrote.

The Joys of Saying Yes

Have young people think of a time when they said yes to God. Explain that their experience of yes might have been simple, such as inviting a classmate they didn't know well to sit at their lunch table. Their yes might have been more complex, such as needing to confront the fear and confusion of being a new student in a new school. Invite young people to tell their ideas to a partner, naming at least one way that their experience of saying yes brought them joy.

Have young people study the fine art on page 225. Say: *The first place God led Mary was to the home of her cousin Elizabeth.* Ask: *How did Mary feel about visiting Elizabeth?* (She was joyful.) Explain that Elizabeth was her cousin and friend. They were both pregnant. They could support each other and share their feelings and experiences. Say: *When we say yes to God, we are led to joyful places. We are given the support we need. We are given companions who understand and encourage us.*

Ask volunteers to take turns reading the two paragraphs in the section Advent Prayer: The Advent Wreath. Have an Advent wreath on display in the room, and ask young people to compare it to the description on the page. Invite volunteers to describe any traditions their families follow with the Advent wreath.

Our Catholic Character

Ask a volunteer to read aloud Our Catholic Character. Distribute Bibles and have young people locate Luke 1:26–45. Invite volunteers to identify the different speakers. Ask: *What does this passage tell us about Mary?* (She is chosen by God. God is with her. Her child will be blessed.)

③ Close

Have young people close their eyes and imagine that Mary has come to visit them in their home. Then pray the Hail Mary aloud as a group. Have young people imagine addressing the words directly to Mary.

Prayer

Guide young people as they participate in a prayer service.

Prepare Pray the prayer on page 226 in advance.

 Pray Explain that Mary's prayer, the *Magnificat*, contains many references to the Old Testament and demonstrates her deep knowledge of the Jewish faith. Explain that a deep knowledge of our Catholic faith helps us follow Mary's example and respond to God with trust.

Invite young people to bring their books to the prayer space. Read aloud the title and paragraph. Assign the role of Leader and organize the group into Side 1 and Side 2. Invite everyone to pray the All and Response parts. Prompt the first All part. Proceed to pray each part as indicated, pausing to allow time for meditation after each one. After young people pray the Response, invite them to offer their own prayers of thanksgiving before praying the final Leader and All parts. Conclude by praying the Sign of the Cross together.

---

① Respond

Mary's prayer praises God for lifting up the lowly. Say: ***During Advent, we look for ways to help those in need.*** Arrange young people in small groups. Have them discuss ways in which they might respond to those in need this Advent season. Afterward, ask members of each group to share their ideas.

② Go in Peace

Pray aloud as young people pray silently: ***Thank you, God, for Advent, when we anticipate the birth of your Son, Jesus. Help us respond to your call as Mary did with joy, courage, and trust. Amen.***

Prayer

God Is Great

Mary's prayer, the *Magnificat*, gives thanks to God and praises him for his wondrous deeds throughout the ages. Advent is a good time to offer our own prayers of thanksgiving as we get ready to welcome the light of Christ on Christmas.

Thanks and Praise to God

All: Praise be to God.

Leader: During this Advent season, we remember Mary's yes to God. Like Mary, we recognize that God has done marvelous deeds throughout history and in our own lives. Let us pray together Mary's *Magnificat* and praise God for all of his wondrous deeds.

All: "My soul proclaims the greatness of the Lord; my spirit rejoices in God my savior. For he has looked upon his handmaid's lowliness; behold, from now on will all ages call me blessed.

Side 1: The Mighty One has done great things for me, and holy is his name. His mercy is from age to age to those who fear him.

Side 2: He has shown might with his arm, dispersed the arrogant of mind and heart.

Side 1: He has thrown down the rulers from their thrones but lifted up the lowly.

Side 2: The hungry he has filled with good things; the rich he has sent away empty.

All: He has helped Israel his servant, remembering his mercy, according to his promise to our fathers, to Abraham and to his descendants forever."

Luke 1:46–55

Response: God has done great things for us!

Offer prayers of thanksgiving. ℞.

Leader: Lord our God, you fill us with good things. Continue to bless us as we prepare to celebrate the coming of your Son, Jesus Christ, who reigns with you and the Holy Spirit, now and forever.

All: Amen.

226 *The Year in Our Church*

IF TIME ALLOWS

Great Things

Arrange young people in small groups and provide them with current newspapers and magazines. Invite group members to look through the publications for at least two events that show that God is working in our world today "doing great things for us." Invite young people to share their examples.

FYI

Coaching Young People to Pray

Remind young people that when they are at a loss for words in prayer, they have options. Suggest they might be silent and listen for God's voice, or they might read and reflect on a Scripture passage such as Mary's *Magnificat*. Assure them of God's presence and his response to their prayers.

Christmas

"... I proclaim to you good news of great joy ..."

Luke 2:10

At Christmas, we celebrate the fulfillment of God's promise to send the world a Savior. We know this Savior to be Jesus, God's own Son. Jesus' birth in Bethlehem brings to the world God's promise of peace and Salvation.

PRAYER

Thank you, God, for the amazing gift of your Son. Help us share this gift with everyone we meet by using words and actions that reflect Jesus' love.

Christmas **227**

MATERIALS: Get Ready for the Session

For this session, you will need Bibles, writing supplies, and a Nativity set. Review any If Time Allows activities you intend to do for additional required materials.

OUTCOMES

▶ Tell Luke's account of the birth of Jesus.

▶ Identify Jesus' birth as the fulfillment of God's promise of Salvation and peace.

① Set the Stage

Invite young people to share stories they've been told about events surrounding their births. Ask: **Why do you think people enjoy hearing or telling these stories?** (Possible answers: It makes them feel special and loved. It connects them to a time before they had their own memories.) Say: **From its very beginning, the Christian community told the story of Jesus' birth for similar reasons. It reminded them of their identity and of God's love for them. It connected them to Jesus and to earlier Christians. At the same time, it passed the Good News forward so that others might believe in Jesus.**

② Get Started

Invite young people to tell the story of Jesus' birth from memory, including as many details as possible. List these details on the board. Invite volunteers to explain what each detail might tell us about Jesus' identity and character or about God's love for us. Say: **In this session, we'll look closely at the version of the Christmas story found in the Gospel of Luke.**

Invite a volunteer to read aloud the Scripture verse in the box. Ask: **Who said these words?** (the angel Gabriel) Then ask a volunteer to read aloud the rest of the text in the box.

 Prayer

Pray the prayer aloud together. Conclude by praying the Sign of the Cross.

① Begin

Distribute Bibles and organize young people into four groups. Assign each group one of the four Gospels. Instruct each group to find the beginning of their assigned Gospel and to take turns telling whether it begins with a narrative of Jesus' birth. Briefly discuss the differences in the way each Gospel begins.

② Connect

Have volunteers read aloud the first two paragraphs of the article. Ask: **Why would Matthew and Luke include different details?** (Possible answer: Each writer appealed to a specific audience at a specific time and made particular points about Jesus as Messiah.) Remind young people that each Gospel was written for a particular community of believers and that each Gospel contributes in a different way to our understanding of Jesus.

Have young people scan Chapters 1 and 2 of the Gospel of Luke in their Bibles. Invite them to identify details about Jesus' birth. Write the details on the board. Then ask volunteers to read aloud the next two paragraphs of the article.

Invite a volunteer to read aloud Luke 2:1–20. Then show young people a Nativity set and tell them that Saint Francis of Assisi is believed to have introduced this common devotion. Observe that many Nativity scenes are a combination of both the Gospels of Matthew and Luke.

Read aloud the next paragraph. Ask: **What prominent message does Luke deliver about Jesus?** (Jesus came into the world humble and poor. He is not a worldly king but our divine king.)

Christmas

The Birth of Jesus

The Nativity, Sir Edward Burne-Jones, ca. 19th century.

MOST of us can tell the story of Jesus' birth by heart, as the story has been told and retold every year. But there is more to understand about the story.

Only the Gospels of Matthew and Luke include the stories of Jesus' birth. While both Gospels have details in common, they also relate unique aspects surrounding Jesus' birth. You might be surprised to learn that only Matthew's Gospel records the visit of the Magi, who are sometimes called the Wise Men. Meanwhile, the account of the angels appearing to shepherds in the fields and announcing that the Messiah had been born is found only in Luke's Gospel. Because these two Gospels highlight different details from Jesus' birth, we will focus only on Luke's Gospel as we consider the mystery we celebrate at Christmas.

Luke's Infancy Narrative begins with the angel's announcement to Zechariah that his wife, Elizabeth, will bear a son (to be named John) in her old age. Luke's Gospel continues with the Annunciation, the angel's announcement of Jesus' birth to Mary, and the Visitation, Mary's visit to her now-pregnant relative, Elizabeth. In this way, Luke's Gospel connects the lives of John the Baptist and Jesus. Immediately after reporting the birth of John the Baptist, Luke tells the story of Jesus' birth.

Luke's Gospel provides historical perspective about the world into which Jesus was born. Caesar Augustus was the Roman emperor, a fact similar to identifying the president of the United States when you were born. Luke notes that a census had been announced, which explains why Mary and Joseph had traveled to Bethlehem, where Jesus was born. Luke's historical perspective reveals that Jesus' birth was an important event for the world, a theme that repeats throughout his Gospel.

The Gospel of Luke delivers the message that from his birth, Jesus was a different kind of king. He was not a king with material possessions; instead, he was a divine king. Jesus came to the world as someone who is poor and lowly. Because there was no room at the inn, Jesus was born in a stable and laid in a manger, which was a feeding trough for animals.

Jesus came for all people, not only the rich and powerful. Angels announced to shepherds in the fields the good news of Jesus' birth. Revealing this news to shepherds is an unexpected detail. Shepherds were simple workers, toiling in the fields and tending to animals. Yet these lowly ones were the first to

---

IF TIME ALLOWS

Nativity Murals

Organize young people into two groups, each responsible for designing a Nativity mural. One mural should reflect the details found in the Gospel of Luke, and the other should reflect the details found in the Gospel of Matthew. Ask them to include only elements found in either Matthew or Luke. When each group is finished, invite them to present their Nativity mural. Ask them to explain the main message about Jesus that each Gospel writer may have been trying to convey.

receive and acknowledge the appearance of the Savior. The shepherds journeyed to Bethlehem and found Mary, Joseph, and Jesus just as the angels had said. They returned from Bethlehem singing praise and glory to God. By including these details, Luke delivers the message that those who responded most faithfully to Jesus' teaching were those least perceived to be chosen by God—those who were poor, sinners, lepers, outcasts, or foreigners.

In the Gospel of Luke, Mary plays a significant role. Mary is central to the mystery of the Incarnation. Because she responded yes to becoming the Mother of God, she is our first model of discipleship and our model of grace and trust in God. After the visit from the shepherds, Mary reflects on everything that has happened in her heart. She shows us a path to finding God in prayer, reflecting on his will, and following in faith.

We are called to respond in prayer to the miracle and mystery of Christmas. We are called to imitate Mary's faithfulness. The Christmas season includes the Solemnity of Mary, a Holy Day of Obligation, on January 1, a feast day that is devoted to remembering Mary's role as Mother of God.

In the account of Jesus' birth in Luke's Infancy Narrative, we find plenty of good news to celebrate. Jesus' birth brings Salvation to the whole world. In particular, Jesus' kingship is inclusive, bringing good news to those who are ignored or held in low esteem by society. During the Christmas season, we are called to pray and reflect on the events surrounding Jesus' birth and the story of Salvation.

The First to be Told About Jesus, Clive Uptton, ca. 20th century.

Our Catholic Character

Angels, spiritual creatures in the Gospels who worship God in Heaven and serve as God's messengers, reveal some of God's plans for Salvation. In Luke's Gospel, angels bring news to Zechariah, Mary, and the shepherds. Eight days after his birth and at his circumcision, Mary gives Jesus his name—the name the angel Gabriel said when he announced that Mary had been chosen to be the mother of the Savior. By including these details, Luke makes clear Jesus' devout Jewish upbringing by Mary and Joseph. Angels in Luke's Gospel give more titles for Jesus when they announce his birth to the shepherds, calling Jesus "a savior," "Messiah," and "Lord."

Christmas **229**

IF TIME ALLOWS

Christmas BLM

The Christmas Story, Retold Provide each young person with the Christmas Blackline Master [T-391] and read aloud the introductory text and the directions. Have young people work in pairs to complete the chart. Encourage them to consult the Gospels of Matthew and Luke as they work. Invite young people to answer the question at the bottom independently. Then ask volunteers to share their ideas.

Angels Among Us

As a group, discuss young people's understanding of angels. Then ask them to draw a picture or write a poem or short story that represents something about their guardian angel or how their guardian angel works in their lives. Invite volunteers to share their completed work with the group.

Invite volunteers to read the next three paragraphs of the article. Say: *Because shepherds are not common in our society, it is easy for us to miss the significance of their role in the Christmas story.* Explain that we might understand this part of the story better if we imagined Jesus being born today. Ask: *If the Christmas story had happened today instead of 2,000 years ago, who might be the shepherds?* (Possible answer: simple workers or those who are poor and have low status in society)

Invite a volunteer to read aloud the last paragraph of the article. Point out that the Christmas season is often so filled with activities and events that it can be difficult to make time to pray. Have young people brainstorm ways to make time to reflect on the mystery of Jesus' birth. Encourage them to choose and enact one of these strategies in the coming days.

Our Catholic Character

Ask a volunteer to read aloud Our Catholic Character. Invite young people to find *Savior*, *Messiah*, and *Lord* in the Glossary and read aloud the definitions. Invite young people to explain what each title tells us about Jesus.

Explain that the Church affirms the existence of angels working in our world today. Encourage young people to pray to their guardian angel for protection and guidance in their daily lives.

③ Close

Have young people close their eyes and silently ask their guardian angel for guidance with a particular problem or issue they are facing. Pray aloud: *God, thank you for the gift of your messengers and for the wonderful news they bring us about your Son.*

Prayer

Guide young people as they participate in a prayer service.

Prepare Pray the prayer on page 230 in advance.

Pray Ask a volunteer to read aloud the title and the paragraph. Then invite young people to bring their books to the prayer space. Say: ***Sometimes we act like Christmas is a one-day celebration, when it is actually a liturgical season.*** Assign the Leader and Reader parts. Organize the group into Side 1 and Side 2. Read aloud the title of the prayer. Remind young people that Jesus is present in this place and encourage reverence and mindful prayer. Prompt the Leader to begin. Pause. Then cue the Reader. After another pause, cue the Leader to pray, followed by the All part. Prompt Side 1 and Side 2 as they alternate praying verses of the psalm. After the All parts, encourage young people to close their eyes briefly for silent meditation. Following the Leader part, pray *Amen* together. Conclude by praying the Sign of the Cross together.

① Respond

Say: ***Jesus was born as one of us and came to the world as one who was poor and lowly. We believe that every person has dignity in the eyes of God.*** Discuss how we obtain dignity. Then discuss simple ways that young people can honor their own dignity every day as well as the dignity of others.

② Go in Peace

Invite young people to pray silently as you pray aloud: ***Thank you, Father, for sending your Son as our Savior. Help us see and honor the dignity in all people. Amen.***

Prayer

Welcome Jesus!

We rejoice at Jesus' birth because he brought Salvation to the whole world. Jesus, the Savior, came for everyone. The angels announced Jesus' birth to poor shepherds, who responded by journeying to Bethlehem to find Jesus. How will we respond to the good news?

He Is Born

Leader: Let us prayerfully reflect on the good news of Jesus' birth. Like Mary, let us ponder this mystery in the stillness of our hearts.

Reader: A reading from the holy Gospel according to Luke.
[Luke 2:1–14]
The Gospel of the Lord.

Leader: Glory to God in the highest.

All: Glory to God in the highest.

Side 1: Sing to the LORD a new song;
sing to the LORD, all the earth.
Sing to the LORD, bless his name;
proclaim his salvation day after day.
Psalm 96:1–2

Side 2: Give to the LORD, you families of nations,
give to the LORD glory and might;
give to the LORD the glory due his name!
Bring gifts and enter his courts;
bow down to the LORD, splendid
in holiness.
Tremble before him, all the earth; . . .
Psalm 96:7–9

Side 1: Let the heavens be glad and the
earth rejoice;
let the sea and what fills it resound;
let the plains be joyful and all that
is in them.

Side 2: Then let all the trees of the forest rejoice
before the LORD who comes,
who comes to govern the earth,
To govern the world with justice
and the peoples with faithfulness.
Psalm 96:11–13

All: Glory to God in the highest.

All: Praise to you, Lord Jesus Christ.

Allow time for silent meditation.

Leader: Let us pray. God sent to us a Savior, Jesus, our Messiah and Lord. He was born as one of us. May we, like the shepherds, give glory to God for the great gift of Salvation. We pray this in Jesus' name.

All: Amen.

230 *The Year in Our Church*

IF TIME ALLOWS

Glory to God

Point out that the psalmist invites the heavens, earth, sea, plains, and trees of the forest to sing glory to God. Pray these verses aloud again. Point out the use of personification, which is giving human characteristics or personality to an object. Ask young people to think of another line that follows the pattern in the psalm, using personification: "Let the [noun] [verb]." For example, "Let the flowers dance" or "Let the mountains shout." Ask young people to work with a partner. Invite volunteers to share their ideas with the group.

FYI

Coaching Young People to Pray

Remind young people that one of the greatest gifts we can give Jesus is our time. Encourage them to set a time and a place for prayer every day. Explain that even a few minutes of daily prayer will strengthen their relationship with Jesus and make them better able to hear his voice at all times.

Lent

> At once the Spirit drove him out into the desert, . . .
>
> *Mark 1:12*

Lent is a season of repentance and renewal. The Holy Spirit guides us to turn away from our sinfulness and to recommit ourselves to following Jesus. Beginning with Ash Wednesday, we spend 40 days fasting and praying, just as Jesus fasted and prayed in the desert before his public ministry.

PRAYER

Thank you, God, for the gift of liturgical seasons and especially for the season of Lent. Help us make the most of this special time with you.

Lent **231**

MATERIALS: Get Ready for the Session

For this session, you will need a photo of an athlete in training, Bibles, ashes from Ash Wednesday, and copies of your parish bulletin. Review any If Time Allows activities you intend to do for additional required materials.

OUTCOMES

▶ Describe Jesus' temptations in the desert.

▶ Explain the Lenten practices of prayer, fasting, and almsgiving.

① Set the Stage

Show young people a photo of an athlete in training. Ask: *What are some things athletes do to prepare for a competition?* (Possible answers: practice sport-specific skills, weight train, eat healthy foods) Explain that just as athletes strengthen their bodies by training, we strengthen our spirits during Lent by practicing certain disciplines. Say: *Lenten practices prepare us to celebrate and appreciate Christ's Resurrection at Easter.*

② Get Started

Explain that many athletes train both alone and as part of a team. Ask: *Why are both kinds of training important?* (Athletes become strong individually, but they must also work well with other members of the team.) Say: *This is true for spiritual training, too. We must strengthen our individual relationships with God as well as our relationships with others.* Explain that the spiritual practices of praying, fasting, and almsgiving help us do both.

Have a volunteer read aloud the Scripture verse and paragraph in the box. Say: *We usually think of a desert as a barren place. But it can also be a place of self-discovery, as it was for Jesus.* Explain that Lent is a time for us to enter our own wilderness situation in order to grow closer to God.

Prayer

Pray the prayer aloud while young people listen and reflect. Pray the Sign of the Cross together.

① Begin

Invite young people to share what they know about a desert environment. Discuss why deserts are challenging places. Explain that in Scripture, deserts are often places of spiritual as well as physical challenges. Ask: *In the Old Testament, when are God's people challenged in the desert?* (in Exodus, when Moses leads the Israelites out of Egypt) Say: *Moses led his people into the desert, away from the physical bondage of slavery. Jesus is also led into the desert so that he can help us escape bondage.* Ask: *From what does Jesus set us free?* (Possible answers: sin, selfish desires)

② Connect

 Invite a volunteer to read aloud the title and first paragraph of the article. Then distribute Bibles and have young people turn to Mark 1:12–13. Ask a volunteer to read aloud the passage. Ask: *Why did Jesus stay in the desert?* (He was committed to the task his Father had given him. His love for us was great.)

Have volunteers read aloud the next four paragraphs. Say: *Jesus received a big message at his baptism. He needed time to prepare to carry out this message.* Ask young people to give examples of "big messages" they have received and how they prepared or responded.

Ask a volunteer to read aloud the section on Prayer under the heading Lenten Practices: Prayer, Fasting, and Almsgiving. Point out that Lenten practices help us prepare to receive the "big message" that occurs on Easter Sunday. Say: *During Lent we seek to convert our hearts. Our hearts learn to pray in faith. Just as Jesus prayed to his Father, he teaches us that what we ask in prayer will be given if we only believe.* Write Matthew 21:22 on the board and discuss what it means: *Whatever you ask for in prayer with faith, you will receive.*

Lent

A Retreat in the Desert

Christ in the Wilderness, Briton Riviere, 1898.

SCRIPTURE tells us that after John the Baptist baptized Jesus in the Jordan River, the Holy Spirit led Jesus into the desert. Jesus prayed to God and fasted for 40 days. He prepared himself for his ministry. During this time, Jesus was tempted by Satan. In the desert's harsh and wild surroundings, angels tended to him. (Mark 1:12–13)

As we journey in faith and grow spiritually, we contemplate Jesus' baptism and retreat to the desert. Since the Second Vatican Council, Catholics recognize the celebration of Lent as a time to prepare for receiving the Sacrament of Baptism or a time to renew our baptismal promises. Jesus' acceptance of baptism from John the Baptist was acceptance of his Father's mission. At Jesus' baptism, a voice from Heaven proclaimed to Jesus, "'You are my beloved Son; with you I am well pleased.'" (Mark 1:11)

Jesus needed to pray about his mission. We, too, need to pray about our actions and the events of our lives to learn what God intends for us. When something happens to us—good or bad—it's helpful to take time to pray and listen for what God is calling us to do.

When we receive ashes on Ash Wednesday, we signal that we accept our dependence on God. The priest, deacon, or lay minister traces the Sign of the Cross on our foreheads with the blessed ashes. As this is done, one of two prayers is prayed. One prayer reminds us that we are mortal beings who will stand before God one day for judgment: "Remember, man, you are dust and to dust you will return." The other prayer reminds us that we are baptized and called to conversion: "Turn away from sin and be faithful to the Gospel."

During Lent, members of the Church commit themselves to following their mission, imitating the footsteps of Jesus as he prepared for his mission in the wilderness of the desert. In order to follow our mission, we incorporate traditional Lenten practices into our lives.

Lenten Practices: Prayer, Fasting, and Almsgiving

Prayer Daily prayer is an important part of Christian life. During the season of Lent, we consider our life of prayer as a personal practice that prepares us for the celebration of Easter. The Church challenges us to renew our commitment to prayer, the central action of our spiritual life. We choose to deepen our commitment by praying for the grace to live out our baptismal promises. We pray for those who are preparing to receive the Sacrament of Baptism at Easter. During this season of conversion, as we change our hearts and turn away from sin, we receive the Sacrament of Penance and Reconciliation and pray for others who are reconciling themselves to God.

232 *The Year in Our Church*

IF TIME ALLOWS

When in Doubt, Pray

Have young people work in groups of two or three. Ask groups to brainstorm personal events that remind them of the importance of prayer. Challenge young people to consider both major events and small, everyday events in their lives. Encourage young people to share their completed lists of events with the whole group.

Discuss whether any event or decision is too small to take to God. Explain that God delights when we invite him into the details of our day, and that if we develop the habit of talking to God frequently, our feelings of security, joy, and well-being will increase.

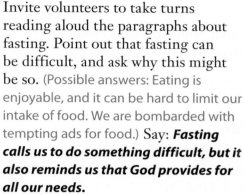

Fasting This spiritual practice increases awareness of our need for penance and conversion. Fasting, or limiting the intake of food and drink for a period of time, reminds us that Jesus fasted during his 40 days in the desert. Catholics between the ages of 18 and 59 are asked to fast on Ash Wednesday and Good Friday. Denying ourselves a full stomach helps make us more aware of our hunger for God and our dependence on him as his children. Fasting also works to remind us of our responsibility to ease the burdens of those who suffer physical, economic, or political hardships.

Catholics 14 years and older are also asked to abstain, or refrain, from eating meat on Ash Wednesday, Good Friday, and on the Fridays of Lent. Eating simple meals links us spiritually to the poor, who often have to do without proper food. Abstaining helps remind us of Lent's purpose.

Catholics both fast and abstain on Ash Wednesday and Good Friday. In addition to these spiritual practices, we might choose our own personal fast or abstinence during Lent. For example, you may choose not to eat candy, or you may give up television during Lent. Doing without some things we enjoy frees us to focus our lives on Jesus Christ alone. During Lent, we look at ways to simplify our lives by leaving behind things that don't really contribute to our fulfillment or to real happiness.

Almsgiving The Lenten practice of almsgiving is prompted by charity. To give alms is to assist those in need, such as an offering of money, possessions, time, or talent. Some people combine almsgiving with their practice of fasting. For example, you might give up buying lunch at the school cafeteria and donate the money that you would have spent on this food to those in need.

Through the spiritual practices of praying, fasting, and almsgiving, we make Lent our own retreat to the desert. Jesus speaks of praying, fasting, and almsgiving in Matthew 6:1–18, teaching us that we should not follow these practices as ways to be recognized, praised, or seen as holy. Instead, Jesus wants us to pray, fast, and give alms for love of God and neighbor. In this way, when it's time for Holy Week and Easter, we'll find ourselves ready to rejoice in the Good News of Jesus' Resurrection.

Past Meets Present

PAST: The Old Testament contains many references to wearing sackcloth and ashes as signs of repentance and as an acknowledgment of sinfulness, including Jeremiah 6:26, Isaiah 58:5, Daniel 9:3, and Jonah 3:6. In the early history of the Church, those seeking forgiveness wore sackcloth and ashes and begged members of the community to pray for them. The custom of distributing ashes arose from witnessing these public penitents. By the end of the 11th century, Pope Urban II called for the distribution of ashes on the Wednesday before Lent.

PRESENT: Receiving ashes, a sacramental, remains a popular devotion that begins the season of Lent. The ashes are made by burning palms that were blessed on the previous Palm Sunday. Some parishes invite parishioners to bring palms for burning to church before the season of Lent begins. Four ancient prayers are prayed in the blessing of the ashes, which are also sprinkled with holy water and perfumed with incense. The Ash Wednesday Scripture readings remind us of our call to conversion.

Lent

 Lent **233**

IF TIME ALLOWS

Lent BLM

Lenten Commitments Provide young people with the Lent Blackline Master [T-392] and read aloud the introductory text and directions. Have young people work independently to complete the activity. Encourage them to choose commitments to which they can realistically remain faithful, and ask volunteers to share their choices. Discuss which commitments might be the most challenging and why.

Commitment Buddies

Ask partners to agree to check in with each other at least once a week to see how their Lenten commitments are going. Encourage young people to be honest during their check in reports and invite them to support one another with congratulations, encouraging notes, texts, or e-mails throughout the week.

Invite volunteers to take turns reading aloud the paragraphs about fasting. Point out that fasting can be difficult, and ask why this might be so. (Possible answers: Eating is enjoyable, and it can be hard to limit our intake of food. We are bombarded with tempting ads for food.) Say: *Fasting calls us to do something difficult, but it also reminds us that God provides for all our needs.*

Have volunteers read aloud the paragraphs about almsgiving. Ask young people how they might practice almsgiving in school. Then distribute copies of your parish bulletin. Have young people browse the bulletin with a partner and brainstorm opportunities in the parish and diocese for almsgiving. Invite volunteers to share concrete ways to participate in almsgiving, including the giving of money, possessions, time, or talent.

✝ *The Poor and Vulnerable*

Past Meets Present

Invite a volunteer to read aloud Past Meets Present. If possible, obtain some ashes from Ash Wednesday to show the group. Ask: *Why are ashes an appropriate symbol for the season of Lent?* (Ashes show our need for God's mercy and forgiveness. They remind us of God's calling to be Kingdom people, not people trapped by false values. Without God's grace and conversion of our hearts, we are lifeless.)

③ Close

Have young people close their eyes and imagine putting the three Lenten practices into action. Say: *One definition of retreat is "a refuge or place of safety."* Ask: *How is God our refuge?* (God loves us infinitely and shelters us as a Father shelters his children.) Say: *God, thank you for leading us through our own desert experiences. Help us grow closer to you.*

Prayer

Guide young people as they participate in a prayer service.

Prepare Pray the prayer in advance.

 **Pray** Ask a volunteer to read the title and opening paragraph. Explain that when we experience a spiritual conversion, our relationship with God shifts. We become less preoccupied with ourselves and more aware of God. Say: *Conversion doesn't happen once and for all. It is an ongoing process in the life of a Christian.*

Invite young people to bring their books to the prayer space. Assign the Leader and Reader parts. Encourage young people to relax and open their hearts and minds for prayer. Remind them that God is present. Prompt the parts of Leader, All, and Reader, pausing briefly after each. Be sure the Leader pauses after each question preceded by a bullet. After brief meditation following the last question, continue with the final Leader and All parts. Conclude by praying together the Sign of the Cross.

Prayer

Renew Our Hearts

During Lent, we acknowledge our dependence on God. To prepare for Jesus' Resurrection, we turn back to God and turn away from sin. As we renew our hearts, we grow more faithful to God's Word. Lent is a good time to pray for the strength to be a better disciple.

Return to God

Leader: The grace of our Lord Jesus Christ be with us, now and forever.

All: Amen.

Leader: During Lent, we follow Jesus' footsteps into the desert. In our prayer and fasting, we remind ourselves of our need for God in our lives. In our almsgiving, we show our commitment to the poor. As we begin this season of Lent, let us ask God to renew our hearts and to help us return to him by following his ways more closely.

Reader: A reading from the Book of Joel.
[Joel 2:12–17]
The Word of the Lord.

All: Thanks be to God.

Leader: As we pray silently, let us consider how we will renew our lives this Lent through the spiritual practices of prayer, fasting, and almsgiving. Tell God what you will do this Lent as you turn away from sin and grow more faithful to the Gospel.

- What can I do to renew my prayer life? (*Pause.*)

- From what can I fast to help me hear what God is asking of me? (*Pause.*)

- What can I do to help those who are in need this Lent? (*Pause.*)

Reflect in the silence of your hearts.

Leader: We pray that God will accept our Lenten sacrifices and give us the strength to persevere in our promises. We ask this through Christ our Lord.

All: Amen.

234 *The Year in Our Church*

① Respond

Invite young people to reflect on the many choices they face every day. Say: *Each choice, large or small, can lead us toward God or away from God.* Encourage young people to carry this idea with them throughout the season of Lent.

② Go in Peace

Invite young people to pray silently as you pray aloud: *Thank you, heavenly Father, for the holy season of Lent. Help us use this time to turn our lives toward you. Amen.*

Lenten Prayer Guides

Make a variety of Lenten prayer guides available to young people, and invite them to look through the guides for a short prayer or invocation that appeals to them. Give young people time to write down the prayer and commit it to memory. Then suggest that young people say the prayer throughout the days of Lent whenever they grow idle or feel confused by choices.

FYI

Coaching Young People to Pray

Remind young people that many athletes use a journal to keep a record of their training and results. Explain that during the "spiritual training" season of Lent, a prayer journal can help them remain faithful to their commitments and can provide a concrete way to ask for help when they falter.

Holy Week

"Father, into your hands I commend my spirit."
Luke 23:46

Holy Week commemorates Jesus' triumphant entry into Jerusalem; his gift of the Eucharist; and his suffering, Death, and Resurrection. The three solemn liturgies on Holy Thursday, Good Friday, and the Easter Vigil are called the Triduum.

PRAYER

Thank you, Father, for inviting us on the journey of Holy Week and for the precious gift of your Son, Jesus, whose steps we follow.

Holy Week **235**

MATERIALS: Get Ready for the Session

For this session, you will need Bibles, writing supplies, art supplies, newspapers, and a crucifix. Review any If Time Allows activities you intend to do for additional required materials.

HOLY WEEK

OUTCOMES

▶ Explain the events that we commemorate during Holy Week.

▶ Explain that through the Paschal Mystery, Jesus calls us into new life.

① Set the Stage

Have young people imagine that they are about to leave their homes to go on a trip. Ask: *What are the very last things you or your family members do before you leave?* (Answers will vary.) Ask: *How are you feeling just before you walk out the door?* (Possible answers: excited, full of anticipation) Say: *Holy Week is also a time of final preparations and great anticipation. Our long-term preparations of prayers, fasting, and almsgiving during Lent will continue but with greater intensity. Palm Sunday is our doorway into the holiest week of the Church year.* Have young people find Holy Week and the days of the Triduum on the *Finding God* poster The Liturgical Year displayed in the room.

② Get Started

Ask: *What objects do we regard as holy?* (Possible answers: holy water, rosaries, the Bible, medals) Say: *Something holy has been set apart for a sacred purpose.* Ask: *What is the purpose of Holy Week?* (to prepare our hearts for the wonder of Easter)

Have a volunteer read aloud the Scripture verse and the paragraph. Say: *During Holy Week, we walk alongside Jesus and pray for greater appreciation of Jesus' sacrifice and recognition of the full extent of his love for us.*

 Prayer

As a group, pray aloud the prayer. Close by praying the Sign of the Cross together.

1 Begin

Share newspaper articles that tell about human suffering. Ask young people how they feel when they hear such stories. Say: **God gave us the ability to feel compassion and a deep awareness of the suffering of others. As Christians, we are called to develop this ability and to make choices based on it.** Ask: **How did Jesus show compassion for others?** (Possible responses: He healed both physical and spiritual suffering.) Say: **Holy Week invites us to remember that compassion is a privilege and duty of our faith.**

2 Connect

Invite a volunteer to read aloud the title and first three paragraphs of the article. Then distribute Bibles and have young people turn to Luke 19:28–48. Ask volunteers to take turns reading aloud the verses.

Then ask young people to imagine that they were present for Jesus' entry into Jerusalem. Ask them to work with a partner to write a headline that summarizes what they saw and heard. Remind young people that at the time, many people, including government officials, viewed Jesus as a threat. Invite partners to share their headlines with the group and to explain how and why they chose the words they did.

Ask a volunteer to read aloud the fourth paragraph. Ask: **What sacrament commemorates Jesus' Last Supper?** (the Eucharist) Say: **Every time we receive the Eucharist, we experience the Real Presence of Jesus Christ.**

Read aloud the last paragraph on the page. Ask: **What do we remember on Good Friday?** (the events of Jesus' Passion and Death) Remind young people that praying the Stations of the Cross can encourage us to carry our crosses in life with grace and hope as disciples of Jesus.

Holy Week

The Holiest Week of the Year

Jesus before Caiaphas, ceiling painting, Golgotha Chapel, Holy Sepulchre, Jerusalem.

AS we make our final preparations for Easter during Holy Week, we commemorate the events that led to Jesus' acceptance of his Death on the Cross for our sins. We remember these events with great hope because we know that death and evil do not triumph. Jesus will rise on Easter morning!

On Palm Sunday, the beginning of Holy Week, we remember that Jesus' journey to the Cross began with his glorious entry into Jerusalem. The crowds received him as their king. They laid out palm branches and shouted,

"Blessed is the king who comes in the name of the Lord.
Peace in heaven and glory in the highest."

Luke 19:38

Some Pharisees urged Jesus to rebuke the crowd for calling him a king, but Jesus would not. Jesus then went to the Temple, where he drove out the merchants and continued to teach. Shortly afterward, the religious leaders began to make plans to arrest Jesus. (Luke 19:28–48)

On Holy Thursday, we recall how Jesus celebrated his Last Supper with his disciples. This was a Passover meal, the Jewish feast that celebrated God's deliverance of Israel from slavery in Egypt. As Jesus celebrated Passover, he gave the feast a new meaning. Jesus said that his Death would begin the New Covenant. He would give his life for the forgiveness of sins.

Following their Passover meal, Jesus and his disciples went to the Mount of Olives. Jesus, knowing his betrayal was imminent, wanted to pray. On Good Friday, we reflect on the events that begin with Jesus' arrest in the garden. Jesus was taken to the house of the high priest, Caiaphas, and tried by the Sanhedrin, which was the council of Jewish elders, chief priests, and scribes. Peter followed Jesus to the courtyard of Caiaphas's house, where he was recognized as one of Jesus' disciples. Just as Jesus had told him, Peter denied even knowing Jesus three times.

236 *The Year in Our Church*

IF TIME ALLOWS

Don't Pass Over Passover

Point out that Passover is observed with a special meal and prayers that recall how God freed the people of Israel from slavery in Egypt. Ask young people to explain how the Lenten practices of praying, almsgiving, fasting, and abstinence can release someone from a kind of slavery; in this sense, a release from something to which he or she is unhappily attached. Invite volunteers to share their thoughts. Encourage young people to continue to look for parallels between the events of their own lives and those they encounter in Scripture.

In the meantime, the Sanhedrin had determined that Jesus was guilty of inciting the people by claiming to be the Messiah and king. The Sanhedrin sent him to the Roman governor, Pontius Pilate. Because the Jews were under Roman rule, only Pilate had the authority to sentence Jesus to death.

At first, Pilate refused to find Jesus guilty of anything. To appease Jesus' accusers, he sent him to King Herod, the Jewish ruler of Galilee. Herod and his court questioned and mistreated Jesus and eventually sent him back to Pilate. Again, Pilate found Jesus free from guilt of the crimes for which he was accused, preferring to have Jesus flogged and released. But Jesus' accusers persisted and the crowd called for his crucifixion. In Jesus' place, they asked for the release of another prisoner, Barabbas. Pilate protested a third time, saying he found no guilt. But Pilate's resolve was not strong, and he gave in to the demands of the people. He released Barabbas and sentenced Jesus to death on the cross.

Jesus was led away and forced to carry a cross to the place of execution, as was the custom. Along the way, a bystander named Simon of Cyrene carried Jesus' Cross for a while. Jesus met some women followers and friends. He stopped to warn them of bad times to come. Finally, between two criminals, Jesus was nailed to the Cross.

As Jesus hung on the Cross, his garments were divided among the soldiers, and he was taunted by the crowd. A mocking inscription was placed above his head that read, "This is the King of the Jews." (Luke 23:38) One of the two criminals crucified with Jesus asked Jesus to remember him when he entered his kingdom. Jesus recognized the man's faith and promised that he would join Jesus in Paradise. Finally, Jesus cried out his last words, "Father, into your hands I commend my spirit," and died. (Luke 23:46)

In his Passion and Death for our sins, Jesus showed the full depth of his love for us. His sacrifice made our eternal life in Heaven a possibility. We remember the events of Jesus' Passion and Death as we also strive to be with Jesus in Paradise at the end of our earthly lives.

Past Meets Present

PAST: The Stations of the Cross originated from the early Christian tradition of making a pilgrimage through Jerusalem to visit and pray along the path of Jesus' journey to the Cross. Along this pilgrimage were 14 stations—places to stop and recall important moments of Jesus' journey.

PRESENT: Praying the Stations of the Cross can take place any time of the year, but they are prayed more frequently during Lent and Holy Week. When we pray the Stations—most churches have depictions of them—we pray as we walk from station to station, recalling Jesus' way to his Crucifixion. Sometimes a 15th Station, the Resurrection of Jesus, is added to the prayer.

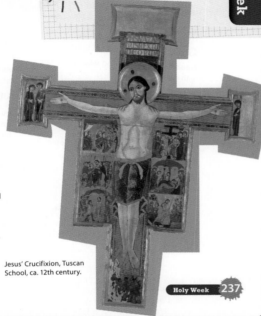

Jesus' Crucifixion, Tuscan School, ca. 12th century.

Holy Week

Holy Week **237**

IF TIME ALLOWS

Holy Week BLM

Were You There? Provide young people with the Holy Week Blackline Master [T-393] and ask a volunteer to read aloud the introductory text and directions. Have young people work independently to complete the activity. Ask volunteers to share ideas and discuss how their understanding of the Stations of the Cross has deepened or changed.

I Was There

Have young people illustrate one of the Stations of the Cross. Encourage them to include themselves as part of the crowd in the scene. Invite young people to render the scene in a surprising or creative way. For example, they might set the scene in a contemporary context or develop a slide-show presentation with reflective music.

Invite volunteers to read aloud the remaining paragraphs in the article on page 237. Ask young people to discuss how the holiest week of the year affects them, even though they've heard the stories many times before. Say: ***Sometimes, our appreciation of a Gospel story deepens if we pay special attention to a single detail.***

Refer young people to the account of Jesus' Passion in Luke 22:7–46. Have them read the account silently, looking for any detail they might not have noticed before. Ask them to close their eyes and visualize the detail. Allow time for young people to meditate briefly on this detail. Afterward, invite them to describe how this single detail gave them new insights into Jesus' experience and his gift of Salvation to us.

Past Meets Present

Invite a volunteer to read aloud Past Meets Present. Say: ***When we pray the Stations of the Cross, we remember Jesus' compassion for us, we feel compassion for his suffering, and we pray to become more compassionate toward others.*** Have young people turn to pages 284–285 of Prayers and Practices to find the Stations of the Cross. If possible, visit the church and have young people pray the Stations.

③ Close

Point out that the Passion of Jesus is remarkable because it shows both his humanity and his perfect divinity. Ask: ***How do the Holy Week Gospel stories reflect both Jesus' human and divine natures?*** (Possible answers: humanity—his physical vulnerabilities, his stumbling, his thirst; divinity—his forgiveness of the thief, his surrender to the Father's will, his winning of Salvation for our sins) Then have young people pray silently for grace to live as Jesus did.

Prayer

Guide young people as they participate in a prayer service.

Prepare Pray the prayer in advance.

 Pray Invite young people to bring their books to the prayer space. Display a crucifix and explain that we revere the Cross because through his Death, Jesus showed us the way to life. Remind young people that petitions are a form of prayer, reviewing pages 272–273 of Prayers and Practices as needed. Read aloud the title of the page and paragraph.

Assign the Reader part. Read aloud the title of the prayer. Prepare young people to pray by asking them to quiet their minds and relax. Remind them that God is present. Begin praying aloud the Leader part, followed by the All part. Continue alternating each part as shown, following the cues and pausing after each part. Conclude by praying *Amen*. Together pray the Sign of the Cross.

① Respond

Remind young people that remembering Jesus' journey teaches us to have compassion for others. Then arrange young people in groups of three and distribute the newspaper articles you shared in the Begin step, one per group. Have group members discuss ways we might respond with compassion to the suffering described in their group's article. Ask volunteers to share their ideas.

② Go in Peace

Invite young people to offer thanksgiving, praying silently as you pray aloud: ***Thank you, heavenly Father, for sending Jesus to reveal to us your great love. Help us show compassion to others as we remember Jesus' Way of the Cross.***

Prayer

We Thank Jesus

We remember the events of Jesus' Passion and Death during Holy Week. We thank him for his abundant love and for his ultimate sacrifice for our Salvation. We also recall Jesus' lesson of forgiveness. "Father, forgive them, they know not what they do." (Luke 23:34)

Our Petitions Before the Cross

Leader: Praise be to God, who fills our lives with love and joy.

All: Praise be to God.

Leader: Jesus died so that our sins might be forgiven. Let us pray that we will one day be received by Jesus in Paradise.

Reader: A reading from the holy Gospel according to Luke.
[Luke 23:33–46]
The Gospel of the Lord.

All: Praise to you, Lord Jesus Christ.

Reflect in the silence of your hearts.

Leader: Remembering all that Jesus has done for us, we offer our petitions to God:

That we follow the example of your only Son who, even as he died on the Cross, forgave those who crucified him, we pray to the Lord.

All: Lord, hear our prayer.

Leader: That we forgive those who do us harm so that we will not be filled with anger but with your love, we pray to the Lord.

All: Lord, hear our prayer.

Leader: Father, we pray to you with a spirit of forgiveness so that we can be free to accept the love you offer. Hear these prayers and the prayers of our heart. We pray through Jesus, your Son, and with the Holy Spirit.

All: Amen.

238 *The Year in Our Church*

IF TIME ALLOWS

Compassion in Action

Have young people discuss ways they might put into action one of the compassionate responses from the Respond step. Work with young people to define a realistic action plan and encourage them to follow through with it.

✝ *Solidarity*

FYI

Coaching Young People to Pray

Remind young people that this prayer service is about Jesus' saving actions and about learning to forgive those who hurt us. Explain that refusing to forgive others hardens our hearts and makes it impossible to be fully open to the love Jesus offers us. Before praying, invite them to ask God for the strength to forgive others.

Easter

"He is not here, but he has been raised."

Luke 24:6

At Easter, we celebrate God's most amazing surprise. Each of the four Gospels tells how the disciples found an empty tomb. Jesus Christ had risen from the dead! He is still with us. We encounter his Real Presence in the Eucharist.

PRAYER

Thank you, God, for surprising us every day with your love. Keep us always open to your surprises and willing to share them with others.

Easter **239**

MATERIALS: Get Ready for the Session

For this session, you will need Bibles and writing supplies. Review any If Time Allows activities you intend to do for additional required materials.

EASTER

OUTCOMES

▶ Describe the discovery of Jesus' empty tomb and the disciples' encounters with the risen Jesus.

▶ Identify the Eucharist as our encounter with the risen Jesus.

① Set the Stage

Have young people remember a time when their sadness or disappointment was unexpectedly turned around. Invite volunteers to describe their experiences. Then say: *When joy follows closely on the heels of sadness, we may feel it even more intensely. Likewise, the sadness of Jesus' friends turned to incredible joy when Jesus appeared to them after his Resurrection.*

② Get Started

Point out the season of Easter on the *Finding God* poster The Liturgical Year. Have young people point out the special days that fall within the season. (Easter Sunday, Ascension, Pentecost)

Ask a volunteer to read aloud the Scripture verse and the text in the box on the page. Then say: *We've heard the Easter story many times. We know how it will end. Therefore, we may have difficulty imagining how surprised Jesus' friends were to discover the empty tomb—and how difficult, at first, it must have been to understand the truth. Once they understood, they were filled with the desire to share the Good News with others.* Ask young people to describe a time when the truth of something dawned on them, and they felt compelled to share it.

 Prayer

Pray the prayer aloud while the group prays silently. Pray the Sign of the Cross together.

① Begin

Invite volunteers to describe their feelings when a close friend or relative moved away. Say: *Losing daily contact with someone you love can cause grief.* Write *grief* on the board, and have young people define it and additional events or situations that can cause it. Say: *Jesus' friends felt many emotions when he died. They believed they had lost him forever.* Read aloud the title Jesus Is Risen.

② Connect

✝ Invite volunteers to read aloud the paragraphs in the left column and the section Amazing News: Jesus' Tomb Is Empty! Then ask a volunteer to read aloud Luke 24:1–12. Arrange young people into two groups. Ask one group to use their imaginations and write what the women might have reported to the other disciples. Ask the other group to write what Peter's report might have been. Remind young people that the women had been advised by the "two men in dazzling garments," while Peter had not, and that this must have influenced the content of their reports. When both groups are ready, have a representative from each share their report. Discuss any differences between the two reports. Ask: *Which report would you have more readily believed? Why?* (Answers will vary.) Say: *The accounts are not identical, but they both contain the crucial truth of Jesus' Resurrection from the tomb.*

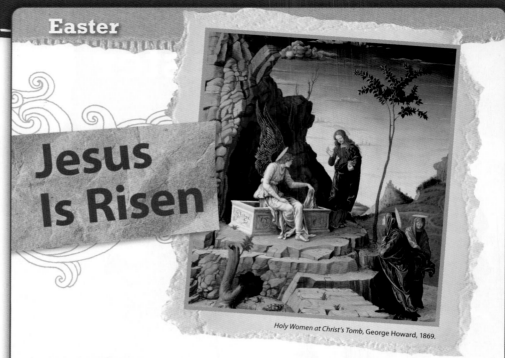

Easter

Jesus Is Risen

Holy Women at Christ's Tomb, George Howard, 1869.

IMAGINE what it must have been like to be Jesus' friend, his disciple, on the day he was put to Death on the Cross. Jesus had been tried as a criminal, found guilty, tortured, and killed in a public and most horrible way.

After witnessing all that had happened, Jesus' friends might have shared intense feelings of sadness, fear, confusion, or anger. They probably tried to comfort one another as Jesus' body was taken from the Cross and placed in the tomb. Saturday, the day after Jesus' Death on Good Friday, was the Jewish Sabbath. The Sabbath laws restricted activities on this day, so no one could visit Jesus' tomb.

Amazing News: Jesus' Tomb Is Empty!

On the day after the Sabbath, some women disciples went to Jesus' tomb with spices to embalm his body. This practice was part of their Jewish custom. However, they returned from the tomb with an amazing report. The stone had been moved from the entrance to the tomb. Jesus' body was not there. And they had seen a vision of two men in white who told them that Jesus had been raised from the dead. (Luke 24:1–7)

The women reported this to other disciples. In first-century Jewish society, women couldn't serve as public witnesses. The men may have thought, "These women are crazy." Luke's Gospel tells us, "[T]heir story seemed like nonsense and they did not believe them." (Luke 24:11) Imagine what it must have been like to be one of those women. Only Peter got up and ran to Jesus' tomb, where he found the burial cloths but not Jesus' body. And Peter left amazed. (Luke 24:12)

240 *The Year in Our Church*

IF TIME ALLOWS

Member, Remember!

✝ Point out that even Jesus' closest friends had faulty memories about who he was. The "men in dazzling garments" had to remind the women at the tomb what Jesus had told them earlier about his fate. Reread Luke 24:6–8 aloud. Then have young people think of a time when they forgot something important and it took another person to remind them. Ask how they felt toward that person. Explain that since none of us is perfect, we need one another's help to stay focused and remember what's important. Explain that this is one of our most vital jobs as members of Christ's Church.

But What Happened?

At first Jesus' disciples considered that Jesus' body had been stolen. That seemed possible, perhaps even logical. But why were the burial cloths found in the tomb? Even grave robbers would keep a dead body wrapped. It took time for the disciples to understand fully that Jesus had been raised from the dead.

What led the disciples to believe that Jesus had been raised from the dead? The angels at the tomb said to the women, "'Why do you seek the living one among the dead? He is not here, but he has been raised.'" (Luke 24:5–6) The angels reminded the women that Jesus had said that he would be put to death by sinners and would rise again on the third day.

The risen Jesus appeared to his disciples. The Gospel of Luke tells us about Jesus' appearance to two disciples on the road to Emmaus, a village about seven miles from Jerusalem. These two disciples engaged in conversation with a stranger. In the course of their conversation, the stranger, who was Jesus, explained and interpreted all that Scripture predicted about the Messiah. While breaking bread together at a meal, the disciples finally recognized that the stranger was Jesus.

Amazed and anxious to share their news, these two disciples returned to Jerusalem. As they gathered with the eleven Apostles and others, imagine their surprise at reports that others had also seen Jesus. "The Lord has truly been raised and has appeared to Simon!" (Luke 24:34) Then the two told those assembled what had happened and how they recognized Jesus in the breaking of the bread.

Our Encounter with Jesus

The amazing news of the risen Jesus didn't end there in Jerusalem. We share in this experience, too, when we encounter Jesus in the celebration of the Eucharist. In the Eucharist, we experience Jesus' Real Presence at the consecration, when the bread and wine become the Body and Blood of Jesus Christ. Every Sunday we celebrate Jesus' Resurrection from the dead. Like the women who found the empty tomb and the disciples who encountered the risen Jesus, we can't help but share this amazing good news with others.

Easter

Our Catholic Character

Alleluia is a Hebrew word used to offer praise to God. During the season of Lent, the word *Alleluia* is not acclaimed during Mass. For instance, the *Alleluia* before the Gospel is replaced with an alternate acclamation. We pray and sing *Alleluia* with extra joy again during the Easter liturgies.

Easter 241

IF TIME ALLOWS

Easter BLM

✝ **"Remember What He Said to You."** Provide young people with the Easter Blackline Master [T-394] and ask a volunteer to read aloud the introductory text and directions. Have young people work independently. Invite volunteers to share their responses.

Empty Yet Full

Point out that similar to the cross, the empty tomb is a powerful symbol of our faith and the responsibility we are given as Christians to share the Good News of Christ's presence among us with other people. Have young people work with a partner to design an empty tomb as a symbol of our Christianity. Invite partners to share their completed designs with the group.

Have volunteers read aloud But What Happened? Then ask a volunteer to read aloud Luke 24:13–25. Ask: **Why did Jesus call the two "foolish"?** (They persisted in their disbelief.) Say: **In spite of the women's report and Peter's report, the disciples remained blinded by grief and confusion.** Ask young people to share times they persisted in disbelieving something they later learned was true. Say: **The truth is often right before our eyes. This was true of the two disciples on the road to Emmaus.** Ask: **Why was it fitting that the disciples recognized Jesus while sharing a meal?** (Possible answer: He shared himself with them at this meal, just as he had done at the Last Supper.)

Point out that just as Jesus was present to the disciples on the road to Emmaus, he is present with us in the Eucharist. Then ask a volunteer to read aloud Our Encounter with Jesus. Challenge young people to recall and recite the priest's and congregation's last words at Mass. (Priest: "Go in peace, glorifying the Lord by your life." Congregation: "Thanks be to God.") Say: **The women who discovered the empty tomb and the Emmaus disciples could not contain themselves; once they realized the truth, they had to share it. We, too, are sent forth from the Mass to share joyfully the Good News of Jesus with all those we meet.**

Our Catholic Character

Invite a volunteer to read aloud the feature. Encourage young people to notice the frequency with which we pray "Alleluia" in our Easter liturgies.

③ Close

Ask young people what changes they see in the sanctuary of the church on Easter Sunday. (Possible answers: flowers, white or gold banners and vestments, an Easter candle) Say: **These visual changes are another way of saying "Alleluia!" They symbolize our joy and the light of Jesus in the world.**

Prayer

Guide young people as they participate in a prayer service.

Prepare Pray the prayer in advance.

Pray Ask young people how they stay in touch with loved ones. Remind them that Jesus is present to us at every Mass. Say: *Once we become aware of Jesus' presence, we are called to pass on the Good News just as the disciples did.* Explain that in this litany we will alternate humble entreaties to God, followed by a response. Assign volunteers the parts of the prayer. Point out the words of the Response and the symbol that reminds them to pray after the designated Leader parts.

Invite young people to bring their books to the prayer space. Ask them to get comfortable and to know that God is present. Cue the Leader to begin and proceed to pray, alternating parts as indicated. Allow a brief time for meditation after each part. Conclude by praying together the Sign of the Cross.

① Respond

Remind young people that Jesus wants us to share his Good News with others through our words and deeds. Have them brainstorm at least 10 specific ways we might do this. Write their responses on the board.

② Go in Peace

Invite young people to pray in thanksgiving for the risen Jesus. Then pray aloud while young people pray silently: *Thank you, God, for raising Jesus from the dead so that we might experience his presence with us. Help us share the message of Jesus' Resurrection with others. Amen.*

Prayer

Alleluia! Jesus Is Risen

Jesus is God of the living. By his Resurrection, all of Jesus' works and teachings are confirmed. By his Death, he saves us from sin. Jesus' Resurrection opens a way for us to share eternal life with him in Heaven. This is why we joyfully pray Alleluia.

A Litany: The Victory of the Cross

Leader: The grace of the risen Jesus Christ be with us all, now and forever.

All: Amen.

Reader: A reading from the holy Gospel according to Luke.
[Luke 24:1–6]
The Gospel of the Lord.

All: Praise to you, Lord Jesus Christ.

Leader: Let us pray together in praise and thanksgiving. Jesus has been raised from the dead! Alleluia! Alleluia!

Response: Alleluia! Jesus is truly risen!

Leader: As the first disciples came to have faith in Jesus' Resurrection from the dead, so too may we have faith in the power of God, who has conquered death. ℟.

Leader: As the hearts of the disciples on the road to Emmaus were set on fire when Jesus talked with them about the Scriptures, so too may we be enlivened when we encounter Jesus through the words of Scripture. ℟.

Leader: As the disciples on the road to Emmaus recognized Jesus in the breaking of the bread, so too may we recognize Jesus' Real Presence in the Eucharist. ℟.

Leader: As the disciples proclaimed the Good News of Jesus Christ's Resurrection to others, so too may we be witnesses of his Resurrection to the world. ℟.

Leader: Lord, hear our prayers and continue to deepen our faith in the power of Christ's Resurrection. We ask this through your Son, who lives and reigns with you and the Holy Spirit for ever and ever.

All: Amen.

242 *The Year in Our Church*

IF TIME ALLOWS

Compassion in Action
Have young people consider the list of words and deeds written on the board during the Respond step. Then have them choose one option or another of their own choice and resolve to live it in the coming week.

FYI

Coaching Young People to Pray

Remind young people that Jesus wants us to act as his children in the world. When we pray humbly to God, asking him for what we need, God hears our prayers. Before praying, encourage young people to ask God for help to deepen their faith in the power of Christ's Resurrection.

Pentecost

And they were all filled with the holy Spirit . . .
Acts of the Apostles 2:4

Before Jesus' Ascension into Heaven, he had promised his disciples that he would not leave them alone. He had promised to send them a helper. So the disciples returned in faith to Jerusalem to wait for Jesus' promise to come true.

PRAYER

Thank you, Jesus, for keeping all your promises to us, especially your promise to send a helper. Make us always aware of your Spirit in our midst.

Pentecost **243**

MATERIALS: Get Ready for the Session

For this session, you will need Bibles. Review any If Time Allows activities you intend to do for additional materials young people may require.

OUTCOMES

▶ Describe the story of the descent of the Holy Spirit at Pentecost.

▶ Explain how the Holy Spirit strengthens us to be Christ's witnesses.

① Set the Stage

Ask young people to recall a time when they were so excited or enthusiastic about something that they couldn't wait to share the news with others. Invite volunteers to describe the experience. Then say: *When the Holy Spirit descended on the disciples, they felt the same way. They were so filled with God's love that they had to proclaim the works of God immediately.*

② Get Started

Draw a time line on the board. To the left, write these events concerning Jesus: *Ascension, Resurrection,* and *Appearances to Disciples.* Ask volunteers to put these three events in chronological order on the time line. (Resurrection, Ascension, Appearances to Disciples)

Invite a volunteer to read aloud the Scripture verse and the text in the box. Say: *Jesus fulfilled his promise to his friends. We call this event Pentecost.* Write *Pentecost* to the right of "Appearances to Disciples" on the time line. Use the *Finding God* poster The Liturgical Calendar to point out that each of these events occurred within the Easter season of the Church year.

Prayer

As a group, pray the prayer aloud slowly and reverently. Close by praying the Sign of the Cross together.

1 Begin

Have young people recall a time when they were left waiting. Invite them to share the experience and their feelings. Point out that waiting can be joyful anticipation, but it can also cause anxiety. Say: *The disciples waited together in Jerusalem for about 10 days after the Ascension. Ten days is a long time to wait when you are excited or anxious.* Ask: *What kinds of things do you think the disciples expected to happen? How might their feelings have changed over the course of the 10 days?* (Answers will vary.)

2 Connect

Read aloud the title. Invite volunteers to read aloud the first two paragraphs. Distribute Bibles and instruct young people to find the ending of the Gospel of Luke and the beginning of the Acts of the Apostles.

Arrange young people in two groups. Ask one group to read Luke 24:36–53 and the other to read Acts of the Apostles 1:1–12. Then invite groups to summarize the passages. After the first group's summary, ask: *How did Jesus prepare his disciples for what would happen next?* (Possible answers: He showed them his hands and feet. He demonstrated that he was real. He "opened their minds to understand the scriptures." He told them that they were witnesses and that they would soon be "clothed with power from on high.") After the second group summarizes, ask: *What does Jesus promise in this account?* (that the disciples will be baptized with the Holy Spirit) Ask: *What additional assurance do the disciples receive after Jesus ascends?* (Two men dressed in white garments promise that Jesus will return.)

Read aloud the first paragraph of The Gift of the Holy Spirit. Ask a volunteer to read aloud Acts of the Apostles 2:1–12 in the Bible as others read silently.

Pentecost

The Beginning of the Church

JESUS' Ascension into Heaven appeared to signal the end of his encounters with his disciples. But they would soon find out that they were part of a new and wonderful beginning. The story of the beginning of the Church is found in the Acts of the Apostles.

The Acts of the Apostles was written by the same person who recorded the Gospel of Luke. The Gospel of Luke tells the story of Jesus' life, Death, Resurrection, and Ascension. The Acts of the Apostles continues the story by telling how the Holy Spirit led the Apostles to preach the message of Jesus throughout the Roman empire.

The Gift of the Holy Spirit

After Jesus was taken to Heaven, the disciples returned to Jerusalem and gathered in the house where they had been staying. These disciples included the twelve Apostles (Matthias had been chosen to replace Judas, Jesus' betrayer), as well as women disciples and Mary, the Mother of Jesus. As this group of Jesus' closest friends gathered on the Jewish feast of Pentecost, an extraordinary thing happened. The Acts of the Apostles tells us that a loud noise, like wind, filled the house. And then it looked as if tongues of fire touched each of them. The disciples felt themselves filled with the Holy Spirit, and they began to speak in different languages. (Acts of the Apostles 2:1–4)

244 *The Year in Our Church*

IF TIME ALLOWS

Pentecost Facts

Share with young people the following information.

• *Pentecost* is the Greek name for *Shavuot,* the Jewish Festival of Weeks, which celebrates God's gift of the five books of Moses—the Pentateuch.

• In the Jewish tradition, Shavuot is celebrated 50 days after Passover.

• Christians celebrate the Feast of Pentecost 50 days after Easter Sunday.

Using either the liturgical calendar on page 221 or the *Finding God* poster The Liturgical Calendar, point out that Ordinary Time is the next season. Explain that Ordinary Time continues through the summer and fall until a new liturgical year begins with Advent.

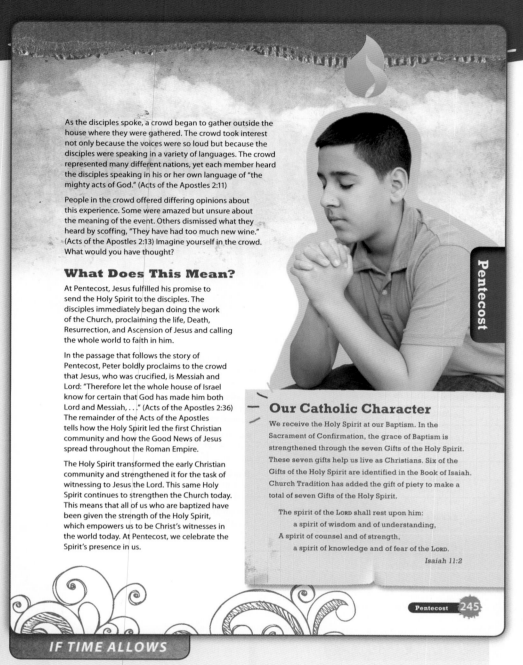

As the disciples spoke, a crowd began to gather outside the house where they were gathered. The crowd took interest not only because the voices were so loud but because the disciples were speaking in a variety of languages. The crowd represented many different nations, yet each member heard the disciples speaking in his or her own language of "the mighty acts of God." (Acts of the Apostles 2:11)

People in the crowd offered differing opinions about this experience. Some were amazed but unsure about the meaning of the event. Others dismissed what they heard by scoffing, "They have had too much new wine." (Acts of the Apostles 2:13) Imagine yourself in the crowd. What would you have thought?

What Does This Mean?

At Pentecost, Jesus fulfilled his promise to send the Holy Spirit to the disciples. The disciples immediately began doing the work of the Church, proclaiming the life, Death, Resurrection, and Ascension of Jesus and calling the whole world to faith in him.

In the passage that follows the story of Pentecost, Peter boldly proclaims to the crowd that Jesus, who was crucified, is Messiah and Lord: "Therefore let the whole house of Israel know for certain that God has made him both Lord and Messiah, . . ." (Acts of the Apostles 2:36) The remainder of the Acts of the Apostles tells how the Holy Spirit led the first Christian community and how the Good News of Jesus spread throughout the Roman Empire.

The Holy Spirit transformed the early Christian community and strengthened it for the task of witnessing to Jesus the Lord. This same Holy Spirit continues to strengthen the Church today. This means that all of us who are baptized have been given the strength of the Holy Spirit, which empowers us to be Christ's witnesses in the world today. At Pentecost, we celebrate the Spirit's presence in us.

Pentecost

Our Catholic Character

We receive the Holy Spirit at our Baptism. In the Sacrament of Confirmation, the grace of Baptism is strengthened through the seven Gifts of the Holy Spirit. These seven gifts help us live as Christians. Six of the Gifts of the Holy Spirit are identified in the Book of Isaiah. Church Tradition has added the gift of piety to make a total of seven Gifts of the Holy Spirit.

> The spirit of the LORD shall rest upon him:
>   a spirit of wisdom and of understanding,
> A spirit of counsel and of strength,
>   a spirit of knowledge and of fear of the LORD.
>
> Isaiah 11:2

Pentecost **245**

IF TIME ALLOWS

Pentecost BLM

Gifts of the Holy Spirit Provide young people with the Pentecost Blackline Master [T-395] and read aloud the introductory text and directions. Have young people work with a partner to develop a short description of each gift, using key words or phrases. Then have them work independently to think of ways to use each gift before they answer the questions at the bottom of the page. Discuss ideas as a group.

Pentecost Word Cloud

Have young people use articles from magazines and newspapers to make a word cloud that represents Pentecost. Challenge them to include unexpected words or phrases and to be prepared to explain how they relate to the coming of the Holy Spirit in their lives. Invite them to use markers or pens to add additional words. Allow volunteers to share their completed word clouds with the group.

Have a volunteer continue reading the remaining paragraphs in The Gift of the Holy Spirit section. Discuss young people's own experiences of large crowds. Ask: **How would you describe the energy generated by a large crowd?** (Possible answers: invigorating, loud, enthusiastic, confusing, anticipatory, chaotic) Ask: **How might the Pentecost gathering have been the same?** (Possible answers: The atmosphere was anticipatory and curious, the crowd was diverse, and people had different opinions about what they were witnessing.)

Invite volunteers to read aloud What Does This Mean? Ask young people to think of a time when they received unexpected strength or courage. Say: **This is what happened at Pentecost. Despite all the fear and uncertainty that came before, the disciples were filled with the desire and ability to speak the truth.** Ask: **What do we celebrate on the Feast of Pentecost?** (the fact that we, too, are filled with the Holy Spirit)

Our Catholic Character

Invite a volunteer to read aloud Our Catholic Character. Ask them to find and circle the seven Gifts of the Holy Spirit. Explain that in the Sacrament of Confirmation, we celebrate the strengthening of the grace we received at Baptism, and we celebrate the Gifts of the Holy Spirit at work in our lives.

③ Close

Remind young people that we can ask the Holy Spirit to work in our lives and in our world. Refer young people to the Prayer to the Holy Spirit on page 275 of Prayers and Practices. Pray the prayer aloud together. Encourage young people to pray this prayer often.

Prayer

Guide young people as they participate in a prayer service.

Prepare Pray the prayer in advance.

Pray Explain that the Gifts of the Holy Spirit help us share the Good News of Jesus through our words and deeds. Ask: *How can we make the Gifts of the Spirit more apparent in our lives?* (Possible answers: We can pray to the Holy Spirit. We can become more mindful of what we do and say.)

Invite young people to bring their books to the prayer space and prepare to pray. Assign the seven Reader parts. Point out the Response and pray it aloud. Remind young people that the symbol following each Reader part tells them to repeat the words of the Response. Read the Leader part, followed by the All part. Continue to alternate parts, pausing briefly for meditation between each one. Conclude the service by praying the Sign of the Cross together.

① Respond

Observe that people who are filled with the Holy Spirit inspire others to follow their example of Christian living. Have young people work in groups of three or four to identify people in our world who give evidence that the Holy Spirit is at work in their lives. Then have them identify concrete ways in which we might follow their example. When all groups are finished, invite them to share their ideas.

② Go in Peace

Pray aloud, asking God to help us remain open to receive the Holy Spirit: *Thank you, God, for the gift of the Holy Spirit. Help us allow the Holy Spirit to strengthen us to be your witnesses in the world. Amen.*

Prayer

Lord, Send Down Your Spirit

Pentecost, from the Hunterian Psalter, ca. 1170.

Just as the Holy Spirit prepared the Apostles to preach God's Word, so does the Spirit encourage us to act as witnesses in the world. On the Feast of Pentecost, we pray that the Holy Spirit strengthens us as we continue the mission of the Church.

Welcome, Holy Spirit

Leader: Let us praise the God of wisdom and grace. Blessed be God forever.

All: Blessed be God forever.

Leader: Just as the Holy Spirit strengthened Jesus' first disciples and enabled them to witness to the Lord, so too may we be strengthened by the Gifts of the Holy Spirit.

Response: Lord, help us be open to your Spirit.

Reader 1: May we receive the gift of wisdom, that we may recognize God's action in our lives. We pray, . . . ℟.

Reader 2: May we receive the gift of fortitude, that we may persevere in our love of God. We pray, . . . ℟.

Reader 3: May we receive the gift of understanding, that our hearts may be open to the message of God's great love. We pray, . . . ℟.

Reader 4: May we receive the gift of knowledge, that we will always seek to know more about God. We pray, . . . ℟.

Reader 5: May we receive the gift of counsel, that we may always show right judgment in the decisions we make. We pray, . . . ℟.

Reader 6: May we receive the gift of piety, that others may see in us a life of faithfulness. We pray, . . . ℟.

Reader 7: May we receive the gift of fear of the Lord, that we may always be in wonder and awe of God's kindness to us. We pray, . . . ℟.

Leader: May the Gifts of the Holy Spirit make us faithful witnesses to Christ and strengthen the Church's mission today. We pray this in Jesus' name.

All: Amen.

246 *The Year in Our Church*

IF TIME ALLOWS

At Work in the World

Have young people work in pairs to scan recent newspapers or magazines for stories that reflect the movement of the Holy Spirit in the world today. When all pairs have found at least one story, invite them to share with the group, explaining why they chose the story.

FYI

Coaching Young People to Pray

Suggest that young people ask the Holy Spirit to strengthen their ability to use each gift in their daily lives. Point out that there are seven gifts, and suggest that they use each day of the week to focus on a different gift when they pray.

All Saints Day

Beloved, we are God's children now; . . .
1 John 3:2

We celebrate the relationship we share with the holy women and men who have gone before us in the faith and who live now with God in Heaven. We honor them on November 1, All Saints Day, and November 2, All Souls Day.

PRAYER

Thank you, God, for giving us the saints as guides in faith. Help us learn from them and follow in their ways.

All Saints Day **247**

MATERIALS: Get Ready for the Session

For this session, you will need Bibles, assorted books about the saints, and writing supplies. Review any If Time Allows activities you intend to do for additional required materials.

OUTCOMES

▶ Describe a saint as someone whose life reveals God's grace.

▶ Explain the Communion of Saints as an important part of Catholic spirituality.

① Set the Stage

Invite young people to think of a person they believe to be holy. Ask them to name traits they have observed in this person. Write young people's responses on the board. Then say: *All these traits are signs of God's grace. A saint is a person who reflects God's grace in their words and deeds and in their relationships with others and with the world.*

② Get Started

Explain that the image shown is a section of the Communion of Saints tapestry in the Cathedral of Our Lady of the Angels. The artist, John Nava, used both old and modern techniques to weave together 135 saints from many different centuries so that people could recognize that "a saint could look like me."

Then have a volunteer read aloud the Scripture verse and the text in the box. Explain that All Saints Day is a Holy Day of Obligation so we celebrate all that God has done for us by attending Mass. If necessary, review the meaning of *Holy Day of Obligation* by referring to it in the Glossary. Ask a volunteer to find All Saints Day on the *Finding God* poster The Liturgical Calendar. Ask: *In which season does this feast day fall?* (Ordinary Time)

Prayer

Pray the prayer aloud as the group prays in silence. Close by praying the Sign of the Cross together.

① Begin

Have young people recall a time when they participated in a sporting event or another performance in front of an audience. Ask about the difference the audience made. Point out that the energy and expectations of an audience can help athletes and performers boost their efforts and do their best. Say: *The saints do the same for us. They give us energy and higher expectations for ourselves. They give us a boost toward God.*

② Connect

Invite a volunteer to read aloud the title Our Fan Club in Heaven and the first two paragraphs. Then have young people think of a time when they prayed for someone else or when they knew someone else was praying for them. Ask: *What difference does prayer make in your life or in the lives of other people?* (Possible answers: Prayer inspires us, it restores our faith, and it helps us recognize the needs of others.)

Say: *Praying for one another is an important part of Catholic spirituality. Because we form one family of God, every prayer we pray for the living, for those who have died and are in Heaven, or for those who have died and are in Purgatory, strengthens the Church and brings us closer to Christ.*

Invite volunteers to read aloud the sections Who Is a Saint? and Litany of the Saints. Arrange young people in two groups and ask each group to list the names of some saints. Invite groups to share their lists. Write the saints' names on the board and brainstorm details related to them.

Distribute books about the lives of the saints, and have young people verify the details they cited and locate new details. Explain that reading about the saints can keep them present in our lives and inspire us to follow Christ more faithfully.

All Saints Day

Our Fan Club in Heaven

PRAYER for one another is an integral part of our Catholic Tradition. We believe prayer is central to our spiritual well-being and our relationship with God. Prayer also benefits the entire Christian community when we pray for one another's needs.

Prayer for one another doesn't end with death. We believe in the Communion of Saints, men and women who have been saved in Jesus Christ, who may be living or dead. Those who have died in friendship with God continue to pray for us and to intercede on our behalf before God. We, the living, pray for the dead in Purgatory who are being prepared to see the face of God. In this way, the living and the dead form one family before God.

Who Is a Saint?

The Church elevates certain individuals whose lives exemplify what it means to love God. The saints are not perfect people, but they are spiritual guides and companions. We believe that a saint has led a holy and virtuous life that models a path for us to follow. Through God's grace, the saints have received what we all hope to receive one day, which is God's promised Salvation. A saint is a person whom the Church believes now lives with God in Heaven. By declaring a person a saint, the Church acknowledges that evidence of God's grace was at work in this person's life as an authentic witness to Christ. Because of the abundance of God's grace in their lives, the saints can intercede before God on behalf of the living.

Litany of the Saints

A litany is a form of prayer in which a number of petitions are offered and the congregation responds. A special form of litany is the Litany of the Saints. In this prayer we ask the saints to pray for us by naming individual saints. This prayer is often prayed as part of the Easter Vigil and at ordinations. However, we might choose to pray this form of prayer anytime we wish to call upon the witness and prayers of those who have gone before us in the faith.

248 *The Year in Our Church*

IF TIME ALLOWS

Saint Q and A

Have young people work with a partner. Ask partners to select a saint from one of the books you distributed, read about the saint's life, and then role-play an interview with the saint. The young person taking the role of the saint may wish to dress for the part. Encourage the interviewer to ask the saint for advice in various situations and ask the saint to respond in a way that is consistent with the facts of that saint's life or the teachings of the Church. Ask volunteers to perform their interviews for the group.

A Calendar Full of Saints

Our Church calendar is filled with the names of saints whom we believe live now with God in Heaven. Many of us know the feast days for some popular saints. For example, March 17 is Saint Patrick's Day, March 19 is Saint Joseph's Day, and December 12 is the Feast of Our Lady of Guadalupe.

By popular devotion, some saints are considered patrons for particular needs or causes, which are usually related to an aspect of his or her life. We take our special needs to patron saints and ask them to intercede to God on our behalf. Saint Francis of Assisi is the patron saint of ecology because of his reverence for God's creation. Saint Frances Xavier Cabrini is the patron saint of immigrants because of all the work she did to help immigrants. Sometimes individuals, organizations, churches, and even countries are placed under the patronage of a particular saint. For example, Mary, the Mother of God, is the patroness of the United States.

We remember all these holy men and women whom the Church recognizes as saints on All Saints Day, November 1. In addition to the saints, there are many individuals who live now with God in Heaven who haven't been officially declared saints by the Church. Many of us remember the life and witness of family members and friends whom we believe to be unofficial saints. On All Saints Day, we also celebrate these undeclared saints, who also pray for us before God.

All Saints Day Is Also Our Feast Day

In his letters to early Christian communities, Saint Paul often addressed the people as "the holy ones" or "the saints" to remind them of their call to holiness. We, too, are called to be saints. We dedicate our lives to God and pray that through his grace we may join the saints in Heaven and live forever in his presence. Devotions to saints, such as pilgrimages to shrines or our use of sacramentals, are practices that deepen our spiritual values and help us learn the path to Salvation.

Day of the Dead altar honoring family ancestors.

All Saints Day

Our Catholic Character

Our Catholic Tradition distinguishes the prayer and worship we offer to God from the veneration and honor we give to Mary and the saints. Prayer is properly directed only toward God. Of all the saints, Mary is given a place of honor, and we offer special devotion to her. When we honor the saints, we ask for their intercession on our behalf with God. The effects of our devotion to the saints come from God's grace alone.

All Saints Day **249**

All Saints Day BLM

Dear Child of God Distribute books about the saints to young people. Then provide young people with the All Saints Day Blackline Master [T-396] and read aloud the introductory text and directions. Before beginning, encourage young people to ask the saint to be with them as they write. Copy the following letter frame on the board and ask them to imagine what the saint would write to them:

Dear _____,

I am writing to tell you _____. I know you are concerned about _____, but I want you to know that _____. From my own experience, I know that _____. Remember that _____ and that God will always _____.

Love,

_____

Have a volunteer read aloud A Calendar Full of Saints. Then ask young people to recall the holy person they thought about in Set the Stage on page 247. Say: *These people may be undeclared saints. On All Saints Day, we remember the witness and example of these unofficial saints as well.*

Distribute Bibles and arrange young people in three groups, assigning each a Scripture passage: Ephesians 1:1–2, Philippians 4:21–23, or 2 Corinthians 1:1–2. Invite volunteers from each group to read their passages aloud. Explain that all three passages are letters written by Saint Paul and that the phrase "holy ones" is another translation for the word *saints*.

Invite a volunteer to read aloud All Saints Day Is Also Our Feast Day. Say: *Just as Saint Paul called the members of the early Christian communities "saints," we too are called to be saints. We are called to pray that people will see in us reflections of Jesus and evidence of God's grace.*

Our Catholic Character

Invite a volunteer to read aloud Our Catholic Character. Ask young people to name prayers that are directed to Mary or the saints. (Possible answers: the Hail Mary; Hail, Holy Queen; Prayer to Saint Joseph; Prayer to Saint Jude; Prayer to Saint Michael the Archangel)

Say: *When we pray to the saints, it is like asking a good friend of Jesus' to pray for us. This kind of prayer is called intercessory prayer.*

③ Close

Provide materials and ask young people to find and pray aloud a prayer of intercession. Encourage young people to continue to pray for those who have died and to offer intercessory prayers to the saints.

Prayer

Guide young people as they participate in a prayer service.

Prepare Pray the prayer in advance.

Pray Invite young people to name favors they might ask of their friends. Say: *When we pray to the saints, we ask them to intercede for us before God. We ask them to add their prayers to our own. We believe this chorus of voices pleases God and strengthens the Body of Christ.*

Invite young people to bring their books to the prayer space. Assign the Leader and Reader parts. Prompt all to pray the Sign of the Cross. Encourage young people to focus on the meaning of the words about to be prayed. Prompt the Leader to begin. Pause and then cue the Reader. After the response by All, have the Leader introduce the litany. Alternate between the Leader and the Response. Invite young people to name favorite saints. Then prompt the Leader to pray the final part. All pray *Amen.* Then conclude by praying the Sign of the Cross.

① Respond

Remind young people that the saints are models of Christian living. Have them write about the life of a saint that they would like to emulate in their own lives. Say: *Consciously practicing a virtuous way to live can lead to lifelong habits.* Invite volunteers to share their ideas with the group.

② Go in Peace

Invite young people to reflect on these words as you pray aloud: *Thank you, God, for raising up among us models of Christian living. Help us imitate these saints in their holiness. Amen.*

Prayer

A Litany of the Saints

On November 1 we celebrate All Saints Day. These holy men and women, recognized by the Church for leading virtuous lives in the service of God, intercede before God on our behalf. The saints in Heaven encourage and inspire us to act as witnesses for Christ.

Pray for Us

All: In the name of the Father and of the Son and of the Holy Spirit. Amen.

Leader: God, you have called us to be your children and have given us the grace to become holy. We thank you for uniting us with the holy men and women who have gone before us in the Communion of Saints. We long for the day when we will see you face to face.

Reader: A reading from the First Letter of John. [1 John 3:1–3] The Word of the Lord.

All: Thanks be to God.

Leader: Let us pray a Litany of the Saints, asking the holy men and women who are with God in Heaven to pray for us.

Response: Pray for us.

Leader: Saint Mary Magdalene ℟.

Leader: Saint Basil ℟.

Leader: Saint Elizabeth ℟.

Leader: Saint Anthony ℟.

Leader: Saint Monica ℟.

Leader: Saint Thomas Aquinas ℟.

All are invited to invoke the names of their favorite saints. ℟.

Leader: May the example of the lives of the saints and their prayers for us lead us to join them one day in the presence of God. We ask this through Christ our Lord.

All: Amen.

250 *The Year in Our Church*

IF TIME ALLOWS

Saintly Connection

Have young people write the invocation "Saint , pray for us" on a strip of construction paper. Then have them loop and tape the strips together to create a paper chain. Remind young people to tape their strips so that each invocation is visible on the outside of the paper link. Have young people arrange the completed chain around the room, in the prayer space, or at the base of a statue of a saint.

FYI

Coaching Young People to Pray

Remind young people that in addition to praying for those who have died, they may ask loved ones who have died to intercede with God on their behalf. Encourage young people to imagine a deceased loved one face-to-face with God, interceding on their behalf. Point out the comfort and assurance we enjoy as one family before God.

Prayers and Practices of Our Faith

Prayers and Practices of Our Faith 251

The following resources from the Young People's Book are reproduced in this section for your convenience.

- **The Bible and You**
- **Formulas of Catholic Doctrine**
- **Praying Our Faith**
- **Celebrating and Living Our Faith**

Prayers and Practices of Our Faith

Luke

John

251

CATECHIST INFORMATION

Encourage young people to reference these pages throughout the year. This resource is divided into four sections: Scripture, doctrine, prayer, and suggestions for celebrating and living our faith.

Prayers and Practices of Our Faith

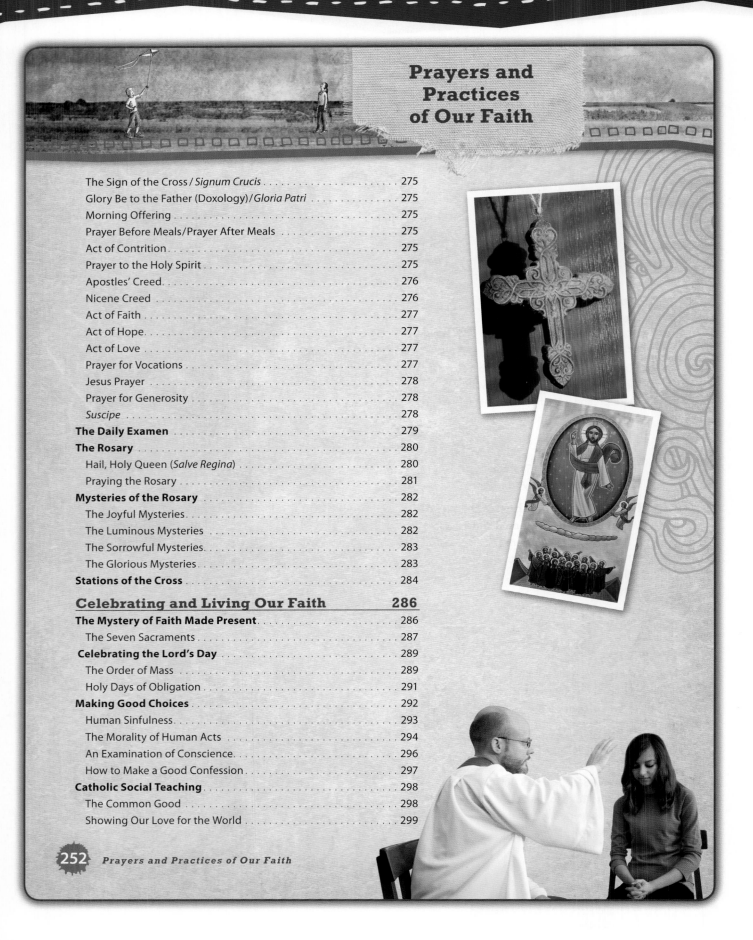

252 *Prayers and Practices of Our Faith*

The Bible and You

The Story of God's Promise

GOD speaks to us in many different ways. One way that he has revealed himself to us is through Scripture. These collected writings make up the Bible. The Scriptures tell the story of God's promise to care for us, especially through his Son, Jesus. At Mass, readings from the Bible are proclaimed during the Liturgy of the Word. Christians all over the world pray with Scripture when they pray the Liturgy of the Hours or read the Bible on their own.

The Bible is not one book; it is a collection of books that is made up of two parts, the Old Testament and the New Testament. The events we read about in the Bible happened over a period of about 2,000 years. The Old Testament tells about events that unfolded over many centuries. The events in the New Testament happened, for the most part, in a single century. These events occurred during Jesus' lifetime and in the lifetime of his followers during the first century A.D.

Many of the stories that are included in the Bible were first developed in oral cultures. The stories were passed on by word of mouth from one generation to the next. Eventually the stories were written down, the earliest writings in the New Testament being Paul's first letter to the Thessalonians. The writings that make up the Bible were inspired by the Holy Spirit and were written by different authors who used various literary styles.

Christ on the Cross, Barthelemy d'Eyck, ca. 1445–50, Louvre, Paris, France.

The Scriptures tell the story of God's promise to care for us.

The Bible and You 253

Two Parts of the Bible

The Bible is made up of two parts: the Old Testament and the New Testament. The Old Testament contains 46 books that tell stories about the Jewish people and their faith in God before Jesus was born.

The New Testament contains 27 books that tell the story of Jesus' life, Death, Resurrection, and Ascension and the experiences of the early Christians. For Christians, the most important books of the New Testament are the four Gospels—Matthew, Mark, Luke, and John.

Finding a Passage

How can you find a passage in the Bible? Bible passages are identified by book, chapter, and verse, such as Genesis 1:28. The name of the book comes first. Sometimes the name is abbreviated. Your Bible's table of contents will help you determine what the abbreviation means. After the name of the book, there are two numbers. The first number identifies the chapter. So for Genesis 1:28, Chapter 1 is being referenced. The number or range of numbers following the colon identifies the verse or verses, which in the example below is verse 28.

Discovering the Truth in the Bible

When we read the Bible, we want to try our best to understand and interpret it accurately. We know that the Bible teaches truth because it is inspired by God. We use the word **inspiration** to explain that God is the author who, through the Holy Spirit, enlightened the minds of human authors while they were writing.

By acting through the authors, the Holy Spirit made sure that they would teach the truth about God with **inerrancy,** which means that the Bible is without error when it tells us a religious truth about God and about God's relationship with us. Religious truth is what we need to know for our Salvation, but it is not necessarily a record of scientific and historic facts.

Even though the Bible is inspired by God and teaches religious truth without error, its message needs to be applied to people in every age and in every situation of life. So the Bible must be interpreted. **Interpretation** is a coming to an understanding of the words of Scripture, combining human knowledge with the wisdom and guidance of the teaching office of the Church.

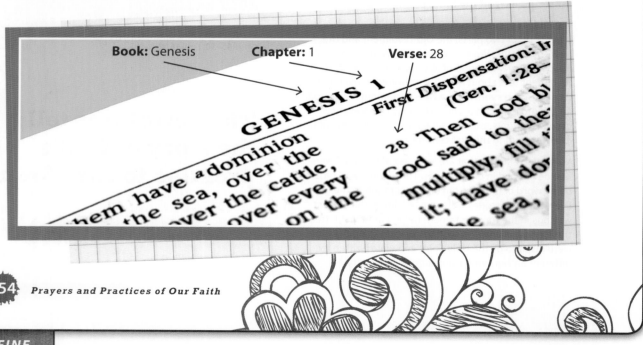

Book: Genesis   **Chapter:** 1   **Verse:** 28

GENESIS 1

First Dispensation: I
(Gen. 1:28–

...hem have a dominion
...the sea, over the
...over the cattle,
...over every
...on the

28 Then God bl
God said to the
multiply; fill
it; have do
...the sea,

DEFINE

Draw young people's attention to the terms *inspiration, inerrancy,* and *interpretation.* Have young people read aloud from the Glossary the definition of each term. Invite volunteers to define the terms in their own words.

Interpreting with Human Knowledge

Historical Perspective One way to use human knowledge to understand the Bible is to know how people lived, thought, and communicated during biblical times. When Jesus walked the earth, Palestine was occupied by Rome, which had conquered it in 63 B.C. In general, Rome respected Jewish religious practices, but the Jewish people resented the Roman taxes, laws, and troops. Jewish men who collected taxes for Rome were despised as traitors. Jews were not allowed to mix with Gentiles, or non-Jews.

The Jews were divided among various religious and political groups. The Pharisees, largely middle-class Jews, often interpreted the Torah strictly and added many regulations for living a life of holiness. The Sadducees were wealthy and politically powerful. Zealots were freedom fighters who sometimes used violence in attempts to overthrow Rome's control over Palestine. The Essenes were separatists who withdrew to the desert and lived simply as an expression of their desire to live the Jewish faith without contamination from other influences.

Literary Forms We recognize many styles of writing, or literary forms, in the Bible. Some of these literary forms are history, epic stories, gospels, proverbs, letters, wisdom sayings, parables, apocalyptic literature, and poetry. Each literary form serves a particular purpose in relaying God's Word. For example, the story of Jonah and the large fish in the Old Testament is not meant to relay historical facts. Instead, it is an inspired parable. The parable's purpose is to teach a lesson in faith that is divinely inspired. The essential religious truths revealed through the Jonah story are what matters, not the story's factual elements. Jesus used parables too. These stories helped listeners connect ordinary ideas or events in their lives in a way that revealed a deep spiritual truth or lesson about what it means to belong to the Kingdom of God.

The variety of literary forms in the Bible accomplishes what any one form cannot do by itself. Therefore, to discover the author's intention, "[T]he reader must take into account the conditions of their time and culture, the literary genres in use at the time, and the modes of feeling, speaking, and narrating then current." (*CCC* 710)

Interpreting with the Church's Magisterium

The key to understanding the Bible is to seek more than what the story says. The most important point is to unlock the story's meaning. In addition to human knowledge, the Church's Magisterium—the bishops in union with the pope and guided by the Holy Spirit—teach us how to interpret the Bible faithfully. As the official teachers of the Church, the Magisterium makes sure that we interpret the Bible faithfully by helping us understand what is essential for us to know for the sake of our Salvation. ✝

The Bible and You **255**

Discovering Jesus in the Scriptures

THE Old Testament contains 46 books that tell stories about the Jewish people and their faith in God before Jesus was born. The sections of the Old Testament are the Pentateuch (called the Torah), the historical books, the wisdom books, and the prophetic books.

The Old Testament as we know it today did not begin to take shape until a period known as the Babylonian Exile (587–537 B.C.). It was in Babylon that members of the priestly class took many of the oral and written accounts of God's saving work and put them together in what we now call the Pentateuch.

The Old Testament

The Pentateuch The first five books of the Old Testament—Genesis, Exodus, Leviticus, Numbers, and Deuteronomy—are referred to as the Torah, meaning "instruction" or "law." The stories from the prehistory of Israel that are in the Book of Genesis were probably the first part of the Old Testament to be written. The author is probably King David's court historian, who wrote the stories around 1000 B.C. The author referred to God as Yahweh and spoke of God in human terms. It was this author who wrote the story of God walking in the Garden with Adam and Eve and the story of God's orderly creation of the world in six days and his rest on the seventh.

King David

256 *Prayers and Practices of Our Faith*

Moses

Torah

Paul

The central story in the Torah is the Exodus. After the Hebrews had been enslaved by the Egyptians, God called Moses to lead them out of Egypt to the Promised Land. During the journey, God gave Moses and the people the Ten Commandments.

The Historical Books The historical books were put together from the court accounts of various kings of Israel and Judah, such as Saul, David, and Solomon. This section of the Old Testament records the story of the Israelites who fought to establish and maintain control of the Promised Land, to which God had delivered them during the Exodus.

The Wisdom Books These books are a collection of the wisdom teachings of the Israelites that surfaced over thousands of years. These writings include wisdom about the time when the people wandered the desert during the Exodus, their time living in the Promised Land, and their struggle during a period of exile known as the Babylonian Exile.

One of the best-known wisdom books is the Book of Psalms. A psalm is a prayer in the form of a poem. Each psalm expresses an aspect, or feature, of the depth of human emotion. Over several centuries, 150 psalms were gathered to form the Book of Psalms. They were once sung at the Temple, the house of worship first built by Solomon in Jerusalem. The psalms have been used in the public worship of the Church since its beginning. We often pray the psalms as part of our private prayer and reflection.

The Prophetic Books A large part of the Old Testament, 18 books, presents the messages and actions of the prophets. These were people called by God to speak for him to urge the Jewish people to be faithful to the Covenant.

The Bible and You **257**

The New Testament

The second part of the Bible, the New Testament, contains 27 books. Even though the most important books of the New Testament are the four writings known as Gospels, in reality, one "gospel" of and about Jesus Christ, runs through the books. While the first three Gospels (Matthew, Mark, and Luke) reveal events of Jesus' life in different ways, the stories are similar enough to be read side by side. Because of this, we call them **synoptic.**

Many books of the New Testament are letters written by early Church leaders such as Paul. In reading about Jesus' public ministry, his Paschal Mystery, and the life of the early Church, we discover our own call to discipleship.

Mark

The Gospel of Mark reveals the nature of true discipleship.

The Gospel of Mark

The Gospel of Mark was most likely written between the years A.D. 65 and 70. These were troublesome years for both Jews and the first Christians in the Mediterranean world. The Church in Rome had just suffered the first large-scale persecution at the hands of the Roman government. The Church in Palestine, still close to its Jewish roots, watched as Roman armies invaded to crush a Jewish uprising. This invasion ended with the conquest of Jerusalem and the destruction of the Temple in the year A.D. 70. Early Christian converts who had embraced Jesus with a great spirit of hope and expectation discovered that they now lived in the midst of suffering and destruction.

In these times of trouble, what message of comfort and hope could be given to Christians? Mark responded by writing the first Gospel account. He proclaimed Jesus as the Son of God sent by the Father to save the human family through service and the sacrifice of his life for our Salvation.

Writing the Gospel From his vantage point as Peter's companion in Rome, Mark collected Jesus' teachings and sayings, the stories and preaching about Jesus, and the stories of the events of the Last Supper and Jesus' Death on the Cross. He then shaped these stories into a larger story to help Christians recognize that Jesus was the Son of God. The Gospel of Mark was written in everyday Greek so it could be read by the mostly Greek-speaking audience. Mark presented Jesus as a dynamic figure who was always on the move, proclaiming the Kingdom of God to all who would listen. Mark's Gospel, being the first one written, strongly influenced the Gospels of Matthew and Luke, whose writings would follow.

Jesus as Healer and Teacher In the Gospel of Mark, Chapters 1—8, Jesus is a powerful healer and preacher. Even as he performs a number of miracles and explains the meaning of his parables, his disciples don't seem to understand the meaning of who he is. (Mark 4:13) After Jesus performs miracles, he orders his disciples not to talk about them, but

258 *Prayers and Practices of Our Faith*

DEFINE

Draw young people's attention to the term *synoptic*. Have a young person read aloud from the Glossary the definition of the term. Invite a volunteer to define the term in his or her own words.

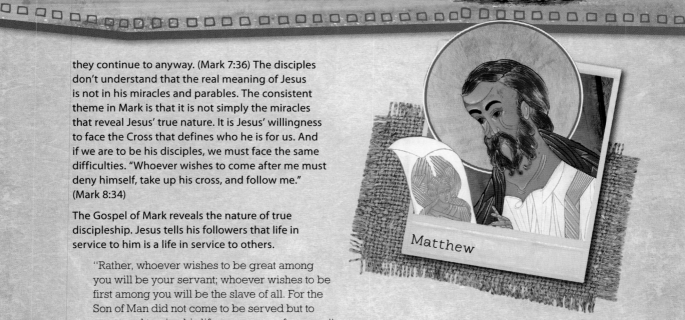

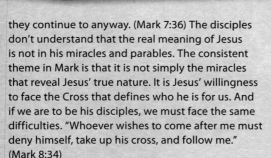

Matthew

they continue to anyway. (Mark 7:36) The disciples don't understand that the real meaning of Jesus is not in his miracles and parables. The consistent theme in Mark is that it is not simply the miracles that reveal Jesus' true nature. It is Jesus' willingness to face the Cross that defines who he is for us. And if we are to be his disciples, we must face the same difficulties. "Whoever wishes to come after me must deny himself, take up his cross, and follow me." (Mark 8:34)

The Gospel of Mark reveals the nature of true discipleship. Jesus tells his followers that life in service to him is a life in service to others.

> "Rather, whoever wishes to be great among you will be your servant; whoever wishes to be first among you will be the slave of all. For the Son of Man did not come to be served but to serve and to give his life as a ransom for many."
>
> *Mark 10:43–45*

The Gospel of Mark describes the Crucifixion and Death of Jesus. When Mark writes that a Roman centurion who is witnessing Jesus' Death recognizes him as the Son of God, we hear Mark's message—we must look to the Cross to understand the depth of God's loving sacrifice for us.

The Gospel of Matthew

The Gospel of Matthew was written in a Jewish-Christian community in Syria about A.D. 70s–80s. One ancient tradition attributes the Gospel to the apostle Matthew. It is more likely that the writer was a leader in the local church, possibly a converted rabbi, who was well-versed in the Scriptures. This Gospel writer faced the challenge of Jewish Christians interacting and worshiping with Gentiles, who were also members of the community. When it became clear that the majority of Jews would not become Christians, Matthew encouraged the Jewish-Christian community to recognize itself as the true heirs of God's promises to Israel.

The message and love of Jesus is not for Jews alone. To include the Gentile members of the community, Matthew showed that Jesus came to save everyone.

Matthew incorporated Gentiles into the very beginning of Jesus' story. He told the story of the Wise Men from the East who were the first to pay homage to Jesus as the Messiah. (Matthew 2:10–11) The Wise Men were not Jews. They were Gentiles, an important segment of Matthew's audience. Matthew stressed that Jesus gave instructions to the disciples to proclaim the Gospel to the entire world, baptizing in the name of the Father, the Son, and the Holy Spirit. (Matthew 28:19–20)

Jesus as the New Moses Matthew presents Jesus as the new Moses. His Gospel describes how Jesus retraced the steps of Moses' journey. Mary and Joseph took the infant Jesus to Egypt to escape the murderous rage of King Herod. They stayed there until Herod's death. Like his Hebrew ancestors, Jesus was called out of Egypt, and he retraced their journey to the Holy Land. (Matthew 2:15)

Exodus chapters 19—20 tells us that Moses went up on Mount Sinai to receive the Law from God. Matthew chapters 5—7 recounts how Jesus went up a mountain not to receive the Law, but to deliver the New Law. Moses spoke with God's authority, but Jesus spoke with his own authority as the Son of God. As the Son of God, Jesus understands and proclaims the true meaning of the Law.

The New Law Matthew had great respect for the Law. He wished to emphasize its continuing validity for the both Jewish and Gentile Christians.

> "Do not think that I [Jesus] have come to abolish the law or the prophets. I have come not to abolish but to fulfill. Amen, I say to you, until heaven and earth pass away, not the smallest letter or the smallest part of a letter will pass from the law, until all things have taken place."
>
> *Matthew 5:17–18*

Jesus also understood and proclaimed the true meaning of the Law. Through their faith in Jesus, Christians followed the true intent of the Law.

Matthew and the Church Matthew viewed the Church as the way to pass on the real meaning of Jesus' identity. He stressed that Peter, as the head of the disciples, was the leader of the Church. (Matthew 10:2) Since Peter was the leader of the Church, he shared Christ's authority. (Matthew 9:8; 10:40) God is united with his people through the Church. (Matthew 28:18–20)

The Gospel of Luke and the Acts of the Apostles

By the year A.D. 85, Christianity was becoming well established in the cities of the Roman empire. Gentile citizens were becoming more interested in the Church, but they still had questions. Some Christians expected Christ to return soon, even within their lifetime. But it was becoming apparent that the Christian journey would continue through time. How could early Christians live by their values in a world dominated by Rome? The Gospel of Luke and the Acts of the Apostles, two different works by one author, are, in part, responses to this question.

The Writer of Luke Early Christian tradition attributes the Gospel of Luke and the Acts of the Apostles to Luke, a Syrian from Antioch. He is mentioned in the New Testament in Colossians 4:14, Philippians 1:24, and 2 Timothy 4:11. The writer of the Gospel of Luke identifies himself as a second-generation Christian who uses other sources to help

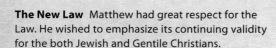

Luke

Luke gives importance to prayer as a way to live a Christian life.

him tell the story. Both the Gospel and the Acts of the Apostles were addressed to Theophilus, which means "friend of God" in Greek. The Gospel of Luke portrays the beginning of the Christian story from the announcement that the Messiah is coming to the Death and Resurrection of Jesus. The Acts of the Apostles starts with the Resurrection and Ascension of Jesus and then continues with events involving the spread of the Church.

Citizens of the Empire Luke sets his story in the Roman empire. Although Jesus was condemned by a Roman magistrate, Luke shows the Romans in a positive light. In Luke 7:9, Jesus says of the Roman centurion seeking a cure for his slave, "I tell you, not even in Israel have I found such faith." (Luke 7:9) Later, in Acts of the Apostles, Cornelius, a Roman centurion in Caesarea, is described as a prayerful, God-fearing man who gave generously to the Jewish people. (Acts of the Apostles 10:1–2) Luke wants his readers to understand that Christianity is compatible with the Roman world.

Guidance of the Holy Spirit The work of the Holy Spirit is highlighted in both the Gospel of Luke and the Acts of the Apostles. Through the power of the Holy Spirit, Mary conceives the Messiah. (Luke 1:35) Elizabeth, inspired by the Holy Spirit, recognizes Mary as the mother of the Messiah. (Luke 1:41)

The Holy Spirit is active in the life of Jesus. The Spirit leads Jesus into the desert. (Luke 4:1) Jesus returns from the desert in the power of the Spirit. (Luke 4:14) When Jesus returns and reads the Scriptures in the synagogue, he identifies himself as the one on whom the Spirit rests. (Luke 4:18)

The Holy Spirit is especially present in the Acts of the Apostles. The Holy Spirit empowers the disciples to preach the Gospel and sends them as missionaries (Acts of the Apostles 2:1–17; 16:6–7) Luke tells these stories to emphasize that the Holy Spirit is always a part of Christian life. The same Holy Spirit leads and guides the Church today.

Prayer Luke stresses the importance of prayer. Salvation is first announced to Zechariah when he is serving in the Temple and the whole assembly is praying. (Luke 3:9–10) Simeon and Anna recognize the infant Jesus as the Messiah as a result of their years of prayer in the Temple. (Luke 2:25–38) Jesus prays before he chooses the 12 Apostles. (Luke 6:12) He prays before the Transfiguration. (Luke 9:29) Active and enthusiastic prayer is also a characteristic of the early Christian community. (Acts of the Apostles 1:13–14; 2:42; 3:1) By telling these stories, Luke gives importance to prayer as a way to live a Christian life.

The Gospel of John

The Gospel of John was written around A.D. 90. This was 50 to 60 years after Jesus' life, Death, Resurrection, and Ascension. Although this Gospel has been attributed to the apostle John, it is more likely to have been written by a few members of the early Christian community. It was common practice to write in the name of a person admired by the community so that people would pay attention to the writing. Since the Gospel was written nearly two generations after Jesus walked the earth, the writer was able to reflect on what had already been written and taught about Jesus.

The Prologue in John 1:1–18 introduces the main theme of the Gospel—God's Revelation. It explains that the Word was with God from the beginning and that the Word of God became man in Jesus. Jesus, in turn, reveals the Father's great love for us. Jesus is fully God, fully man.

Reborn in Baptism through the power of the Holy Spirit, we participate in the divine nature of Jesus Christ. God dwells in us, and we become witnesses to his presence in the world. In Jesus, God's glory is revealed as a sign of his everlasting love.

The Book of Signs John's Gospel is divided into two major sections: the Book of Signs and the Book of Glory. The Book of Signs, John 1:19—12:50, recounts Jesus' wondrous deeds. Jesus transforms the water into wine at Cana not only to save his friends the embarrassment of running out of wine. The abundance of wine that Jesus provides is a sign that the kingdom has come in the person of Jesus.

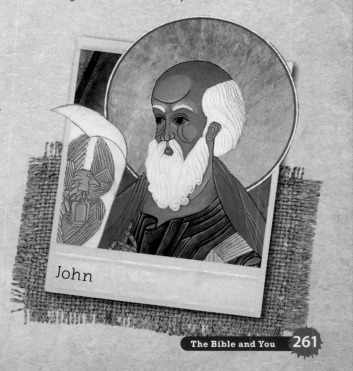

John

St. Paul the Apostle, Claude Vignon, 17th century.

Chapter 3 of the Gospel of John tells about the Jewish leader Nicodemus, who comes in the night to speak with Jesus. He does not want to be recognized by his peers. Nicodemus is coming out of the darkness and into the light of Jesus. Jesus speaks to Nicodemus about faith and baptism. He tells Nicodemus that he has come because of the Father's great love for the world. Jesus has come to save the world.

The Book of Glory The second major section of John's Gospel, John 13:1 through 20:31, is known as the Book of Glory. These chapters recount the Last Supper and Jesus' Passion and Death. John shows how Jesus reverses the values of the world. Crucifixion was a Roman punishment, a horrible and slow death inflicted on those despised by the government. Instead of being a sign of shame, John reveals the glory of God through Jesus' victory of the Cross Through Jesus' ultimate sacrifice, we come to realize that we might be saved.

Before he returns to the Father, Jesus tells his disciples to be hopeful. Jesus promises that he will not leave them alone in the world. He will send an Advocate, the Holy Spirit, to be with them and to guide them. As time went on, the disciples experienced the glory of Jesus' presence, especially when they were persecuted for proclaiming the Good News. Jesus did not leave them orphans, and neither does he leave us.

The Letters of Paul

The apostle Paul was the greatest of the early Christian missionaries. But before he did great work for God, he was a Pharisee and an early opponent of the Christian Church. Paul believed in the strict observance of God's Law, both for himself and for all Jews. While journeying to Damascus, Paul had an encounter with the risen Christ. (Acts of the Apostles 9:1–19) Paul became convinced that fellowship with the risen Jesus Christ, not the observance of the Law, was all that was needed to receive God's promise for Salvation. (Galatians 1:11–12; 3:1–5)

Paul's Writings Thirteen Epistles bear Paul's name. However, scholars do not believe that he wrote them all. Paul was the author of 1 Thessalonians, 2 Thessalonians, Galatians, Philippians, 1 Corinthians, 2 Corinthians, Romans, and Philemon. The letters to the Ephesians, Colossians, Titus, 1 Timothy, and 2 Timothy bear Paul's name, but scholars believe that these were written after Paul's death. The writers of these letters were likely disciples of Paul who continued his teaching. Whoever the authors of these Epistles were, the writings have been accepted as inspired by the Holy Spirit and are part of the New Testament.

Centrality of Jesus Christ The most profound day in Paul's life was when he met the risen Jesus Christ. Paul was well respected by the Jewish community and his peers. But he gave it all up for Christ. "More than that, I even consider everything as a loss because of the supreme good of knowing Christ Jesus my Lord." (Philippians 3:8)

Paul realized that Jesus had been sent by the Father to bring Salvation for all. He taught that we are united with Christ in faith and Baptism. "We were indeed buried with him through baptism into death, so that, just as Christ was raised from the dead by the glory of the Father, we too might live in newness of life." (Romans 6:4)

Justification Paul believed that the justice of God was saving justice at its best. God is faithful, fulfilling the promises made in the Covenant with his people. God has taken the initiative to call the human family back to him through Christ. This process of reuniting the human family with God is called justification. (Romans 3:21–31)

We cannot justify ourselves; we can only be justified by being united in faith with Jesus Christ and by accepting the grace won by Christ. (Romans 5:1–2) Christians can only be made right with God and set free from a life of immorality by accepting God's reconciling grace. Christians recognize that when they are united with and justified by Christ, they are given the grace needed to overcome sin and to live moral lives. (Galatians 5:16–26)

Life in the Spirit Paul teaches that it is through the Holy Spirit that the love of God has been poured out to us. (Romans 5:5) The Holy Spirit is the source of all love, and the Spirit creates a bond between ourselves and God like children bound to a father. (Romans 8:14–16) Even though we are weak, the Holy Spirit helps us live faithfully within that relationship. (Romans 8:26–27) It is through the Holy Spirit that we can live in love with all people. (1 Corinthians 13:3–7)

Other Epistles and the Book of Revelation

The remaining letters include the letters of Peter, which reflect the concerns of the Church in Rome; the letter to the Hebrews, a homily on early Christian themes; the letter of Jude; the letters of John; and the Book of Revelation. Revelation is an example of apocalyptic literature, a type of writing popular in Judaism at the time. Revelation presents a vision of the end of the world in which the good and just triumph. It was written to address a crisis—the persecution of Christians by the Roman emperor Domitian. Revelation offered encouragement to the people to endure during this difficult time and was not intended to be interpreted literally. †

The Bible and You **263**

Understanding the Time Line

Biblical scholars have assigned the most likely dates to indicate when the various books of the New Testament were put into writing. Some dates on the Time Line of the New Testament may seem confusing because more than one year or a range of years is given. The manuscripts that the scholars have to work with are copies from later generations. We do not have original texts from the writers of the books of the New Testament. So scholars have to give their best estimates as to when the books were originally recorded.

The early Church predates the writing of the New Testament Scripture. Jesus taught with the spoken word. His disciples would listen to, remember, and discuss his teachings. The Apostles, inspired by the Holy Spirit, shared the Good News by word of mouth, and many Christian communities developed. As long as there were eyewitnesses in the world, or someone who personally knew an eyewitness, it wasn't necessary to write down Jesus' words and deeds.

This established tradition of spreading Jesus' teachings by word of mouth worked well enough. Eventually, though, as the Apostles and other eyewitnesses died, an official written record was needed to keep Jesus' teachings alive.

About 20 years after Jesus' Resurrection, Saint Paul's missionary work resulted in the formation of many early Christian communities. His letters to the Thessalonians are the earliest examples of New Testament writing, soon to be followed by letters to many other communities.

The Gospel of Mark followed Paul's letters about 15 years later. We presume that the apostolic writings in the possession of an early Christian community were publicly shared in religious assemblies, and in this way, the collections of inspired writing grew among the widely separated Church communities. The canon of the New Testament, which is the Church's collection of sacred books, developed over a period of time.

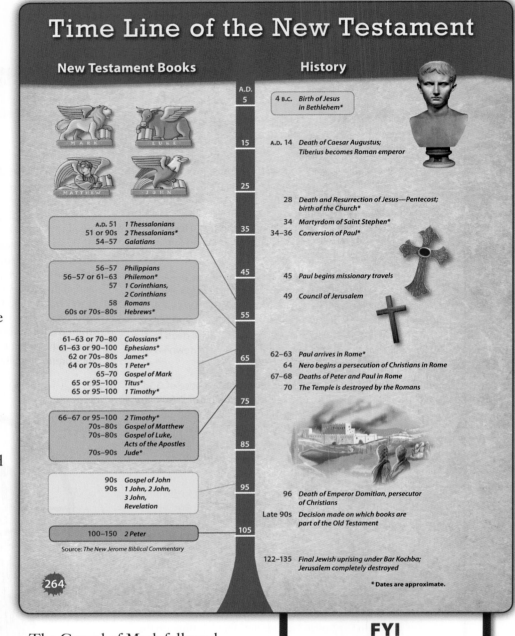

Time Line of the New Testament

New Testament Books

A.D. 51	1 Thessalonians
51 or 90s	2 Thessalonians*
54–57	Galatians
56–57	Philippians
56–57 or 61–63	Philemon*
57	1 Corinthians, 2 Corinthians
58	Romans
60s or 70s–80s	Hebrews*
61–63 or 70–80	Colossians*
61–63 or 90–100	Ephesians*
62 or 70s–80s	James*
64 or 70s–80s	1 Peter*
65–70	Gospel of Mark
65 or 95–100	Titus*
65 or 95–100	1 Timothy*
66–67 or 95–100	2 Timothy*
70s–80s	Gospel of Matthew
70s–80s	Gospel of Luke, Acts of the Apostles
70s–90s	Jude*
90s	Gospel of John
90s	1 John, 2 John, 3 John, Revelation
100–150	2 Peter

Source: *The New Jerome Biblical Commentary*

264

History

4 B.C.	Birth of Jesus in Bethlehem*
A.D. 14	Death of Caesar Augustus; Tiberius becomes Roman emperor
28	Death and Resurrection of Jesus—Pentecost; birth of the Church*
34	Martyrdom of Saint Stephen*
34–36	Conversion of Paul*
45	Paul begins missionary travels
49	Council of Jerusalem
62–63	Paul arrives in Rome*
64	Nero begins a persecution of Christians in Rome
67–68	Deaths of Peter and Paul in Rome
70	The Temple is destroyed by the Romans
96	Death of Emperor Domitian, persecutor of Christians
Late 90s	Decision made on which books are part of the Old Testament
122–135	Final Jewish uprising under Bar Kochba; Jerusalem completely destroyed

Time line A.D. marks: 5, 15, 25, 35, 45, 55, 65, 75, 85, 95, 105

* Dates are approximate.

FYI

Time Line

Use this explanatory text to help young people understand the time line and the dates of the written accounts of the New Testament. You may wish to share this information when displaying the *Finding God* poster Time Line of the New Testament.

Saint Paul's Missionary Journeys

First Missionary Journey
(A.D. 47–49)

Second Missionary Journey
(A.D. 49–52)

Third Missionary Journey
(A.D. 53–58)

Journey to Rome
(A.D. 60–61)

The Bible and You **265**

Formulas of Catholic Doctrine

What Every Catholic Should Know

The Great Commandment

The Ten Commandments are fulfilled in Jesus' Great Commandment.

"You shall love the Lord your God with all your heart, with all your soul, with all your mind, and with all your strength. . . . You shall love your neighbor as yourself."

Mark 12:30–31

The New Commandment

Before his Death on the Cross, Jesus gave his disciples a new commandment.

"[L]ove one another. As I have loved you, so you also should love one another."

John 13:34

The Golden Rule

"Do to others whatever you would have them do to you."

Matthew 7:12

266 *Prayers and Practices of Our Faith*

The Beatitudes

The Beatitudes are the teachings of Jesus in the Sermon on the Mount. Jesus teaches us that if we live according to the Beatitudes, we will live a happy Christian life. The Beatitudes fulfill God's promises made to Abraham and his descendants. Jesus' guidelines describe the rewards that will be ours in this life and eternal joy in the next as faithful followers of Christ.

"Blessed are the poor in spirit,
 for theirs is the kingdom of heaven.
Blessed are they who mourn,
 for they will be comforted.
Blessed are the meek,
 for they will inherit the land.
Blessed are they who hunger and thirst
  for righteousness,
 for they will be satisfied.
Blessed are the merciful,
 for they will be shown mercy.
Blessed are the clean of heart,
 for they will see God.
Blessed are the peacemakers,
 for they will be called children of God.
Blessed are they who are persecuted
  for the sake of righteousness,
 for theirs is the kingdom of heaven."

Matthew 5:1–10

Sermon on the Mount,
Laura James.

The Ten Commandments

As believers in Jesus Christ, we are called to a new life and asked to make moral choices that keep us united with God. With the help and grace of the Holy Spirit, we can choose ways to act to keep us close to God, to help other people, and to be witnesses to Jesus.

The Ten Commandments guide us in making choices that help us live as God wants us to live. The first three commandments tell us how to love God. The other seven tell us how to love our neighbor.

1. I am the Lord your God: you shall not have strange gods before me.
2. You shall not take the name of the Lord your God in vain.
3. Remember to keep holy the Lord's Day.
4. Honor your father and your mother.
5. You shall not kill.
6. You shall not commit adultery.
7. You shall not steal.
8. You shall not bear false witness against your neighbor.
9. You shall not covet your neighbor's wife.
10. You shall not covet your neighbor's goods.

Precepts of the Church

The Precepts of the Church provide the faithful with a foundation for living a Catholic life. These rules describe the minimum effort we must make in prayer and in living a moral life. All Catholics are called to move beyond the minimum by growing in love of God and love of neighbor. The Precepts of the Church are as follows:

† attendance at Mass on Sundays and Holy Days of Obligation

† confession of sins at least once a year

† reception of the Eucharist at least once a year during the Easter season

† observance of the days of fast and abstinence on prescribed days and times of the Church year as a way to grow in holiness through self-sacrifice

† providing for the needs of the Church. This includes supporting the Church with our talents, gifts, service, and financial assistance.

The Four Last Things

The end of human life is the beginning of eternal life. Immediately upon death, we are rewarded according to our deeds and faith. At death, Christ gives a judgment and destination for each soul.

The four last things describe the end of human life for all:

death   judgment   Heaven   Hell

Virtues

Virtues are gifts from God to do what is right and good. They lead us to live in a close relationship with God. Virtues are like good habits. They need to be practiced; they can be lost if they are neglected.

Theological Virtues

The three most important virtues are called Theological Virtues because they are gifts from God and lead to God. God gives us the Theological Virtues so we can live as his children and merit eternal life.

faith   hope   charity

Cardinal Virtues

The Cardinal Virtues are human virtues that can be acquired by education and good actions. *Cardinal* comes from *cardo*, the Latin word for "hinge," meaning "that on which other things depend."

prudence   justice   fortitude   temperance

Prudence This virtue helps us discern good from evil and abide by our conscience.

Justice Justice is the strong will to rightly give what is due to God and neighbor.

Fortitude Fortitude is the strength and courage to face difficulties and do what is right.

Temperance This is a virtue of moderation in pleasures, providing balance in the use of material goods.

Gifts of the Holy Spirit

The Holy Spirit makes it possible for us to do what God asks of us by giving us these many gifts.

wisdom   understanding   counsel   piety
fortitude   knowledge   fear of the Lord

Fruits of the Holy Spirit

The Fruits of the Holy Spirit are signs of the Holy Spirit's action in our lives.

love   joy   peace
patience   kindness   generosity
faithfulness   gentleness   self-control

Church Tradition also includes goodness, modesty, and chastity as Fruits of the Holy Spirit.

Formulas of Catholic Doctrine **269**

Works of Mercy

Mercy is a virtue that influences a person's compassion for another. Mercy influences the will to ease another's misfortunes or suffering in either body or soul. The Corporal and Spiritual Works of Mercy are charitable actions that extend God's compassion and mercy to those in need.

However, the Works of Mercy are more than gestures or obligations. To gain merit in Heaven, the actions must be performed as acts of love for our neighbor as a response to our deep love for God. The Corporal and Spiritual Works of Mercy work together as paths to Salvation. They give Christians ways to live according to Jesus' Great Commandment.

Corporal Works of Mercy

The Corporal Works of Mercy are kind acts by which we help our neighbors with their material and physical needs:

† feed the hungry

† shelter the homeless

† clothe the naked

† visit the sick and imprisoned

† bury the dead

† give alms to the poor

Spiritual Works of Mercy

The Spiritual Works of Mercy are acts of compassion by which we help our neighbors with their emotional and spiritual needs:

† instruct

† advise

† console

† comfort

† forgive

† bear wrongs patiently

"... 'Amen, I say to you, what you did not do for one of these least ones, you did not do for me.'"

Matthew 25:45

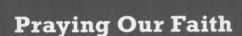

Praying Our Faith

Prayer and Forms of Prayer

GOD is always with us. He wants us to talk to him and to listen to him. In prayer we raise our hearts and minds to God. We are able to speak to and listen to God because through the Holy Spirit, God teaches us how to pray.

What Is Prayer?

Being a Christian requires that we believe all that God has revealed to us, that we celebrate it in the liturgy and the sacraments, and that we live what we believe. All of this depends on a vital and personal relationship with the living and true God. This relationship is found in prayer.

Prayer is, first of all, a gift from God. We can pray because God first seeks us out and calls us to meet him. We become aware of our thirst for God because God thirsts for us. Prayer arises from our heart, beyond the grasp of reason. Only the Spirit of God can understand the human heart and know it fully. Prayer is the habit of being with God—Father, Son, and Holy Spirit. This communion with God is always possible because through our Baptism we are united with Christ. Christian prayer is communion with Christ that branches out to all the members of his Body, the Church.

Meditate and Contemplate

To **meditate** is to think about God and to focus your attention on him alone. You may use Scripture, prayer books, or icons (religious images) to help you concentrate and to spark your imagination. Another way to pray is to **contemplate.** To contemplate is to rest quietly in God's presence.

Get Ready to Pray

You can get ready to pray by resting your body in a comfortable position. You might close your eyes and fold your hands comfortably in front of you. Concentrating on your breathing, slowly breathing in and out, helps quiet your thoughts.

Avoid Distractions

If distracting thoughts remove your focus from God, go back to thinking about your breathing. After some practice, you will be able to avoid distractions, pray with your imagination, and spend time with God in your heart and mind.

DEFINE

Draw young people's attention to the terms *meditate* and *contemplate*. Have young people read aloud from the Glossary the definition of each term. Invite volunteers to define the terms in their own words.

The Five Basic Forms of Christian Prayer

The Holy Spirit teaches us to pray. Our conversation with God can take different forms.

Blessing

To bless someone is to acknowledge his or her goodness. The prayer of blessing, or adoration, is our response to God's goodness because of all the gifts he has given us. In the prayer of blessing, God's gifts and our acceptance of them come together.

Petition

In prayers of petition, we do more than ask God for things we want or need. We express our relationship with God as our Creator and Father and we as his children, who depend on him for all good things. When we sin and turn away from God, we can turn back toward him and petition for forgiveness.

Intercession

In prayers of intercession, we ask God for something on behalf of another. Intercession is a prayer of petition that leads us to pray as Jesus did. Throughout his life on earth, Jesus interceded with the Father on behalf of all people. To pray in this way means that our hearts are turned outward, focused on the needs of others.

Thanksgiving

Thanksgiving as a form of prayer is especially realized in the Eucharist. *Eucharist* means "thanksgiving." Through his Death and Resurrection, Christ has reconciled us to God. His sacrifice is made present in the Eucharist. When we receive the Eucharist, we become a people of thanksgiving.

Praise

Praise is a form of prayer that recognizes God and gives him glory. Praise goes beyond thanking God for what he has done for us. A prayer of praise gives God glory simply because he is. Praise embraces the other forms of prayer and carries them to God, who is the source of all that is. ✝

Prayers to Take to Heart

WE can pray with any words that come to mind. Sometimes, when we find that choosing our own words is difficult, we can use traditional prayers. Likewise, when we pray aloud with others, we rely on traditional prayers to unite our minds, hearts, and voices. Memorizing traditional prayers such as the following can be very helpful. When we memorize prayers, we take them to heart, meaning that we not only learn the words but also try to understand and live them.

Pope Benedict XVI has identified four prayers that are shared by the universal Church. If they are learned in Latin, they can be prayed as a sign of the universal nature of the Church. Catholics throughout the world would be praying in the same language. The Latin versions of these four prayers are included across from each of them.

Lord's Prayer

Our Father, who art in heaven,
hallowed be thy name;
thy kingdom come,
thy will be done
on earth as it is in heaven.
Give us this day our daily bread,
and forgive us our trespasses,
as we forgive those who trespass against us;
and lead us not into temptation,
but deliver us from evil.
Amen.

Pater Noster

Pater noster, qui es in caelis,
sanctificetur nomen tuum.
Adveniat regnum tuum.
Fiat voluntas tua,
sicut in caelo et in terra.
Panem nostrum quotidianum da nobis hodie,
et dimitte nobis debita nostra
sicut et nos dimittimus debitoribus nostris.
Et ne nos inducas in tentationem,
sed libera nos a malo.
Amen.

Hail Mary

Hail Mary, full of grace,
the Lord is with you.
Blessed are you among women,
and blessed is the fruit of your womb, Jesus.
Holy Mary, Mother of God,
pray for us sinners,
now and at the hour of our death.
Amen.

Ave Maria

Ave Maria, gratia plena,
Dominus tecum.
Benedicta tu in mulieribus,
et benedictus fructus ventris tui, Iesus.
Sancta Maria, Mater Dei,
ora pro nobis peccatoribus,
nunc, et in hora mortis nostrae.
Amen.

The Sign of the Cross

In the name of the Father, and of the Son,
and of the Holy Spirit.
Amen.

Glory Be to the Father (Doxology)

Glory be to the Father, and to the Son, and to
the Holy Spirit. As it was in the beginning, is
now, and ever shall be, world without end.
Amen.

Morning Offering

My God, I offer you my prayers, works, joys
and sufferings of this day in union with the
holy sacrifice of the Mass throughout the world.
I offer them for all the intentions of your
Son's Sacred Heart, for the salvation of souls,
reparation for sin, and the reunion of Christians.
Amen.

Prayer Before Meals

Bless us, O Lord, and these your gifts
which we are about to receive from your goodness.
Through Christ our Lord.
Amen.

Prayer After Meals

We give you thanks
for all your gifts,
almighty God,
living and reigning
now and for ever.
Amen.

Signum Crucis

*In nomine Patris, et Filii,
et Spiritus Sancti.
Amen.*

Gloria Patri

*Gloria Patri, et Filio, et Spiritui Sancto.
Sicut erat in principio, et nunc, et semper,
et in saecula saeculorum.
Amen.*

Act of Contrition

My God,
I am sorry for my sins with all my heart.
In choosing to do wrong
and failing to do good,
I have sinned against you
whom I should love above all things.
I firmly intend, with your help,
to do penance,
to sin no more,
and to avoid whatever leads me to sin.
Our Savior Jesus Christ
suffered and died for us.
In his name, my God, have mercy.

Prayer to the Holy Spirit

Come, Holy Spirit, fill the hearts of your faithful.
And kindle in them the fire of your love.
Send forth your Spirit and they shall be created.
And you will renew the face of the earth.
Let us pray.

Lord,
by the light of the Holy Spirit
you have taught the hearts of your faithful.
In the same Spirit
help us to relish what is right
and always rejoice in your consolation.
We ask this through Christ our Lord.
Amen.

Praying Our Faith 275

Apostles' Creed

I believe in God,
the Father almighty,
Creator of heaven and earth,
and in Jesus Christ, his only Son, our Lord,
who was conceived by the Holy Spirit,
born of the Virgin Mary,
suffered under Pontius Pilate,
was crucified, died and was buried;
he descended into hell;
on the third day he rose again from the dead;
he ascended into heaven,
and is seated at the right hand of God
   the Father almighty;
from there he will come to judge the living
   and the dead.

I believe in the Holy Spirit,
the holy catholic Church,
the communion of saints,
the forgiveness of sins,
the resurrection of the body,
and life everlasting. Amen.

Nicene Creed

I believe in one God,
the Father almighty,
maker of heaven and earth,
of all things visible and invisible.

I believe in one Lord Jesus Christ,
the Only Begotten Son of God,
born of the Father before all ages.
God from God, Light from Light,
true God from true God,
begotten, not made, consubstantial
   with the Father;
through him all things were made.
For us men and for our salvation
he came down from heaven,
and by the Holy Spirit was incarnate of the
   Virgin Mary,
and became man.

For our sake he was crucified under
   Pontius Pilate,
he suffered death and was buried,
and rose again on the third day
in accordance with the Scriptures.
He ascended into heaven
and is seated at the right hand of the Father.
He will come again in glory
to judge the living and the dead
and his kingdom will have no end.

I believe in the Holy Spirit, the Lord,
   the giver of life,
who proceeds from the Father and the Son,
who with the Father and the Son is adored
   and glorified,
who has spoken through the prophets.

I believe in one, holy, catholic and
   apostolic Church.
I confess one Baptism for the forgiveness of sins
and I look forward to the resurrection of the dead
and the life of the world to come. Amen.

Act of Faith

O my God, I firmly believe that you are one God in three divine Persons, Father, Son, and Holy Spirit. I believe that your divine Son became man and died for our sins, and that he will come to judge the living and the dead. I believe these and all the truths which the holy Catholic Church teaches, because you have revealed them, who can neither deceive nor be deceived.
Amen.

Act of Hope

O my God, relying on your infinite mercy and promises, I hope to obtain pardon of my sins, the help of your grace, and life everlasting, through the merits of Jesus Christ, my Lord and Redeemer.
Amen.

Act of Love

O my God, I love you above all things with my whole heart and soul, because you are all good and worthy of all my love. I love my neighbor as myself for the love of you. I forgive all who have injured me and I ask pardon of those whom I have injured.
Amen.

Prayer for Vocations

God, in Baptism you called me by name
and made me a member of your people, the Church.
Help all your people to know their vocation in life,
and to respond by living a life of holiness.
For your greater glory and for the service
    of your people,
raise up dedicated and generous leaders
who will serve as sisters, priests,
brothers, deacons, and lay ministers.

Send your Spirit to guide and strengthen me
that I may serve your people
following the example of your Son, Jesus Christ,
in whose name I offer this prayer.
Amen.

Praying Our Faith 277

Jesus Prayer

Lord Jesus Christ, Son of God,
   have mercy on us sinners.

Prayer for Generosity

Eternal Word, only begotten Son of God,
Teach me true generosity.
Teach me to serve you as you deserve.
To give without counting the cost,
To fight heedless of wounds,
To labor without seeking rest,
To sacrifice myself without thought of any reward
Save the knowledge that I have done your will. Amen.

Suscipe

Take, Lord, and receive all my liberty,
my memory, my understanding,
and my entire will.
All I have and call my own.

You have given all to me.
To you, Lord, I return it.

Everything is yours; do with it what you will.
Give me only your love and your grace.
That is enough for me.

The Daily Examen

SAINT Ignatius of Loyola gave the Church a great gift—the Spiritual Exercises. Praying with the Spiritual Exercises helps us discover God's plan for us.

The Daily Examen is an important part of the Spiritual Exercises. When we pray the Daily Examen, we reflect on the events of the day so that we can discover God's presence and discern his will for us. The Daily Examen helps us recognize God's presence in our everyday lives.

The following steps are a version of the Daily Examen that we can use in our personal prayer.

Saint Ignatius of Loyola, 1882, engraving, London, England.

1. **Become aware of God's presence.** Take a moment to reflect on all the blessings you have received from God throughout the day. Ask yourself, "How did God reveal himself to me in the events I experienced and the people I met?"

2. **Review the day with gratitude.** Take a moment to thank God for the joys and delights you have experienced throughout the day. Ask yourself, "What joys have I experienced in my interactions with others? What sights, sounds, and smells have filled me with delight?"

3. **Pay attention to your emotions.** Reflect on the feelings you have experienced throughout the day. Ask yourself, "Have any of my emotions drawn me closer to God or led me away from him? What might God be telling me through my emotions?"

4. **Choose one feature of the day and pray with it.** Ask the Holy Spirit to help you identify something from your day that seems especially important. It may be a feeling, an encounter, or a recurring thought you've had. Spend a moment reflecting on the experience and pray a prayer from your heart.

5. **Look toward tomorrow.** Ask God for the grace to help you remain faithful to the call of discipleship. Then ask him to open your mind and heart so that you can continue to discover his presence in your everyday experience.

By praying this version of the Daily Examen, you can become more aware of God's action in your life so that you can find God in all things.

The Rosary

THE Rosary helps us pray to Jesus through the intercession of Mary. When we pray the Rosary, we think about the special events, or mysteries, in the lives of Jesus and Mary.

The Rosary is made up of a string of beads and a crucifix. We hold the crucifix in our hands as we pray the Sign of the Cross. Then we pray the Apostles' Creed.

Hail, Holy Queen
(Salve Regina)

Hail, holy Queen, Mother of mercy,
hail, our life, our sweetness, and our hope.
To you we cry, the children of Eve;
to you we send up our sighs,
mourning and weeping in this land of exile.
Turn, then, most gracious advocate,
your eyes of mercy toward us;
lead us home at last
and show us the blessed fruit of your womb, Jesus:
O clement, O loving, O sweet Virgin Mary.

Next to the crucifix, there is a single bead, followed by a set of three beads and another single bead. We pray the Lord's Prayer as we hold the first single bead and a Hail Mary at each bead in the set of three that follows. Then we pray the Glory Be to the Father. On the next single bead, we think about the first mystery and pray the Lord's Prayer.

There are five sets of 10 beads; each set is called a decade. We pray a Hail Mary on each bead of a decade as we reflect on a particular mystery in the lives of Jesus and Mary. The Glory Be to the Father is prayed at the end of each set. Between sets is a single bead on which we think about one of the mysteries and pray the Lord's Prayer.

In his apostolic letter *Rosary of the Virgin Mary*, Pope John Paul II wrote that the Rosary could take on a variety of legitimate forms adapted to different spiritual traditions and different Christian communities. "What is really important," he said, "is that the Rosary should always be seen and experienced as a path of contemplation." With this in mind, it is traditional in some places to pray the Hail, Holy Queen after the last decade.

We end our prayer by holding the crucifix in our hands as we pray the Sign of the Cross.

280 *Prayers and Practices of Our Faith*

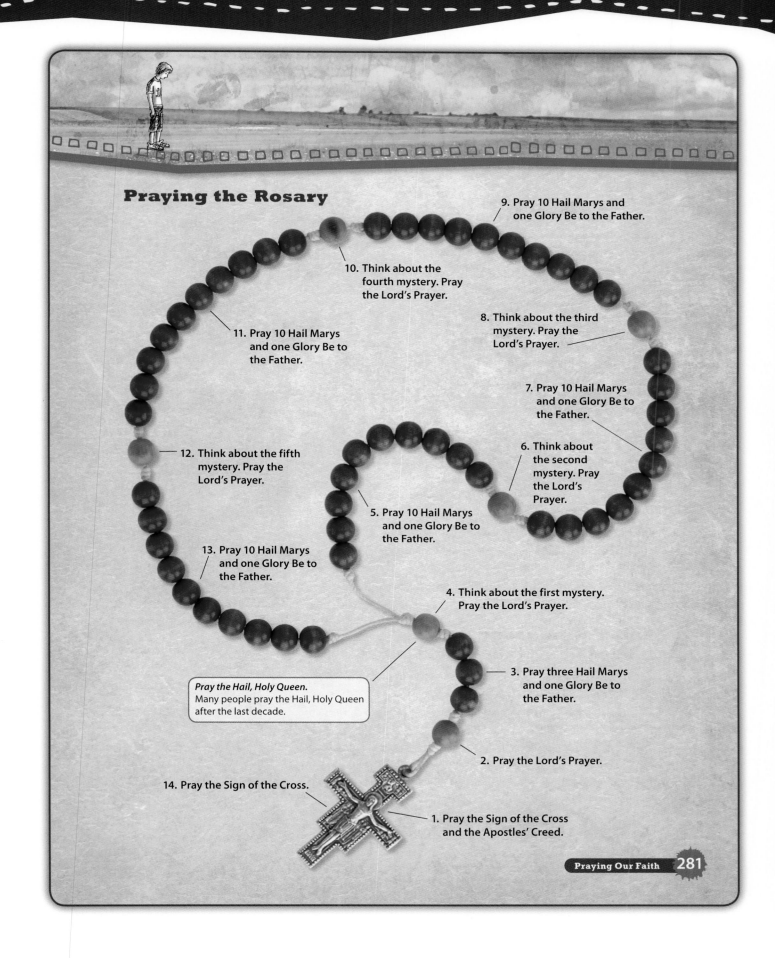

Praying the Rosary

9. Pray 10 Hail Marys and one Glory Be to the Father.

10. Think about the fourth mystery. Pray the Lord's Prayer.

11. Pray 10 Hail Marys and one Glory Be to the Father.

8. Think about the third mystery. Pray the Lord's Prayer.

7. Pray 10 Hail Marys and one Glory Be to the Father.

12. Think about the fifth mystery. Pray the Lord's Prayer.

6. Think about the second mystery. Pray the Lord's Prayer.

5. Pray 10 Hail Marys and one Glory Be to the Father.

13. Pray 10 Hail Marys and one Glory Be to the Father.

4. Think about the first mystery. Pray the Lord's Prayer.

Pray the Hail, Holy Queen. Many people pray the Hail, Holy Queen after the last decade.

3. Pray three Hail Marys and one Glory Be to the Father.

2. Pray the Lord's Prayer.

14. Pray the Sign of the Cross.

1. Pray the Sign of the Cross and the Apostles' Creed.

Mysteries of the Rosary

THE Church has used three sets of mysteries for many centuries. In 2002, Pope John Paul II proposed a fourth set of mysteries—the Luminous Mysteries, which are also called the Mysteries of Light.

According to his suggestion, the four sets of mysteries might be prayed on the following days: the Joyful Mysteries on Monday and Saturday, the Sorrowful Mysteries on Tuesday and Friday, the Glorious Mysteries on Wednesday and Sunday, and the Luminous Mysteries on Thursday.

The Joyful Mysteries

1. The Annunciation Mary learns that she has been chosen to be the mother of Jesus.

2. The Visitation Mary visits Elizabeth, who tells her that she will always be remembered.

3. The Nativity Jesus is born in a stable in Bethlehem.

4. The Presentation Mary and Joseph take the infant Jesus to the Temple to present him to God.

5. The Finding of Jesus in the Temple Jesus is found in the Temple, discussing his faith with the teachers.

The Annunciation

The Luminous Mysteries

1. The Baptism of Jesus in the River Jordan God proclaims that Jesus is his beloved Son.

2. The Wedding Feast at Cana At Mary's request, Jesus performs his first miracle.

3. The Proclamation of the Kingdom of God Jesus calls all to conversion and service to the kingdom.

4. The Transfiguration of Jesus Jesus is revealed in glory to Peter, James, and John.

5. The Institution of the Eucharist Jesus offers his Body and Blood at the Last Supper.

Wedding Feast at Cana

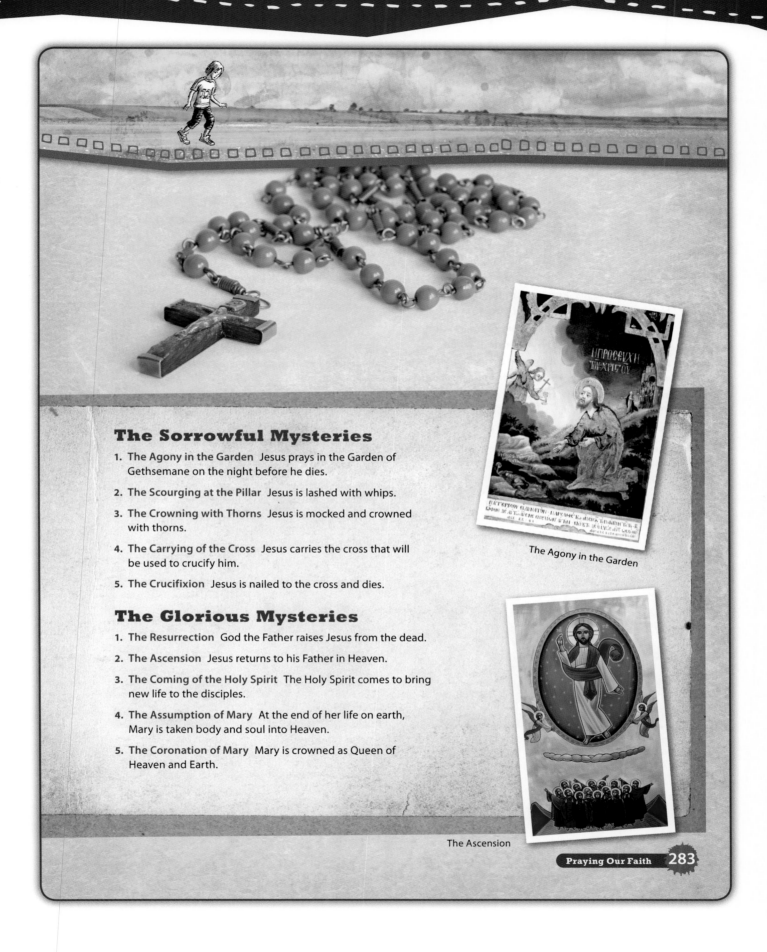

The Sorrowful Mysteries

1. **The Agony in the Garden** Jesus prays in the Garden of Gethsemane on the night before he dies.

2. **The Scourging at the Pillar** Jesus is lashed with whips.

3. **The Crowning with Thorns** Jesus is mocked and crowned with thorns.

4. **The Carrying of the Cross** Jesus carries the cross that will be used to crucify him.

5. **The Crucifixion** Jesus is nailed to the cross and dies.

The Glorious Mysteries

1. **The Resurrection** God the Father raises Jesus from the dead.

2. **The Ascension** Jesus returns to his Father in Heaven.

3. **The Coming of the Holy Spirit** The Holy Spirit comes to bring new life to the disciples.

4. **The Assumption of Mary** At the end of her life on earth, Mary is taken body and soul into Heaven.

5. **The Coronation of Mary** Mary is crowned as Queen of Heaven and Earth.

The Agony in the Garden

The Ascension

Praying Our Faith 283

Stations of the Cross

THE 14 Stations of the Cross represent events from Jesus' Passion and Death. Even before the Gospels were in written form, the followers of Jesus told the story of his Passion, Death, Resurrection, and Ascension. When people went on pilgrimages to Jerusalem, they were anxious to see the sites where Jesus lived and died. Eventually, following in the footsteps of the Lord on the way to his Death on the Cross became an important part of the pilgrimage.

The stations that we pray today came about when it was no longer easy or even possible to visit the holy sites in Palestine. In the 1500s, villages all over Europe started making replicas of the Way of the Cross, setting up small shrines commemorating the places along the route in Jerusalem. Eventually, these shrines became the 14 stations we now reflect on.

The first thing to remember about the Stations of the Cross is that they are a prayer. They are not an exercise in remembering events from the past. They are an invitation to make present the final hours of Jesus' life and to experience who Jesus is. When we pray the Stations of the Cross and open our hearts to be touched by prayer, we can respond fully to Jesus' sacrifice on the Cross. Praying the stations moves our hearts and helps us know Jesus' love for us.

As we follow the Lord's footsteps on his way to the Cross, we use our senses and our imagination to reflect prayerfully on Jesus' suffering, Death, and Resurrection. The stations allow us to visualize the meaning of his sacrifice and lead us to gratitude. They can also lead us into a sense of solidarity with people around the world, especially those who suffer, who are unjustly accused or victimized, who sit on death row, who carry difficult burdens, or who face terminal illnesses.

Jesus Is Condemned to Death.
Pontius Pilate condemns Jesus to death.

Jesus Takes Up the Cross.
Jesus willingly accepts and patiently bears the cross.

Jesus Falls the First Time.
Weakened by torments and by loss of blood, Jesus falls beneath the cross.

Jesus Meets His Sorrowful Mother.
Jesus meets his mother, Mary, who is filled with grief.

5

Simon of Cyrene Helps Jesus Carry the Cross.
Soldiers force Simon of Cyrene to carry the cross.

6

Veronica Wipes the Face of Jesus.
Veronica steps through the crowd to wipe the face of Jesus.

7

Jesus Falls the Second Time.
Jesus falls beneath the weight of the cross a second time.

8

Jesus Meets the Women of Jerusalem.
Jesus tells the women not to weep for him but for themselves and for their children.

9

Jesus Falls the Third Time.
Weakened almost to the point of death, Jesus falls a third time.

10

Jesus Is Stripped of His Garments.
The soldiers strip Jesus of his garments, treating him as a common criminal.

11

Jesus Is Nailed to the Cross.
Jesus' hands and feet are nailed to the cross.

12

Jesus Dies on the Cross.
After suffering greatly on the cross, Jesus bows his head and dies.

13

Jesus Is Taken Down from the Cross.
The lifeless body of Jesus is tenderly placed in the arms of Mary, his mother.

14

Jesus Is Laid in the Tomb.
Jesus' disciples place his body in the tomb.

The closing prayer—sometimes included as the 15th station—reflects on the Resurrection of Jesus.

Praying Our Faith **285**

Celebrating and Living Our Faith

The Mystery of Faith Made Present

THE word *church* means "convocation of all those who are gathered together in assembly" for the People of God. The apostle Paul describes the Church by calling it the Body of Christ. "As a body is one though it has many parts, and all the parts of the body, though many, are one body, so also Christ." (1 Corinthians 12:12)

The First Letter of Peter states that through faith and Baptism, Christians belong to the People of God. "But you are 'a chosen race, a royal priesthood, a holy nation, a people of his own, so that you may announce the praises' of him who you called out of darkness into his wonderful light." (1 Peter 2:9) Jesus Christ is the head of the Church.

"He is before all things,
     and in him all things hold together.
He is the head of the body, the church."

Colossians 1:17–18

In the Letter to the Ephesians, the Church is vividly described as the bride of Christ, who "loved the church and handed himself over for her to sanctify her, cleansing her by the bath of water with the word, that he might present himself to the church in splendor, without spot or wrinkle or any such thing, that she might be holy and without blemish." (Ephesians 5:25–28).

The Church was revealed to the world with the coming of the Spirit on Pentecost. This gift of the Spirit ushered in a new era in the history of Salvation. This era is the age of the Church in which Christ makes present and communicates his work of Salvation through the liturgy of his Church. The Church, as Christ's Body, is the first sacrament, the sign and instrument through which the Holy Spirit dispenses the mystery of Salvation. In this age of the Church, Christ lives and acts through the sacraments.

286 *Prayers and Practices of Our Faith*

The Seven Sacraments

Jesus touches our lives through the sacraments. In the sacraments physical objects or actions—water, bread and wine, oil, laying on of hands, and others—are signs of Jesus' presence.

Sacraments of Initiation

These sacraments lay the foundation for our Christian life.

Baptism In Baptism we are born into new life in Christ. Baptism takes away Original Sin and makes us members of the Church. Its sign is the pouring of water.

Confirmation Confirmation seals our life of faith in Jesus. Its signs are the laying on of hands on a person's head, most often by a bishop, and the anointing with oil. Like Baptism, it is received only once.

Eucharist The Eucharist nourishes our life of faith. We receive the Body and Blood of Christ often. Its signs are bread and wine.

Sacraments of Healing

These sacraments celebrate the healing power of Jesus.

Penance and Reconciliation Through Penance we receive God's forgiveness. Forgiveness requires being sorry for our sins. In Penance we receive Jesus' healing grace through absolution by the priest. The signs of this sacrament are our confession of sins, our repentance and satisfaction, and the words of absolution.

Anointing of the Sick This sacrament unites a sick person's suffering with Jesus'. Its signs are the laying on of hands by a priest and anointing with oil, which is a symbol of strength.

Importance of Baptism

The Church teaches us that, if God has called you to know the fullness of the truth about Jesus and his Church, you will not be saved if you refuse to believe. As Jesus said, "He who believes and is baptized will be saved; whoever does not believe will be condemned" (Mark 16:16). This does not mean that people who are not Christian will be condemned. People who search for the truth honestly and with a sincere heart, even if they are not called to God to the fullness of faith in Jesus, can be saved. But for us who are called, believing in Jesus Christ and in the one who sent him is necessary for Salvation. In the unfortunate circumstance of children dying before they have been baptized, the Church entrusts them to the mercy of God and prays for their Salvation.

From the earliest times the Church has practiced infant Baptism. The Church has celebrated this practice, recognizing Baptism is a gift of grace from God that is not connected to any human merit. By receiving this grace, children are more capable of fighting tendencies to be envious of others, and they can trust in God more completely.

Sacraments at the Service of Communion

These sacraments help members serve the community.

Matrimony In Matrimony, a baptized man and woman are united with each other as a sign of the unity between Jesus and his Church. Matrimony requires the consent of the couple, as expressed in the marriage promises. The couple are the sign of this sacrament.

Holy Orders In Holy Orders, men are ordained priests to be leaders of the community or deacons to be reminders of our baptismal call to serve others. The signs of this sacrament are the laying on of hands and the prayer by the bishop asking God for the outpouring of the Holy Spirit. ✝

Chastity and the Sacraments at the Service of Communion

Baptism challenges us to follow Christ, the model of chastity. Chastity is the essential virtue that helps us live out our sexuality in a proper manner. A chaste person is someone who is in control of his or her emotions and keeps them directed toward what is good for him or her.

Chastity is practiced differently by people according to their circumstances. Those who choose religious vocations take vows of chastity, which enable them to give themselves fully to God alone. For single people who are not in a religious order, chastity means learning to express sexuality in ways other than physical intimacy. For married couples, chastity means doing all those things that will help both the husband and the wife remain faithful to each other. It also means not practicing morally unacceptable means of birth control.

Celebrating the Lord's Day

THE Sabbath, the day on which God rested after creating the world, represents the completion of Creation. Saturday has been replaced by Sunday for Christians because it recalls the beginning of the new creation through the Resurrection of Jesus Christ.

The Sunday celebration of the Lord's Day is at the heart of the Church's life. That is why on Sundays and Holy Days of Obligation, we are required to participate in the Mass. We also rest from work, take time to enjoy our families, enrich our cultural and social lives, and perform Works of Mercy. On Sunday, people from all over the world gather at God's Eucharistic table.

The Order of Mass

The Mass is the high point of Catholic life, and it always follows a set order.

Introductory Rites—preparing to celebrate the Eucharist

Entrance Chant
We gather as a community and praise God in song.

Greeting
We pray the Sign of the Cross. The priest welcomes us.

Penitential Act
We remember our sins and ask God for mercy.

Gloria
We praise God in song.

Collect
We ask God to hear our prayers.

Liturgy of the Word—hearing God's plan of Salvation

First Reading
We listen to God's Word, usually from the Old Testament.

Responsorial Psalm
We respond to God's Word in song.

Second Reading
We listen to God's Word from the New Testament.

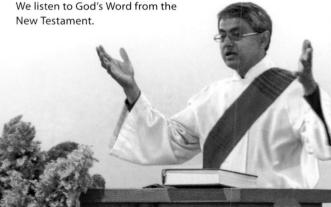

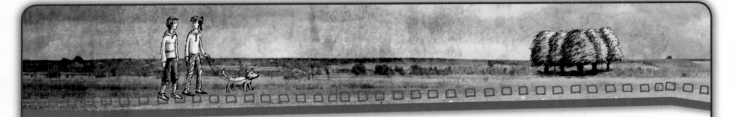

Gospel Acclamation
We sing "Alleluia!" to praise God for the Good News. During Lent we use a different acclamation.

Gospel Reading
We stand and listen to the Gospel of the Lord.

Homily
The priest or the deacon explains God's Word.

Profession of Faith
We proclaim our faith through the Nicene Creed.

Prayer of the Faithful
We pray for our needs and the needs of others.

Liturgy of the Eucharist—celebrating Christ's presence in the Eucharist

Presentation and Preparation of the Gifts
We bring gifts of bread and wine to the altar.

Prayer over the Offerings
The priest prays that God will accept our sacrifice.

Eucharistic Prayer
This prayer of thanksgiving is the center and high point of the entire celebration.

✝ **Preface**—We give thanks and praise to God.

✝ **Holy, Holy, Holy**—We sing an acclamation of praise.

✝ **Institution Narrative**—The bread and wine become the Body and Blood of Jesus Christ.

✝ **The Mystery of Faith**—We proclaim the mystery of our faith.

✝ **Amen**—We affirm the words and actions of the Eucharistic Prayer.

Communion Rite—preparing to receive the Body and Blood of Jesus Christ

The Lord's Prayer
We pray the Lord's Prayer.

Sign of Peace
We offer one another Christ's peace.

Lamb of God
We pray for forgiveness, mercy, and peace.

Communion
We receive the Body and Blood of Jesus Christ.

Prayer after Communion
We pray that the Eucharist will strengthen us to live as Jesus did.

Concluding Rites—going forth to glorify the Lord by our lives

Final Blessing
We receive God's blessing.

Dismissal
We go in peace, glorifying the Lord by our lives.

Holy Days of Obligation

The Holy Days of Obligation are the days other than Sundays on which we celebrate the great things God has done for us through Jesus and the saints. On Holy Days of Obligation, Catholics attend Mass.

Six Holy Days of Obligation are celebrated in the United States.

January 1—
Mary, Mother of God

40 days after Easter—
Ascension

August 15—Assumption of the Blessed Virgin Mary

November 1—All Saints Day

December 8—
Immaculate Conception

December 25—Nativity of Our Lord Jesus Christ

Making Good Choices

OUR conscience is the inner voice that helps us know the law God has placed in our hearts. Our conscience helps us judge the moral qualities of our own actions. It guides us to do good and avoid evil.

The Holy Spirit can help us form a good conscience. We form our conscience by studying the teachings of the Church and following the guidance of our parents and pastoral leaders.

God has given every human being freedom of choice. This does not mean that we have the right to do whatever we please. We can live in true freedom if we cooperate with the Holy Spirit, who gives us the virtue of prudence. Prudence helps us recognize what is good in every situation and make correct choices. The Holy Spirit gives us the gifts of wisdom and understanding to help us make the right choices in life in relationship to God and others. The gift of counsel helps us reflect on making correct choices in life.

The Ten Commandments help us make moral choices that are pleasing to God. We have the grace of the sacraments, the teachings of the Church, and the good example of saints and fellow Christians to help us make good choices.

Making moral choices involves the following steps:

1. Ask the Holy Spirit for help.

2. Think about God's law and the teachings of the Church.

3. Think about what will happen as a result of your choice. Ask yourself, "Will the consequences be pleasing to God? Will my choice hurt someone else?"

4. Seek advice from someone you respect and remember that Jesus is with you.

5. Ask yourself how your choice will affect your relationships with God and others.

Making moral choices takes into consideration the object of the choice, our intention in making the choice, and the circumstances in which the choice is made. It is never right to make an evil choice in the hope of gaining something good.

292 *Prayers and Practices of Our Faith*

Human Sinfulness

When we sin, we offend God. We choose to turn away from him. Saint Augustine defines it as "an utterance, a deed, or a desire contrary to the eternal law."

Original Sin

Tempted by Satan in the Garden, Adam and Eve let their trust in their Creator die in their hearts and abused their freedom by choosing to disobey God. They chose themselves over God. They believed Satan and chose to "be like God." All subsequent sin would be disobedience toward God and lack of trust in his goodness. Adam and Eve committed a personal sin, but this sin affected the human nature that they would then transmit to humanity. Human nature would now be deprived of the original holiness and justice that God had intended. Original Sin is not a sin we commit but a state we are born into. Baptism, by giving us the life of Christ's grace, erases Original Sin and turns us back toward God. But the consequences of our nature, weakened and inclined to evil, remain in us.

Mortal Sin

Mortal sin destroys the love of God in our heart. A conversion of heart, through the Sacrament of Penance and Reconciliation, is necessary to experience God's mercy again. For a sin to be mortal, three conditions must be met: First, the matter of the sin must be serious. Second, mortal sin requires full knowledge of the seriousness of the act. Finally, there must be complete consent. In other words, the sin is really a personal choice.

Venial Sin

Venial sin allows the love of God to remain in our heart, but it offends and wounds that love. One commits a venial sin when the offense is of a less serious matter or, if the matter is serious, it is chosen without full knowledge or complete consent. Venial sin weakens love within us. It interferes with our practice of the virtues, makes it harder to do good, and can lead us to mortal sin. Venial sin is forgiven through the Sacrament of Penance and Reconciliation, the practice of good works, and reception of the Eucharist.

Capital Sins

Saint John Cassian and Saint Gregory the Great distinguished seven sins that they called Capital Sins because they produce other sins and other vices.

pride	covetousness	envy	anger
lust	gluttony	sloth	

Adam and Eve Driven Out of Paradise, Siegfried Detler Bendixen, 20th Century.

Celebrating and Living Our Faith 293

The Morality of Human Acts

Human beings are able to act morally only because we are free to decide how we act. If we were not free to decide what to do, our acts could not be good or evil. Human acts that are freely chosen after a judgment of conscience can be morally evaluated. They are either good or evil.

The morality of human acts depends on

✝ the object chosen;

✝ the end in view or the intention; and

✝ the circumstances of the action.

For an act to be good, what you choose to do must be good in itself. If the choice is not good, the intention or the circumstances cannot make it good. You cannot steal a digital camera because it is your father's birthday and it would make him very happy to have one. But a good act done with a bad intention is not necessarily good as well. Participating in a hunger walk to impress a teacher from whom you want a good grade instead of out of genuine concern for those who are poor is not necessarily a good act. Circumstances can affect the morality of an act. They can increase or lessen the goodness of an act. Acting out of fear of harm lessens a person's responsibility for an act.

When Jesus gave us the Beatitudes in the Sermon on the Mount, he was teaching us to live in a healthy relationship with God and with others. Jesus wants us to respect other people and to treat their lives as sacred. It is good to think about our Christian values regarding people and their lives.

Life

Jesus and his Church teach us that every person is created in the image and likeness of God. The life of every single person, therefore, is holy because God created that life and wants it to exist.

Many plots in police dramas center on a murder taking place. Killing is depicted so often that it almost becomes an afterthought. Because murder is the deliberate taking of another person's life, it shows great disrespect for life and for the Lord of Life. God condemns murder because it goes against the dignity of the person and the holiness of God who made that person. Sometimes, however, someone will kill another person in self-defense. That is not murder, and it is not sinful if it is the only way to defend oneself.

Abortion

Protection of human life includes the life of the unborn. Every child has the right to life from the moment he or she is conceived. You might watch a movie or a TV show in which a woman who is expecting a baby has an **abortion.** Such an action is gravely wrong, and Catholic mothers who have abortions and those who aid them receive the severe penalty of excommunication. This means that the person is no longer part of the Church community and cannot receive the sacraments or participate in Church activities.

DEFINE

Draw young people's attention to the term *abortion*. Have a young person read aloud from the Glossary the definition of the term. Invite a volunteer to define the term in his or her own words.

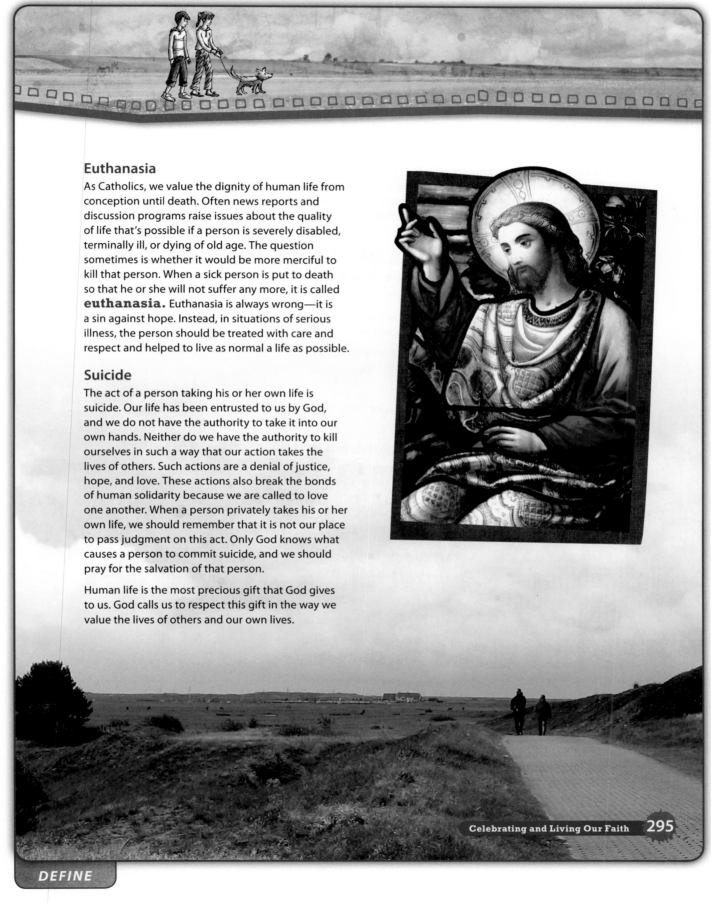

Euthanasia

As Catholics, we value the dignity of human life from conception until death. Often news reports and discussion programs raise issues about the quality of life that's possible if a person is severely disabled, terminally ill, or dying of old age. The question sometimes is whether it would be more merciful to kill that person. When a sick person is put to death so that he or she will not suffer any more, it is called **euthanasia.** Euthanasia is always wrong—it is a sin against hope. Instead, in situations of serious illness, the person should be treated with care and respect and helped to live as normal a life as possible.

Suicide

The act of a person taking his or her own life is suicide. Our life has been entrusted to us by God, and we do not have the authority to take it into our own hands. Neither do we have the authority to kill ourselves in such a way that our action takes the lives of others. Such actions are a denial of justice, hope, and love. These actions also break the bonds of human solidarity because we are called to love one another. When a person privately takes his or her own life, we should remember that it is not our place to pass judgment on this act. Only God knows what causes a person to commit suicide, and we should pray for the salvation of that person.

Human life is the most precious gift that God gives to us. God calls us to respect this gift in the way we value the lives of others and our own lives.

Celebrating and Living Our Faith **295**

DEFINE

Draw young people's attention to the term *euthanasia*. Have a young person read aloud from the Glossary the definition of the term. Invite a volunteer to define the term in his or her own words.

An Examination of Conscience

An examination of conscience is the act of looking prayerfully into our hearts and asking how we have hurt our relationships with God and other people through our thoughts, words, and actions. We reflect on the Ten Commandments and the teachings of the Church. The questions below help us in our examination of conscience.

My Relationship with God

☐ What steps am I taking to grow closer to God and to others? Do I turn to God often during the day, especially when I am tempted?

☐ Do I participate at Mass with attention and devotion on Sundays and Holy Days of Obligation?

☐ Do I pray often and read the Bible?

☐ Do I use God's name and the names of Jesus, Mary, and the saints with love and reverence?

My Relationships with Family, Friends, and Neighbors

☐ Have I set a bad example through my words or actions? Do I treat others fairly? Do I spread stories that hurt other people?

☐ Am I loving toward those in my family? Am I respectful of my neighbors, my friends, and those in authority?

☐ Do I value human life? Do I do what I can to promote peace and end violence? Do I avoid talking about others in ways that could harm them?

☐ Do I show respect for my body and for the bodies of others? Do I keep away from forms of entertainment that do not respect God's gift of sexuality?

☐ Have I taken or damaged anything that did not belong to me? Have I cheated or copied homework?

☐ Have I told the truth even when it was difficult?

☐ Do I show concern for the poor and offer assistance to them in the ways I am able? Do I show concern for the environment and care for it as God has asked?

☐ Do I quarrel with others just so I can get my own way? Do I insult others to try to make them think they are less than I am? Do I hold grudges and try to hurt people who I think have hurt me?

How to Make a Good Confession

An examination of conscience is an important part of preparing for the Sacrament of Penance and Reconciliation. The Sacrament of Penance and Reconciliation includes the following steps:

1. The priest greets us, and we pray the Sign of the Cross. He invites us to trust in God. He may read God's Word with us.

2. We confess our sins. The priest may help and counsel us.

3. The priest gives us a penance to perform. Penance is an act of kindness or prayers to pray, or both.

4. The priest asks us to express our sorrow, usually by praying the Act of Contrition.

5. We receive absolution. The priest says, "I absolve you from your sins in the name of the Father, and of the Son, and of the Holy Spirit." We respond, "Amen."

6. The priest dismisses us by saying, "Go in peace." We go forth to perform the act of penance he has given us.

Celebrating and Living Our Faith **297**

Catholic Social Teaching

THE Catholic Church has developed a large body of teaching on social justice issues because action on behalf of justice to shape a more just world is an essential part of preaching the Gospel.

The major development of the social doctrine of the Church began in the 19th century when the Gospel encountered modern industrial society. There were new structures for the production of consumer goods, new concepts of society, new types of states and authorities, and new forms of labor and ownership.

Since that time the Church has been making judgments about economic and social matters that relate to the basic rights of individuals and communities.

The Common Good

A core principle of Catholic Social Teaching since the beginning has been that society as a whole is responsible for building up the common good. The common good is not the good for the greatest number of people. That would leave out some people. Rather every person must participate in the common good, not just the smartest, the most powerful, or the luckiest.

Following the principles of the common good means that people have the right to develop their talents and skills to become the best individuals they can be. The political, social, economic, and cultural environment must produce conditions that enable everyone to do this. The principles of the common good are best dealt with at the local level by the people most directly involved with the social issues.

The Church's social teaching is a rich treasure of wisdom about how to build a just society and live holy lives amid the challenges of the modern world.

Showing Our Love for the World

In the story of the Good Samaritan (Luke 10:29–37), Jesus makes clear our responsibility to care for those in need. The Catholic Church teaches this responsibility in the following themes of Catholic Social Teaching.

Life and Dignity of the Human Person

All human life is sacred, and all people must be respected and valued over material goods. We are called to ask whether our actions as a society respect or threaten the life and dignity of the human person.

Call to Family, Community, and Participation

Participation in family and community is central to our faith and to a healthy society. Families must be supported so that people can participate in society, build a community spirit, and promote the well-being of all, especially the poor and vulnerable.

Rights and Responsibilities

Every person has a right to life as well as a right to those things required for human decency. As Catholics, we have a responsibility to protect these basic human rights in order to achieve a healthy society.

Option for the Poor and Vulnerable

In our world, many people are very rich, while at the same time, many are extremely poor. As Catholics, we are called to pay special attention to the needs of the poor by defending and promoting their dignity and by meeting their immediate material needs.

The Dignity of Work and the Rights of Workers

The basic rights of workers must be respected: the right to productive work, fair wages, and private property; and the right to organize, join unions, and pursue economic opportunity. Catholics believe that the economy is meant to serve people and that work is not merely a way to make a living but an important way in which we participate in God's creation.

Solidarity

Because God is our Father, we are all brothers and sisters with the responsibility to care for one another. Solidarity is the attitude that leads Christians to share spiritual and material goods. Solidarity unites rich and poor, weak and strong, and helps build a society that recognizes that we all depend on one another.

Care for God's Creation

God is the Creator of all people and all things, and he wants us to enjoy his creation. The responsibility to care for all God has made is a requirement of our faith. ✝

Glossary and Index

The following resources and the acknowledgments are reproduced in this section for your convenience.

- **Young People's Book Glossary**
- **Young People's Book Index**
- **Young People's Book Acknowledgments**

Glossary

A

Abba the Aramaic word for "father" but more like the informal "papa" or "daddy." When Jesus spoke to God the Father, he called him "Abba." [Abba]

abortion the deliberate ending of a pregnancy that results in the death of the unborn child. The Church teaches that since life begins at conception, abortion is a serious crime against life and is gravely against the moral law. [aborto]

Abraham the model of faith and trust in God in the Old Testament. God made a covenant with Abraham, promising him land and many descendants. He became the father of the Chosen People. [Abrahán]

absolution the forgiveness we receive from God through the priest in the Sacrament of Penance and Reconciliation. Absolution places us in a state of grace and prepares us to receive other sacraments. [absolución]

abstain the choice to avoid certain foods or activities. Abstaining is a form of fasting that helps remind us that God comes first in our lives and that we are dependent on God for everything. [abstenerse]

Acts of the Apostles the second volume of Luke's two-volume work. Written for a Greek Christian audience, it continues the story of Jesus' Resurrection and Ascension and reports the beginnings of the Church at Pentecost. It then tells stories of the Apostles, including Paul, and how their evangelism spread the Church from Jerusalem to the ends of the earth. [Hechos de los Apóstoles]

actual grace the gift of God, freely given, that unites us with the life of the Trinity. Actual grace helps us make the choices that conform our lives to God's will. (See *grace, habitual grace,* and *sanctifying grace.*) [gracia actual]

adoration the act of giving reverence to God by recognizing and worshiping the Real Presence of Jesus Christ in the Blessed Sacrament, displayed in a monstrance. [adoración]

adultery a sin of unfaithfulness to one's marriage vows that injures the bond of the marriage covenant. It occurs when two people have sexual relations while at least one of them is married to another person. The Sixth Commandment forbids adultery because it undermines the institution of marriage and is harmful to children, who need the stability of their parents' marriage commitment. [adulterio]

Advent the four weeks before Christmas. It is a time of joyful preparation for the celebration of the Incarnation, Jesus' birth as our Savior, and a time for anticipating the coming of Jesus Christ at the end of time, which is known as the Second Coming. [Adviento]

Advocate Jesus' name for the Holy Spirit. The Holy Spirit comforts us and makes Jesus present to us. [Defensor]

Age of Enlightenment the shift in worldview that took place during the 1700s. The Age of Enlightenment included great advances in science and scientific understanding but also led to questions about religion, morality, and the existence of God. [Ilustración, la]

age of reason the age one must reach in order to receive Confirmation, usually around seven years old. The Church also requires that one reach the age of reason before celebrating the Sacraments of Reconciliation and the Eucharist. [edad de la razón]

Agony in the Garden the time Jesus spent in fervent prayer in the Garden of Gethsemane the night before his Crucifixion. Jesus' Agony in the Garden reminds us to remain true to our identity as sons and daughters of God, especially when we are tempted to run away from God. [Oración de Jesús en el Huerto, la]

All Saints Day November 1, the day on which the Church honors all who have died and now live with God as saints in Heaven. This group includes those who are officially recognized as saints as well as people who have not been officially declared saints but now live in God's presence in Heaven. The feast celebrates our union with those who have gone before us and points to our ultimate goal of union with God. [Día de Todos los Santos]

All Souls Day November 2, the day on which the Church prays that all who have died in friendship with God may rest in peace. Those who have died may need purification in Purgatory before living fully in God's presence. Our prayers and good works can help them in this process. Along with All Saints Day, this feast reminds us that all who love God, living and dead, are united with Jesus Christ and one another in the Communion of Saints. [Día de los Fieles Difuntos]

Glossary

Alleluia │ asceticism

Alleluia a prayer of praise to God. It is usually sung as the Gospel Acclamation before the proclamation of the Gospel Reading at Mass except during Lent. [Aleluya]

almsgiving the offering of money, possessions, time, or talent to those in need. Along with fasting and prayer, almsgiving is an important spiritual practice during Lent. [limosna, dar]

altar the table in the church on which the priest celebrates Mass, where the sacrifice of Christ on the Cross is made present in the Sacrament of the Eucharist. The altar represents two aspects of the mystery of the Eucharist. It is the place where Jesus Christ offers himself for our sins and where he gives us himself in the Eucharist as food for eternal life. [altar]

ambo a raised stand from which a person proclaims the Word of God during Mass [ambón]

Amen the Hebrew word used to conclude Jewish and Christian prayers. It means "This is true," "So be it," or "Let it be so." We end prayers with *Amen* to show that we mean what we have just said. [amén]

angel a spiritual creature who worships God in Heaven. Angels serve God as messengers. They tell us God's plans for our Salvation. [ángel]

Angelus a Catholic devotion recited three times a day—morning, noon, and evening. The devotion reflects on the mystery of the Incarnation—the coming of the angel to Mary, her acceptance of the invitation to be the mother of Jesus, and the Word made flesh. [Ángelus]

anger an emotion that is not in itself wrong, but when not controlled can harden into resentment and hate, becoming one of the seven capital sins (See *capital sins*.) [ira]

annulment a finding by a Church tribunal that at least one essential element for a marriage was not present on the day of the wedding. The Church can declare that the Sacrament of Matrimony did not take place if one of the parties did not freely choose to marry, had been married before and that marriage was not annulled, or was not open to having children. An annulment cannot be considered until after a person is divorced. Catholics who receive an annulment are free to marry in the Church. [anulación]

Annunciation the announcement to Mary by the angel Gabriel that God had chosen her to be the mother of the Messiah. She would conceive a child through the Holy Spirit and name him Jesus. The Feast of the Annunciation is celebrated on March 25, nine months before Christmas. [Anunciación]

Anointing of the Sick one of the seven sacraments. In this sacrament a seriously ill person is anointed with holy oil and receives the strength, peace, and courage to overcome the difficulties associated with illness. Through this sacrament, Jesus brings the sick person spiritual healing and forgiveness of sins. If it is God's will, healing of the body is given as well. [Unción de los Enfermos]

antiphon one or more psalm verses sung in response during the liturgy. Although the Mass also uses antiphons, they are used in the Liturgy of the Hours to pray about the central events of the Christian faith. [antífona]

apocalyptic literature a form of writing that uses symbolic language and imagery to describe the eternal struggle between good and evil. The Book of Revelation is an example of apocalyptic literature. [literatura apocalíptica]

apologist a defender of the faith. Apologists defend Christianity against critics and proclaim the truths of the faith. [apologista]

Apostle one of the twelve chosen men who accompanied Jesus in his ministry and were witnesses to the Resurrection. *Apostle* means "one sent." These were the men sent to preach the Gospel to the whole world. [Apóstol]

Apostles' Creed a statement of Christian belief that developed out of a creed used in Baptism in Rome. The Apostles' Creed lists simple statements of belief in God the Father, Jesus Christ the Son, and the Holy Spirit. The profession of faith used in Baptism today is based on it. [Credo de los Apóstoles]

apostolic the Mark of the Church that indicates that Jesus continues to lead the Church through the pope and the bishops. The pope and the bishops are the successors of the Apostles. (See *Marks of the Church*.) [apostólico]

Ark of the Covenant the sacred box that God commanded Moses to build out of acacia wood to hold the restored tablets of the Law (Exodus 25:10–16) [Arca de la Alianza]

Ascension the entry of Jesus into God's presence in Heaven. In the Acts of the Apostles, it is written that Jesus, after his Resurrection, spent 40 days on earth, instructing his followers. He then returned to his Father in Heaven. [Ascensión]

asceticism the practice of self-denial and spiritual discipline as a way of training and forming oneself for the service of God and others. Asceticism can take many forms such as abstinence, fasting, celibacy, and prayer. [ascetismo]

Ash Wednesday the first day of Lent, on which we receive ashes on our foreheads. The ashes remind us to prepare for Easter by repenting and showing sorrow for offending God and hurting our relationships with others. [Miércoles de Ceniza]

assembly the People of God when they are gathered together to worship him [asamblea]

Assumption when Mary was taken into Heaven, body and soul. Mary had a special relationship with her Son, Jesus, from the very beginning when she conceived him. Because of this relationship, she enjoys a special participation in Jesus' Resurrection and has been taken into Heaven where she now lives with him. We celebrate this event in the Feast of the Assumption on August 15. [Asunción]

atone to make amends for sin. Jesus' obedience to God the Father by dying on the Cross atoned for the sins of the whole world. [expiar]

B

Baptism the first of the seven sacraments. Baptism frees us from Original Sin and is necessary for Salvation. Baptism gives us new life in Jesus Christ through the Holy Spirit. The celebration of Baptism consists of immersing a person in water while declaring that the person is baptized in the name of the Father, the Son, and the Holy Spirit. [Bautismo]

baptismal font the water vessel where the Sacrament of Baptism is celebrated. The baptismal font may be located in a separate baptistry, near the entrance of the church, or in the midst of the community. [pila bautismal]

basic rights the human rights a government should protect, such as religious liberty, personal freedom, access to necessary information, right to life, and protection from terror and torture [derechos básicos]

basilica the term used to designate a certain church of historical significance in a local area. Major basilicas are in Rome and are designated churches of ancient origin that serve as places of pilgrimage. Minor basilicas are designated churches that have historical or devotional importance in local areas throughout the world. [basílica]

beatified recognized by the Church as having lived a life of great Christian virtue and declared to be in Heaven. Beatified persons are referred to as *Blessed* and can be publicly venerated by the Church. [beatificado]

Beatitudes the teachings of Jesus in the Sermon on the Mount in Matthew's Gospel. The Beatitudes are eight guidelines for Christlike living that lead to happiness in this life and eternal joy in the next. They are the fulfillment of the Ten Commandments given to Moses. [Bienaventuranzas]

Bible the collection of books that contains the truths of God's Revelation. These writings, inspired by the Holy Spirit and written by different authors using different styles, are the Word of God. The Bible is made up of 46 books in the Old Testament and 27 books in the New Testament. [Biblia]

bishop a man who has received the fullness of Holy Orders. As a successor to the original Apostles, he cares for the Church and is a principal teacher in it. [obispo]

blasphemy any word, thought, or action done in hatred or defiance against God. It extends to using language that disrespects the Church, the saints, or holy things. It is also blasphemy to use God's name as an excuse to enslave people, to torture them, or to put them to death. Using God's name to do these things can cause others to reject religion. [blasfemia]

Blessed Sacrament the Eucharist that has been consecrated by the priest at Mass. It is kept in the tabernacle to adore and to be taken to those who are sick. [Santísimo Sacramento]

blessing a prayer that calls for God's power and care upon some person, place, thing, or special activity [bendición]

Body and Blood of Christ the Bread and Wine that has been consecrated by the priest at Mass. In the Sacrament of the Eucharist, all the risen Lord Jesus Christ—body, blood, soul, and divinity—is present in the consecrated Bread and Wine. [Cuerpo y Sangre de Cristo]

Bread of Life a title that Jesus gives himself in John 6:33–35. Jesus is food for the faithful. [Pan de Vida]

Buddhism a religion based on the teaching of Siddhartha Gautama, who was known as the Buddha, which means "Enlightened One." The Buddha was born to a royal family in northern India about five and a half centuries before Jesus. At age 29 he became disillusioned with life and left his comfortable home to find an answer to the question of why humans suffer. [Budismo]

Glossary

Glossary 303

Canaan | chasuble

C

Canaan the name of the land between Syria and Egypt in which the Israelites settled [Caná]

calumny (slander) a false statement about someone's reputation that makes others think bad of that person. Calumny is a sin against the Eighth Commandment. [calumnia]

canon the official list of the 73 books that make up the Old and New Testaments of the Bible [canon]

canonization the process by which someone is declared a saint. The process ensures that the person who is a candidate for canonization lived an exemplary Christian life and can serve as a model for Christians around the world. [canonización]

canonize to declare that a Christian who has died is already a saint in Heaven and may be looked to as a model of Christian life who may intercede for us [canonizar]

capital sins those sins that can lead to more serious sin. They are pride, covetousness, envy, anger, gluttony, lust, and sloth. [pecados capitales]

Cardinal Virtues the four virtues that lead a person to live in relationship with God and with others. Prudence, justice, fortitude, and temperance can be acquired by education and good actions. (See *fortitude, justice, prudence,* and *temperance.*) [virtudes cardinales]

cast lots to throw down small stones or pebbles called lots to help determine a decision needing divine guidance. Lots were cast to choose the disciple to replace Judas in the Acts of the Apostles 1:23–26. Roman soldiers also cast lots to divide Jesus' clothing among them as in John 19:24. [echar a suertes]

catechism a collection or summary of Church teachings for the education of the faithful. The current *Catechism of the Catholic Church* provides a contemporary summary and explanation of the Catholic faith. [catecismo]

catechumen a person being formed in the Christian life through instruction and by the example of the faith community. Through conversion and maturity of faith, a catechumen is preparing to be welcomed into the Church at Easter through the Sacraments of Baptism, Confirmation, and the Eucharist. [catecúmeno]

catechumenate the process of becoming a Christian. In the early Church, the process took several years. [catecumenado]

cathedral the main church in a diocese where a bishop presides and where the bishop's *cathedra,* or chair, is located. The *cathedra* represents the bishop's authority as the main teacher of the faith in the diocese. [catedral]

catholic one of the four Marks of the Church. The Church is catholic because Jesus is fully present in it, because it proclaims the fullness of faith, and because Jesus has given the Church to the whole world. The Church is universal. (See *Marks of the Church.*) [católica]

Catholic Social Teaching the body of teaching on social justice issues, action on behalf of justice, and work toward a more just world. The Church makes judgments about economic and social matters that relate to the basic rights of individuals and communities. The Church's social teaching is a rich treasure of wisdom about how to build a just society. [enseñanza social católica]

celebrant a bishop or priest who leads the people in praying the Mass. A deacon who baptizes or witnesses a marriage is also a celebrant. [celebrante]

celebrate to worship, praise, and thank God for what he has done for us with prayers and songs, especially in the celebration of the Eucharist [celebrar]

census a systematic counting of the citizens of a particular place. In addition to the census taking place when Jesus was born, the Bible records several censuses, including two in the Book of Numbers and one by King David. [censo]

character a permanent spiritual mark. Character shows that a person has a new relationship with Jesus and a special standing in the Church. Baptism, Confirmation, and Holy Orders each have a specific permanent character and therefore may be received only once. [carácter]

charism a special gift of the Holy Spirit given for the service of others, the good of the world, and particularly for the building up of the Church [carisma]

charity a virtue given to us by God that helps us love God above all things and our neighbor as ourselves. (See *Theological Virtues.*) [caridad]

chastity the integration of our physical sexuality with our spiritual nature. Chastity helps us be completely human, able to give to others our whole life and love. All people, married and single, are called to practice chastity. [castidad]

chasuble the visible liturgical vestment worn by the bishop or priest at Mass. A newly ordained priest receives a chasuble as part of the ordination ritual. [casulla]

Chosen People | **contemplative**

Chosen People the people set apart by God to have a special relationship with him. God first formed a Chosen People when he made a covenant, or solemn agreement, with Abraham. He reaffirmed the Covenant through Moses at Mount Sinai. The Covenant is fulfilled in Jesus and his Church. [Pueblo Elegido]

Chrism a perfumed oil, consecrated by a bishop, that is used in the Sacraments of Baptism, Confirmation, and Holy Orders. Anointing with Chrism signifies the call of the baptized to the threefold ministry of priest, prophet, and king. [crisma]

Christ a Greek version of the Hebrew word *Messiah*, or "anointed one." It is another name for Jesus as priest, prophet, and king. [Cristo]

Christian the name given to all those who have been anointed through the gift of the Holy Spirit in Baptism and have become followers of Jesus Christ [cristiano]

Christmas the feast of the birth of Jesus (December 25) [Navidad]

Church the people of God throughout the whole world, or diocese (the local Church), or the assembly of those called together to worship God. The Church is one, holy, catholic, and apostolic. [Iglesia]

clergy those men who are set apart as sacred ministers to serve the Church through the Sacrament of Holy Orders [clero]

commandment a standard, or rule, for living as God wants us to live. Jesus summarized all the commandments into two: love God and love your neighbor. [mandamiento]

common good the sum total of the social conditions that allow people, individually and as a group, to reach their full potential. The common good requires peace, security, respecting everyone's rights, and meeting everyone's spiritual and worldly needs. People have a responsibility to contribute to the good of the entire society. It is one of the basic principles at the center of Catholic Social Teaching. [bien común]

communal prayer the worship of God together with others. The Liturgy of the Hours and the Mass are the main forms of communal prayer. [oración comunitaria]

Communion of Saints the unity of all, dead or living, who have been saved in Jesus Christ. The Communion of Saints is based on our one faith, and it is nourished by our participation in the Eucharist. [Comunión de los Santos]

community Christians who are gathered in the name of Jesus Christ to receive his grace and live according to his values [comunidad]

compassion God's fundamental attitude toward his people. This is best seen in Jesus' reaching out to heal those in need. Acting with compassion and mercy toward those in need identifies a person as belonging to God. [compasión]

confession the act of telling our sins to a priest in the Sacrament of Penance and Reconciliation. The sacrament itself is sometimes referred to as confession. [confesión]

Confirmation the sacrament that completes the grace we receive in Baptism. It seals, or confirms, this grace through the seven Gifts of the Holy Spirit that we receive as part of Confirmation. This sacrament also makes us better able to participate in worship and the apostolic life of the Church. [Confirmación]

conscience the inner voice that helps each of us judge the morality of our own actions. It guides us to follow God's Law by doing good and avoiding evil. [conciencia]

consecrate to make a thing or a person to be special to God through a prayer or blessing. At Mass the priest's words at the consecration transform the bread and wine into the Body and Blood of Jesus Christ. People or objects set apart for God in a special way can also be consecrated. For example, men or women living in religious communities consecrate themselves to God through the evangelical counsels. [consagrar]

consubstantial the doctrine affirming that Jesus, the Son of God, assumed human nature while maintaining the same divine nature as God the Father. The Nicene Creed was written in part to make clear that Jesus is consubstantial with the Father. [consustancial]

consumerism giving undue value to the acquisition of material goods, acting in a way that puts things at the center of one's life where God alone should be [consumismo]

contemplate to focus on God while quieting and emptying our minds of all other distractions [contemplar]

contemplation the act of prayerfully and continuously focusing on God. Many religious communities and spiritualities in the Church are devoted to contemplation. [contemplación]

contemplative the character of an activity or a way of life that is prayerful and continuously focused on God. Many religious communities in the Church are devoted to contemplative life. [conemplativo]

Glossary 305

contrition | **deacon**

contrition the sorrow we feel when we know that we have sinned, followed by the decision not to sin again. Contrition is the most important act of the penitent preparing to celebrate the Sacrament of Penance and Reconciliation. (See *imperfect contrition* and *perfect contrition*.) [contrición]

conversion a radical or serious change of the whole life, a turning away from sin and toward God. The call to change of heart is a key part of the preaching of Jesus. Throughout our entire lives, Jesus calls us to change in this way. [conversión]

convert one who embraces a new faith or religion. At the beginning of the Church, whether Gentile converts needed to observe Jewish law was a major controversy resolved at the Council of Jerusalem. [converso]

convocation a gathering of people called together. We are called together in the Church as a convocation to work for the Salvation of all people. [asamblea]

Corporal Works of Mercy kind acts by which we help our neighbors with their everyday material needs. Corporal Works of Mercy include feeding the hungry, finding a home for the homeless, clothing the naked, visiting the sick and those in prison, giving alms to the poor, and burying the dead.
[obras de misericordia corporales]

Council of Jerusalem the name of the meeting around A.D. 50 that is described in Acts of the Apostles. The meeting was the result of a disagreement between Paul and his followers and the Jewish Christian followers of James, the leader of the Jerusalem Church. James felt that those who became Christians should also observe Jewish customs. Paul said that there should be no such necessity. [Concilio de Jerusalén]

counsel one of the seven Gifts of the Holy Spirit. Counsel helps us make correct choices in life through reflection, discernment, consultation, and advisement. (See *Gifts of the Holy Spirit*.) [consejo]

Covenant, the in the Old Testament, the solemn agreement between God and the Chosen People, Israel, that involved mutual commitments. God made covenants with Noah, Abraham, and Moses and prepared his people for Salvation. In the New Testament, God's new and final Covenant was established through Jesus' life, Death, Resurrection, and Ascension. *Testament* is another word for *covenant*. [Alianza]

covet to desire something belonging to someone else out of envy or jealousy. Coveting something is a desire that becomes an obsession. We are forbidden by the Ninth and Tenth Commandments from coveting others' spouses or possessions. [codiciar]

covetousness having a craving for wealth or for another's possessions (See *capital sins*.) [avaricia]

creation God's act of making everything that exists outside himself. Creation also refers to everything that exists. God said that all of creation is good. [creación]

Creator God, who made everything that is and whom we can come to know through everything he created [Creador]

crèche a Nativity scene depicting the birth of Christ. Crèches are popular ways to observe Advent and Christmas, and they can be found in homes, churches, and public places. [belén]

creed a brief statement of faith. The word *creed* comes from the Latin *credo*, meaning "I believe." The Nicene Creed and the Apostles' Creed are the most important summaries of Christian beliefs. [credo]

crosier the staff carried by a bishop that shows he cares for us in the same way that a shepherd cares for his sheep. It also reminds us that a bishop represents Jesus, the Good Shepherd. [báculo]

crucified the way in which Jesus was put to death, nailed to a cross. As the crucified one, Jesus died for the sake of the world. [crucificado]

Crucifixion refers to Jesus' Death on the Cross. In the ancient method of crucifixion used by the Romans, the victim was tied or nailed to a wooden cross and left to hang until dead, usually from suffocation. The cross with an image of the crucified Jesus on it is called a crucifix. [Crucifixión]

culture the activity of a group of people that includes their music, art, language, and celebrations. Culture is one of the ways people experience God in their lives. [cultura]

D

Daily Examen a prayer from the Spiritual Exercises that helps us become aware of God's presence, give thanks for the day we are given, pay attention to how we feel about our actions, and resolve to act more intentionally in the future. [examen diario de conciencia]

deacon a man ordained through the Sacrament of Holy Orders to the ministry of service in the Church. Deacons help the bishops and priests by serving the various charitable ministries of the Church. They help by proclaiming the Gospel, preaching, and assisting at the Liturgy of the Eucharist. Deacons can also celebrate Baptisms, witness marriages, and preside at funerals. [diácono]

detraction the act of talking about the faults and sins of another person to someone who has no reason to hear this and who cannot help the person. Detraction damages the reputation of another person without any intent to help that person. [detracción]

dignity of the human person a basic principle at the center of Catholic Social Teaching. It is the starting point of a moral vision for society because human life is sacred and should be treated with great respect. The human person is the clearest reflection of God among us. (See *Catholic Social Teaching*.) [dignidad de la persona humana]

dignity of work a basic principle at the center of Catholic Social Teaching. Since work is done by people created in the image of God, it is not only a way to make a living but also an important way we participate in God's creation. In work, people fulfill part of their potential given to them by God. All workers have a right to productive work, decent and fair wages, and safe working conditions. (See *Catholic Social Teaching*.) [dignidad del trabajo]

diocese the members of the Church in a particular area, united in faith and the sacraments, and gathered under the leadership of a bishop [diócesis]

disciple a person who has accepted Jesus' message and tries to live as he did, sharing his mission, suffering, and joys [discípulo]

discipleship for Christians, the willingness to answer the call to follow Jesus. The call is received in Baptism, nourished in the Eucharist, strengthened in Confirmation, and practiced in service to the world. [discipulado]

discrimination the act of mistreating other people because of how they look or act or because they are different [discriminación]

Dismissal the part of the Concluding Rites of the Mass in which the people are sent forth by the priest or deacon to do good works and praise and bless God (See *The Order of Mass*.) [despedida]

divine law the moral law as revealed by God in the Bible [ley divina]

Divine Praises a series of praises beginning with "Blessed be God," traditionally prayed at the end of the worship of the Blessed Sacrament in Benediction [alabanzas de desagravio]

Divine Providence the guidance of God over all he has created. Divine Providence exercises care for all creation and guides it toward its final perfection. [divina providencia]

Doctor of the Church a man or a woman recognized as a model teacher of the Christian faith [doctor(a) de la Iglesia]

doctrine the teachings that help us understand and accept the truths of our faith as revealed by Jesus and taught by the Church [doctrina]

dogma a teaching that the Church assures Catholics is true and that Catholics are obliged to believe. Papal infallibility, the Assumption, and the Immaculate Conception are all dogmas of the Church. [dogma]

domestic church the Christian home, which is a community of grace and prayer and a school of human virtues and Christian charity [iglesia doméstica]

doxology a Christian prayer praising and giving glory to God, often referencing the three divine Persons of the Trinity. The Glory Be to the Father and the *Gloria* at Mass are two common doxologies. [doxología]

E

Easter the celebration of the bodily raising of Jesus Christ from the dead. Easter is the festival of our redemption and the central Christian feast, the one from which other feasts arise. [Pascua]

Easter Vigil the celebration of the first and greatest Christian feast, the Resurrection of Jesus. It occurs on the first Saturday evening after the first full moon of spring. During this night watch before Easter morning, catechumens are baptized, confirmed, and receive the Eucharist for the first time. [Vigilia Pascual]

Eastern Catholic Churches a group of Churches that developed in the Near East in countries such as Lebanon and are in union with the Roman Catholic Church. These Churches have their own liturgical, theological, and administrative traditions. They show the truly catholic nature of the Church, which takes root in many cultures. [iglesias católicas orientales]

ecumenical council a gathering of Catholic bishops from the entire world, meeting under the leadership of the pope or his delegates. Ecumenical councils discuss pastoral, legal, and doctrinal issues. There have been 21 ecumenical councils recognized by the Catholic Church. The first was the First Council of Nicaea in 325. The most recent was the Second Vatican Council, which took place between 1962 and 1965. [concilio ecuménico]

Glossary

ecumenism | *Exsultet*

ecumenism the movement to bring unity among Christians. Christ gave the Church the gift of unity from the beginning, but over the centuries, that unity has been broken. All Christians are called by their common Baptism to pray and to work to maintain, reinforce, and perfect the unity Christ wants for the Church. [ecumenismo]

Emmanuel a Hebrew name from the Old Testament that means "God with us." In Matthew's Gospel, Jesus is called Emmanuel. [Emanuel]

encyclical a letter written by the pope and sent to the whole Church and sometimes to the whole world. It expresses Church teaching on some specific and important issue. [encíclica]

envy a feeling of resentment or sadness because someone has a quality, a talent, or a possession that we want. Envy is one of the seven capital sins, and it is contrary to the Eighth Commandment. (See *capital sins*.) [envidia]

epiphany an event in the life of Christ when Jesus' divinity revealed itself. The Church recognizes four epiphanies: the Nativity, the adoration of the Magi, Jesus' baptism, and Jesus' sign at the wedding feast at Cana. [epifanía]

Epistle a letter written by Saint Paul to a group of Christians in the early Church. Twenty-one books of the New Testament are letters written by Paul or other leaders. The second reading at Mass on Sundays and holy days is usually from one of these books. [epístola]

eternal life living happily with God in Heaven when we die in grace and friendship with him. Jesus calls all people to eternal life. [vida eterna]

Eucharist, the the sacrament in which we give thanks to God for the Body and Blood of Christ. The Eucharist nourishes our life of faith. We receive the Body and Blood of Christ in the consecrated Bread and Wine. [Eucaristía, la]

Eucharistic liturgy the public worship, held by the Church, in which the bread and wine are consecrated and become the Body and Blood of Jesus Christ. The Sunday celebration of the Eucharistic liturgy is at the heart of Catholic life. [Liturgia Eucarística]

Eucharistic Prayer during the Mass the liturgical expression of praise and thanksgiving for all that God has done in creation and in the Paschal Mystery (Christ's dying and rising from the dead) and through the Holy Spirit (See *The Order of Mass*.) [Plegaria Eucarística]

euthanasia an act with the intent to cause the death of a person who is handicapped, sick, or dying. Euthanasia is considered murder and is gravely contrary to the dignity of the human person and to the respect due to the living God, our Creator. [eutanasia]

evangelical counsels the virtues of poverty, chastity, and obedience that help men and women live holy lives in accordance with the Gospel. All Christians are called to live the evangelical counsels, although members of religious communities consecrate themselves by making vows to live according to the evangelical counsels. [consejos evangélicos]

Evangelist one of the writers of the four Gospels: Matthew, Mark, Luke, and John. The term is also used to describe anyone engaged in spreading the Gospel. Letters in the New Testament and in the Acts of the Apostles list Evangelists, along with Apostles and prophets, as ministers of the Church. [evangelista]

evangelization the declaration by word and example of the Good News of Salvation we have received in Jesus Christ. It is directed both to those who do not know Jesus and to those who have become indifferent about him. Those who have become indifferent are the focus of what is called the New Evangelization. [evangelización]

examination of conscience the act of prayerfully thinking about what we have said or done in light of what the Gospel asks of us. We also think about how our actions may have hurt our relationship with God and with others. An examination of conscience is an important part of our preparing to celebrate the Sacrament of Penance and Reconciliation. [examen de conciencia]

Exile the period in the history of Israel between the destruction of Jerusalem in 587 B.C. and the return to Jerusalem in 537 B.C. During this time many of the Jewish people were forced to live in Babylon, far from home. [Exilio]

Exodus God's liberation of the Hebrew people from slavery in Egypt and his leading them to the Promised Land. It is also one of the first five books in the Bible. [Éxodo]

Exsultet an Easter hymn of praise sung during the Service of Light that begins the Easter Vigil [Exsultet]

F

faith a gift of God that helps us believe in him. We profess our faith in the Creed, celebrate it in the sacraments, live by it through our good conduct of loving God and our neighbor, and express it in prayer. It is a personal adherence of the whole person to God, who has revealed himself to us through words and actions throughout history. (See *Theological Virtues*.) [fe]

fasting a spiritual practice of limiting the amount we eat for a period of time to express sorrow for sin and to make ourselves more aware of God's action in our lives. Adults ages 18–59 fast on Ash Wednesday and Good Friday. The practice is also encouraged as a private devotion at other times of penitence. [ayuno]

fear of the Lord one of the seven Gifts of the Holy Spirit. This gift leads us to a sense of wonder and awe in the presence of God because we recognize his greatness. (See *Gifts of the Holy Spirit*.) [temor de Dios]

feast day important liturgical celebrations in the life of the Church that mark an event in the life of Jesus or the life of a particular saint [día de fiesta]

Feast of Our Lady of Guadalupe feast day during the Advent season that celebrates Mary's appearance to Juan Diego. Widely celebrated on December 12, this feast is an important religious day for Catholics, especially those from Mexico and other parts of Latin America. [Solemnidad de Nuestra Señora de Guadalupe]

Feast of the Holy Family celebrated on the Sunday that falls within the octave of Christmas or, if no Sunday falls within the octave, on December 30. The feast celebrates the family of Jesus, Mary, and Joseph as a model for all Catholic families. [Fiesta de la Sagrada Familia]

forgiveness the willingness to pardon those who have hurt us but have then shown that they are sorry. In the Lord's Prayer, we pray that since God will forgive us our sins, we are able to forgive those who have hurt us. [perdón]

fortitude the strength to choose to do the right thing even when that is difficult. Fortitude is one of the seven Gifts of the Holy Spirit and one of the four central human virtues, called the Cardinal Virtues, by which we guide our conduct through faith and the use of reason. (See *Cardinal Virtues* and *Gifts of the Holy Spirit*.) [fortaleza]

four last things our belief in the four realities of death, judgment, Heaven, and Hell. The Church invites us to think about how the choices we make each day have consequences now and in the future. [los novísimos]

free will the ability to choose to do good because God has made us like him. Our free will is what makes us truly human. Our exercise of free will to do good increases our freedom. Freely choosing to sin makes us slaves to sin. [libre voluntad]

Fruits of the Holy Spirit the demonstration through our actions that God is alive in us. Saint Paul lists the Fruits of the Holy Spirit in Galatians 5:22–23: love, joy, peace, patience, kindness, generosity, faithfulness, gentleness, and self-control. Church Tradition has added goodness, modesty, and chastity to make a total of 12. [frutos del Espíritu Santo]

fundamentalist a person who believes the Bible is literally true, word for word. Fundamentalists fail to recognize that the inspired Word of God has been expressed in human language, under divine inspiration, in different literary forms, by human authors possessed of limited capacities and resources. [fundamentalista]

G

Garden of Eden a garden created by God, filled with trees and lush vegetation, where God first placed Adam and Eve and from which they were later expelled [Jardín del Edén]

genealogy a listing of a person's ancestors through generations. Jesus' genealogy is listed in Matthew 1:1–17. [genealogía]

Gentile the name given by the Jews after the Exile to a foreign person. Gentiles were considered to be nonbelievers who worshiped false gods. They stand in contrast to the Jewish people who received God's Law. [gentil]

genuflect to show respect in church by touching a knee to the ground, especially before the Blessed Sacrament in the tabernacle [genuflexión]

gesture the movements we make, such as the Sign of the Cross or bowing, to show our reverence during prayer [gestos]

gift of peace the peace that Jesus gives to us that flows from his relationship with his Father. This is the peace that the world cannot give, for it is the gift of Salvation that only Jesus can give. [don de la paz]

Gifts of the Holy Spirit the permanent willingness, given to us through the Holy Spirit, that makes it possible for us to do what God asks of us. The Gifts of the Holy Spirit are drawn from Isaiah 11:1–3. They include wisdom, understanding, counsel, fortitude, knowledge, and fear of the Lord. Church Tradition has added piety to make a total of seven. [dones del Espíritu Santo]

Glossary

gluttony | **Holy Day of Obligation**

gluttony excessive indulgence in food or drink (See *capital sins.*) [gula]

God the Father, Son, and Holy Spirit, one God in three distinct Persons. God created all that exists. He is the source of Salvation, and he is Truth and Love. [Dios]

godparent a witness to Baptism who assumes the responsibility for helping the baptized person along the road of Christian life [padrino/madrina]

Good News the meaning of the word *Gospel* in Greek. The spreading of the Good News began on Pentecost and continues today in the ministry of the Church. [Buena Nueva]

Gospel the Good News of God's mercy and love that we experience by hearing the story of Jesus' life, Death, Resurrection, and Ascension. The story is passed on in the teaching ministry of the Church as the source of all truth and right living. It is presented to us in four books in the New Testament: the Gospels according to Matthew, Mark, Luke, and John. [Evangelio]

grace the gift of God, given to us without our meriting it. Grace is the Holy Spirit alive in us, helping us live our Christian vocation. Grace helps us live as God wants us to live. (See *actual grace, habitual grace,* and *sanctifying grace.*) [gracia]

Great Commandment Jesus' commandment that we are to love both God and our neighbor as we love ourselves. Jesus tells us that this commandment sums up everything taught in the Old Testament. [mandamiento mayor]

Great Commission Jesus' command to the Apostles to spread the Good News to all people. Jesus commissioned the disciples before his Ascension. [misión de los discípulos]

Great Schism a split in the Church during the Middle Ages when two and then three men all claimed to be pope. The split began because the papal court had moved between Rome and Avignon, France. The schism was resolved at the Council of Constance (1414–1418) with the election of Martin V. [Gran Cisma]

Gregorian chant a form of liturgical music that began its development during the time of Pope Gregory the Great [canto gregoriano]

guardian angel the angel who has been appointed to protect, pray for, and help a person live a holy life [ángel de la guarda]

H

habit the distinctive clothing worn by members of religious orders. It is a sign of the religious life and a witness to poverty. [hábito]

habitual grace another name for sanctifying grace, as it refers to our God-given inclination and capacity for good. Habitual grace is a participation in God's own spirituality. (See *actual grace, grace, and sanctifying grace.*) [gracia habitual]

Heaven union with God the Father, Son, and Holy Spirit in life and love that never ends. Heaven is a state of happiness and the goal of the deepest wishes of the human heart. [cielo]

Hebrew a descendant of Abraham, Isaac, and Jacob, who was enslaved in Egypt. God helped Moses lead the Hebrews out of slavery. [Hebreo]

Hell a life of total separation from God forever. In his infinite love for us, God can only desire our Salvation. Hell is the result of the free choice of a person to reject God's love and forgiveness once and for all. [infierno]

herald a messenger who announces important news. Angels served as the heralds of the birth of Christ. [heraldo]

heresy a false teaching that distorts a truth of the Catholic faith. Many of the Church councils have taught against heresies about the Trinity, Jesus, or the faith of the Church. [herejía]

holiness the fullness of Christian life and love. All people are called to holiness, which is made possible by cooperating with God's grace to do his will. As we do God's will, we are transformed more and more into the image of the Son, Jesus Christ. [santidad]

holy the Mark of the Church that indicates that the Church is one with Jesus Christ. Holiness is closeness to God, and therefore the Church is holy because God is present in it. (See *Marks of the Church.*) [santo]

Holy Communion the consecrated Bread and Wine that we receive at Mass, which is the Body and Blood of Jesus Christ. It brings us into union with Jesus and his saving Death and Resurrection. [Comunión]

Holy Day of Obligation a principal feast day, other than Sundays, of the Church. On Holy Days of Obligation, we celebrate the great things that God has done for us through Jesus and the saints. Catholics are obliged to participate in the Eucharist on these days, just as we are on Sundays. [día de precepto]

Holy Family the family of Jesus as he grew up in Nazareth. It included Jesus; his mother, Mary; and his foster father, Joseph. [Sagrada Familia]

Holy of Holies the holiest part of the Temple in Jerusalem. The High Priest entered this part of the Temple once a year to address God and ask his forgiveness for the sins of the people. [Sanctasanctórum]

Holy Orders the sacrament through which the mission given by Jesus to his Apostles continues in the Church. The sacrament has three degrees: deacon, priest, and bishop. Through the laying on of hands in the Sacrament of Holy Orders, men receive a permanent sacramental mark that calls them to minister to the Church. [sacramento del Orden]

Holy Spirit the third Person of the Trinity, who is sent to us as our helper and, through Baptism and Confirmation, fills us with God's life. Together with the Father and the Son, the Holy Spirit brings the divine plan of Salvation to completion. [Espíritu Santo]

Holy Thursday the Thursday of Holy Week on which the Mass of the Lord's Supper is celebrated, commemorating the institution of the Eucharist. The season of Lent ends with the celebration of this Mass. [Jueves Santo]

holy water water that has been blessed and is used as a sacramental to remind us of our Baptism [agua bendita]

Holy Week the celebration of the events surrounding Jesus' establishment of the Eucharist and his suffering, Death, and Resurrection. Holy Week commemorates Jesus' triumphal entry into Jerusalem on Palm Sunday, the gift of himself in the Eucharist on Holy Thursday, his Death on Good Friday, and his Resurrection at the Easter Vigil on Holy Saturday. [Semana Santa]

Homily the explanation by a bishop, a priest, or a deacon of the Word of God in the liturgy. The Homily relates the Word of God to our lives as Christians today. (See *The Order of Mass*.) [homilía]

honor giving God or a person the respect that they are owed. God is given this respect as our Creator and Redeemer. All people are worthy of respect as children of God. [honrar]

hope the confidence that God will always be with us, make us happy now and forever, and help us live so that we will be with him forever (See *Theological Virtues*.) [esperanza]

human condition the general state of humankind. While the human family is created in the image and likeness of God, it is also wounded by sin and often rejects the grace won by Jesus Christ. So while called by God to the highest good, too often human behavior leads to personal and social destruction. [condición humana]

I

idolatry the act of worshiping something other than God. Originally idolatry meant the worship of statues or other images of gods, but the pursuit of money, fame, or possessions can become forms of idolatry. (See *consumerism*.) [idolatría]

Immaculate Conception the Church teaching that Mary was free from Original Sin from the first moment of her conception. She was preserved through the merits of her Son, Jesus, the Savior of the human race. Declared a dogma of the Catholic Church by Pope Pius IX in 1854, the Feast of the Immaculate Conception is celebrated on December 8. [Inmaculada Concepción]

imperfect contrition Sorrow for sin that is motivated by reasons other than loving God above all else. Imperfect contrition comes from fear of punishment or other consequences of our sin. Contrition is the most important act of the penitent preparing to celebrate the Sacrament of Penance and Reconciliation. (See *contrition* and *perfect contrition*.) [contrición imperfecta]

incarnate to take human form. The word *incarnate* comes from a Latin term meaning "to become flesh" and describes what happened in the mystery of the Incarnation when the Son of God, Jesus, became man, conceived and born of Mary. [encarnar]

Incarnation Jesus Christ, the Son of God, is God made flesh. The Son of God, the Second Person of the Trinity, is both true God and true man. [Encarnación]

indulgence a lessening of temporal punishment gained through participation in prayer and works of charity. Indulgences move us toward our final purification, after which we will live with God forever. [indulgencia]

Industrial Revolution the rapid economic change beginning at the end of the 18th century and continuing into the 19th century that resulted in a shift away from homemade and agricultural production and toward industry and manufacturing. [Revolución industrial]

inerrancy the absence of error in the Bible when it tells us a religious truth about God and his relationship with us. The Church teaches the inerrancy of Scripture on moral and faith matters. [inerrancia]

Glossary

infallibility | **justice**

infallibility the inability to be in error or to teach something that is false. On matters of belief and morality, the Church is infallible because of the presence and guidance of the Holy Spirit. [infalibilidad]

infallible the quality of Church teachings in areas of faith and morals that have been proclaimed by the pope and the bishops, in their role as the Magisterium and guided by the Holy Spirit, to be without error [infalible]

Infancy Narrative an account of the infancy and childhood of Jesus that appears in the first two chapters of Matthew's and Luke's Gospels. Matthew's Infancy Narrative reveals Jesus as the fulfillment of prophecies. Luke's Infancy Narrative reveals Jesus as a Savior who came for everyone, not the privileged few. The intention of these stories is to proclaim Jesus as Messiah and Savior. [narración de la infancia]

inspiration the quality that explains God as the author who, through the Holy Spirit, enlightened the minds of human authors while they were writing the books of the Bible. God blessed the writers of Scripture with inspiration that enabled them to record religious truths for our Salvation. [inspiración]

inspired influenced by the Holy Spirit. The human authors of Scripture were influenced by the Holy Spirit. The creative inspiration of the Holy Spirit made sure that the Scripture was written according to the truth God wants us to know for our Salvation. [inspirado]

Institution Narrative the words prayed by the priest at the Eucharist that recall Jesus' words and actions at the Last Supper. During the Institution Narrative, the bread and wine become the Body and Blood of the risen Christ. [narración de la institución]

intercession a form of prayer on behalf of others. We ask for the intercession of those in Heaven, such as Mary and the saints, or those still with us here on earth. [intercesión]

intercessor a person who prays for the needs of others. An intercessor can be someone still alive on earth or a saint in Heaven. [intercesor]

interpretation coming to an understanding of the words of Scripture, combining human knowledge with the wisdom and guidance of the teaching office of the Church [interpretación]

interreligious dialogue the ongoing discussions between Christians and those of other faiths [diálogo interreligioso]

Islam the third great religion, along with Judaism and Christianity, that professes belief in one God. *Islam* means "submission" to that one God. [islamismo]

Israelite a descendant of Abraham, Isaac, and Jacob. God changed Jacob's name to "Israel," and Jacob's twelve sons and their children became the leaders of the twelve tribes of Israel. (See *Hebrew*.) [israelita]

J

Jerusalem the city conquered by David in 1000 B.C. to serve as his capital. David also made it the center of worship by bringing in the Ark of the Covenant, which held the tablets of the Law. [Jerusalén]

Jesse Tree an Advent activity that helps us prepare to celebrate Jesus' birth. A small or an artificial tree is decorated with images of Jesus' ancestors. The image is based on Isaiah 11:1, "But a shoot shall sprout from the stump of Jesse, / and from his roots a bud shall blossom." [tronco de Jesé]

Jesus the Son of God, who was born of the Virgin Mary and who died and was raised from the dead for our Salvation. He returned to God and will come again to judge the living and the dead. *Jesus* means "God saves." [Jesús]

Jews the name given to the Hebrew people, from the time of the Exile to the present. The name means "the people who live in the territory of Judah," the area of Palestine surrounding Jerusalem. [judíos]

Joseph the foster father of Jesus who was engaged to Mary when the angel announced that Mary would have a child through the power of the Holy Spirit. In the Old Testament, Joseph was the son of Jacob, who was sold into slavery in Egypt by his brothers and then saved them from starvation when famine came. [José]

Jubilee Year a holy year in which the pope calls people to witness to their faith in specific ways. Pope John Paul II announced that 1985 was a Jubilee Year. [Año jubilar]

Judaism the name of the religion of Jesus and all the people of Israel after they returned from exile in Babylon and built the second Temple [judaísmo]

justice the virtue that guides us to give to God and others what is due them. Justice is one of the four Cardinal Virtues by which we guide our Christian life. (See *Cardinal Virtues*.) [justicia]

312 *Glossary*

justification the action of the Holy Spirit that cleanses us from sin in Baptism and that continually gives us the grace to walk in right relationship with God. Justification is the saving action of God that restores the right relationship between God and an individual. [justificación]

K

Kingdom of God God's rule over us, announced in the Gospel and present in the Eucharist. The beginning of the kingdom here on earth is mysteriously present in the Church, and it will come in completeness at the end of time. [Reino de Dios]

Kingdom of Heaven the term for the Kingdom of God in Matthew's Gospel. The Beatitudes help us enter into the Kingdom of Heaven by guiding us in ways to live according to the values of Jesus. [Reino de los cielos]

knowledge one of the seven Gifts of the Holy Spirit. This gift helps us perceive what God asks of us and how we should respond. (See *Gifts of the Holy Spirit.*) [ciencia]

L

laity those who have been made members of Christ in Baptism and who participate in the priestly, prophetic, and kingly functions of Christ in his mission to the whole world. The laity is distinct from the clergy, whose members are set apart as ordained ministers to serve the Church. [laicado]

Lamb of God the title for Jesus that emphasizes his willingness to give up his life for the Salvation of the world. Jesus is the Lamb without blemish or sin who delivers us through his sacrificial Death. [Cordero de Dios]

Last Judgment the final judgment of all human beings that will occur when Christ returns in glory and all appear in their own bodies before him to give an account of all their deeds in life. In the presence of Christ, the truth of each person's relationship with God will be laid bare, as will the good each person has done or failed to do during his or her earthly life. At that time, God's kingdom will come into its fullness. [Juicio Final]

Last Supper the meal Jesus ate with his disciples on the night before he died. At the Last Supper, Jesus instituted the Sacrament of the Eucharist. [Última Cena]

lectio divina a reflective way of praying with Scripture. *Lectio divina* is Latin for "sacred reading" and is an ancient form of Christian prayer. It involves four steps: sacred reading of a Scripture passage, meditation on the passage, speaking to God, and contemplation or resting in God's presence. [*lectio divina*]

Lectionary for Mass the official book that contains all the Scripture readings used in the Liturgy of the Word [*Leccionario*]

Lent the 40 days before Easter (not counting Sundays) during which we prepare through prayer, fasting, and almsgiving to change our lives and live the Gospel more completely [Cuaresma]

Light of the World a name that helps us see that Jesus is the light that leads us to the Father. Jesus lights up our minds and hearts, replacing sin and darkness with the knowledge of God. [luz del mundo]

litany a prayer that consists of a series of petitions, often including requests for the intercession of particular saints [letanía]

literary forms the different styles of writing found in the Bible. Some forms are history, proverbs, letters, parables, Wisdom sayings, and poetry. They all have as their purpose the communication of the truth found in God's Word. [géneros literarios]

liturgical year the celebration throughout the year of the mysteries of the Lord's birth, life, Death, Resurrection, and Ascension. The cycle of the liturgical year constitutes the basic rhythm of the Christian's life of prayer. [año litúrgico]

liturgy the public prayer of the Church that celebrates the wonderful things God has done for us in Jesus Christ, our High Priest, and the way in which he continues the work of our Salvation. The original meaning of *liturgy* was "a public work or service done for the people." [liturgia]

Liturgy of the Eucharist the part of the Mass in which the bread and wine are consecrated and become the Body and Blood of Jesus Christ. We then receive Christ in Holy Communion. [Liturgia de la Eucaristía]

Liturgy of the Hours the public prayer of the Church to praise God and sanctify the day. It includes an office of readings before sunrise, morning prayer at dawn, evening prayer at sunset, and prayer before going to bed. The chanting of psalms makes up a major portion of this prayer. [Liturgia de las Horas]

Liturgy of the Word the part of the Mass in which we listen to God's Word from the Bible and consider what it means for us today. The Liturgy of the Word can also be a public prayer that is not followed by the Liturgy of the Eucharist. [Liturgia de la Palabra]

Glossary

living wage | Messiah

living wage the amount of income that is enough to support a person and a family in reasonable comfort. Pope Leo XIII defined what a living wage was in his encyclical *On the Condition of Labor*. [salario digno]

Lord a title that indicates the divinity of God. *Lord* replaced *Yahweh*, the name God revealed to Moses and was considered too sacred to pronounce. The New Testament uses the title *Lord* for both the Father and for Jesus, recognizing him as God himself. (See *Yahweh*.) [Señor]

lust the excessive craving for or indulgence of bodily pleasure that makes the other a victim of our desires (See *capital sins*.) [lujuria]

M

Magi, the the men who came from the East to Bethlehem by following a star. They were the first Gentiles to believe that Jesus was the Messiah. [Reyes Magos]

Magisterium the living, teaching office of the Church. This office, through the bishops and with the pope, provides an authentic interpretation of God's Revelation. It ensures faithfulness to the teaching of the Apostles in matters of faith and morals. [Magisterio de la Iglesia]

Magnificat Mary's song of praise recorded in the Gospel of Luke. Sung before Jesus' birth, the *Magnificat* shows Mary's understanding of Jesus' mission and her role as a disciple. [*magníficat*]

manna the food provided by God when the Israelites were in the desert [maná]

marginalized those who are viewed as unimportant or powerless in society. We find Jesus among the marginalized, such as people who are poor, mistreated, discriminated against, and the victims of war. [marginados]

Marks of the Church the four most important aspects of the Church found in the Nicene Creed. According to the Nicene Creed, the Church is one, holy, catholic, and apostolic. (See *apostolic, catholic, holy*, and *one*.) [atributos de la Iglesia]

martyr one who has given his or her life for the faith. *Martyr* comes from the Greek word for "witness." A martyr is the supreme witness to the truth of the faith and to Christ to whom he or she is united. In chapter 7 of Acts of the Apostles, the death of the first martyr, the deacon Stephen, is recounted. [mártir]

Mary the mother of Jesus. She is called blessed and "full of grace" because God chose her to be the mother of the Son of God, the Second Person of the Trinity. [Virgen María]

Mass the most important sacramental celebration of the Church, established by Jesus at the Last Supper as a remembrance of his Death and Resurrection. At Mass we listen to God's Word from the Bible and receive Jesus Christ in the consecrated Bread and Wine that are his Body and Blood. [Misa]

Matrimony a solemn agreement between a woman and a man to be partners for life, for their own good and for bringing up children. Marriage is a sacrament when the agreement is properly made between baptized Christians. [Matrimonio]

meditate to focus the mind prayerfully on an image or a word in order to experience God and understand God's will [meditar]

meditation a form of prayer using silence and listening. Through imagination, emotion, and desire, it is a way to understand how to adhere and respond to what God is asking. By concentrating on a word or an image, we move beyond thoughts, empty the mind of contents that get in the way of our experience of God, and rest in simple awareness of God. [meditación]

memorial a remembrance of events that have taken place in the past. We recall these events because they continue to affect us since they are part of God's saving plan for us. Every time we remember these events, we make God's saving action present. [memoria]

Mendicant Order a unique variety of religious order that developed in the 13th century. Unlike monks who remain inside a monastery, members of Mendicant Orders have ministries of preaching, teaching, and witnessing among people. They are called mendicant from the Latin word for "begging," which is their major means of supporting themselves. The two main Mendicant Orders are the Dominicans, founded by Saint Dominic de Guzman, and the Franciscans, founded by Saint Francis of Assisi. [orden mendicante]

mercy the gift to be able to respond with care and compassion to those in need. The gift of mercy is a grace given to us by Jesus Christ. [misericordia]

Messiah a title that means "anointed one." It is from a Hebrew word that means the same thing as the Hebrew word *Christ*. Messiah is the title given to Jesus as priest, prophet, and king. [Mesías]

ministry service or work done for others. All those baptized are called to a variety of ministries in the liturgy and in service to the needs of others. [ministerio]

miracle a sign or an act of wonder that cannot be explained by natural causes and that is the work of God. In the Gospels, Jesus works miracles as a sign that the Kingdom of God is present in his ministry. [milagro]

mission the work of Jesus Christ that is continued in the Church through the Holy Spirit. The mission of the Church is to proclaim Salvation through Jesus' life, Death, Resurrection, and Ascension. [misión]

missionary a person sent by Church authority to spread the Gospel through evangelization and catechesis. Missionaries may serve in areas where few people have heard about Jesus or in small, underserved communities of isolated believers. [misionero]

monastery a place where men or women live out their solemn vows of poverty, chastity, and obedience in a stable community. People who live in monasteries spend their days in public prayer, work, and meditation. [monasterio]

monasticism a form of religious life in which men and women live out their vows of poverty, chastity, and obedience in a stable community. The goal of monasticism is to pursue a life of public prayer, work, and meditation under the guidance of a rule for the glory of God. Saint Benedict of Nursia, who died about 550, is considered the father of Western monasticism. [monacato]

monstrance a vessel that holds the Blessed Sacrament for adoration and Benediction [custodia]

moral choice a choice to do what is right or not to do what is wrong. We make moral choices because they help us grow closer to God and because we have the freedom to choose what is right and avoid what is wrong. [decisión moral]

moral law a rule for living that has been established by God and people in authority who are concerned about the good of all. Moral laws are based on God's direction to us to do what is right and avoid what is wrong. Some moral laws are "written" in the human heart and can be known through our own reasoning. Other moral laws have been revealed to us by God in the Old Testament and in the new law given by Jesus. [ley moral]

mortal sin a serious decision to turn away from God by doing something that we know is wrong. For a sin to be mortal, it must be a very serious offense, the person must know how serious it is, and the person must freely choose to do it anyway. [pecado mortal]

Mother of God the title for Mary proclaimed at the Council of Ephesus in 431. The council declared that Mary was not just the mother of Jesus, the man. She became the Mother of God by the conception of the Son of God in her womb. Because Jesus' humanity is one with his divinity, Mary is the mother of the eternal Son of God made man, who is God himself. [Madre de Dios]

Muslim a follower of the religion of Islam. *Muslim* means "one who submits to God." [musulmán]

mystery a religious truth that we can know only through God's Revelation and that we cannot fully understand. Our faith is a mystery that we profess in the Creed and celebrate in the liturgy and the sacraments. [misterio]

mystic a person who has a special understanding of God from intense, private experiences [místico]

Mystical Body of Christ the members of the Church formed into a spiritual body and bound together by the life communicated by Jesus Christ through the sacraments. Christ is the center and source of the life of this body. In it, we are all united. Each member of the body receives from Christ gifts fitting for him or her. [Cuerpo Místico de Cristo]

N

Nativity the mystery of Jesus' birth as told in the Gospels of Matthew and Luke. Although the two Nativity stories focus on different details, they relate the same truth that Jesus is the promised Savior. [Natividad]

natural law the moral law that is "written" in the human heart. We can know natural law through our own reason because the Creator has placed the knowledge of it in our hearts. It can provide the solid foundation on which we can make rules to guide our choices in life. Natural law forms the basis of our fundamental rights and duties and is the foundation for the work of the Holy Spirit in guiding our moral choices. [ley natural]

neighbor according to Jesus, this includes everyone, as each person is made in God's image. We are all meant to develop mutually supportive relationships. [prójimo]

neophyte a person who has recently been initiated into the Church through the Sacraments of Initiation [neófito]

New Evangelization the work of missionaries in traditionally Christian areas with people who may already know about Jesus and the Gospel [nueva evangelización]

Glossary

New Testament | Palm Sunday

New Testament the 27 books of the Bible that tell of the teaching, ministry, and saving events of the life of Jesus. The four Gospels present Jesus' life, Death, and Resurrection. Acts of the Apostles tells the story of Jesus' Ascension into Heaven. It also shows how Jesus' message of Salvation spread through the growth of the Church. Various letters instruct us in how to live as followers of Jesus Christ. The Book of Revelation offers encouragement to Christians living through persecution. [Nuevo Testamento]

Nicene Creed the summary of Christian beliefs developed by the bishops at the first two councils of the Church held in A.D. 325 and 381. It is the Creed shared by most Christians in the East and the West. [Credo Niceno]

novena a Catholic tradition repeated over a set number of days, usually nine, in devotion to a particular mystery or saint [novena]

novice a monk or nun who has not yet taken vows. Novices deepen their faith and learn about the customs, practices, and obligations of the religious life. [novicio]

O

obedience the act of willingly following what God asks us to do for our Salvation. The Fourth Commandment requires children to obey their parents, and all people are required to obey civil authority when it acts for the good of all. To imitate the obedience of Jesus, members of religious communities make a special vow of obedience. [obediencia]

obey to follow the teachings or directions given by God or by someone who has authority over us [obedecer]

oil of catechumens the oil blessed by the bishop during Holy Week and used to anoint catechumens. This anointing strengthens them on their path to initiation into the Church. Infants are anointed with this oil right before they are baptized. [óleo de los catecúmenos]

oil of the sick the oil blessed by the bishop during Holy Week and used in the Sacrament of the Anointing of the Sick, which brings spiritual and, if it is God's will, physical healing [óleo de los enfermos]

Old Testament the first 46 books of the Bible, which tell of God's Covenant with the people of Israel and his plan for the Salvation of all people. The first five books are known as the Torah or Pentateuch. The Old Testament is fulfilled in the New Testament, but God's Covenant presented in the Old Testament has permanent value and has never been revoked. [Antiguo Testamento]

one the Mark of the Church that indicates the unity of the Church as a community of Christian believers as well as the unity of all the members with Christ (See *Marks of the Church*.) [una]

option for the poor the principle of Catholic Social Teaching that holds that Christians must promote social justice and serve those who are poor (See *Catholic Social Teaching*.) [opción por los pobres]

ordained men who have received the Sacrament of Holy Orders so that they may preside at the celebration of the Eucharist and serve as leaders and teachers of the Church [ordenado]

Order of Mass, The the sequence of the prayers, gestures, readings and Eucharistic rites of the Mass [Ordinario de la Misa, el]

Order of Penitents a group of people within the Church, practicing intense repentance. The Order of Penitents first began in the early centuries of the Church, and many of the practices of Lent, including the use of ashes, come from the Penitents. [orden de penitentes]

Ordinary Time the longest liturgical season of the Church. It is divided into two periods—the first after the Christmas season and the second after Pentecost. The first period focuses on Jesus' childhood and public ministry. The second period focuses on Christ's reign as King of Kings. [Tiempo Ordinario]

ordination the rite of the Sacrament of Holy Orders by which a bishop gives to men, through the laying on of hands, the ability to minister to the Church as bishops, priests, and deacons [ordenación]

Original Sin the consequence of the disobedience of the first human beings. Adam and Eve disobeyed God and chose to follow their own will rather than God's will. As a result, human beings lost the original blessing God had intended and became subject to sin and death. In Baptism we are restored to life with God through Jesus Christ, although we still experience the effects of Original Sin. [pecado original]

Orthodox Church the Eastern Churches that split with the Roman Catholic Church in 1054. These Churches are distinct from the Roman Catholic Church in their liturgy and some of their traditions. [Iglesia Ortodoxa]

P

Palm Sunday the celebration of Jesus' triumphant entry into Jerusalem on the Sunday before Easter. Today it begins a week-long commemoration of the saving events of Holy Week. [Domingo de Ramos]

pantheism the belief that rejects a personal God and instead considers that God and the universe are identical. Pantheism was condemned in the *Syllabus of Errors*. [panteísmo]

parable one of the stories that Jesus told to show us what the Kingdom of God is like. Parables present images drawn from everyday life. These images show us the radical choice we make when we respond to the invitation to enter the Kingdom of God. [parábola]

Paraclete another name for the Holy Spirit. Jesus promised to send a Consoler and Advocate who would help the Apostles continue his mission. [Paráclito]

parish a stable community of believers in Jesus Christ who meet regularly in a specific area to worship God under the leadership of a pastor [parroquia]

participation one of the seven principles of Catholic Social Teaching. All people have a right to participate in the economic, political, and cultural life of society. It is a requirement for human dignity and a demand of justice that all people have a minimum level of participation in the community. (See *Catholic Social Teaching*.) [participación]

particular judgment Christ's judgment made of every person at the moment of death that offers either entrance into Heaven (after a period of purification in Purgatory if needed) or immediate and eternal separation from God in Hell. At the moment of death, each person is rewarded by Christ in accordance with his or her works and faith. [juicio individual]

Paschal Mystery the work of Salvation accomplished by Jesus Christ through his Passion, Death, Resurrection, and Ascension. The Paschal Mystery is celebrated in the liturgy of the Church, and we experience its saving effects in the sacraments. In every liturgy of the Church, God the Father is blessed and adored as the source of all blessings we have received through his Son in order to make us his children through the Holy Spirit. [Misterio Pascual]

Passion the suffering and Death of Jesus. The Passion is part of the Paschal Mystery that accomplished Jesus Christ's saving work and that we celebrate and remember in the Eucharist. [Pasión]

Passover the Jewish festival that commemorates the delivery of the Hebrew people from slavery in Egypt. In the Eucharist, we celebrate our passover from death to life through Jesus' Death and Resurrection. [pascua]

pastor a priest who is responsible for the spiritual care of the members of the parish community. It is the job of the pastor to see that the Word of God is preached, the faith is taught, and the sacraments are celebrated. [párroco]

patriarch, Catholic the title used by leaders of certain Eastern Catholic Churches [patriarca, católico]

patriarch, Old Testament a leader of a family or clan within ancient Israel. More specifically, in biblical studies, the patriarchs are the founders of the Hebrew people described in Genesis chapters 12–50. Prominent among the patriarchs are Abraham, Isaac, Jacob, and Jacob's twelve sons. [patriarca, Antiguo Testamento]

patriarch, Orthodox the title used by leaders of Orthodox Churches. The bishop of Constantinople is known as the Ecumenical Patriarch. [patriarca, ortodoxo]

peacemaker a person who teaches us to be respectful in our words and actions toward one another [paz, los que trabajan por la]

penance the turning away from sin with a desire to change our life and live more closely the way God wants us to live. We express our penance externally by praying, fasting, and helping those who are poor. Penance is also the name of the action that the priest asks us to take or the prayers that he asks us to pray after he absolves us in the Sacrament of Penance and Reconciliation. (See *Sacrament of Penance and Reconciliation*.) [penitencia]

Penance and Reconciliation, Sacrament of the sacrament in which we celebrate God's forgiveness of sin and our reconciliation with God and the Church. This sacrament includes sorrow for the sins we have committed, confession of sins, absolution by the priest, and doing the penance that shows our willingness to amend our ways. [sacramento de la Penitencia y de la Reconciliación]

Penitential Act a formula of general confession asking for God's mercy at Mass. The priest may lead the assembly in praying the *Confiteor* ("I confess to almighty God . . .") or a threefold invocation echoed by "Lord have mercy . . . Christ have mercy . . . Lord have mercy" in English or in Greek. (See *The Order of Mass*.) [acto penitencial]

Pentecost the 50th day after Jesus was raised from the dead. On this day the Holy Spirit was sent from Heaven, and the Church was born. It is also the Jewish feast, called *Shavuot* in Hebrew, that celebrated the giving of the Ten Commandments on Mount Sinai 50 days after the Exodus. [Pentecostés]

People of God another name for the Church. In the same way that the people of Israel were God's people through the Covenant he made with them, the Church is a priestly, prophetic, and royal people through the new and eternal Covenant with Jesus Christ. [Pueblo de Dios]

Glossary **317**

perfect contrition | priest

perfect contrition the sorrow for sin that arises from a love of God above all else. Perfect contrition is the ideal act of the penitent preparing to celebrate the Sacrament of Penance and Reconciliation. (See *contrition* and *imperfect contrition*.) [contrición perfecta]

personal prayer the kind of prayer that rises up in us in everyday life. We pray with others in the liturgy, but also we can listen and respond to God through personal prayer every moment of our lives. [oración personal]

personal sin a sin we choose to commit, whether serious (mortal) or less serious (venial). Although the consequences of Original Sin leave us with a tendency to sin, God's grace, especially through the sacraments, helps us choose good over sin. [pecado personal]

petition a request to God, asking him to fulfill a need. When we share in God's saving love, we understand that every need is one that we can ask God to help us with through petition. [petición]

Pharaoh the Egyptian word for "Great House," referring to the royal palace of the king of Egypt. The reference to Pharaoh became known for the king himself, just as "White House" might refer to the president. Pharaoh was both the political and religious leader of Egypt. [faraón]

Pharisee a member of a party or sect in Judaism that began more than 100 years before Jesus. Pharisees saw Judaism as a religion centered on the observance of the Law. The Gospels depict tension between Jesus and the Pharisees. Pharisees were later found in the Christian community in Jerusalem. (Acts of the Apostles 15:5) Before his conversion, Paul was proud to call himself a Pharisee. [fariseo]

piety one of the seven Gifts of the Holy Spirit. It calls us to be faithful in our relationships both with God and with others. Piety helps us to love God and to behave responsibly and with generosity and affection toward others. (See *Gifts of the Holy Spirit*.) [piedad]

plague a natural calamity or disease that is seen as being inflicted by God as a remedial event to make people more conscious of their duties toward God and one another. In the Book of Exodus, the plagues inflicted on the Egyptians are seen as the means by which God convinced the Egyptians to free the Hebrew people from slavery. [plaga]

pope the Bishop of Rome, successor of Saint Peter, and leader of the Roman Catholic Church. Because he has the authority to act in the name of Christ, the pope is called the Vicar of Christ. The pope and all the bishops together make up the living, teaching office of the Church, the Magisterium. [papa]

poverty the quality of living without attachment to material goods. All baptized persons, not only those called to religious life, are called to live a holy life by practicing the virtues of chastity, obedience, and poverty. [pobreza]

praise the expression of our response to God, not only for what he does, but also simply because he is. In the Eucharist, the whole Church joins with Jesus Christ in expressing praise and thanksgiving to the Father. [alabanza]

prayer the raising of our hearts and minds to God. We are able to speak to and listen to God in prayer because he teaches us how to pray. [oración]

prayer of intercession a prayer of petition in which we pray as Jesus did to the Father on behalf of people. Asking on behalf of others is a characteristic of a heart attuned to God's mercy. Christian intercession recognizes no boundaries. Following Jesus' example, we pray for all people—for those who are rich, for political leaders, for those in need, and even for persecutors. [oracione de intercesión]

Precepts of the Church those positive requirements that the pastoral authority of the Church has determined are necessary to a moral life. The Precepts of the Church ensure that all Catholics move beyond the minimum by growing in the love of God and neighbor. [mandamientos de la Iglesia]

precursor a title for John the Baptist as the immediate forerunner of Jesus, the Messiah. John the Baptist is considered the last of the prophets. [precursor]

presbyter a word that originally meant "an elder or a trusted advisor to the bishop." From this word comes the English word *priest*, one of the three degrees of the Sacrament of Holy Orders. All the priests of a diocese under the bishop form the presbyterate. [presbítero]

pride a false image of ourselves that goes beyond what we deserve as God's creation. Pride puts us in competition with God. It is one of the seven capital sins. (See *capital sins*.) [soberbia]

priest a man who has accepted God's call to serve the Church by guiding it and building it up through the ministry of the Word and the celebration of the sacraments [sacerdote]

318 *Glossary*

priesthood all the people of God who have been given a share of the one mission of Christ through the Sacraments of Baptism and Confirmation. The ministerial priesthood, which is made up of those men who have been ordained bishops and priests in Holy Orders, is essentially different from the priesthood of all the faithful because its work is to build up and guide the Church in the name of Christ. [sacerdocio]

Promised Land the land first promised by God to Abraham. It was to this land that God told Moses to lead the Chosen People after they were freed from slavery in Egypt and received the Ten Commandments at Mount Sinai. [Tierra Prometida]

prophecy a divine communication that comes through a human person. Prophecy in the Old Testament often tells of the coming of Jesus or conveys an important message to God's people. [profecía]

prophet one called to speak for God and to call the people to be faithful to the Covenant. Eighteen books of the Old Testament present the messages and actions of the prophets. [profeta]

prudence the virtue that directs us toward the good and helps us choose the correct means to achieve that good. When we act with prudence, we carefully and thoughtfully consider our actions. Prudence is one of the Cardinal Virtues that guide our conscience and influence us to live according to the Law of Christ. (See *Cardinal Virtues*.) [prudencia]

psalm a prayer in the form of a poem, written to be sung in public worship. Each psalm expresses an aspect of the depth of human prayer. Over several centuries, 150 psalms were assembled into the Book of Psalms in the Old Testament. Psalms were used in worship in the Temple in Jerusalem, and they have been used in the public worship of the Church since its beginning. [salmo]

Purgatory a possible outcome of particular judgment following death. Purgatory is a state of final cleansing after death of all our human imperfections to prepare us to enter into the joy of God's presence in Heaven. [purgatorio]

R

racism the opinion that race determines human traits and capacities and that a particular race has an inherent, or inborn, superiority. Discrimination based on a person's race is a violation of human dignity and a sin against justice. [racismo]

rationalist a person who regards human reason as the principal source of all knowledge. Rationalism was developed by René Descartes and dominated European thought in the 17th and 18th centuries. Rationalists recognize as true only those religious beliefs that can be explained rationally and stress confidence in the orderly character of the world and in the mind's ability to make sense of this order. [racionalista]

Real Presence the way in which the risen Jesus Christ is present in the Eucharist in the consecrated Bread and Wine. Jesus Christ's presence is called real because in the Eucharist his Body and Blood, soul and divinity, are wholly and entirely present. [Presencia Real de Cristo]

reconciliation the renewal of friendship after that friendship has been broken by some action or lack of action. In the Sacrament of Penance and Reconciliation, through God's mercy and forgiveness, we are reconciled with God, the Church, and others. [reconciliación]

Redeemer Jesus Christ, whose life, sacrificial Death on the cross, and Resurrection from the dead set us free from the slavery of sin and bring us redemption [Redentor]

redemption our being set free from the slavery of sin through the life, sacrificial Death on the cross, and Resurrection of Jesus Christ. [redención]

reform to put an end to a wrong by introducing a better or changed course of action. The prophets called people to reform their lives and return to being faithful to their Covenant with God. [reforma]

refugee a person who flees his or her home country because of a natural or a manmade disaster. Jesus was a refugee when Joseph and Mary escaped to Egypt to keep Jesus safe from King Herod. [refugiado]

relic a piece of the body of a saint, something that belonged to a saint. The first relics were from the bodies of martyrs and were enshrined in Christian basilicas and churches. [reliquia]

religious life a state of life recognized by the Church. In religious life, men and women freely respond to a call to follow Jesus by living the vows of poverty, chastity, and obedience in community with others. [vida religiosa]

repentance our turning away from sin, with a desire to change our lives and live more closely as God wants us to live. We express our penance by prayer, fasting, and helping those who are poor. [arrepentimiento]

Resurrection the bodily raising of Jesus Christ from the dead on the third day after his Death on the cross. The Resurrection is the crowning truth of our faith. [Resurrección de Cristo]

Glossary

Glossary **319**

Revelation | Sacrifice of the Mass

Revelation God's communication of himself to us through the words and deeds he has used throughout history to show us the mystery of his plan for our Salvation. This Revelation reaches its completion in his sending of his Son, Jesus Christ. [Revelación]

righteousness an attribute of God used to describe his justice, his faithfulness to the Covenant, and his holiness in the Old Testament. As an attribute of humans, righteousness means being in a right relationship with God through moral conduct and observance of the Law. We have merit in God's sight and are able to do this because of the work of God's grace in us. Paul speaks of righteousness in a new way that is no longer dependent on observance of the Law. It comes through the faith in Jesus and his saving Death and Resurrection. To be made righteous in Jesus is to be saved, vindicated, and put right with God through his grace. [rectitud]

rights and responsibilities an important idea within Catholic Social Teaching. All people have the right to the necessities for a full and decent life, such as dignified work, health care, and education. All people also have responsibilities to promote the common good and to help others. (See *Catholic Social Teaching*.) [derechos y responsabilidades]

rite one of the many forms followed in celebrating liturgy in the Church. A rite may differ according to the culture or country where it is celebrated. A rite is also the special form for celebrating each sacrament. [rito]

Rite of Christian Initiation of Adults (RCIA) the process through which unbaptized adults join the Church. Catechumens receive instruction in preparation for their initiation into the Church. Lent marks the beginning of the catechumens' final period of preparation. During Lent they participate in the Rite of Election, during which their sponsors stand as witnesses to their faith, moral character, and desire to join the Church. During the Easter Vigil on Holy Saturday, the Elect profess their faith in Christ and the Church, and they promise to live as Jesus' disciples in the world. They are welcomed into the Church through the Sacraments of Initiation. [Ritual de la Iniciación Cristiana de Adultos]

Rosary a prayer in honor of the Blessed Virgin Mary. When we pray the Rosary, we meditate on the mysteries of Jesus Christ's life while praying the Hail Mary on five sets of ten beads and the Lord's Prayer on the beads in between. In the Latin Church, praying the Rosary became a way for ordinary people to reflect on the mysteries of Christ's life. [Rosario]

S

Sabbath the seventh day, when God rested after finishing the work of creation. The Third Commandment requires us to keep the Sabbath holy. For Christians the Sabbath became Sunday, the Lord's Day, because it was the day that Jesus rose from the dead and the new creation in Jesus Christ began. [sabbat]

sacrament holy, visible signs that signify a divine reality. Through the sacraments, Christ acts in us to save us. Grace received through the Holy Spirit enables us to carry out our mission as disciples. [sacramento]

sacramental an object, a prayer, or a blessing given by the Church to help us grow in our spiritual life [sacramental]

sacramental seal the obligation of priests to keep absolutely secret the sins confessed during the Sacrament of Penance and Reconciliation [sello sacramental]

Sacraments at the Service of Communion the Sacraments of Holy Orders and Matrimony. These two sacraments contribute to the personal Salvation of individuals by giving them a special way to serve others. [sacramentos al Servicio de la Comunidad]

Sacraments of Healing the Sacraments of Penance and Reconciliation and Anointing of the Sick, by which the Church continues Jesus' healing ministry of body and soul [sacramentos de la Curación]

Sacraments of Initiation the sacraments that are the foundation of our Christian life. We are born anew in Baptism, strengthened by Confirmation, and receive in the Eucharist the food of eternal life. By means of these sacraments, we receive an increasing measure of the divine life and advance toward the perfection of charity. [sacramentos de la Iniciación]

sacrifice a ritual offering of animals or produce made to God by the priest in the Temple in Jerusalem. Sacrifice was a sign of the people's adoration of God, giving thanks to God, or asking for forgiveness. Sacrifice also showed union with God. The great High Priest, Christ, accomplished our redemption through the perfect sacrifice of his Death on the Cross. [sacrificio]

Sacrifice of the Mass the sacrifice of Jesus on the Cross, which is remembered and made present in the Eucharist. It is offered in reparation for the sins of the living and the dead and to obtain spiritual or temporal blessings from God. [sacrificio de la Misa]

saint a holy person who has died united with God. The Church has said that this person is now with God forever in Heaven. [santo]

Salvation the gift, which God alone can give, of forgiveness of sin and the restoration of friendship with him [Salvación]

sanctify to make holy. Sacramentals and other Church practices make holy the everyday events and objects in our lives. [santificar]

sanctifying grace the gift from God, given to us without our earning it, that introduces us to the intimacy of the Trinity, unites us with its life, and heals our human nature, wounded by sin. Sanctifying grace helps us respond to our vocation as God's adopted children, and it continues the work of making us holy that began at our Baptism. (See *actual grace, grace,* and *habitual grace.*) [gracia santificante]

sanctuary a holy place to worship God. A sanctuary in church is the place where a religious rite is celebrated. [santuario]

Sanhedrin the Jewish court that ruled on matters of faith and practice among Jews. The Sanhedrin was the only Jewish court allowed to inflict the death penalty. [Sanedrín]

Satan a fallen angel and the enemy of anyone attempting to follow God's will. Satan tempts Jesus in the Gospels and opposes his ministry. In Jewish, Christian, and Muslim thought, Satan is associated with those angels who refused to bow down before human beings and serve them as God commanded. They refused to serve God and were thrown out of Heaven as a punishment. Satan and the other demons tempt human beings to join them in their revolt against God. [Satanás]

Savior Jesus, the Son of God, who became man to forgive our sins and restore our friendship with God. *Jesus* means "God saves." [Salvador]

scriptorium the room in a monastery in which books were copied by hand. Often beautiful art was added to the page to illustrate a story. [scriptorium]

Scriptures the holy writings of Jews and Christians, collected in the Old and New Testaments of the Bible [Sagradas Escrituras]

seal of confession also called the sacramental seal. It declares that the priest is absolutely forbidden to reveal under any circumstances any sin confessed to him in the Sacrament of Penance and Reconciliation. (See *sacramental seal.*) [sigilo sacramental]

Second Coming the return in glory of Jesus Christ to the world. The Church looks forward to the Second Coming with joy. [Segunda Venida]

Second Vatican Council the 21st and most recent ecumenical council of the Catholic Church. It met from October 11, 1962, to December 8, 1965. Its purpose, according to Pope John XXIII, was to renew the Church and to help it promote peace and unity among Christians and all humanity. [Concilio Vaticano Segundo]

seminary a school for the training and spiritual formation of priests. Seminaries first became widespread in the Church during the renewals of the 1500s. [seminario]

seraphim the heavenly beings who worship before the throne of God. One of them purified the lips of Isaiah with a burning coal so that he could speak for God. (Isaiah 6:6–7) [serafín]

Sermon on the Mount the words of Jesus, written in Chapters 5–7 of the Gospel of Matthew, in which Jesus reveals how he has fulfilled God's law given to Moses. The Sermon on the Mount begins with the eight Beatitudes and includes the Lord's Prayer. [Sermón de la Montaña]

sexism a prejudice or discrimination based on sex, especially discrimination against women. Sexism leads to behaviors and attitudes that foster a view of social roles based only on sex. [sexismo]

Sign of Peace the part of the Mass in which we offer a gesture of peace to one another as we prepare to receive Holy Communion. This signifies our willingness to be united in peace before we receive the Lord. (See *The Order of Mass.*) [Rito de la Paz]

Sign of the Cross the gesture we make that signifies our belief in God the Father, the Son, and the Holy Spirit. It is a sign of blessing, a confession of faith, and a way that identifies us as followers of Jesus Christ. [Señal de la Cruz]

signs events in the world that point to a deeper reality. The first half of the Gospel of John presents seven signs that reveal the glory of God and give us a glimpse of what the Kingdom of God is like. [signos]

sin a deliberate thought, word, deed, or failure to act that offends God and hurts our relationships with other people. Some sin is mortal and needs to be confessed in the Sacrament of Penance and Reconciliation. Other sin is venial, or less serious. [pecado]

Glossary

sloth a carelessness of heart that leads a person to ignore his or her development as a person, especially spiritual development and a relationship with God. Sloth is one of the seven capital sins, and it is contrary to the First Commandment. (See *capital sins*.) [pereza]

social justice the fair and equal treatment of every member of society. It is required by the dignity and freedom of every person. The Catholic Church has developed a body of social principles and moral teachings described in papal and other official documents issued since the late 19th century. This teaching deals with the economic, political, and social order of the world. It is rooted in the Bible as well as in the traditional theological teachings of the Church. [justicia social]

social sin social situations and institutions that are against the will of God. Because of the personal sins of individuals, entire societies can develop structures that are sinful in and of themselves. Social sins include racism, sexism, structures that deny people access to adequate health care, and the destruction of the environment for the benefit of a few. [pecado social]

solidarity the attitude of strength and unity that leads to the sharing of spiritual and material goods. Solidarity unites rich and poor, weak and strong, to foster a society in which all give what they can and receive what they need. The idea of solidarity is based on the common origin of all humanity. (See *Catholic Social Teaching*.) [solidaridad]

Son of God the title revealed by Jesus that indicates his unique relationship to God the Father. The revelation of Jesus' divine sonship is the main dramatic development of the story of Jesus of Nazareth as it unfolds in the Gospels. [Hijo de Dios]

soul the part of us that makes us human and an image of God. Body and soul together form one unique human nature. The soul is responsible for our consciousness and our freedom. The soul does not die and will be reunited with the body in the final resurrection. [alma]

Spiritual Exercises a spiritual retreat written by Ignatius of Loyola, designed to help people become aware of the presence of God in all things. The Spiritual Exercises are a major part of Ignatian spirituality. [Ejercicios Espirituales]

spirituality our growing, loving relationship with God. Spirituality is our way of expressing our experience of God in both the way we pray and the way we love our neighbor. There are many different schools of spirituality. Examples of these schools are Franciscan and Jesuit.

These are guides for the spiritual life and have enriched the traditions of prayer, worship, and living in Christianity. [espiritualidad]

Spiritual Works of Mercy the kind acts through which we help our neighbors meet the needs that are more than material. The Spiritual Works of Mercy include instructing, advising, consoling, comforting, forgiving, and bearing wrongs with patience. [obras de misericordia espirituales]

Stations of the Cross a prayer for meditating on the final hours of Jesus' life, from his condemnation by Pontius Pilate to his Death and burial. We pray the Stations by moving to each representation of 14 incidents, based on events from Jesus' Passion and Death. [Vía Crucis]

stewardship the careful and responsible management of something entrusted to one's care, especially the goods of creation, which are intended for the whole human race. The sixth Precept of the Church makes clear our part in stewardship by requiring us to provide for the material needs of the Church, according to our abilities. [corresponsabilidad]

subsidiarity the principle that the best institutions for responding to a particular social task are those closest to it. The responsibility of the closest political or private institution is to assist those in need. Only when issues cannot be resolved at the local level should they be resolved at a higher level. [subsidiaridad]

Summa Theologiae a work of Christian theology in five volumes written by Saint Thomas Aquinas. In the *Summa Theologiae*, Aquinas asks questions about thousands of theological topics that continue to influence Christian theology today. [*Summa Theologiae*]

superior the leader of a community of consecrated religious men or women [superior]

swaddling wrapping an infant in strips of cloth for warmth and comfort. Jesus' swaddling clothes symbolized the humility and poverty of his birth and foreshadowed the shroud he would be wrapped in after his Crucifixion. [envolver en pañales]

Syllabus of Errors a document issued by Pope Pius IX condemning false claims and ideas about the nature of God and the world. The condemned views included claims related to pantheism, socialism, communism, the rights of the Church, and many other topics. [Syllabus Errorum]

synagogue the Jewish place of assembly for prayer, instruction, and study of the Torah. After the destruction of the Temple in 587 B.C., synagogues were organized as places to maintain Jewish faith and worship. Jesus attended the synagogue regularly for prayer and to teach. When visiting a city, Paul would first visit the synagogue. The synagogue played an important role in the development of Christian worship and in the structure of Christian communities. [sinagoga]

synod a meeting of bishops from all over the world to discuss doctrinal or pastoral matters. Synods offer suggestions to the pope, which may or may not become official teachings at a later time. [sínodo]

synoptic the way in which three of the four Gospels—Matthew, Mark, and Luke—tell similar stories in similar ways about the life and Death of Jesus. The Gospel of John's structure and stories are often different from the other three. Although none of the Gospels agree on every detail, each one conveys unique truths from their own perspectives about Jesus' life and mission. [sinóptico]

T

tabernacle the container in which the Blessed Sacrament is kept so that Holy Communion can be taken to those who are sick and dying. It is also the name of the tent sanctuary in which the Israelites kept the Ark of the Covenant from the time of the Exodus to the construction of Solomon's Temple. [sagrario]

temperance the Cardinal Virtue that helps us control our attraction to pleasure so that our natural desires are kept within proper limits. This moral virtue helps us choose to use goods in moderation. (See *Cardinal Virtues*.) [templanza]

Temple the house of worship of God, first built by Solomon. The Temple provided a place for the priests to offer sacrifice, to adore and give thanks to God, and to ask for forgiveness. It was destroyed and rebuilt. The second Temple was also destroyed and was never rebuilt. Part of the outer wall of the Temple mount remains to this day in Jerusalem. [Templo]

temptation an attraction, from outside us or inside us, that can lead us to disobey God's commands. Everyone is tempted, but the Holy Spirit helps us resist temptation and choose to do good. [tentación]

Ten Commandments the 10 rules given by God to Moses on Mount Sinai that sum up God's law and show us what is required to love God and our neighbor. By following the Ten Commandments, the Hebrews accepted their Covenant with God. [Diez Mandamientos]

theologian an expert in the study of God and his Revelation to the world [teólogo]

Theological Virtues the three virtues of faith, hope, and charity that are gifts from God and not acquired by human effort. The virtue of faith helps us believe in God, the virtue of hope helps us desire eternal life and the Kingdom of God, and the virtue of charity helps us love God and our neighbor as we should. [virtudes teologales]

Torah the Hebrew word for "instruction" or "law." It is also the name of the first five books of the Old Testament: Genesis, Exodus, Leviticus, Numbers, and Deuteronomy. [Torá]

Tradition the beliefs and practices of the Church that are passed down from one generation to the next under the guidance of the Holy Spirit. What Christ entrusted to the Apostles was handed on to others both orally and in writing. Tradition and Scripture together make up the single deposit of faith, which remains present and active in the Church. [Tradición católica]

Transfiguration an event witnessed by the apostles Peter, James, and John that revealed Jesus' divine glory. Jesus' face shone like the sun, his clothes became dazzlingly white, and he spoke with Elijah and Moses on the mountain. [Transfiguración]

transubstantiation the unique change of the bread and wine in the Eucharist into the Body and Blood of the risen Jesus Christ, while retaining their physical appearance as bread and wine [transubstanciación]

trespasses unlawful acts committed against the property or rights of another person or acts that physically harm a person [ofensas]

Triduum a Latin word meaning "three days" that refers to Holy Thursday, Good Friday, and Holy Saturday. The liturgies of the Triduum are among the most solemn celebrations of the Catholic faith. [Triduo Pascual]

Trinity the mystery of the existence of God in three Persons—the Father, the Son, and the Holy Spirit. Each Person of the Trinity is God, whole and entire. Each Person is distinct only in the relationship of each to the others. [Trinidad, Santísima]

Truce of God an act of the Church in the 11th century that banned fighting on Sundays and that was eventually extended to more than half the year [tregua de Dios]

Glossary

Glossary 323

U

understanding one of the seven Gifts of the Holy Spirit. This gift helps us make the right choices in life and in our relationships with God and with others. (See *Gifts of the Holy Spirit.*) [consejo]

universal Church the entire Church as it exists throughout the world. The people of every diocese, along with their bishops and the pope, make up the universal Church. (See *catholic.*) [Iglesia universal]

V

venerate to show respect for someone or something. Although only God should be worshiped, Christians venerate the saints and objects associated with them to show respect for God's work in their lives. [venerar]

venial sin a choice we make that weakens our relationship with God or with other people. Venial sin wounds and lessens the divine life in us. If we make no effort to do better, venial sin can lead to more serious sin. Through our participation in the Eucharist, venial sin is forgiven when we are repentant, strengthening our relationship with God and with others. [pecado venial]

viaticum the Eucharist that a dying person receives. It is spiritual food for the last journey we make as Christians, the journey through death to eternal life. [viático]

Vicar of Christ the title given to the pope who, as the successor of Saint Peter, has the authority to act in Christ's place. A vicar is someone who stands in for and acts for another. (See *pope.*) [Vicario de Cristo]

virtue an attitude or a way of acting that enables us to do good [virtud]

Visitation one of the Joyful Mysteries of the Rosary, a reference to Mary's visit to Elizabeth to share the good news that Mary is to be the mother of Jesus. Elizabeth's greeting of Mary forms part of the Hail Mary. During this visit, Mary sings the *Magnificat,* her praise of God. [Visitación]

vocation the call each of us has in life to be the person God wants us to be and the way we each serve the Church and the Kingdom of God. Each of us can live out his or her vocation as a layperson, as a member of a religious community, or as a member of the clergy. [vocación]

vow a deliberate and free promise made to God by people who want especially to dedicate their lives to God. Their vows give witness now to the kingdom that is to come. [voto]

Vulgate the Latin translation of the Bible by Saint Jerome from the Hebrew and Greek in which it was originally written. Most Christians of Saint Jerome's day no longer spoke Hebrew or Greek. The common language, or vulgate, was Latin. [Vulgata]

W

Way, the what Saint Paul called the early faith and those who follow Jesus. Like the disciples on the road to Emmaus, our life is a journey of faith on "the Way" for which Jesus gives strength in the Eucharist. [Camino, el]

wisdom one of the seven Gifts of the Holy Spirit. Wisdom helps us understand the purpose and plan of God and live in a way that helps bring about this plan. It begins in wonder and awe at God's greatness. (See *Gifts of the Holy Spirit.*) [sabiduría]

Wisdom Literature the Old Testament books of Job, Proverbs, Ecclesiastes, Song of Songs, Wisdom, and Ben Sira. The purpose of these books is to give instruction on ways to live and how to understand and cope with the problems of life. [literatura sapiencial]

witness the passing on to others, by our words and our actions, the faith that we have been given. Every Christian has the duty to give witness to the good news about Jesus Christ that he or she has come to know. [testimonio]

worship the adoration and honor given to God in public prayer [culto]

Y

Yahweh the name of God in Hebrew, which God told Moses from the burning bush. *Yahweh* means "I am who am" or "I cause to be all that is." [Yavé]

Index

Index

Index

Index

Acknowledgments

Excerpts from the *New American Bible, revised edition* © 2010, 1991, 1986, 1970 Confraternity of Christian Doctrine, Washington, D.C., and are used by permission of the copyright owner. All rights reserved. No part of the *New American Bible* may be reproduced in any form without permission in writing from the copyright owner.

The English translation of the Act of Contrition from *Rite of Penance* © 1974 International Commission on English in the Liturgy Corporation (ICEL); the English translation of Prayer to the Holy Spirit and Hail, Holy Queen *(Salve Regina)* from *A Book of Prayers* © 1982, ICEL; the English translation of Prayer Before Meals and Prayer After Meals from *Book of Blessings* © 1988, ICEL; the English translation of Nicene Creed and Apostles' Creed from *The Roman Missal* © 2010, ICEL. All rights reserved.

Excerpts from the English translation of the *Catechism of the Catholic Church, Second Edition* for the United States of America © 2000 United States Catholic Conference, Inc.—Libreria Editrice Vaticana.

Excerpt from *Economic Justice for All: Pastoral Letter on Catholic Social Teaching and the U.S. Economy* © 1986 United States Conference of Catholic Bishops, Washington, D.C. All rights reserved. Used by permission.

Excerpt from *Faithful Citizenship: A Catholic Call to Political Responsibility* © 2003 United States Conference of Catholic Bishops, Washington, D.C. All rights reserved. Used by permission.

Excerpt from *Forming Consciences for Faithful Citizenship* © 2007, 2011 United States Conference of Catholic Bishops, Washington, D.C. All rights reserved. Used by permission.

Excerpts from papal encyclicals and other Vatican documents are © Libreria Editrice Vaticana. All rights reserved.

The Prayer for Generosity and the *Suscipe* are from *Hearts on Fire: Praying with Jesuits* by Michael Harter, S.J. © 2005 Loyola Press.

Loyola Press has made every effort to locate the copyright holders for the cited works used in this publication and to make full acknowledgment for their use. In the case of any omissions, the publisher will be pleased to make suitable acknowledgments in future editions.

Art and Photography

When there is more than one picture on a page, positions are abbreviated as follows: **(t)** top, **(c)** center, **(b)** bottom, **(l)** left, **(r)** right, **(bg)** background, **(bd)** border.

Photos and illustrations not acknowledged are either owned by Loyola Press or from royalty-free sources including but not limited to Art Resource, Alamy, Bridgeman, Corbis/Veer, Getty Images, iStockphoto, Jupiterimages, Media Bakery, PunchStock, Shutterstock, Thinkstock, and Wikipedia Commons. Loyola Press has made every effort to locate the copyright holders for the cited works used in this publication and to make full acknowledgment for their use. In the case of any omissions, the publisher will be pleased to make suitable acknowledgments in future editions.

Frontmatter: i Rafael Lopez. **ii–iii** iStockphoto/Thinkstock. **iii** (t) © iStockphoto.com/keeweeboy. **iii** (c) The Crosiers/Gene Plaisted, OSC. **iii** (b) Jupiterimages/Creatas/Thinkstock. **iv** (t) Zvonimir Atletic/Shutterstock.com. **iv** (bl) © iStockphoto.com/hadynyah. **iv** (br) © iStockphoto.com/botsman141.

© iStockphoto.com: 4 (t) Jbryson. **6** (t) -Mosquito-. **6–7, 21, 31** (t, b) blue67. **8** (t) Maica. **12** (t) TonyBaggett. **15** (t) blue67; (br) Luseen. **21** (cl) lawcai; (cr) Allkindza; (cl, bc) deeAuvil; (bc) Crisma. **22** (bl) iStockphoto. **30** (tl) blue67; (b) Auki. **32** (t) eyecrave. **37** (bc) alexsl. **38** (bl) Liliboas. **44** (tr) evilclown.

46 (t) mixformdesign. **48** (b) ranplett. **58** (t) Chelnok; (bl) kryczka. **64–67** (tl, b) blue67. **64** Hogie. **65** (c) Hogie. **72** (bl) ranplett. **76** (t) arieliona. **82–83** (bd) blue67. **87** (t) ChrisSteer; (b) jabejon. **88** (t) peepo. **100** (bd) trigga; (b) Fos4o. **102** (bd) ChuckStryker. **108–109** (b) artplay711. **110** (bd) ChuckStryker. **118** (tl, tr, b) blue67. **123** (cb) iStockphoto.com. **126–127** (b) Beastfromeast. **128** (b) blue67. **132** (t) hadynyah; (b) Vardhan. **134** (t) keeweeboy; (b) javarman3. **138–139** (b, t) Beastfromeast. **139** (cr) kryczka. **145** (cr) LokFung. **146** (br) diane555. **147** (br) bubaone. **148** (c) Beastfromeast. **154–155** (c, br) LokFung. **161** (cr) blue67; (b) Beastfromeast. **163** (t) stdemi. **167** (cr) aldegonde. **167–169** (b) Beastfromeast. **168** (t) duncan1890. **168–169** (b) Beastfromeast. **170** (t) abzee; (c) aleksandarvelasevic. **171** (br) elsen029. **176** (t) JennaWagner; (bl) lisafx; (br) kali9. **178** (c) cstar55. **181** (br) princessdlaf. **183** (b) blue67. **184** (t) Slonov; (c) blue67. **196** (bd) abzee. **204** (t) Beastfromeast; (b) svetikd. **205–206** (b, tl) Beastfromeast. **219** (t) HeikeKampe; (b) OllieMac. **221** (tr) 7io; (bg) Jasmina007. **222** (bl) beastfromeast. **224** (bd) kamisoka. **225** (b) huronphoto. **229** (b) chankimlungistock. **230** (c) blue67. **233** bopshops. **234** (c) blue67. **242** botsman141. **244** (t) javarman3. **246** (bd) kentarcajuan. **248** (b) kulicki. **251** (t, bd) Jasmina007; (tr) WPChambers. **252** (ct) ankh-fire; (cr) beastfromeast. **253** (bd) makkayak. **254** blue67. **257** (t) duncan1890; (bl) jgroup; (br) ZU_09. **270** (cb) kevinruss. **272–273** (bg) Trifonov_Evgeniy. **273** grandriver. **274** livjam. **275** blue67. **277** (b) beastfromeast. **283** (t) ajt. **287** teekid. **290** duckycards. **296** AndrisTkachenko. **298** LeggNet; eyedear. **300** (c) MariaAngelaCiucci.

Thinkstock: 4 (t) iStockphoto. **43** (tl) Jupiterimages/Creatas. **52** (b) iStockphoto. **56–57** (b) iStockphoto. **72** (c) PhotoObjects.net/Hemera Technologies. **112** (t) Jupiterimages/Creatas. **138** (t) Jupiterimages/Photos.com. **144** (bd) Hemera. **184** (b) Brand X Pictures. **198** (c) iStockphoto. **199** (bd) Brand X Pictures. **212** (bd) iStockphoto. **212–213** (r, t) iStockphoto. **215** (bd) Brand X Pictures. **216** (t) iStockphoto. **221** (t) iStockphoto. **236** (b) iStockphoto.

Unit 1: 1 (t) Andrew R. Wright. **2** (br) Andrew R. Wright. **3** (t) Ocean Photography/Veer. **5** (tr) Susan Tolonen; (br) Scala/Art Resource, NY. **7** (cr) AgnusImages.com. **9** (t) Loyola Press Photography; (b) James Woodson/Digital Vision/Getty Images. **11** (t) OJO Images Photography/Veer. **13** (tr) The Crosiers/Gene Plaisted, OSC; (br) AgnusImages.com. **14** (t) Don Hammond/Design Pics/Corbis. **15** (bc) Fotosearch. **16** (t) Fancy Photography/Veer. **19** (t) Blend Images Photography/Veer. **20** (t) Detail: Murillo, Bartolome Esteban (1618–1682) The Nativity. Pen and brown ink, brush and brown wash, over traces of leadpoint or soft black chalk. 10-3/4 x 9 in. (27.3 x 22.9 cm). Purchase, Clifford A. Furst Bequest, by exchange, and Harry G. Sperling Fund, 1995 (1995.375). The Metropolitan Museum of Art, New York, NY, U.S.A. Photo Credit: Image copyright © The Metropolitan Museum of Art/Art Resource, NY; (b) SuperStock/Getty Images. **22** (t) Rui Vale de Sousa/Shutterstock.com; (br) Alinari/The Bridgeman Art Library International. **23** (t) Olga Kushcheva/Jupiterimages; (t) The Crosiers/Gene Plaisted, OSC; (br) The Crosiers/Gene Plaisted, OSC. **24** (t) Alloy Photography/Veer. **27** (t) Corbis Photography/Veer. **28** (t) Scala/Art Resource, NY; (b) Daily Mail/Rex/Alamy. **29** (cr) The Crosiers/Gene Plaisted, OSC; (br) Giraudon/The Bridgeman Art Library International. © 2013 Artists Rights Society (ARS), New York/ADAGP, Paris. **30** (t) Blend Images Photography/Veer. **31** (t) Jupiterimages. **35** (cr) Image Source Photography/Veer. **36** (t) Fancy Photography/Veer; (b) Royalty-free image. **38** (t) The Crosiers/Gene Plaisted, OSC; (cl) Jupiterimages; (cr) The Crosiers/Gene Plaisted, OSC. **39** (b) Fine Art Photographic Library/Corbis. **40** (b) Ocean Photography/Veer. **41** Mark Poulalion. **43** (bl) Wikimedia public domain. **44** (b) Warling Studios.

Unit 2: 45 (t) Andrew R. Wright. **46** (c) Museu Nacional d'Art de Catalunya, Barcelona, Spain/The Bridgeman Art Library International; (br) Andrew R. Wright. **47** (t) Blend Images Photography/Veer. **48** (t) The Crosiers/Gene Plaisted, OSC. **49** (tr) Zvonimir Atletic/Shutterstock.com; (br) The Crosiers/Gene Plaisted, OSC. **50** (t) Corbis Photography/Veer. **51** (tr) Warling Studios; (br) Michael O'Brien. **52** (t) Ocean Photography/Veer. **55** (t) Fancy Photography/Veer. **56** (t) The Crosiers/Gene Plaisted, OSC. **57** (tr) The Crosiers/Gene Plaisted, OSC; (bc) Private Collection/The Bridgeman Art Library International. **59** (t) W.P. Wittman Limited; (br) Phil Martin Photography. **60** (t) Monkey Business Images/Veer. **63** (t) Blend Images Photography; (t) Laurence Mouton/PhotoAlto/Corbis. **64** (tr) The Crosiers/Gene Plaisted, OSC. **64, 68, 80** (tr) Jupiterimages. **65** (t) The Crosiers/Gene Plaisted, OSC. **66** (tl) Jupiterimages; (t) The Crosiers/Gene Plaisted, OSC; (t) SeDmi/Veer. **67** (tr) Jesus Mafa/© Look and Learn/The Bridgeman Art Library International. **68** (t) Alloy Photography/Veer. **71** (t) moodboard Photography/Veer. **72** (t) Ocean Photography/Veer; (bl) AgnusImages.com. **73** (cr) The Crosiers/Gene Plaisted, OSC. **74** (t) Corbis Photography/Veer. **75** (cr) W.P. Wittman Limited; (br) Alinari/The Bridgeman Art Library International. **79** (c) The Crosiers/Gene Plaisted, OSC. **80** (t) Warling Studios; (br) W.P. Wittman Limited. **81** (br) The Crosiers/Gene Plaisted, OSC. **82** (t) The Crosiers/Gene Plaisted, OSC; (br) Private

Collection/The Bridgeman Art Library International. **83** (br) Private Collection/The Bridgeman Art Library International. **84** (t) Alloy Photography/Veer; (b) Photodisc Object Series. **88** (b) Echo/Cultura/Getty Images.

Unit 3: 89 (t) Andrew R. Wright. **90** Jupiterimages; (t) Andrew R. Wright. **91** (t) is/Veer. **92** (t) The Crosiers/Gene Plaisted, OSC; (b) National Gallery, London, UK/The Bridgeman Art Library International. **93** (br) The Crosiers/Gene Plaisted, OSC. **94** (tr) Private Collection/The Bridgeman Art Library International; (c) Bettmann/Corbis. **95** (br) Erich Lessing/Art Resource, NY. **96** (t) Oliver Rossi/Corbis. **99** (t) Barbara Reddoch/Veer. **100** (t) The Crosiers/Gene Plaisted, OSC. **101** (tr) The Crosiers/Gene Plaisted, OSC; (bl) Cameraphoto Arte Venezia/The Bridgeman Art Library International. **102** (tr) W.P. Wittman Limited. **103** (br) Alessandra Cimatoribus. **104** (t) Alloy Photography/Veer. **105** Jim Wright. **107** (t) Corbis Photography/Veer. **108** (t) Private Collection/The Bridgeman Art Library International; (bd) SeDmi/Veer. **109** (br) Media Bakery. **110–111** (t) Rafael Lopez. **110** (br) Giraudon/The Bridgeman Art Library International. **111** (br) The Crosiers/Gene Plaisted, OSC. **113** Loyola Press Photography. **115** (t) Blend Images Photography/Veer. **116** The Palsied Man Let Down Through the Roof, illustration for 'The Life of Christ', c.1886–94 (gouache on paper), Tissot, James Jacques Joseph (1836–1902)/Brooklyn Museum of Art, New York, USA/The Bridgeman Art Library International. **117** (br) Warling Studios. **118** (t) The Crosiers/Gene Plaisted, OSC. **119** (cr) Greg Kuepfer; (bl) Private Collection/The Bridgeman Art Library International. **120** (t) Sean Justice/Corbis. **123** (ct) Jupiterimages. **124** The Crosiers/Gene Plaisted, OSC. **125** (tr) W.P. Wittman Limited; (br) Giraudon/The Bridgeman Art Library International. **126** (tl) Jupiterimages; (tr) Maria Laughlin; (c) Jupiterimages. **127** (t) Warling Studios. **128** (t) Warling Studios. **129** Loyola Press Photography. **131** (t) Warling Studios; (b) Blend Images Photography/Veer.

Unit 4: 133 Andrew R. Wright. **134** (br) Andrew R. Wright. **135** Lisafx/Veer. **136** Jupiterimages; (t) Regional Art Museum, Zaporizhia, Ukraine/The Bridgeman Art Library International; (br) Rafael Lopez. **137** (t) AgnusImages.com; (br) Judy McGrath. **140** (t) SW Productions/Media Bakery. **141** (t) Loyola Press Photography. **143** (t) OJO Images Photography/Veer. **144** (t) The Crosiers/Gene Plaisted, OSC. **145** (br) Nocturne (Gethsemane) 1915 (oil on canvas), Rouault, Georges (1871–1958)/Allen Memorial Art Museum, Oberlin College, Ohio, USA/© DACS/R.T. Miller, Jr. Fund/The Bridgeman Art Library International. © 2013 Artists Rights Society (ARS), New York/ADAGP, Paris. **146** (t) Floresco Productions/Media Bakery. **147** (t) Courtesy of the Archives of the Sisters of the Blessed Sacrament, Bensalem, PA. **148** (t) Auslöser/Media Bakery. **151** (t) Walter Lockwood/Media Bakery. **152** (t) The Crosiers/Gene Plaisted, OSC; (b) Bill Perry/Shutterstock.com. **153** (br) Galleria degli Uffizi, Florence, Italy/The Bridgeman Art Library International. **154** (t) The Crosiers/Gene Plaisted, OSC; (bd) St. Peter's, Vatican, Rome, Italy/The Bridgeman Art Library International. **156** (t) Media Bakery. **159** (t) Ocean Photography/Veer. **160** (t) The Crosiers/Gene Plaisted, OSC; (t) Jupiterimages; (br) Nic Neufeld/Shutterstock.com. **161** (t) Image Source Photography/Veer. **162** (t) Alessandra Cimatoribus; (c) Jupiterimages. **163** (cr) W.P. Wittman Limited; (br) Image by Elizabeth Wang, Code: T-00535-OL-V2, Copyright © Radiant Light 2000, Title: "At the Mass, if we unite ourselves with Christ's self-offering, we are like jewels on His robe." **164** (t) Don Hammond/Media Bakery. **165** Carrie Gowran. **168** (t) © The Trustees of the Chester Beatty Library, Dublin/The Bridgeman Art Library International. **169** (t) Photodisc/Getty Images. **170** (tr) He Qi, www.heqigallery.com. **172** (t) Tim Pannell/Media Bakery. **175** (t) W.P. Wittman Limited; (b) W.P. Wittman Limited.

Unit 5: 177 Andrew R. Wright. **178** (l) Jupiterimages; (r) Andrew R. Wright. **179** moodboard Photography/Veer. **180** (t) Warling Studios; (br) He Qi, www.heqigallery.com. **182** (t) Image Source Photography/Veer; (bd) Jupiterimages; (br) Wikipedia. **187** cultura Photography/Veer **188** (t) The Crosiers/Gene Plaisted, OSC. **190** (t) W.P. Wittman Limited; (br) Musee Nat. Picasso La Guerre et la Paix, Vallauris, France/The Bridgeman Art Library International. © 2014 Estate of Pablo Picasso/Artists Rights Society (ARS), New York. **191** (b) The Crosiers/Gene Plaisted, OSC. **192** (t) Image Source Photography/Veer **195** Blend Images Photography/Veer. **196** (t) The Crosiers/Gene Plaisted, OSC. **197** (t) The Crosiers/Gene Plaisted, OSC; (b) Scala/Art Resource, NY. **198** (t) Klaus Mellenthin/Getty Images; (b) The Crosiers/Gene Plaisted, OSC. **199** (tr) The Crosiers/Gene Plaisted, OSC. **200** (t) PT Images/Veer. **203** (t) Ian Lishman/Juice Images/Corbis **205** (cr) Bible Society, London, UK/The Bridgeman Art Library International. **206** (tr) The Crosiers/Gene Plaisted, OSC; (b) bokononist/Shutterstock.com. **207** (br) The Crosiers/Gene Plaisted, OSC. **208** (t) Warling Studios. **211** (r) Ben Blankenburg/Corbis. **212** (l) © Radiant Light/The Bridgeman Art Library International. **213** (br) © Museumslandschaft Hessen Kassel Ute Brunzel/The Bridgeman Art Library International. **214** Ivan Vdovin/

Alamy. **215** (t) Tim Pannell/Corbis; (b) The Crosiers/Gene Plaisted, OSC. **220** (t) Corbis Photography/Veer; (b) cultura Photography/Veer.

The Year in Our Church: 221 (cl) Jupiterimages; (cl) Plush Studios/Digital Vision/Getty Images; (cr, clockwise) Andrew R. Wright; (br) SeDmi/Veer. **222** (t) The Crosiers/Gene Plaisted, OSC; (ct) The Crosiers/Gene Plaisted, OSC; (cb) The Crosiers/Gene Plaisted, OSC; (br) The Crosiers/Gene Plaisted, OSC. **223** Warling Studios. **224** (t) © British Library Board. All Rights Reserved/The Bridgeman Art Library. **225** (br) Rafael Valls Gallery, London, UK/The Bridgeman Art Library. **226** The Crosiers/Gene Plaisted, OSC. **227** Private Collection/The Bridgeman Art Library. **228** (t) Birmingham Museums and Art Gallery/The Bridgeman Art Library; (bd) Phecsone/Shutterstock.com. **229** (t) © Look and Learn/The Bridgeman Art Library. **230** (tr) The Crosiers/Gene Plaisted, OSC. **231** Warling Studios. **232** (tr) © Guildhall Art Gallery, City of London/The Bridgeman Art Library; (bd) Jupiterimages. **233** (tr) Warling Studios; Stockdisc Classic/Alamy. **234** (tr) Warling Studios. **235** Copyright 2001 TheoLogic Systems, Inc. All rights reserved. Usage subject to license agreement. **236** (tr) The Crosiers/Gene Plaisted, OSC. **237** Galleria degli Uffizi, Florence, Italy/The Bridgeman Art Library. **238** (tr) ReligiousStock/Alamy. **239** The Crosiers/Gene Plaisted, OSC. **240** (tr) Private Collection/The Bridgeman Art Library. **241** (c) Warling Studios. **243** The Crosiers/Gene Plaisted, OSC. **244** (tr) The Crosiers/Gene Plaisted, OSC; (bc) ColonialArts.com **245** Warling Studios. **246** (tr) © Glasgow University Library, Scotland/The Bridgeman Art Library. **247** John Nava/Los Angeles Cathderdral of Our Lady of the Angels. **248** (tr) Werner Forman/Art Resource, NY. **249** (cl) Charles O. Cecil/Alamy; (cr) Siede Preis/Photodisc; (b) Siede Preis/Photodisc. **250** (tr) National Gallery, London, UK/The Bridgeman Art Library; (bd) Thunderstorm.

Prayers and Practices of Our Faith: 251–300 (bd) Greg Becker. **251** (cl) © Hermitage Art, Inc./Reproductions at www.Bridgebuilding.com; (cr) © Hermitage Art, Inc./Reproductions at www.Bridgebuilding.com. **251** (b) Steph Fowler/Media Bakery. **252** (cb) The Crosiers/Gene Plaisted, OSC; (b) Warling Studios. **253** (c) Giraudon/The Bridgeman Art Library. **255** (c) Michael Runkel Ethiopia/Alamy. **256** Lebrecht Music and Arts Photo Library/Alamy. **258** (c) © Hermitage Art, Inc./Reproductions at www.Bridgebuilding.com; (b) SeDmi/Veer. **259** (c) © Hermitage Art, Inc./Reproductions at www.Bridgebuilding.com. **260** (c) © Hermitage Art, Inc./Reproductions at www.Bridgebuilding.com. **261** (c) © Hermitage Art, Inc./Reproductions at www.Bridgebuilding.com. **262** (c) Alinari/The Bridgeman Art Library; (b) **263** (b) The Crosiers/Gene Plaisted, OSC. **264** (tl, b) Bill Wood; (tr) Bettmann/Corbis; (br) Bill Wood. **265** (c) Bill Wood. **266** Corbis Photography/Veer **267** (b) Private Collection/The Bridgeman Art Library. **268** (b) Christina Balit. **269** ImageZoo/Corbis. **270** (c) Warling Studios. **271** (b) KidStock/Media Bakery. **272** (c) Rick Becker-Leckrone/Shutterstock.com; (bd) Jupiterimages. **276** The Crosiers/Gene Plaisted, OSC. **277** (br) Warling Studios. **278** (b) Fancy Photography/Veer; (br) Warling Studios. **279** (c) Engraving from; Jesuits; Loyola; Saint Ignatius; The Illustrated Globe Encyclopaedia of Universal Knowledge; Vol. V (London 1882). **279** (b) Jupiterimages. **280** (cr) The Crosiers/Gene Plaisted, OSC. **281** Greg Kuepfer. **282** (c) The Crosiers/Gene Plaisted, OSC; (b) The Crosiers/Gene Plaisted, OSC. **283** (cr) The Crosiers/Gene Plaisted, OSC; (br) The Crosiers/Gene Plaisted, OSC. **284** (l) James, Laura/Private Collection/The Bridgeman Art Library; (cl) James, Laura/Private Collection/The Bridgeman Art Library; (cr) James, Laura/Private Collection/The Bridgeman Art Library; (r) James, Laura/Private Collection/The Bridgeman Art Library. **285** Top left to right (a) James, Laura/Private Collection/The Bridgeman Art Library. (b) James, Laura/Private Collection/The Bridgeman Art Library; (c) James, Laura/Private Collection/The Bridgeman Art Library; (d) James, Laura/Private Collection/The Bridgeman Art Library; (e) James, Laura/Private Collection/The Bridgeman Art Library; (f) James, Laura/Private Collection/The Bridgeman Art Library; (g) James, Laura/Private Collection/The Bridgeman Art Library; (h) James, Laura/Private Collection/The Bridgeman Art Library; (i) James, Laura/Private Collection/The Bridgeman Art Library; (j) James, Laura/Private Collection/The Bridgeman Art Library. **286** (cr) The Crosiers/Gene Plaisted, OSC. **287–288** Alessandra Cimatoribus. **289** (t) AgnusImages.com; (b) W.P. Wittman Limited. **291** (tl) The Crosiers/Gene Plaisted, OSC; (tc) Private Collection/The Bridgeman Art Library; (tr) Louvre, Paris, France/Giraudon/The Bridgeman Art Library; (bl) © Radiant Light/The Bridgeman Art Library; (bc) The Crosiers/Gene Plaisted, OSC; (br) Photo © Boltin Picture Library/The Bridgeman Art Library. **292** (cr) Granger Wootz/Media Bakery. **293** (br) © Look and Learn/The Bridgeman Art Library. **294–295** chbaum/Shutterstock.com. **295** (tr) The Crosiers/Gene Plaisted, OSC. **297** (cr) Warling Studios; (cr) Warling Studios; (cr) Warling Studios; (b) Warling Studios. **299** (cr) Alex Mares-Manton/Asia Images/Getty Images. **300** (br) Safia Fatimi/Taxi/Getty Images.

CD Scripts

Faith comes alive through the dramatized Scripture stories and recorded guided reflections contained on the *Finding God* CDs. While listening to the Scripture stories, young people can visualize themselves in the scene. The guided reflections encourage young people to lead a more prayerful life.

The following scripts from the program CDs appear in this section for your convenience.

- **Recorded Scripture Story Scripts**
- **Recorded Guided Reflection Scripts**

The Feeding of the 5,000 *based on Mark 6:34–44*

Narrator: Jesus was meeting with his disciples right after they had returned from a journey where they healed and helped people. After they had reported what they had done, Jesus told them that they needed some rest. They went off in their boat to a quiet place so they could relax and get away from the crowds of people that followed Jesus everywhere he went. But the people were persistent. Thousands of them walked around the shoreline to the place where Jesus and his disciples docked their boat.

Disciple #1: I can't believe this. Where are they all coming from?

Disciple #2: So much for getting a little rest and relaxation.

Narrator: Jesus was quiet as he gazed out at all those faces. His eyes glistened a little, filling with tears. The disciples nearest him heard him murmur.

Jesus: They're like sheep wandering without a shepherd. There's no one guiding them or taking care of them.

Narrator: And right away, Jesus found a little hill to stand on, and he began to teach. He stood there for hours as the sun slid toward the western horizon.

Disciple #2: Jesus, we need to wrap this up and send everybody home. It's getting late, and they're getting hungry. And, if they're lucky, they'll be able to find food in some of the towns and villages they pass through on their way home, but they have to start before dark.

Jesus: I don't want to send them away hungry; I'm afraid that they'll collapse on the way. You should feed them.

Narrator: The disciples looked at him in disbelief. Finally, one of them spoke.

Disciple #3: But we're in the middle of nowhere. Even if we could come up with an enormous amount of money this minute, we'd still have to send a huge group to the nearest town and hope that their bakers had enough bread to feed everybody.

Narrator: The disciples laughed a little at that idea, but Jesus wasn't laughing.

Jesus: What food do we already have?

Narrator: He looked at them, eyebrows raised, and they looked back at him, speechless.

Jesus: Go find out how much bread we have.

Narrator: They split up and looked through the crowd for whatever food was on hand. They returned to Jesus feeling worse then ever.

Disciple #1: All we can come up with are five loaves of bread—and two fish.

Jesus: OK. Get everyone seated, in groups of 50 and 100.

Narrator: By now, the disciples were completely confused, but they did what they were told. While they were getting the people settled on the grass, Jesus held up the basket with its five loaves and two fish and said a blessing over it. Then he divided the loaves of bread and the fish into 12 baskets. He gave a basket to each disciple.

Jesus: Pass it out to all the people.

Narrator: The disciples walked up to the first groups of people, feeling very uncertain but also strangely excited. Jesus had never let them down. They began to move from one group to the next, giving the food to the people. As the people took the loaves of bread and the fish, the disciples reached back into their baskets and there was more food! The more they gave to the people, the more food they found in the baskets.

Disciple #2: Unbelievable! Glory to God!

Narrator: That day, Jesus fed 5,000 men and their families. When everyone was full, the disciples collected the food that had not been eaten. The leftovers filled all 12 baskets. †

The Man Born Blind *based on John 9:1–38*

Narrator: Jesus did good things wherever he went. Unfortunately, people didn't always like the way he did things or understand him. For instance, one day Jesus and his disciples met a man who had been born blind. The disciples couldn't understand how something as severe as blindness could happen to a good person.

Disciple: So what did he do to deserve being born blind? I mean, his parents must have sinned, right, and then God punished them by letting their baby be blind.

Narrator: Jesus responded right away.

Jesus: Your heavenly Father does not work that way. This blindness has nothing to do with sin. Sometimes it is through great difficulty that we discover God. This is an opportunity.

Narrator: Jesus spat on the ground and mixed his saliva with the dirt to make a muddy paste. Then he spread the mud on the man's eyes while everybody watched in shock.

Jesus: Brother, go wash that mud off in the pool over there.

Narrator: One of the disciples helped the man over to the pool, where he splashed water on his eyes to clean off the mud. He was surprised at what Jesus had just done to him. But when the mud was off, the man could see, just like that. Everyone turned to look when the man started whooping and hollering and dancing around. He ran up to people and grabbed them and looked into their faces, yelling, "I can see! I can see!" And people who were his neighbors and who knew his family tried to make sense of it.

Person #1: Isn't that the blind guy?

Person #2: Can't be. That guy isn't blind, but he does look like him.

Person #1: No, it's definitely him. What's going on?

Micah: It's really me. The teacher put mud on my eyes, told me to wash it off, and now I can see.

Narrator: This happened on the Sabbath, and the crowd took the man to their leaders at the synagogue and told the story. The leaders got upset.

Leader: What happened?

Micah: The teacher gave me my sight.

Leader: If he's healing on the Sabbath—which is against the law—then he's a sinner, not a miracle worker.

Micah: All I know is that I was blind before I met him, and I can certainly see now. He is a prophet.

Narrator: That made the leaders even more angry. They refused to believe that the man had been blind since birth. They called for his parents and began grilling them too.

Leader: Your son is telling quite a story. Was he ever truly blind?

Mother: Of course—he was born that way. We don't know what happened. But he can definitely see now. If you want to know the details, talk to him. He's a grown man and can speak for himself.

Narrator: The man's parents were on the defensive because they knew that Jesus was controversial, and they didn't want to be associated with him. If they disagreed with their leaders, they could be punished by being kicked out of the synagogue. So the leaders turned to the man again.

Leader: Remember that you speak with God as your witness. This man Jesus is a sinner, one who breaks our holy laws. Now tell us what really happened.

Micah: I don't know whether Jesus is a sinner or a holy man. I already told you what happened, but you refused to listen! All I can tell you is that today, for the first time in my life, I can see. And my sight came to me after Jesus spit in the dirt and put mud on my eyes. When I washed off the mud, I could see. You can figure out all the religious legal problems for yourselves. I know what I know. Now that you have seen what Jesus can do, perhaps you want to be one of his disciples too?

Narrator: His question made the leaders furious, and they threw him out of the synagogue. Jesus heard about it and went to talk with him privately.

Micah: Who are you? What is it that you have done to me that now I can see?

Jesus: Do you believe in the Son of Man, the one sent by God to save the world?

Micah: Who is he, sir? I want to believe in him.

Jesus: I am the one God sent to help you and the whole world.

Micah: Sir, I believe you. I really do.

Narrator: The man knelt down and worshipped Jesus. †

The Transfiguration *based on Matthew 17:1–9*

Narrator: After the enthusiastic days following Pentecost, Peter, James, and John finally took time to share some memories. The memory that was most on their mind was when they followed Jesus up a mountainside and experienced his divine glory.

James: We've been quiet about this for a long time, mainly because we didn't know what to think about it or what to do about it.

John: Jesus told us not to tell anybody, at least not then. But time has passed now, and what we've seen and heard might help people have more faith, now that Jesus has returned to the Father.

Peter: He is still with us, John—always, and in a more wonderful way than when everyone knew him as a teacher.

James: You're right about that, Peter. I'm still learning to think about Jesus in this new way—you know, seeing him as not just the teacher and miracle worker, but as the Lord. We'd get into a lot of trouble for calling him that, but we know it's true.

John: James, I think we all knew in our hearts that he was more than just a teacher, even before we went up that mountain with him.

James: I thought I knew it, but seeing what happened to him there lead me to believe at a whole new level.

Peter: Yeah, it did for all of us. That day, I thought it would be just another little retreat away from the crowds. It wasn't unusual for Jesus to take us off to a quiet place to rest and to pray or to talk about what was happening in our lives. But we climbed higher than usual, up to where the winds roar and could nearly blow us off the side of the mountain and into the valley below.

John: I was tired by the time we got to the top. I sort of collapsed, tried to catch my breath, and just sat there and looked out at the countryside.

James: I was digging around in our bags for something to eat. When Jesus' appearance began to change, I had a loaf of bread in my hands. It's unbelievable to think that while this divine thing was happening to my friend, I was worried about my stomach! Peter, you were standing right next to him.

Peter: At first I was just gazing across the rocky wilderness. Then I saw that he had become very calm and still. His eyes were closed and he seemed to be concentrating, the way he did sometimes when he was in prayer.

John: I know what you mean. He would get so focused and quiet. And his breathing would change a little. You saw it too, didn't you James?

James: All I know is that I looked up, and he was glowing. Glowing! Like an angel, or what I suppose an angel would look like. He got so bright I could barely see you, Peter.

Peter: To be honest, I wondered if my eyes were playing tricks on me. But then I saw the other two men standing there too. The two elders from another time, glowing beside him.

James: How did you know they were Moses and Elijah, Peter?

Peter: I didn't at first. But as they began to talk with Jesus, certain things they said stood out and reminded me of what I'd learned from the Scriptures.

John: I couldn't hear them that well from where I was standing. And I know this sounds strange, but I knew right away who they were. It was as if I was recognizing people I'd seen before. I just knew that I knew.

Peter: It was so overwhelming. The holiness in that place—all I could think was how we were in the presence of God's faithful servants, our forefathers, the ones who established our whole religion and way of life.

James: I wanted to run away. I mean, you don't just walk up to holiness and stand there—do you? When Peter suggested we build shelters for them, it seemed like the perfect thing to do.

John: And then that voice came and thundered over us, out of the cloud. "This is my Son, the Beloved; with him I am well pleased; listen to him!"

Peter: I may have passed out then—I don't remember the next few minutes.

James: I think we all did. The next thing I remember is that I was huddling on the ground with the two of you. The power of that voice. It seemed like it could have crushed us or could have burned us up in an instant.

John: But it was a gentle voice, even though it boomed. I can't think of that moment without breaking down. Our heavenly Father spoke to us. And Jesus walked over to us, helped us get up, and told us not to be afraid.

Peter: And Moses and Elijah were gone.

James: And that was that. Jesus told us not to say anything until after the Son of Man would be raised from the dead. I'm ashamed to say that even then I didn't understand what he meant by that—the raising from the dead part.

John: No worry, James, none of us understood until later.

Peter: But all of us believed, even without understanding. How can you not believe, deep down in your soul, when God has allowed you to hear his voice? †

On the Road to Emmaus *based on Luke 24:13–35*

Narrator: Just three days after Jesus died on the cross, two of his followers left Jerusalem and headed home to a town called Emmaus, about seven miles away. It was a long walk, but they had a lot on their minds. It helped to be able to talk as they walked, and they tried to make sense of what had happened.

Disciple #1: Just a few days ago we walked into Jerusalem in the middle of that wonderful parade, following Jesus as he entered the city.

Disciple #2: And now we're leaving, and who would have ever believed how much the situation would change?

Disciple #1: I still can't believe it—all that's happened, and in such a short time. I . . . I can't believe he's really gone.

Disciple #2: Well, if what the women said is true, he isn't really gone—is he?

Disciple #1: I don't know what to think of all that. Maybe in their grief they were hallucinating and thought they saw Jesus.

Disciple #2: But he said something about Resurrection, didn't he?

Disciple #1: I keep thinking that if only we had done something differently. If we had stuck closer to him, maybe things wouldn't have fallen apart the way they did.

Disciple #2: How could everyone turn on him like that? He was a good man, a holy man! I don't understand how everything got so mixed up.

Disciple #1: He was a holy man. No matter what they say about him now that he's gone, we know what we know. I heard his teaching for three years with my own ears.

Disciple #2: We saw for ourselves how he treated people. He was not a criminal.

Narrator: Just then, a man walked up beside them. He, too, was coming from the direction of Jerusalem.

Jesus: Hello.

Disciple #2: You startled us. We were talking so intensely, I guess we didn't notice you.

Jesus: Yes, I couldn't help but hear some of what you were saying. Both of you seem very upset.

Disciple #1: Well, who wouldn't be, given what's happened to our teacher, our friend, in the past few days?

Jesus: I'm afraid you'll have to fill me in.

Narrator: The two disciples stopped and stared at the man in disbelief.

Disciple #1: Are you the only person around here who doesn't know what's happened this week?

Jesus: And what is that?

Disciple #2: All the things that happened to Jesus of Nazareth—you know? The great teacher and holy man? He worked wonders and spoke like a prophet.

Disciple #1: The chief priests and rulers turned him over to the Romans, and the Romans sentenced him to death!

Disciple #2: They crucified him! And he hadn't done anything—not anything at all!

Narrator: The stranger walked with them quietly, listening.

Disciple #1: And we were so sure he was the promised one—the one who would bring peace and justice to Israel at last.

Disciple #2: Not only that, now there are strange rumors. He was buried three days ago, but some of the women from our group went to the tomb early this morning, and his body was gone. The women claim that angels appeared to them and told them Jesus is alive.

Disciple #1: So some others went to the tomb to check it out—and they were right: there was no body.

Narrator: Then they noticed a change in the man's features. He shook his head thoughtfully, his eyes still fastened upon them.

Jesus: How clueless can you be?

Disciple #1: Excuse me? Did you call us clueless?

Jesus: What does it take for you to get it? None of this should surprise you. The prophets have said from the beginning that the Messiah would suffer.

Disciple #2: I can't believe you! How could you be so heartless?

Disciple #1: Wait! Let's hear him out. Please . . . explain what you mean.

Narrator: So the stranger began with the stories of Moses and patiently explained how, through the Scriptures, the suffering of the Messiah was foretold. By then, they had come to the crossroad where the two disciples had to turn to go home. It looked as if the stranger was continuing on the main path.

Disciple #2: Please! We can't end the discussion here. And it's getting late. Come stay with us. Share our evening meal, and we can talk some more.

Narrator: So the stranger went with them to an inn. When the meal was prepared he offered to bless the food. He broke the bread and blessed it. And right then, in that moment, both of the disciples recognized the man as Jesus. They had no sooner recognized him that he vanished from their sight.

Disciple #1: I can't believe we didn't know it was him! We should have known the moment he began to talk with us.

Disciple #2: I felt it, deep down in my soul, when he explained the Scriptures—did you?

Disciple #1: Yes, it was like my heart was on fire. Like my whole body was responding to words that were totally true and right.

Narrator: This excited them so much that even though it was now dark, they walked all the way back to Jerusalem. They searched for and found the other disciples and told them all that had happened—and how they had recognized Jesus in the breaking of the bread. †

Paul Writes to Philemon *based on The Letter to Philemon*

Narrator: Philemon was a disciple of Jesus and a friend of the apostle Paul. But like many of Paul's friendships, the relationship relied mainly on letters because Paul traveled so much. Sometimes years would pass before he could see his friends in person again. In the case of Philemon, something else connected the two friends—Philemon's slave Onesimus.

Paul was in prison for teaching the Christian faith. One day, his cell door opened, and two men walked in. One was a leader from a local group of Christian believers. Whenever the believers could, they sent someone to the prison to take food and other necessities to Paul. Paul greeted the leader warmly and then turned to Onesimus, the young man with him.

Paul: Don't I know you from somewhere? What's your name, son?

Narrator: The young man looked embarrassed, but he cleared his throat and answered Paul, barely looking him in the eye.

Onesimus: I'm Onesimus, sir. We . . . you met me at the home of Philemon, in Colossae.

Narrator: Paul stared for a moment or two while he tried to pull together his memories. A look of realization slowly came to his face.

Paul: Yes . . . I do remember you. You are his servant, aren't you?

Narrator: Onesimus looked at the ground and struggled to answer.

Onesimus: I—I did work for him, yes. There was some trouble, and I left.

Paul: You left? But a slave doesn't just leave. A slave has to be dismissed by his master. Otherwise, he is a runaway.

Jared: When Onesimus first came to us, he was in a bad way. But when he heard the message of our Lord Jesus, about God's love for us, he went through an astounding change of heart. He wishes to learn more about Jesus the Christ. So I have brought him to you.

Narrator: Paul continued to study Onesimus, trying to decide how to approach this sensitive situation. By law, a runaway slave was a fugitive. But Onesimus wanted to know Jesus, and Paul didn't want to turn him away.

Jared: We have been discussing what Onesimus must do. Of course, Philemon must be notified that his servant has been found. We just . . . well, I'd hate to send away a person who is so new to the faith.

Paul: Onesimus, I'd like your help.

Onesimus: Yes. Of course, I'll do whatever you need. It's so unfair for you to be locked up like this. I'd like to help however I can. And I hope to learn from you—that is if you don't mind. There's so much to understand about this life with Jesus.

Paul: I think we can wait a little longer before sending you back home. Philemon is a true brother in Christ, and he will be more than happy for any of his servants to help me in my ministry.

Narrator: So Onesimus spent the next days and weeks helping the apostle Paul in whatever way he could. And his faith grew quickly. Paul discovered that the young man's heart was truly turned toward Jesus. He finally baptized him. But one day, Paul had a difficult discussion with Onesimus.

Paul: Son, I'm sending you back to Philemon in a few days.

Onesimus: I . . . I trust that you know what's best, and I'll go willingly.

Narrator: Paul could see the fear in the young man's face.

Paul: I'm writing a letter to your master. He is a good man, a true Christian and a friend of mine.

Onesimus: Yes sir, I know he's a good man. When I served him before, I was not such a good man.

Paul: But you are a new man now, aren't you? The old Onesimus is dead and gone, and now you are a new creation in Christ. Your name, Onesimus, means "useful." I will remind Philemon that you were useless to him in your former life. But now in your new life in Christ you can be useful to both your master and me.

Onesimus: Yes, sir. Unfortunately, I am still a runaway slave.

Paul: This is what I have written to Philemon: "I am sending him, that is, my own heart, back to you. I should have liked to retain him for myself, so that he might serve me on your behalf in my imprisonment for the gospel, but I did not want to do anything without your consent, so that the good you do might not be forced but voluntary. Perhaps this is why he was away from you for a while, that you might have him back forever, no longer as a slave but more than a slave, a brother, beloved especially to me, but even more so to you, as a man and in the Lord. So if you regard me as your partner, welcome him back as you would me. And if he has done you any injustice or owes you anything, charge it to me."

Onesimus: I can't thank you enough.

Paul: You belong to Jesus, Onesimus, and your life has moved far beyond being a slave or even a young man in this particular time and place.

Onesimus: I know now that God gives us the strength for everything we face. So I'm ready to face Philemon, and I trust he'll be ready to face me. †

Living in Relationship

Take a moment to get comfortable. Make sure there is enough space around you so you won't be distracted or disturb others. Close your eyes and turn your attention inward. *(Pause.)* Allow yourself to grow still. *(Pause.)*

Begin to focus on your breathing. Breathe slowly and deeply, in and out, in and out, slowly and steadily. As you breathe, let your body relax. Relax your arms, legs, neck, and shoulders. *(Pause.)*

Now imagine you are walking through your favorite park on a summer day. What, if anything, is happening at the park? Is it quiet or full of activity? As you walk, you notice two benches underneath a big tree. They look inviting in the shade, so you stop to sit on one of them. As you're sitting, you look around. What do you see? flowers? a lake? maybe a trail? *(Pause.)* You look up into the tree branches overhead and notice that the leaves make a pattern against the sky. *(Pause.)*

When you look down again, you notice the other bench is occupied. An old woman is there. You smile a pleasant acknowledgement to each other. As you look at the woman, you somehow know that she's had a full life in which she's given and received love. You wonder about this for a moment. *(Pause.)*

As you reflect, you hear the happy voices of people greeting one another. A group approaches the woman on the bench. A small girl runs forward, arms outstretched, and hugs the woman. A younger woman follows. As she steps closer, the older woman stands and embraces her. *(Pause.)* You can see from their faces that they are mother and daughter. As you continue to watch, an older man approaches. When he reaches the group he hugs his granddaughter, greets his daughter warmly, and kisses his wife of many, many years. *(Pause.)*

The four people sit together, enjoying one another's company. You see their affection for one another, but you also notice something deeper. Somehow you understand that these people belong together. *(Pause.)* You see the small child looking at her grandmother with a joy that comes from being loved. The daughter of the older woman watches her mother with an admiration and affection. *(Pause.)* When the older man looks at his wife you somehow know he's recalling their long life together. He's remembering this woman as his bride and the mother of his children. He smiles and he thinks about all these things. *(Pause.)* The granddaughter knows the woman in yet a different way—as someone who enjoys playing with her. This woman is different things to different people. *(Pause.)*

You think about this as you look away. How can someone be so many different things to different people and yet be totally herself? *(Pause.)* How is it for you? Do different people know *you* in different ways? *(Pause.)* Is there one thing about you that is unchanging that everyone can see in you? *(Pause.)*

HOW TO USE THE REFLECTION

A special approach to prayer in Unit 1, Session 1, is a recorded guided reflection "Living in Relationship" (CD 1, Track 1). Listen prayerfully to the recording before sharing the reflection with young people. Then when you play the recording during the session, join young people in reflective prayer.

Another option is to pray aloud, using the script of the reflection. Prepare to share the guided reflection with young people by listening to the recording beforehand. During the session, you may wish to use the script as is, or adapt it as you wish. When leading the reflection, play reflective music softly in the background to enhance the sense of prayerfulness.

SENSITIVITIES

Before praying the guided reflection with young people, consider

- their awareness of what it means to speak to God in their hearts.
- their experience with reflective prayer.
- the variety of family structures within the group.
- those with special needs.

HINTS

When leading the guided reflection yourself,

- establish eye contact and use appropriate volume.
- be aware of your voice quality, pacing, and the message.
- speak with expression.
- allow young people time to reflect by pausing where indicated throughout the reflection.
- gradually decrease the volume of the reflective music before turning off the CD.

REFLECTIVE RESPONSES

Help young people continue the reflection by examining their own responses to either the recording or the prayerful recitation of the script. Say: **Answer the following questions in the silence of your heart.** Ask: **How does it feel to know that God recognizes every hair on your head?** (Pause.) **How reassuring is it to know that his love for you is constant and unchanging?** (Pause.) **How can you strengthen your relationship with God?** Encourage young people to maintain a spirit of prayerfulness as they reflect on the questions.

As you think about these things, you hear footsteps and notice a young man approaching. *(Pause.)* You recognize him right away. It's Jesus. *(Pause.)* He asks if you'd like to walk with him awhile, so you leave your bench and go with him. *(Pause.)* You tell Jesus about the woman and her family. *(Pause.)* Jesus tells you how much he enjoys sharing in the love that people have for one another, just as you enjoyed watching the woman and her family. *(Pause.)* As he tells you this, you're aware of the love Jesus has for you. Take a moment to really absorb this. *(Pause.)*

Jesus asks you to share with him who is special to you. Who do you name? *(Pause.)* He then asks you to name the people who care about you. *(Pause.)* Spend some time with Jesus thinking about what it's like to know that you're loved by them. *(Pause.)* Jesus reminds you that he too knew what it was like to love and be loved.

Then Jesus asks if you feel you know his Father well. What do you say? *(Pause.)* As you're thinking, Jesus invites you to go with him to spend some time with his Father. You agree, and as you come into God's presence, you sense that you are known, accepted just as you are, and that you are loved. Let this feeling sink in for a few moments. *(Pause.)* Then share with God whatever is in your heart. And if no words come, God understands and knows what's in your heart. It's enough just to be with him. Allow yourself to just be still in his presence. *(Pause.)*

And now you begin to sense it's time to go. You take a moment to thank God for this time with him and then you let Jesus know that you're ready to go. *(Pause.)* You return to the park bench and sit down. You look across to the other bench and once more acknowledge the old woman. *(Pause.)*

Now take a moment to leave the park, bring your attention back to the here and now, and return to this room. *(Pause.)* When you're ready, open your eyes and stretch if you'd like. Look around and become aware of the others in the room. Be still and honor the prayer time you have just experienced. We're all back now. ✝

Called by Name

Take a moment and get comfortable. Make sure that you have enough space so that you won't be distracted or cause a distraction for others. *(Pause.)* Now close your eyes and let your thoughts turn inward. *(Pause.)* Allow yourself to let go of any inner chatter and to begin to grow still. *(Pause.)*

Now turn your attention to your breathing. Be aware of your breath as you inhale and exhale. Breathe fully and deeply. Let the air fill your lungs and then release it. *(Pause.)* Do this slowly, over and over. Inhale and exhale. *(Pause.)*

As you breathe, notice any places where there is tension in your body. Maybe it's your neck and shoulders or perhaps your jaw, arms, or legs. *(Pause.)* Wherever the tension is, feel your muscles begin to relax with each deep breath you take. *(Pause.)*

Now, imagine that you're offered the opportunity to take lessons in anything you want. What would you choose? Horseback riding? Singing? Parachuting? Moviemaking? Think about it for a moment. *(Pause.)* What about this activity excites you? *(Pause.)*

Now imagine yourself at the first class. The instructor asks you why you want to be here. What do you say? *(Pause.)* Then the instructor tells you that while you're in this class, you can choose whatever name you'd like to go by. The only rule is that you must choose a name that describes why you're in this class. What name do you choose? *(Pause.)* How does this name indicate what you dream of being able to do? *(Pause.)*

When the first class is over, you think about what you've already learned. You wonder how long it will take you to master the skills you're learning. You smile to yourself as you reflect on this. *(Pause.)* One of the other students in the class comes up to you and walks alongside you. He asks you what you're smiling at. You share with him what you've been thinking about. *(Pause.)* He smiles too and tells you that he also knows what the feeling of mastering a new skill is like. As you share this moment of understanding, you realize that you're talking to Jesus. *(Pause.)* It feels so natural for you to be talking together. You know that Jesus understands what you're thinking. *(Pause.)*

Now Jesus asks you a question: If you could call yourself by any name in your everyday life, what it would be? What name really describes who you are in your heart? *(Pause.)* Is it a conventional name like John or Emily? Or maybe a descriptive name like Storm or Diamond? Think about the name that describes your most authentic self. *(Pause.)* Share with Jesus why you chose this name. Explain to him what makes it the perfect description of who you know yourself to be. *(Pause.)*

Then Jesus asks you to think about what this name says about you as one of his disciples. Does your new name have anything to do with being a faithful, good, or holy person? *(Pause.)* Is there another name that would describe you better? *(Pause.)*

HOW TO USE THE REFLECTION

A special approach to prayer in Unit 2, Session 7, is a recorded guided reflection "Called by Name" (CD 2, Track 3). Listen prayerfully to the recording before sharing the reflection with young people. Then when you play the recording during the session, join young people in reflective prayer.

Another option is to pray aloud, using the script of the reflection. Prepare to share the guided reflection with young people by listening to the recording beforehand. During the session, you may use the script as is, or adapt it as you wish. When leading the reflection, play reflective music softly in the background to enhance the sense of prayerfulness.

SENSITIVITIES

Before praying the guided reflection with young people, consider

▶ their awareness of what it means to speak to God in their hearts.

▶ their experience with reflective prayer.

▶ those with special needs.

HINTS

When leading the guided reflection yourself,

▶ establish eye contact and use appropriate volume.

▶ be aware of your voice quality, pacing, and the message.

▶ speak with expression.

▶ allow young people time to reflect by pausing where indicated throughout the reflection.

▶ gradually decrease the volume of the reflective music before turning off the CD.

REFLECTIVE RESPONSES

Help young people continue the reflection by examining their own responses to either the recording or the prayerful recitation of the script. Say: **Answer the following questions in the silence of your heart.** Ask: **How do you feel when someone accepts you exactly the way you are?** (Pause.) **How can accepting everything about yourself lead you to closer discipleship?** (Pause.) **When have you known God's unconditional love for you?** Encourage young people to maintain a spirit of prayerfulness as they reflect on the questions.

Jesus asks you to think about how much your true self has to do with following him. (*Pause.*) You become more aware that being true to yourself as a follower of Jesus sometimes requires you to be different from the world around you. (*Pause.*) Sometimes it might seem that you're challenged to move out of your comfort zone in order to do what's right. You might have to make choices that are different from the ones your peers make or to stand up for others who are teased, ridiculed, or misunderstood. (*Pause.*)

And now Jesus asks you if you'd like to spend some time with the Father. You say yes and almost immediately, you become aware of his unconditional love for you. You understand that God knows your true self better than anyone and longs for you to know and accept yourself in the same way. (*Pause.*) Sit quietly with God and absorb his love for you. Feel the comfort of knowing he accepts you deeply and totally. (*Pause.*)

Gradually you begin to sense that it's time to leave. If some of this is new for you, you might want to spend more time thinking about it. Jesus reminds you that you can always return to spend time with the Father and that his love is always there for you, especially when life gets confusing. (*Pause.*)

As you leave to walk with Jesus back to the lunchroom, you feel grateful for this time with Jesus and the Father. Thank Jesus for being with you and for leading you to the Father. (*Pause.*) Ask him to help you remember your new name and what it says about you, especially when things get tough. (*Pause.*)

When you are ready, bring your attention back to the present and return to this room. (*Pause.*) Open your eyes and stretch if you'd like. (*Pause.*) Look around and become aware of the others in the room. We're all back now. ✝

Paying the Price

Make yourself comfortable and take a moment to look around. Silently acknowledge with a nod or a smile those who are sitting near you. Now close your eyes and turn your thoughts inward. Free yourself of the day's concerns and focus on your breathing. *(Pause.)* Breathe deeply, in and out, in and out. Let go of the tension in your muscles. Feel the tightness leave your body. Relax. Continue breathing slowly, in and out, in and out. *(Pause.)*

Now picture yourself, walking down the hallway at school with a group of friends. Because it's nearly noon, you're headed for the lunchroom. It's been a long morning and a long time since breakfast, and you're getting really hungry. *(Pause.)*

During a lull in the conversation, someone shares a tidbit of gossip— something about one of your friends, something that shouldn't have been shared. Some in your group are shocked. Others are troubled. Still others are enjoying the gossip. How do you feel? *(Pause.)* Think for a moment about the people and activities that have been gossiped about in your school before. What are the things that make people talk? *(Pause.)* Think about the damage that's done to the people talked about. . . to the people gossiping. *(Pause.)*

You know that if this bit of gossip is true, then your friend is in trouble. You also know how scared and lonely you would feel if your friends were talking and laughing about you, especially if no one stuck up for you. *(Pause.)*

You know that what's being rumored is out of character for your friend. The more you think about it, the more you realize it can't be true. Your friend was with you when it was supposed to be happening. You feel the need to set the record straight. *(Pause.)*

By this time you've all reached the lunchroom and are settled at a table. As everyone is giggling and making fun of your friend, you say, "I know that what you're saying isn't true." At first no one listens to you, so you say again, "I know that what you're saying isn't true."

Now everyone is silent, looking at you, staring. How does that make you feel? *(Pause.)* You try to explain yourself, to defend your friend, to stop the gossiping. *(Pause.)* Some in the group say they don't believe you, that if you were with your friend, then you must be guilty of doing the same thing. How do you react to that? Do you feel angry, maybe a bit confused? *(Pause.)* You even try to make a joke about your innocence. Everyone's staring makes you uncomfortable and you just want to get away, so you give them a credible excuse and leave. *(Pause.)*

As you move toward the lunchroom door, you notice someone alone at another table smiling at you. He speaks your name, so you stop. As your eyes meet, you immediately know that it's Jesus. You sit at the table with him, feeling great relief and acceptance. *(Pause.)* Somehow you know that Jesus wants to know why you're leaving, what just happened with you and

HOW TO USE THE REFLECTION

A special approach to prayer in Unit 3, Session 13, is a recorded guided reflection "Paying the Price" (CD 1, Track 5). Listen prayerfully to the recording before sharing the reflection with young people. Then when you play the recording during the session, join young people in reflective prayer.

Another option is to pray aloud, using the script of the reflection. Prepare to share the guided reflection with young people by listening to the recording beforehand. During the session, you may use the script as is, or adapt it as you wish. When leading the reflection, play reflective music softly in the background to enhance the sense of prayerfulness.

SENSITIVITIES

Before praying the guided reflection with young people, consider

- their awareness of what it means to speak to God in their hearts.
- their experience with reflective prayer.
- those with special needs.
- those who may have been harmed by gossip.

HINTS

When leading the guided reflection yourself,

- establish eye contact and use appropriate volume.
- be aware of your voice quality, pacing, and the message.
- speak with expression.
- allow young people time to reflect by pausing where indicated throughout the reflection.
- gradually decrease the volume of the reflective music before turning off the CD.

REFLECTIVE RESPONSES

Help young people continue the reflection by examining their own responses to either the recording or the prayerful recitation of the script. Say: **Answer the following questions in the silence of your heart.** Ask: **How have you responded to suffering in your life?** (Pause.) **When have you been silent instead of speaking up for what is right?** (Pause.) **How can you develop courage to make good choices?** Encourage young people to maintain a spirit of prayerfulness as they reflect on the questions.

your friends. Talk with Jesus for a few moments, telling him what you think about gossip, what you fear about rumors, and how hard it is to stand up for what you value. *(Pause.)*

Jesus listens and you know that he understands your fear. *(Pause.)* But you wonder, how can this be? What could Jesus know about being ridiculed or made fun of? *(Pause.)* And then you remember. How could you forget? In his time of suffering, Jesus was abandoned by his own apostles. He prayed alone in the garden and hung alone on the Cross. *(Pause.)*

Jesus reminds you that you live in an imperfect world, that suffering is a part of life. You know that, but you need to think about it for a while. Take the time now. *(Pause.)* Think about how gossip, whether true or not true, can cause suffering. *(Pause.)* Have there ever been times when you suffered innocently . . . or when you were the cause of someone else's suffering? *(Pause.)*

Jesus wants you to know that while we can't always control when or how we suffer, we can always control how we respond to suffering. You can tell he wants to know what you think. *(Pause.)* Are you sometimes afraid to do what you know is right? afraid of what your friends might think? *(Pause.)* Do you struggle with the choices you have to make? *(Pause.)* Talk with Jesus about these things. It's all right if you don't have the words to say what you want. Jesus knows what you think and feel. Open your heart to him. *(Pause.)*

Jesus invites you to go with him to God the Father. You get up and follow him out of the lunchroom. As you walk, Jesus reminds you that the Father created all people with hearts that long for love and goodness, that even though we make mistakes or wrong choices, the Father loves us beyond imagining. You go with Jesus to the Father. *(Pause.)*

In God's presence, you feel complete understanding, compassion, and total acceptance. Let your worries and fears rest with God for a while; nothing is too much for him. You smile as you think about this. You know it's true, but you so often forget. Now just take time to enjoy being with God. No more words are needed. *(Pause.)*

Sensing it's time to go, you thank the Father for his loving presence and understanding, and you look over at Jesus. He's waiting and walks you back to the table in the lunchroom where you sat with him. *(Pause.)* He reminds you that he calls blessed all those who suffer and all those who work to end suffering. You really don't want to suffer, but you know that doing what is right comes with a cost, just as making wrong choices does. *(Pause.)* Tell Jesus how much you appreciate the time you spent together and arrange to meet with him again. *(Pause.)* As you say goodbye to Jesus, he reminds you that he has faith in you and he loves you always.

It's time to return to class, so you walk slowly and thoughtfully from the lunchroom to your next class. You know that you will still have to deal with difficulties, but you also know that Jesus is always with you to help you. *(Pause.)*

Now slowly bring yourself back to this room. *(Pause.)* Once again become conscious of your breathing. *(Pause.)* When you are ready, open your eyes. Look around. *(Pause.)* Stretch if you'd like. *(Pause.)* Welcome back. ✝

Face to Face

Make yourself comfortable, sit in a way that helps you relax. Notice who you're sitting next to. Silently acknowledge their presence, and then close your eyes and turn your focus inward. *(Pause.)* Turn all your thoughts, cares, and distractions over to God and let them go. *(Pause.)*

Become aware of your breathing. Feel your breath as it flows in and out. Breathe slowly and deeply, in and out, in and out. Breathe from the deepest part of yourself. *(Pause.)* Notice your muscles beginning to relax. As you relax, place your hands comfortably with your palms facing upward, ready to receive God's blessings. *(Pause.)*

Imagine now that you are standing in front of a full-length mirror. You're alone, and you spend some time looking closely at your reflection. *(Pause.)* What are the first things you notice? your clothes? your face? your posture? *(Pause.)*

Now take a moment to look even more closely. What does the expression on your face reveal about your thoughts? *(Pause.)* What does your posture tell others about your spirit? *(Pause.)* As you look more closely at your reflection in the mirror, does it reveal more about yourself than your appearance? Think about this for a while. *(Pause.)* We know that we are creatures of body, mind, and spirit, but how are we certain? How do you become aware of yourself as more than just a physical being? *(Pause.)*

As you continue looking in the mirror, hold your hands up to it and examine them closely. Can you see the veins carrying blood to your fingers? Look closely and see the swirl of your unique fingerprints, the structure of your bones, and the width of your knuckles. *(Pause.)* Are your hands the calloused hands of a worker? or maybe the long, slender hands of a musician? What do your hands tell you about yourself? *(Pause.)*

As you look at your hands, you sense that someone is walking up behind you and your eyes move from your hand to the face that is reflected in the mirror. The face you see is the face of Jesus. You smile and greet Jesus by name. *(Pause.)* He smiles back as he says your name. You look into his eyes, and it seems as if he can see into your heart. What is it that helps you to know who he is? *(Pause.)*

Then Jesus asks you to tell him about the things that you think make you who you are. What do you say? *(Pause.)* How much of who you are is about your appearance? *(Pause.)* How much of who you are is about how you think, what you feel, how you show love and concern for others? *(Pause.)* You may want to ask his help to get to know yourself as you really are. And if you can't find the words, it's OK, Jesus knows what you're thinking. Just be open to what Jesus wants you to know. *(Pause.)*

Then Jesus reminds you that while he was here on earth, he taught us about his Father. He invites you to spend some time now with the Father. *(Pause.)* As you come into God's presence, you are flooded with a sense of being loved unconditionally. *(Pause.)* Spend some time resting in God's presence. Enjoy letting your true self be known and loved by God, who created you. *(Pause.)*

HOW TO USE THE REFLECTION

A special approach to prayer in Unit 4, Session 18, is a recorded guided reflection "Face to Face" (CD 1, Track 3). Listen prayerfully to the recording before sharing the reflection with young people. Then when you play the recording during the session, join young people in reflective prayer.

Another option is to pray aloud, using the script of the reflection. Prepare to share the guided reflection with young people by listening to the recording beforehand. During the session, you may use the script as is, or adapt it as you wish. When leading the reflection, play reflective music softly in the background to enhance the sense of prayerfulness.

SENSITIVITIES

Before praying the guided reflection with young people, consider

▶ their awareness of what it means to speak to God in their hearts.

▶ their experience with reflective prayer.

▶ those with special needs.

▶ the group's attitudes and values concerning personal appearance.

HINTS

When leading the guided reflection yourself,

▶ establish eye contact and use appropriate volume.

▶ be aware of your voice quality, pacing, and the message.

▶ speak with expression.

▶ allow young people time to reflect by pausing where indicated throughout the reflection.

▶ gradually decrease the volume of the reflective music before turning off the CD.

REFLECTIVE RESPONSES

Help young people continue the reflection by examining their own responses to either the recording or the prayerful recitation of the script. Say: **Answer the following questions in the silence of your heart.** Ask: **What can you tell about a person by his or her appearance?** (Pause.) **When can appearances get in the way of knowing your true self?** (Pause.) **When can appearances get in the way of knowing others? How would you describe who you really are?** Encourage young people to maintain a spirit of prayerfulness as they reflect on the questions.

You begin to be aware that it'll soon be time to return your attention to this room; so as you're ready, prepare to leave God's presence. *(Pause.)* Thank him for all his gifts to you, especially the gift of his only Son, Jesus. Sense his love deep within you as you and Jesus leave. *(Pause.)*

Now you and Jesus walk together back toward the mirror. *(Pause.)* As you approach, you again look closely at the reflection of your face. You take a moment to see yourself as God sees you. *(Pause.)*

Now it's time to go. Thank Jesus for this time together and for bringing you to the Father. *(Pause.)*

Slowly bring your attention back to this room. *(Pause.)* When you're ready, open your eyes and stretch. *(Pause.)* Look around and become aware of the others in the room. We're all back now. †

God's Dream for Us

Relax so that you can be attentive to prayer. Take a moment to get comfortable and settle in. Let go of any tension in your arms and legs, your neck and shoulders. *(Pause.)* Set aside for the moment the events and distractions of your day, and then let any concerns or plans just drift off. *(Pause.)*

Close your eyes and begin to focus on your breathing. *(Pause.)* Breathe slowly and deeply, in and out. *(Pause.)* Inhale deeply, then slowly breathe out. Continue this pattern of breathing slowly and deeply. *(Pause.)* Notice the tension leaving your body and allowing you to become more relaxed. *(Pause.)*

Now imagine that you are sitting in the most beautiful church you've ever seen. *(Pause.)* You look around in wonder. What do you see? Are there stained-glass windows with vivid colors? Perhaps there are candles burning in various places. *(Pause.)* Can you detect the fragrance of incense? What kind of artwork is here? Do you see the tabernacle? Spend some time looking around at everything in this beautiful church. *(Pause.)*

As you look around, someone begins to play the organ. The music is beautiful, and you feel it deep inside. *(Pause.)* You stop and absorb the beauty of the music and the place. *(Pause.)* As you relax, you begin to think about the job or career you'd like to have when you've finished school. Since anything is possible in your imagination and in your dreams, you imagine that for this moment in time you've already become what you always wished you would be. What did you choose? *(Pause.)* What is it that makes your chosen career special to you? What is it about this choice that fills you with hope? Think about it for a while. *(Pause.)*

Now you become aware of someone sitting with you. You realize that Jesus has been observing you. *(Pause.)* You look at Jesus' face. He looks at you with loving understanding in his eyes. *(Pause.)* Jesus asks you to share the dream you have for yourself. He wants to know all about it. Take some time to share with Jesus. *(Pause.)*

Now Jesus asks you to think about something else. What dreams might God have for you? *(Pause.)* What might God see in you, and what might God hope for you? *(Pause.)* Do you wonder if God's hopes and dreams for you are the same as yours? Spend some time talking with Jesus about this. *(Pause.)*

Jesus reminds you that God has a dream for each of us. God's dream for us involves serving the Kingdom of God. When you serve the Kingdom of God, you use your natural gifts and talents to help make the world a better place, a place where life is respected, the poor are cared for, the sick are healed. Think about this for a moment. Is there room for this kind of service in the life you are dreaming of? *(Pause.)*

Jesus knows that you can't do the hard things alone. He reminds you that the Holy Spirit is always with you to encourage and strengthen you. Sit quietly for a while and let this truth sink in. *(Pause.)* Think about how

HOW TO USE THE REFLECTION

A special approach to prayer in Unit 5, Session 22, is a recorded guided reflection "God's Dream for Us" (CD 2, Track 1). Listen prayerfully to the recording before sharing the reflection with young people. Then when you play the recording during the session, join young people in reflective prayer.

Another option is to pray aloud, using the script of the reflection. Prepare to share the guided reflection with young people by listening to the recording beforehand. During the session, you may use the script as is, or adapt it as you wish. When leading the reflection, play reflective music softly in the background to enhance the sense of prayerfulness.

SENSITIVITIES

Before praying the guided reflection with young people, consider

▶ their awareness of what it means to speak to God in their hearts.

▶ their experience with reflective prayer.

▶ those with special needs.

HINTS

When leading the guided reflection yourself,

▶ establish eye contact and use appropriate volume.

▶ be aware of your voice quality, pacing, and the message.

▶ speak with expression.

▶ allow young people time to reflect by pausing where indicated throughout the reflection.

▶ gradually decrease the volume of the reflective music before turning off the CD.

REFLECTIVE RESPONSES

Help young people continue the reflection by examining their own responses to either the recording or the prayerful recitation of the script. Say: **Answer the following questions in the silence of your heart.** Ask: **What are your hopes and dreams for the future?** *(Pause.)* **How can you tell if God's hopes and dreams for you are the same?** *(Pause.)* **What are some ways that you can use your gifts and talents to benefit others?** Encourage young people to maintain a spirit of prayerfulness as they reflect on the questions.

you might be called to make the world a better place with the Spirit's help. *(Pause.)* Share with Jesus what you think you can do to continue the work he began on earth. Would this be part of your dream for yourself, for your future? *(Pause.)* Perhaps you've never thought about it much before. You wonder. *(Pause.)*

As you reflect on this, Jesus invites you to spend time with God the Father. You accompany Jesus into his presence. Instantly you sense the love and concern he has for you. *(Pause.)* You feel completely known and accepted. *(Pause.)* Take some time to enjoy the feeling of knowing that God loves you. *(Pause.)*

After a while, Jesus reminds you that your time with him and the Father is drawing to an end. *(Pause.)* You know that you can always spend more time with God. You can think more about your hopes and dreams and how you might work together with Jesus to make them come true. He tells you that you can call on him whenever you want. *(Pause.)*

Look once more around the church and listen to the beautiful music. As you prepare to leave, you feel the stirring of a breeze. The breeze seems to be pulling you forward, and you're ready to go. *(Pause.)*

Now take a moment to leave the church and bring your attention back to this room. *(Pause.)* Open your eyes and stretch if you'd like. Look around and become aware of the others in the room, honoring the silence and the prayer experience you've shared together. *(Pause.)* We're all back now. ✝

Blackline Masters

Reproducible blackline masters appear in this section.

- **Session BLMs**
- **Unit Assessment BLMs**
- **Seasonal BLMs**
- **Answer Key**
- **Catechist Guide Acknowledgments**

These BLMs, Session Assessment BLMs, and answers can be accessed at www.findinggod.com.

Name _____   Date _____

Nature Sketches

God's gift of creation is a constant reminder of his bountiful love and care. Slow yourself down and witness nature with a renewed sense of awe and appreciation during your nature hike.

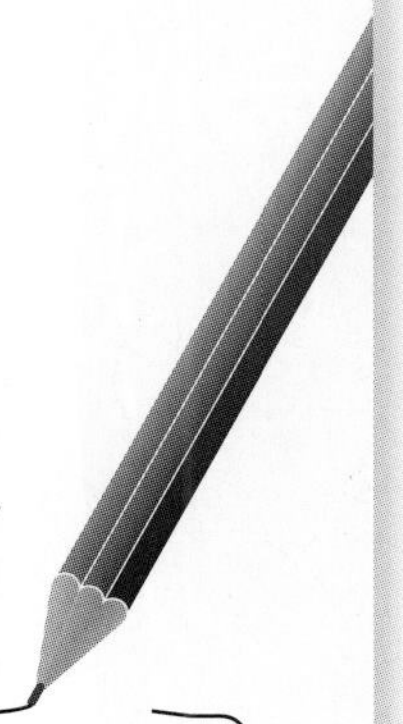

Directions: Use the space below to sketch items in nature that you find beautiful. Be prepared to share your sketches and reasons why you chose each item.

© LOYOLAPRESS.

Jupiterimages

Name _____   Date _____

Mark the Evangelist—The Lion

Each of the four Evangelists—Matthew, Mark, Luke, and John—is represented by an animal that symbolizes his Gospel style. Mark is represented by a lion, a symbol of strength and courage. Mark's Gospel begins with John the Baptist proclaiming Jesus as "one mightier than I."

Directions: Look up the following passages from the Gospel of Mark that depict Jesus acting and speaking with strength and courage.

1:17 "Come after me, and I will ___ ___ ___ ___ you fishers of men."

1:15 "Repent, and ___ ___ ___ ___ ___ ___ in the gospel."

2:17 "I did not come to call the ___ ___ ___ ___ ___ ___ ___ but sinners."

4:9 He added, "___ ___ ___ ___ ___ ___ has ears to hear ought to hear."

5:34 He said to her, "___ ___ ___ ___ ___ ___ ___, your faith has saved you. Go in peace and be cured of your affliction."

2:11 He said to the ___ ___ ___ ___ ___ ___ ___ ___, "I say to you, rise, pick up your mat, and go home."

10:25 "It is easier for a ___ ___ ___ ___ to pass through [the] eye of [a] needle than for one who is rich to enter the kingdom of God."

1:34 He cured many who were ___ ___ ___ with various diseases, and he drove out many demons.

8:34 "Whoever wishes to ___ ___ ___ after me must deny himself, take up his cross, and follow me."

4:39 He woke up, rebuked the ___ ___ ___, and said to the sea, "Quiet! Be still!"

What do the circled letters spell out?

_____

_____

Which of these passages speaks to you the most about courage? Why?

_____

_____

_____

Grade 7 • Unit 1 • Session 2

Name _____   Date _____

Grand Genes

Genealogy is very important in Matthew's Gospel. Matthew uses Jesus' genealogy to show a largely Jewish Christian audience that Jesus fulfills God's promise to send his people a Messiah, or Savior.

Directions: Use your Bible to locate the Scripture passage in which the promise is made and write out the verse(s) in the center column. Then do the same for the passages in the right column. These passages identify some of Jesus' ancestors and show how God fulfilled the promises he made in the Old Testament.

Person	Promise	Fulfillment
Abraham	Genesis 22:18	Matthew 1:1
Judah	Micah 5:1	Matthew 1:2
Jesse	Isaiah 11:1	Matthew 1:6
David	2 Samuel 7:12	Matthew 1:1

Answers: For complete answers, see page T-397.   **T-351**

Name _____   Date _____

Cardinal Virtues

We have an ongoing need for God's intervention. Virtues are gifts from God. They are like good habits that need to be practiced. The three most important virtues are faith, hope, and charity, called the Theological Virtues. We need actual grace in daily life because of our human weakness and sin. We use this grace as help to practice the Cardinal Virtues, which are human virtues we acquire by making decisions and repeating actions that are moral and good.

Directions: Write the letter of the description that best matches each of the Cardinal Virtues.

_____ **prudence**   _____ **justice**   _____ **fortitude**   _____ **temperance**

A. gives us courage to do the right thing despite difficulty, fear, or temptation

B. helps us control our desire to own or take pleasure in earthly goods

C. guides us to give to God and others what is due them

D. guides recognition of the true good in each circumstance and the choice of the right means to achieve that good

- -

Directions: Write a brief example of each Cardinal Virtue on separate note cards. Identify the virtue on the back. Working in small groups, shuffle all the cards, leaving the example sides faceup. Take turns reading a card and identifying the virtue, giving one point for each correct answer. An example card is done for you.

As stewards of God's creation, we should simplify our lifestyles in order to conserve energy, reduce pollution, and lessen our carbon footprint.

PRUDENCE

© Loyola Press.   www.findinggod.com   Grade 7 • Unit 1 • Session 4

T-352   **Answers:** prudence–D, justice–C, fortitude–A, temperance–B. Note cards will vary.

istockphoto.com/blue67

Name _____ Date _____

Saint Thérèse of Lisieux

Think about what you read about Saint Thérèse of Lisieux, her discipleship, and ours.

Directions: Choose a statement from the idea bank. Write a paragraph that explains why you agree or disagree with it. You can use Scripture, ideas from the article, your own experience or ideas, or facts gathered from research to support your argument.

> Love of God and others is a worthy vocation.
>
> Making small sacrifices is an ineffective way to practice your faith.
>
> Saints can help us learn how to be a disciple of Jesus Christ.
>
> Writing an autobiography is the best way for Saint Thérèse to praise God.

_____

_____

_____

_____

_____

_____

_____

_____

_____

_____

_____

_____

_____

_____

Yoshi Miyake

Answers will vary.

Name _____ Date _____

Unit 1 Assessment

A. Circle the letter of the choice that best completes each sentence.

1. Beliefs and practices of the Church that were given to us by Jesus and passed down by the Apostles are
   a. Original Sin.
   b. Tradition.
   c. Gospels.
   d. Trinity.

2. For Saint Augustine, a child who was emptying the sea with a seashell prompted his moment of faith about the
   a. Mysteries of the Rosary.
   b. meaning of a sacramental.
   c. mystery of the Holy Trinity.
   d. symbol of a clover.

3. The Gospel of Matthew begins with a genealogy, which is a
   a. message from the prophets.
   b. story about King David.
   c. promise to Abraham.
   d. listing of ancestors.

4. One of the Corporal Works of Mercy is to
   a. shelter the homeless.
   b. console a friend.
   c. instruct someone.
   d. forgive a sibling.

5. Jesus' command to the Apostles to spread the Good News to all people is his
   a. Ordinary Time.
   b. convocation.
   c. liturgical calendar.
   d. Great Commission.

6. A basic principle of Catholic Social Teaching that allows people to reach their full potential is called
   a. catholic.
   b. common good.
   c. covenant.
   d. free will.

7. God revealed himself by sending his own Son to establish the
   a. canon of the Bible.
   b. Catholic Social Teachings.
   c. New Covenant.
   d. Spiritual Works of Mercy.

8. Grace that helps us make choices to live as God wants us to live is called
   a. sanctifying grace.
   b. actual grace.
   c. habitual grace.
   d. covenant grace.

9. The four Gospels in the New Testament are
   a. Moses, Abraham, Isaac, and Jacob.
   b. James, Peter, John, and Jude.
   c. Matthew, Mark, James, and Peter.
   d. Matthew, Mark, Luke, and John.

10. The name *Jesus* means
    a. "my son."
    b. "anointed one."
    c. "God saves."
    d. "New Covenant."

T-354 Answers: **1.** b; **2.** c; **3.** d; **4.** a; **5.** d; **6.** b; **7.** c; **8.** b; **9.** d; **10.** c

Name _____ Date _____

Unit 1 Assessment

B. Write the word or words that best complete each sentence.

11. The most powerful mystery of our Christian faith is the _____.

12. A person who has accepted Jesus' message and tries to live as he did, sharing his mission, his suffering, and his joys is a _____.

13. Baptism frees us from _____, which is the consequence of Adam and Eve's disobedience when human beings lost God's blessing.

14. When we pray the Hail Mary, we are asking for Mary's _____.

15. The Old Testament tells how God revealed himself through the _____, who are the descendants of Abraham, Isaac, and Jacob.

16. We celebrate the lives of the _____ because they are examples of how to respond to Jesus' call.

17. The teachings of the Church that guide us in ways to build a just society and live holy lives in a modern world are called _____.

18. The angel Gabriel's announcement to Mary that she was chosen to become Jesus' mother is called the _____.

19. A _____ is a solemn agreement between God and his people.

20. The word *Gospel* means _____.

21. Jesus began his public life on the banks of the Jordan River when John _____ him.

22. God's _____, communicated to us throughout the ages, shows us the mystery of his plan for our Salvation.

23. The _____ proclaims that Mary was free of Original Sin from the moment of her conception.

24. A gift from God called _____ helps us believe in him.

25. Bearing wrongs patiently is one of the _____ Works of Mercy.

©LOYOLAPRESS.

Answers: 11. Trinity; **12.** disciple; **13.** Original Sin; **14.** intercession; **15.** Israelites; **16.** saints; **17.** Catholic Social Teaching; **18.** Annunciation; **19.** covenant; **20.** "good news"; **21.** baptized; **22.** Revelation; **23.** Immaculate Conception; **24.** faith; **25.** Spiritual

Name _____ Date _____

Unit 1 Assessment

Show What You Know

C. Describe each Person of the Holy Trinity. How does the Trinity strengthen our faith?

_____

_____

_____

_____

_____

_____

_____

_____

_____

_____

_____

_____

_____

_____

_____

_____

_____

_____

Beliefs and Attitudes

D. As Catholics, we are on a faith journey. Where are you on the path to discover the one true faith? Where do you feel you still need to go? How have you been challenged along the way? What has brought you joy and happiness? Describe your faith journey in three to six paragraphs on a separate sheet of paper.

www.findinggod.com   Grade 7 • Unit 1 Assessment • page 3 of 3

© LOYOLAPRESS.

T-356   All BLMs and possible answers can be found at www.findinggod.com.

Name _____ Date _____

John the Evangelist—The Eagle

John's Gospel is represented by an eagle because of the soaring and lofty style he uses to describe Jesus. The Prologue reminds us that Jesus became one of us.

> And the Word became flesh
>   and made his dwelling among us, . . .
>
>   *John 1:14*

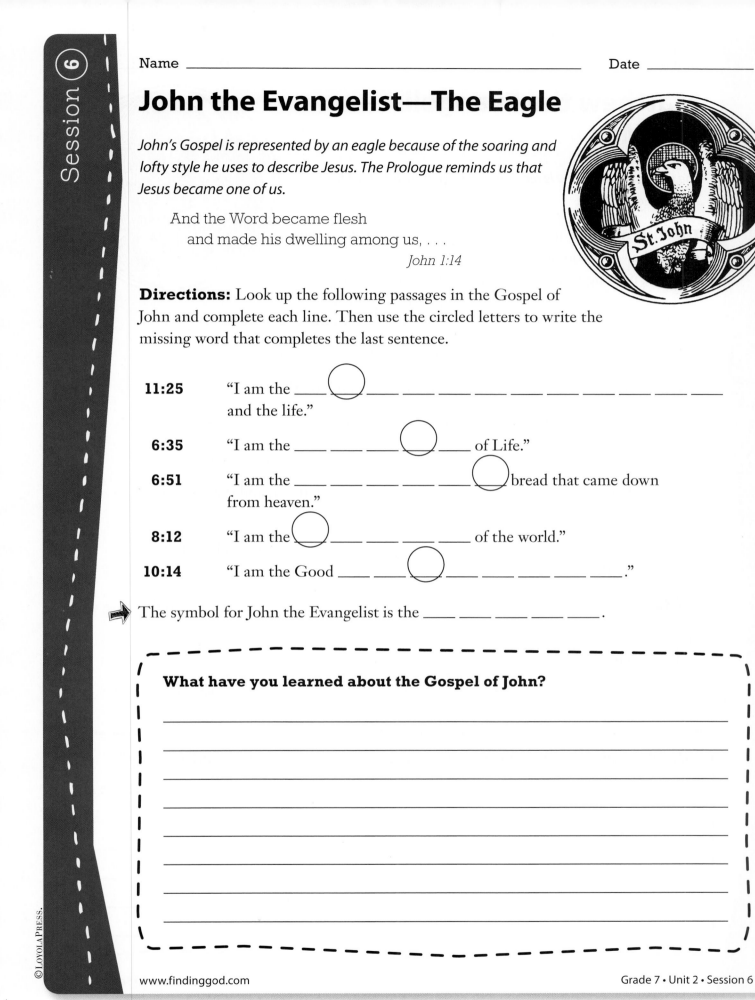

Directions: Look up the following passages in the Gospel of John and complete each line. Then use the circled letters to write the missing word that completes the last sentence.

11:25   "I am the ___ ⃝ ___ ___ ___ ___ ___ ___ ___ ___ ___ ___ ___ ___ and the life."

6:35   "I am the ___ ___ ___ ⃝ ___ of Life."

6:51   "I am the ___ ___ ___ ___ ___ ⃝ bread that came down from heaven."

8:12   "I am the ⃝ ___ ___ ___ ___ of the world."

10:14   "I am the Good ___ ___ ⃝ ___ ___ ___ ___ ___ ."

→ The symbol for John the Evangelist is the ___ ___ ___ ___ ___ .

What have you learned about the Gospel of John?

_____

_____

_____

_____

_____

_____

_____

_____

www.findinggod.com

Grade 7 • Unit 2 • Session 6

Name _____ Date _____

Matthew the Evangelist— The Man

The Gospel of Matthew is represented by a man. It tells us that Jesus is God with us.

Directions: Look up the following passages in the Gospel of Matthew and complete each line. Use the circled letters to spell the missing word that completes the last sentence.

1:18 Now this is how the birth of ____◯____ ___ ___ Christ came about.

20:34 ___◯___ ___ ___ ___ with pity, Jesus touched their eyes.

14:25 He ___ ___◯___ toward them, walking on the sea.

4:2 He fasted for forty days and forty nights, and ___◯___ ___ ___ ___ ___ ___ ___ ___ he was hungry.

8:15 He touched her ___ ___◯___, the fever left her, and she rose and waited on him.

8:26 Then he got up, ___ ___ ___ ___◯___ ___ the winds and the sea, and there was great calm.

13:55 "Is he not the ___ ___ ___ ___◯___ ___ ___ ___' ___ son?"

17:2 His face shone ___◯___ ___ ___ the sun and his clothes became white as light.

➤ Jesus is called ___ ___ ___ ___ ___ ___ ___, which means, "God with us."

Which passage do you believe best demonstrates Jesus' humanity? Why?

_____

_____

_____

_____

_____

Name _____   Date _____

Luke the Evangelist—The Ox

Luke's Gospel is represented by an ox because it begins with Zechariah offering a sacrifice in the Temple. The ox represents Jesus, the ultimate sacrifice for our sins. In Jesus' time wealthy people owned oxen. Oxen were considered precious animals for sacrifice since the goal of sacrifice was to give back to God your very best.

Directions: Look up the following passages in the Gospel of Luke and complete each line. Use the circled letters to write the missing word that completes the last sentence.

9:48 "For the one who is ___ ___ ___◯___ among all of you is the one who is the greatest."

8:54 But he took her by the ___◯___ ___ and called to her, "Child, arise!"

15:23–24 "Then let us◯___ ___ ___ ___ ___ ___ ___ ___ with a feast, because this son of mine was dead, and has come to life again; he was lost, and has been found."

7:50 But he said to the woman, "___ ___ ___◯faith has saved you; go in peace."

10:33 But a ___ ___ ___ ___ ___◯___ ___ ___ traveler who came upon him was moved with compassion at the sight.

6:32 "For ___◯you love those who love you, what credit is that to you?"

18:16 "Let the ___ ___ ___◯___ ___ ___ ___ ___ come to me and do not prevent them; for the kingdom of God belongs to such as these."

19:5 When he ___ ___ ___◯___ ___ ___ the place, Jesus looked up and said to him, "Zacchaeus, come down quickly, for today I must stay at your house."

4:19 "The Spirit of the Lord is upon ___◯___, because he has anointed me to bring glad tidings to the poor."

➡ Jesus is the ultimate ___ ___ ___ ___ ___ ___ ___ ___ for our sins.

Which passage is most meaningful to you? Why?

_____

_____

© Loyola Press.

Name _____ Date _____

Big Dreams

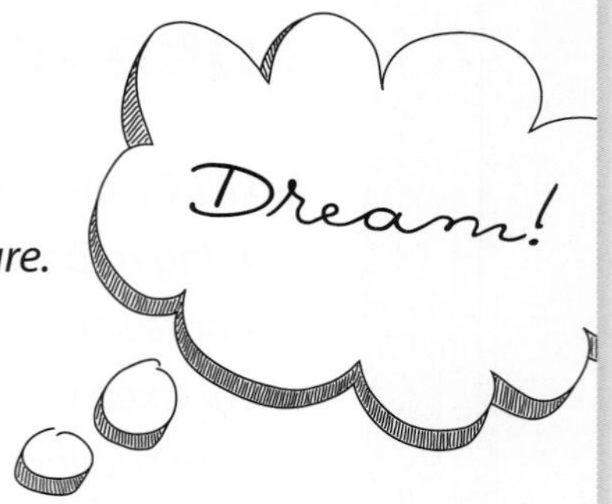

Just as dreams play a significant role in many Bible stories, they also play a role in your life. Think about the dreams or goals that you have for your future.

Dream!

Directions: Fill in the boxes with your ideas and action plan. Use them as a springboard to make your dreams come true.

My Dream for the Future

What My Life Is Like—Family, Home, Friends, Career

How I Will Reach My Dream—Step 1

How I Will Reach My Dream—Step 2

How I Will Reach My Dream—Step 3

Directions: What can you do to keep your dream alive when you face challenges? Write your ideas on the lines.

_____

_____

_____

_____

Name _____   Date _____

The Gospels Tell the Story

Directions: Read the stories of Jesus' birth in Matthew 1:18–25, Matthew 2:1–12, and Luke 2:1–20. Read each description in the first column. Draw a star in the column to indicate where the item is found in the Bible.

Description	Matthew	Luke	Both
1. gold, frankincense, and myrrh	_____	_____	_____
2. the town of Bethlehem	_____	_____	_____
3. angels praising God	_____	_____	_____
4. an angel talking with Joseph	_____	_____	_____
5. visit from the shepherds	_____	_____	_____
6. swaddling clothes	_____	_____	_____
7. visit from the Magi	_____	_____	_____
8. King Herod	_____	_____	_____
9. the star	_____	_____	_____
10. the manger	_____	_____	_____

istockphoto.com/ultra generic

Answers: For complete answers, see page T-398.   **T-361**

Unit 2 Assessment

A. Circle the letter of the choice that best completes each sentence.

1. The Roman emperor at the time of Jesus' birth was
   a. King Solomon.
   b. Julius Caesar.
   c. King Herod.
   d. Caesar Augustus.

2. The season that marks the start of the Church's liturgical year is
   a. Christmas.
   b. Ordinary Time.
   c. Advent.
   d. Lent.

3. Jesus opened a new way for us to relate to God the Father by teaching us the
   a. Lord's Prayer.
   b. Hail Mary.
   c. Great Commandment.
   d. Nicene Creed.

4. On December 8, we remember that Mary was born without Original Sin as we celebrate her
   a. Assumption.
   b. Coronation.
   c. Ascension.
   d. Immaculate Conception.

5. The Council of Nicaea affirmed our Catholic belief that Jesus was
   a. the Sacred Heart.
   b. human.
   c. true God and true man.
   d. the Third Person of the Trinity.

6. Jesus began to understand his mission from the Father when he
   a. gave the Sermon on the Mount.
   b. prayed to the Father as Abba.
   c. was baptized by John the Baptist.
   d. stayed in the Temple with the Jewish elders.

7. A person sent by Church authority to spread the Gospel through evangelization and catechesis is a
   a. saint.
   b. missionary.
   c. novice.
   d. refugee.

8. When a Christian family prays in faith together, it becomes a
   a. synagogue.
   b. domestic church.
   c. heresy.
   d. miracle.

9. Because Jesus' birth was announced to shepherds, Luke shows that
   a. Jesus came to save everyone.
   b. shepherds were held in high esteem.
   c. Jesus was an earthly king.
   d. Jesus was food for the world.

10. God's divine communication through a human being is called a
   a. novena.
   b. prediction.
   c. prophecy.
   d. heresy.

© LOYOLAPRESS.

Answers: 1. d; **2.** c; **3.** a; **4.** d; **5.** c; **6.** d; **7.** b; **8.** b; **9.** a; **10.** c

Unit 2 Assessment

B. Write the word or words that best complete each sentence.

11. An account of the infancy and childhood of Jesus in the Gospels is called an
_____.

12. Saint Margaret Mary Alacoque spread the Catholic devotion to Jesus'
_____, reminding us of his human nature and his love
for humanity.

13. The _____ were the first Gentiles to believe that Jesus was
the Messiah.

14. A false teaching of Catholic faith is called a _____.

15. The Catholic Social Teaching described as strength and unity that leads to the
sharing of spiritual and material goods is _____.

16. Blessed Marie Guyart instructed young women in the convent who had not yet
taken vows, who were called _____.

17. Referring to Jesus as _____ is a key statement of faith,
"God is with us."

18. The Jewish place of assembly for prayer, instruction, and study of the Torah is
called a _____.

19. The name _____ is the English version of the Greek for the
Hebrew name *Yeshua*.

20. We joyfully celebrate the birth of Jesus at _____.

21. Jesus told his disciples "Love one another as I love you," which is the
_____.

22. A _____ is a Catholic prayer that is prayed for nine days in a row.

23. Special days to celebrate the great things that God has done through Jesus and
the saints are called _____.

24. A vessel that holds the Blessed Sacrament for adoration is called a
_____.

25. Mary wrapped Jesus in _____ clothes, a symbol of his humility.

©LOYOLAPRESS.

Answers: 11. Infancy Narrative; **12.** Sacred Heart; **13.** Magi; **14.** heresy; **15.** solidarity; **16.** novices; **17.** Emmanuel;
18. synagogue; **19.** Jesus; **20.** Christmas; **21.** Great Commandment; **22.** novena; **23.** Holy Days of Obligation;
24. monstrance; **25.** swaddling

T-363

Unit 2 Assessment

Show What You Know

C. Think about the choices that Blessed Marie Guyart made during her life. How did she imitate the life of Jesus?

_____

_____

_____

_____

_____

_____

_____

_____

_____

_____

_____

_____

_____

_____

_____

_____

_____

_____

_____

_____

Beliefs and Attitudes

D. During Jesus' early life, he grew in wisdom and a deeper understanding of his Father's plan for him. Through good times and bad, Jesus' family stood by him. The family is the first place where we learn tolerance, respect, patience, acceptance, forgiveness, and love. How has your family helped strengthen these virtues in you? When have you learned something from a family member? Write your ideas in three to six paragraphs on a separate sheet of paper.

Unit 2 Assessment

Name _____ Date _____

Jesus' Baptism

At his baptism, Jesus accepts his mission as Messiah. Our Baptism commits us to reach out to others, witnessing to God's love and proclaiming the Good News of Jesus Christ to everyone we meet.

Directions: Use a Bible to read the Gospel accounts of Jesus' baptism. Then complete the chart.

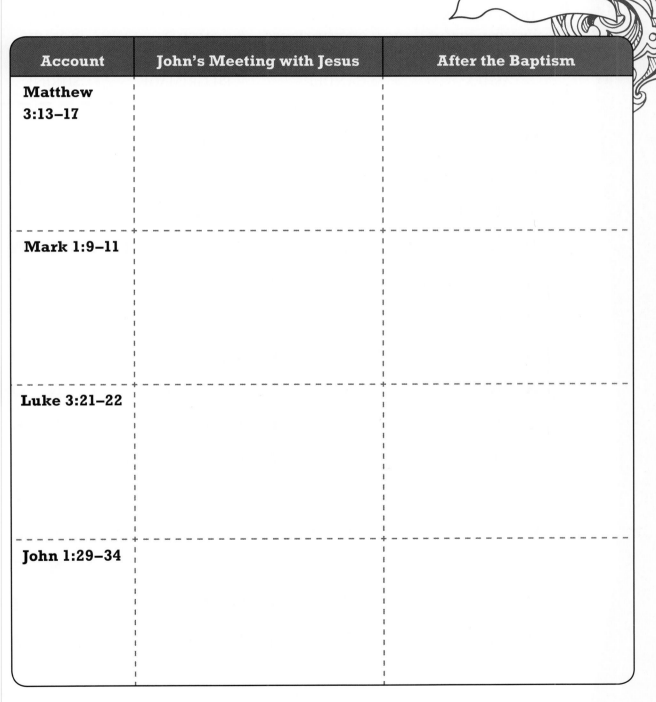

Account	John's Meeting with Jesus	After the Baptism
Matthew 3:13–17		
Mark 1:9–11		
Luke 3:21–22		
John 1:29–34		

© Loyola Press.

istockphoto.com

Grade 7 • Unit 3 • Session 11

Name _____ Date _____

Sacramentals Word Search

Sacramentals are gestures, objects, prayers, or blessings that remind us that God is near. They act as aids in the expression of our Catholic beliefs.

Directions: Find and circle the sacramentals. Answers may be spelled forward or backward and placed horizontally, vertically, or diagonally.

HOLY WATER	STATUE	CRUCIFIX	FASTING
GENUFLECTION	SIGN OF THE CROSS	MEDAL	ROSARY
INCENSE	SCAPULAR	BENEDICTION	OIL
ASHES	CANDLE	PILGRIMAGE	SHRINE

```
M  Y  M  O  S  F  E  T  U  E  C  U  R  L  A
T  U  R  W  G  L  G  D  N  L  H  R  N  T  C
Y  C  E  I  D  T  N  N  O  N  I  O  L  P  U
E  R  T  N  C  R  U  C  I  F  I  X  G  C  W
S  C  A  P  U  L  A  R  T  T  S  C  A  A  I
R  C  W  S  E  I  O  S  C  N  S  U  R  C  F
E  C  Y  S  O  X  N  I  E  U  T  A  T  S  W
A  N  L  R  S  R  D  E  L  C  N  F  F  N  O
S  S  O  R  C  E  H  T  F  O  N  G  I  S  E
C  T  H  I  N  C  I  T  U  L  Y  R  L  I  L
U  E  E  E  S  N  E  C  N  I  I  A  A  L  I
O  L  B  I  S  L  E  L  E  E  D  L  S  X  E
P  I  L  G  R  I  M  A  G  E  T  F  S  N  S
F  O  I  U  I  E  R  N  M  M  Y  S  F  L  H
A  L  D  E  S  C  G  N  E  N  I  R  H  S  R
```

© LOYOLAPRESS.

Punchstock.com

Name _____   Date _____

Entering the Kingdom of God

*Jesus teaches us that we need to have the qualities of
a child if we want to live as members of God's Kingdom.*

Directions: Use a Bible to write the Scripture passages in the space provided.
On the line before each passage, write the letter of the quality it best represents.

_____ **1.** Psalm 47:2 _____
_____
_____

_____ **2.** Luke 10:35 _____
_____
_____

_____ **3.** Joel 3:1 _____
_____
_____

_____ **4.** Ephesians 5:4 _____
_____
_____

_____ **5.** Matthew 20:33 _____
_____
_____

_____ **6.** Proverbs 15:26 _____
_____
_____

_____ **7.** Isaiah 55:6 _____
_____
_____

_____ **8.** John 15:4 _____
_____
_____

A. closeness to God

B. gratefulness

C. caring

D. loyalty

E. jubilation

F. eagerness

G. spiritual openness

H. imagination

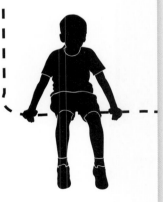

www.findinggod.com

Grade 7 • Unit 3 • Session 13

Hemera/Thinkstock.com

Name _____ Date _____

The Deadly Seven

Sin is an obstacle that prevents us from growing closer to Jesus. Seven sins are considered such great obstacles that they are called the capital, or deadly, sins.

Directions: Use a dictionary to look up the definitions of each capital sin listed below. Write the definitions in the spaces. Then complete the maze that guides you around the deadly sins and leads you to Jesus.

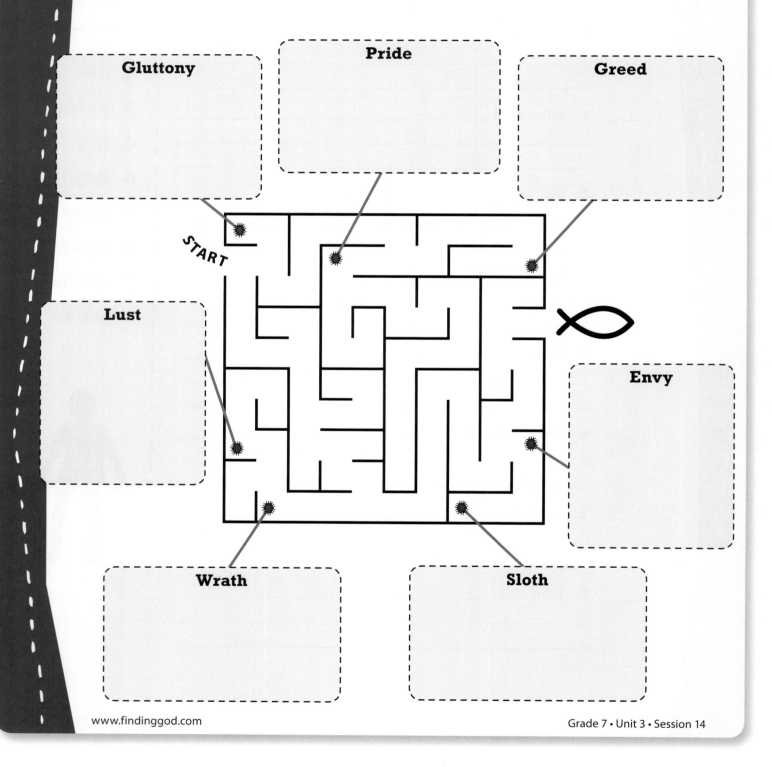

Gluttony

Pride

Greed

Lust

Envy

Wrath

Sloth

© LOYOLAPRESS.

Name _____ Date _____

Lost and Found

We are always lost in some way or another; this is part of being human. When we are fully "found," we will be fully united with God.

Directions: Use a Bible to read each Scripture passage listed below. Then complete the chart.

Scripture Passage	In this passage, God is compared to . . .	Human beings are compared to . . .	I am like one of these because . . .
Luke 15:1–7			
Luke 15:8–10			
Luke 15:11–32			

Which parable do you find the most comforting? Why?

_____

_____

_____

© LOYOLA PRESS.

istockphoto.com/Auki

Answers: For complete answers, see page T-399.

Name _____ Date _____

Unit 3 Assessment

A. Circle the letter of the choice that best completes each sentence.

1. The service or work that Jesus did for others is called his
   a. parable.
   b. epiphany.
   c. ministry.
   d. sacrifice.

2. Jesus' first miracle took place at
   a. Cana.
   b. the Temple.
   c. Bethlehem.
   d. his Resurrection.

3. All the Gospels were written
   a. simultaneously.
   b. over a period of time.
   c. by the Second Vatican Council.
   d. by Peter, the first pope.

4. We call Jesus' special instructions from the top of a mountain the
   a. Ten Commandments.
   b. Gospels.
   c. Spiritual Works of Mercy.
   d. Sermon on the Mount.

5. The sacraments are Baptism, Confirmation, the Eucharist, Penance and Reconciliation,
   a. Anointing of the Sick, Matrimony, and Holy Orders.
   b. Anointing of Holy Orders, Matrimony, and Repentance.
   c. Matrimony and Holy Orders.
   d. Anointing of the Sick and Holy Orders.

6. The Church brings God's care and concern to those who are seriously ill in the celebration of the
   a. Sacraments at the Service of Communion.
   b. Anointing of the Sick.
   c. Spiritual Works of Mercy.
   d. Kingdom of God.

7. Jesus' guidelines for Christlike living that lead to happiness are called the
   a. Church's Tradition.
   b. Ten Commandments.
   c. Magisterium.
   d. Beatitudes.

8. Saint Paul says the best way to embrace your Baptism is to imitate
   a. Christ.
   b. the Apostles.
   c. John the Baptist.
   d. Mary.

9. Any word, thought, or action done in hatred or defiance against God is
   a. contrition.
   b. blasphemy.
   c. repentance.
   d. absolution.

10. After the Holy Spirit was sent from Heaven, the Church was born
    a. at Jesus' baptism.
    b. at Jesus' Crucifixion.
    c. on Pentecost.
    d. at Jesus' Resurrection.

©LOYOLAPRESS.

Answers: **1.** c; **2.** a; **3.** b; **4.** d; **5.** a; **6.** b; **7.** d; **8.** a; **9.** b; **10.** c

Name _____   Date _____

Unit 3 Assessment

B. Write the word or words that best complete each sentence.

11. Moses encountered God on Mount Sinai and received the
_____.

12. Jesus multiplied five _____ and two
_____ so that about 5,000 people could eat.

13. For _____ days, Jesus remained in the desert, living among
wild animals.

14. The sorrow we feel when we know that we have sinned, followed by the decision
not to sin again, is called _____.

15. Limiting the amount of food you eat on certain days during Lent is a practice
called _____.

16. In the Sacrament of Penance and Reconciliation, we confess our sins
to a priest, perform a penance, show repentance, and hear words of
_____.

17. Jesus was _____ by Satan three times in the desert.

18. Jesus told _____, which are stories that taught God's truth.

19. Lent is a season of preparation for Jesus Christ's _____.

20. Serious decisions to turn away from God by doing things known to be wrong
are called _____ sins.

21. The Gospel writers, also called the _____, wanted to
preserve the teachings of Jesus for future generations.

22. The liturgical season of Lent begins on _____.

23. A sacrament is a sacred _____, a ceremonial religious act
that is a sign of God's love and presence in our lives.

24. The Good News is passed on today by the Apostles' successors, the
_____ and the _____.

Answers: 11. Ten Commandments; **12.** barley loaves, fish; **13.** 40; **14.** contrition; **15.** fasting; **16.** absolution;
17. tempted; **18.** parables; **19.** Resurrection; **20.** mortal; **21.** Evangelists; **22.** Ash Wednesday; **23.** rite;
24. bishops, pope

Name _____ Date _____

Unit 3 Assessment

Show What You Know

C. The Gospels answered many questions about the public life of Jesus. Think about the stories and messages that the Gospels teach us. How would you answer these questions: "Who is Jesus?" "What does he teach?"

_____

_____

_____

_____

_____

_____

_____

_____

_____

_____

_____

_____

_____

_____

_____

_____

Beliefs and Attitudes

D. Jesus' first miracle at the wedding at Cana reminds us that opportunities to serve may come when we do not expect them. Think about a time when you unexpectedly helped someone or made a difference in an unexpected way. Describe the experience and tell how Jesus worked through you. How do you think the person you helped felt? How did you feel after your service? Write your answer in three to six paragraphs on a separate sheet of paper.

www.findinggod.com   Grade 7 • Unit 3 Assessment • page 3 of 3

T-372 All BLMs and possible answers can be found at www.findinggod.com.

Name _____   Date _____

Jesus Teaches at Meals

The Jewish people viewed eating meals together as a way of expressing and strengthening relationships with one another under God's covenant. It's no coincidence that some of Jesus' teachings and miracles took place at meals.

Directions: Read the passages from the Gospel of Luke and write your responses in each column.

Passage	Who is present?	What takes place?
Luke 5:27–31		
Luke 7:36–50		
Luke 9:10–17		
Luke 14:7–14		
Luke 22:7–38		
Luke 24:36–53		

Tony Rothberg

Name _____ Date _____

Making Moral Choices

Moral choices often require us to choose between competing values. They can be difficult decisions to make, and there may be more than one way to respond in a morally responsible way.

Directions: Read each situation below. If it requires a moral choice, circle the number and write one morally correct way to respond.

1. You see $10 lying on the ground in front of you at the grocery store.

   _____

   _____

2. You decide to buy a new pair of shoes with your birthday money.

   _____

   _____

3. You see a friend bully someone.

   _____

   _____

4. You consider telling your parents that you don't feel well so you can avoid going to Mass.

   _____

   _____

5. You finish your homework on time.

   _____

   _____

6. Someone is intentionally left out of the group at lunchtime every day.

   _____

   _____

7. A friend likes to gossip.

   _____

   _____

©LOYOLAPRESS.

©iStockphoto.com/Maydaymayday

Name _____   Date _____

Who Is Jesus?

We need to articulate who Jesus is if we are to know and understand him as true disciples.

Directions: Put a check mark in front of each word or phrase that reveals Jesus' true identity.

_____ truly man   _____ the Anointed One

_____ God's beloved Son   _____ the Messiah

_____ the Christ   _____ Elijah

_____ the Mystical Body of Christ   _____ Lamb of God

_____ the suffering servant   _____ Son of God

_____ a centurion   _____ earthly king

_____ a blasphemer   _____ truly divine

Directions: Describe a hardship or suffering in your life that is easier to bear because of Jesus' selfless example of love.

_____

_____

_____

_____

_____

_____

_____

_____

_____

_____

_____

_____

©LOYOLAPRESS.

Session 19

Name ______________________ Date ____________

Jesus Is Everywhere

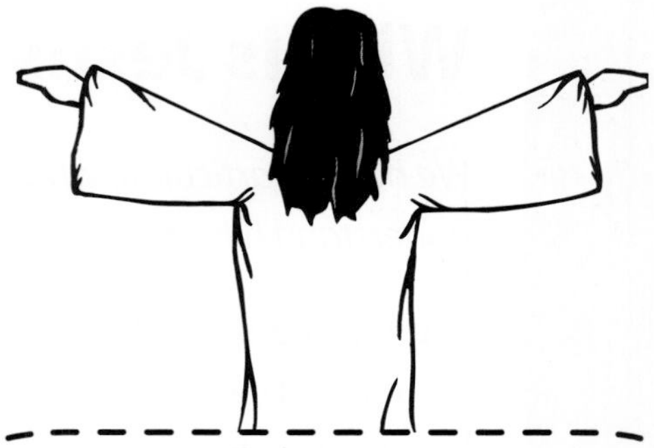

We often encounter Jesus but fail to recognize him. Jesus is present in many places and among many people.

Directions: Fill in each blank square with a short description or sketch of where you recognize Jesus.

In nature

In his Church

In work and play

In the community

Among strangers

Answers will vary.

Name _____ Date _____

Scenes from Holy Week

The stories of Holy Week present us with many powerful images of Jesus' suffering, Death, Resurrection, and Ascension. Imagine that you have been asked to design a cover for your parish's Holy Week program or bulletin.

Directions: In the spaces below, draw or describe some of the images from Jesus' life that we reflect on during Holy Week.

Jesus' Arrest
(Mark 14:43–52)

Peter's Denial
(Mark 14:66–72)

The Crucifixion
(Mark 15:21–32)

Jesus' Resurrection
(Mark 16:1–8)

www.findinggod.com

Grade 7 • Unit 4 • Session 20

Jupiterimages

Artwork will vary.

T-377

Name _____ Date _____

Unit 4 Assessment

A. Circle the letter of the choice that best completes each sentence.

1. Jesus and his disciples shared bread and wine during Jesus'
   a. Sermon on the Mount.
   b. Agony in the Garden.
   c. Institution Narrative.
   d. Last Supper.

2. We remember Jesus' sacrifice on the Cross for us on
   a. Holy Thursday.
   b. Good Friday.
   c. Holy Saturday.
   d. Palm Sunday.

3. The core mystery of Christian faith is
   a. Baptism.
   b. Jesus' Death.
   c. Jesus' Resurrection.
   d. the Eucharist.

4. The Gospel of Luke tells us that Jesus asked his disciples to stay awake while he prayed fervently to his Father at the
   a. Last Supper.
   b. Agony in the Garden.
   c. Easter Vigil.
   d. Sermon on the Mount.

5. For Christians, the cross is a universal sign of
   a. hope.
   b. despair.
   c. patience.
   d. death.

6. We prepare for Easter during
   a. Mass in Ordinary Time.
   b. Holy Days of Obligation.
   c. Holy Week.
   d. the Institution Narrative.

7. Jesus asked his disciples to break bread
   a. to prove their holiness.
   b. as penance for sins.
   c. in memory of him.
   d. whenever they were hungry.

8. When Jesus was put to Death on the Cross, he
   a. refrained from speaking.
   b. humiliated his disciples.
   c. condemned his persecutors.
   d. forgave his persecutors.

9. The fair and equal treatment of every member of society that keeps us faithful to the Kingdom of God is called
   a. doxology.
   b. social justice.
   c. marginalization.
   d. Rite of Christian Initiation of Adults.

10. In First Corinthians, Paul explained that when we sin against our brothers and wound our conscience, we are
    a. sinning against Christ.
    b. only hurting ourselves.
    c. making moral decisions.
    d. acting as good disciples.

Answers: **1.** d; **2.** b; **3.** c; **4.** b; **5.** a; **6.** c; **7.** c; **8.** d; **9.** b; **10.** a

Name _____ Date _____

Unit 4 Assessment

B. Write the word or words that best complete each sentence.

11. Jesus and the Father sent the _____ to teach, guide, and aid us in understanding all that Jesus had done to save us.

12. _____ was a happy and celebratory occasion at which the Jewish people recalled the liberation of the Israelites from captivity in Egypt.

13. Jesus' appearance changed before the disciples' eyes, his face shining like the sun and his clothes as white as light, at the _____.

14. The three days leading up to Easter are called the _____.

15. After the Passover meal, Jesus and his followers went to a garden called _____ so Jesus could pray.

16. We find Jesus in church every time the community gathers to celebrate _____.

17. We remember Jesus' triumphant entry into Jerusalem on _____.

18. Jesus' words at the Last Supper instituted the Sacrament of the _____.

19. In First Corinthians, Christ is called our paschal _____, a symbol of sacrifice and redemption.

20. At the Easter Vigil, we hear the story of our Salvation, beginning with Creation and leading up to the discovery of Jesus' empty _____.

21. In order to make good moral decisions, we need a fully formed _____.

22. The three Sacraments of Initiation are _____, Confirmation, and the Eucharist.

23. During World War II, Saint _____ was taken to a concentration camp called Auschwitz.

24. The Gospel of Mark tells us how to be a _____ of Jesus.

25. Making a _____ choice means choosing to do what is right or choosing not to do what is wrong.

©LOYOLAPRESS.

Answers: 11. Holy Spirit; **12.** Passover; **13.** Transfiguration; **14.** Triduum; **15.** Gethsemane; **16.** Mass; **17.** Palm Sunday; **18.** Eucharist; **19.** lamb; **20.** tomb; **21.** conscience; **22.** Baptism; **23.** Teresa Benedicta of the Cross; **24.** disciple; **25.** moral

Unit 4 Assessment

Show What You Know

C. Jesus' suffering and Death on the Cross taught us that suffering is present in the world to release love. What do you think this means? How does Jesus want us to respond to the suffering in our lives?

_____

_____

_____

_____

_____

_____

_____

_____

_____

_____

_____

_____

_____

_____

_____

_____

_____

_____

Beliefs and Attitudes

D. In Jesus' Agony in the Garden, he was tempted to avoid suffering and Death but remained faithful to God. When have you been tempted to turn away from God? What did you decide to do? What was the outcome of your choice? Write your response in three to six paragraphs on a separate sheet of paper.

Unit 4 Assessment

T-380   All BLMs and possible answers can be found at www.findinggod.com.

Name _____   Date _____

Patron Saint Search

Saints responded to God's invitation to use their gifts and talents. Knowing about the saints can help you figure out your life's work. By popular devotion, some Catholic saints are considered patrons for particular causes and life situations. We can take our special needs to them and ask them to intercede with God on our behalf.

Directions: Research and write the cause or causes for which we pray to each patron saint.

Patron Saint	Cause
Saint Joseph	_____
Saint Matthew	_____
Saint Elizabeth of Hungary	_____
Saint Monica	_____
Saint Francis of Assisi	_____
Saint Thomas Aquinas	_____
Saint Maximilian Mary Kolbe	_____
Saint Scholastica	_____
Saint Lucy	_____
Saint Lawrence	_____
Saint Thomas More	_____
Saint Eligius	_____
Saint Maria Goretti	_____
Saint Albert the Great	_____
Saint John Vianney	_____
Saint Frances Xavier Cabrini	_____

Directions: On a separate sheet of paper, write a prayer to your patron saint, asking for guidance in responding to your calling in life.

www.findinggod.com

Grade 7 • Unit 5 • Session 21

Kathryn Seckman Kirsch

Name _____   Date _____

Understanding God's Will

One spiritual practice of prayerful reflection is called the virtuous circle. It begins with reflection, leads to gratitude, which leads to service. Service leads us back to reflection.

Directions: Think deeply about an area of your life in which you have questions about God's will for you. Pray for guidance. Write your thoughts on the lines below.

Virtuous Circle

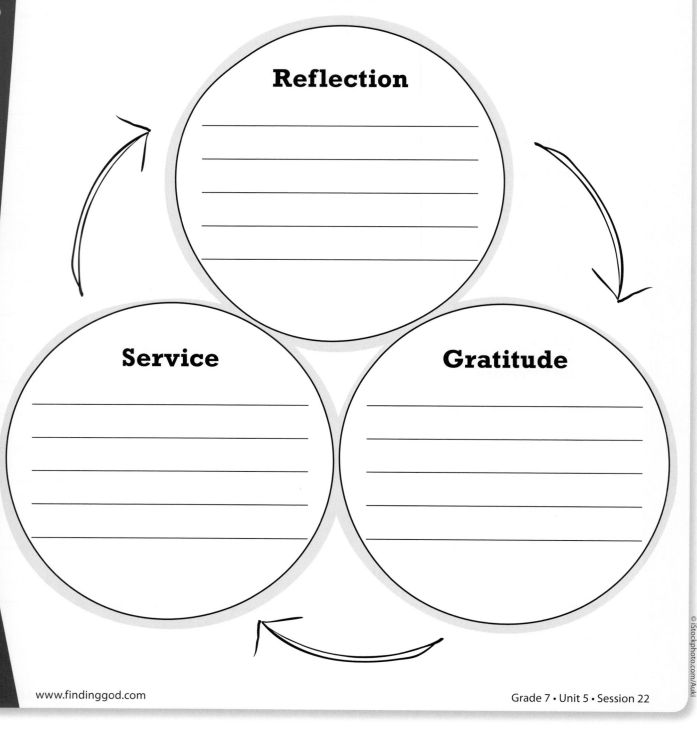

Reflection

Service

Gratitude

© iStockphoto.com/Auki

T-382   Answers will vary.

Name _____   Date _____

Then and Now

Saint Paul wrote about issues that still interest the world today.

Directions: Read each topic that Paul addressed in his letters to early Christian communities. Complete the chart with a current situation that shows how it remains relevant today.

joy	
jealousy	
the poor and vulnerable	
love	
faith	

©LOYOLAPRESS.

www.findinggod.com

Grade 7 • Unit 5 • Session 23

©iStockphoto.com/diane555

Answers will vary.

T-383

Name _____ Date _____

Assumption of Mary, the Blessed Mother

Mary is God's guarantee that the promises he makes will be fulfilled for us as well.

Directions: Read the words in the word bank. Find and circle them in the puzzle. Answers may appear forward, backward, or diagonally.

ASSUMPTION	MARY	HEAVEN	MOTHER OF GOD
INTERCEDE	SAINTS	BODY	SOUL
PROMISE	ETERNAL LIFE	SALVATION	HOLY SPIRIT

```
L I W D L N B E B S M R Y S S
D H L K T O S O K Y S T R F V
W W L C D I F I Q R A S K E T
Y L V Y M T G E M A Y A E F E
V Q O O N P S D K X D L M I F
C Z R Q A M M E E Y E V R L W
F P F L I U L C S H N A M L W
P T S M C S P R Q X R T D A V
P H Z S K S W E Y M A I C N E
L U O S A A U T J Y T O M R G
H G I E K I S N H H V N T E X
H E A V E N N I U H S P F T H
I A R Z A V S T Q R C L F E V
U M L N H O L Y S P I R I T H
D P D O G F O R E H T O M L V
```

Grade 7 • Unit 5 • Session 24

© Loyola Press.

Yoshi Miyake

Answers: For complete answers, see page T-400.

Name _____   Date _____

Symbols of the Holy Spirit

In the Old Testament, God's presence is often associated with fire. God first spoke to Moses in the form of a burning bush (Exodus 3). Later, God guided the Chosen People to the Promised Land as a column of fire at night (Exodus 13:21). At Pentecost, God again used the symbol of fire as he gifted us with his loving presence in the Holy Spirit.

Directions: God is also associated with wind or breath. Read the following Scripture verses in the Bible and put a check mark in the appropriate column.

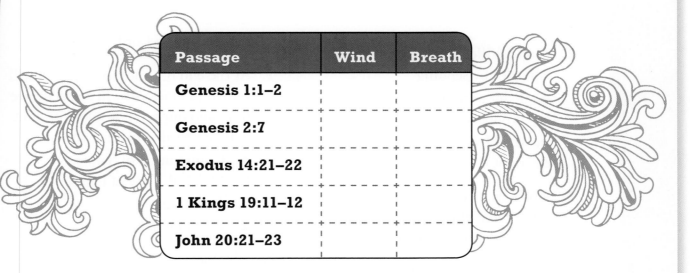

Passage	Wind	Breath
Genesis 1:1–2		
Genesis 2:7		
Exodus 14:21–22		
1 Kings 19:11–12		
John 20:21–23		

Directions: We've read how the Holy Spirit worked in the early Christian Church. Using the lines below, write a short paragraph that explains how the Holy Spirit works in the Church today.

_____

_____

_____

_____

_____

_____

_____

_____

_____

_____

© LOYOLAPRESS.

© iStockphoto.com

Answers: For complete answers, see page T-401.   **T-385**

Name _____ Date _____

Unit 5 Assessment

A. Circle the letter of the choice that best completes each sentence.

1. Catholics recognize that the Bible contains many styles of writing, which are called
   a. literary forms.
   b. factual.
   c. literal events.
   d. novels.

2. God fulfilled Jesus' promise to the Apostles by sending
   a. Peter as pope.
   b. prophets.
   c. the Holy Spirit.
   d. the Good News.

3. The entrance of Jesus' humanity into divine glory as he was lifted up in a cloud is called the
   a. Passion.
   b. Eucharist.
   c. Assumption.
   d. Ascension.

4. The permanent dispositions within us to discover God's will for us and to follow his will throughout our lives are the
   a. Spiritual Works of Mercy.
   b. Gifts of the Holy Spirit.
   c. Beatitudes.
   d. Theological Virtues.

5. Living without an attachment to material goods is called
   a. righteousness.
   b. obedience.
   c. poverty.
   d. chastity.

6. The seven Gifts of the Holy Spirit are wisdom, understanding, counsel, fortitude, knowledge, piety, and
   a. faith.
   b. prudence.
   c. temperance.
   d. fear of the Lord.

7. At the end of time, Jesus Christ will return in glory, all will stand before him, and our relationship with him will be revealed to all at the
   a. Communion of Saints.
   b. Mystical Body of Christ.
   c. Assumption.
   d. Last Judgment.

8. The Easter season ends on
   a. Easter Sunday.
   b. Pentecost Sunday.
   c. Palm Sunday.
   d. the Epiphany.

9. The Commandment that teaches us not to desire what belongs to our neighbors is the
   a. Sixth Commandment.
   b. Eighth Commandment.
   c. Ninth Commandment.
   d. Tenth Commandment.

10. The levels of Holy Orders are
    a. deacons, priests, bishops, and the pope.
    b. priests, bishops, and cardinals.
    c. deacons, priests, and bishops.
    d. deacons, bishops, and the pope.

Answers: **1.** a; **2.** c; **3.** d; **4.** b; **5.** c; **6.** d; **7.** d; **8.** b; **9.** c; **10.** c

Name _____ Date _____

Unit 5 Assessment

B. Write the word or words that best complete each sentence.

11. The Holy Spirit descended on the _____ at Pentecost.

12. We celebrate Pentecost as the _____ of the Catholic Church.

13. Saul _____ the Jewish followers of Jesus in Jerusalem before his conversion.

14. We call the letters written by Saint Paul to Christians in the early Church the _____.

15. Guided by the _____, we are able to know the truth and be true to our calling as disciples of Jesus.

16. On November 1, we remember all holy men and women who are recognized by the Church as _____.

17. The lure of _____ is putting material goods at the center of our lives when the center is the place where God alone should be.

18. The Book of Revelation, written to encourage Christians enduring persecution, contains _____ language and imagery, not literal events.

19. We serve the Kingdom of God and grow in holiness when we use the gifts received from the _____.

20. _____ holds an exalted place in the Communion of Saints.

21. Jesus, who learned carpentry from Joseph, understood the sense of purpose and achievement that comes from doing work well, which is called the _____.

22. During World War II, Saint _____ hid 2,000 Jews from Nazi persecution.

23. Mary was taken into Heaven, body and soul, an event called the _____.

24. In order to receive the Sacrament of _____, a person must be in a state of grace and profess his or her belief in the Catholic faith.

25. The Sacrament of _____ is a sign of the union between Christ and his Church.

©LOYOLAPRESS.

Answers: 11. disciples (or Apostles); **12.** birthday; **13.** persecuted; **14.** Epistles; **15.** Holy Spirit; **16.** saints; **17.** consumerism; **18.** symbolic; **19.** Holy Spirit; **20.** Mary; **21.** dignity of work; **22.** Maximilian Mary Kolbe; **23.** Assumption; **24.** Confirmation; **25.** Matrimony

T-387

Name _____   Date _____

Unit 5 Assessment

Show What You Know

C. Jesus proclaimed the Kingdom of God in his words and actions. He told us how to build the kingdom right now so that we might participate in its fullness in eternal life. How did Jesus help us understand what the Kingdom of God is like?

_____

_____

_____

_____

_____

_____

_____

_____

_____

_____

_____

_____

_____

_____

_____

_____

_____

_____

Beliefs and Attitudes

D. If Jesus appeared to you as he did to the two disciples on the road to Emmaus and asked you to come with him, would you follow him? Why or why not? Could you follow him without even knowing where you were going? Explain your beliefs in three to six paragraphs on a separate sheet of paper. Support your beliefs with specific reasons, details, or explanations.

Name _____ Date _____

The Liturgical Calendar

The liturgical calendar shows us the feasts and seasons of the Church year.

Directions: Label the calendar with each season and feast day. Using the *Lectionary for Mass*, find and write a Scripture reading specific to each Church season.

© LOYOLAPRESS.

Answers: For a completed calendar, refer to page 221.

T-389

Name _____   Date _____

Circle of Life

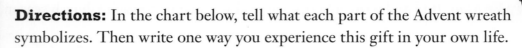

Each element of the Advent wreath has a special meaning and reminds us of the gifts God gives us, not just during Advent but in all times and seasons.

Directions: In the chart below, tell what each part of the Advent wreath symbolizes. Then write one way you experience this gift in your own life.

Wreath Element	What It Symbolizes	How I Experience this Gift
Circle		
Greenery		
Four Candles		
Purple Candles		
Pink Candle		
Light from Candles		

Name _____ Date _____

The Christmas Story, Retold

Casting ancient stories in a contemporary light can help us understand them better. Imagine the Christmas story taking place today.

Directions: For each element of the Nativity listed below, write a modern-day equivalent. Then give a reason for your choice.

Element	Modern-Day Equivalent	Reason for Choice
Mary		
Shepherds		
Swaddling Clothes		
Manger		
King Herod		
Angels		
Star		

Imagine yourself as a modern-day Magi. What gift would you offer baby Jesus? Why?

_____

_____

_____

_____

Answers will vary.

Name _____ Date _____

Lenten Commitments

Our Lenten commitments may seem easier to keep when we perform them in solidarity with others.

Directions: Write your commitment to each Lenten practice. Then identify a person(s) or group with whom you stand in solidarity as you live out the practice.

1. **The Practice of Praying**

   This Lent, I commit to _____ [type of prayer] from _____ to _____ [times of day] on _____ [days of week]. I will do this to stand in solidarity with the following person(s) or group: _____.

2. **The Practice of Fasting**

   This Lent, I commit to fasting or abstaining from _____ _____. I will do this to stand in solidarity with the following person(s) or group: _____.

3. **The Practice of Almsgiving**

   This Lent, I commit to give _____ [amount of money, time, possession, or talent] to _____ [recipient] on _____ [days and times]. I will do this to stand in solidarity with the following person(s) or group: _____.

   Signature: _____

Name _____   Date _____

Were You There?

Accompanying Jesus with compassion throughout the events of his Passion helps us experience the Holy Week journey in a deeper, more complete way.

Directions: Imagine the events from Jesus' Passion. Respond to each question on a separate sheet of paper and describe an event from your own life that helps you accompany Jesus with compassion.

1. Jesus Is Condemned to Death.
   When did you hear bad news?

2. Jesus Takes Up His Cross.
   When did you take a deep breath and do something hard?

3. Jesus Falls the First Time.
   When did you grow tired or lose hope?

4. Jesus Meets His Sorrowful Mother.
   When did you see someone you love in pain?

5. Simon of Cyrene Helps Jesus Carry the Cross.
   When did you receive badly needed help?

6. Veronica Wipes the Face of Jesus.
   When did someone treat you tenderly and with compassion?

7. Jesus Falls a Second Time.
   When did you find yourself struggling to finish something?

8. Jesus Meets the Women of Jerusalem.
   When did you help someone understand something, even when you were tired or distracted?

9. Jesus Falls the Third Time.
   When did you find yourself ready to give up?

Continue walking with Jesus with compassion by writing the remaining Stations of the Cross, Stations 10–14, asking questions that parallel the events in some way in your own life, and responding to these questions.

© LOYOLAPRESS.

© iStockphoto/HelenaOhman

Answers will vary.   **T-393**

Name _____ Date _____

"Remember What He Said to You."

Reflecting on the empty tomb can help us remember some important things about ourselves and our calling as disciples of Christ. Invite young people to reread Luke 24:1–12.

Directions:

▶ In the mouth of the tomb, write a Christian action or attitude that can be hard for you to show or to live.

▶ On the boulder, write what keeps you from living this way.

▶ On the lines, write what the two angels said in Luke 24:1–12.

_____

_____

_____

_____

_____

_____

www.findinggod.com   Grade 7 • The Year in Our Church • Easter

T-394   **Answers:** For complete answers, see page T-401.

Tony Rothberg

Name _____   Date _____

Gifts of the Holy Spirit

The Gifts of the Holy Spirit were meant not only for the disciples gathered together on Pentecost, but for us too.

Directions: Write a brief description of each Gift of the Holy Spirit. Then write one way you can use the gift in your daily life.

Wisdom: _____

   To use this gift, I can _____.

Understanding: _____

   To use this gift, I can _____.

Counsel: _____

   To use this gift, I can _____.

Fortitude: _____

   To use this gift, I can _____.

Knowledge: _____

   To use this gift, I can _____.

Fear of the Lord: _____

   To use this gift, I can _____.

Piety: _____

   To use this gift, I can _____.

Which Gift of the Holy Spirit seems most abundant in your life? Why?

_____

_____

Which Gift of the Holy Spirit might you pray for help to develop further? Why?

_____

_____

Answers will vary.

Name _____ Date _____

Dear Child of God

Thinking like a saint can help us act like one, which can help us become one.

Directions: Read about the life of a saint who interests you. Then put yourself in his or her place. Write a letter from the saint to you. In the letter, offer advice about confusing or challenging issues in your life. As you write, keep the saint's life and works in mind.

Dear _____ ,

_____

_____

_____

_____

_____

_____

_____

_____

_____

_____

_____

_____

_____

_____

_____

_____

Love,
Saint _____

Session 2

Name _____ Date _____

Mark the Evangelist—The Lion

Each of the four Evangelists—Matthew, Mark, Luke, and John—is represented by an animal that symbolizes his Gospel style. Mark is represented by a lion, a symbol of strength and courage. Mark's Gospel begins with John the Baptist proclaiming Jesus as "one mightier than I."

Directions: Look up the following passages from the Gospel of Mark that depict Jesus acting and speaking with strength and courage.

1:17 "Come after me, and I will M A K E you fishers of men."

1:15 "Repent, and B E L I E V E in the gospel."

2:17 "I did not come to call the R I G H T E O U S but sinners."

4:9 He added, "W H O E V E R has ears to hear ought to hear."

5:34 He said to her, "D A U G H T E R, your faith has saved you. Go in peace and be cured of your affliction."

2:11 He said to the P A R A L Y T I C, "I say to you, rise, pick up your mat, and go home."

10:25 "It is easier for a C A M E L to pass through [the] eye of [a] needle than for one who is rich to enter the kingdom of God."

1:34 He cured many who were S I C K with various diseases, and he drove out many demons.

8:34 "Whoever wishes to C O M E after me must deny himself, take up his cross, and follow me."

4:39 He woke up, rebuked the W I N D, and said to the sea, "Quiet! Be still!"

What do the circled letters spell out?
MIGHTY LION

Which of these passages speaks to you the most about courage? Why?
_____
_____

www.findinggod.com   Grade 7 • Unit 1 • Session 2

Session 3

Name _____ Date _____

Grand Genes

Genealogy is very important in Matthew's Gospel. Matthew uses Jesus' genealogy to show a largely Jewish Christian audience that Jesus fulfills God's promise to send his people a Messiah, or Savior.

Directions: Use your Bible to locate the Scripture passage in which the promise is made and write out the verse(s) in the center column. Then do the same for the passages in the right column. These passages identify some of Jesus' ancestors and show how God fulfilled the promises he made in the Old Testament.

Person	Promise	Fulfillment
Abraham	Genesis 22:18 "... and in your descendants all the nations of the earth shall find blessing—all this because you obeyed my command."	Matthew 1:1 The book of the genealogy of Jesus Christ, the son of David, the son of Abraham.
Judah	Micah 5:1 But you, Bethlehem-Ephrathah, least among the clans of Judah, From you shall come forth for me one who is to be ruler in Israel. . . .	Matthew 1:2 Abraham became the father of Isaac, Isaac the father of Jacob, Jacob the father of Judah and his brothers.
Jesse	Isaiah 11:1 But a shoot shall sprout from the stump of Jesse, and from his roots a bud shall blossom.	Matthew 1:6 . . . Jesse the father of David the king. David became the father of Solomon, whose mother had been the wife of Uriah.
David	2 Samuel 7:12 When your days have been completed and you rest with your ancestors, I will raise up your offspring after you. . . .	Matthew 1:1 The book of the genealogy of Jesus Christ.

www.findinggod.com   Grade 7 • Unit 1 • Session 3

Session 6

Name _____ Date _____

John the Evangelist—The Eagle

John's Gospel is represented by an eagle because of the soaring and lofty style he uses to describe Jesus. The Prologue reminds us that Jesus became one of us.

And the Word became flesh
and made his dwelling among us, . . .
John 1:14

Directions: Look up the following passages in the Gospel of John and complete each line. Then use the circled letters to write the missing word that completes the last sentence.

11:25 "I am the R E S U R R E C T I O N and the life."

6:35 "I am the B R E A D of Life."

6:51 "I am the L I V I N G bread that came down from heaven."

8:12 "I am the L I G H T of the world."

10:14 "I am the Good S H E P H E R D."

➡ The symbol for John the Evangelist is the E A G L E.

```
What have you learned about the Gospel of John?
Answers will vary. _____
_____
_____
_____
_____
```

www.findinggod.com   Grade 7 • Unit 2 • Session 6

Session 7

Name _____ Date _____

Matthew the Evangelist—The Man

The Gospel of Matthew is represented by a man. It tells us that Jesus is God with us.

Directions: Look up the following passages in the Gospel of Matthew and complete each line. Use the circled letters to spell the missing word that completes the last sentence.

1:18 Now this is how the birth of J E S U S Christ came about.

20:34 M O V E D with pity, Jesus touched their eyes.

14:25 He C A M E toward them, walking on the sea.

4:2 He fasted for forty days and forty nights, and A F T E R W A R D S he was hungry.

8:15 He touched her H A N D, the fever left her, and she rose and waited on him.

8:26 Then he got up, R E B U K E D the winds and the sea, and there was great calm.

13:55 "Is he not the C A R P E N T E R ' S son?"

17:2 His face shone L I K E the sun and his clothes became white as light.

➡ Jesus is called E M M A N U E L, which means, "God with us."

```
Which passage do you believe best demonstrates Jesus' humanity? Why?
Answers will vary. _____
_____
_____
_____
```

www.findinggod.com   Grade 7 • Unit 2 • Session 7

Session 8

Name _____ **Date** _____

Luke the Evangelist—The Ox

Luke's Gospel is represented by an ox because it begins with Zechariah offering a sacrifice in the Temple. The ox represents Jesus, the ultimate sacrifice for our sins. In Jesus' time wealthy people owned oxen. Oxen were considered precious animals for sacrifice since the goal of sacrifice was to give back to God your very best.

Directions: Look up the following passages in the Gospel of Luke and complete each line. Use the circled letters to write the missing word that completes the last sentence.

9:48 "For the one who is L E A **S** T among all of you is the one who is the greatest."

8:54 But he took her by the **H** A N D and called to her, "Child, arise!"

15:23–24 "Then let us **C** E L E B R A T E with a feast, because this son of mine was dead, and has come to life again; he was lost, and has been found."

7:50 But he said to the woman, "Y O **U** R faith has saved you; go in peace."

10:33 But a S A M A R I T **A** N traveler who came upon him was moved with compassion at the sight.

6:32 "For I **F** you love those who love you, what credit is that to you?"

18:16 "Let the **C** H I L D R E N come to me and do not prevent them; for the kingdom of God belongs to such as these."

19:5 When he R E A **C** H E D the place, Jesus looked up and said to him, "Zacchaeus, come down quickly, for today I must stay at your house."

4:19 "The Spirit of the Lord is upon M **E**, because he has anointed me to bring glad tidings to the poor."

➡ Jesus is the ultimate S A C R I F I C E for our sins.

Which passage is most meaningful to you? Why?

_____

_____

Session 10

Name _____ **Date** _____

The Gospels Tell the Story

Directions: Read the stories of Jesus' birth in Matthew 1:18–25, Matthew 2:1–12, and Luke 2:1–20. Read each description in the first column. Draw a star in the column to indicate where the item is found in the Bible.

Description	Matthew	Luke	Both
1. gold, frankincense, and myrrh	★		
2. the town of Bethlehem			★
3. angels praising God		★	
4. an angel talking with Joseph	★		
5. visit from the shepherds		★	
6. swaddling clothes		★	
7. visit from the Magi	★		
8. King Herod	★		
9. the star	★		
10. the manger		★	

Session 11

Name _____ **Date** _____

Jesus' Baptism

At his baptism, Jesus accepts his mission as Messiah. Our Baptism commits us to reach out to others, witnessing to God's love and proclaiming the Good News of Jesus Christ to everyone we meet.

Directions: Use a Bible to read the Gospel accounts of Jesus' baptism. Then complete the chart.

Account	John's Meeting with Jesus	After the Baptism
Matthew 3:13–17	John doesn't want to baptize Jesus; Jesus insists and is baptized.	Heavens open. The Holy Spirit descends as a dove. A voice from the heavens speaks.
Mark 1:9–11	Jesus is baptized by John.	Heavens are torn open. The Holy Spirit descends upon Jesus like a dove. A voice from the heavens speaks to Jesus.
Luke 3:21–22	Jesus is baptized by John.	Heaven opens. The Holy Spirit descends upon Jesus as a dove. A voice from heaven speaks to Jesus.
John 1:29–34	John calls Jesus the Lamb of God, who takes away the sin of the world. Jesus is baptized by John.	John describes how he saw the Holy Spirit descend as a dove upon Jesus. John had been told that the one on whom the Spirit rests will baptize with the Holy Spirit.

Session 12

Name _____ **Date** _____

Sacramentals Word Search

Sacramentals are gestures, objects, prayers, or blessings that remind us that God is near. They act as aids in the expression of our Catholic beliefs.

Directions: Find and circle the sacramentals. Answers may be spelled forward or backward and placed horizontally, vertically, or diagonally.

HOLY WATER	STATUE	CRUCIFIX	FASTING
GENUFLECTION	SIGN OF THE CROSS	MEDAL	ROSARY
INCENSE	SCAPULAR	BENEDICTION	OIL
ASHES	CANDLE	PILGRIMAGE	SHRINE

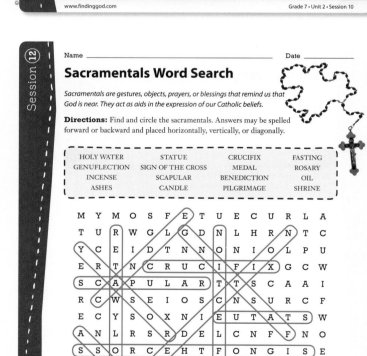

Session 13

Entering the Kingdom of God

Jesus teaches us that we need to have the qualities of a child if we want to live as members of God's Kingdom.

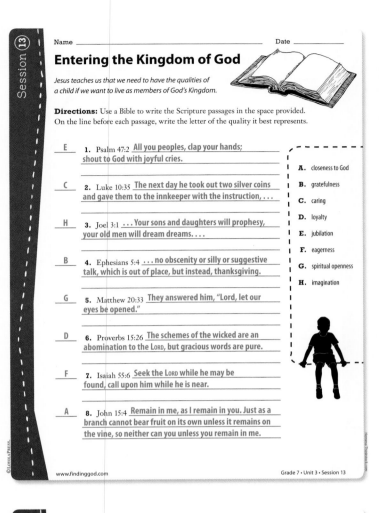

Directions: Use a Bible to write the Scripture passages in the space provided. On the line before each passage, write the letter of the quality it best represents.

E   **1.** Psalm 47:2   All you peoples, clap your hands; shout to God with joyful cries.

C   **2.** Luke 10:35   The next day he took out two silver coins and gave them to the innkeeper with the instruction, . . .

H   **3.** Joel 3:1   . . . Your sons and daughters will prophesy, your old men will dream dreams. . . .

B   **4.** Ephesians 5:4   . . . no obscenity or silly or suggestive talk, which is out of place, but instead, thanksgiving.

G   **5.** Matthew 20:33   They answered him, "Lord, let our eyes be opened."

D   **6.** Proverbs 15:26   The schemes of the wicked are an abomination to the Lord, but gracious words are pure.

F   **7.** Isaiah 55:6   Seek the Lord while he may be found, call upon him while he is near.

A   **8.** John 15:4   Remain in me, as I remain in you. Just as a branch cannot bear fruit on its own unless it remains on the vine, so neither can you unless you remain in me.

A. closeness to God
B. gratefulness
C. caring
D. loyalty
E. jubilation
F. eagerness
G. spiritual openness
H. imagination

www.findinggod.com   Grade 7 • Unit 3 • Session 13

Session 14

The Deadly Seven

Sin is an obstacle that prevents us from growing closer to Jesus. Seven sins are considered such great obstacles that they are called the capital, or deadly, sins.

Directions: Use a dictionary to look up the definitions of each capital sin listed below. Write the definitions in the spaces. Then complete the maze that guides you around the deadly sins and leads you to Jesus.

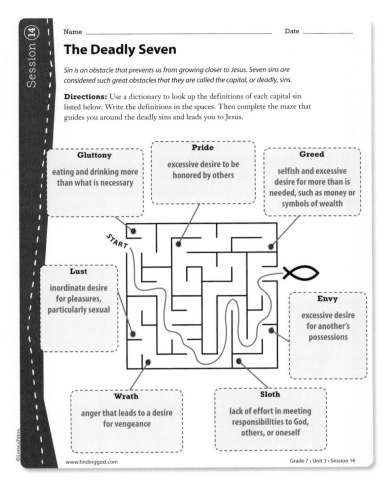

Gluttony — eating and drinking more than what is necessary

Pride — excessive desire to be honored by others

Greed — selfish and excessive desire for more than is needed, such as money or symbols of wealth

Lust — inordinate desire for pleasures, particularly sexual

Envy — excessive desire for another's possessions

Wrath — anger that leads to a desire for vengeance

Sloth — lack of effort in meeting responsibilities to God, others, or oneself

www.findinggod.com   Grade 7 • Unit 3 • Session 14

Session 15

Lost and Found

We are always lost in some way or another; this is part of being human. When we are fully "found," we will be fully united with God.

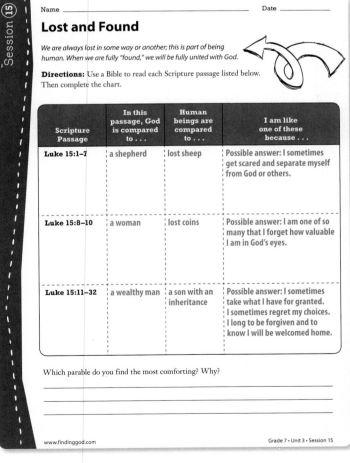

Directions: Use a Bible to read each Scripture passage listed below. Then complete the chart.

Scripture Passage	In this passage, God is compared to . . .	Human beings are compared to . . .	I am like one of these because . . .
Luke 15:1–7	a shepherd	lost sheep	Possible answer: I sometimes get scared and separate myself from God or others.
Luke 15:8–10	a woman	lost coins	Possible answer: I am one of so many that I forget how valuable I am in God's eyes.
Luke 15:11–32	a wealthy man	a son with an inheritance	Possible answer: I sometimes take what I have for granted. I sometimes regret my choices. I long to be forgiven and to know I will be welcomed home.

Which parable do you find the most comforting? Why?

_____

_____

www.findinggod.com   Grade 7 • Unit 3 • Session 15

Session 16

Jesus Teaches at Meals

The Jewish people viewed eating meals together as a way of expressing and strengthening relationships with one another under God's covenant. It's no coincidence that some of Jesus' teachings and miracles took place at meals.

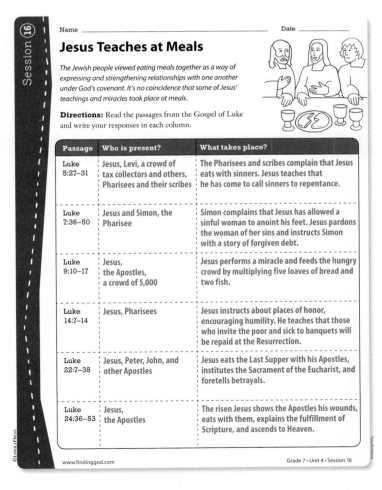

Directions: Read the passages from the Gospel of Luke and write your responses in each column.

Passage	Who is present?	What takes place?
Luke 5:27–31	Jesus, Levi, a crowd of tax collectors and others, Pharisees and their scribes	The Pharisees and scribes complain that Jesus eats with sinners. Jesus teaches that he has come to call sinners to repentance.
Luke 7:36–50	Jesus and Simon, the Pharisee	Simon complains that Jesus has allowed a sinful woman to anoint his feet. Jesus pardons the woman of her sins and instructs Simon with a story of forgiven debt.
Luke 9:10–17	Jesus, the Apostles, a crowd of 5,000	Jesus performs a miracle and feeds the hungry crowd by multiplying five loaves of bread and two fish.
Luke 14:7–14	Jesus, Pharisees	Jesus instructs about places of honor, encouraging humility. He teaches that those who invite the poor and sick to banquets will be repaid at the Resurrection.
Luke 22:7–38	Jesus, Peter, John, and other Apostles	Jesus eats the Last Supper with his Apostles, institutes the Sacrament of the Eucharist, and foretells betrayals.
Luke 24:36–53	Jesus, the Apostles	The risen Jesus shows the Apostles his wounds, eats with them, explains the fulfillment of Scripture, and ascends to Heaven.

www.findinggod.com   Grade 7 • Unit 4 • Session 16

Session 17

Name _____ **Date** _____

Making Moral Choices

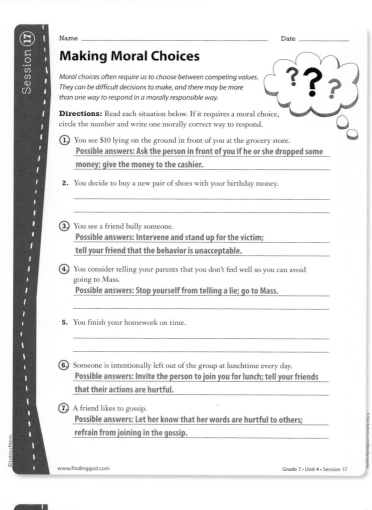

Moral choices often require us to choose between competing values. They can be difficult decisions to make, and there may be more than one way to respond in a morally responsible way.

Directions: Read each situation below. If it requires a moral choice, circle the number and write one morally correct way to respond.

1. You see $10 lying on the ground in front of you at the grocery store.
   Possible answers: Ask the person in front of you if he or she dropped some money; give the money to the cashier.

2. You decide to buy a new pair of shoes with your birthday money.
   _____

3. You see a friend bully someone.
   Possible answers: Intervene and stand up for the victim; tell your friend that the behavior is unacceptable.

4. You consider telling your parents that you don't feel well so you can avoid going to Mass.
   Possible answers: Stop yourself from telling a lie; go to Mass.

5. You finish your homework on time.
   _____

6. Someone is intentionally left out of the group at lunchtime every day.
   Possible answers: Invite the person to join you for lunch; tell your friends that their actions are hurtful.

7. A friend likes to gossip.
   Possible answers: Let her know that her words are hurtful to others; refrain from joining in the gossip.

Session 18

Name _____ **Date** _____

Who Is Jesus?

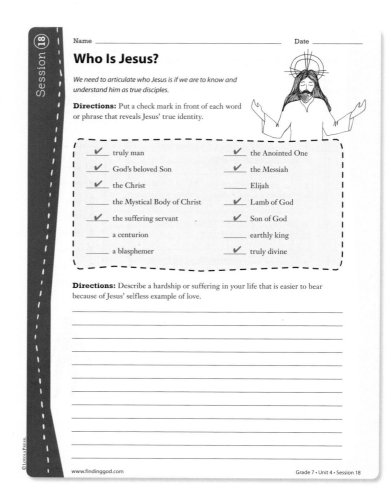

We need to articulate who Jesus is if we are to know and understand him as true disciples.

Directions: Put a check mark in front of each word or phrase that reveals Jesus' true identity.

- ✔ truly man
- ✔ God's beloved Son
- ✔ the Christ
- ___ the Mystical Body of Christ
- ✔ the suffering servant
- ___ a centurion
- ___ a blasphemer
- ✔ the Anointed One
- ✔ the Messiah
- ___ Elijah
- ✔ Lamb of God
- ✔ Son of God
- ___ earthly king
- ✔ truly divine

Directions: Describe a hardship or suffering in your life that is easier to bear because of Jesus' selfless example of love.

_____
_____
_____
_____
_____
_____
_____
_____
_____
_____

Session 21

Name _____ **Date** _____

Patron Saint Search

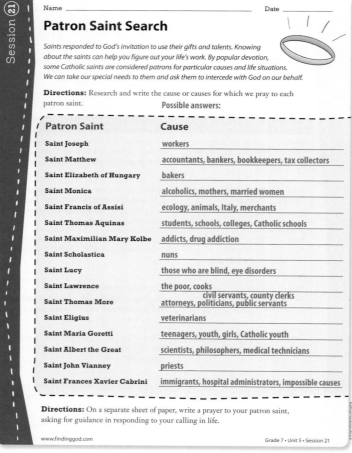

Saints responded to God's invitation to use their gifts and talents. Knowing about the saints can help you figure out your life's work. By popular devotion, some Catholic saints are considered patrons for particular causes and life situations. We can take our special needs to them and ask them to intercede with God on our behalf.

Directions: Research and write the cause or causes for which we pray to each patron saint.

Possible answers:

Patron Saint	Cause
Saint Joseph	workers
Saint Matthew	accountants, bankers, bookkeepers, tax collectors
Saint Elizabeth of Hungary	bakers
Saint Monica	alcoholics, mothers, married women
Saint Francis of Assisi	ecology, animals, Italy, merchants
Saint Thomas Aquinas	students, schools, colleges, Catholic schools
Saint Maximilian Mary Kolbe	addicts, drug addiction
Saint Scholastica	nuns
Saint Lucy	those who are blind, eye disorders
Saint Lawrence	the poor, cooks
Saint Thomas More	civil servants, county clerks attorneys, politicians, public servants
Saint Eligius	veterinarians
Saint Maria Goretti	teenagers, youth, girls, Catholic youth
Saint Albert the Great	scientists, philosophers, medical technicians
Saint John Vianney	priests
Saint Frances Xavier Cabrini	immigrants, hospital administrators, impossible causes

Directions: On a separate sheet of paper, write a prayer to your patron saint, asking for guidance in responding to your calling in life.

Session 24

Name _____ **Date** _____

Assumption of Mary, the Blessed Mother

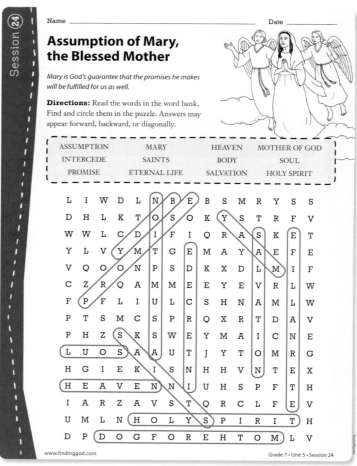

Mary is God's guarantee that the promises he makes will be fulfilled for us as well.

Directions: Read the words in the word bank. Find and circle them in the puzzle. Answers may appear forward, backward, or diagonally.

ASSUMPTION MARY HEAVEN MOTHER OF GOD
INTERCEDE SAINTS BODY SOUL
PROMISE ETERNAL LIFE SALVATION HOLY SPIRIT

```
L I W D L N B E B S M R Y S S
D H L K T O S O K Y S T R F V
W W L C D I F I Q R A S K E T
Y L V Y M T G E M A Y A E F E
V Q O O N P S D K X D L M I F
C Z R Q A M M E Y E V R L L F
F P F L I U L C S H N A M L W
P T S M C S P R Q X R T D A V
P H Z S K S W E Y M A I C N E
L U O S A A U T J Y T O M R G
H G I E K I S N H H V N T E X
H E A V E N N I U H S P F T H
I A R Z A V S T Q R C L F E V
U M L N H O L Y S P I R I T H
D P D O G F O R E H T O M L V
```

Session 25

Name _____ Date _____

Symbols of the Holy Spirit

In the Old Testament, God's presence is often associated with fire. God first spoke to Moses in the form of a burning bush (Exodus 3). Later, God guided the Chosen People to the Promised Land as a column of fire at night (Exodus 13:21). At Pentecost, God again used the symbol of fire as he gifted us with his loving presence in the Holy Spirit.

Directions: God is also associated with wind or breath. Read the following Scripture verses in the Bible and put a check mark in the appropriate column.

Passage	Wind	Breath
Genesis 1:1–2	✔	
Genesis 2:7		✔
Exodus 14:21–22	✔	
1 Kings 19:11–12		✔
John 20:21–23		✔

Directions: We've read how the Holy Spirit worked in the early Christian Church. Using the lines below, write a short paragraph that explains how the Holy Spirit works in the Church today.

www.findinggod.com   Grade 7 • Unit 5 • Session 25

Advent

Name _____ Date _____

Circle of Life

Each element of the Advent wreath has a special meaning and reminds us of the gifts God gives us, not just during Advent but in all times and seasons.

Directions: In the chart below, tell what each part of the Advent wreath symbolizes. Then write one way you experience this gift in your own life.

Wreath Element	What It Symbolizes	How I Experience this Gift
Circle	God's unending love	Answers will vary.
Greenery	new life that Jesus will bring to us	
Four Candles	each Sunday of Advent	
Purple Candles	the liturgical color for Advent	
Pink Candle	reminds us to rejoice because the Lord is near	
Light from Candles	the light of Jesus that came into the world at his birth	

www.findinggod.com   Grade 7 • The Year in Our Church • Advent

Easter

Name _____ Date _____

"Remember What He Said to You."

Reflecting on the empty tomb can help us remember some important things about ourselves and our calling as disciples of Christ. Invite young people to reread Luke 24:1–12.

Directions:
► In the mouth of the tomb, write a Christian action or attitude that can be hard for you to show or to live.
► On the boulder, write what keeps you from living this way.
► On the lines, write what the two angels said in Luke 24:1–12.

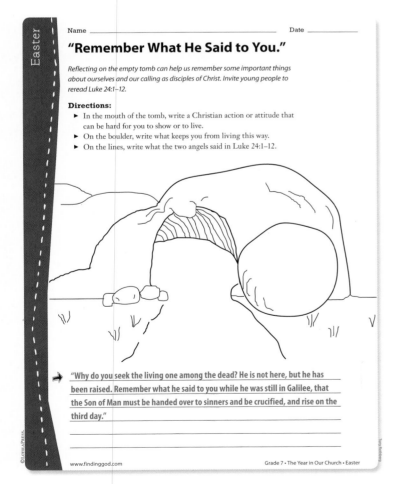

"Why do you seek the living one among the dead? He is not here, but he has been raised. Remember what he said to you while he was still in Galilee, that the Son of Man must be handed over to sinners and be crucified, and rise on the third day."

www.findinggod.com   Grade 7 • The Year in Our Church • Easter

Answer Key   **T-401**

Acknowledgments

Excerpts from the *New American Bible, revised edition* © 2010, 1991, 1986, 1970 Confraternity of Christian Doctrine, Washington, D.C., and are used by permission of the copyright owner. All rights reserved. No part of the *New American Bible* may be reproduced in any form without permission in writing from the copyright owner.

Excerpts from the English translation of the *Catechism of the Catholic Church, Second Edition* for the United States of America © 2000 United States Catholic Conference, Inc.— Libreria Editrice Vaticana.

Excerpts from papal encyclicals and other Vatican documents are © Libreria Editrice Vaticana. All rights reserved.

The *Suscipe* is from *Hearts on Fire: Praying with Jesuits* by Michael Harter, S.J. © 2005 Loyola Press.

Loyola Press has made every effort to locate the copyright holders for the cited works used in this publication and to make full acknowledgment for their use. In the case of any omissions, the publisher will be pleased to make suitable acknowledgments in future editions.

Spoken Word and Reflective Music CDs

All CDs were produced and developed by Loyola Press in partnership with Loyola Productions, Los Angeles, California.

Executive Producer: Loyola Press
Executive Producers for Loyola Productions:
Edward J. Siebert, S.J.; Paul Brian Campbell, S.J.
Producer: Javier Ruisanchez
Production Coordinator: Mirabai Rose
Instrumental music: Nathanael Lew
CDs edited, mixed & mastered by: Nathanael Lew

Dramatized Scripture Stories
Voice-Over Actors
Jessica Bogart: Ruth, Orpah, Mother
Nathan Carlson: Paul, Micah, Father, James
Cam Clarke: Onesimus, Disciple, John, Thomas, Disciple 3
Edward Cunningham: Jared, Boaz, Rabbi, Disciple 2
Jennifer Darling: Naomi, Person 2
Abner Genece: Peter, Worker
Wendy K. Gray: Narrator
Elijah Runcorn: Asa, Person 1
Lloyd Sherr: Leader, Grandfather, Disciple 1
R. Todd Torok: Jesus

Guided Reflections
Narrators
Cam Clarke
Jennifer Darling

Art and Photography

When there is more than one picture on a page, positions are abbreviated as follows: **(t)** top, **(c)** center, **(b)** bottom, **(l)** left, **(r)** right, **(bg)** background, **(bd)** border.

Photos and illustrations not acknowledged are either owned by Loyola Press or from royalty-free sources including but not limited to Art Resource, Alamy, Bridgeman, Corbis/Veer, Getty Images, iStockphoto, Jupiterimages, Media Bakery, PunchStock, Shutterstock, Thinkstock, and Wikipedia Commons. Loyola Press has made every effort to locate the copyright holders for the cited works used in this publication and to make full acknowledgment for their use. In the case of any omissions, the publisher will be pleased to make suitable acknowledgments in future editions.

Catechist Guide

i Raphael Lopez. **ii** Greg Becker. **OV-1** Greg Becker. **OV-2** Greg Becker. **OV-3** Greg Becker. **OV-4** cardboard border: © iStockphoto.com/sorendls. **OV-4** torn paper: Jupiterimages. **OV-5** (t) © iStockphoto.com/kryczka. **OV-5** (tc) Somos Photography/Veer. **OV-5** (bc) Corbis Photography/Veer. **OV-5** (b) Buccina Studios/Thinkstock. **OV-9** Warling Studios. **OV-19** (t) © iStockphoto.com. **OV-22** (b) © Stockbyte. **OV-23** (t) Sandra Gligorijevic/Shutterstock.com. **OV-23** (t) iStockphoto/Thinkstock. **OV-30** Sterling Hundley. **EC-1** © iStockphoto.com/EricHood. **EC-2** iStockphoto/Thinkstock. **EC-3** iStockphoto/Thinkstock. **EC-4** (b) Hemera/Thinkstock. **EC-4** (t) © iStockphoto.com/MarieC2. **EC-4** (b) Loyola Press Photography. **EC-5** Hemera Technologies/PhotoObjects.net/Jupiterimages. **EC-6** (t) © iStockphoto.com/Maica. **EC-6** (b) © www.imagesource.com. **EC-7** Polka Dot Images/Thinkstock. **EC-8** Stockbyte/Thinkstock. **EC-9** Huntstock/Thinkstock. **EC-10** (t) © iStockphoto.com/nico_blue. **EC-10** (b) James Woodson/Getty Images. **EC-11** (t) George Doyle/Stockbyte/Thinkstock. **EC-11** (b) iStockphoto/Thinkstock.

1a Andrew R. Wright. **45a** Andrew R. Wright. **89a** Andrew R. Wright. **133a** Andrew R. Wright. **177a** Andrew R. Wright. **221b** (t) © iStockphoto.com/nazarethman. **221b** (c) © iStockphoto.com/botsman141. **221b** (b) © iStockphoto.com/timurka.

Young People's Book acknowledgments begin on page 331.